PERSONAL INCOME DISTRIBUTION

PERSONAL INCOME DISTRIBUTION

Proceedings of a Conference held by the
International Economic Association
Noordwijk aan Zee, Netherlands
April 18–23, 1977

Edited by

WILHELM KRELLE
ANTHONY F. SHORROCKS

1978

NORTH-HOLLAND PUBLISHING COMPANY – AMSTERDAM · NEW YORK · OXFORD

© NORTH-HOLLAND PUBLISHING COMPANY – 1978

All rights reserved. No part of this publication may be reproduced, stored in a retrieval system, or transmitted in any form or by any means, electronic, mechanical, photocopying, recording or otherwise, without the prior permission of the copyright owner.

Publishers
NORTH-HOLLAND PUBLISHING COMPANY
AMSTERDAM · NEW YORK · OXFORD

Distributors for the U.S.A. and Canada
ELSEVIER NORTH-HOLLAND, INC.
52 VANDERBILT AVENUE
NEW YORK, N.Y. 10017

Library of Congress Cataloging in Publication Data
Main entry under title:
Personal income distribution.

  Bibliography: p.
  Includes index.
  1. Income distribution – Congresses.
I. Krelle, Wilhelm. II. Shorrocks, Anthony F.
III. International Economic Association.
HC79.I5P473   339.2   78-14053
ISBN 0-444-85220-4

PRINTED IN THE NETHERLANDS

CONTENTS

Foreword — ix
List of Participants — xi
Opening Addresses — xiii
   Mr. Boersma, Minister for Social Affairs, The Netherlands
   Mr. Kruijtbosch, The Netherlands Economic Society
Introduction: The Theory of Personal Income Distribution — 1
   Wilhelm Krelle

PART I: ETHICAL ASSESSMENT OF INCOME DIFFERENTIALS

1 Equitable Distribution: Definition, Measurement, Feasibility — 35
    Jan Tinbergen
   Discussion — 51
2 The Ethical Justification of Income Inequalities — 59
    P.J. Roscam Abbing
   Discussion — 78
3 Ethical Measurement of Inequality: Some Difficulties — 81
    Amartya Sen
   Discussion — 95

PART II: MEASUREMENT OF INCOME INEQUALITY

4 Annual Income, Lifetime Income and other Income Concepts in Measuring Income Distribution — 101
    C.C. von Weizsäcker
   Discussion — 106
5 The Perception of Income Inequality — 113
    Bernard van Praag
   Discussion — 137
6 On Comparisons of Distribution Processes — 141
    Michael Wagner
   Discussion — 159

PART III: DATA ON INCOME DISTRIBUTION

7 Our Shaky Data Base — 167
  Peter Wiles
  Discussion — 193
8 Size-Distribution of Household Incomes and Earnings in Developed Socialist Countries — 199
  Jan M. Michal
  Discussion — 226
9 Patterns of the Distribution of Earnings in Poland — 229
  Egon Vielrose
  Discussion — 239
10 Income Distribution in Less Developed Countries: Methodological Problems — 241
  Christian Morrisson
  Discussion — 260
  Longevity and Income Distribution: Discussion — 264

PART IV: THEORIES OF PERSONAL INCOME DISTRIBUTION

11 Equality, Taxation and Inheritance — 271
  Joseph E. Stiglitz
  Discussion — 300
12 Entropy and the Analysis of Income Distribution — 305
  Bertil Naslund
  Discussion — 314
13 Production and the Appropriation of Personal Incomes — 317
  Louis Lévy-Garboua
  Discussion — 330
14 The Role of Power in the Distribution of Personal Income: Some Illustrative Numbers — 335
  Jan Pen
  Discussion — 353
15 A General Market Model of Labour Income Distribution: An Outline — 359
  W.H. Somermeyer
  Discussion — 376

PART V: THE DISTRIBUTION OF EARNINGS

16 The Relative Influence of Inheritable and Environmental Factors and the Importance of Intelligence in Earnings Functions — 381
  Paul Taubman
  Discussion — 395

17	The Influence of Substitution and Technical Progress on Income Differences between Graduate and other Labour *K. Groenveld and S.K. Kuipers*	399
	Discussion	415
18	Labour Market Duality and Income Distribution: The Case of the UK *George Psacharopoulos*	421
	Discussion	441
19	The Effect of Collective Bargaining on Wages *R. Layard, D. Metcalf and S. Nickell*	445
	Discussion	465

PART VI: ECONOMIC POLICY AND INCOME DISTRIBUTION

20	Growth Policy and the Distribution of Income *Carmel Ullman Chiswick*	471
	Discussion	488
21	Transfer Policy and Changes in Income Distribution *Hans-Juergen Krupp*	493
	Discussion	513

Index   519

FOREWORD

One of the outstanding activities of the International Economic Association (I.E.A.) consists of organising symposia on topics which are in the centre of contemporary scientific and political interest. Personal income distribution is one of those topics where new insights have been reached in the last decade and substantial political efforts have been made. Thus it was only natural that in February 1976 the I.E.A. took up the offer of the Dutch Economic Association to host a conference on personal income distribution in the Netherlands scheduled for the spring of 1977. Income distribution has already been the topic of an I.E.A. symposium in Palermo, Italy, in September 1964; the proceedings are published in Jean Marchal and Bernard Ducros, *The Distribution of National Income*, Macmillan, London, 1968. But the emphasis of the Palermo Conference was on the functional distribution of income, not the personal distribution. And, more importantly, the years from 1964 to 1977 have been a period of rapid development in this field. Thus it was time for a symposium again. In February 1976 I was asked to organise the conference with Professor Jan Tinbergen as co-chairman and Professors Bentzel (Uppsala), Bombach (Basel), Gollas (Mexico), Kuipers (Groningen), Lecaillon (Paris) and Mileykovsky (Moscow) as members of the programme committee. I should like to thank Professor Tinbergen and all members of the programme committee, especially Dr. Kuipers, for their invaluable advice and help in getting together those scholars who have been most active and influential in this field. Dr. Kuipers also served as the local organiser, together with Mr. Kruijtbosch and Professor Misset. Anyone who has ever done that job knows how much time and effort has to be spent to create a real "symposium" rather than just a simple conference. I am sure I express the feelings of all conference participants when I thank them heartily for their work.

Originally the conference was planned to cover a broader field. Scholars from socialist countries had been invited to discuss income distribution in their countries and to compare it with that in other countries. Unfortunately, neither Professor Mileykovsky (Moscow), Professor Rimashevskaya (Moscow) nor Dr. Eltetö (Budapest) were able to come and present their papers. Only Professor Vielrose (Warsaw) was able to participate in the conference.

As to income distribution in developing countries, the first conference plan included this topic. But in order to focus the discussion the executive committee of the I.E.A. decided not to deal extensively with this problem at the conference. Thus only one paper was scheduled in this area.

For personal reasons, Professor Bombach and Professor Näslund were unable to come to the conference. The paper by Näslund was introduced and discussed by Professor v. Weizsäcker and is included in this volume. Professor Bombach's paper "The Conflict between Equality and Efficiency" was not available at the conference and is, therefore, not included in this volume.

All the papers were discussed at some length. Many new ideas and aspects came up during these lively and active discussions. Dr. Shorrocks with the assistance of Mr. Bartels prepared an admirable summary of these discussions. I wish to thank them for their efforts on behalf of all the participants.

The conference was opened by Mr. Boersma, the Dutch Minister for Social Affairs. His address, as well as the welcoming speech of Mr. Kruijtbosch on behalf of the Netherlands Economic Society, is included in this volume.

I should like to join Mr. Kruijtbosch in thanking all those people and institutions whose financial contributions made the conference possible: the Dutch Ministers for Social and Economic Affairs, for Culture and Welfare, and for Education and Science; the Netherlands Bank; and the Trustfund for Social Sciences of the Erasmus University, Rotterdam. Thanks are also due to the Board of the Netherlands Economic Society and to the Executive Board of the Rijksuniversiteit te Leiden for the receptions arranged for the conference participants.

Last, but not least, I want to extend my gratitude to Professor Malinvaud, President of the I.E.A., and Professor Luc Fauvel, Secretary General of the I.E.A., for their advice and suggestions and to Miss Crook and Mrs. Majid for doing an excellent job in organising the conference details.

Wilhelm Krelle

LIST OF PARTICIPANTS

Professor P.J. Roscam ABBING, University of Groningen, Netherlands
Professor H. ABELE, Université de Fribourg, Switzerland
Professor Irma ADELMAN, University of Maryland, USA
Mr. C.P.A. BARTELS, University of Groningen, Netherlands
Professor Ragnar BENTZEL, University of Uppsala, Sweden
Mr. Jorge BUENROSTRO-HERNANDEZ, Sistema Nacional para el Desarrollo Integral de la Familia, Mexico
Professor Carmel Ullman CHISWICK, University of California, Berkeley, USA
Professor Paul COULBOIS, Université de Paris, France
Professor Luc FAUVEL, International Economic Association, Paris, France
Professor Manuel GOLLAS, El Colegio de México, Mexico
Mr. K. GROENVELD, University of Groningen, Netherlands
Mr. J. HARTOG, Erasmus University, Rotterdam, Netherlands
Professor W.P. HOGAN, University of Sydney, Australia
Professor Wilhelm KRELLE, Bonn University, Federal Republic of Germany
Professor H.J. KRUPP, Johann Wolfgang Goethe University, Frankfurt, Federal Republic of Germany
Dr. S.K. KUIPERS, University of Groningen, Netherlands
Mr. R. LAYARD, London School of Economics, UK
Professor Jacques LECAILLON, Université de Paris, France
Professor LEVY-GARBOUA, Centre de Recherches et de Documentation sur la Consommation, Paris, France
Professor Edmond MALINVAUD, International Economic Association, Paris, France
Professor M.A.G. van MEERHAEGHE, University of Gent, Belgium
Professor Jan M. MICHAL, State University of New York at Binghamton, USA
Professor Christian MORRISSON, Université de Paris, France
Dr. G.R. MUSTERT, University of Tilburg, Netherlands
Professor J. PEN, University of Groningen, Netherlands
Professor Bernard van PRAAG, University of Leiden, Netherlands
Dr. G. PSACHAROPOULOS, London School of Economics, UK
Sir Austin ROBINSON, Cambridge University, UK
Professor Amartya SEN, London School of Economics, UK
Dr. A.F. SHORROCKS, London School of Economics, UK
Professor W.H. SOMERMEYER, Erasmus University, Rotterdam, Netherlands
Professor Joseph E. STIGLITZ, Oxford University, UK
Professor Paul TAUBMAN, University of Pennsylvania, USA

Dr. H. THOMAS, Institute of Social Studies, The Hague, Netherlands
Professor Jan TINBERGEN, The Hague, Netherlands
Professor E. VIELROSE, University of Warsaw, Poland
Dr. Michael WAGNER, Institute for Advanced Studies, Vienna, Austria
Professor C.C. von WEIZSACKER, Bonn University, Federal Republic of Germany
Professor Peter WILES, London School of Economics, UK
Professor P. de WOLFF, Advisory Council on Scientific Policy, Heemstede, Netherlands

OPENING ADDRESSES

Address by Mr. BOERSMA, Netherlands Minister for Social Affairs

It is with great pleasure that I am here today to open your Congress. The subject concerns one of the main items of policy for which I am primarily responsible as Minister of Social Affairs in the Netherlands.

Incomes policy has national, European and global aspects. It is concerned with industry to a limited extent and, to a larger extent, with the entire working population. It presents itself to us not only as a question of the distribution of personal incomes, in the sense of the share of disposable national income to which each individual is entitled, but also as a problem of costs in the productive sphere and, consequently, as an important factor in the development of employment. I shall revert to these interrelationships later on.

In my opinion it is beyond question that, of all the efforts directed towards obtaining a proper perspective of our world and its population, the socio-economic objectives are the predominant ones. For, after all, the fulfilment of the right to work and to earn an income are two important conditions governing the quality of life. Many of the other social and cultural objectives cannot be realised until the first two have been met.

Therefore, considering the ultimate political shape which we would like our society to have, high priority should be assigned to these socio-economic objectives.

I fully realise, however, that at a global level the developments still differ very widely and there is still great disparity in the distribution of employment and income.

But precisely because, in the formulation of national priorities, there should be scope for contributing towards a better distribution of incomes on a global scale, it is good to discuss these questions internationally. Moreover, in many parts of the world we are now confronted with structural problems in which questions of employment and incomes play an important part. A meeting, as the one we are having here, provides us with a very useful opportunity to exchange views with this guiding principle in mind and to gain inspiration for a new approach.

The Netherlands Government has once more indicated the importance they attach to an acceptable distribution of incomes in a publication entitled "Interim Note on Income Policy", which was issued nearly two years ago. This memorandum should be seen as forming part of a policy directed towards the spreading of power, property, incomes and knowledge. Efforts have been made to establish a link with social developments and changing views on income differentials in the public and scientific discussions of the past few years.

The first guiding principle is that all men are equal and that there are no reasons for assuming *a priori* that people should have disparities in income. Differences in work performance should be recognised as such, if they are to lead to acceptable differences in income. This is very clearly an ethical approach, which has met with a wide response, both inside and outside politics.

Income differentials should be based on the effort with which the income is earned or the sacrifices involves in earning an income. In this connection we consider the hours of work, unpleasant work (such as stench, noise and dirt), responsibility, etc., in such a way that these factors can be interpreted quantitatively with the aid of job evaluation systems. Here we can speak of compensatory income differentials, to use Professor Tinbergen's term.

Income differentials compensate for differences in sacrifices and efforts involved in earning an income, and help to increase the supply of manpower available for this type of work.

There is a second category of income differentials, namely those arising from factors such as aptitude and training. As a matter of fact, these are not valid grounds for compensatory income differentials, as they cannot always be regarded as worthy of merit and are, consequently, more difficult to justify from an ethical point of view. Nevertheless, they cannot automatically be equated with non-compensatory income differentials.

Income differentials arising from aptitude and training call for a special approach, as they fulfil a function in balancing the supply and demand for workers, and the element of scarcity clearly plays a part in this respect. I endorse the view of Professor Tinbergen and others, who advocate an increase in supply through training facilities, thus decreasing the quasi-rent.

Non-compensatory differences refer to factors such as social environment, knowing the right people, etc. In my opinion differences arising from these factors are not acceptable. Incomes policy should in the first place be directed towards reducing these non-compensatory differences.

Finally, the power factor plays an important part in income determination, particularly when the income differentials cannot be based on differences in effort, unpleasant work or training, and it has been found that in spite of this there are great differences in remuneration. For this reason I would give priority to spreading power within the framework of incomes policy. However, attention should also be paid to the reduction of income differentials.

In a recent article the Dutch Professors Pen and Tinbergen showed, by a great variety of criteria, how substantially the income distribution in the Netherlands has been levelled since 1938. One of their conclusions, arising from the most important criteria, is that income differentials between 1938 and 1972 have on average been halved. If the tertiary distribution is also taken into account, the percentage reduction would even exceed 50%.

This trend has continued in the last few years, influenced also by government policy. Some of the major results are an increase in minimum wages and the minimum wage of young workers, and the raising of national insurance benefits up to the level of the net minimum wage. The increase in minimum wages may have been a major factor in reducing the gap between the minimum wage and top salaries in industry. The statistics of the earnings of 75% of all adult workers reveal that earnings in the highest income bracket (the 98½th to 99½th, percentile) has decreased as a multiple of the (gross) minimum wage from 4.8 in 1972 to 3.9 in 1976.[1] Apart from raising the minimum wage, moderation at the top through increases in guilders rather than percentage increases may also have been a contributory factor.

Apart from the ethical aspect there is the reality of economic life. Incomes policy will have to be pursued in conjunction with other socio-economic policy objectives. Without pretending to be complete, I would like to elucidate this statement on a few points.

An excessive policy of reducing income differentials might lead to a shortage of supply for activities which are felt to be difficult or unpleasant, and surpluses in the supply available for easier and more attractive activities. This leads to difficulties in bringing the supply and demand for workers into line with one another and, consequently, to employment problems. This means that the problem of scarcity forms an integral part of the incomes problem.

In addition, there is the burning question of unemployment resulting from insufficient overall demand for labour. The incomes policy should be prevented from leading to wage increases which in the longer run exceed productivity, as this would result in a further loss of employment opportunities. In this connection I would point to the unbalanced international competitive position and to the substitution of manpower by capital, phenomena which in many countries have led to unemployment.

Moreover, any increases in wage costs that are in excess of increases in productivity will inevitably raise prices. This leads us to ask ourselves whether incomes policy should be enlisted in support of the fight against inflation.

Now we are faced with the dilemma that it is impossible, or very difficult indeed, to combine the fight against inflation with full employment and free wage-determination, as long as no progress has been made in the field of incomes policy.

An essential factor is the reaction among workers and employers. Social acceptance is very important and it is, therefore, problematic to interfere in wage-determination without the consent of the parties concerned.

Other very important groups are the self-employed and the liberal professions. A great drawback is that these groups may continue to fix their incomes more or less as they please, although the Prices Act makes provision for the possibility of enforcing certain tariffs and prices. The effect of such intervention is only partial, and it does not solve the problem of how to arrive at an acceptable distribution of incomes. On the contrary, it merely becomes clearer that a solution cannot be reached without the cooperation of the parties concerned.

---

[1] The figures above are based in data furnished by half-yearly wage surveys carried out periodically by the Central Statistical Office for the years 1972 up to and including 1976. The surveys cover gross weekly earnings in industry and in the service sector for employees aged 23 and older. In these sectors approximately 3 million workers are employed. The figures indicate the ratio of incomes of wage-earners in the 98.5th to 99.5th percentile to the minimum wage before deduction of taxes and social insurance contributions. The development from 1972 to 1976 was as follows: 1972, 4.8; 1973, 4.4; 1974, 4.2; 1975, 4.0; 1976, 3.9 (preliminary).

In the development of incomes policy, workers' and employers' organisations and other social groups will be able and willing to perform an important role. I am convinced that, by means of a workable consultation arrangement, the fight can be waged against non-compensatory differences in incomes. Special legislation directed towards the publication of job incomes has been placed before Parliament. In my opinion this legislation will make for a better understanding of the relationship between occupations and earnings.

In this connection there is a need for broader legislation, particularly a legislative framework concerned with the formation of incomes, directed towards extending and deepening consultations between and with the "social partners" and other special interest groups in society and towards improving the coordination of government policy in the matter of incomes. This legislation has now been delayed by the recent Cabinet crises. I should like to avail myself of this opportunity, however, to explain some ideas on this point.

With regard to a legislative framework for the formation of incomes, I am specifically thinking of a statutory framework.

Consultative bodies will have to be shaped as the social need becomes apparent. Gradually, more detailed attention will have to be given to the way in which the groups concerned can participate in the consultative bodies in a representative way.

The scope to which the legislative framework relates will have to be comprehensive. Specifically, consultations will have to take place with those concerned about all subjects directly affected by the incomes aspect.

In this connection the following items may be mentioned:

(1) regulations in the field of labour relations (work in paid employment);
(2) other acts and decrees having consequences for primary incomes;
(3) the social insurance acts;
(4) the taxation system;
(5) other government measures influencing the incomes position.

At present government policy does take the possibility of incomes effects into account, but coordination via government policy is still inadequate.

This appears, amongst other things, in the irregular marginal burden of taxation, premiums and subsidies, when considering the difference between primary and tertiary incomes. This irregular marginal burden presents a certain problem.

In recent publications, cases are mentioned in which the marginal burden on incomes due to taxation and social security contributions, together with the marginal burden resulting from reductions in rent subsidies, grants to students, etc., reaches excessive levels, in some cases over 100%. However, it must be borne in mind that these figures are based on heroic assumptions.

This is not the crux of the matter but it illustrates the complicated problems which can only be solved by a more fundamental harmonisation of all elements that are of importance for the determination of incomes.

It must be emphasised that each Minister should be responsible for his own policy, including the incomes policy aspect. In addition, coordination must be ensured. This can be achieved by giving the Minister in charge of incomes a coordination position in the Cabinet, comparable to the accountability of the

Finance Minister or the planning responsibility of the Minister of Public Housing and Physical Planning.

This first of all applies to the consultations on the incomes aspects of any measures to be taken within the framework of the legislation mentioned above. The initiative may be taken by the Minister who is primarily responsible, who also invites the parties concerned to take part in the consultations. The Minister in charge of incomes should in principle have to take part in these consultations, so that he can judge the coherence of the overall policy and make suggestions, if necessary.

The desire to gain goods and earn income forms one of man's primary motives, derived on the one hand from the need to feel secure and on the other from the urge to assert oneself, which to a greater or lesser degree is characteristic of all of us. Any incomes policy should allow for this, otherwise there is great risk of opposition, either active or passive, which could frustrate any goal directed at an acceptable distribution of incomes. In my opinion the representative organisations of employers and workers, representatives of those practising the liberal professions, consumers' organisations and other social interest groups are to a very large extent responsible for the incomes structure and the incomes distribution.

In these consultations the government can and should play a part, in particular by guarding the rights of those who, because they are not economically active, are not represented and are not in a position of power.

The task of the government is primarily to maintain equilibrium and make suggestions for long-term policy. The imposition of direct measures without the consent of the consultative bodies should, therefore, be seen as "ultimum remedium", a last resort, which should only be applied in exceptional cases, when the national economy is at stake.

A well-balanced spread of power should result in a democratic process of decision-making which gives all groups involved a voice in the matter. In that case the incomes structure will be accepted as compensatory to a far greater degree than at present. This would solve a considerable part of the problems connected with incomes policy.

The primary distribution, however, does not make sufficient allowance for the the elements of need and solidarity. Adjustments through redistribution would be necessary to achieve this. These elements may take the form of income-transfers to family budgets: national insurance schemes, benefits under the social security acts, benefits under the National Assistance Act, etc., as a result of which an acceptable standard-of-living can be ensured for those who do not take part in economic activity and for those who are not sufficiently capable of making their own likelihood.

These income-transfers, too, may be the subject of consultation. The same applies to subsidies lowering prices, charges made by public services, etc.. A considerable problem in this connection is the use made of free public services by the different social groups. This differs widely and is not always in proportion to the income. This tertiary distribution, therefore, differs from the secondary distribution and not always in the way intended. It should also be possible to discuss these points.

It it may be assumed that compensatory differences are adequately reflected in the primary distribution, it may be unnecessary in the future to modify the distribution because the primary distribution is unacceptable. This can never be entirely the case as matters now stand. Insofar as an acceptable distribution of incomes has not yet been achieved, income taxation may be a means of achieving this, in view of the fact that compensatory wage differentials need no further correction. In the long run, contributions to public revenue may be based on the principle of ability to pay, which, after all, maintains income differentials to the greatest possible extent, taking account of the marginal utility of money.

Progressive taxation could be moderated to a considerable extent, while maintaining a high rate at the top if necessary, should there be reason to assume that the principle of compensatory differences is unworkable at the top.

The elements determining the secondary and tertiary distribution are being dealt with by Parliament more often than the elements determining the primary distribution. This should be ascribed to the fact that, for the secondary and tertiary distribution, measures are involved which need the approval of Parliament. Nevertheless, it will be a good thing if they were made the subject of consultation with social groups, if only to enable Parliament to learn how policy decisions effect the parties concerned. Of course it should not result in Parliament only having to ratify what the parties concerned have agreed upon in their consultations with the government.

In order that the results of the consultations are widely accepted, it is necessary that the representative character of the organisations concerned should be satisfactory. Specifically, it is necessary to encourage social interest groups to organise themselves so they can have a voice in the consultations on incomes and be recognised as representative.

An organisation, however, need not take part in all forms of consultation. Representation confined to one or more areas of consultation is possible and desirable.

I have already mentioned the legislative framework on the formation of incomes which is now being prepared. My intention is that the consultants on incomes and income distribution should cover all sources, namely:

(1) primary income distribution, which includes wages, profits, income derived from interest, rent and rentals;
(2) secondary income distribution, which covers incomes or income-transfers to family budgets after the levying of taxes and payment of social insurance contributions by families, and
(3) tertiary income distribution, which takes into account the effect of public expenditure on the income distribution (e.g. prices kept artificially low (administered prices); subsidies tending to lower prices; free services, for instance in the form of training courses etc.).

I make a distinction between general consultations and consultations on certain aspects of the determination of incomes.

(a) *General consultation*
Representative organisations of all groups concerned, including the government, take part in the general consultations. The aim of general consultations

is to give all groups concerned a voice in the consultations regarding permissable rises in income. I am thinking of structuring the consultations with employers' and workers' organisations, with those practising the liberal professions and also with other organisations, a structure which will make it possible to discuss matters with each other in the same way as is done in Parliament. It may be hoped that the onesided emphasis on the results of the wage negotiations can be avoided, both preventing disproportionately large wage increases and avoiding one-sided wage measures.

(b) *Consultations on certain aspects of the formation of incomes*

These consultations include, for instance, wage negotiations for one sector of industry, negotiations on the fees of certain groups of professional people and negotiations on rents or rentals. In principle, taxes, social insurance contributions and benefits may also be the subject of these consultations. For this purpose, sufficient scope should be allowed for the future extension of consultations into various fields. The idea is to ensure that the results of these consultations will fit into the overall arrangements to be made in the general framework of consultations.

Through a proper planning of consultations, a well-balanced spread of power may be obtained, and the weakest partners in the consultation may be given support by the government, if their point of view is reasonable. Perhaps it will be possible in this way to ensure that the principle of compensatory differences will finally be applied as a basis for the determination of incomes. It is clear that in this exercise the proposed publication of earned incomes plays an important role as a guiding principle for the determination of the compensatory differences. This legislative framework and the Act on the Publication of Incomes should therefore be seen as instruments which are necessary to complement each other.

I am very glad that the I.E.A. has decided to hold a conference on the distribution of personal incomes. The scientific contribution essentially inspires the policy to be pursued. In this connection it is important to mention that in the Netherlands there are plans for setting up an advisory board for questions of incomes policy, to ensure that the scientific approach to incomes policy can be given maximum scope.

I hope that the ideas I have just explained to you may contribute towards achieving this aim. I am absolutely certain that, in this intricate field of incomes policy, a contribution will have to be made by political, industrial and scientific circles in close cooperation.

Address by E.D.J. KRUIJTBOSCH on behalf of the Netherlands Economic Society (*Abstract*)

In 1973 the first postwar government of the Netherlands with a progressive majority took office and gave first priority to the objective of minimising income differentials. Because of its topicality the Netherlands Economic Society devoted its 1973 annual meeting to this problem. This annual meeting was a great success and it was decided to try to internationalise the scientific discussion about personal income distribution. The Netherlands Economic Society took the initiative to arrange an international conference in the Netherlands for two reasons:

(1) the prime importance attached to this problem by the government in power,
(2) the growing interest in the Netherlands of both older and younger economists, and scientists from other disciplines, in problems related to income distribution.

A group consisting of Van Eijk, Kruijtbosch, Kuipers, Misset and Tinbergen formulated a possible programme of the conference and made suggestions about potential participants. The proposal was submitted to the Executive Committee of the I.E.A. and finally led to the actual organisation of this conference.

Apart from intellectual inputs, financial inputs are also necessary to hold such a conference.

Mr. Boersma, we are very grateful to the subsidy provided by your ministry, which made this conference possible. Would you please be so kind to also convey our thanks to your colleagues for Economic Affairs, Culture and Welfare, and Education and Science for their financial contributions.

Important grants were also given by the Trustfund for social sciences of the Erasmus University of Rotterdam and the Netherlands Bank. The latter implicitly agreed to our philosophy that an incomes policy can be effected more easily if people feel that the income distribution is equitable, with beneficial effects for the stability of the guilder. Finally "De Baak" was willing to offer a special price for food and lodging of the participants.

May I conclude by expressing the hope that you will together reach some agreement that will form a basis for further policy in this field and that your discussions will stimulate younger economists to continue research on this difficult but very attractive subject.

INTRODUCTION: THE THEORY OF PERSONAL INCOME DISTRIBUTION

WILHELM KRELLE

Income distribution may be viewed in two different ways: from the *normative aspect* (what should income distribution be like? What is an equitable income distribution?) and the aspect of *economic theory* (how can the actual income distribution be explained? What would be the effects of different measures of economic policy on income distribution?). The normative side has an old tradition in ethics going back to classical philosophy; it has been taken up by welfare economics. The papers of Tinbergen and Abbing in this volume belong to this normative side. In the first part of this introduction I shall try to integrate their ideas into the general context of ethics and utility theory.

In the second part of this introduction I shall develop a general theory which unites the different strands of thought on personal income distribution to be found in the papers in this volume. It is unsatisfactory that the same phenomenon (personal income distribution) will be explained by such diverse factors as natural endowment, schooling, inheritance, human capital, political power, chance, etc. without any indication of how all these factors are related to each other and to ordinary macroeconomic variables such as wage income and profit income.

I. The ethics of personal income distribution: Which distribution could be called equitable?

I.1. *The foundation of ethics. Transition to preference orderings*

The basic question in ethics is: where do the ethical evaluations of individual or social actions come from? Or to put it in another way: whose authority validates ethical value judgements? There are two possible answers: somebody or something outside the subjective beliefs of the ordinary human beings or just those subjective beliefs themselves. In the first "objective" case a theological or a philosophical foundation of ethics is possible. In theology, ethical evaluations derive their validity and authority from God as far as his will is revealed in holy scriptures as the Bible, or in the words and writings of prophets and other men inspired by God. In philosophy an *a priori* ethics is founded on the conception of a basic structure of thought or of human existence yielding guidelines for what men should do. The categoric imperative of Kant or the natural law of medieval theologicans and philosophers are examples of this kind of thinking.

In the second case the only authority of a value judgement is the man who states that judgement. Of course, if two men differ in their value judgements, one cannot say whose judgement is "right" and whose is "wrong". There may be decision rules for a society; e.g. the majority rule. But if there are contradictions in the value judgements of people there is no way out of the dilemma that, whatever society decides, some people may find it "wrong". Since their judgement has the same validity as the judgement of those who find it "right", the ethical dilemma cannot be resolved. There is no "final authority" – God or natural law or reason – nor is majority will sufficient justification for rightness in the ethical sense.

This seems to be the basic problem in ethics, from classical antiquity until now. In Plato's dialogue "Protagoras", Socrates begins with the assertion that virtue cannot be taught (or, in other words, that there is no ethical system independent of individual beliefs) whereas Protagoras holds the opposite view. At the end of the dialogue the two interlocators have changed their positions completely: now Socrates asserts that virtue can be perceived by contemplation whereas Protagoras – unwillingly – is forced to defend Socrates' former position. In Plato's dialogue "Theaetetus", Socrates attacks Protagoras' dictum that man is the judge of all things. Why should the pig or the ape not be the judge of all things? Why should he (Socrates) be forced to be a judge despite his limited insight? In chapter 2 of this volume Professor *Abbing* states the two opposite positions; he is on the "objective" side. In section I.2 he says that "...ethical statements need to have general validity. It is not simply a matter of taste for which we cannot objectively account." On the other hand (section II.1) he states: "Concerning the norm one should be aware that ... it is more or less a product of its own time and class and its own individual development and circumstances." Professor Abbing hopes that "scholarly ethical reflection" may determine which part of the actual norm belongs to "objective" ethics.

Professor *Tinbergen* is on the "subjective" side of the issue (chapter 1, sections I.1 and I.2). He takes it for granted that normative statements are subjective in character. Thus he defines his own notion of equity, hoping that his concept will be accepted by others and knowing that it is a purely subjective one and that he cannot force anybody by pure logic to accept his choice. In Professor *Sen's* approach (chapter 3) the basic ethical problem does not appear explicitly. It is hidden behind the concept of a social welfare function. If there exists a social welfare function which is accepted by all members of society the ethical problem is settled *for all practical purposes:* situation A is "better" than situation B if and only if the social welfare index of A is higher than that of B. But does a social welfare function also exist when the individual preferences of members of society differ? This is left open. And even if it exists, will it conform to some "objective" ethical structure? Naturally, if there are no "objective" ethics, the last question disappears.

Let us try to find a solution to the basic ethical question from the standpoint of science. Of course, this leaves out the religious foundation of ethics, which is not subject to scientific judgement. Science starts from observation or from basic axioms. There seems to be one *basic principle* for all possible human systems of individual and social life: *all propositions of ethics should be such that (if universally adopted) human life could be preserved on earth.* The value judgement behind this principle is that the human race is of positive value in itself.

This principle limits all possible ethics, though these limits may be very broad and sometimes fuzzy. Nevertheless, they exist. For instance a "social welfare function" (even if it is unanimously adopted by all members) stating that all members of other societies should be killed, contradicts the "objective" ethical structure indicated by the basic principle and therefore does not qualify as an ethical system. But within these broad limits all possible ethics must be accepted in principle as indistinguishable from the "objective" point of view.

Individual values are subject to change due to spontaneous inner events (Saul becomes Paul), which may be considered from the scientific viewpoint as stochastic processes resulting from the environment. In this respect, learning and information systems are of greatest importance. Individual value judgements may be represented by partial, weak, possibly intransitive, individual preference orderings. They might not be compatible with "objective" ethics.

Each society needs rules for arriving at decisions valid for all members, in case individuals have different opinions (as they usually do) as to the best social decision. It may be that the rules are agreed upon unanimously, but this will not generally be the case. Anyway, each existing society has institutional rules laid down in constitutions, standards of behaviour, the power structure of social groups etc. determining how individual preferences are transformed into social preferences. Of course, these rules are changed gradually or suddenly in the political process. But that is not our subject here. In each period there are rules determining how decisions are made on behalf of the society as a whole. This process may again be reflected in a partial, weak, possibly intransitive social preference ordering. This ordering may again not be compatible with "objective" ethics.

For simplicity, and as a starting point, nice differentiable utility functions may be taken to represent individual and social preference orderings. For some theoretical problems the ethical content of these functions may be left open, i.e. no assumptions are made as to the shape of the function in detail, apart from some very general features such as concavity. This is done, for instance, in the contributions of *Sen* (chapter 3) and *v. Weizsäcker* (chapter 4). For recommendations about individual or social actions these details of the utility function are crucial: one has really to state which kinds of action should be preferred. The contributions of *Tinbergen* (chapter 1) and *Abbing* (chapter 2) deal with this problem.

I.2. *Equitable income distribution*

If there are more narrowly defined objective ethical norms in the sense of Professor *Abbing* it should be possible to discover them by comparing Abbing's three principles of equitable income distribution with others found in the literature, especially in the field of theological ethics. There should be some sort of general agreement on the content of objective ethical norms, if this approach really differs from the subjective one.

Professor *Tinbergen's* approach should also be compared with other "subjective" norms. Since he does not claim objective validity, personal judgement (in this introduction, my judgement) is the ultimate subjective criterion. Of course, other people may reach other conclusions. But also here there is an extended discussion in the literature under the heading of "utilitarianism" which may be consulted.

I.2.1. Theological ethics[1]

It is fundamental to all theological ethics that its unconditional claim for legitimacy is derived from divine authority. No agreement exists as to the details of this ethic and to the sources of this authority. The *catholic ethic* starts from the Bible, the Early Fathers and the saints (especially *Thomas Aquinas*), the resolutions of the councils, and the encyclicals of the popes. In addition, natural law, interpreted in different ways, has played an important role ever since *Thomas Aquinas* took up *Aristotles*' ideas on this. But this foundation leaves some freedom for individual interpretations and the ideas of different writers in this field.

As to the problem of income distribution in the Middle Ages and partly up to the 19th century, the idea of a "standesgemäßer Lebensunterhalt" was prominent in catholic ethics: everybody should get income according to his status in society. Since this status, as well as the income associated with it, was well defined and generally accepted in these times, an income distribution was considered to be equitable if it corresponded to the ranking by status. This rather conservative approach was modified with the encyclical of *Pope Leo XIII* "*Rerum Novarum*" (1891), which considered the new social conditions of an industrialised capitalist society. In contrast to socialism Leo XIII regarded the right of private property to be a basic natural law; but, in contrast to capitalism, he also stated as natural law that ownership of a product belongs to the worker who produced it. No practical conclusions can be drawn from this general statement – understandably, since this principle cannot be invoked in an industrialised economy with division of labour. "*Suum cuique*" (everybody should get as much as his due) is stated as a basic principle of income distribution instead. What this exactly means is left open, except for the requirement that the basic needs of workers must be satisfied and that all possible means should be applied to improve the economic situation of the worker. Differences in natural endowments, skills, diligence and position in society are recognised as just reasons for income inequality.

This line of thought was further developed in favour of the workers and lower income classes by *Pope Pius XI* in "*Quadragesimo Anno*" (1931) and especially by *Johannes XXIII* in "*Mater et Magistra*" (1961). In the latter encyclical Johannes XXIII demanded that income from labour should not be determined by market conditions. It should be such that the worker reaches a really human standard of living, sufficient to meet his obligations to his family. Within these limits his contribution to production, the repercussions of the wage level on employment and social welfare in general should be taken into account.

Catholic moral ethics stays within these limits as a rule. The more economically minded authors stress the contribution to output as the prime measure of equitable income. This income should be corrected afterwards according to social status,

---

[1] I intend to discuss only christian theology, as an example.

family responsibilities etc. (Tautscher (1957)). The more theologically minded authors reverse this order. Some declare that there is no unique solution to the problem of equity in income distribution (von Nell–Brenning (1960)). Böckle (1966) goes even further by stating that there is no invariant natural law of ethics. "Der Mensch ist und gibt sich selbst sein Gesetz" (man is, and gives himself, his own law). Thus the historic character of all statements on equitable income distribution is recognised.

The protestant ethic takes the Bible alone as the basis of theological reasoning and, as an additional help (in questions of doubt and as a guideline), the writings of the reformers. As a rule, there are more "radical" and more "egalitarian" traits in protestant ethics (sometimes of a romantic type along the lines of "ideal" society of farmers and artisans) due to the origins of protestantism as a movement against religious secularisation and against oppression of the lower classes by the nobility and clergy. The radical and sometimes even utopian character of some variants of protestant ethics is intensified by Saint Augustinus' idea of divine inspiration (Luther was an Augustinian monk) in contrast to Thomas Aquinas's emphasis on rationality and natural law. On the other hand Luther's doctrine of the two realms (the Kingdom of Heaven and the order of this world) and the pietistical movement in protestantism encourage indifference towards economic and political problems, since these are not of special importance sub specie aeternitatis any way. As there is no supreme authority in protestantism on matters of belief, the range of ideas is much wider here.

Luther himself[2] was not only an outstanding theologian but also an eminent political personality. He made public his opinions on all the important political and social questions of his time in the form of letters to the princes and other influential persons, pamphlets, books and public discussions. Taking the Bible (as he understood it) as the basis for his decisions, he was always absolutely sure of the justness of his opinion. This also applies to his ideas on equitable income, which he made public on several occasions. In his main work on this subject ("Von Kaufhandlung und Wucher", On Buying and Usury, 1524) he states that the government should fix all prices so that everybody gets his appropriate income ("ziemliche Nahrung") – an opinion not very different from medieval ethics. Unfortunately, the government does not do this. In that case the "perfectly competitive market price" (to put it in modern language) should be taken by tradesmen as an equitable price. If there is none, the tradesmen should estimate the time, effort and risk needed to get the merchandise and compare that to the wage of a usual worker. This would result in a just price. In other words, an equitable income distribution is defined as being proportional to the amount of labour and the risk involved in an occupation; of course, this should result in a reasonable income for everybody including his family (an "appropriate income"). Moreover, Luther was opposed to all luxury, to large companies, financial business, interest payments, imports and unnecessary commodities, striving for profits – in short, against the

---

[2] It is not possible here to review the ideas of the other reformers. In many respects they did not coincide with Luther's ideas.

origins of capitalism in his time. But all this lies on a secondary level. A real christian does not care much for wordly goods; he has his treasure in heaven.

After Luther there was a long silence on problems of social ethics in the protestant churches, due to the fact that the protestant princes became heads of the protestant churches and to the dominant pietistical tendencies. Only at the end of the 19th century, and especially after the first World War when the protestant churches had been separated from the states in Germany, did a new social ethical movement come to life on the protestant side. Wünsch (1927) was the first to continue along the lines of Luther. Wages should be related to effort, diligence, the quality and difficulty of work and to the costs of acquiring the necessary skills. The total payment should be such as to guarantee an income according to a person's needs and position in society ("standesgemäßes Einkommen"). Social ethics demands that the income should also provide a reasonable living standard for the family; this contradicts individual ethics, which requires that income should be proportional to effort. But social ethics should be dominant. Similar to Luther, Wünsch's ideal is a modest economy which satisfies everybody's basic needs but no more. He is against the profit motive, against economic growth divorced from the satisfaction of basic needs. Brunner (1939, 1943) is more in line with the existing free enterprise system. There must be compromises in order to improve equity in practice. The individual and the community have their rights. Income should take into account the actual effort in production as well as the needs of the family. Individualistic capitalism and collectivistic communism must be rejected. Thielicke (1965), on the basis of the two realms doctrine of Luther (which is changed to a two aions doctrine), does not care much for income distribution. There is no "christian economy" anyway. Different starting points (because of differences in natural endowments or wealth) are inevitable and one has to face the facts. Equality is not feasible in this world. The real ethical problem is the *use* of income.

Whereas Thielicke might be grouped on the "right" of protestant ethics, Barth (1954 and other publications)[3] stays on the left. He denies all autonomy of special sides of the society. All ethical questions are basically settled by Christ's teaching and his life and death. All employment of labour to make money is wrong. Competition, as well as monopoly, stem from corrupt unchristian behaviour. Christian ethics means challenging everything existing. Only an attempt at this is possible. The church should always be "leftist", i.e. on the side of the proletariat and the handicapped, and for some sort of socialism. This does little to illuminate what an equitable income distribution means in any economic system. But this "leftist side" of protestantism has now taken up neo-marxist ideas and thus reversed the sequence of Luther's two realms: *first* comes this world and perhaps *afterwards* the heavenly one. This is now the dominent philosophy in the World Ecumenical Council as far as ethics is concerned (see the reports on the plenary meetings in Uppsala 1968 and Nairobi 1975). But until now it has produced no new ideas in the ethics of personal income distribution.

Professor Abbing's contribution (chapter 2) should be looked at before this review. He postulates that, in a society where people are optimally assigned to

---

[3] A review of Barth's ideas in other works may be found in Weber (1970) and Kramer (1973).

jobs, everyone will be equally satisfied. Hopefully, such a state exists; I would doubt that. In general there will be too many people thinking that they are better qualified for the highest positions and therefore feel dissatisfied in lower positions. But given that such a state exists, everybody should get equal payment. The only three ethically acceptable reasons for income differentials are then: more effort, worse working conditions (compared to the generally accepted standard) and family needs. This is a further egalitarian development of Lutheran thought, but neglects all productivity effects of the work on income – only exceptional contributions will be considered. This contradicts both the catholic ethical position as put forward in "Mater et Magistra" and all the protestant positions mentioned above. Professor Abbing is more egalitarian and more "utopian" in his demands for equity than Wünsch, Brunner and Thielicke, but less utopian and much more realistic (and therefore more christian, in my opinion) than Barth. Ethical agnosticism and utopian radicalism does not help to change the world to the advantage of the poor and the handicapped, which after all is the ultimate goal of christian ethics.

I.2.2. Conclusions: Can theological ethics help in defining equitable income distribution?

Looking back to the development of theological ethics as sketched in the subsection above, one cannot help wondering how these different and conflicting views could be expressed with the same claim to universal validity. It should be stated honestly and modestly that all ethical demands, however they may be derived, are products of human thought which develops over time. There is no specific rule of ethical behaviour valid for all time. The Bible does not give guidance specific enough to provide a well defined set of rules valid for all time. Man is left free and responsible for his own decisions and actions in this respect.

But leaving aside this false claim, there are many valuable ideas and hints to be found in theological ethics. The ever changing list of factors which should be taken into account to make income distribution equitable, the degree of egalitarism or, to put it in another way, the natural or historical differences which should be accepted as given and not compensated for, all these challenge personal judgement but do not take away the burden of personal decision.

I.2.3. Utility and Utilitarianism. The static approach

Theological and philosophical ethics[4] impose moral rules for individual and social behaviour which are taken (or supposed to be taken) from outside: either from divine revelation or from philisophical reflection or both. Utilitarianism tries to derive ethics from the individual judgements of all people in a society regarding the desirability of different social states. That means it tries to transform ethics into a

---

[4] I shall not deal with philosophical ethics here since there was no paper on that at the Noordwijk conference.

science, the propositions of which may be tested. The basic assumption of this approach is that man is able to express his preferences (wherever they come from) in the form of a transitive weak preference ordering of all relevant individual and social states. Under some additional assumptions this ordering may be represented by an individual utility function which, *in the static case* of a society consisting of n "normal" individuals, may be written:

$$u_i = f_i(z), \quad i = 1, \ldots, n, \tag{1}$$

and $f_i(z^*) > f_i(z)$, if and only if z^* is preferred to z by individual i.

Here $z = (y_1, \ldots, y_N, \bar{y}_1, \ldots, \bar{y}_M)$ is a vector describing the state of the society, $y = (y_1, \ldots, y_N)$ is the vector of endogenous variables (which may be changed by the actions of members of society) and $\bar{y} = (\bar{y}_1, \ldots, \bar{y}_M)$ is the vector of exogenous variables (which are given for the society, such as weather, natural endowments). Of course, the social state z must be attainable, not just imaginary:

$$z \in Z, \tag{1a}$$

where Z is the set of feasible social states. Bentham (1789) and John Stuart Mill (1863) took "preference" to mean "pleasure" more or less in the physical sense (along the lines of the old hedonists like Epikuros), but this is an obsolete psychology and does not concern us here.

Assume further that all utilities u_i are measured on the same scale (which requires interpersonal comparability of utilities). Now *utilitarianism* asserts that there is a *social utility function*

$$U = F(u_1, \ldots, u_n) \tag{2}$$

having the individual utilities as arguments, which assumes the form of an arithmetic mean[5]

$$U(z) = \sum_{i=1}^{n} u_i(z) \cdot w_i, \quad u_i(z) = f_i(z) \text{ in (1)}, \quad w_i > 0, \quad \sum w_i = 1, \tag{3}$$

where w_i are "weights" for the individuals. In a democratic society

$$w_i = \frac{1}{n}. \tag{3a}$$

Now a social state z^* is better than a social state z if $U(z^*) > U(z)$, and the ethical requirement is to choose a social or individual action which transforms z to z^* (if there is any).[6]

The utilitarian formula (3) may be derived from (2) by applying the biblical principle: treat other people in the same way you would like to be treated by them,

---

[5] This yields a consistent social preference ordering; see Krelle (1968). Pareto optimality is preserved. Arrow's impossibility theorem does not apply because of the assumption of interpersonal comparability of utilities; see Arrow (1951).

[6] Of course, no cheating is allowed on the part of the individuals in stating their utilities. Otherwise the weights w_i have to be chosen in such a way as to correct for that. This problem is a difficult one if people know that a social action will be taken as a result of their revealed preferences, but is not unsoluable; see Groves and Ledyard (1977).

cf. *Harsanyi* (1953, 1955, 1958, 1976). It makes explicit what the old utilitarians, in a misleading way, expressed as "the greatest happiness for the greatest number of people". There are obvious variations of (3), for example,

$$U(z) = \sum_{i=1}^{n} \log u_i(z) \cdot w_i, \qquad u_i(\cdot) > 0, \quad w_i > 0, \tag{4}$$

and

$$w_i = \frac{1}{n}. \tag{4a}$$

which still may be subsumed under utilitarianism. But utilitarianism proper is abandoned if other *special decision criteria* are postulated, even if based upon individual utility functions (1).

The following rules have been proposed:

(1) *Tinbergen's equal utility proposition* ("equal welfare for all individuals"); see Tinbergen (1975).

$$U = \max u(z) \text{ such that } u_1(z) = \ldots = u_n(z) = u(z). \tag{5}$$

This proposition has been substantially changed in Tinbergen's contribution to this book (see chapter 1) by applying the principle to social groups rather than to individuals. It is obvious that this decision rule does not yield pareto-optimal results in general. Equality in utility terms is the ultimate goal of society however large the sacrifices in general welfare may be.

(2) *Rawls maximin principle* of ethics; that social state z^* is the best among all possible social states in the set Z, when the utility of the least fortunate individual is largest; see Rawls (1971).

$$z^* \leftarrow \max_z \left[\min \left(u_1(z), \ldots, u_n(z) \right) \right], \qquad z \in Z. \tag{6}$$

But there are some obvious counter examples showing that this rule cannot be universally applied (e.g. almost all schooling efforts should be directed to the most handicapped and retarded individuals where the results are minimal; see Harsanyi (1973, 1974). Rawls defence is not convincing; see Rawls (1974).

(3) *The majority rule*: that social state $z^* \in Z$ is best which defeats all other social states in a voting process

$$z^* \leftarrow \#\tilde{u}(z^*) \geq \#\tilde{u}(z), \qquad z^*, z \in Z. \tag{7}$$

where $\#\tilde{u}(z^*)$ means the number of individuals preferring z^* over z. It is well known that this criterion may lead to inconsistent social preference orderings; see Krelle (1968). It is not universally applicable, therefore.

There are other criteria also, for instance *Selten's equity core*; see Selten (1976).

All these special criteria seem to be inferior to the utilitarian formula (3) or (4) in general, but satisfactory as approximations in special cases. But the static approach as in (3) or (4) is much too simple a guideline for personal or social ethics.

In the following section I should like to sketch a dynamic extension of the utilitarian theory which comes closer to practical applicability.

I.2.4. *The dynamic utilitarian approach in ethics*

To use the utilitarian approach in practice, "normality" has to be defined. Not all human beings can be included in those whose preference orderings are taken into account when forming the ethical rules of society. Children, the mentally ill, those with preference orderings which if generally applied would destroy mankind (such as sadists, drug addicts etc.) have to be excluded. (This takes care of the "basic principle" of objective ethics in section I.1 above). There is no clear cut line of division, of course. All people whose preference orderings are excluded from consideration are nevertheless members of the society. Their actions as well as their welfare have also to be considered. We shall further assume, that society has decided on a future discount rate $\rho > 0$ and that there is no uncertainty.[7] In this case the utilitarian approach suggests that a sequence of social states $z(0), z(1), \ldots$ should be evaluated according to the discounted social utility

$$\bar{U}(z) = \sum_{t=0}^{\infty} U_t(z(t)) \cdot \left(\frac{1}{1+\rho}\right)^t ,^8 \tag{8}$$

where

$$U_t(z(t)) = F_t(u_1(t), \ldots, u_{n_t}(t)), \qquad \text{cf. (2)}, \tag{8a}$$

$$u_i(t) = f_{it}(z(t)), \qquad i = 1, \ldots, n_t, \qquad \text{cf. (1)}, \tag{8b}$$

$$z(t) = (y(t), \bar{y}(t)) \tag{8c}$$

$$y(t) = (y_1(t), \ldots, y_{N_t}(t)), \qquad \text{the vector of endogenous variables}, \tag{8d}$$

$$\bar{y}(t) = (\bar{y}_1(t), \ldots, \bar{y}_{M_t}(t)), \qquad \text{the vector of exogenous variables.}^9 \tag{8e}$$

The endogenous variables $y(t)$ describe the characteristics of each person in society (e.g. income, type of employment, mental state) which can be influenced by actions of members of the society. The exogenous variables $\bar{y}(t)$ indicate those facts which cannot be influenced (e.g. the weather conditions, world market conditions (in certain situations) etc.). $z(t)$ is the vector of all these state variables. The vector of the endogenous variables depends on the decision vector x_g of the society as a whole ($=$ government), on the decision vector x_p of all people in the society (including those whose judgement does not count) in the current and past periods, and on the social state z in past periods:

---

[7] It is not difficult to introduce risk if everybody accepts the von Neumann–Morgenstern axioms of rational behaviour under risk.
[8] For practical purposes ∞ has to be replaced by some finite time horizon T.
[9] Note that in the social utility function F_t, as well as in the individual utility functions f_{it}, the number n_t of people whose judgements are included when defining ethical rules, and the number N_t and M_t of endogenous and exogenous variables, may vary over time. There are theories about changes in the utility functions; see Krelle (1968, 1973), for example.

Introduction

$$y(t) = G_t(z(t-1), z(t-2), \ldots, x_g(t), x_g(t-1), \ldots, x_p(t), x_p(t-1), \ldots, \bar{y}(t)). \tag{8f}$$

Let us assume temporarily that there are behaviour functions for each individual depending on the state of society, the decisions of the government (such as tax and expenditure rates), previous individual decisions and the exogenous variables:

$$x_p(t) = H_t(z(t-1), z(t-2), \ldots, x_g(t), x_g(t-1), \ldots, x_p(t-1), x_p(t-2), \ldots, \bar{y}(t)) \tag{8g}$$

They describe the *actual* behaviour of the members of the society whatever may happen. By substituting back, the vector $z(t)$ of all state variables may be expressed as function of former states, of decisions, and of the exogenous variables:

$$z(t) = \varphi_t(z(t-1), \ldots, x_g(t), x_g(t-1), \ldots, x_p(t-1), \ldots, \bar{y}(t), \bar{y}(t)).^{10} \tag{8h}$$

It is obvious that government and private decisions should be such as to maximise social utility. Thus from the point of view of utilitarian ethics a sequence $x_g^*(0), x_g^*(1), \ldots, x_p^*(0), x_p^*(1), \ldots$ of decisions yielding a sequence $z^*(0), z^*(1), \ldots$ of social states is better than another sequence yielding $z(0), z(1), \ldots$ if and only if

$$\bar{U}(z^*) > \bar{U}(z). \tag{8i}$$

In order to get the best possible sequence of government decisions, the control theoretical problem

$$\bar{U}(z) = \max_{x_g(0), x_g(1), \ldots} \tag{9}$$

subject to (8h) and to $x_g(0) \in X_g(0), x_g(1) \in X_g(1), \ldots$

has to be solved, where $X_g(t)$ denotes the set of feasible government actions. This is called *act utilitarianism* in the literature (see Brandt (1959), Harsanyi (1976)), because the consequences of the acts of *one* decision maker (in this case, the government) are considered, whereas all other people only passively respond. Social welfare is determined by the "average judgement" of all "normal" persons (as it will be at the time when the government action is formulated) and future judgements are discounted: the judgement of this generation on the action of the present government counts more than the judgement of future generations.

For individual ethics, *act utilitarianism* is defined in the same way: now individuals act so as to maximize the social utility function. In their decision they take account of the possible reactions of other agents. For instance, person i solves problem (9) with respect to his decision variables $x_i(0), x_i(1), \ldots$ In most cases the solution to this problem will not maximise the personal utility of agent i:

$$\bar{u}_i(z) = \sum_{t=0}^{\infty} u_i(t) \cdot \left(\frac{1}{1+\rho_i}\right)^t, \quad u_i(t) = f_{it}(z(t)), \tag{9a}$$

$$\rho_i = \text{time discount rate of person } i,$$

$$i = 1, \ldots, n_t,$$

---

[10] A special form of (8h) is an econometric forecasting model.

under the constraint that everybody else behaves as before, which means that (8g) holds for everybody except person i. This may be expressed as

$$x_i(t) = H_t^{(i)}(\cdot). \tag{9b}$$

Moreover, the actions $x_i(t)$ have to be chosen from a set of feasible actions $X_i(t)$:

$$x_i(t) \in X_i(t), \quad t = 0, 1, \ldots, \quad i = 1, \ldots, n_t. \tag{9c}$$

Actions of this kind cannot be called "moral", in general. They may be selfish and lead to very undesirable social states. Stealing, murdering, breaking contracts, blackmail et cetera may be rewarding from the individual point of view.

Act utilitarianism as defined by (9) is not subject to this type of criticism. But there are other shortcomings: according to this principle promises should be broken or even persons killed if such measures would increase social utility even to the slightest degree. Moreover, if the agents disregard the strategic interdependencies of their actions, the actual outcome of true moral actions may be far from optimal. For these reasons *rule utilitarianism* has been proposed (see Brandt (1959), Harsanyi (1976)), suggesting that *rules of behaviour* rather than single actions should be the arguments of the social utility function. Each person should choose a rule of action so as to maximise social utility under the assumption that everybody else uses the same rule. The rules have to be defined broadly enough to allow for individual differences in the actual decisions. If the decision rules are derived that way, each person should act according to these rules irrespective of whether his action would appear to be optimal in the specific situation.

In equations (8f)–(8h) and (9) the vectors $x_g(t)$ and $x_p(t)$ should now be interpreted as vectors of decision rules of the government and private persons such as "do not break promises unless keeping the promise would reduce person i's utility by more than $\bar{u}_i$," or "give money to person i if his discounted utility after the transfer would be higher by at least $\bar{v}_i$ times the amount your discounted utility would be lower." Thus the rule decision vector of person j in period t may be expressed as $x_j(t) = (\bar{u}_{j1}(t), \ldots, \bar{u}_{jn}(t), \bar{v}_{j1}(t), \ldots, \bar{v}_{jn}(t), \ldots)$. Under *rule utilitarianism* person j solves the ethical problem:

$$\bar{U}(z) = \max_{x_j(0), x_j(1), \ldots} \tag{10}$$

subject to $z(t) = f_t(z(t-1), \ldots, x_1(t), x_1(t-1), \ldots, x_n(t), x_n(t-1), \ldots, \bar{y}(t), \bar{y}(t-1), \ldots)$
and to

$$x_i(0) = x_j(0), x_i(1) = x_j(1), \ldots, \forall i \in \{1, \ldots, n\}, j \in \{1, \ldots, n\}, i \neq j$$

$$x_j(0) \in X_j(0), x_j(1) \in X_j(1), \ldots$$

Rule utilitarianism is very similar to the Kantian proposition that one should act in such a way that the principle of that action could be made a general rule for society.

But rule utilitarianism has some drawbacks. There are infinitely many conceivable "rules" governing the same type of action. Thus the most attractive feature of utilitarianism, its operationality, is lost; moreover, the outcome depends heavily on the way the rules are defined. Take the example of table 1a where two persons

A and B decide on the "principle of action" 1 and 2 (e.g. whether a promise should be broken if the utility loss by keeping the promise is low (= principle 1) or high (= principle 2)). The entries are the social utilities. Only the figures on the diagonal are taken into account in rule utilitarianism. Thus the principle 2 is morally accepted. The combination (2, 2) is reached, though the combination (1, 2) yields a higher social utility. This could be alright: keeping promises might be worth sacrificing some social utility. But if the "principle of action" is specified as in table 1b which indicates that a person in situation A and a person in situation B should adopt different combinations of conditions under which promises should be broken, the optimal combination (1, 2) turns out to be morally best. Thus there must be "rules for defining rules" in order to get definite results.

Table 1a. Social utilities.

Rule of behaviour of person A	Rule of behaviour of person B	
	1	2
1	1	4
2	2	3

Table 1b. Social utilities [a]

Rule of behaviour of person A	Rule of behaviour of person B			
	1' = (1,1)	2' = (1,2)	3' = (2,1)	4' = (2,2)
1' = (1,1) [b]	1	–	–	–
2' = (1,2)	–	4	–	–
3' = (2,1)	–	–	2	–
4' = (2,2)	–	–	–	3

[a] Dashes (–) indicate "not defined".
[b] (i, j) = combination of rule i for person A and rule j for person B in table 1a.

In our context of the ethics of income distribution, operationality is of primary importance. Therefore we shall use a variant of act utilitarianism called *simultaneous act utilitarianism,* under which social utility is maximised *simultaneously* with respect to the actions of all agents, including the government:

$$\bar{U}(z) = \max_{x_1(0), x_1(1),\ldots,x_n(0),x_n(1),\ldots} \tag{10a}$$

subject to $z(t) = f_t(z(t-1), \ldots, x_1(t), x_1(t-1), \ldots, x_n(t), x_n(t-1), \ldots, \bar{y}_t, \bar{y}_{t-1}, \ldots)$

and to

$$x_i(\tau) \in X_i(\tau), \quad i = 1, \ldots, n; \quad \tau = 0, 1, \ldots.$$

For simplicity we restate the last feasibility constraint as

$$\underline{x}_i(\tau) \leq x_i(\tau) \leq \bar{x}_i(\tau).$$

The solution $x_1^*(0), x_1^*(1), \ldots, x_n^*(0), x_n^*(1), \ldots$ of this control theoretic problem defines the ethically acceptable actions under simultaneous act utilitarianism. Of course, an individual will not be able to solve (10a), in general. Usually he is only able to judge his own affairs. Therefore ethical demands should be imposed on the individual in the form of constraints on his admissible actions. Thus ethics may be defined as a set of constraints $\underline{x}_i^*, \bar{x}_i^*$ for each person i such that personal utility maximisation according to (9a) under the constraints $\underline{x}_i^*, \bar{x}_i^*$ for each person i, yields the same results as the solution of (10a):

$$\bar{u}_i(z) = \max_{x_i(0), x_i(1), \ldots} \tag{10b}$$

subject to $z(t) = f_t(\cdot)$ and to

$$\underline{x}_i^*(\tau) \leq x_i(\tau) \leq \bar{x}_i^*(\tau), \qquad \tau = 0, 1, \ldots; \quad i = 1', \ldots, n.$$

With appropriately chosen ethical constraints $\underline{x}_i^*, \bar{x}_i^*$, the simultaneous solution of (10b) for all persons $1, \ldots, n$ (forming a Nash-equilibrium point) coincides with the solution of (10a).

Tables 2a and 2b illustrate this procedure. Table 2a gives an example for a two-person society in which everybody has three potential actions.

Table 2a.

Action of person A	Action of person B		
	1	2	3
1	10,10	7,12	4,13
2	12,7	9,9	5,10
3	13,4	10,5	6,6[a]

[a] Nash-equilibrium point.

The entries are the personal utilities of person A (left figure) and person B (right figure). The utilities may be interpreted, for example, as incomes. Table 2b gives the social utilities of the different states under the assumption that the arithmetic mean yields the social utility (cf. (3)).

Table 2b.

Action of person A	Action of person B		
	1	2	3
1	10	9.5	8.5
2	9.5	9	7.5
3	8.5	7.5	6

The entries are the social utilities.

In table 2a the strategies (3, 3) form a Nash-equilibrium point: nobody can deviate from this strategy when the other keeps to it, without substantially worsening his situation. This is the solution for unconstrained personal utility maximisation. If actions 2 and 3 are "forbidden" by the accepted ethical standards (1, 1) will be the new Nash-point and therefore the solution; and this coincides with social utility maximisation.

Simultaneous act utilitarianism states the ethical demand that everybody restrains his set of possible actions in such a way that, by maximising individual utilities under these constraints, the best possible social outcome results.

I.2.5. *Conclusions: Does utilitarian ethics help in defining equitable income distribution?*

The advantage of utilitarian ethics is that it reaches definite conclusions about equitable income distribution. Take the *static approach* as the simplest example and assume that utilitarianism is accepted in the form given by (4) under the constraint (1a). Let us simplify further and assume $u_i(z)$ to have the form $u_i(A_i, C_i)$, where A_i = labour, C_i = real income of person i, $w_i = 1/n$, $\partial u_i/\partial A_i < 0$, $\partial^2 u_i/\partial A_i^2 < 0$, $\partial u_i/\partial C_i > 0$, $\partial^2 u_i/\partial C_i^2 < 0$. The constraint (1a) is the production function $\sum_{i=1}^{n} C_i = f(A_1, \ldots, A_n)$, $\partial f/\partial A_i > 0$, $\partial^2 f/\partial A_i^2 < 0$. In this case optimal income distribution is determined simultaneously with optimal labour input and optimal production by solving

$$\tilde{U} = \sum_{i=1}^{n} \log u_i(A_i, C_i) = \max_{C_1, \ldots, C_n, A_1, \ldots, A_n} \tag{11a}$$

under the constraint

$$g = -\sum_{i=1}^{n} C_i + f(A_1, \ldots, A_n) = 0. \tag{11b}$$

The necessary and sufficient optimality conditions are

$$\frac{1}{u_i} \partial u_i/\partial C_i = \lambda: \tag{11c}$$

each person should get an income such that the *relative* marginal utilities of income are equal (i.e. those who have a high utility of income should get more in absolute terms).[11]

$$[-(1/u_i)\partial u_i/\partial A_i]/[\partial f/\partial A_i] = \lambda: \tag{11d}$$

each person should work until the *relative* marginal disutilities of labour, weighted by the marginal products of labour, are equal (i.e. those whose disutility of labour (or marginal labour effort) is high should work less, so that the marginal product of their labour also becomes large).

---

[11] $\lambda > 0$ is a Lagrangian multiplier.

Equating (11c) and (11d) yields

$$\partial u_i/\partial C_i = -[\partial u_i/\partial A_i]/[\partial f/\partial A_i]: \tag{11e}$$

an equitable income distribution is reached if everybody's marginal utility of income equals his marginal labour effort relative to the marginal product of his labour.

Thus it is evident that a person's factual contribution to society as well as his personal effort and his ability to enjoy income has to be taken into account if an income distribution is to deserve the name "equitable". Equality of income or of utility is not equity from the point of view of utilitarian ethics.

Professor *Sen*'s paper (chapter 3 of this volume) comes to a similar but more radical conclusion: greater inequality may lead to higher social welfare, since "equality" and "social welfare" are two quite distinct concepts. Moreover, Professor *v. Weizsäcker* (chapter 4) shows that simply taking actual income distribution as a measure of the welfare distribution may yield wrong results, due to different individual income profiles over the lifetime and to different degrees of risk involved in different occupations.

Professor *van Praag* (chapter 5) is able to derive individual utility functions of income from household surveys. These functions are of the cumulative log-normal form. If one accepts his type of measurement, the calculations suggested in equations suggested in equations (11a) to (11e) may be carried out numerically.

It is not possible to treat the dynamic case in a similar way, due to lack of space. Only some obvious results can be given.

(1) In changing income distributions, not only the direct impact (e.g. the poor get more, the rich get less) but all temporary and future indirect effects have to be taken into account; for example, those on employment, the rate of inflation, the rate of growth.
(2) The best intentions of those who initiate the change do not count ethically. What counts are the real social consequences as judged by all "normal" persons.
(3) The consequences have not only to be judged according to our preferences but also according to the preferences of all future generations. Since they are not yet living, we have to act for them as well.
(4) Ethics means the sacrifice of some freedoms (e.g. the freedom to steal, to rob, to break promises, to cheat). In the case of income distribution it means the sacrifice of the right to extract more income (profit or labour income) if this results in a worse social state in the future.

In order to be more specific, the necessary and sufficient conditions for the solution of the dynamic systems (9) and (10) have to be derived. It is surprising to find that the results of the static approaches and the "general principles" (1)–(4) above are not very far from theological ethics as stated in the "Mater and Magistra" of Johannes XXIII and from some of the ideas of Wünsch, Brunner and others on the protestant side, though very different from "radical" protestant ethics.

II. The theory of personal income distribution

We now leave the normative aspect of income distribution and turn to the factual side. The aim here is to integrate the different strands of thought to be found in later chapters of this volume into one general coherent theory of personal income distribution, and to link this theory to macroeconomics in such a way that personal income distribution may be explained simultaneously with the functional income distribution and other macroeconomic phenomena using, say, an econometric forecasting system.

II.1. The conceptual framework: A complete system of income distribution measures

II.1.1. The necessary microdata

Real knowledge about personal income distribution requires a consistent system of statistical data available at regular time intervals. All theories on personal income distribution are purely speculative unless they can be tested against reality. Unfortunately, Professor *Wiles* (chapter 7) is absolutely right to emphasise the deficiency of our knowledge in this field. The first step towards improving the situation is devising a suitable conceptual framework which should be used in statistical data collection. The necessary data must come from two sources: micro-surveys and the system of national accounts. Both statistics have to be conceptually compatible. In this section we deal with the micro-data base.

A sample of all private households in the economy should be questioned each year concerning:

(α) *The characteristics of the household*
  (1) The sector of the economy from which the household gets its main income or to which the household belongs (e.g. agriculture, engineering or student, pensioner). This classification by sector must be consistent with the classification used for macrodata from GNP, employment and other statistics.
  (2) Type of employment of the main income recipient of the household (e.g. self-employed with $0, 1-10, 11-50, \ldots$ employees; employed as a manager, executive, clerical worker, skilled worker, unskilled worker ...). This classification must again be consistent with that of macroeconomic statistics.
  (3) Household composition number (sex, and age of household members ...).
  (4) Educational background of the members of the household (primary school, secondary school, university ...).
  (5) Number of hours worked by each member of the household.

(β) *The type and size of income of each household member*
  (1) Income from self-employment before and after tax and social insurance
  (2) Wage income of each income earner of the household, before and after tax and social insurance
  (3) Unearned income from savings accounts, bonds, shares, land, ...
  (4) Transfer income from social insurance, other insurance, pensions, trusts, ...

(γ) *Household expenditure and saving*
   (1) Expenditure on insurance (excluding social insurance), for food, clothing, housing, private cars, other consumer durables, ...
   (2) Savings (or dissavings) on current accounts, savings accounts, bonds, shares, property, ...

II.1.2. *Measures of income distribution*

The microdata of section II.1.1 above cannot be used directly, as a rule. They must be summarised by distributional characteristics to be of practical use in the theory of personal income distribution. There are different measures of income inequality which may be grouped into two categories: functional (or economic) indices and heuristic (or purely statistical) indices.

(α) *Functional (or economic) indices of income inequality*
   These are measures derived from social utilities: income inequality is measured by its effect on social welfare. This approach is equivalent to the functional price and quantity indices suggested by Frisch (1936), Samuelson and Swamy (1974) and others. In the context of personal income distribution the Dalton and the Atkinson measures are used; see Dalton (1920), Atkinson (1970, 1975). Both measures are discussed in this volume in the contributions of *Sen* (chapter 3), *v. Weizsäcker* (chapter 4), *van Praag* (chapter 5) and others. The main problem is, of course, to determine the social welfare function. Since this is a difficult problem it may be wise to stick to the conventional inequality measures of the heuristic indices, at least for the time being.

(β) *Heuristic (or purely statistical) indices of income inequality*
   There are several well known general statistical measures of location and dispersion; e.g. the mean, variance, skewness, kurtosis, and different moments about the mean. Different percentiles are also used, mostly quintiles and deciles. In addition there are specific statistical measures in the income distribution literature, such as the Pareto α, the Gini coefficient, the Theil coefficient, the Kolm measure and others. Professor *van Praag* (chapter 5) and *Michal* (chapter 8) deal with these. Professor Michal suggests a new type of index – a marginal utility weighted Gini coefficient of income inequality – thus blending the two approaches. Most of these indices are used in the empirical chapters of this book; see part III, chapters 7–10.
   For our purposes it is not necessary to specify exactly which measures of inequality should be used. The different moments about the mean, the Gini coefficient and the upper and lower deciles would all be equally satisfactory, in my opnion. The same measures should be used for other household characteristics such as consumption and savings ratios, age, years of schooling etc..

II.1.3. *The connection between micro- and macrodata: The complete system of income distribution measures*

Distribution theory has to be fully integrated into general economic theory and not just loosely attached to it as a sort of supplement. The relationship between functional and personal income distribution and the repercussions of personal income distribution on the most important macroeconomic variables, such as GNP, employment, and the rate of growth, have to be analysed. In this subsection the conceptual framework for that is developed.

We start with the first two columns in table 3 which show the value added by productive sector i broken down into payments W for different kinds of labour input and imputed or real payments Q, for profits, and R, for different kinds of interest and rent payments. The income of self-employed persons is subdivided into labour income W^s and profit income Q^s by imputing the same wage income to a self-employed person as the wage income W^e of an equivalently employed person would have been. The subdivision of the economy into sectors, and the subdivision of different types of employment, self-employment and interest and rent payments, should be the same as used in macrodata collection.

The set of all private households is subdivided into subsets according to the main income source of the household. The subset of households whose main income stems from employment or self-employment in production sector i will be attached to that sector (see third column of table 3). All other households (e.g. those of students, pensioners) are subdivided according to other criteria and treated in the same way. From microdata the information reproduced in the following columns of table 3 may be obtained. *Labour income* $Y^e_{i\mu}(L)$ of the household attached to employment type μ of sector i ($\mu = 1, \ldots, m$) consists of the main labour income $W^e_{i\mu}(i\mu e)$ from employment in subsector μ of production sector i, of other labour income $W^{ee}_{i\mu}$ from employment in other sectors and from labour income $W^{se}_{i\mu}$ from self-employment in all sectors. Labour income $Y^s_{i\mu}(L)$ of a household whose main income stems from self-employment of type μ in sector i is subdivided into similar parts. The *profit income* $Y^e_{i\mu}(Q)$ of households whose main income stems from employment consists of profit income $Q^{se}_{i\mu}$ from self-employment in all sectors and from other interest and rent receipts $Z^e_{i\mu}$. Profit income $Y^s_{i\mu}(Q)$ of households whose main income $Q^s_{i\mu}(i\mu s)$ stems from self-employment of type μ in sector i consists of this income and income $Q^{ss}_{i\mu}$ from self-employment in other sectors and from interest and rent receipts $Z^s_{i\mu}$. Factor income is defined as the sum of labour and profit income. Adding transfer income $T^e_{Ri\mu}$ and $T^s_{Ri\mu}$ yields total money income $Y^e_{i\mu}(\text{tot})$ and $Y^s_{i\mu}(\text{tot})$, respectively. Subtracting social insurance contributions and taxes $T^e_{i\mu}$ and $T^s_{i\mu}$ gives disposable income $Y^e_{i\mu}(\text{disp})$ and $Y^s_{i\mu}(\text{disp})$. For welfare analyses, income in kind $Y^e_{Ki\mu}$ and $Y^s_{Ki\mu}$ should be added to yield net income $Y^e_{i\mu}(\text{net})$ and $Y^s_{i\mu}(\text{net})$ respectively.

The bottom line of table 3 gives the sum of the corresponding columns. The notation is self-explanatory.

Let $L^e_{i\mu}$, $L^s_{i\mu}$ be the number of hours worked in sector i by employed or self-employed persons of type μ; $B^e_{i\mu}$, $B^s_{i\mu}$ the number of persons employed or self-employed; and $B^c_{i\mu}$ a measure of the total productive units in category $i\mu$. Now the

Table 3.

	Factor payments of productive sector i, $i=1,\ldots,n$		Set of households attached to sector i, employment types $1,\ldots,m$	Income of households attached to production sector i, $i=1,\ldots,$	
	Labor income	Profit income		Labour income	Profit income
Types of employment	W^e_{i1} $\vdots$ W^e_{im}		$\leftrightarrow \{H^e_{i1}\}$ $\vdots$ $\leftrightarrow \{H^e_{im}\}$	$\leftrightarrow Y^e_{i1}(L) = W^e_{i1}(i1e) + W^{ee}_{i1} + W^{se}_{i1}$ $\vdots$ $\leftrightarrow Y^e_{im}(L) = W^e_{im}(ime) + W^{ee}_{im} + W^{se}_{im}$	$Y^e_{i1}(Q) = Q^{se}_{i1} + Z^e_{i1}$ $\vdots$ $Y^e_{im}(Q) = Q^{se}_{im} + Z^e_{im}$
Types of self-employment	W^s_{i1} $\vdots$ W^s_{im}	Q^s_{i1} $\vdots$ Q^s_{im}	$\leftrightarrow \{H^s_{i1}\}$ $\vdots$ $\leftrightarrow \{H^s_{im}\}$	$\leftrightarrow Y^s_{i1}(L) = W^s_{i1}(i1s) + W^{es}_{i1} + W^{ss}_{i1}$ $\vdots$ $\leftrightarrow Y^s_{im}(L) = W^s_{im}(ims) + W^{es}_{im} + W^{ss}_{im}$	$Y^s_{i1}(Q) = Q^s_{i1}(i1s) + Q^{ss}_{i1} + Z^s_{i1}$ $\vdots$ $Y^s_{im}(Q) = Q^s_{im}(ims) + Q^{ss}_{im} + Z^s_{im}$
Types of productive corporations belonging to sector i		Q^c_{i1} $\vdots$ Q^c_{im}			
Types of interest and rent payments	R_{i1} $\vdots$ R_{im}				
Sum or set	W_i	Q_i	$\{H_i\}$	$Y_i(L) = W_i(i) + W^e_i + W^s_i$	$Y_i(Q) = Q^s_i + Q^{s'}_i + Z_i$
Value added by sector i	$= Y_i$		Set of all households not attached to sector i $\{H_k\}$	$Y_k(L) = W^0_k + W^0_k$	Income of households k not attached to $Y_k(Q) = Q^0_k + Z^0_k$
			Sum of all household incomes	$Y(L) = \sum_i Y_i(L) + \sum_k Y_k(L)$	$Y(Q) = \sum_i Y_i(Q) + \sum_k Y_k(Q)$

average wage rate w per hour and wage income $\bar{w}$ per person may be defined

$$w^r_{i\mu} = W^r_{i\mu}/L^r_{i\mu}; \qquad \bar{w}^r_{i\mu} = W^r_{i\mu}/B^r_{i\mu}, \qquad r \in \{e,s\}. \tag{12a}$$

This applies to the first two columns of table 3.

Similarly, let $L^e_{hi\mu}, L^s_{hi\mu}$ be the number of hours worked of type μ by members of a household $h \in \{H^e_{i\mu}\}, \{H^s_{i\mu}\}$ getting its main income $W^e_{hi\mu}(i\mu e), W^s_{hi\mu}(i\mu s)$ from labour in section $i\mu$. Let $B^e_{hi\mu}, B^s_{hi\mu}$ be the number of household members getting this income and $\bar{B}^e_{hi\mu}, \bar{B}^s_{hi\mu}$ the number of household members in adult equivalent units. Now the wage rates w_h per hour and the wage income $\bar{w}_h$ per person may be defined with respect to household h:

$$w^r_{hi\mu} = W^r_{hi\mu}(i\mu r)/L^r_{hi\mu}; \qquad \bar{w}^r_{hi\mu} = W^r_{hi\mu}(i\mu r)/B^r_{hi\mu}, \qquad r \in \{e,s\}. \tag{12b}$$

Factor income	Total money income	Disposable income	Net income including Income in kind
$Y_{i1}^e = Y_{i1}^e(L) + Y_{i1}^e(Q)$	$Y_{i1}^e(\text{tot}) = Y_{i1}^e + T_{Ri1}^e$	$Y_{i1}^e(\text{disp}) = Y_{i1}^e(\text{tot}) - T_{i1}^e$	$Y_{i1}^e(\text{net}) = Y_{i1}^e(\text{disp}) + Y_{Ki1}^e$
$\vdots$	$\vdots$	$\vdots$	$\vdots$
$Y_{im}^e = Y_{im}^e(L) + Y_{im}^e(Q)$	$Y_{im}^e(\text{tot}) = Y_{im}^e + T_{Rim}^e$	$Y_{im}^e(\text{disp}) = Y_{im}^e(\text{tot}) - T_{im}^e$	$Y_{im}^e(\text{net}) = Y_{im}^e(\text{disp}) + Y_{Kim}^e$
$Y_{i1}^s = Y_{i1}^s(L) + Y_{i1}^s(Q)$	$Y_{i1}^s(\text{tot}) = Y_{i1}^s + T_{Ri1}^s$	$Y_{i1}^s(\text{disp}) = Y_{i1}^s(\text{tot}) - T_{i1}^s$	$Y_{i1}^s(\text{net}) = Y_{i1}^s(\text{disp}) + Y_{Ki1}^s$
$\vdots$	$\vdots$	$\vdots$	$\vdots$
$Y_{im}^s = Y_{im}^s(L) + Y_{im}^s(Q)$	$Y_{im}^s(\text{tot}) = Y_{im}^s + T_{Rim}^s$	$Y_{im}^s(\text{disp}) = Y_{im}^s(\text{tot}) - T_{im}^s$	$Y_{im}^s(\text{net}) = Y_{im}^s(\text{disp}) + Y_{Kim}^s$
$Y_i^f = Y_i(L) + Y_i(Q)$	$Y_i^{\text{tot}} = Y_i^f + T_{Ri}$	$Y_i^{\text{disp}} = Y_i^{\text{tot}} - T_i$	$Y_i^{\text{net}} = Y_i^{\text{disp}} + Y_{Ki}$

any productive sector, $k = n + 1, \ldots, z$

$Y_k^f = Y_k(L) + Y_k(Q)$	$Y_k^{\text{tot}} = Y_k^f + T_{Rk}$	$Y_k^{\text{disp}} = Y_k^{\text{tot}} + T_k$	$Y_k^{\text{net}} = Y_k^{\text{disp}} + Y_{Kk}$
$Y^f = \sum_i Y_i^f + \sum_k Y_k^f$	$Y^{\text{tot}} = \sum_i Y_i^{\text{tot}} + \sum_k Y_k^{\text{tot}}$	$Y^{\text{disp}} = \sum_i Y_i^{\text{disp}} + \sum_k Y_k^{\text{disp}}$	$Y^{\text{net}} = Y^{\text{disp}} + Y_K$

This applies to the fourth column of table 3.

As a rule, the average wage rates of households belonging to subsector $i\mu$, calculated from (12b), will differ from the average wage rates of subsector $i\mu$ in (12a). To restore consistency the income and employment figures have to be adapted.

Similarly, all other income concepts may be related to the number of working hours, the number of household members getting the income in question and the number of household members in adult equivalent units. Important variables in this context are disposable income y_h^{disp} and the net income per household member:

$$y_h^{\text{disp}} = Y_h^{\text{disp}}/\bar{B}_h; \quad y_h^{\text{net}} = Y_h^{\text{net}}/\bar{B}_h \text{ for household } h \tag{12c}$$

We now define the *complete system of income distribution measures*. Let $D(Z)$ be a vector of distribution measures for a vector Z of grouped multidimensional data. The measures may be chosen from those discussed in section II.1.2 above. The vector $D(Z)$ covers distributions within each group, as well as distributions between the groups (and unions of groups), for each dimension of the data set. Consider income distribution from the aspect of factor payments (the first two columns of table 3). Let

$$Z = \begin{cases} (W, Q) = \text{the vector of all elements of the first two columns in table 3,} \\ (W/L) = \text{the vector of wage rates,} \\ (W/B) = \text{the vector of per capita labour incomes,} \\ (Q^s/B^s) = \text{the vector of per capita profit incomes from self-employment,} \\ (Q^c/B^c) = \text{the vector of profit incomes per unit size.} \end{cases}$$

(13a)

Now $D(Z)$, for all definitions of Z according to (13a), constitutes a complete system of income distribution measures from the viewpoint of production.

Alternatively define Z, from the fourth to the last column of table 3, to be:

$$Z = \begin{cases} (Y_h, W_h, Q_h, Z_h, T_{Rh}, T_h) = \text{the vector of all elements from the fourth to the last column in table 3,} \\ (W_h/L_h) = \text{the vector of wage rates,} \\ (W_h/B_h) = \text{the vector of per capita labour incomes,} \\ (Q^s_h/B^s_h) = \text{the vector of per capita profit incomes,} \\ (Y^f_h/\bar{B}_h) = \text{the vector of factor income per standardised household member,} \\ (Y^{tot}_h/\bar{B}_h) = \text{the vector of total money income per standardised household member,} \\ (Y^{disp}_h/\bar{B}_h) = \text{the vector of disposable income per standardised household member,} \\ (Y^{net}_h/\bar{B}_h) = \text{the vector of net income per standardised household member.} \end{cases}$$

(13b)

$D(Z)$, for all definitions of Z according to (13b), constitutes a complete system of income distribution measures from the household side. The dimensions of the income distributions are types of income; types and number of income receiving households; types, number, age, sex, educational background (e.g. years of schooling),... of income receiving persons. Of course, different distribution measures are sometimes related; e.g. for distributions in one dimension and for independent normal distributions, the mean of the sum of all observations equals the sum of the means of observations within a group, and the same applies to the variances.

Unfortunately, a complete system of income distribution measures is not known for any economy. But at least some distributions are known in some dimensions. In this volume Professor *Wiles* (chapter 7) provides figures for the distribution of total money income and disposable income in the U.S., Canada and the U.K., by household size. Professor *Morrison* (chapter 10) gives distribution figures for the total income of persons and household (and income by age group and type of employment) in some developed and less developed countries. Professor *Michal* (chapter 8) estimates distribution indices for the per capita household income of different types of households in Hungary, Czechoslovakia, Poland and the GDR. He also gives figures for average earnings of employed people of different types from the production aspect. Professor *Vielrose* (chapter 9) provides distribution figures for total money income and disposable income in Poland, as well as for wages for different types of employment in various production sectors and for total money income of people with different levels of education. Thus at least some hints are given as to the actual income distribution.

II.2. *The theory of personal income distribution*

Economics must not stop at the description of facts. Observed facts have to be explained, a theory of personal income distribution must be developed. On the one hand this theory should explain the distribution of the different types of income (labour income, profit income, total money income, disposable income, net income). This includes theories on different means of redistribution and their effects. On the other hand, a distribution theory should also analyse the repercussions of income distribution on other economic variables such as the level and rate of growth of GNP, labour supply and demand, productivity of labour and the rate of inflation. We shall consider these different branches of distribution theory below, but only the theory of the earnings distribution will be dealt with in some detail.

II.2.1. *Statistical theories of income distribution*

These theories do not go into the details of the economic process of income generation but try to capture the statistical laws. Gibrat (1931) was the first to suggest this approach by assuming a "law of proportionate effect": $x_t = x_{t-1}(1 + v_t)$, where x_t is income in period t and v_t is a normally distributed random variable. He proved that this stochastic process generates a log-normal distribution.

Dr. *Wagner* (chapter 6) extends this approach by considering a Markov-process where the transition probabilities from one income class to another depend on the income class in a more complicated way and are different in the upward and downward directions. This could apply to all the income concepts above, but the verbal interpretation given by Wagner seems to suggest that he wants to apply the theory to the distribution of labour income rather than other types of income.

Professor *Näslund* (chapter 12) derives the income distribution by maximising the entropy $H(p) = -\sum_i p_i \ln p_i$ under a constraint $p \in C$, where p_i is the probability of an income in the range i and C is given by a system of equations determining the income distribution from propensities to save, along the lines of Kaldor. This theory could be applied to all types of income distributions but seems to be best applied to the distribution of profit income.

The attractive feature of these types of theories is that they look at the distribution as a stochastic process, which it is in reality. The disadvantage is the small economic content in it: almost all economic factors governing the income generating process are neglected.

II.2.2. *The theory of the distribution of earnings*

Since labour income is the most important type of income, this theory will be dealt with here in more detail. Professor *Somermeyer* (chapter 15) offers a complete theory of this type based on neoclassical production and utility functions. Wages are determined by equalising demand and supply for different kinds of labour. In this way the income distribution can be derived. Basically we follow the same approach here but go into more detail and relax the assumption of perfect competition.

α. *Labour demand.* Consider a representative firm in sector i producing a product x_i under a neoclassical, linear homogeneous production function, with Harrod-neutral technical progress:

$$x_i = f_i(\tau_{i1}L_{i1}, \ldots, \tau_{im}L_{im}, K_{i1}, \ldots, K_{in}), \quad i = 1, \ldots, n, \tag{14a}$$

where $\tau_{i1}, \ldots, \tau_{im}$ are technical progress terms and $K_{i1}, \ldots, K_{1n}$ amounts of capital goods of type $1, \ldots, n$. Let w_μ be the wage rate for labour $L_{i\mu}$ and p_v be the user cost of capital K_{iv}. Minimising cost with respect to $L_{i1}, \ldots, L_{im}, K_{i1}, \ldots, K_{in}$,

$$\sum_\mu w_\mu L_{i\mu} + \sum_v p_v K_{iv} = \min! \tag{14b}$$

under the constraint (14a) yields the system of *demand functions* for labour and capital where the price ratios enter as arguments and output x_i enters in a multiplicative way. The labour demand function may be written

$$L_{i\mu} = F_{i\mu}\left(\frac{w_i}{w_\mu}, \ldots, \frac{w_m}{w_\mu}, \frac{p_1}{w_\mu}, \ldots, \frac{p_n}{w_\mu}, \tau_{i1}, \ldots, \tau_{im}\right) x_i, \quad \begin{array}{l}\mu = 1, \ldots, m,\\ i = 1, \ldots, n.\end{array} \tag{15a}$$

In industry i, demand for labour of type μ, $L_{i\mu}$ hours, is transformed into labour demand $B_{i\mu}$ ($B^e_{i\mu}$ employed + $B^s_{i\mu}$ self-employed) by

$$B_{i\mu} = L_{i\mu}/T_\mu, \tag{15b}$$

where T_μ is the average number of hours worked by those employed in that type of work. T_μ will be explained below.

Total demand for labour of type μ may then be written

$$B_\mu = \sum_i B_{i\mu}, \quad L_\mu = \sum_i L_{i\mu}. \tag{15c}$$

β. *Labour supply.* Unfortunately, the theory of labour supply is much more complicated than the theory of labour demand.

Let $B^e_{hi\mu}$, $B^s_{hi\mu}$ be the number of persons in household h attached to sector i and

Introduction

able to offer labour of type μ for employment or self-employment in sector i. As far as they are employed or self-employed they get the income $W^e_{hi\mu}(i\mu e)$, $W^s_{hi\mu}(i\mu s)$, respectively. Let $\bar{B}^e_{hi\mu}$, $\bar{B}^s_{hi\mu}$ be the number of employed or self-employed people (or equivalent adults) in the same household h able to offer labour of the same type μ to other sectors. Now the total labour of type μ available in the economy amounts to

$$\bar{B}^\mu = \sum_h \sum_i (B^e_{hi\mu} + B^s_{hi\mu} + \bar{B}^e_{hi\mu} + \bar{B}^s_{hi\mu}). \tag{16a}$$

With total available labour $\bar{B} = \sum_\mu \bar{B}^\mu$, the proportion α^μ of labour μ to total labour $\bar{B}$ is given by

$$\bar{B}^\mu = \alpha^\mu \cdot \bar{B} \tag{16b}$$

Total labour $\bar{B}$ available in the country depends on the population N:

$$\bar{B} = \eta \cdot N \tag{16c}$$

where η is a function of the age distribution $D(a)$, the distribution $D(b)$ of the beginning b and the distribution $D(c)$ of the end of the working life in the population and other factors:

$$\eta = \eta(D(a), D(b), D(c), \ldots) \tag{16d}$$

From the total $\bar{B}^\mu$ only a fraction β^μ will actually be offered, yielding the labour supply of type μ (in the number of persons):

$$B^\mu = \beta^\mu \cdot \bar{B}^\mu, \quad 0 \leq \beta^\mu \leq 1. \tag{16e}$$

β^μ will be explained below together with the average working time T^μ per person supplying labour of type μ. Thus total labour of type μ (in hours worked) amounts to:

$$L^\mu = T^\mu \cdot B^\mu \tag{16f}$$

Now total labour supply is defined by

$$B = \sum_\mu B^\mu; \quad L = \sum_\mu L^\mu. \tag{16g}$$

B^μ and T^μ follow from maximising a utility function for a representative household

$$U = U(B^1, \ldots, B^m, T^1, \ldots, T^m, C_1, \ldots, C_n, \bar{C}, \sigma_1, \ldots, \sigma_N), \tag{16h}$$

with respect to all arguments under its control, subject to the constraints:

$$\sum_j B^j T^j \frac{w_j}{w_\mu}(1 - t_j) + [\bar{Y}(Q) + \bar{T}_R] \sum_i \gamma_i \frac{p_i}{w_\mu} - \sum_i C_i \frac{p_i}{w_\mu} - \bar{C} \sum_i \gamma_i \frac{p_i}{w_\mu} = 0 \tag{16i}$$

$$B^j \leq \bar{B}^j, \quad \underline{T}^j \leq T^j \leq \bar{T}^j. \tag{16k}$$

C_i denotes real consumption of commodity i, $\bar{C}$ future real consumption, $\bar{Y}(Q)$ net real profit and $\bar{T}_R$ transfer income of the household; $\sigma_1, \ldots, \sigma_N$ are parameters of the utility functions which may change over time; $\sum_i \gamma_i p_i$ is the price level of consumption goods; t_j is the tax rate on wage income of type j.

Equation (16i) is the budget constraint (including saving, which is taken as future consumption) divided by the wage rate $w_\mu, \mu \in \{1,\ldots,m\}$. (16k) are constraints for available manpower and for variations in the number of hours worked.

The solution of the programming problem (16h) to (16k) yields the supply functions:

$$B^\mu = G^\mu\left(\frac{w_1}{w_\mu},\ldots,\frac{w_m}{w_\mu},\frac{p_1}{w_\mu},\ldots,\frac{p_n}{w_\mu},\sigma_1,\ldots,\sigma_N,t_1,\ldots,t_m,\bar{Y}(Q),\bar{T}_R,\bar{B}^1,\ldots,\bar{B}^m,\right.$$

$$\left. \underline{T}^1,\ldots,\underline{T}^m,\bar{T}^1,\ldots,\bar{T}^m\right), \tag{16l}$$

$$T^\mu = H^\mu\left(\frac{w_1}{w_\mu},\ldots,\bar{T}^m\right). \tag{16m}$$

Thus

$$\beta^\mu = \frac{1}{\bar{B}^\mu} G^\mu(\cdot), \qquad \mu = 1,\ldots,m. \tag{16n}$$

Let us arrange the m types of labour available in the economy according to their quality q on a quality scale:

$$\mu \leftrightarrow q_{\mu-1}. \tag{17a}$$

Thus there are qualities $q_0,\ldots,q_M$ of labour, q_0 being unskilled labour, $M \geq m-1$.

Consider a representative person. Let $f(x,\ldots)$ be the probability that this person has labour quality x, $x = 0, 1, \ldots, M$. This probability depends on the person's natural endowments d, years of schooling sch, years of on-the-job training l (or environmental influences, or "learning by doing", often simply measured by age), and on other factors:

$$f(x,\ldots) = \varphi(x, d, sch, l, \ldots). \tag{17b}$$

For example, if there is an equal basic probability π of moving up one step on the quality scale and if there are exactly M chances of moving, $f(x)$ becomes the binomial distribution

$$\varphi(x_j\ldots) = C_x^M \pi^x (1-\pi)^{M-x}, \qquad 0 < \pi < 1, \quad x = 0, 1, \ldots, M, \tag{17c}$$

$$C_x^M = M!/x!(M-x)!$$

The probability π is derived from innate probability $\pi_0 = d$, called "natural endowments", on the years of schooling sch, on environmental influences (or learning by doing, or age) l and other factors ε. In the linear case

$$\pi = \pi_0 + \alpha \cdot sch + \beta \cdot l + \varepsilon, \tag{17d}$$

α and β being learning coefficients which may be considered part of the natural endowment.

Figure 1 shows the quality distribution (17c) for 6 levels of labour quality ($M = 5$) under the assumptions: $\pi_0 = 0.05$, $\alpha = 0.030$, $\beta = 0.010$, $\varepsilon = 0$, and ten years each of schooling and practical experience.

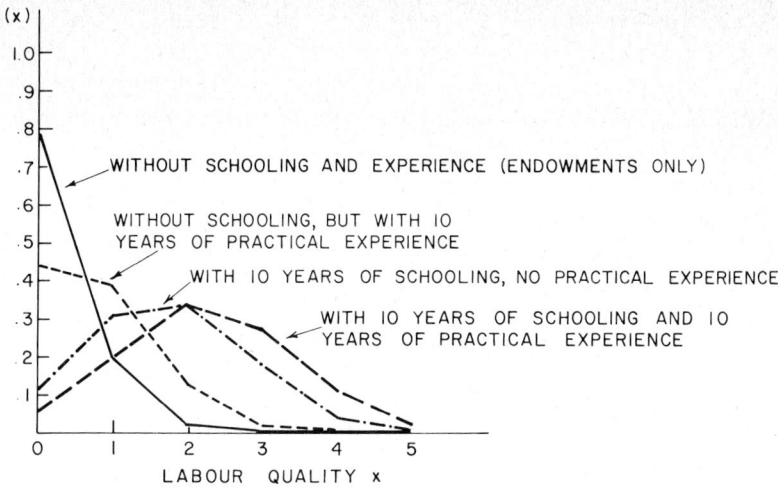

Figure 1. Probability distribution for the labour quality x attained.

Now consider people with different natural endowments, years of schooling and years of experience.

Let $v(d_j, sch_j, l_j, \ldots, \alpha_j, \beta_j)$ be the probability that a particular person has natural endowments d_j, years of schooling sch_j, years of practical experience l_j and learning coefficients α_j, β_j. Let $\varphi(x, d_j, sch_j, l_j, \ldots)$ be the probability of this person attaining labour quality x. Labour quality x is now found in society with probability $F(x)$ given by

$$F(x) = \sum_j \varphi(x, d_j, sch_j, l_j, \ldots) \cdot v(d_j, sch_j, l_j, \ldots, \alpha_j, \beta_j). \tag{17e}$$

$F(x)$ is observable, since

$$F(\mu - 1) = \alpha^\mu, \mu = 1, \ldots, m, \tag{17f}$$

cf. equation (16b). Thus the number of persons $\bar{B}^\mu$ with labour quality μ is given by

$$\bar{B}^\mu = F(\mu - 1) \cdot \bar{B}. \tag{18a}$$

This number depends on natural endowments, the school system, the number of years of on the job training and other factors, in a way made explicit in (17e).

Considering equations (16b) to (16f), the supply function ϕ^μ for labour of type μ (in terms of persons) may be written

$$B^\mu = \phi^\mu\bigg(\frac{w_1}{w_\mu}, \ldots, \frac{w_m}{w_\mu}, \frac{p_1}{w_\mu}, \ldots, \frac{p_n}{w_\mu}, \sigma_1, \ldots, \sigma_N, t_1, t_m, \bar{Y}(Q), \bar{T}_R, \underline{T}^1, \ldots,$$
$$\underline{T}^n, \bar{T}^1, \ldots, \bar{T}^m, F(0), \ldots, F(\mu - 1), \eta(\cdot), N\bigg). \tag{18b}$$

In terms of hours worked (cf. (16f) and (16m)),

$$L^\mu = \psi^\mu\left(\frac{w_1}{w_\mu}, \ldots, N\right). \tag{18c}$$

γ. The theory of wages: The earnings function. In a free labour market, equating labour supply L^μ and demand L_μ for each type of labour, given prices $p_1, \ldots, p_n$ and production $x_1, \ldots, x_n$, would yield the money wage rates $w_1^*, \ldots, w_m^*$ (cf. equations (15a)–(15c) and (18c)):

$$L_\mu = \sum_i F_{i\mu}\left(\frac{w_1}{w_\mu}, \ldots, \frac{w_m}{w_\mu}, \frac{p_1}{w_\mu}, \ldots, \frac{p_n}{w_\mu}, \ldots\right) \cdot x_i$$

$$= L^\mu = \psi^\mu\left(\frac{w_1}{w_\mu}, \ldots, \frac{w_m}{w_\mu}, \frac{p_1}{w_\mu}, \ldots, \frac{p_n}{w_\mu}, \ldots\right), \quad \mu = 1, \ldots, m,$$

$$\rightarrow w_1^*, \ldots, w_n^*. \tag{19a}$$

This is the approach of Professor *Somermeyer* (chapter 15), which conforms to a general equilibrium framework. But as Professor *Pen* (chapter 14) and Professor *Lévy-Garboua* (chapter 13) point out, and Mr. *Layard* shows econometrically (chapter 19), unionisation and other institutional factors frequently have a substantial effect on the money wage rate. The wage rate is determined by bargaining in such a way that supply may deviate from demand. But, of course, demand and supply still have some influence. Thus we have to postulate a system of wage functions:

$$w_\mu = H_\mu(L_\mu, L^\mu, p_1, \ldots, p_n, \bar{U}_\mu, \ldots), \quad \mu = 1, \ldots, m, \tag{19b}$$

where $\bar{U}_\mu$ is an index of administrative and union power in the determination of wages of type μ, e.g. measured by the coverage. The solution of (19b) yields the wage rates $w_1^*, \ldots, w_m^*$. For econometric estimation, a dynamic version of equation (19b) should be preferred. Taking rates of growth, equation (19b) becomes a Phillips curve, with a great number of shift variables.

Using (19b) and (18c), for any household h total earnings W_h from employment and self-employment is determined by:

$$W_h = \sum_\mu w_\mu L_h^\mu = \sum_\mu H_\mu(L_\mu, L^\mu, \ldots, \bar{U}_\mu, \ldots) \cdot \psi_h^\mu(\ldots, F_h(0), \ldots, F_h(\mu-1), \ldots), \tag{20}$$

where

$$F_h(x) = \varphi_h(x, d, sch, l, \ldots), \quad \text{see (17c).}$$

Equation (20) is the earnings function; W_h equals $Y(L)_h$ in column 4 of table 3 above. By linearising this function, the influence of genetic endowments d, schooling sch and learning on the job or environment l may be estimated econometrically, assuming an appropriate microdata sample is available. This is done by Professor *Taubman* (chapter 16) using statistical data on monozygotic twins. He arrives at the conclusion that about 50% of the variance of earnings is due to genetic endowments. From Professor *Pen*'s three types of power (political, economic and administrative), two come in at this stage: economic and administrative power, both represented here by $\bar{U}_\mu$. Mr. *Layard* (chapter 19) concentrates on the measurement of the union influence of $\bar{U}$ on the earnings function ($\bar{U}$ interpreted as union power and measured by the coverage), but also considers schooling and different environmental factors. Dr. *Psacharopoulos* (chapter 18) also estimates earnings functions to find out whether segmentation exists in the labour market.

Following Becker (1975), schooling may be considered as investment in human capital. In this case the variable *sch* should be measured in terms of the cost of schooling rather than the time spent at school. Professor *Stiglitz* (chapter 11), Professor *Lévy-Garboua* (chapter 13), and Professor *Chiswick* (chapter 20) use this approach.

Under uncertainty (not considered here) schooling has a screening function: people with better natural endowments d and higher abilities l to learn (and therefore higher productivity on the job, in general) are distinguished from those with lower ones; see Stiglitz (1975).

Using equation (20) the distributional effect of a change in the labour supply of a certain kind may be estimated. If total labour supply is divided into two kinds L^1 and L^2 (e.g. academically trained and other labour), the elasticity of substitution σ between the first and the second kind of labour determines whether the income distribution changes in favour ($\sigma > 1$) or to the disadvantage ($\sigma < 1$) of academically trained labour, or whether it remains unchanged ($\sigma = 1$), when the wage rate of acedemically trained people decreases relatively. Let W^1 be earnings of academically trained labour and W^2 earnings of other labour. Let $\{h^1\}$, $\{h^2\}$ be the set of all households supplying labour of type 1 and 2, respectively. From equation (20)

$$W^i = \sum_{h \in \{hi\}} W_h = F^i(L^i, \ldots), \qquad i = 1, 2, \ldots. \tag{21a}$$

If $F^i(L^i, \ldots)$ takes the special form

$$F^i(L^i, \ldots) = e^{\alpha_i + \beta_i t} \cdot (L^i)^\gamma, \tag{21b}$$

we get

$$\ln \frac{W^1}{W^2} = \alpha + \beta t + \gamma \ln \left(\frac{L^1}{L^2}\right), \qquad \text{where } \alpha = \alpha_1 - \alpha_2; \quad \beta = \beta_1 - \beta_2. \tag{21c}$$

In this case the elasticity of substitution of earnings with respect to labour supply becomes

$$\sigma = \frac{d(W^1/W^2)}{d(L^1/L^2)} \frac{L^1/L^2}{W^1/W^2} = \gamma. \tag{21d}$$

Professor *Kuipers* (chapter 17) tries to determine σ in this way. Assuming that the average time worked T^μ is constant, he uses B^μ rather than L^μ. Looking at the simplifying assumption (21b), it is understandable that the results obtained are difficult to interpret.

II.2.3. *The theory of the distribution of unearned income*

The distribution of unearned income depends on the distribution of wealth which in turn (starting from a historically given distribution) depends on personal savings, personal wealth transfers of all kinds (especially inheritance), price changes, wealth losses arising from natural deterioration and decay of goods, bankruptcies, taxation and other influences. There is no simple generally accepted theory of the distribution of unearned income including all these factors. Time and space do not permit presentation of a theory as detailed as that on labour income. In this volume only chapter 11 written by Professor *Stiglitz* is devoted to this problem. Professor Stiglitz shows that an inheritance tax may not equalise the distribution of unearned income – it may perhaps lead to greater inequality. But it may have a sizeable effect on growth, instead.

II.2.4. *The redistribution of income by taxes, transfer payments, and transfers in kind*

Recently substantial efforts have been made to develop a theory on this subject, under the name of *Grants Economics*. The names of Professor Boulding and Pfaff are important here; see Pfaff (1976) as an example. But, unfortunately, no coherent theory has yet emerged. The subject lies on the borderline between economics and political science and is surely difficult to analyse. In this volume Professor *Pen* (chapter 14) deals with this subject under the heading of "political power". The paper of Professor *Krupp* (chapter 21) sheds some light on another side of the problem, namely, to what extent transfer payments change the inter-group income distribution. Though the main effect of the system of transfer payments, at least in Germany, seems to be a redistribution of income within the social groups, there is evidence for at least some inter-group redistribution.

II.3. *The effect in changes in personal income distribution on other economic variables*

Personal income distribution is not a loose end of the network of economic relations, where the chain of mutual influences terminates. There are repercussions on almost all other economic variables, especially on consumption and investment demand. It is a question of the proper division of labour among economic theorists, or (to put it another way) a question of the appropriate grouping of different branches of economic theory, whether these repercussions should be analysed under the heading of distribution theory or under the heading of the specific theories where the influence is felt, e.g. in consumption or investment demand, or in labour productivity. The latter arrangement seems to be more appropriate. There is now a growing concern about the repercussions of income distribution on other variables, e.g. on the trade-off between equality and efficiency; see Okun (1975). In this volume the paper of Professor *Chiswick* (chapter 20) deals with the influence of income distribution on the rate of growth in the dual economy of a less developed country. Professor *Stiglitz* (chapter 11) analyses the influence of an inheritance tax on the optimal choice between investment in human and physical capital. Of course, similar effects are also mentioned in other chapters.

III. Concluding remarks

The theory of personal income distribution has made substantial progress in the last few years. The main reasons for that are the availability and the econometric analysis of microdata files, and the extension of general economic theory to education. The use of microdata files enables a large number of economic and non-economic factors to be examined for their effects on wages, labour supply, earnings and other variables at the individual or household level, which previously went unnoticed. The human capital and screening approaches opened up a new field which proved to be fruitful in distribution theory as well. Further developments in production and utility theory also had an important impact on distribution theory. The chapters in this book indicate the frontiers of research in the different areas of distribution theory during these years. Of course, there are omissions in the coverage of the different areas in this volume, and, more importantly, certain aspects are neglected in research in general. By providing a kind of "general theory" of income distribution, this introduction should connect the different strands of thought in the different chapters of this volume, as well as hint at these "blind spots" in research. They lie mostly on the borderline between economics, political science and sociology, and may be roughly identified with the theory of transfer payments and transfers in kind ("grants economics"), the theory of taxation and the influence of power on wages and income. Perhaps the extension of economic theory to these fields may prove to be as fruitful as the extension of economic theory to education. But this remains to be seen.

References

Arrow, K., *Social Choice and Individual Values*, New York, London, 1951.
Atkinson, A.B., "On the Measurement of Inequality", *Journal of Economic Theory*, 1970.
Atkinson, A.B., *The Economics of Inequality*, Oxford, 1975.
Barth, K., *Der Römerbrief*, 2. Aufl., Zürich 1954.
Becker, G., *Human Capital*, 2nd ed., New York 1975.
Bentham, J., *An Introduction to the Principles of Morals and Legislation*, London, 1789.
Böckle, F., ed., *Das Naturrecht im Disput*, Düsseldorf, 1966.
Brandt, R.B., *Ethical Theory*, Englewood Cliffs, 1959.
Brunner, E., *Das Gebot und die Ordnungen*, 4. Aufl., Zürich 1939.
Brunner, E., *Gerechtigkeit. Eine Lehre von den Grundgesetzen der Gesellschaftsordnung*, Zürich, 1943.
Dalton, H., "The Measurement of the Inequality of Income", *Economic Journal*, 1920.
Frisch, R., "Annual Survey of General Economic Theory. The Problem of Index Numbers", *Econometrica*, 1936.
Gibrat, R., *Les inégalités économiques*, Paris, 1931.
Groves, T. and Ledyard, J., "Optimal Allocation of Public Goods: A Solution to the 'Free Rider' Problem", *Econometrica*, 1977.
Harsanyi, J.C., "Cardinal Utility in Welfare Economics and the Theory of Risk-Taking", *Journal of Political Economy*, 1953.
Harsanyi, J.C., "Cardinal Welfare, Individualistic Ethics, and Interpersonal Comparison of Utility", *Journal of Political Economy*, 1955.

Harsanyi, J.C., "Ethics in Terms of Hypothetical Imperatives", *Mind*, 1958.
Harsanyi, J.C., "Can the Maximin Principle Serve as a Basis for Morality? A Critique of John Rawls's Theory", Working Paper Nr. CP-351, Center for Research in Management Science, University of California, Berkeley, June 1973.
Harsanyi, J.C., "A Further Note on Rawls's Theory", Working Paper Institute of Mathematical Economics, Universität Bielefeld, July 1974.
Harsanyi, J.C., "Rule Utilitarism and Decision Theory", Working Paper CP-384, Center for Research in Management Science, University of California, Berkeley, June 1976.
Kramer, R., *Die christliche Verantwortung in der sozialen Marktwirtschaft*, Stuttgart, 1973.
Krelle, W., *Präferenz- und Entscheidungstheorie*, Tübingen, 1968.
Krelle, W., "Dynamics of the Utility Function", in J.H. Hicks and W. Weber (ed.), *Carl Menger and the Austrian School of Economics*, Oxford, 1973.
Mill, J.S., *Utilitarianism*, London, 1863.
von Nell-Breuning, O., "Der Lohn als Erwerbsmittel und Eigentumsquelle", in: *Eigentum und Eigentümer in unserer Gesellschaftsordnung, Veröffentlichungen der Walter-Raymond-Stiftung*, Bd. 1, Köln und Opladen, 1960.
Okun, A.M., *Equality and Efficiency, The Big Trade-off*, Washington, D.C., 1975.
Pfaff, M. (ed.), *Grants and Exchange*, Amsterdam, New York, Oxford, 1976.
Rawls, J., *A Theory of Justice*, Cambridge/Mass., 1971.
Rawls, J., "Some Reasons for the Maximin Criterion", *American Economic Review, Papers and Proceedings*, May 1974.
Samuelson, P.A. and Swamy, S., "Invariant Economic Index Numbers and Canonical Duality: Survey and Synthesis", *American Economic Review*, 1974.
Selten, R., "The Equity Principle in Economic Behavior", Working Paper Nr. 46, Institute of Mathematical Economics, Universität Bielefeld, July 1976.
Stiglitz, J.E., "The Theory of 'Screening', Education, and the Distribution of Income", *American Economic Review*, 1975.
Tautscher, A., *Wirtschaftsethik, Handbuch der Moraltheologie*, Band 11, München, 1957.
Thielicke, H., *Theologische Ethik*, Tübingen, 1965.
Tinbergen, J., *Income Distribution, Analysis and Policies*, Amsterdam, Oxford, New York, 1975.
Weber, H., *Theologie, Gesellschaft, Wirtschaft. Die Sozial- und Wirtshaftsethik in der evangelischen Theologie der Gegenwart*, Göttingen, 1970.
Wünsch, G., *Evangelische Wirtschaftsethik*, Tübingen, 1927.

PART I

ETHICAL ASSESSMENT OF INCOME DIFFERENTIALS

1 EQUITABLE DISTRIBUTION: DEFINITION, MEASUREMENT, FEASIBILITY

JAN TINBERGEN

I. Definition

I.1. *Introduction: Distribution of what?*

Although the emphasis of this paper will be on income distribution the reader must be warned in advance that distributional problems cannot be discussed properly when restricted to the distribution of only one variable, in this case income. The distribution of income is necessarily interconnected with the distribution of other variables which describe the position of individuals (or other units) in society. Thus, the jobs performed by the individuals studied is clearly related to the important component of income called labour income or earnings. Also the taxes to be paid, and the benefits received in one form or another, are connected with income components. Hence, our subject is wider than income distribution alone.

A second preliminary remark seems appropriate. A discussion on equity must, by definition, be of a normative and hence subjective character: it is based on a value judgement. In order to avoid misunderstandings, the value judgement chosen must be made clear from the start.

Thirdly it seems proper to announce, in this introductory section, the structure of the paper. It consists of four sections. Section I deals with the chosen definition of equity in distribution. Section II attempts to further develop the theory of utility on which this definition of equity is based. Economic science has been based on utility concepts for at least a century, but several aspects of these concepts are not sufficiently developed for the purposes of this paper. Guided somewhat by the theoretical development offered, attempts at measuring utility are discussed in section III; this is necessary for the application of the concept of equity chosen in section I. Finally, section IV deals with the feasibility of an equitable distribution as defined in section I. In other words, section IV tries to answer the question whether an equitable distribution can be attained, and if so, under what conditions and by means of what socio-economic policy.

I.2. *Quantitative aspects of equity*

The value judgement on which this paper is based is that a situation of equity or equitable distribution is defined as a situation of equal welfare for all social groups considered. Welfare of a group is supposed to be identical to the welfare of representative individuals in that group. For reasons to be discussed in section I.6 some groups will have to be excepted from the definition; groups in some physiological sense "too abnormal". The use of representative individuals in fact means that elements of a purely individual character, such as religious feelings, love, friendship, etc. are left out of consideration, as far as they cannot be affected by the social order, or, in other words, are not "organisable". The number of groups considered determines the degree of precision of the study made. Clearly it is desirable that the number be as large as possible. The absolute minimum is two, since otherwise no groups are introduced. An example of the use of only two groups is a macro-Marxian grouping of the population into capitalists and workers; another is a division into rural and urban population. Clearly such coarse subdivisions of society are much too crude to admit conclusions about the size distribution of incomes and other elements.

An essential pre-condition for the application of our definition is the measurability of welfare or satisfaction – for which concept economists often use the word utility. As long ago as 1896 Pareto, to avoid restrictive interpretations of the latter expression, proposed a concept "ophelimity", supposed to be more neutral, but also broader, than a narrow interpretation of the phrase "utility". Most economists doubt whether welfare can be measured, but the trend is changing again. Other social scientists are also divided on the issue, but the rising interest in social indicators shows that attempts at measuring welfare are increasing. Any measurement may profit from an explicit theory of welfare and we will attempt to contribute to such a theory in section II.

I.3. *Qualitative aspects of equity and welfare*

It seems odd to discuss qualitative aspects after quantitative ones, since any quantity refers to some quality of an object after measurement. In this paper, qualitative aspects refer to some dimensions of equity which we do not discuss in depth, since we consider them self-evident. Such self-evidence is not warranted at all in many nations, however, and this paper therefore is not meant to cover the subject of equity for such nations: for them it only covers part of the subject. Many of the qualitative aspects we are going to avoid are important components of the concept of human rights, such as equality under the law, voting rights, and so on. This paper's orientation may be said to take it for granted that the social order should grant these most fundamental human rights to its citizens.

Yet, the method developed to measure welfare may be of some relevance to these qualitative aspects. It is a natural development in science that qualitative concepts progress to be quantitative concepts. Thus, voting rights may be extended to larger numbers of individuals or to larger numbers of voting procedures. The present paper applies this mode of thinking to some elements of welfare where the process of measurement has progressed but is not yet sufficiently advanced.

I.4. *Comparison of our definition with some alternatives*

In today's political discussions, three alternative definitions of an equitable distribution are frequently used. One, to be called liberalist, defines equity as equality between an individual's income and his productive contribution to society. We reject this definition in its general form, since an individual's productive contribution may reflect rare innate capabilities whose distribution by nature over individuals need not necessarily be equitable. Nature is in many respects very cruel and the human mind, in its better moments or manifestations, tries to reduce cruelty. It is in this context that the human mind may try to reduce or eliminate differences in income due to innate capabilities rather than conscious efforts.

We said that we reject the definition quoted in its general form. By this we want to suggest the possibility that, under circumstances different from those now prevailing, the value attached to rare capabilities may become such that the welfare of all individuals is equalised. If such a pricing system becomes possible – we will discuss this in section IV – the liberalist definition might coincide with ours.

Another alternative definition of equitable distribution is that certain minimum needs can be satisfied by all. This definition "creates a floor to the income distribution" but leaves out of consideration how incomes above this base level are distributed. Again we reject this definition, but we have to recognise that situations are conceivable in which our definition and the one now discussed both apply. In our view equity also requires a more precise choice for incomes above the chosen minimum, even if it is relatively high.

A third alternative definition of equitable distribution is equality of incomes. We disagree with this definition as well, but again it is conceivable that the other determinants of welfare are chosen in such a way as to reconcile the two definitions. Thus, one can imagine varying working hours to compensate for the degree of attractiveness of work: shorter hours for disagreeable work. Also, an individual, weaker than a colleague, may be permitted to work less. Income equality is a rather arbitrary choice and may be difficult to organise if these sorts of compensations are desired. In section IV questions of this type will be taken up in more detail.

I.5. *Equitable versus optimal distribution*

It should be clear that equity is not the only aim of a social order and socio-economic policy. Most communities want to attain a combination of aims, including, in addition to a distributional objective, targets referring to the average level of welfare, equivalent to a target for total welfare. If the state of welfare of the population at large can be expressed in something often called social or total welfare, the objective, as a synthesis, is maximum social welfare. This maximum need not coincide with equality of welfare among individuals. In more concrete terms, full employment, stable prices and other objectives may be components of social welfare; and it is perfectly possible that equity can only be attained at the cost of lower employment, unstable prices or, for that matter, a lower total production of goods and services. Equity and optimality are not synonymous therefore. Again, in some situations, equity may, by coincidence, be attained in the optimal situation (cf. Tinbergen (1975)).

I.6. *Excluded groups*

In our definition of equitable distribution we introduced individuals representative of various groups in the population, each of them more homogeneous than the population at large. We added that some groups may have to be excluded from the definition. These groups are various types of physically or mentally handicapped individuals. Their handicap can be so serious that no social compensation is able to make them satisfied in a way comparable to the physically or mentally normal. Here again nature's cruelty is such that no human intervention can compensate for the handicap. The problem of these groups can only be partly alleviated; and there remain alternative choices. As a subject of socio-economic policy the situation constitutes an insoluble problem; and we know there are such problems.

Another restriction to our definition, or at least the way we are going to apply it, is that we exclude groups whose socio-economic situation is subject to rapid change. Formulated another way, we want to concentrate our attention on gradual changes towards more equity. The reason is that quick changes bring disturbances which are often harmful and can be avoided. They are harmful not only to those whose position suddenly deteriorates, but also because that deterioration is able to cause reactions harmful to all.

II. **A theory of utility or welfare**

II.1. *Successive approximations*

If we accept as the definition of equitable distribution a distribution such that, for the socio-economic groups considered, welfare is equal, we presuppose its measurability. Measurement can be facilitated and made more systematic if we start from a theory of the determinants of welfare or utility. As already observed, utility functions have now been used for at least a century in economic theory; but in many respects the concept has been a rather meagre picture of what welfare really involves. Utility has been presented mainly as something determined by the quantities of goods consumed; sometimes the quantity of labour supplied has been added and in a few cases other determinants. Psychologists have gone into much more detail and introduced some of the less material and more subtle determinants of a person's welfare. On many of these, extensive discussions in psychology and related sciences have developed, most of them not finished and not a matter of consensus (yet). It is natural for economists to introduce into their research only, or mainly, the more self-evident among the determinants under discussion. It is also natural for econometricians to start in an even simpler way and introduce determinants for which figures are already available; even to first introduce the most relevant ones and stepwise to add others. This is somewhat similar to what is known as successive approximations, a method even used in mathematics, if a complete analysis is found to be too difficult.

II.2. *Parameters, variables, mathematical shape, coefficients*

Before considering, by successive approximations, the determinants and their impact on welfare, a subdivision of the determinants into two categories will be discussed, followed by a discussion of the mathematical shape of utility functions. We propose to speak of parameters of an individual's welfare function if determinants are discussed which are (approximately) constant for the individual considered and hence characterise it. When strictly constant over a long period we may even call them innate features of the person in question. For shorter-term purposes the parameters may be used to indicate features which can only be changed slowly, for instance as the result of a learning process, including the level of education attained, or the experience on a job. Parameters may also characterise the individual's general health condition (disregarding temporary illness or the effect of an accident). Some relevant elements of taste are also parameters. For shorter-run problems family size may be added.

Variables, then, are determinants subject to relatively quick changes. Such changes may result from the individual's own choice and the most relevant example is a change of job, with the accompanying changes in efforts and in income. Other changes in variables may be independent of the individual's preferences: his income may vary as a consequence of a change in a collective agreement on income, or a change in taxes.

Parameters and variables together are what we call the determinants of welfare; mathematicians may prefer the word "arguments" here. The way in which they affect welfare is represented by the mathematical shape of the welfare or utility functions. Within some limits this shape can be chosen freely; one of the conditions it should satisfy being, as is well known, that indications of rising welfare must be reflected in increased values of the function. The simplest mathematical form conceivable is an additive (linear) function. The impact of each determinant on welfare can be seen from the coefficient attached to that determinant in such a formula. More complicated formulae will be necessary as soon as a joint effect of two or more determinants is found to exist (so-called interaction terms, whose simplest form is a product of two determinants preceded by a coefficient). Joint effects can also be represented by saying that, for example, "income corrected for effort" enters into the function as an expression $x - c_0 s$, where x is disposable income (income minus taxes plus transfers), s a measure of effort and c_0 a coefficient indicating how much income is required to compensate for an additional unit of effort. The way in which this corrected income affects utility may then be chosen in different ways; a rather well-known form of the utility function being $\ln(x - c_0 s)$

and another $(x - c_0 s)^v$; there are others, such as Van Praag's $N(\log X; \mu, \sigma)$, where N denotes the normal distribution function of $\log X$, with mean μ and standard devitation σ, and X may be our previous $x - c_0 s$ (Van Praag (1971)).

II.3. *Concrete determinants; disposable income*

We now propose to discuss the actual determinants which we will introduce, starting with the most relevant as we see them and adding others as announced in section II.1. We admit that the order in which we present the successive approximations is not necessarily the only one conceivable or the best one. As long as we agree on what finally will be taken as determinants, this order is irrelevant. Substantive differences of opinion may arise on the importance of determinants; and agreement on such differences must essentially be based on empirical evidence.

The first determinant we propose to discuss is disposable income. We choose it as a general variable representing consumption possibilities, instead of quantities of individual commodities consumed per time unit. Our reason for aggregating all consumption is that we are not interested in differences in tastes for individual commodities. Far more interesting differences in tastes occur in what could be called the productive sphere of a person's life, to be discussed below. Disposable income need not be spent entirely on consumption within the time period considered. Part of it may be saved. Also consumption in the time period considered includes consumption of services of durables bought earlier, whereas the durables bought in that period are only partly consumed. Thus, part of disposable income represents future consumption. Income coincides with earnings only for those who supply labour as a factor of production. In other cases part of income may be income from capital (in the widest sense).

II.4. *Wealth*

Accumulated savings, together with inherited wealth, constitute another determinant of welfare since they provide a feeling of security and the possibility of being less dependent on short-term opportunities for work. One form of wealth consists of a right to an old-age pension or rights to social benefits, an important phenomenon in Western mixed and Eastern communist societies. Most forms of wealth involve the acceptance of certain risks, a fact of some relevance in a discussion on equitable distribution and to be taken up later.

II.5. *Job characteristics and productive personality traits*

We now arrive at the complex of parameters and variables which are connected with the individual's productive situation. For a long time over-simplified, in the last twenty years this subject has been the focus of an enormous amount of research. This is based on job evaluation, or function analysis, by which the capabilities –

and hence efforts – required for the proper execution of a large number of jobs is described by a series of numbers, each constituting a measure of the degree to which a number of skills must be found in the person doing the job. As economists we may call this the demand side of the labour market or, more generally, the factor market. Somewhat later, comparable research has begun on the evaluation of performance by people at their job. In its most developed form this research resulted in career planning for personnel members of (usually the larger) enterprises or government services. The least developed aspect is probably the contribution to welfare made by the relationships between individuals in neighbouring jobs – colleagues, and those higher up and lower down in the hierarchy.

In the language used in section II.2, the job characteristics or requirements enter into the welfare function as variables, together with income, whereas performance is based on personality traits which are partly parameters (if they are more or less innate, or the effect of a long learning process) and partly variables (when more easily adaptable to circumstances by the individual). A particular aspect is the work rate, which can be influenced by wage incentives.

An important question in actual applications is how many mutually independent characteristics are needed to describe the job, as well as the person doing the job, in order to explain most of the variance in earnings or in welfare. With the aid of factor analysis, a mathematical–statistical technique, this number can be estimated and, as a rule, four to six independent characteristics will do. Various systems are in use and the nature of the characteristics differs among them. Two broad categories are apparent in most systems; one prevailing in the lower income groups and related to manual dexterity; and one prevailing at higher labour incomes, related to various aspects of intelligence. In most cases a capability described as leadership also plays an important role in the high earnings range; but here several approaches have been attempted by different firms and different labour psychologists. Each of them considers various components of leadership. One system uses the concepts of independence, the ability to organise, to supervise, to convince others, a sense of responsibility; another system speaks of the power of analysis, imagination, a sense of reality and an integrated concept referred to as the "helicopter quality" (Muller (1970)).

II.6. *Age, experience, health*

Basically physiological determinants, but of some relevance also for productive capabilities, are those of age and health. Physical, as well as mental power, increase with age up to some point from which they decline. The shape of this profile depends on the individuals, the type of job held and health. Early maxima are found for physical strength and mathematical ability, to quote two examples; later maxima are characteristic for the ability to handle both human relations and complex situations. Experience has been specified as experience in a given job, or as work experience after the formal learning process of schooling. Health not only affects the ability to work hard, but clearly also the general feeling of well-being.

II.7. *Capacity to enjoy leisure*

Considerable differences exist between individuals in the satisfaction they derive from leisure. For the mass of the population of working age this aspect of welfare played no role during the early phases of industrialisation, since they had no spare time. With increased general productivity and a corresponding reduction in working hours, this phenomenon has become increasingly important for welfare, although not necessarily through productive capabilities. Essentially three groups of individuals can be distinguished: group A use any spare time to do odd jobs in order to earn more; group B have hobbies and enjoy leisure through the satisfaction derived from them; group C do not know what to do in their spare time and have to be amused by recreation industries, otherwise they get bored and in recent years boredom has spread. Part of today's cultural crisis is due to this boredom, which is the cause of many criminal activities.

II.8. *Family size*

In a general way we have already stated that among the parameters there are those which reflect needs and possibly tastes. A major determinant of needs is family size; but in the longer run family size is not a parameter: it can be regulated by a married couple and thus becomes a variable.

III. Actual attempts at measuring utility

III.1. *Based on verbal enquiries*

For a long time it has been understood that there are at least two sources of information about human satisfaction and future action. One is to ask people what they feel, think or plan and the other is to observe people's behaviour. An example outside the subject of this paper is how a higher income will be spent. Often people think they will spend a higher income in a way in which, once they have the higher income, they do not. For our present problem, the measurement of welfare, the first method consists of asking them which verbal welfare category corresponds best to their situation. Van Praag (1971, 1973, 1975) used ten expressions of ascending welfare: from "very badly off" to "very good". One quantitative element introduced into his enquiries was a question asking respondents to indicate the incomes which would make them feel "very badly off", "very good" etc. Another quantitative element he, as the analyst, added was the figure attached to each of the verbal categories. He gave to these figures the values of 0.1, 0.2 etc. up to 1.0, in other words a scale between zero and one. As a result he found welfare ω to be the cumulated lognormal function $N(\log X; \mu, \sigma)$ of income X. He could have given a different number to each of the verbal categories and obtained, for instance, a welfare function $\omega' = \log X$. For our problem of equity this doesn't make any difference. For the construction of a social welfare function Ω it makes a great deal of difference; for instance $\Omega = \sum \omega$ is quite different from $\sum \omega'$, if we define social welfare as the sum of all individual welfares – which is not the only possible definition, of course. Since the social optimum requires Ω to be a (conditional) maximum, that optimum depends very much on what we choose Ω to be.

An evident weakness of the method described is that we must assume that the words chosen have the same meaning to all respondents. Since there was no immediate interest involved for them, systematic misrepresentation may be ruled out. Moreover, the remarkable similarity in the curves $\omega(X)$ found by Van Praag strengthens his method. Even so we must be aware of the likelihood that *ceteris paribus* a given degree of affluence may give less satisfaction to a demanding individual than to a modest one and that, for instance, people with more education, or with more educated parents, may be more demanding. This is the reason why many economists doubt whether one man's welfare can be compared to that of another. On the other hand it is important to state that it is a voluntary answer about each person's welfare which is the basis of Van Praag's material.

III.2. *Based on behaviour: Revealed preference*

An alternative method of measurement is, as we observed, the one derived from observed behaviour. While this may avoid the difficulty inherent in the method just discussed – the possible divergence between intentions and behaviour – it needs complementary information if it is to be used. It is in this method that we need the concept of parameters as distinct from variables; when carried to their logical core, the difference between unchangeable characteristics and characteristics subject to choice. In words well known to economists we can also use the concept of non-competing groups: people with different parameters cannot compete with regard to their parameters. Yet we find that people with the same value of parameters choose different jobs. Within that group of jobs we assume them to be perfectly mobile and this must imply that they are equally satisfied. Income differences between these jobs are only compensation for voluntarily chosen differences in efforts.

Starting at the lower end of the job-income distribution we can first consider the set of jobs open to the people with similar parameter values. Consequently we know how the variables involved enter into the utility function, namely in such a way as to not change the level of utility. Since we are dealing with small variations in the variables, we may use a linear formula for utility expressed in terms of the variables. As the simplest example take $\omega = x - c_0 s$, the expression mentioned in section II.2, where the income increase that compensates for one unit of additional effort is c_0. Now we shift to the next higher portion of the job-income set and repeat the procedure. If we find the same value for c_0, we maintain the formula just mentioned. If the value of c_0, changes, we will have to opt for a curvilinear expression in s, for instance by adding a term in s^2. In this way we continue until all groups of jobs-incomes have been dealt with. Thus we will have found how ω depends on the variables considered. The number of variables can be chosen so as to cover all relevant variables. Starting with only two, as we did, illustrates the process of successive approximation mentioned above.

The procedure may be illustrated by table 1.1. Again, using successive approximations, we start by assuming that there is only one parameter and, apart from income x, only one variable, again called effort s. Columns contain jobs held by people with the same parameter value w for the characteristic described as leadership.

Table 1.1. Incomes y (in Hfl 1000 of 1973) of higher employees of AKZO[a] for various levels of effort s and leadership w.

Meaning of s	s	$w = 11$	25	40	54
Modern secondary educ.	28	8.3			
Classical secondary educ.	40	12.4	16.2		
Higher technical educ.	60		33.6	37.4	
Full university educ.	93		51.8	55.6	59.3

[a] AKZO is the name of a large chemical concern with its seat in Velp (NL).

These figures, calculated with the aid of equation (1), are close to observed figures for the firm mentioned: the formula used explains 78 per cent of the observed variance. The levels of w are chosen in the following way: $w = 25$ constitutes the average score for leadership in the firm's job evaluation system; $w = 11$ is one standard deviation lower, $w = 40$ one, and $w = 54$ two, standard deviations higher. The figures for s are indicated by the education required for the jobs considered. The material includes higher employees only. The assumptions underlying the table are that differences in education requirements are indicative of a choice open, within limits, to each group with a given value of w. Since in this case the linear equation explains a remarkable portion of income variance, it was assumed to be an acceptable representation of the income structure. The equation runs:

$$y = 0.338x_1 + 0.673x_2 + 0.260x_{11} - 3.9, \qquad (1)$$

where x_1 is the score for required basic education, x_2 the one for required specialised education and x_{11} is identical to w in the table. The values of s are equal to $0.338x_1 + 0.673x_2$, showing that higher weights have to be given to the scores for specialised education than to those for basic education requirements.[1]

Using our assumption that s can be chosen freely, the term in the utility function referring to the variables is $y - 0.338x_1 - 0.673x_2$. The question then remains whether terms referring to parameters should be added. The fundamental difficulty of this second method of measuring utility is that people cannot change parameters, and that observation of behaviour here can only be obtained from experiments with their incomes. Such experiments require a comparison over different time

---

[1] The scales applied to education are as follows, where p stands for points: *Basic education*: 2 years of lower general education, 4p; 2 years of medium-level general education, 8p; 3 years of the same, 12 p; 4 years, 16p; 5 years of higher general education (i.e. secondary), 28p; 6 years of preparatory scientific education (i.e. classical secondary), 40p. *Specialised education*: 3 years of lower technical education, 8p; chemical specialist A, 5p; chemical specialist A + B, 10p; higher technical education completed, 32p; book-keeping diploma, or social academy, 32p; complete university education BA or BSc), 53p; chemical engineer, 53p.

periods or countries. An example is given by Burck (1976) who shows that the chief executives he studied accepted, between 1952 and 1976, a relative decline (in comparison to average non-farm wages) of 30 per cent. This may be interpreted to mean that they preferred to continue as executives at a relatively lower pay than in 1952 and that their satisfaction depended positively on w. An unknown positive term in w should then be added to the expression in the variables, $y - 0.338x_1 - 0.673x_2$. Neglecting this term implies underestimation of the executives' satisfaction. Assuming that the Dutch executive of 1973 is in the same position as the American executive of 1952, his money income should be complemented by a psychic income of some 43 per cent $((1/0.7) - 1)$. The conclusion to be drawn from table 1.1 is then that income differences compensating for effort s between $s = 28$ and $s = 93$ amount to some Hfl 40,000. Total income differences calculated as 59.3–8.3 or Hfl 51,000 are underestimated, since 59.3 may have to be raised to 85 to reflect psychic income. Total income differences then amount to 77 or almost twice the compensatory income differences.

III.3. *A comparison of some results obtained with the two methods*

Van Praag's material can be used to compare the two methods described above: his own method of direct enquiry with the people concerned and the indirect method of establishing an earnings or income equation and leaving out the terms corresponding to the parameters. In the comparison on which we are going to report in this sub-section, an arbitrary decision will be made on which determinants are considered as parameters. We come back to this choice in the next section (III.4).

An appropriate source for the proposed comparison is Bouma, Van Praag and Tinbergen (1976) where (on page 190) five pairs of equations are shown. Each pair consists of an income equation expressing income after tax, or its logarithm, in terms of various determinants. All five pairs use as determinants a "degree of independence" w comparable to the "leadership" used in section III.2, age t and one or two education determinants. The latter will again be assumed to represent effort. In the paper under discussion completed education has been expressed in terms of years of schooling. Sometimes actual years of schooling v have been used, sometimes a dummy s for years of schooling required, for which either the lower quartile of v in each occupational group or its median was taken. The second equation of each pair was derived from the equity definition, in other words assuming utility ω constant and equal to the average of the sample of 2663 persons. The direct method enables us to derive from the second equation, for average values of the parameters w and t (both happen to be equal to 2), the equitable income ratio for individuals with 18 and 6 years of education respectively – hence the terminology third and first level. Table 1.2 shows the equations for equitable income distribution in the five cases for each of the two methods, as well as the equitable income ratios of third to first level of education for average values of the parameters.

It may be interesting to compare these figures with two ratios obtained for the

Netherlands 1962 using the different model appearing in Pen and Tinbergen (1977): these are 1.33 and 1.32, respectively. The overestimation of the ratios obtained with the indirect method (due to neglecting satisfaction from higher values of w) finds support in these figures.

Table 1.2. Equations for equitable incomes after tax X_E, X'_E (Netherlands, 1971, in Hfl) at various levels of education s or v (in years) for average values of parameters w and t (both $= 2$), and ratios between incomes at the third and first level of education.

Case[a]	Equation for direct method	Equation for indirect method	Ratios	
			D	I
1–11	$\log X_E = 9.36 + 0.27 \log v$	$\log X'_E = 8.73 + 0.44 \log v$	1.34	1.62
2–12	$\log X_E = 9.74 + 0.144 \log s$	$\log X'_E = 8.97 + 0.38 \log s$	1.17	1.52
6–16	$\log X_E = 9.46 + 0.245 \log s$	$\log X'_E = 8.52 + 0.54 \log s$	1.31	1.81
4'–34'	$X_E/1000 = 22.52 + 0.23 v$	$X'_E/1000 = 7.88 + 0.54 v$	1.12	2.61
9–39	$X_E/1000 = 22.59 + 0.238 v$	$X'_E/1000 = 10.27 + 0.67 v$	1.12	1.56
		Average ratio	1.2	1.8

[a] Numbering of Cases as in Bouma (1976).

III.4. *Increasing the number of parameters and variables*

The examples given so far are over-simplified, because not all relevant parameters and variables have been introduced. Moreover, they suffer from the uncertainty surrounding the determinants used: are some of them really parameters or are they variables, and vice versa.

A number of other determinants have been measured by other authors, for instance Duncan, Featherman and Duncan (1968), Taubman (1974, 1975, 1976) and Hartog (1977). Research is in progress to repeat what has been done in sections III.2 and III.3. In addition, using some of the material mentioned, I made alternative assumptions as to whether a given determinant should be considered a parameter or a variable. A corresponding variety of answers can be given to the question of what portion of income differences is justifiable or equitable (cf. Tinbergen (1976b)).

These answers can only be very tentative since too little material is available about the relevant determinants of income. Even though several authors have now collected and published information on the relevant job characteristics, their counterparts, the corresponding personality characteristics, have very seldom been included in this research. So far, the only material giving such information is the AKZO material used in table 1.1. However, the "counterparts" of s have not yet been used. This is being planned for a publication by Berkouwer (1978).

IV. Feasibility of an equitable distribution

IV.1. *Introduction; Some assumptions*

We will now discuss whether the equitable distribution as defined in this paper can possibly be attained and if so, by what policies. We will discuss this problem in a comparative-static framework. This implies that we consider long-term developments without major cyclical components or sudden changes. We are not going to list explicitly all the implied assumptions but they can be regarded as requiring that the future need for, say, academically trained manpower, is anticipated satisfactorily, so a sufficient number of students at lower levels, with the correct specialisation, are present at each point of time.

Another assumption is that the recommended policies are adopted internationally. Hence we exclude difficulties that could arise if policies were adopted by a single small country in a world following a different course.

IV.2. *Determinants of incomes*

To answer the question posed, we have to know with a reasonable degree of certainty what the most relevant determinants of incomes will be for the next few decades. The theoretical basis chosen is the one described in earlier publications (Tinbergen (1975, 1976a)) and further developed in collaboration with Professor Pen (Pen and Tinbergen (1977)), a collaboration on which this paper has drawn heavily, thanks to my colleague's generosity. The name we use to describe our theory is the theory of relative scarcity, and it goes without saying that we are indebted to many colleagues for discussions with them, both public and private. We cannot be complete in our list of those from whose contributions we have profited; among others we think of J. Berkouwer, V. Halberstadt and C.A. de Kam, J. Hartog, R.H. Haveman, G.R. Mustert, P. Taubman, B.M.S. van Praag and Mrs. Chiswick.

The theory has also been called the multifactor theory because we feel that the demand and supply for a number of human capabilities, say six or eight, have to be included. Our data base over longer periods, however, does not permit them all to be taken into account. Our own attempts to partly test the theory using time series are based only on evidence regarding education, the degree of independent decision making and the capital available per head, and we try to make a distinction between the demand and supply for each. At the core of our theory we consider the "race between technological development and education", described in Tinbergen (1975a, ch. 6) and a forthcoming study on the decline in the share of capital. The outcome of the race has so far been that educated people of various types have become considerably less scarce and will presumably continue to be so for the next few decades. The share of capital in national income has fallen and this may continue. The relative scarcity of leadership has similarly decreased, as reflected in the relative fall in executives' earnings already mentioned for the USA, but also applying in the Netherlands. However, we do not approve of the extreme fall in profits around 1975 and do not base our expectations on this recession effect, whether cyclical or structural.

IV.3. *Prospective scarcity of third-level manpower and its impact*

As a model has been elaborated for the Netherlands (Pen and Tinbergen (1977)) enabling us to specify the reduction in the relative scarcity of third-level manpower needed to attain an equitable income distribution between groups with different levels of education, we will concentrate on the Dutch figures. This model has been used to estimate what percentage of the active population should have third and second-level education in order that differences in income after tax are reduced to the differences compensating for differences in effort, as determined by a utility function estimated in a previous publication (Tinbergen (1975)). The percentages are 6.3 for third and 9.8 for second-level education compared with actual figures of 3.0% and 5.9% in 1962. These figures assume constant technology for which a correction will be discussed later. Let us first compare the percentages required with those already observed in 1973: the latter amount to 9% and 14% and are the consequence of the steep rise in the participation in education which took place in the "sixties". Since only the younger part of the active population present in 1973 had participated, we can expect – without a further rise in this participation – that by 1990 both figures will have risen further. We estimate the percentage in the third level will become 16.8 which is well above the 6.3% required for equity.

We must take into account, however, the probability of further technological development. If we do this in the same way as previously (Tinbergen (1975a, ch. 6)) we find that demand for third-level personnel will rise by a factor of 1.88 between 1962 and 1990; hence the percentage of the active population with third level education required for an equitable income distribution will become $6.3 \times 1.88 = 11.8\%$, still well below 16.8%. We can even assume a decline in participation in higher education, although this is not necessary to account for the increased "effort": this is already taken into consideration in the calculation of the figures 6.3% (without technological development) and 11.8% (including such development).

IV.4. *Prospective scarcity of leading or independent manpower*

In an analysis as yet unpublished (Tinbergen (1977)) we estimate that if independent manpower increases by 1% of the total active population, their relative income will fall by 2.3%. This result is obtained from a production function and hence represents the demand effect. Since in comparable countries independents constitute about 15% of the active population, the demand elasticity is approximately -3; however, for the U.S. a figure of -1 was found. To this result we add the assumption that it is possible to train extra leadership manpower; hence leadership is not entirely an innate capability. We base this assumption on the growth in the number of management courses organised by business as well as public authorities (business schools, for instance).

Taken together no clear picture of the prospects of the leadership élite evolves. Much research remains to be done on its possible contribution to less income inequality. However, the American figure for the fall in relative incomes of important business executives is remarkable.

IV.5. Possible changes in technological development

Until a decade ago most technological development was labour-saving. Since it meant the elimination of heavy physical effort or repetitive work, it was a positive contribution to human welfare as long as widespread unemployment could be avoided. Today, different trends are apparent. Pollution and other "new scarcities" are forcing industrialised communities to push legislation directed towards a new orientation in technological research: increasingly we have to save on energy and maintain or improve the quality of the environment. This may imply that the labour-saving aspect loses importance and that the increase in competition for jobs requiring more education may be even stronger than estimated in section IV.3. As far as the intellectual élite is concerned, the possibility exists that by market forces alone – if permitted to work – income differences may become equitable (in the sense we define it) before the year 2000. Whether anything comparable can be expected for the leadership élite is difficult to say (cf. section IV.4).

References

Berkouwer, J., doctoral dissertation, forthcoming 1978.
Bouma, N., B.M.S. van Praag and J. Tinbergen, "Testing and Applying a Theory of Utility", *European Economic Review* (1976).
Burck, C.G., "A Group Profile of the Fortune 500 Chief Executive", *Fortune*, May 1976.
Chiswick, B.R., *Income Inequality*, New York, 1974.
Chiswick, C.U., "The Growth of Professional Occupations in the American Labour Force: 1900–1963", World Bank paper based on Columbia University dissertation, Washington D.C. 1972. A revised version is published in *Research in Human Capital and Development*, Volume 1, 1977.
Duncan, O.D., D.L. Featherman and B. Duncan, *Socio-Economic Background and Occupational Achievement: Extensions of a Basic Model*, Washington, 1968.
Halberstadt, V. and C.A. de Kam, "Belastingpolitiek en inkomensverdeling", Verslag van het Congres ter ere van Prof. Mr. H.J. Hofstra, Leiden, 1976.
Hartog, J., doctoral dissertation, forthcoming 1977.
Haveman, R.H., "Jan Tinbergen's Income Distribution: Analysis and Policies, A Review Article", to appear in *Human Resources* and *De Economist*, 1977.
Muller, H., *The Search for the Qualities Essential to Advancement in a Large Industrial Group*, Utrecht, 1970.
Mustert, G.R., "Van dubbeltjes en kwartjes", een uitgave van de Wetenschappelijke Raad voor het Regeringsbeleid in de reeks Voorstudies en Achtergronden, Den Haag, 1976.
Pareto, V., *Cours d'économie politique*, Lausanne, 1896/7.
Pen, J. and J. Tinbergen, *Naar een rechtvaardiger inkomensverdeling*, Amsterdam, 1977.
Taubman, P. and T. Wales, *Higher Education: An Investment and a Screening Device*, New York, 1974.
Taubman, P., *Sources of Inequality of Earnings*, Amsterdam, 1975.
Taubman, P., "The Determinants of Earnings: Genetics, Family and Other Environments; A Study of White Male Twins", *American Economic Review* (1976).
Tinbergen, J., *Income Distribution: Analysis and Policies*, Amsterdam, 1975.
Tinbergen, J., *Income Differences: Recent Research*, Amsterdam (1976a).

Tinbergen, J., "Equitable Income Distribution: a Quantitative Challenge", in: Cairncross, A. and M. Puri (eds), *Employment, Income Distribution and Development Strategies: Problems of the Developing Countries,* London, 1976b.

Van den Doel, J., C. de Galan and J. Tinbergen, "Pleidooi voor een geleide loonpolitiek", *Economisch Statistische Berichten* (1976).

Van Praag, B.M.S., "The Welfare Function of Income in Belgium: An Empirical Investigation", *European Economic Review* (1971).

Van Praag, B.M.S. and A. Kapteyn, "Further Evidence on the Individual Welfare Function of Income: An Empirical Investigation in the Netherlands", *European Economic Review* (1973).

Van Praag, B.M.S., *De verdeling van Inkomen en Macht,* Leiden, 1975.

1 DISCUSSION

PAPER BY JAN TINBERGEN

Professor Krelle said that the paper discusses three main issues: the problem of equity, the determinants of income differences, and forecasts for the degree of inequality in the future. He intended to concentrate on the equity aspect. In his book, Tinbergen defines equity as "equal utility for all individuals". In the paper equity is regarded as "equal utility for all social groups", with the social groups defined fairly broadly. For example, all educated people are taken as one social group. The earlier definition is clearly the more basic as this implied "equal utility for all social groups", but the converse is not true.

He suggested considering the problem as follows. Suppose the utility of the ith individual is a function of his income y_i, variables x_{ij} under the control of person i representing "efforts", and parameters z_{ij} not under the control of person i, which can be regarded as endowments

$$u_i = f(y_i, x_{i1}, \ldots, x_{im}, z_{i1}, \ldots, z_{ih}), \qquad i = 1, \ldots, n. \tag{1}$$

There is a constraint due to the production function,

$$Y = \sum_{i=1}^{n} y_i = F(x_{11}, \ldots, x_{nm}, z_{11}, \ldots, z_{nh}, \ldots) \tag{2}$$

Aggregate real income equals total net production and is the sum of individual incomes, which are functions of all the individual efforts and endowments. There is a further constraint which is not mentioned explicitly in Professor Tinbergen's paper. Individual incomes are generated by a kind of earnings function

$$y_i = y_i(x_{i1}, \ldots, x_{im}, z_{i1}, \ldots, z_{ih}, \alpha_1, \ldots, \alpha_k, \ldots) \tag{3}$$

which includes parameters α_j determined by the government. The problem facing the government is to choose values of α_j in such a way that the u_i given in equation (1) are equalised under the constraints (2) and (3). The solution to this problem may involve a very low utility level, perhaps even lower than the minimum utility which would occur when utilities are not equalised. It may therefore be more appropriate to describe the outcome as Pareto pessimal rather than Pareto optimal.

Professor Krelle doubted whether this corresponded to our notions of equity, or to Professor Tinbergen's intentions. However a number of related problems are raised. He argued that suitable values of the α_j will not always exist, for example if some individuals are severely handicapped. But where should the line be drawn?

If the severely handicapped are excluded then perhaps the moderately handicapped should also be left out of consideration, together with those with strange perceptions, and those who are too demanding. In fact we may wish to neglect all whose needs can be satisfied only at very high cost. Otherwise the discontented, those in depressions, the egoists, people who are insatiable, will get the bulk of the GNP. Secondly, how are the individual utility functions obtained, even assuming they are measurable? They can be derived from questionnaires only if people do not know why the questions are being asked. If they understand the consequences of answering a question such as "When are you exceedingly well-off?", they will lie. In practice questioning is not feasible without elaborate precautions.

A third problem arises from Professor Tinbergen's individualistic concept of equity, which is distinguished from well being. Professor Krelle argued that more account should be taken of society as a whole. Equity in the sense used by Professor Tinbergen may involve a very high sacrifice for everybody, both in the current generation and in the future. He suggested that Professor Tinbergen's ideas could be taken up within the framework of the papers by Professors Abbing and Sen, where a balance is struck between individuals and society. It would be better to have a social preference function whose aruments are the individual utilities. Adopting an axiomatic approach, with the Nash axioms of Cooperative Game Theory, the social utility function is linear in the logarithms of individual utilities:

$$U = \sum_{i=1}^{n} \log u_i(\cdot), \tag{4}$$

where

$$u_i(\cdot) = u_i(C_i, L_i, \ldots), \quad \partial u_i/\partial C_i > 0, \quad \partial u_i/\partial L_i < 0, \quad u_i \text{ concave.} \tag{5}$$

The production constraint is:

$$\sum_i C_i - f(L_1, \ldots, L_n, \ldots) = 0, \tag{6}$$

where C = real consumption, L = labor, $\partial f/\partial L_i > 0$, f concave.

Maximizing U with respect to C_i, L_i under constraint (6) yields

$$\frac{1}{u_i}\frac{\partial u_i}{\partial C_i} = \lambda, \quad \frac{1}{u_i}\frac{\partial u_i}{\partial L_i} = -\lambda\frac{\partial f}{\partial L_i}, \quad \lambda \text{ a Lagrangian multiplier.} \tag{7}$$

The optimal distribution then involves equalising relative marginal utilities rather than absolute utilities.

Regarding the practical computations, he found it heroic that people with the same parameters should be at the same utility level regardless of their educational background. Essentially it assumes that people choose their education and occupation freely. This is not the case in Germany where the system determines where people end up, and it is frequently not an individual decision. Finally he found Professor Tinbergen's final remarks optimistic: that equity will be achieved before the year 2000. He also doubted whether the utilities of individuals could be maintained at roughly the same level in the long run. With higher average income, people become more sensitive to all kinds of differences.

Professor Somermeyer thought that Professor Krelle's remarks had been illuminating but not entirely fair. The paper states that the number of population sub-groups should be chosen as large as possible, so the distinction between "equal utilities for all individuals" and "equal utilities for all social groups" may not be very marked. In addition, after individuals have adjusted *optimally* to the constraints they face, utility differences will be reduced and the "efforts" become endogenous, with the values determined simultaneously with income.

Professor Sen found the paper stimulating and the approach useful. He agreed that the equity and optimality issues were not identical and that equity relates more to the characteristics of personal welfare than to income as such. He also agreed with the multi-factor approach to the relative scarcity theory, but, as Professor Krelle had pointed out, its application is somewhat easier when the groups are chosen fairly broadly. He was also a little worried about the use of the relative scarcity approach to income derived from capital ownership, where the approach suggests that we may need a lot of capital. Instead, we may have to consider the question of social ownership of capital, if we were placing much emphasis on equity.

On other issues he may differ from Professor Tinbergen. On the definition of equity there are two issues: (i) the space on which we define equity, and (ii) whether we define it in terms of an optimal point *or* in terms of a ranking. He agreed with Professor Tinbergen's choice of space, the space of personal welfares. However, if we define equity as a single ("most equitable"), point the rest of the space remains unordered. An equity ranking identifies the point of equity as a maximum. There is the further problem of ranking points which are not at the top and it is here that different approaches to the problem of attacking equity may typically surface. This also relates to the comment in the paper that the individual welfare function chosen – whether those estimated by Professor van Praag or not – would make little difference. The function chosen may not affect the equity point, but it will usually affect rankings elsewhere in the space. He personally had more sympathy with the approach of Professor van Praag than with the more common approach based on revealed preference, since actual choices may reflect a compromise of considerations, and furthermore (as Professor Krelle had pointed out) some of the options may not be available in actual choices. There is also the problem of cardinalisation which is inherently more difficult in the revealed preference approach than in that followed by van Praag, where the cardinalisation is natural.

Professor Sen also wondered about the handling of variations outside these broad social groups. The paper cites the problems of "organisability" and "insolvability" as justification for neglecting individual differences. He found the former perfectly acceptable. Consider the case in which we know that there are individual differences but not which way they go. As Abba Lerner and others have indicated, if you do not know which way they go, for a broad class of social welfare functions you will do better assuming these distinctions away rather than introducing them arbitrarily.

He had doubts about the insolvability question: the argument that for the physically or mentally handicapped it is impossible to raise them to the same welfare level. With a *ranking* of the welfare space it may be possible to *improve* equity without necessarily succeeding in getting to the point of complete equality.

Finally, he was stimulated by Professor Tinbergen's concern for going into the qualitative aspects of equity and welfare which is central to our judgement of the good society. Economists should have a lot to say on this question but typically neglect to say it. Tinbergen raises the question of individual rights, which is a very important problem. Frequently this is overlooked, or posed in terms of bogus contrasts. For example the contrast between liberty and equity, much discussed in the literature, is a bogus contrast because they are fundamentally after dissimilar things. Liberty is, in some ways, like income: it is, as it were, a good thing – a desired object. Just as there is a problem of distributing a good thing like income, there is the problem of distributing the good thing "liberty". The reason why emphasis on liberty often has right-wing associations is that some champions of liberty have tended to be concerned with liberty without considering its distribution. In fact, if we pursued this line of thought further, we could think of the problem of liberty being embedded in a general problem of equity, going into the distribution of good things – both income and rights. Income gives you freedom to choose what you buy and what kind of life you lead, and in this sense the analogy with liberty is, of course, striking. Equity in the distribution of liberty (in the sense of non-restraint) has thus as much a claim to our attention as income distributional equity.

Professor Stiglitz wondered why Professor Tinbergen's notion of equity differed from that of Rawls and how the problem of intertemporal equity between generations was to be resolved. Pursuing the conventional distinction between equity and efficiency, he asked whether Tinbergen had an ethical framework in which both these problems could be embedded. The question was raised partly because, if you are a Utilitarian, it can be shown that, in general, you will not want an equitable distribution in the way specified. For example, if everyone had exactly the same utility functions and the only form of taxation is income taxation (i.e. distortionary taxation, not lump-sum taxation), then, under fairly weak conditions, social welfare is maximised with an unequal income distribution. So we have inequality even though everybody is the same *ex ante*. The reason for this is that, with distortionary taxation, the mathematical structure is changed and we are faced with a non-concavity which results in inequality being optimal.

He was less convinced than Professors Sen and Krelle that individual utilities could be compared, and about the ability to measure individual utility functions. To take one example, most Americans feel that health problems are more severe than, say, those in India, who see themselves as quite healthy. If you were to allocate medical resources on the basis of those perceptions, peculiar results would occur. He disputed Professor Sen's remark that there was less problem of cardinalisation. He pointed out that, in addition to the estimation problems already raised concerning compensatory variations in income, it also has to be assumed that people have identical tastes. There is a substantial literature on labour supply, demonstrating that cross section estimates of supply elasticities do not measure those of any representative individual.

Professor Wiles approved of what he called "the Dutch School of income distribution" to which the conference had been exposed. But he noted the curious identification of the inequality of income with the inequality of power, which came out most clearly in the Minister's address. However, bureaucrats have relatively equal incomes but very unequal powers. The Dutch School also seems to have declared war on the market payment for scarce talent. With this he agreed, but it raised the question of how scarce talent was then to be allocated. He suspected that this would be done by administrative power, which would cease to be identified at all with wealth.

He warned against excessive emphasis on education; as Professor Taubman would later show, there is a great return on natural talent over and above education. Again the Dutch obsession with earned income and the disutility of labour neglected many other elements in distribution, for example the inheritance of capital and the family itself. Finally he did not believe in the Dutch theory of the convergence of capitalism and communism; all the recent evidence on the communist side was of a reversion to Stalinist practice. Even the equality of income, so much superior to ours, was being called into question again.

Professor von Weizsäcker suggested that the forecasts for increasing income equality in Holland may not extend to other countries. Germany had experienced only a rather slow movement towards equality. During the recent recession, unemployment had been higher than at any other time since the reconstruction of the German economy after the last war. The structure of unemployment was also interesting. There had been a shortage of skilled workers together with a surplus of university graduates and unskilled workers, particularly women. The shortage of skilled workers was due in part to the wage squeeze which had caused the wages of unskilled workers to rise above their productivity, but the educational process was also at fault. It had not converted unskilled workers to skilled workers as required, but rather to graduates. So the job structure had not changed to the same extent as the training pattern. People may get the income corresponding to their characteristics on the Tinbergen scale if such jobs existed, but they have a danger of being unemployed, particularly the higher income earners, and this affects their liberty to choose jobs.

Mr. Layard supported those who had argued against concentrating on pretax incomes. He also pointed out that the link between low earnings and the poorest households (measured in per adult equivalent terms) was rather weak. Of adult workers in the lowest 5% of the hourly wage distribution, only one in eight is in the lowest 5% of the distribution of income per adult equivalent. Low earnings are not, therefore, a major cause of household poverty. It should also be noted that two years of flat rate incomes policy in the U.K. has had almost no effect on the earnings distribution, except at the very top.

In his opinion, the role of income expectations, as opposed to actual income received, was given too little attention by welfare economists. He suggested that politicians act as if there is a kink in the utility function at about the current expected level of income, with the marginal utility of increments smaller than the utility loss from a corresponding income reduction. This illustrates one of the main difficulties in implementing redistributive policies; however desirable they appear to be, account must be taken of those who lose out in the process.

Dr. Wagner suggested that the discussion of equity should not concentrate on extreme examples of income distributions. It may be more rewarding to examine the way in which income distributions change in a general egalitarian direction. Less inequality certainly does not solve all social problems, but there is no need to be too anxious about new problems arising from less inequality, since substantial changes in the distribution will cause significant reinforcing changes in the perception of inequality.

Professor Tinbergen said the concept of equity proposed in the paper was, of course, a normative one and hence a subjective choice. It attempted to give a concrete scientific meaning to a word often used in political discussions. The definition implies that some types of labour income differences are acceptable from his point of view, whilst others are not – for example, scarcity premiums paid to talented individuals. The concept should be applied to groups of similar people to reduce the effect of irrelevant personal differences, in so far as these are randomly distributed.

He agreed with all those who said that a situation of equity may differ from one of optimality (maximum social welfare) and that for practical reasons (especially the allocation of scarce talent) the optimum must then be preferred. In his book *Income distribution: Analysis and policies* (Amsterdam, 1975, ch. 7), where the optimum was analysed, he felt that earnings equations had not been overlooked, as Professor Krelle feared. There, he did attempt to derive earnings equations from the demand and supply for various types of labour. Professor Sen had been right to point out that the paper did not discuss the ranking of distributions other than those which are equitable. Professor Sen's own paper in this volume would be helpful if such a ranking was thought to be necessary.

Professor Tinbergen said his definition of equity does require measurement of utility and in the paper he discusses two types of measurement: (i) asking people themselves to indicate their level of utility and (ii) derivation of utility levels from observed behaviour. The danger of misrepresentation raised by Professor Krelle only occurs with type (i), for instance with Professor van Praag's method. But its impact may be reduced considerably by using the answers to the questionnaire for tax purposes as well as for acquiring a desired job. Moreover, in scientific enquiries a guarantee that names will be deleted before the answers are used, helps a good deal to avoid misrepresentation.

His own preference was slightly in favour of (ii), but it does require additional assumptions, as indicated in the paper. Method (ii) also requires some freedom of choice for people with the same parameters, and he disagreed with Professor Krelle that no such freedom exists at all. Table 1.1 only assumes a limited range of choice and this seemed to him to be realistic.

He agreed with Mr. Layard that income expectations should be considered, and in a forthcoming dissertation by Mr. Jan Berkouwer some attention is devoted to that topic. Income from capital had also been neglected in this paper, but it is examined in the forthcoming book by Pen and Tinbergen.

Professor Tinbergen continued by saying that he felt the feasibility of an equitable income distribution to be less of an illusion than others may think. It largely depends on whether education can make certain personal qualities less scarce. For cognitive qualities he thought a fair degree of success was possible – even though he shared Professor Wiles' view that the impact of education on income is often overestimated. Evidence for Holland seemed to indicate a movement towards an equitable income distribution, as far as the incomes of people with different levels of education are concerned. Whether this is also true of incomes for different levels of managerial ability is another question. This depends on the degree to which these abilities can be learned, and this is not yet known. It is a most important area for further research.

Finally, he agreed that the theory of convergence (between East and West) has not, so far, been confirmed by the facts; but we should perhaps allow a longer period of time for the trends to emerge.

2 THE ETHICAL JUSTIFICATION OF INCOME INEQUALITIES

P.J. ROSCAM ABBING

I. Introduction

Every economist has encountered ethical points of view in his profession. But ethics is not just a different science, it is an essentially different kind of science. Epistomologically, as a moral philosopher, I am a stranger among economists. Thus you may wish to know the status of ethics and the nature of the relationship between economics and ethics. I shall not pass too lightly over questions on these matters. In addition, it will be seen that some anthropological concepts are required, so I shall deal with anthropology and its status as well.

I.1. *Economics*

Economics is one of the *descriptive* sciences. These sciences, to which primarily the natural sciences belong, give *ontological judgements*. They describe, ascertain, explain, predict.

Different descriptive sciences have different objectives. Economics is the study of how mankind organises production and consumption activities. A more elaborate definition is "economics is the study of how men and society end up *choosing*, with or without the use of money, to employ scarce productive resources which could have alternative uses, to produce various commodities and distribute them for consumption, now or in the future, among various people and groups in society" (Samuelson (1955)). One advantage of this more detailed definition is that it shows human choice to be the starting-point. Economics resembles the natural sciences, but it may also be considered one of the humanities. Even if man possessed freedom of choice, his actions and their effects would be embedded within a world determined by cause and effect.

Personal income distribution is one of the many separate subjects studied by economists. Economic science searches for possible means of measuring income distribution to provide statistical facts. From there it proceeds to analyse and explain the actual situation. It then goes on to study the ways in which movements towards some ideal state can be brought about.

I.2. Ethics

Ethics is not a descriptive, but a *normative* science. It gives no ontological judgements, but *value-judgements*. It aims at differentiating, not between appearance and reality, but between good and bad. Therefore it has a specific status, which is examined by the so-called meta-ethics.

What is the foundation of ethical statements? We begin by giving two negative answers. First of all, it should be clear that norms cannot be derived from facts. Those who think this can be done are guilty of the well known "naturalistic fallacy". It is not valid to argue from "is" to "ought". Secondly, natural scientists are inclined to see the ethical as a sort of characteristic, just as an object has characteristics, like those of being large or green. In other words, adherents of one discipline think in the terms and categories of their own science rather than in those of another. Furthermore, reducing the ethical, not to the objective characteristic of things but to the subjective opinions of people, will lead us nowhere. Ethical statements are then seen as expressions of emotions. This so-called *emotivism* neglects the fact that ethical statements need to have general validity. It is not simply a matter of taste for which we cannot objectively account.

Let us now consider the definition of ethics. Ethics is the science concerned with *man's positive and constructive response to requests made upon him by his fellow-man*. Objects, including the object-quality of man, convey a language to us and we respond with the natural sciences. However our fellow-man, as a human being, speaks a language which makes us feel a responsibility towards him and the study of ethics is directed towards this notion of responsibility. The starting-point in considering "the good", is the positive response to the appeal of our fellow-man, affirming and confirming his existence. Man is not only *homo faber* or *homo civis*, but also *homo respondens*.

It would seem then that the ethical cannot be reduced to the non-ethical. This is not a secondary, but a primary fact. It is no epiphenomenon, but a basic phenomenon. Those who see everything in objective terms cannot understand why one man should feel compassion towards another, unless such compassion can be subsumed under instincts of self interest. Those who do not remain impartial, but who are aware of and concerned about the appeal made by their fellow-man, clearly feel they should be compassionate towards him. Thus, the ethical is based upon *evidence* which is both apparent and authoritative. Every science starts from certain basic data or axioms; ethics, as a science, starts from this evidence.

How can we obtain norms that determine what is good and what is bad? Again we start by giving two negative answers. It is not sufficient to say *teleologically* that the result of our actions is determinate and that the desired result is derived from the actual needs of man, as they are defined by *hedonism* and *eudemonism*. The effect of human actions does matter, but the ethical question concerns what is right for the other person. Nor is it enough to hold the *deontological* view, which presumes that only the will of the individual concerned can be right and that this will is right if man acts, not according to disposition, but according to obligation. The intentions of human action are indeed relevant in ethical judgements, but they do not result in a criterion for ethically correct action.

Norms are produced in a relationship between two people based on *responsibility*. I shall mention four of the norms that are thus produced and that are, in any case, essential.

Firstly, we should act with reverence or *respect* towards our fellow-man. He is the value that determines the norm. In every respect he is the objective, not the means, of our action. That is why we respect his individuality, his freedom, his conviction. Secondly, we should act *reliably* and speak truthfully. The relationship with him should involve communication, so we can take each other seriously and rely upon one another. Thirdly, we should act in *mercy*. If our fellow-man needs our help, we should not refuse, for his need makes our help necessary. Finally, we should act in *justice*. Every man is, in principle, equal and it is not ethically right to discriminate, to prefer one person to another.

Ethics covers many topics. One of them is the ethics of income distribution. In this the norm of justice is dominant. That which can be distributed among people should be justly distributed. In my opinion, there are mainly three items to be distributed: *income, freedom* and the *opportunity to share responsibility*. Although we shall pay particular attention to a just distribution of income, it is clear that we cannot disregard the just distribution of freedom and responsibility.

Income is not just a matter of wages, but of possessions and the physical and mental effects of an environment. But we shall first consider income in the form of wages. By a just distribution among everyone, we include future generations as well as the current generation and view justice in international, rather than national, terms. However, we shall develop our analysis in terms of national distributions.

I.3. *Anthropology*

Anyone who is seriously concerned with ethics must consider man seriously. Ethics implies anthropology. The converse is also true – they are interrelated. Anthropology makes use of the techniques of various sciences. Fundamentally, however, it is a philosophical discipline. Philosophy searches for answers to final questions. Its quest is for the essence, the meaning.

One of the branches of philosophy is philosophical anthropology. What is its concern? Because we are now dealing with final issues, evidence is more important than logical proofs. Thus we proceed on the principle that man is not merely a complicated thing, nor a disguised god. But what is man? Many answers are possible. One account is the following:

Man is an entity with several dimensions. Certain dimensions are more essential and specific to him than others. The following four dimensions are progressively essential. Man is an *object*, spatially, physically, with particular form, structure and weight; as such he is determinate, subject to cause and effect. Yet man is even more *subject*, he is I, making choices; as such he is not without a certain amount of freedom. Furthermore he is *relative*, living primarily in relation with the outside world, with his fellow-men, with values, with God. In the relationship with his fellow-man, as in other respect, he can act either for good or for evil. Finally and fundamentally man is *history*, living in the present, making history. This is one reason why man is morally responsible for his actions.

The question whether man is good or evil cannot be answered, because good and evil are not objective qualities. While choosing or acting, he can behave well or badly. He who lives without consideration for his fellow-man, has chosen a course of action that shows concern for the wrong things. However such behaviour is rarely consistent or continuous.

Another anthropological question concerns the fundamental aim of man. What is the meaning of his life? Numerous answers are provided by the various philosophies, world-view and religions. I, as a Christian, would answer that man finds the meaning of his life if he lives within, and on the basis of, a good relationship with the true God – but others will answer differently. Fortunately these specific answers need not be relevant for the ethics of income distribution. Social justice does not prohibit any pluriform culture. On the contrary, if freedom is also distributed fairly, everyone will be entitled to hold and practice worldly and religious convictions. Within the framework of the ethics of income distribution we cannot escape the anthropological question concerning the relationship between the individual and the community.

In what respect is one individual related to other individuals, to the community (of the nation and ultimately of mankind)? Again we must first remove two misconceptions.

The other person is no secondary entity. The community does not result from adding individuals together. Individuals do not primarily form their own entities, to be then joined together in a community. Such *ontological individualism* always leads to ethical individualism.

The converse, the community being primary and the individual secondary, is not true either. If that were the case society would be like a tree and the individuals its leaves, which have a function but which can be pruned off to increase the tree's vigour. Individuals would then have a secondary value and could be sacrificed to the welfare of society. Such *ontological collectivism* or *vitalism* always leads to ethical collectivism or vitalism, by which individuals may be sacrificed.

In principle, man is communal, so his fellow-man is no secondary entity. Neither society nor the individual is secondary. There is a synchronism and a *mutual relationship*.

Each individual is related to the community, which in turn is related to each individual. This ontological aspect correlates with the ethical. Each individual should be aware of the interest of all the community – and the community should be aware of the interest of each constituent individual. Later we shall discuss the difficult issue of how this should be translated into social organisation, which leads to the notion of income distribution.

II. Ethical principles of income distribution

II.1. *Deduction and induction*

In ethics one must try to bring *norm* and *fact* closely together. The norm is the deductive element in the argument, analysis of facts the inductive element. They require each other, but they do not follow from one another.

Concerning norms, one should be aware that often the current norm has not been chosen consciously, but is more or less a product of its own time and class, and its own individual development and circumstances. A considerable volume of cognitive sociology, including ethical sociology as well as developmental psychology and psycho-analysis, can assist in removing unconsciousness, to clarify what is really evident. Scholarly ethical study can help to differentiate between what, by tradition, is apparently evident and what, objectively, is really evident.

With regard to *reality-analysis*, one encounters reality at a certain moment in a historical context. It is the last picture in a series which together shows the film of history. An analysis of the present may benefit from an analysis of the past that led to the present. Yet one should guard against a historical philosophy, as well as against the idea that the historical process develops in accordance with immutable laws. With such an idea in mind one frequently discovers laws when there are no laws, or assumes developments which are far from certain; and one pretends to be able to discover from reality which are the right developments, so that one thinks that norms can be derived from facts and trends.

II.2. *The ideal and reality*

We have discussed the problem of bringing together norm and reality, the deductive and the inductive. We can reduce it to the denominators of the ideal and the real. Ethics examines how something should be ideally and how it can be in reality.

Both the terms "ideally" and "in reality" can refer to several concepts at the same time. It is necessary to distinguish these. I shall mention three:

(i) In a very broad sense we can distinguish between the *abstract* and the *concrete*, a norm being an abstract thing and a fact concrete.

(ii) The contrast mentioned above becomes more precise if we understand by "ideally" a very *simplified* situation and by "reality" a *complicated* situation, such as is customary among people. In the ethics of income distribution it is indeed useful to consider first what the distribution would be like if all men performed the same kind of work and attached the same value to it, if all men had the same needs and satisfied these in the same way, and if all men had the same abilities – with the additional assumptions that all have maximum social concern and that the organisation that settles these matters is perfect. If one gradually drops these unreal assumptions and introduces complications, one can determine step by step what the income distribution should be in the

complex real world. In this way one applies the method of diminishing abstraction, which is often used in economics as well as ethics.
(iii) It is necessary to distinguish further the sorts of complications that arise. On the one hand there is the problem that men have different needs and abilities. This is no logical embarrassment, but it makes the problem rather complicated. On the other hand there exists harsh reality which, in more than one respect, impedes the realisation of what is truly just. As an example of such obstacles I mention first the fact that every organisation is defective, unstable; and secondly the fact that the disposition of the men concerned is often defective as well, since it includes elements of egoism. Thus the contrast may either be between *perfect* and *defective* or between *good* and *evil*.

II.3. *Equality and inequality*

Let us consider first *in abstracto* a most simplified situation. If all men were equal in all respects and if all of them were to carry out the same work during the same period of time under similar circumstances, it would be taken for granted that everyone would receive the same wages. I can think of no reason why one should earn more than another. Our starting point should thus be the notion that all men must have the same income if there are no variables that generate unequal incomes. For convenience we shall neglect the fact that not everyone can receive income from work, for example children, the aged and sick. Nor shall we take into account the position of the housewife who works, although her work is not regarded as an occupation. We shall limit our consideration to the person who is employed and we state that he has a right to income.

We must now introduce actual differences one by one to see whether these should ideally involve a difference in reward. For the sake of brevity we shall move on to a situation in which objectively the nature, duration and circumstances of the work vary, and subjectively the abilities and tastes of the worker vary as well. For the time being we shall assume that an ideal organisation can direct the right man to the right place, so that every person will be employed according to his abilities and liking – or to what he dislikes least. Then all will be equally satisfied and should receive equal payment.

To be more realistic we now assume that not everybody is equally satisfied with the work he is supposed to do. Certain variations in work are inevitable and these do not simply correspond to differences in the preferences of workers. Moreover workers themselves may live in different circumstances which make differing expenditures necessary or desirable.

Thus there are in my opinion three ethically acceptable reasons why rewards should vary. Firstly, it is just that those who *work harder* should earn more than those who do not; so those who are willing to work overtime should be allowed to receive extra payment. Secondly, those who accept *unpleasant working conditions* should be allowed some compensation for this more unpleasant work; so those whose work is dirty or unduly strenuous or involves greater responsibility, should earn more than those whose work does not include such features. Finally the amount of income should correspond to certain *elements of need;* in this, one can include professional needs, and also the extra expenditure associated with a large family or periods of illness.

In general there is agreement as regards the ethical acceptability of these three variables; exertion, unpleasant working conditions and special needs. A good deal has already been provided in our society, although one of the weak points is that very unpleasant work is often paid the least (work for which we in Western Europe attract immigrant workers, who are underpaid).

If one asks to what extent wages should be allowed to differ in view of the first and second variables, I would say that this cannot be established in general terms because the mechanism of a really free labour market, without the power of monopolies, should itself solve this problem. If, for instance, extra work should be done by a few members of a group, all of whom are capable of doing this extra work, it is in principle not only efficient and economical, but also fair, to determine the reward by "auction". For the pleasure of increased potential consumption will offset the displeasure of extra work.

For those who think in conventional terms, the difficulty lies not in the existence of these three variables, but in the non-existence of other variables. In our present society many other factors play a part in income differentials. Even now *tradition* plays a major role, for example the tradition that intellectual professions should be paid more than other professions. Hitherto *power* has also played a considerable part. Each year collective labour agreements are determined by a trial of strength between employers and employees; nothing can guarantee, or even make it seem probable, that the group that wins has justice on its side. In this matter our Western world has up to now been a jungle, in which the law of the jungle prevails – a situation which must worry each of us. Furthermore, being endowed with a *scarce talent*, for which there is an economic need, plays an enormous part. Thus the person who has been gifted with such a scarce talent can sell himself on the labour market at a high price, as long as the system pays according to the economic value of the work performed. In so far as that talent has not been formed by extra exertion, but was endowed at birth, it is simply unjust if such an arbitrary and fortunate factor assures a high income.

There is also the problem of *unearned income*. If one person owns more than another, he has an extra source of income from interest, rent or dividends. The principle of interest is not necessarily wrong and it performs an economically useful function, because it directs scarce resources to where they are most remunerative. However it further increases unjust differences in wealth. These differences are indeed unjust if they derive from inheritance or from saving out of an income which is already too high. All in all it is clear that we should strive for a society in which all the factors that determine differences in income are eliminated as much as possible.

One factor I have not mentioned is *risk-taking*. Those who are involved in free enterprise, either the self-employed – a farmer, shopkeeper, commercial agent – or producers – whether an individual, a group or an organisation – always take risks. They either lose or win, in each case to a greater or lesser extent. To judge this factor in a truly ethical way we should distinguish at least six different types of risk. This would take more space than is available here. But among those who have to live by profit, there are always people who are victims and those who are profiteers through circumstances they do not control. Ethically this is a bad thing. Therefore the starting-point remains that each should receive a certain income that corresponds to the nature of his work in the service of the community.

II.4. *Organisation and incentive*

If we are seeking to create a labour-system in which the only variations in wages are those which have been accepted above, then an organisation is required which can help to achieve it. If, for convenience, we think in national terms for the present, it will be simplest if everyone can work in one big national production and service organisation. Then it will be easy to establish one system of payments with standardised wages, set up on pure principles. The mangement of that national business will be in government hands, a government appointed, controlled and supported by an excellent democracy. It is clear, however, that such a mammoth organisation has its disadvantages, if only the dangers of inefficiency, bureaucracy, costliness because of the number of civil servants, inertia of central decision making, rigidity and so on. At the very least there should be some decentralisation, so that certain units, such as business companies, will receive relative autonomy, controlled on the one hand by the internal democracy of the workers involved and on the other by the external democracy of government and nation.

In practice one also needs to make other concessions. There is not only the problem of organisation, but also the selfishness of many of the workers. It will almost inevitably be necessary to introduce, for example, incentives which stimulate extra exertion and discourage slackness. In this way one must also provide encouragement to take justifiable risks. It is not possible to elaborate on these matters here.

II.5. *Justice and other criteria*

In all these matters we should realise that the achievement of social justice cannot be our sole aim. If insistence on strict justice crippled all production, the final result would be that only a small cake would be distributed in an extremely fair way, while it would be more advantageous to all if a large cake were divided more randomly. If that is true, one should make at least five demands upon the socio-economic structure of any society. The social structure should be such that: a large national product will be produced; there will be growth, if that is justifiable and desired; there will be a pleasant living environment; the ethos will be such that all concerned are encouraged to adopt a social rather than an egotistic attitude; and finally, of course, social justice will be realised to the greatest possible extent.

The order in which I have listed these five criteria is arbitrary, but it is clear that there can be conflicting claims among the five and in some cases one criterion must dominate another.

In the above we have gradually introduced various real phenomena, but the whole approach has remained rather theoretical. We shall now try to look at these questions more closely, considering economic and legal aspects in particular.

III. Applied ethics of income distribution: Socio-political systems

III.1. *Selfishness*

In section II we introduced, in general terms, the realism that is necessary. We ended by admitting the fact that people can be selfish. To give full weight to realism – and thus to guard ethics against the appearance of being irrelevant, romantic or utopian – we shall begin with that most realistic fact, the selfishness of the average person. For convenience we shall start from the principle that each person, to some extent at least, will serve his own interest. This raises the question whether it will be possible to prevent society from becoming a fight of all against all.

Will the only alternative, then, be that each person will have a policeman assigned to him, who will forbid him to do anything that may damage the interest of his fellow-man and who will oblige him to do what is in the interest of all? And must there be a soldier behind each policeman to watch this policeman, and so on?

Fortunately social reality need not look quite so grim. The fact that society is not a fight of all against all is largely a result of mysterious and inbuilt harmony mechanisms. The Classical liberals even started from the principle of this harmony dogma: if each person serves his own interest, then all will serve the interest of all. It is not quite as simple as that. Nevertheless, discovering and guarding these precious harmony elements is of great importance. We shall examine each of them briefly.

III.2. *Forms of harmony between self-regarding action and altruistic effect*

It can happen that an individual, in serving his own interest, simultaneously serves the interest of others – perhaps more often unintentionally. It may also happen that an individual is encouraged to serve the interest of others as well as his own, or to moderate striving for his own interest in the short term, because that will benefit him in the longer run. Both possibilities will be examined separately.

III.2.1. *Socially beneficial pursuit of self interest*

So far as I can discover, there are five situations in which the pursuit of self-interest serves the interest of others at the same time.
(i) *Exchange:* If *A* and *B* want to exchange two goods voluntarily, not under pressure of need or with unequal access to market information, each of them serves both his own interest and the interest of the other in this transaction. From this viewpoint one can approve of the working of the market. Indeed

the market mechanism, operating in the goods and service markets as well as the labour market or even the money market, is an invaluable system for which it is difficult to suggest a substitute. It is well known that in practice there are very serious defects associated with this mechanism, particularly since one market group can be stronger than another and can therefore exercise power. The consequences can then be socially disastrous. However, the remedy should not be rejection of the market mechanism, but elimination of the detrimental side effects.

(ii) *Co-operation:* In certain circumstances two people can together achieve more than double what each of them could have achieved separately. Then both *A* and *B* relies on co-operation with the other to pursue his own interest. This is the basis for widespread co-operation on which our affluence depends to a great extent. It is recognised that there are difficulties here also, particularly since one person may be stronger than the other and it is possible for the employer to exploit his employee. Again the objective should not be the destruction of the system of co-operation, but mitigation of the detrimental side effects.

(iii) *Enjoyment of work:* The man who takes pleasure in his job and regards his work as a kind of hobby, may work for his own enjoyment and at the same time perform a job which is socially useful. Unfortunately this situation seldom arises. However it is important that we try to enable everyone to derive as much enjoyment from their work as possible.

(iv) *The need for mutual affection:* If a woman longs to have children, it may be considered primarily a selfish desire. But the mystery is that her desire is directed towards giving affection to another person. This need for mutual affection, or at least having good relations with others, is a most useful factor in society. However this harmony factor can also work in reverse, for affection for one's own family or group sometimes means a dislike for others outside that group.

(v) *Profit to third parties:* Activities which fully reflect self-interest can be important to third parties. If an employer makes an investment by extending his factory, construction workers and others will benefit by it. The flow of money, even for evil purposes, enables others to benefit. This argument has often been abused, when it is said that the poor should be grateful for the existence of the rich. The motivation varies, but the theme remains the same. In the past it was argued that the rich were useful because they could be charitable to the poor; later it was said that the very rich spent money which would generate activity among tradespeople. Then it was suggested that the wealthy were necessary to provide the capital that business companies need to finance investments. Nowadays one hears the argument that the rich are useful because they contribute a large part of the taxes which enable a government to provide services for all, including the poor.

Though many of these arguments may have some validity, they do not explain why differences between the rich and poor should continue. One would rather conclude that it is a condemnation of any form of society which compels the poor to be grateful to the rich.

All in all we should remember that these five harmony elements are of great importance. In practice it is very surprising that, in so many situations, pursuit of one's own interest also serves the interest of others.

III.2.2. *Relationships of interdependence*

There are also situations in which *A* can only serve his own interest by deliberately taking into account the interest of *B*, either by serving *B*'s interest to some extent, or by avoiding doing too much damage to *B*'s interest. This is likely to occur most often with *relationships of interdependence*. In this section we started from the principle that *A*'s relationship with *B* is both autonomous and autarchic. It may also happen that there is an interdependence between *A* and *B*, and this introduces a whole new mechanism.

In so far as *A* is dependent of *B*, he may feel obliged to keep on good terms with *B* in his own interest. If *A* simply plays off his own interest against *B*, it may happen that *B* – for instance if he is employed by *A* – avoids *A* or shakes his fist at *A* or obstructs *A*. Thus it is important that *A* adopts a positive psychological, as well as economic, relationship towards *B*. *B* may be an employee of *A* but he can adopt a position more distant from *A*, so the full effects of *A*'s relation to *B* may only become apparent retrospectively in the long run. Thus employers may damage their own interests if they allow their employees to become so poor and ill that they cannot work properly; or if they pay such low wages that employees will not have the spending capacity to purchase the products of the employers; or if they keep the developing countries in such an underdeveloped state that in the long run it will be impossible to continue trading with them.

Alternatively, if employees manage to increase their wages to such a high level that it is unprofitable to employ them, they harm themselves as a group. The so-called "well-informed self interest" of both should ensure that they will not do great damage to each other's interests.

Such a situation may occur in almost any of the five cases mentioned above. If there is a perfectly competitive market, each producer will be forced by his competitors to offer a product as good and cheaply as possible. The situation provides an incentive for rendering good service and prevents attempts to cheat or trick customers. As regards co-operation, we have just shown that employers and employees are dependent on each other in many respects.

III.2.3. *Balance of powers*

One can go a step further and recall that there are also cases when *A* and *B* are well matched in power and in this situation one cannot damage the other too much without being harmed by the other. Then the *"countervailing powers"* come into play, about which R. Niebuhr has already written and from which Galbraith expects a great deal. Certain groups should preferably have powers which match the power of other groups. According to this idea, employers' organisations and trade unions, as well as consumer associations, etc., should each have about the same amount of power. In the usual tug of war, for instance the negotiation of collective labour agreements, the result will be that one party cannot unilaterally impose his will upon the other.

It will be recognised that such a balance of power is always unstable and hazardous. Thus the question arises concerning the appropriate power a government should have to enable it in promote social justice and, in particular, a fair distribution of incomes, for the whole population rather than just one group. The mechanisms which we have discussed in this section do not adequately remedy social injustice. They will have to be used, but a great deal more will have to be done to achieve a close approximation to a just distribution of incomes.

IV. The law

IV.1. *Legislation, pragmatism and ethos*

In the last section we concentrated our attention on what is involved in well-informed self interest. We assumed only a pragmatic disposition in the individual citizen. Fortunately, this will take us a long way, but not quite far enough.

A second possibility is that the citizen has a more *ethical disposition*. Then, from an ethical sense of responsibility, he will personally strive for what is socially just and take no more than his share would be in a perfectly just society. Thus he will help those who are in difficulty even if this conflicts with his own interest. Such an ethos is of great value. Nevertheless in our desire for a just society we cannot use that ethos as a basis in addition to pragmatism. In fact this would mean a return to charity instead of progress towards justice. Moreover we would be speculating on a characteristic which is only occasionally found among individual citizens; yet we require such an ethos of social purpose to be present in a majority of the population. In a democracy the citizen should direct government policy. Thus there should be at least a majority of the people who want the government to promote not so much the interest of their own group as the equal interest of all.

Indeed the government with its legislation should be a third factor, enforcing what is necessary in a decisive way. In addition to *pragmatism* and *ethos*, *legislation* is also indispensable.

IV.2. *Legislation to maintain the purity of harmony elements*

The least the law can do is to foster the harmony-elements described above, removing the disadvantages as far as possible. Thus one can try to prevent the creation of excessive market power by means of anti-trust legislation, for instance. Following such a policy, one can create advisory bodies, in which common sense will identify the mutual interests of conflicting parties. To promote a balance of power, one can help a weak partner become strong among the strong by means of, say, a government–sponsored consumers' association. In this very indirect way a great deal needs to be done, but it will be immediately obvious that this is only patchwork, because interdependent relationships are practically always asymmetrical and the balance of power is always unstable. The harmony-elements are the most indispensable and therefore must be preserved; but they need to be purged as completely as possible.

IV.3. *Social legislation*

Social legislation and compulsory social insurance are more directly effective in the service of those who are weak and deprived. One can also adopt a policy to make access to better paid jobs open to everyone in principle, regardless of their background and financial standing.

Requiring employers to pay minimum wages to all those who work full-time is an even more direct method. I could mention other examples. But it is clear that all this is only patchwork and does not affect the major injustices.

IV.4. *More radical legislation*

Anyone who really wants to overcome all those factors which cause differences in income, apart from the three factors which we have identified as ethically acceptable, ought to be prepared to give more power to the government and should approve stricter legislation. The man who is endowed with a scarce talent that is capable of being made economically remunerative, should no longer be allowed to sell himself at the highest price on the labour market. The men who has capital (how did he acquire it?) should not use it to provide an additional source of income. Still less should he be allowed to influence business companies because of his capital. The government should have the power to fix wages and prices and to have authority over companies. Such brief statements immediately raise many questions, however. How far should the authority of the government go? What is its objective? These questions are so important that we must consider them separately.

V. **The government**

As indicated earlier, for the sake of convenience we shall limit consideration to national government rather than world government, which we may contemplate or even seek to achieve. A true government is one of a united state. There should be one central authority over a given territory. This central authority is necessary to enforce justice, among other things, in all parts of that country.

V.1. *Structure*

This government should be chosen democratically, and then supported and regulated. By the democratic method we understand – with Schumpeter – an institutional arrangement by which individuals secure the power to make political decisions by competing for the votes of the population. The more authority the government possesses, the better the parliamentary democracy must work. A fair distribution, not only of consumption but also of freedom and the opportunity to share responsibility, necessarily involves democracy, including political democracy. This implies that every form of dictatorship has been rejected.

The government should recognise the limits of its power. Basic rights of the individual citizen should be guaranteed in the constitution. Various forms of freedom – not just religious freedom – must be ensured. This implies that the totalitarian state has been rejected. Conversely, the government must have far-reaching powers to produce prosperity and to secure fair distribution. Thus reduction to a police state, which merely maintains order, has also been rejected.

At an earlier point we looked at man as an object, as a subject, as a relation. In that connection we discussed his consumption requirements, his freedom, his responsibilities. Accordingly the government must concern itself with consumption, prosperity and its fair distribution, and at the same time respect rights of freedom and recognise democratic responsibility.

The thing which particularly interests us, in the present context, is the way in which such a state should take care of prosperity and its fair distribution.

V.2. *Individual and community*

What is the basis for the notion that the government should be responsible for prosperity and justice? To be comprehensive we should say responsible for prosperity, including growth; for welfare, to the extent that it involves a healthy and pleasant environment and a satisfactory educational system; and for justice, bearing in mind the five criteria that we thought important in our appraisal of a social system. Although nowadays relatively few people dispute the responsibility of a government in this field, it is important to discuss its background, so this responsibility is seen to be well founded and its consequences accepted. Therefore we shall direct our attention to the following points:

(a) A popular community is a community of people who, to some extent at least, feel concern for one another. Together they decide not to allow one person to perish helplessly. It would seem that we feel responsible, up to a point, for each other's opportunities in life. In that respect a national population somewhat resembles a family. In a much weaker sense one might call it a community of mutual affection. In my opinion this is not merely a romantic statement; it is a realistic statement, as it should be. And it has been valid to a great extent ever since we became an affluent state, a welfare state, a social state.

(b) Mutual care for one another assumes give and take. It assumes certain obligations and rights for each individual person. In Western countries the constitutional liberties have been won from autocratic authorities. Because of this the liberties of the individual citizen have been given primary emphasis. Emphasis on these liberties is a good thing, but it is one sided. A citizen has not only community rights but obligations as well. In the constitutions of Eastern

European countries there is more emphasis on obligations. It seems to me that this is correct; at least that the rights and obligations of liberty should supplement each other.

(c) Behind this difference between the contents of the constitutions in Western European and Eastern European countries there lies a difference in the concept of the relationship between the individual and society. We have already argued that, as a matter of principle, every strict individualism and collectivism should be rejected. However this merely poses, rather than solves, the problem. In the East, as in the West, the interest of the individual is acknowledged and the responsibility of the individual is recognised. Moreover, recall that we have concentrated exclusively on socio-economic issues. We are only concerned here with the living conditions of the people, divorced from whatever else each person makes of his life in terms of his own freedom and exercising his own responsibility. The question of income distribution has to be considered from this aspect.

The Western World has a liberal past. This is apparent from the fact that in Western constitutions the emphasis lies on each individual person's freedom. In practice this appears to come down to the fact that each person is expected to serve his own interest and that, representing the community, the government's task is to ensure that the resulting differences do not become too large. The government makes *corrections* ex post, regulating high incomes by progressive taxation, for instance, and increasing low incomes by means of social security, scholarships and the like. Production depends mainly on free enterprise, under which each company is assumed to serve its own interest. The government, however, levies taxes on profits and tries increasingly to control the companies by means of social legislation.

In Eastern Europe the framework is different. There are nationalised companies; there is a planned economy; in principle everyone is a civil servant. This is based on the idea that society should be responsible for everyone's welfare and a fair distribution. The whole framework has therefore been centrally organised. In practice, however, *concessions* are made, such as a degree of decentralisation and wage incentives, which lead to significant differences in earnings.

However, strict liberalism, with a completely free economy, is in practice nowhere to be found in the Western World. Nor can strict communism, with a completely centrally planned economy, be found anywhere in the Eastern World. The West has long been busy diluting its liberalism and imposing social constraints on free enterprise. And the East has long been busy liberalising in the socio-economic field. Tinbergen has developed a convergence theory, according to which the West will become increasingly socialised and the East increasingly liberalised. So far as I can see, his conception of this matter, and his view of the most favourable regime, is right in practice. Nevertheless I think that, both methodologically and in principle, some starting-point should be chosen.

The communist starting-point seems to me ethically right. On the other hand the starting-point of liberalism does not seem ethically right. Elsewhere I have written: "the communist ethic is positive: let each individual serve all, then the community will serve him; the liberal ethic is negative: let no one be a burden on his fellow man, then the community will not be a burden on him. Besides this positive and negative distinction, there is the difference between the concept of the individual as a member of the community and the individual as monad. Communism sees the individual in his relation to the community: the individual has an obligation towards the community, is dependent on the community and is itself the goal of the community. Liberalism is interested primarily in the individual apart from the community and only secondly in communal interests. The former is right; the latter is at least incomplete.

It is right to create a social structure that encourages community service and the awareness than the state stands beside me and should be supported by me. And it is wrong to create social structures in which community service is achieved only indirectly at best, and in which the government is my opponent and restricts my freedom. It is right to make social justice a primary objective, to make this objective the responsibility of the government and to give the government the powers required to achieve that goal. It is wrong to choose a starting-point in which this is not a primary ambition. It is inherently right that capital goods should be owned by the community and it is wrong to reject this on ethical grounds. It is right to make concessions to the harsh and selfish reality only when this is strictly necessary, and it is wrong to start from that reality and make concessions only when it is ethically inevitable".

To avoid any misunderstanding I want to make it clear that, in the above, I have been concerned only with the socio-economic system, not with the cultural and political environment. Moreover it is exclusively concerned with the best system in an *ideal* situation. In addition, it concerns solely the starting-point for thought. Finally, the issue is only that of a fundamental choice of position, quite apart from the question of where in practice the most just society, as judged by the five above criteria, is to be found.

V.3. *Policy*

If the previous argument is correct, it follows that, if we were free to build a society from scratch, we should not ask which companies should be nationalised, but which companies should be run privately. The nationalised company is fundamentally right, although it may be better for practical reasons to let certain companies belong to groups of individuals. The community can control production, wages and prices through government bodies – again democratically chosen, regulated and supported. The government and its representatives should determine wages by professional analysis of the variables (exertion, unpleasant working conditions and special needs) related to the nature of the work and the employer.

Various things will be needed to preserve the harmony elements mentioned earlier. It stands to reason that co-operation is indispensable. A planned economy has even the claim to be able to make such co-operation optimal. But it is particularly important that the free market and competition are preserved. This is true not only of the markets for goods and services, but also (to a limited extent) of the labour and money markets. There are many who think that to combine a planned economy with a free market is the equivalent of trying to square the circle. However, certain neo-socialist economists argue that a planned economy can be most advantageous for a free market, because there are no private monopolies. I know that these matters are not as simple as I am now making them. Nevertheless such a system is definitely no mere utopia; it is becoming more and more capable of realisation.

Nevertheless, no doctrinaire solution should be imposed. If harsh reality requires concessions, then these *concessions* must indeed be made. As harsh reality we must consider two factors which I have mentioned earlier: defects of organisation and defects in the attitude of workers.

As regards organisation, there will have to be insistence on decentralisation. With decentralisation top management becomes less expensive; certain decisions can be made quicker; internal democracy can be given more scope; and more account can be taken of local circumstances. However decentralisation contains an element of concession as a rule, because both conflicts and injustices may arise between decentralised units.

Concessions will also have to be made to defects in the attitude of the workers. Creating systems in which self-regarding action has no anti-social effect and may even be socially beneficial, is not always fully effective. At least for the time being, it is probably impossible to pay according to exertion with such a delicate precision that inadequate exertion will be limited or reflected in lower wages, and the acquisition of skills will be encouraged and reflected in higher wages, when (and only when) acquisition of those skills has entailed extra exertion. Perhaps separate payments should be made for risk-taking. All this we cannot and need not work out in detail. It is the viewpoint from which one should regard all this that is most important. The view taken of the possibly inevitable concessions is also relevant here, limiting the claims of justice in the interest of efficiency, real wages, pleasant working conditions, or rewards for special responsibility.

V.4. *No attempt to minimise government authority in the socio-economic field*

From all this it appears that we certainly do not argue for minimising government powers in the socio-economic field. Adherents of certain theories on the nature and function of government do so. One of the weak points of these theories – which here we cannot discuss further – is that such a government is unable to achieve social justice.

To avoid misunderstanding we shall repeat once more that we have in mind a government that has been democratically chosen, supported and regulated (there is no dictatorship) and possessing an authority that covers only the socio-economic field (it is no totalitarian state).

VI. Postscript

There are two reasons for breaking the rule, that I have followed here, of quoting no one, to mention Rawls and his *Theory of Justice* (1973) and explain briefly my position in relation to him. The first reason is that he had been invited to write this paper, before I was asked. The second is that his book is well-known, important and has been discussed on many occasions. This short comment will have little value for those who do not know his book. Therefore I am only going to discuss it as a postscript.

Rawl's method is different from my own. He lets imaginary spirits, who know about earthly relationships and opportunities but do not know what part they will have to play on earth after their incarnation, set up a social contract. He assumes that everyone, mindful of his own interest, will choose a socio-economic system in which all have equal rights, to avoid the danger of belonging to the most deprived group of people. Critics have pointed out, rightly in my opinion, that at least one moral postulate lies hidden in this: the norm of impartiality. Neither a myth of social contractors nor the concept of an "ideal observer" can remove the necessity of making the demand for impartiality explicit. That is why it is better to make this ethical demand for impartiality openly, as I have done.

Moreover a distinction must be made between what is ideal and what can be done in reality. This distinction is not made by Rawls in a satisfactory, systematic way. He argues that social and economic inequalities should be such that they are both (a) reasonably expected to be to everyone's advantage, and (b) attached to positions and offices open to all. In my opinion this well-known indifference principle can only be applied if the socio-economic order is incapable of being so arranged that these inequalities do not arise. Rawls fails to show that a situation, to which his principle applies, cannot be improved or prevented. Nor does he show that it involves, at most, a concession to obstinate reality. In my opinion this is a methodological mistake with serious practical consequences: social inequalities will be justified far too readily and with it all kinds of social injustice will be tolerated. I myself have indicated that various concessions may be inevitable, in most cases for the time being, in other cases permanently. For a number of reasons "in reality" will never coincide with "ideally". A detailed, mainly economic, analysis of real facts and opportunities (to which he devotes too little attention) is necessary to establish, in general terms, what should ideally be regarded as injustice, what injustices can be overcome in the present state of our knowledge and ability, and what steps we can now take towards a more just society. I myself have not attempted any such calculations. However my argument does require additional quantitative evidence.

References

Abbing, Roscam P.J., *Ethiek van de inkomersverdeling*, Deventer, 1973.
Brandt, R.B., *Ethical Theory*, Englewood Cliffs, 1959.
Brunner, E., *Gerechtigkeit*, Zürich, 1943.
Frankema, W.K., *Ethics*, Prentice Hall, 1963.
Hospers, J., *Human Conduct*, New York, 1961.
Lerner, A.P., *Economics of Control*, New York, 1946.
McCloskey, H.J., *Meta-ethics and Normative Ethics*, Den Haag, 1969.
Pen, J., *Income Distribution*, London, 1971.

Rawls, J., *A Theory of Justice*, 1973.
Reiner, H., *Die philosophische Ethik*, Heidelberg, 1964.
Samuelson, P.A., *Economics*, 1955.
Tinbergen, J., *Income Distribution*, Amsterdam, 1975.
Veldhuis, R., *Realism versus Utopianism?*, Assen, 1975.
Weddigen, W., *Wirtschaftsethik*, Berlin, 1951.

2 DISCUSSION

PAPER BY P.J. ROSCAM ABBING

Professor Bentzel thought the paper had raised a central question regarding the harmony between selfishness and altruism. There was also much to be discussed regarding the concrete political conclusions, for example the supposed benefits of wage regulation by the state. However, he intended to stick to the central theme contained in the second part of the paper, namely the problem of finding ethical principles for the determination of the optimal income distribution. These ethical principles can be based either on welfare economic considerations or on considerations of justice. The former provides us with little guidance since the problems of distribution are systematically side-stepped by modern welfare economics. On the other hand, the alternative basis of principles of justice runs into similar difficulties. Justice is a subjective concept and there are many different opinions. Perhaps a few generally acceptable postulates can be formulated, for instance the principle of "equal treatment of equals". But generally acceptable postulates are unlikely to give us interesting conclusions about the welfare distribution.

The paper illustrates this problem clearly. Although Professor Bentzel was sympathetic to the postulates given in the paper, he imagined that many individuals would dispute them. Thus, when the strong subjective element is recognised, it seems unlikely that principles of justice can form the basis for the ethics of welfare distribution.

He pointed out that Professor Abbing's paper resembled the writings of Rawls, in the sense that they have constructed their postulates so the results agree with their original conception of the optimal distribution, rather than the other way around. However, we should not be looking for an *ex post* rationalisation of our original prejudices. Instead, we should look for one or more general rules from which we can draw conclusions about the optimal distribution.

He had some difficulties accepting Professor Abbing's statement that the magnitude of those wage differentials regarded as justifiable, should be indicated by the labour market itself. Principles of justice ought to be independent of the labour market mechanism. It is important to make a clear distinction between considerations of justice (or welfare), positive economics and politics. The question of optimal distribution is a matter of justice (or welfare). The analysis of the economic consequences of the optimal distribution is a matter of positive economics; and the problem of finding a compromise between the optimal distribution and the fulfillment of economic goals is a matter of politics.

Although the welfare economic approach to optimal distribution has its deficiencies, he argued that it compared favourably with the justice approach. A major advantage is its ability to specify the problems in such a way that suitable economic and political measures can be found.

In his opinion it is the distribution of individual welfares – and not the distribution of incomes – which is the appropriate policy objective. The welfare of individuals, itself dependent on consumption in different periods and perhaps other variables, can be regarded as forming the arguments of a social welfare function of the Bergsonian type. This social welfare function should be required to satisfy the simple but appealing property that an income transfer from an individual at a higher welfare level to an individual at a lower level increases the value of the function, provided that individuals have identical welfare functions. This simple rule has very important implications. In fact, all three postulates formulated by Professor Abbing follow logically from this principle.

If the assumption of identical welfare functions is abandoned, the situation is more complicated. We can certainly follow Abba Lerner and treat individuals *as if* they had identical welfare functions, even if we know this is not true, but this procedure is not generally applicable. For instance, it seems unreasonable to assume that old people have the same welfare functions as the young, so the welfare effects of transfers from economically well off young people to less well off old people has to be considered with great caution. It is far from clear that such a transfer will increase social welfare.

Another problem concerns the treatment of public consumption, since it is unlikely that the optimal welfare distribution is independent of the size and structure of the public sector. There are also complications arising from wealth holdings, which give owners two types of benefits: a stock of potential future consumption and a degree of security and independence. Finally the choice of time horizon has to be considered – the question whether welfare over the whole lifetime or a shorter period should be our concern.

Professor Sen concentrated on two points on which he disagreed with Professor Abbing. He felt that rather different approaches were being put together and this is seen most sharply when considering the reward to talent. In section II.3 it seems to be argued that it is unjust if a talented person is paid more, but that this is acceptable if the extra talent comes from extra exertion. This raises the question whether people have the same ability to exert. The opportunities to exert may, for example, depend in part on characteristics innately born. The circumstances in which we may exert may also not be within our control. The crucial issue here is controllability, and when this is introduced it becomes very difficult to justify a reward to talent in any way.

There is an alternative approach based on natural freedom. In its simplest form if someone picks up some clay and makes a jug by his own effort, then the jug is his. Extending this to social production it is possible to go in different directions. On the Marxist interpretation the jug was his *because* it was his labour which produced it. This leads to a theory of claims based on labour. In a more neo-classical approach the generalisation takes a different direction: the jug is his *because* he caused the jug to be produced. Extending this interpretation to social production suggests that the person has a right to what he causes to be produced, and this can be seen in terms of some notion of marginal product. (There remains, of course, the additional issue of justifying ownership and inheritance.) Although they are quite different generalisations, the two theories of deserts are both based on the idea of natural freedom and it seems difficult to capture either type of approach within Professor Abbing's concept of justice.

Referring to the appendix where Rawls is discussed, Professor Sen questioned whether the main criticism is a fair one. There it states "it is better to make the demand for impartiality openly". Whilst he agreed with this demand, it still leaves the question of what the content of impartiality should be. His interpretation of Rawls' "original position" was that it was an open use of the notion of impartiality, namely if you did not know which person you were going to be, which society would you choose? So there is no conflict between Professor Abbing and Rawls on this issue.

Professor Abbing, replying to Professor Bentzel, said the crucial issue was whether ethics is a science. Most economists consider economics to be a science but regard ethics as a subjective method or a matter of taste. Although he may differ from Rawls in a number of ways this is no indication that ethics is a matter of personal choice, just as the variety of opinions to be found on economics is no reflection as to whether or not is is scientific. In fact differences of opinion demonstrate that the science is progressing – that there is a need for further discussion. If it were true that his principles of justice were designed merely to rationalise his own prejudices, this provided an opportunity to improve the basic postulates and hence progress.

It had been argued that a distinction should be made between the principles of justice and rules for application in specific instances. He agreed with this and with the necessity to begin with the formulation of general principles, before deriving practical rules. He also agreed that the distribution of welfare, rather than income, was the appropriate objective, although he would stress the role of *needs* in the determination of welfare.

In response to the points raised by Professor Sen, Professor Abbing admitted that it is impossible to measure precisely the degree to which individuals exert themselves, particularly in connection with training and the acquisition of skills. He agreed that people may differ in their ability to exert. However exertion cannot be measured according to simple objective standards: ten hours work for one person may be a relatively easy and light load, for another it may be difficult and strenuous. So a physical and psychological measure of the degree of exertion is required. If ten hours work was a great exertion for one individual, he has a right to a greater reward than one for whom it was little exertion. Although it is difficult to determine exactly the degree of exertion, in many situations we can make some approximate estimate. And in any case we must surely agree at the outset that it would be just to try and measure exertion in this way, regardless of whether practical problems forbid the realisation of this ideal.

Finally he questioned whether there was no conflict between Rawls and himself concerning the demand for impartiality. This may be true of the conclusion, but not of the method by which the conclusion is reached. A fictional human ghost might well choose to take the risk of having less if there was also the opportunity to get more. So why not show directly what *évident* impartiality involves?

3 ETHICAL MEASUREMENT OF INEQUALITY: SOME DIFFICULTIES

*AMARTYA SEN**

I. Introduction

In studies of the language of morals it is common to distinguish between a "prescriptive" term, which has prescriptive meaning "whether or not is has descriptive meaning", and an "evaluative" term, which has "both kinds of meaning" (Hare (1952, 1963)). That it is not easy to view "inequality" as a purely descriptive concept seems to be widely accepted by now;[1] it relates to the notion of "equity", which – as Tinbergen points out in his paper in this volume – must be seen to be "normative", being "based on a value judgement". But, at the same time, inequality cannot be seen to be a *purely* prescriptive concept either, since it also has descriptive meaning from which the concept cannot be easily divorced.[2] I shall try to show in section II that this duality has very damaging consequences for the "ethical measurement" of inequality, initiated by Dalton (1920), and recently widely explored in a number of contributions, most notably in the path-breaking and elegant paper of Atkinson (1970).

There is a second issue closely related to this. In one of the traditional formulations of the Bergson–Samuelson social welfare function, social welfare W is taken to be a function of the vector of individual utilities (see Samuelson (1947) and Graaff (1967)).[3]

$$W = f(U_1, \ldots, U_n). \tag{1}$$

---

* My greatest debt is to Tony Atkinson, since my thinking on this subject has been largely inspired by his contributions, even though this has led me to a position rather different from his.

[1] For an engaging (and illuminating) dissent, see Wiles (1974), who feels able "to banish *welfare economics from the process of measurement*, and to restore the strictest objectivity to our actual measures" (page xi).

[2] See Bentzel (1970), Sen (1973), Wiles (1974), Hansson (1977) and Atkinson (1976).

[3] There is an ambiguity in the form of this representation (1) since it is possible to take W and $(U_1, \ldots, U_n)$ not to be a real number and a vector of real numbers respectively, but to be a real-valued function and an n-tuple of real-valued functions respectively, each defined over the environment X of social states. The distinction turns out to be crucial in assessing the applicability of Arrow-like impossibility theorems to the Bergson–Samuelson social welfare functions (see Sen (1977a)). It seems clear, however, that this interpretation of $f(.)$ as a "functional" is not intended in the formulations in question (see the operations in Samuelson (1947, p. 246, equation (31)) and Graaff (1967, p. 51, figure 7(b))). However, these impossibility theorems arise only when interpersonal comparisons of utility are ruled out, which makes rather little sense for ethical measures of inequality, and leads to disastrous results (see Hammond (1976a)).

While it is not possible in general to split up the ethical judgements implicit in $f(\cdot)$ into assessment of total *size* and that of *distribution*, under special circumstances such identifications are possible. Since – to quote Tinbergen again – "equity is not the only aim of a social order", it is not really surprising that a measure of inequality that is derived from *over-all* ethical judgements may incorporate the influence of size in addition to that of distribution. What may be less obvious is that, under some specified circumstances when the size-distribution split up is possible and the ranking of size is exactly the opposite of the ranking of distribution, the ethical measures of inequality may reflect the ranking of size only, ignoring distribution altogether.

It is possible to use *personal* welfare functions rather than *social* welfare functions in inequality assessment. This may not necessarily lead to a complete measure (i.e. a measure that generates a complete ordering over all distributions of income). On the other hand, under standard assumptions, it certainly does generate an important partial ordering (see section III), and permits us to focus directly on the question of the distribution of personal welfares. Interpersonal comparisons of utility need be no more than *ordinal* for this purpose.

Finally, the question is raised as to whether it is sensible to think of social welfare as a function of individual welfares only, i.e. to assume what I have elsewhere called "welfarism" (Sen (1977a)). Concepts of rights implicit in such diverse notions as liberty and exploitation militate against a welfarist approach. If welfarism is abandoned, the consequent broadening of the ethical framework raises some additional difficulties in the ethical measurement of inequality. These are briefly discussed in section IV.

II. Contradictions

First a description of the ethical measures of inequality. Let social welfare be taken to be an increasing, symmetric and quasi-concave function $g(\cdot)$ of the vector of individual incomes:[4]

$$W = g(y_1, \ldots, y_n). \qquad (2)$$

The level of inequality of a given vector y of incomes can be measured under the normative approach

either (i) by comparing the level of social welfare generated by y with the social welfare that would be generated if the same total income were equally distributed (the Dalton measure);

or (ii) by comparing the total income of y with the total income that would generate the same social welfare if it were equally distributed (the Atkinson measure).

---

[4] These assumptions are not strictly necessary for the approach to be used. It is sufficient that, for each total income, social welfare should be maximised by equal distribution. For this, S-concavity of function $g(.)$ is sufficient (see Kolm (1972) and Dasgupta, Sen and Starrett (1973)).

Ethical measurement

In fact, Atkinson also assumed additionally that $g(\cdot)$ was an additively separable function of individual incomes, and Dalton went further in assuming that g must be strictly utilitarian (and there were no externalities):[5]

$$W = \sum_{i=1}^{n} U(y_i), \quad \text{with } U(\cdot) \text{ concave.} \tag{3}$$

We do not *need* these additional assumptions for the use of the Dalton–Atkinson ethical approach and their measures can be translated into the general form of (2). But, of course, utilitarianism is perfectly *compatible* with the approach, and since it will simplify the presentation of the point at issue, we may as well begin with this case.

To simplify further, let the individual utility function be of the following form (with constant elasticity of marginal utility):[6]

$$U = C + \frac{1}{\eta}(y_i)^\eta, \quad \text{with } \eta < 1. \tag{4}$$

Atkinson's measure of inequality A can be now seen to be given by:

$$A = 1 - \frac{e}{m}, \tag{5}$$

when m is the mean income of the individual incomes vector, and e is "the equally distributed equivalent income":

$$e = \left[\frac{1}{n}\sum_{i=1}^{n}(y_i)^\eta\right]^{1/\eta}. \tag{6}$$

We now have to check how this ethical measure relates to our ideas on the descriptive notion of inequality. The descriptive notion of inequality is not, however, unambiguous in many comparisons, and therefore we have to concentrate on those special cases in which there is no ambiguity in the descriptive ranking of inequality.

Two types of variations may now be considered:
(I) variations of the income distribution vector given the degree of concavity of the utility function $g(\cdot)$;
(II) variations of the degree of concavity of $g(\cdot)$ given the income distribution vector.
Contradictions between the ethical measures and descriptive features of inequality have been noted for variations of type (I) in Sen (1973) and for variations of type (II) in Hansson (1977). The problems in question are analysed below.

An unambiguous case of an increase in income inequality arises when there is

---

[5] Atkinson's formulation looks similar to (3), but the set of U-values need not be interpreted as "utilities".

[6] This class of utility functions was much explored in contributions to the optimum growth literature in the sixties (see Chakravarty (1970)). Note that with $\eta < 0$, the second term on the right hand side of (4) must always be negative, and the responsibility for making total utility non-negative for the relevant values of y_i falls on C being positive and sufficiently large. In fact the "subsistence" level may then be defined by y^*:

$$y^* = (-C\eta)^{1/\eta}. \tag{4'}$$

a transfer of income from a poorer to a richer person. This obviously also leads to an increase in the inequality of personal welfares if both persons share the same increasing utility function relating personal welfare to personal income. It is clearly reasonable to require that this must lead to an increase in the measure of inequality, and this is indeed the so-called "Pigou–Dalton criterion". This mild test is, in fact, passed by the ethical measure A for $\eta < 1$. But if $\eta = 1$ (a possibility admitted above and by Atkinson (1970)), we do have a violation, since this would make $e = m$, and the Atkinson measure of inequality becomes zero for all distributions. Contradictions of this type between the ethical and the descriptive notions of inequality are worrying, since "it would be odd to describe (0, 10) and (5, 5) as having the same degree of inequality" (Sen (1973)).

One can argue that the source of this problem lies in ignoring the difference between the two following statements:
(A) "there *is no social welfare loss* from inequality",
(B) "there *is no* inequality".
Ethical measures of the class specified by Dalton and Atkinson take the two statements to be the same, but in an obvious sense (A) and (B) are saying quite different things.

If the difficulty in question were confined only to the extreme case of $\eta = 1$, then one might try to dismiss it as merely a curiosum. But the problem is much deeper. As the value of η is raised parametrically, the impact of the transfer (from the poor to the rich) on the ethical measure becomes smaller and smaller until it vanishes altogether in the extreme case of $\eta = 1$. On the other hand, the impact on inequality enhancement in income terms remains the same (obviously so, since we keep looking at the *same* income transfer), and the impact on inequality enhancement in terms of personal welfares goes on *increasing*. Thus as the welfare inequality responds *more and more* to the transfer of income, the ethical measure of inequality responds *less and less*.

The reason for this difference is not far to seek. In the case of a transfer from the poor to the rich, the impact on social welfare, with which the ethical measure is concerned, is given under utilitarianism by:

$$\text{social welfare loss} = U'(y_p) - U'(y_r), \tag{7}$$

where $U'(y_p)$ and $U'(y_r)$ are the marginal utility of income of the poor and rich respectively. On the other hand, the extent of enhancement of personal welfare inequality between the rich and the poor is given *not* by the *difference* between the marginal utilities, but by their *sum*:

$$\text{enhancement of inequality} = U'(y_p) + U'(y_r). \tag{8}$$

It is, therefore, not surprising that as the social value of η is raised, the reduction of social welfare loss is accompanied by an increase in inequality enhancement. The extreme case of $\eta = 1$, which yields the minimal social welfare loss of 0 and the maximal enhancement of inequality of 2, is simply the end of this chain of a perverse relationship. The problem is fundamental and *not* a curiosum.

I turn now to Hansson's problem, *viz.*, the effect of variations of type (II) on the extent of inequality of a *given* distribution of income. As the value of η is raised towards unity, the ethical measure of inequality *goes down* monotonically. But since the rise of η leads to a *widening* of the range of, and the gaps between, the welfare values, in an obvious sense the inequality of the welfare distribution is *increased*. Thus as the degree of concavity is changed through variation of η, the ethical measure of inequality seems to head in the opposite direction to the description of inequality.

The contrast can be brought out graphically by taking a two-person case with a given income distribution, say y_p and y_r with $y_p < y_r$. In diagram 3.1 three alternative values of η are considered, and as η is raised, the value of the parameter C is reduced to keep $U(y_p)$ unchanged. (It may be remarked that the value of C does not affect the value of the ethical measure A given by (5) and (6).) It is clear that the inequality of personal utilities *increases* as η is raised, and in the extreme case of linearity ($\eta = 1$), the welfare inequality for the given income distribution reaches its peak. In contrast, the ethical measure of inequality *goes down* monotonically, becoming zero with $\eta = 1$.

This contrast can, of course, arise even when the utility function is not of the constant elasticity form, but takes some other form, e.g. that obtained by van Praag (1968, 1971) and van Praag and Kapteyn (1973). In fact, what the preceding discussion shows is that *even within the family of constant-elasticity utility functions*, we can find two utility functions such that a change from one to the other unambiguously *increases* inequality of personal welfares, while the ethical measure records a clear *decline*.

Furthermore, these conflicts are not confined only to utilitarian social welfare functions. It is easy to find non-utilitarian and non-additively-separable social welfare functions $f(\cdot)$ that also show a directional contradiction between the ranking of inequality by the ethical measures and the descriptive rankings of inequality of personal welfares.

The attempt to identify "greater inequality" with "lower social welfare" leads to contradictions arising from the fact that both inequality and social welfare are "primitive" notions, and they cannot be arbitrarily declared to be identical without some genuine loss of meaning. The ranking of "social welfare" of alternative distributions cannot be simply *defined* to be the ranking of "equality", since they stand for distinct concepts. There is, of course, an often-articulated view that anyone is free to define anything as he likes. But people's interest in the measurement of inequality depends on the accepted meaning of inequality, and will not necessarily survive if the term inequality were redefined. (If that view about the absolute freedom to define were to be accepted, I would in any case like to exercise my right – given by that view – to define craziness as the holding of that view.)

While the contradictions between ethical measures and descriptions of inequality are not confined to utilitarian social welfare functions, they are particularly acute under utilitarianism. This is because utilitarianism is concerned only with the utility *sum* irrespective of distribution of that sum.[7] Thus, when the ethical measures are combined with utilitarianism, this produces a peculiarly perverse situation:

---

[7] On the far-reaching implications of this feature of utilitarianism, see Sen (1973). For some controversies on this, see Harsanyi (1975), Sen (1976c), Harsanyi (1977), Sen (1977b).

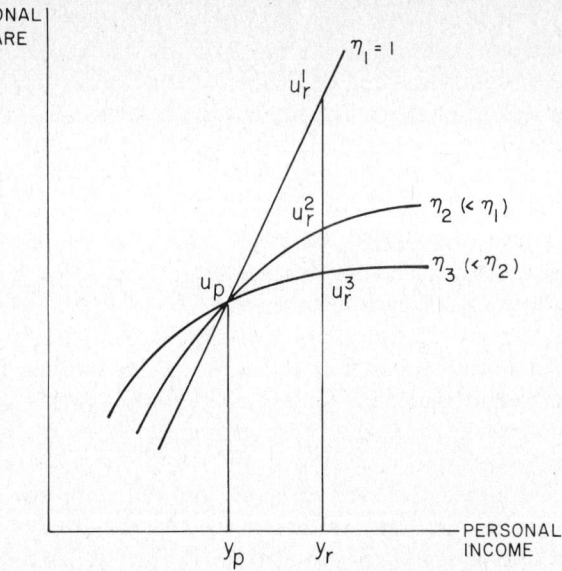

Figure 3.1.

"inequality" ranking is defined entirely in terms of the "social welfare" ranking, and the "social welfare" ranking is entirely unconcerned with distribution as such! This is why in the example considered earlier with a given income distribution, as η was raised and the personal welfare distribution turned more and more unequal while the loss of welfare *sum* from inequality became less and less, the ethical measure of inequality based on utilitarianism recorded an *unequivocal* decline (despite growing inequality of welfare levels). While the difficulty in identifying the inequality ranking with the social welfare ranking is present in any case, it becomes especially severe when the social welfare ranking couldn't care less about distribution as such and puts all its weight on total *size* only.

III. Description and prescription: minimal partial orderings

Following the publication of Robbins' classic discussion of interpersonal comparisons of utility (see Robbins (1938)), the fashionable view among economists was, for a long time, that such comparisons must be based on value judgements. The conceptual confusion implicit in that view has been discussed by Little (1950) and others, and it is fair to say that that view is not so common now. Had that view been adhered to, it would have been, of course, absurd to seek a *descriptive* measure of interpersonal welfare inequality. Quite a number of contributions in recent years have been concerned with the meaning and use of interpersonal welfare comparisons, defined frequently in terms of hypothetical choices about being one person rather than another (see, among many others, Vickrey (1945), Harsanyi (1955), Rawls (1958, 1971), Suppes (1966), Kolm (1969, 1972), Sen (1970, 1973,

1976b, 1977a), Hammond (1976b, 1976c), Maskin (1976), d'Aspremont and Gevers (1977), Deschamps and Gevers (1976a), Roberts (1976), and Arrow (1977)).

Nevertheless, there are difficulties in applying descriptive measures of inequality to personal welfare data, since the extent of measurability of welfare information is typically taken to be much weaker than that of income data. Depending on the type of "invariance restriction" applied to the welfare information, particular mathematical operations to which the magnitudes of incomes may be subjected may or may not be usable for personal welfare data (see Sen (1977a)). Perhaps the most difficult case arises when it is taken that welfare comparisons – whether for the same person or between persons – must be purely *ordinal*. This would rule out the use of the standard descriptive measures of inequality (e.g. the variance) for expressing welfare inequality. Would this at all permit any interesting statements to be made about descriptive inequality of personal welfares? Would such statements not be entirely arbitrary?

Before turning to answering these questions, it may be useful to note that statements on even ethical measures of inequality tend to have an element of arbitrariness arising from the difficulty of choosing a particular social welfare function $g(\cdot)$ from a wide class.[8] It is to avoid this problem of arbitrariness that a number of recent contributions have been concerned with the question of generating a partial ordering of ethical measures that would correspond to the entire class of plausible social welfare functions satisfying certain general properties (see Kolm (1969), Atkinson (1970), Sheshinski (1972), Dasgupta, Sen and Starrett (1973), Rothschild and Stiglitz (1973), Sen (1973), and others). The "unambiguous" ethical measurement that emerges from these works is confined to the case of Lorenz-dominance only. It transpires that if income distributions y Lorenz-dominates income distribution x, then y must have a lower ethical measure of inequality than x for all social welfare functions $g(\cdot)$ that satisfy symmetry and strict quasi-concavity (more weakly – and therefore more generally for this sufficiency theorem – strict S-concavity). Furthermore, we can be sure that y has a lower ethical measure of inequality than x *only if* y Lorenz-dominates x, when all we know about the social welfare function $g(\cdot)$ is that it satisfies symmetry and strict quasi-concavity (more strictly – and therefore more generally for this necessity theorem – symmetry, strict concavity and additivity). Thus, for the familiar class of social welfare functions (even when rather narrowly defined), the only "safe" ethical ranking of inequality is the Lorenz partial ordering.

Is there a similar "safe" partial ranking for the descriptive measurement of inequality of personal welfares, even when no more than *ordinal* comparisons of utility are permitted? The answer is: yes, and it is exactly the same partial ordering, *viz.*, that given by the Lorenz-dominance relation.

Consider a ranking of four utility values in the following order: $a > b \geq c > d$. There is clearly no "cardinal" assumption involved in declaring that the pair (a, d) has more inequality of welfare than (b, c). This type of comparison of "ordinal

---

[8] Note, however, that there is no one-to-one correspondence between ethical measures of inequality and social welfare functions (see Esteban (1976)). There are, however, more complex correspondences (see Blackorby and Donaldson (1977)).

intensity" permits us to rank alternative distributions without using anything other than *ordinal* welfare information (see Sen (1976c)).

It is easy to combine the above requirement with the condition that a permutation of utility numbers among persons must not change the descriptive measure of inequality. And it can also be combined with a requirement of "separability" so that the presence of other welfare numbers (when matched in terms of "indifference") should not affect the description of inequality.[9] Thus if two n-vectors of utility x and y match each other exactly except for two numbers each (say, x_1, x_2, and y_1 and y_2), and these remaining numbers are ranked $x_1 > y_1 \geq y_2 > x_2$, or $x_1 > y_2 \geq y_1 > x_2$, then x is more unequal than y.

This criterion was called "strengthened two-person ordinal inequality criterion" – STOIC for short – in Sen (1976c), and the ordinal inequality ranking was denoted θ^* (i.e. $y\theta^*x$, in the above case). The transitive closure of θ^* was denoted θ^{**}, which is the "ancestral" inequality ranking under ordinal comparisons. The symmetry assumption used in the *ethical* measurement of inequality has its counterpart in the descriptive framework in the assumption that everyone shares the same personal utility function $U(\cdot)$, and furthermore $U(\cdot)$ is assumed to be a monotonically increasing function of the income of the person in question.

The following result holds: the ranking of descriptive inequality of personal welfares obeying STOIC must incorporate the relation of Lorenz-dominance (see (T.1) in Sen (1976c)).[10] For any two distributions x and y of the same total income, y Lorenz dominates x if an only if $y\theta^{**}x$.

In an important sense it can, therefore, be said that the non-controversial part of the descriptive ranking of welfare inequality is exactly as extensive as the non-controversial part of the ethical ranking. While $U(\cdot)$ is taken to be an increasing function of personal income, it can be *any* increasing function, and nothing more than *ordinal* comparisons are used. In fact, no assumption of *concavity of any kind* is needed for the descriptive theorem, and even increasing marginal utility (if measurable) will not affect the result one iota.

This coincidence of ethical measurement of inequality with the description of welfare inequality happens to hold only for the case of Lorenz-dominance. Even here description and ethical measurement may contradict each other in terms of the relative *sensitivity* of inequality measures to transfers, as discussed in section II. (Remember that "Pigou–Dalton" transfers are covered by the Lorenz-dominance relation.) The coincidence is only of the *ordering* properties of the inequality measures applied to alternative distributions with *given* personal and social welfare functions, and it holds only for the "unambiguous" *partial* ordering implicit in each.[11]

---

[9] For a critical evaluation of this type of "separability" in the context of social choice, see Deschamps and Gevers (1976b).

[10] The theorem follows essentially from an elementary result noted by Hardy, Littlewood and Polya (1934) that y Lorenz-dominates x (as we define this term) if and only if y can be obtained from x by a non-empty and finite sequence of transfers from a higher to a lower income; see Sen (1976c). In fact, the theorem on the ethical measure of inequality in terms of social welfare involving Lorenz-dominance also follows from exactly the same property.

[11] In fact, as discussed in section II, under utilitarianism with $\eta = 1$, which is a permitted case, this Lorenz-dominance strict partial ordering would not, in fact, be incorporated in the ethical measurement of inequality. But this is an extreme case at the end of a perverse chain (see section II).

When cases not covered by Lorenz-dominance are considered, the exercise of ethical measurement and that of description part company, and much will then depend on the exact social welfare function chosen and the exact personal utility function and descriptive measure selected. There is, of course, quite a wide family of descriptive measures,[12] which can be combined with a particular specification of personal utility functions (e.g. obtained by quantifying parameters C and η for the constant-elasticity functions (4), or μ and σ for van Praag's formulation). However, depending on the "invariance requirements" imposed by the measurability conditions of personal welfare, some particular measures may be rendered inadmissible (see Sen (1977a)). The relationship between these "invariance requirements" and admissible measures of welfare inequality will not be further pursued in this paper. The important point to note in the present context is that once the Lorenz-dominance relation has been separated out, any *additional* ranking based on ethical measurement can coincide with descriptive ranking only accidentally, since the two types of exercises are essentially unlike each other (see section II).

IV. Welfare and welfarism

In section II we considered parametric variations in the personal utility function in the form of changes in the value of η and examined its consequences on (i) ethical and descriptive measures of inequality for a *given distribution* of income, and (ii) the sensitivity of these measures to a *given transfer* of income. The discussion having been rather formal, one might wonder what is the real content of this type of exercise.

Perhaps an illustration will help. Suppose a utilitarian economist has sent around a questionnaire of the type used by van Praag (1971), and it has turned out that the answers lead to a good estimation of C and η. (I am sticking to the constant-elasticity form since it is easier to interpret.) Suppose also that calculations reveal a rather rapid move towards "satiation" thanks to a low value of η. The boss of the research project promptly uses equations (5) and (6) to obtain the ethical measure of inequality A, and the result is, of course, reported in The Times.

Then, suddenly, it transpires that some mistake was made in the calculation, and – after firing the old research assistant (without changing the income distribution) – it is now estimated that η is, in fact, much higher, and satiation takes place much more slowly than was thought earlier. The utilitarian boss promptly recalculates the ethical measure of inequality A and it is, of course, now substantially lower. The correction is duly published in The Times with the following explanation: "The recalculation shows that satiation from income increments is reached more slowly. Hence the rich are, in fact, quite efficient in transforming income into utility (happily, their own). So the loss of aggregate welfare from inequality is less than we thought earlier. Obviously, there is less inequality in this country."

The research assistant, who is now a man of leisure, writes a letter to his former boss saying that since the interpersonal gaps in levels of well-being have been

---

[12] See Atkinson (1970), Sen (1973, Chapter 2), Muellbauer (1974), Mehran (1976), Stoft (1975).

revised *upwards* by the change, there clearly must be *more* inequality, not less. "Isn't there a mistake?" The boss feels vindicated in having fired the former assistant, since the poor chap clearly does not understand that the increase in welfare gaps between persons has got *nothing* to do with the measure of inequality A! ("Probably reading a lot of Wiles!", the boss was overheard to mutter.)

The contradiction between the directions of movement of the ethical and descriptive measures arises in this case out of a cognitive revision, *viz*, that concerning facts about satiation and the true personal welfare function. Exactly a similar contrast will hold between the assessment of inequality increase arising from a *transfer* from a poorer to a richer person under these circumstances. After η has been revised upwards, a lower impact of the transfer on social welfare will now be observed (see (7)) and the ethical measure A will be less affected by it. On the other hand, the extent of enhancement of welfare gaps by such transfers will now be larger (see (8)), suggesting the opposite in terms of description of inequality of personal welfares. These contrasts reflect contradictory responses to a factual revision.

It is worth noting in this context that while a social welfare function is essentially an ethical concept, the same is not true of personal welfare functions. Whatever arbitrariness there may be in the latter, it is an arbitrariness of description rather than of prescription. The revision of parameters like η (or van Praag's μ and σ) are factual corrections. It is the contradictory handling of such factual corrections that is at the root of the inability of ethical measures of "inequality" to reflect inequality as description.

The contrast is, of course, most sharp with a utilitarian social welfare function since under that approach $f(U)$ is concerned only with the utility *sum*. If the form of the function is made more unfavourably inclined to features of inequality captured in descriptive measures of welfare inequality, the contradictions will, obviously, tend to be reduced. But the question of the right ethical approach raises a more fundamental issue: should social welfare W be at all taken to be a function *only* of personal utilities?

I have tried to argue elsewhere that a function $f(U)$ is *informationally* very restrictive (Sen (1977a)). It assesses social states *entirely* in terms of the *personal welfare* features of the respective states; the approach may thus be described as "welfarism".[13] Such ethical concepts as "exploitation", "justice" and "liberty", cannot be accommodated in $f(U)$, since they typically require information that go beyond personal welfare data, e.g. dated labour inputs, past promises, specification of "personal" protected spheres, etc. To take the notion of "exploitation" as an illustration, two *identical* distributions of personal welfares may receive *different* treatments in the Marxian system depending on how the personal incomes are related to the respective labour inputs.[14] Similarly, the formulation of the "liberty" to do certain things requires detailed specification of pairs of social states over which a person is given freedom to choose. Two *identical* distributions of personal

---

[13] In collective choice theory, this is the condition of "neutrality" (see Arrow (1963), Sen (1970, 1977a)).

[14] See Marx (1887). The purely welfaristic approach, Marx reserved exclusively for the "ultimate stage of communism" (see Marx (1875)).

welfares may receive *different* treatments in a framework granting the right to personal liberty, if one case involves the violation of that liberty and the other does not.[15]

While these non-welfaristic concepts have great relevance to political discussions and practical judgements, they are completely left out in those Bergson–Samuelson social welfare functions which make social welfare a function only of the personal welfare data. It is important for the progress of normative economics, and – in particular – the analysis of distributive justice, that attention be paid to acknowledgement of "rights", involving such notions as "claim" (see Kanger (1957, 1972), Hart (1961), and Dworkin (1977)).[16]

The enrichment of the ethical framework involved in this broadening of the informational base will militate against both welfarism ($W = f(U)$) and the treatment of social welfare as a function of the vector of individual incomes ($W = g(y)$). But if such a "broader" social welfare function is used, then two vectors of individual incomes cannot be compared with each other in terms of social welfare *without* bringing in further information, and the ethical measures would cease to be well-defined. One would no longer be able to answer clearly such questions as: what total income, if distributed equally, would lead to just as much social welfare as the current income distribution? The answer can be quite different depending on a variety of factors that have not been specified (e.g. what types of production structure, what systems of remuneration, what types of redistribution policy, etc., will be used to bring about the counter-factual equal distribution of income).

This basic difficulty is analytically most damaging to the approach of ethical measurement of inequality. But it only accentuates what we knew already (see section II), *viz*, the ethical approach involves an identification, in specified contexts, of two quite distinct "primitive" concepts, *viz*, "social welfare" and "equality". While the latter is an important constituent of the former (in terms of prevailing notions of social welfare), it is not the only constituent, even when we focus our attention on the distribution of a given total income. (Indeed, for some ethical systems, particularly utilitarianism, there is no role given to equality of personal *utilities*, and even the role of *income* equality in enhancing social welfare is not intrinsic but entirely context-dependent.) Thus, even under welfarism and even when W is taken to be a function of y, the ethical measurement of "inequality" can go totally against the notion of inequality as a description of the distribution of personal incomes and of personal welfares.

V. Concluding remarks

It is certainly true that the descriptive notion of inequality is not an exact one, and we may often have to settle for a partial ordering based on the intersection of the orderings generated by a set of descriptive criteria. What is at issue is whether

---

[15] See Sen (1970, 1976a), Rawls (1971), Nozick (1974).
[16] For a helpful exposition of the analytical formulations involved, see Lindahl (1977).

this incompleteness should lead us to use instead a complete "ethical" ordering obtainable from a specified social welfare function. It must be recognised, however, that there is ambiguity also in the "ethical" measurement arising from the choice of a particular social welfare function out of an "acceptable" family, and the "unambiguous" partial ordering corresponding to the usual ethical restrictions is not more extensive than the "unambiguous" partial ordering of description of inequality (see section III).

But this is not the only difficulty in using the ethical approach. A more fundamental difficulty arises from the fact that our ethics, when more fully specified, may incorporate elements that go well beyond a concern for reducing inequality, even when we examine alternative distributions of a given total income, which does not, of course, imply a given *sum* of personal welfares. The extra-egalitarian concerns are patent with utilitarian ethics (see section II), as well as with many others, e.g. those involving concepts of rights, dealing with such issues as non-exploitation and liberty (see section IV). This makes the ethical approach yield in many cases clearly perverse results from the point of view of description of inequality (section II), while in other cases the ethical measure is rendered unusable (section IV).

The idea of measuring inequality on the basis of an over-all social welfare function is fundamentally misconceived. It leads to a clearcut answer but to a question different from the one that was posed.

References

Arrow, K.J., *Social Choice and Individual Values*, second edition. New York: Wiley, 1963.
Arrow, K.J., "Extended Sympathy and the Possibility of Social Choice", *American Economic Review*, 1977.
Atkinson, A.B., "On the Measurement of Inequality", *Journal of Economic Theory*, 1970.
Atkinson, A.B., *The Economics of Inequality*. Oxford: Clarendon Press, 1976.
Bentzel, R., "The Social Significance of Income Distribution Statistics", *Review of Income and Wealth*, 1970.
Blackorby, C. and D. Donaldson, "Measures of Relative Equality and Their Meaning in Terms of Social Welfare", *Journal of Economic Theory*, 1977.
Burk, R. and W. Gehrig, "Indices of Income Inequality and Societal Income, An Axiomatic Approach", mimeographed, Universität Karlsruhe, 1976.
Chakravarty, S., *Capital and Development Planning*, Cambridge, Mass.: M.I.T. Press, 1970.
Dalton, H., "The Measurement of the Inequality of Incomes", *Economic Journal*, 1920.
Dasgupta, P., A.K. Sen and D. Starrett, "Notes on the Measurement of Inequality of Incomes", *Journal of Economic Theory*, 1973.
d'Aspremont, C. and L. Gevers, "Equity and the Informational Basis of Collective Choice", *Review of Economic Studies'* 1977.
Deschamps, R. and L. Gevers, "Leximin and Utilitarian Rules: A Joint Characterization", *Journal of Economic Theory*, forthcoming, 1976a.
Deschamps, R. and L. Gevers, "Separability, Risk-bearing and Social Welfare Judgements", mimeographed, 1976b.
Dworkin, R., *Taking Rights Seriously*. London: Duckworth, 1977.
Esteban, J.M., "Social Welfare Functions and Inequality Measures", mimeographed, Economia W.P. 76, Universitat Autónama de Barcelona, 1976.
Gevers, L., "On Interpersonal Comparability and Social Welfare Orderings", mimeographed, Faculté des Sciences Économiques et Sociales, Namur, 1976.
Graaff, J. de V., *Theoretical Welfare Economics*. Cambridge: Cambridge University Press, 1967.
Hammond, P.J., "Why Ethical Measures of Inequality Need Interpersonal Comparisons", *Theory and Decision*, 1976a.

Hammond, P.J., "Equity, Arrow's Conditions and Rawls' Difference Principle", *Econometrica*, 1976b.
Hammond, P.J., "Dual Interpersonal Comparisons of Utility and the Welfare Economics of Income Distribution", *Journal of Public Economics*, forthcoming 1976c.
Hansson, B., "The Measurement of Social Inequality", text of invited lecture at the Congress of Logic, Philosophy and Methodology of Science, London, Ontario, 1975; in R. Butts and J. Hintikka (eds.), *Logic, Methodology and Philosophy of Science*. Dordrecht: Reidel, 1977.
Hardy, G., J. Littlewood and G. Polya, *Inequalities*, London: Cambridge University Press, 1934.
Hare, R.M., *The Language of Morals*, Oxford: Clarendon Press, 1952.
Hare, R.M., *Freedom and Reason*, Oxford: Clarendon Press, 1963.
Hart, H.L.A., *The Concept of Law*, Oxford: Clarendon Press, 1961.
Harsanyi, J,. "Cardinal Welfare, Individualistic Ethics and Interpersonal Comparisons of Utility", *Journal of Political Economy*, 1955.
Harsanyi, J., "Non-linear Social Welfare Functions, or Do Welfare Economists have a Special Exemption from Bayesian Rationality", *Theory and Decision*, 1975.
Harsanyi, J., "Non-linear Social Welfare Functions: A Rejoinder to Professor Sen", in R. Butts and J. Hintikka (eds.), *Logic Methodology and Philosophy of Science*. Dordrecht: Reidel, 1977.
Kanger, S., *New Foundations for Ethical Theory*, Part 1, Stockholm, 1957.
Kanger, S., "Law and Logic", *Theoria*, 1972.
Kanger, S. and H. Kanger, "Rights and Parliamentarism", *Theoria*, 1966.
Kolm, S-Ch., "The Optimum Production of Social Justice", in J. Margolis and H. Guitton (eds.), *Public Economics*, London: Macmillan, 1969.
Kolm, S-Ch., *Justice et equite*, Paris: CNRS, 1972.
Kolm, S-Ch., "Unequal Inequalities", *Journal of Economic Theory*, 1976.
Little, I.M.D., *A Critique of Welfare Economics*, Oxford: Clarendon Press, 1950.
Lindahl, L., *Position and Change: A Study in Law and Logic*, Dordrecht: Reidel, 1977.
Marx, K., *Critique of the Gotha Programme*, 1875. English translation in K. Marx and F. Engels, *Selected Works, vol. II*. Moscow: Foreign Languages Publishing House, 1958.
Marx, K., *Capital: A Critical Analysis of Capitalist Production*, vol. I. London: Sonnenschein, 1887. Republished London: Allen & Unwin, 1938.
Maskin, E., "Decision-making under Ignorance with Implications for Social Choice", mimeographed, Jesus College, Cambridge, 1976.
Mehran, F., "Linear Measures of Income Inequality", *Econometrica*, 1976.
Muellbauer, J., "Inequality Measures, Prices and Household Composition", *Review of Economic Studies*, 1974.
Nozick, R., *Anarchy, State and Utopia*. Oxford: Blackwell, 1974.
Rawls, J., "Justice as Fairness", *Philosophical Review*, 1958.
Rawls, J., *A Theory of Justice*. Cambridge, Mass: Harvard University Press and Oxford: Clarendon Press, 1971.
Robbins, L., "Interpersonal Comparisons of Utility", *Economic Journal*, 1938.
Roberts, K.W.S., "Interpersonal Comparability and Social Choice Theory", mimeographed, St. John's College, Oxford, 1976.
Rothschild, M. and J.E. Stiglitz, "Some Further Results on the Measurement of Inequality", *Journal of Economic Theory*, 1973.
Samuelson, P.A., *Foundations of Economic Analysis*. Cambridge, Mass.: Harvard University Press, 1947.
Sen, A.K., "The Nature and Classes of Prescriptive Judgements", *Philosophical Quarterly*, 1967.
Sen, A.K., *Collective Choice and Social Welfare*. San Francisco: Holden Day and Edinburgh: Oliver and Boyd, 1970.
Sen, A.K., *On Economic Inequality*. Oxford: Clarendon Press and New York: Norton, 1973.
Sen, A.K., "Liberty, Unanimity and Rights", *Economica*, 1976a.
Sen, A.K., "Interpersonal Comparisons of Welfare", mimeographed, forthcoming in a festschrift for Tibor Scitovsky. 1976b.
Sen, A.K., "Welfare Inequalities and Rawlsian Axiomatics", text of invited lecture at the Congress of Logic, Philosophy and Methodology of Science, London, Ontario, 1975, in *Theory and Decision*, 1976c; also in R. Butts and J. Hintikka (eds.), *Logic, Methodology and Philosophy of Science*. Dordrecht: Reidel, 1977.
Sen, A.K., "On Weights and Measures: Informational Constraints in Social Welfare Analysis", *Econometrica*, 1977a.
Sen, A.K., "Non-linear Social Welfare Functions: A Reply to Professor Harsanyi", in R. Butts and J. Hintikka (eds.), *Logic, Methodology and Philosophy of Science*, Dordrecht: Reidel, 1977b.

Sheshinski, E., "Relation between a Social Welfare Function and the Gini Index of Income Inequality", *Journal of Economic Theory*, 1972.
Stoft, S., "A New Positive Measure of Inequality", mimeographed, University of California, Berkeley, 1975.
Suppes, P., "Some Formal Models of Grading Principles", *Synthese*, 1966; reprinted in P. Suppes, *Studies in the Methodology and Foundations of Science*, Dordrecht: Reidel, 1969.
Tinbergen, J., "A Positive and Normative Theory of Income Distribution", *Review of Income and Wealth*, 1970.
Van Praag, B.M.S., *Individual Welfare Functions and Consumer Behaviour*, Amsterdam: North-Holland, 1968.
Van Praag, B.M.S., "The Welfare Function of Income in Belgium: An Empirical Investigation", *European Economic Review*, 1971.
Van Praag, B.M.S. and A. Kapteyn, "Further Evidence on the Individual Welfare Function of Income: An Empirical Investigation in the Netherlands", *European Economic Review*, 1973.
Vickrey, W., "Measuring Marginal Utility by Reactions to Risk", *Econometrica*, 1945.
Wiles, P., *Distribution of Income: East and West*, Amsterdam: North-Holland, 1974.

3 DISCUSSION

PAPER BY AMARTYA SEN

Professor Tinbergen said the paper displayed the skilful scientific strategy we have come to expect from the author. He thought it was worthwhile mentioning a number of points on which they were in agreement. He agreed that the formulation of an individual welfare function does not imply a value judgement, in contrast to the formulation of a social welfare function by a theorist. He also agreed that social welfare functions should not be "welfaristic", depending solely on individual welfare functions, although such social welfare functions may be used for purposes of illustration. He wondered whether Professor Sen supported his inclusion of other variables, such as efforts or sacrifices, in both personal and social welfare functions. These represent counterparts to income, sometimes negative counterparts in the case of disutilities and sometimes positive contributions as may arise in satisfaction from labour.

He felt it would be useful for Professor Sen and Dr. Mustert to exchange views on the paper's last remark that "the idea of measuring inequality on the basis of an overall social welfare function is fundamentally misconceived". Dr. Mustert had recently derived such a measure from a social welfare function for the Netherlands, based on a public opinion poll. He was inclined to regard this exercise, which came down in favour of the Theil coefficient, as useful.

The paper argues that the ethical measurement of inequality and the description of welfare inequality coincide when the criterion of Lorenz dominance is considered. He wondered whether this implied that the Gini ratio, for example, is an acceptable measure of inequality "from the ethical viewpoint". Finally he believed it was unreasonable to set $\eta = 1$, and this may weaken the argument based on examples where this value was chosen, even as a limiting case.

Professor van Meerhaeghe said that Professor Sen avoids discussion of value judgements and believes in the possibility of interpersonal comparison of utilities, which he believed to be impossible.

In common with the two earlier papers, there is an obsession with levelling down, inspired by the myth that for someone to have more, someone else must have less. This was based on what Harry Johnson had called "the historical Western inheritance of the Judaic-Christian tradition: the equality of man before God" and "a naive and basically infantile anthropomorphism". Professor van Meerhaeghe believed that the issues under discussion made emotional elements and value judgements unavoidable. He had expected some papers to favour more inequality, as well as those biased towards more equality. At least in Western Europe, more and more people were aware that income redistribution had gone too far. Without sufficient income differentials there is no incentive to work and no progress. Even in the Soviet Union the official viewpoint regarded levelling down as the enemy of social equality. *L'Humanité*, the French communist daily, believed that a policy too egalitarian for the Swedish electorate caused the defeat of the Swedish socialist party. And he agreed with the view of *The Economist* that

> the real trouble in Britain ... is not that there are still a very few thousand exceedingly rich families clinging to their ancestral piles by acting as park-keepers to day-trippers or through having dodged inheritance tax since Lloyd George. It is that it is very difficult for anybody to build up even a moderate fortune in Britain today by thrift, successful work and risk-taking. The result is that Britain is losing the dynamic that needs to be provided by risk-taking investors and has become a land of risk-fleeing disinvestors instead.

Professor Bentzel found the analysis convincing and agreed that measures derived from social welfare functions could not be regarded as inequality measures. However, he thought they could be considered as measures of distributional efficiency in creating welfare, provided we accept additive functions. On the question of introducing a number of other variables into the social welfare function, he asked whether it might not be more natural to incorporate them directly into the individual utility functions.

Professor Wiles had had great pleasure reading the paper, particularly footnote 1 and section V, and had come to the conclusion that he had been right; that welfare economics must be banished from the measurement of inequality. He wondered if this was the correct interpretation. He had earlier believed that the use of a single number to describe inequality was a bad habit derived from statisticians, but now thought that welfare economists may have been responsible. He emphasised that distributions are too complicated to be summarised in one number. Finally, in the welfare context, he asked whether it is necessary any longer to use a concave welfare function. It seems that we no longer need the perfectly equal distribution to be the ultimately desirable one, even in this context.

Professor Krelle agreed with the paper but not its conclusion. He felt that welfare loss was one legitimate approach to the measurement of inequality. The objections contained in the paper were not really objections but rather the implications of measuring inequality that way. These should be borne in mind, but do not provide sufficient justification for abandoning this approach.

Professor von Weizsäcker said that economists are not concerned with the colour of consumer durables since, even if it were a problem, economists would have little to say on this particular topic. Inequality, however, was the concern of economists. He argued that the case $\eta = 1$ was analogous to the colour of consumer durables; the problem of the distribution of income or welfare would cease to be of interest to economists. Consequently he did not find the comparison of different utility functions for the same distribution very convincing.

Dr. Wagner said that the use of inequality measures was simply a way of organising data for the purpose of comparing different distributions of income.

Mr. Layard thought the Atkinson approach could be justified on the basis of the efficiency–inequality trade-off which it makes explicit and which is the focus of attention in many policy issues. He felt that Professor Sen wanted to make a further subdivision, so that the contribution attributable to a concave social welfare function defined over individual utilities could be separated from the effects of the concave individual utilities themselves. He did not see how this might be done and felt that in the meantime the simple efficiency–inequality distinction was still useful, with inequality referring to the inequality of incomes rather than the inequality of individual welfares.

Dr. Kuipers pointed out that identical utility functions are assumed for all individuals. He asked how this might be justified and what consequences would follow from allowing the utility functions to differ amongst individuals.

Mr. Bartels asked whether the Pigou–Dalton criterion was "clearly reasonable" on purely normative or ethical grounds.

Professor Sen thanked Professor Tinbergen for his kind comments. He pointed out that the $\eta = 1$ case was allowed in the Atkinson system and led to transparently perverse results. Similar problems arise with other values of the parameter but the perverseness is not quite as obvious. On the question of the Gini coefficient, his paper in *Econometrica* (1976) presents an axiomisation of this measure and the axioms required are rather strong. Essentially it corresponds to a rank order weighting system.

He was happy that his paper had provided the occasion for Professor van Meerhaeghe to make his remarks, although they had little relevance to the paper. He admitted he did have an obsession with inequality but this was not revealed in the paper. In fact he had been arguing in favour of descriptive measures which provide common ground for economists, regardless of their views on the desirability of further redistribution. He agreed very much with the comments of Professor Bentzel. The Atkinson index measures the distributional deficiency of the income distribution, and this applies even when the social welfare function is non-additive.

On the question of why social welfare cannot be defined as a function of individual utilities only, there were other considerations which he felt individual utilities could not capture when ethical or prescriptive judgements are made. Suppose, for example, a taxi is hired to take a person to Amsterdam but delivers him instead to the Hague. The driver asks for the fare but payment is refused. He then enquires whether his passenger is a utilitarian, and points out that he is poorer and will still be poorer, even if payment is made. They agree they have the same concave utility functions. There is then no welfare basis for refusing to pay – the argument that the passenger has been delivered to the wrong destination is not valid since that is now a historical fact. Of course the passenger may deny that he is a utilitarian, but a similar argument applies for any social welfare function defined only over individual utilities, since it fails to incorporate concepts of claims and rights. Similarly, whilst disutility from working can be captured in personal welfares, this is not the case with notions related to natural freedom, e.g. that a person has a right to what he has produced by his own efforts.

He felt there may have been some partial reconciliation of his own views and those of Professor Wiles. However, he would still argue that inequality measures could not be purely descriptive, just as they could not be purely prescriptive. In reply to Professor Krelle he suggested that if they agreed that an index was a measure of distributional efficiency then they should call it such, and not an index of inequality, which it patently is not. A similar remark applied to the comments of Professor von Weizsäcker. If we are not concerned about the colour of an object, it does not imply that there is no difference. The statements "we *are not interested* in the colour difference" and "there *is no* colour difference" remain distinct, and there is no advantage in asserting the latter when one means the former. Furthermore, even with $\eta = 1$, the problem of equity does in fact remain, since inequalities of personal welfares are of interest for principles of equity, and $\eta = 1$ does nothing to eliminate that. He also disputed the suggestion that comparisons of the same distribution with different values of the parameter η were not legitimate. Systematic revisions of the value of η may occur for a number of reasons, so it is important that the corresponding inequality values reflect the changes in an appropriate way.

In reply to Professor Kuipers he agreed that in many contexts the assumption of identical personal utility functions was not a good assumption, but he used it here because he was criticising the approach in which it is commonly used. To the question raised by Mr. Bartels, he said that he thought the Pigou–Dalton criterion made sense as a description of inequality: a transfer from a richer to a poorer person does reduce inequality in an obvious descriptive sense. Whether or not it made sense in a normative context he could not say; it depends partly on the choice of social welfare function and partly on whether a "welfaristic" approach is adopted.

Professor Tinbergen drew Professor van Meerhaeghe's attention to the second paragraph of his paper which explicitly states that his definition of equity is normative, and hence subjective. His definition attempted to give concrete scientific meaning to a word often used in political discussions. On the basis of this definition, certain income differences (for example, compensatory variations) are acceptable, whilst others are not – scarcity premiums paid to talented individuals, for instance. It is not true that all income differentials are rejected, as Professor van Meerhaeghe seemed to suggest.

Consideration had also been given earlier to the feasibility of an equitable income distribution, and he had indicated his belief that this could not be established immediately. If imposed it may damage the optimal allocation of manpower. But he felt it may be possible to attain an equitable distribution with the aid of what the Germans call "marktkonforme(n) Methoden".

Finally, in his opinion, certain income differentials have occasionally become too narrow. However, according to an opinion poll, a majority of the Dutch population feel that income differences are still too large in the Netherlands.

PART II

MEASUREMENT OF INCOME INEQUALITY

4 ANNUAL INCOME, LIFETIME INCOME AND OTHER INCOME CONCEPTS IN MEASURING INCOME DISTRIBUTION

C.C. VON WEIZSÄCKER

Friedman's (1957) Permanent Income Hypothesis or Modigliani's (1954) Life Cycle Hypothesis are theories of consumption and savings behaviour which presuppose the existence of only one budgetary constraint within the lifetime of a decision maker. All consumption decisions in the lifetime of a decision maker are made with the same marginal utility of money as the representative of opportunity costs of consumption. The welfare of a person conforming to this model is not determined by his current income but rather by his lifetime income. The relevant variable to be looked at from the point of view of distribution is lifetime income.

On the other hand, empirical research on income distribution concentrates on current annual income. It is known that current annual income has a different distribution compared to lifetime income. It is therefore quite important to ask, whether current annual income is a good proxy for personal distribution of welfare. Should we not rather take life income as the better indicator of welfare distribution? In this note, I want to make a small contribution to this issue.

Let us assume that it is impossible to shift consumption from one unit period to the next for an individual. His consumption and utility thus are determined by his income in the current unit period. Obviously, this assumption is rather unrealistic for very short unit periods like seconds or minutes or days, weeks. Even for years the assumption is not particularly realistic in present day economies.

Following Atkinson (1970) a measure of inequality is associated with each quasi utility function $U(y)$ and each income distribution $y_1, y_2, \ldots y_n$ for individuals $1, 2, \ldots n$. It is defined by the equality equivalent $\hat{y}$ and the average income $\bar{y}$ in the following way. Let

$$W = \frac{1}{n} \sum_{i=1}^{n} U(y_i).$$

Then the equality equivalent is defined by the equation

$$U(\hat{y}) = \frac{1}{n} \sum_{i=1}^{n} U(y_i).$$

Let

$$\bar{y} = \frac{1}{n} \sum_{i=1}^{n} y_i.$$

Then the Atkinson measure of inequality is defined by

$$A = 1 - \frac{\hat{y}}{\bar{y}}.$$

Its usefulness and flexibility is due to the fact that it builds explicitly on society's value judgements concerning the distribution of incomes.

Let us now, for simplicity, look at an economy which is in a stationary state. At a given moment of time, the different income recipients can be indexed also according to their age. This indexation as such does not change anything. Alternatively, we can look at one age cohort and consider all the incomes $y_{1i}, y_{2i}, \ldots y_{mi}$ any individual i of the cohort has received or will receive in his lifetime, i.e. through a sequence of m unit periods. If we treat the same individual in different periods as different individuals, the Atkinson index of inequality is

$$A = 1 - \frac{\hat{y}}{\bar{y}},$$

where

$$\bar{y} = \frac{1}{mn} \sum_{i=1}^{n} \sum_{t=1}^{m} y_{ti},$$

$$U(\hat{y}) = \frac{1}{mn} \sum_{i=1}^{n} \sum_{t=1}^{m} U(y_{ti}).$$

In a stationary system this measure of inequality roughly is the same as the measure of inequality of unit period current income of the whole population.

But let us now change our point of view and treat an individual living through a life of m unit periods as one individual. What would then correspond to his welfare. Taking the same quasi utility function $U(y)$, the person's individual welfare would correspond to an equal income in each period of $\hat{y}_i$ given by the equation

$$U(\hat{y}_i) = \frac{1}{m} \sum_{t=1}^{m} U(y_{ti}).$$

The measure of inequality would now be given by

$$A' = 1 - \frac{\hat{y}}{\bar{y}'},$$

where

$$\bar{y}' = \frac{1}{n} \sum_{i=1}^{n} \hat{y}_i$$

and

$$U(\hat{y}) = \frac{1}{n} \sum_{i=1}^{n} U(\hat{y}_i)$$

$$= \frac{1}{nm} \sum_{i=1}^{n} \sum_{t=1}^{m} U(y_{ti}).$$

Given that U is concave, it is easily seen that

$$A' \leq A$$

for $\hat{y}_i \leq 1/m \sum_{t=1}^{m} y_{ti}$, because U is concave, and therefore

$$\bar{y}' \leq \bar{y}.$$

Indeed, it is not difficult to derive a formula relating A and A'. Let a_i be the individual index of inequality defined by

$$a_i = 1 - \frac{\hat{y}_i}{\bar{y}_i},$$

where

$$\bar{y}_i = \frac{1}{m} \sum_{t=1}^{m} y_{ti}.$$

We then have

$$A = 1 - \frac{\hat{y}}{\bar{y}} = 1 - \frac{\hat{y}}{\bar{y}'} \frac{\bar{y}'}{\bar{y}} = 1 - (1 - A') \frac{\bar{y}'}{\bar{y}}.$$

But

$$\frac{\bar{y}'}{\bar{y}} = \frac{\frac{1}{n}\sum_{i=1}^{n} \hat{y}_i}{\frac{1}{n}\sum_{i=1}^{n} \bar{y}_i} = \frac{\sum_{i=1}^{n} \frac{\hat{y}_i}{\bar{y}_i} \bar{y}_i}{\sum_{i=1}^{n} \bar{y}_i} = \frac{\sum_{i=1}^{n} (1 - a_i)\bar{y}_i}{\sum_{i=1}^{n} \bar{y}_i}$$

$$= \sum_{i=1}^{n} (1 - a_i)\gamma_i,$$

where

$$\gamma_i = \frac{\bar{y}_i}{\sum_{i=i}^{n} \bar{y}_i}$$

is the share of person i in lifetime income. Hence

$$A = 1 - (1 - A') \sum_{i=1}^{n} (1 - a_i)\gamma_i.$$

Thus A or rather $1 - A$ can be expressed as the product of two components; one is $1 - A'$, the inequality index of individual welfare indexes and the other is a weighted average of inequality of intra-individual unit period incomes.

If any one of the two measures is an appropriate measure of inequality, then it is A', the measure of inter-individual inequality. To express a total measure of inequality as the sum or the product of two components (by taking logarithms a product can of course easily be transformed into a sum) one of which is a proper expression of inequality, whereas the other picks up a spurious inequality, is an idea which can be applied in other contexts.

Thus, for example, risk-taking may be an activity which leads to a kind of inequality which is quite appropriate and thus should not be reckoned as a genuine inequality. In a very simplified model, we can try to be more specific. Let us assume that there are two economic activities between which economic agents can choose: call them self-employment and contract employment. People who choose contract employment are employed by others. They bear no risk but receive a wage according to their ability, n. Thus let

$$w(n) = xn,$$

where x is to be determined by market equilibrium conditions. Self-employment is risky and the income a self-employed person can expect is a random variable $y(n)$ depending on his ability, where

$$y(n) = Z\bar{z}n.$$

The random variable Z has expected value of one: $E\{Z\} = 1$. The value of $\bar{z}$ will be determined by market equilibrium conditions.

We can assume that there exists a production function $F(S, C)$ with self employed (S) and contract employed (C) labour as inputs, which is homogeneous of degree one and whose marginal products determine the equilibrium values of x and $\bar{z}$. Assuming that the incomes of the self-employed are stochastically independent random variables, the model generates a certain equilibrium income distribution. Take as an example identical preferences of all agents with respect to risk and a given constant relative risk aversion. This implies that there is no reason to assume an upward or downward ability bias among those who are self-employed, as compared to the contract employed people. We then have a certain distribution of contract incomes derived from the density function $f(n)$ of the ability distribution. The expected values of incomes of self-employed people have a similar distribution derived from the density function except that the multiplier here is not x but $\bar{z}$. In the case of risk aversion the equilibrium level of $\bar{z}$ is greater than x. The ex post distribution of incomes of self-employed people of course has greater inequality, being the product of two distributions: the ability distribution and the distribution of the random variable determining individual self-employed incomes.

Let us look at the particular case where the Atkinson quasi-utility function $U(y)$ and the von Neumann–Morgenstern utility function $U(y)$ are the same. Using the Atkinson measure of inequality, we get a measure which indicates greater inequality for the total distribution than for the distribution of contract income. This can be seen as follows: by the construction of the example, everybody is, in equilibrium, indifferent between self-employment and contract employment. Hence, the certainty equivalent of a self-employed person is just equal to the wage rate he could earn under contract employment. But given that, in this case, the Atkinson quasi utility function just expresses the degree of risk aversion for the group of the self-employed, their equality equivalent is just equal to the equality equivalent of the contract employed. Hence, the equality equivalent of the total population equals the equality equivalent of the contract employed. On the other hand, the average income, given risk aversion, in the population is greater than the average income of the contract employed people. Therefore, the Atkinson measure indicates greater inequality for the whole population than for the contract employed population.

But instead we can separate the intrinsic inequality due to differences in endowments from the inequality effect of risk taking, the latter being a kind of inequality for which those who suffer from it (as a group) are compensated by a higher expected income. We thus might take an ex ante view of income distribution, at least in this case where the representative individual needs not expose himself to any risk. We would then look at the distribution of certainty equivalents of income expectations. In the example at hand, these certainty equivalents have the same distribution as the incomes of contract employed people. Thus in terms of certainty equivalents the modified Atkinson index has the same value for the total population as for the contract employed part of the population.

We can derive again a similar formula, where the Atkinson index can be decomposed into two factors, one giving inequality of ex ante incomes in terms of certainty equivalents and the other giving the average "intrapersonal inequality" i.e. the average degree of inequality of *ex post* incomes for any given ex ante certainty equivalent.

If income can be transferred from one period to the next without difficulties, lifetime income is probably an appropriate measure for income distribution. This has to be somewhat modified when uncertainty about future income is important.

If transferring income from one period to another is costly but not impossible, things become complicated. This issue will have to be treated in another paper.

References

Atkinson, A., "On the Measurement of Inequality", *Journal of Economic Theory*, 1970.
Friedman, M., *A Theory of the Consumption Function*, Princeton, 1957.
Modigliani, F. and F. Brumberg, "Utility Analysis and the Consumption Function: an Interpretation of Cross Section Data", in: *Post-Keynesian Economics*, K. Kurihara (ed.), New Brunswick, 1954.

4 DISCUSSION

PAPER BY C.C. VON WEIZSÄCKER

Mr. Layard began by saying why he agreed with the suggestion that lifetime income is the appropriate basis for welfare comparisons. To illustrate his argument he gave an example of two societies with the same contemporaneous consumption distribution. Each society contains one individual of each age and type. People live for two periods and their needs are the same in each period. The lifetime consumption profiles are given as follows:

	Society I		Society II	
	Age 1	Age 2	Age 1	Age 2
Type A	2	1	2	2
Type B	2	1	1	1

Although both societies exhibit the same inequality at any point in time, there is no lifetime inequality in society 1 but a great deal in society 2.

According to the paper there is inequality in society 2, but society 1 is completely equal. He agreed with this assessment. In society 1 there may be a problem of efficiency arising from consumption differences in two periods, but there is no problem of equity. The fact that consumption decreases between the two periods may increase the efficiency problem. However, it is still not a problem of equity. Exactly the same problem might arise in a Robinson Crusoe economy in which equity considerations are clearly irrelevant.

Whilst agreeing in general with the approach adopted in the paper, he felt that it relied too much on an additive utilitarian framework. Instead, he suggested using a social welfare function of the form

$$W = \sum_i V(U_i),$$

where $V(\cdot)$ is some concave function. As before $\hat{y}_i$ is defined implicitly by

$$U(\hat{y}_i) = \frac{1}{m} \sum_t U(y_{ti}).$$

But the cross section measure of inequality becomes

$$A = 1 - \frac{\tilde{y}}{\bar{y}},$$

where

$$V[U(\tilde{y})] = \frac{1}{nm} \sum_i \sum_t V[U(y_{ti})].$$

The interpersonal inequality index has to be defined as

$$A' = 1 - \frac{\tilde{y}'}{\bar{y}'},$$

with $\bar{y}' = 1/n \sum_i \hat{y}_i$, as earlier, and

$$V[U(\tilde{y}')] = \frac{1}{n} \sum_i V[U(\hat{y}_i)]$$

$$= \frac{1}{n} \sum_i V\left[\frac{1}{m} \sum_t U(y_{ti})\right]$$

$$> \frac{1}{n} \sum_i \frac{1}{m} \sum_t V[U(y_{ti})], \quad \text{by concavity of } V,$$

$$= V[U(\tilde{y})].$$

Thus $\tilde{y}' > \tilde{y}$ and we now find

$$A = 1 - \frac{\tilde{y}'}{\bar{y}'} \cdot \frac{\bar{y}'}{\bar{y}} \cdot \frac{\tilde{y}}{\tilde{y}'} = 1 - (1 - A') \sum_i (1 - a_i)\gamma_i \frac{\tilde{y}}{\tilde{y}'}.$$

So the cross-section equality measure $(1 - A)$ equals lifetime equality $(1 - A')$ *times* inter-lifetime equality (less than unity) *times* a term (also less than unity) representing the greater apparent unfairness of annual as against lifetime income.

Mr. Layard went on to raise the question of how differences in the length of life of individuals should be dealt with. He hoped he was right in supposing that Professor von Weizsäcker would measure lifetime welfare by $\sum_{t=1}^{m} (U(y_{ti})/m)$, regardless of the length of life m. If lifetime welfare were defined instead to be just the sum of the sub-period utilities, then people who live for a long time in poverty turn out to have a relatively high lifetime welfare.

Finally he pointed out that the computation of lifetime welfares can be made directly from data on consumption profiles or inferred from data on income profiles, if capital markets are perfect. There are, however, serious problems if only income data are available and capital markets are imperfect. For example, if the same discount rate is to be applied to all individuals, it is sometimes the case that the appropriate rate is lower than the lowest rate faced by any individual investor.

Dr. Psacharopoulos expressed reservations about the diminishing importance attached to cross-section inequality. It was no good, he suggested, telling people currently on low incomes that they will be better off in ten years time.

Professor Sen saw the force of the criticism of cross-section inequality but did not accept the alternative. He suggested that society 1 in Mr. Layard's example was not equal in anything but a very narrow sense. From a descriptive point of view there is inequality at any point of time and this should be reflected in the inequality measure. In a normative context, which is the main concern of the paper, problems arise if transfers between different points of the life are not costless and from uncertainty about the future, which may lead to under or over provision. In real life there is considerable evidence to suggest that such planning failures exist and to ignore them (or to assume that they are the "fault" of the individuals themselves) he found unacceptable. Mr. Layard's agreement on these issues confirmed what he had always suspected, viz. that Mr. Layard regards *King Lear* to be not a Shakespearean tragedy but a Shakespearean "efficiency exercise". If people live in relative prosperity for most of their lives but suffer extreme hardship towards the end, he was strongly opposed to dismissing the problem as merely one of efficiency. He therefore resisted the notion that cross-section inequality was entirely spurious and of little relevance to the problem of equity. The two notions of equity supplemented each other, reflecting two different aspects of it.

Professor van Praag did not feel that life-time inequality was a substitute for short period cross-section inequality. He agreed with the earlier discussants who regarded these as two distinct aspects. He suggested that it might be useful to decompose life-time inequality in order that the separate age-group contributions could be identified. He also suggested that a decomposition of, say, the Atkinson measure across occupational groups would enable an estimate to be made of the inequality due to uncertainty in earnings. For example this might be done by comparing inequality within the civil service group, which can be assumed to have no earnings uncertainty, with that of the self-employed. Finally, he believed that the computation of life-time income required the time preference of individuals to be taken into account.

Professor Somermeyer believed there was an important link between life-time income and expectations, since life-time income represents the present value of the *expected* flow of future income, and to a certain extent is therefore arbitrary. Nevertheless, he considered life-time income as a valuable concept, by virtue of its comprehensiveness over time. For analysing its distribution, however, he preferred the variance or the Theil coefficient to the Atkinson measure, since the former two measures, unlike the latter, can be simply decomposed into within-group and between-group contributions to total inequality.

Professor Stiglitz was very sympathetic towards the general approach. One advantage is that some differences in consumption due to different individual savings propensities cancel out over the life-time and to this extent some of the cross-section inequality is spurious. This is one reason why the distribution of annual incomes exaggerates the true degree of inequality. He pointed out that income is taken as an exogenous variable except in the last part of the paper where risk-taking is considered. The fact that income depends in part on the number of hours worked, and that individuals differ in their labour-leisure choice, provides a further source of spurious inequality. Moreover the approach to the measurement of inequality adopted in the paper essentially asks how much society would be willing to pay to eliminate inequality. If income is endogenous and the mechanism for income redistribution is a distortionary tax (like income tax) there is a cost associated with the reduction of inequality. This is another reason why the degree of cross-section inequality is exaggerated. Other arguments suggests reasons for the Atkinson measure to be biased downwards, but it is unlikely that these factors will dominate the upward biases.

He went on to comment on the role of markets in determining inequality, particularly when there are elements of risk-taking. Suppose all individuals face a risky income stream and do not have the choice of selecting a certain income stream instead. With a complete set of security markets they could all have the same present value of income. Whatever way individuals choose to distribute their consumption over the different periods, there is a sense in which it can be said that this society is completely equal. If a complete set of markets does not exist, it can be argued that some of the observed inequality is real inequality and not merely a problem of efficiency. Finally he asked whether there was any method of identifying the choice and non-choice contributions in total inequality.

Professor Vielrose pointed out that the formula on the bottom of page 2 did not take into account the fact that some people die. He also emphasised the difficulties involved in estimating life-time incomes. Ideally observations are required for a cohort throughout the period of its economic life, although it may be possible to make use of cross-section data and construct an artificial pattern. Even if these computations were made, he could see no useful practical application.

Professor Bentzel was also sceptical about the practical value of evidence on life-time income inequality. He did not see how it could be incorporated within the framework normally used to analyse welfare. He did not feel that the horizon of young people extended to the end of their life, and therefore suggested that future incomes should be discounted rather heavily.

Professor Taubman mentioned two US studies which might be relevant to the discussion. In one study for white males it was found that 80 per cent of the variation in annual earnings reflected variations in long-run earnings. The other study concerned individuals over 25 years old, with the earnings distribution split into three equal parts. More than half of the people remained in the same part of the distribution in 13 out of 17 consecutive years.

Professor Krupp thought a critical issue was whether life-time incomes were more equally distributed than annual incomes. He was not sure that the evidence indicated that this was so. There were some indications that the life-time distribution was more unequal than the annual distribution. Studies at his Institute suggested that the answer to this question depended very heavily on the future incomes projected for the youngest age group.

Professor Wiles said he had constructed a life-time earnings distribution for Canada in 1960 and compared it with the distribution of annual earnings. The decile ratios for the two distributions were almost identical. There was a marked tendency for the earnings of young professionals to increase as they get older and this draws the life-time P_{90} upwards, offsetting the upward movement of P_{10}. Of course the same would not apply to P_{99}. Having himself tried to make these computations he shared Professor Vielrose's doubts as to whether they would ever have any practical use. In particular, how should estimates be made of life-time earnings for both women and children?

Professor Michal said there was evidence from Czeckoslovakia that life-time incomes were more unequal than annual incomes. This situation arose because, with small earnings differentials, differences in the length of working lives becomes critical in determining life-time inequality.

Dr. Shorrocks said there was a formal statement of the circumstances in which life-time income would be less unequal than annual income. Suppose we take a generalised Atkinson measure based on a strictly quasi-concave social welfare function. If inequality in each age group is the same then, when everyone has the same length of life, inequality in life-time income cannot exceed that of annual income; and they are identical only when the relative incomes of individuals remain invariant over the life-span.

Professor Robinson said the discussion had not yet touched on various practical problems, for example how future responsibilities, as well as income, might be taken into account. It seemed to be assumed that this could be incorporated within the utility function in some way. The computation of life-time incomes was also complicated by the existence or absence of pensions.

Professor von Weizsäcker began by saying that the quasi-utility function used in the paper was not an individual utility function but an indication of the relative *social* preference for equality. This was consistent with his interpretation of the original Atkinson article. The extension proposed by Mr. Layard suggested an explicit relationship between the social welfare function and individual utilities, and for this reason he was not entirely happy with the change. Nor was he convinced that differences in the length of life should be treated in the way that Mr. Layard suggested; the problem might be dealt with in a number of ways and he had not yet decided which was the most appropriate.

Several people had been sceptical about the use of life-time income as a measure of individual welfare, and a number of separate arguments could be identified. The "King Lear" argument emphasises variations in well being at different points of life, but assuming perfect capital markets etc. there is no problem as long as individuals attempt to maximise the sum of the single period utilities. The argument therefore rests on the empirical question whether utilities can be aggregated over periods, rather than on any ethical or normative question. Another argument suggests that people make irrational intertemporal decisions. Professor von Weizsäcker was convinced that in societies which let people make their own decisions, people act more or less rationally. If this were not the case, society would withold this freedom, as it does for children and the mentally retarded. A third argument which had been raised was that the expectation of higher incomes in the future was of no benefit to those currently poor. But low income at this moment of time is reflected in a low value for current utility, so this aspect is not neglected. Lastly he dealt with the question of imperfect capital markets. These present no problem unless there is uncertainty and insurance opportunities are inadequate, in which case uncertain future income needs to be discounted in some appropriate way. However this is not an argument against lifetime income as a concept, merely against the use of too naive a variable to represent lifetime income.

Finally he turned to the questions concerning the second part of the paper. If there is risk but no insurance, there will, in a statistical sense, be inequality due to risk. But if individuals are free to avoid this risk there is no point in taking this inequality into account, since the risk is already compensated by the higher expected income. It is not the kind of inequality which we want to see reduced.

5 THE PERCEPTION OF INCOME INEQUALITY

BERNARD VAN PRAAG

I. Introduction

One of the prominent issues in economics is the measurement of income inequality. When the income distribution is described by a continuous density function $f(y)$ on $(0, \infty)$, it is clear that summarising such a density in just *one* number will always imply a loss of information. If the inequality measure is denoted by $I(f)$, any given value of $I(f)$ will correspond to a variety of income distributions $f_1, f_2, \ldots$.

If an inequality measure indicates that two distributions f_1, f_2 are equally unequal ($I(f_1) = I(f_2)$) and this is against an individual's (political) value judgement, he will dismiss that inequality measure I, as it does not conform to his value judgement. This suggests that it is futile to search for *the* measure of inequality, because it does not exist. The choice of an inequality measure *is* essentially a political value judgement. Kolm (1976) recognised this when constructing rightist and leftist inequality measures.

A political value judgement also seems to be the main reason why so many people in the Western world consider present inequality to be similar to that observed before World War II or even in the 19th century, although, for instance, Pen and Tinbergen (1976) show that (Dutch) income inequality has fallen according to any one of a score of well-known inequality measures.

There seem to be four major problems:

(a) If people express a value judgement as to the inequality of the income distribution, it is basically not an assessment of *income* differences but one of *welfare* differences. We shall attack this problem using the log-normal individual welfare function and our empirical estimates of that function derived from several large-scale surveys. The estimation method will be outlined in section II and the resulting estimates discussed in section III.
It turns out that individuals have different welfare functions depending on their individual circumstances, particularly income received and the size of their family.
(b) Once the individual welfare function is defined, it becomes possible to examine the welfare distribution corresponding to any specific income distribution. The second problem is then to define a measure of inequality for that distribution. We choose the variance of the logarithm of marginal utility. This will be considered in section IV.
(c) Since individual welfare functions differ among individuals, the inequality

of the income distribution is perceived and evaluated differently by different people. In this preliminary analysis we shall characterise the individual by his income alone. Then it becomes possible to study differences in inequality perception (according to this measure) between various income brackets. It sheds new light on a problem raised by Kolm (1976). This will be the subject of section V.

(d) Fourthly, by recognising individual perceptions, an additional problem is created – how to construct an aggregate measure reflecting individual opinions on inequality. Here we have to consider the way and the extent to which interpersonal welfare comparisons are involved. This will be examined in section VI.

In section VII we insert the estimated welfare function into two well-known inequality measures, the Dalton and Atkinson measures. Since our individual welfare function differs among individuals, the Dalton and Atkinson measures are "individualised". Their behaviour will be analysed.

In section VIII we will present our conclusions.

II. The individual welfare function of income

In this paper we shall make extensive use of the individual welfare function of income as defined in Van Praag (1968). It bears a superficial similarity to the old-fashioned cardinal utility function of income. We do not intend to go into details here concerning the differences between our concept and the Edgeworthian concept; for a theoretical background the reader is referred to the above monograph. Here we restrict ourselves to the following short (and admittedly superficial) introduction.

Let y be the level of the individual's annual income, assumed to be constant over time. This level can be evaluated by the individual as "bad", "insufficient", "sufficient", "good", etc. This applies not only to the individual's actual income, but to all income levels. In fact, the individual evaluates income levels by comparing them with the best and worst income levels he can imagine. (We assume the worst level to be zero and the best level to "equal" ∞). The evaluation can be recorded on a *numerical* scale. Denoting the evaluation of income level y by $U(y)$, it would be fairly natural to assign 0 to the worst income level, $U(0)$, and 1 to the best, $U(\infty)$.

This is also the way in which, for instance, students are graded; evaluations "good", "bad", etc. are translated into numbers on a finite scale. It is not really necessary to confine the scale to the interval $[0, 1]$; it could just as well be $[0, 10]$ or any other finite interval. It is only necessary that it should be bounded, reflecting the psychological reality that every individual assesses his income by comparing it with a worst position and a position of complete satiation, although any finite amount of money may not be sufficient to attain such a situation. Assuming that $U(y)$ takes values in the interval $[0, 1]$, the shape of $U(y)$ is typically expected to be like that sketched in fig. 5.1; we call $U(y)$ the *individual welfare function of income*. For the theoretical and philosophical basis of this concept we refer to

Van Praag (1968), but one point should be mentioned here. The individual welfare function of income does not indicate any objectively measurable property of income, only the *relative welfare* as perceived by the individual; it is measured as the ratio of the welfare attained to that of the best imaginable situation. It is determined up to a positive linear transformation. (We call it a *neo-cardinal* concept, for reasons which become clear if the concept is embedded in a world with a variable number of commodities). In the above monograph it was shown that, under fairly general conditions, $U(y)$ may be approximated by a lognormal distribution function, i.e.

$$U(y) = \Lambda(y; \mu, \sigma) = \frac{1}{\sigma\sqrt{2\pi}} \int_{-\infty}^{\ln(y)} \exp\left(-\tfrac{1}{2}(t-\mu)^2/\sigma^2\right) dt.$$

The values of the parameters μ and σ are determined for each individual. So the welfare function of income can be different for each *individual*, even though it is always approximately lognormal.

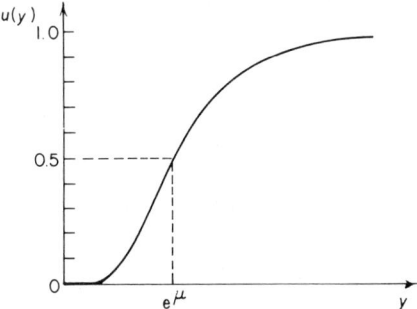

Figure 5.1. Individual welfare function of income.

An individual welfare function of the lognormal type $\Lambda(y; \mu, \sigma^2)$ has the shape sketched in figure 5.1. The function takes the value 0.5 when $y = e^\mu$, and σ (> 0) determines the shape of the function about e^μ. In the limiting case, as σ approaches zero, the function tends to the stepfunction $\Lambda(y) = 0$, $y \leq e^\mu$; $\Lambda(y) = 1$, $y > e^\mu$. We call σ the individual's *welfare sensitivity* and e^μ the "natural unit" by which the individual evaluates income levels. The function tends to one[1] as $y \to \infty$.

We have

$$\Lambda(y; \mu, \sigma) = N(\ln y; \mu, \sigma) = N\left(\frac{\ln y - \mu}{\sigma}; 0, 1\right)$$

where N represents the normal distribution function.[2] The dependence on the unit of account is easily examined. Let the monetary unit be divided by ten, so an income level y in the old system is equivalent to an amount $\tilde{y} = 10y$ in the new system. If the real value is to remain the same, we have

[1] For details about the term "natural unit" see Van Praag (1968).
[2] For more information on the lognormal distribution see Aitchison and Brown (1957).

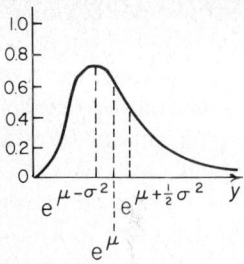
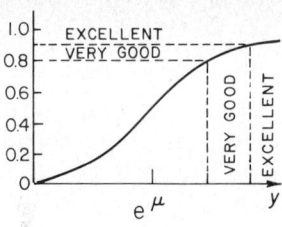

Figure 5.2.a. Lognormal welfare density function.

Figure 5.2.b. Lognormal welfare function.

$$\frac{\ln y - \mu}{\sigma} \equiv \frac{\ln \tilde{y} - \tilde{\mu}}{\tilde{\sigma}},$$

at all income levels y. This identity holds if and only if $\tilde{\sigma} = \sigma$ and $\tilde{\mu} = \mu + \ln(10)$. In general, if prices rise by a factor $(1 + \alpha)$, e^μ also increases by the factor $(1 + \alpha)$.

The individual welfare function is, of course, a theoretical construct, since no individual is able to assess income levels on a *continuous* scale. However, people are able to decide whether a specific income range is "good", "sufficient", "excellent", "bad", etc. Conversely, after some consideration an individual is able to suggest income intervals that correspond in his view to certain qualitative descriptions. We exploited this ability by asking individuals the following question.[3]

Taking into account your own family and job situation, you would call your net-income (including fringe benefits and after substracting social security contributions)

	week	A
per	month	B
	year	C
excellent	if it were above	f 45,000
good	if it were between	f 35,000 and 45,000
amply sufficient	if it were between	f 30,000 and 35,000
sufficient	if it were between	f 25,000 and 30,000
barely sufficient	if it were between	f 22,000 and 25,000
insufficient	if it were between	f 20,000 and 22,000
very insufficient	if it were between	f 17,000 and 20,000
bad	if it were between	f 12,000 and 17,000
very bad	if it were below	f 12,000

In this way the individual provides us with a partition of the income range into intervals $(0, y_2], (y_2, y_3], \ldots, (y_n, \infty)$. Comparing different answers it is clear that these are not given in a random way. (For instance, the extreme intervals are always wider than those in the middle.) In fact, it is likely that the individual attempts to provide as reliable information as possible about his individual welfare function.

---

[3] The figures inserted (in roman) are those of a typical answer. See Van Praag (1971) and Van Praag and Kapteyn (1973) for details.

Obviously, he is unable to characterise it exactly, because he can only answer a finite set of questions, while the function itself is continuous. Nevertheless, he tries to answer in such a way that inaccuracy is minimised.

This "inaccuracy" concept can be defined more precisely. Consider the specific answer indicated above. The welfare value attached to an income in the interval (25, 30], labelled "sufficient" is on average

$$\tfrac{1}{2}[U(25) + U(30)] = U(\bar{y}_6).$$

This implicitly defines $\bar{y}_6$. But we cannot say that all income levels in the interval (25, 30) have the welfare value $U(\bar{y}_6)$. The *average inaccuracy* of this evaluation can be measured by

$$\int_{25}^{30} [U(y) - U(\bar{y}_6)]^2 \, dU(y).$$

For the partition $(0, y_2], (y_2, y_3], \ldots, (y_n, \infty)$ the *total average inaccuracy* is, by definition,

$$\sum_{i=1}^{n} \int_{y_i}^{y_{i+1}} [U(y) - U(\bar{y}_i)]^2 \, dU(y). \tag{1}$$

The separate integrals increase with the variation of U over $(y_i, y_{i+1}]$ and the interval length $(y_{i+1} - y_i)$. Hence the individual selects narrow brackets where U is steep, and wide brackets where it increases slowly. In mathematical terms, the individual attempts to choose the value of y_i in such a way that (1) is minimised.

Applying the "integral transformation" $z = U(y)$, we replace minimisation of (1) by the equivalent problem

$$\min_{z_2,\ldots,z_n} \sum_{i=1}^{n} \int_{z_i}^{z_{i+1}} \tfrac{1}{2}(z - \bar{z}_i)^2 \, dz,$$

where $z_i = U(y_i)$, $\bar{z}_i = \tfrac{1}{2}(z_i + z_{i+1})$, $z_1 = 0$ and $z_{n+1} = 1$. Integration yields

$$\min_{z_2,\ldots,z_n} \sum_{i=1}^{n} (z_{i+1} - z_i)^3,$$

subject to $\sum_{i=1}^{n} p_i = 1$, where $p_i = (z_{i+1} - z_i) > 0$. The unique solution is $p_i = 1/n$, which implies $z_i = U(y_i) = (i - 1)/n$.

This result states that *the individual partitions the income range into intervals corresponding to equal percentile intervals of the welfare function*. In our survey, the question gives nine intervals, so y_i is the $(i - 1) \times 11.1$ percentile of the distribution, as defined by the distribution function U.

The definition (1) of the average inaccuracy is somewhat arbitrary, but any other reasonable criterion yields the same solution, $p_i = 1/n$.[4]

---

[4] See Kapteyn (1977) who shows that the same solution applies if a wider class of criterion functions is chosen.

By the method described, we have found a sequence of points $\{y_i, U(y_i)\}_{i=2}^{9}$ for an individual, which have to be on the graph of his welfare function. The question now is whether the assumption that the individual welfare function is lognormal is reasonable, and how the parameters μ and σ may be estimated. We solve this problem by making a scatter of the points on *lognormal* paper, where the horizontal axis has a logarithmic scale and the vertical axis measures $x = N^{-1}(.; 0, 1)$, where $N(.; 0, 1)$ is the standard-normal distribution function. If the points $\{y_i, U(y_i)\}$ lay on the graph of the distribution function $\Lambda(y; \mu, \sigma)$, it would be the case that

$$U(y_i) = N(\ln(y_i); \mu, \sigma) = N\left(\frac{\ln(y_i) - \mu}{\sigma}; 0, 1\right).$$

We know that the logarithms of the y_i given in answer to the survey, are 11.1 percentiles (say, $u_2, \ldots, u_9$) of the normal distribution. Hence

$$\frac{\ln(y_i) - \mu}{\sigma} = u_i,$$

or

$$\ln(y_i) = \sigma u_i + \mu, \quad \text{for } i = 2, \ldots, 9. \tag{2}$$

Obviously, the individual answers will not satisfy (2) exactly, but we assume that (2) is approximately true. Then μ, σ are estimated from the linear model

$$\ln(y_i) = \sigma u_i + \mu + \varepsilon_i$$

where ε_i is a random disturbance term. We assume that the ε_i are independently and identically distributed with expectation zero.

Applying ordinary least squares regression to the eight observations (y_i, u_i) from the questionnaire, we obtain estimates for μ and σ. If the individual has not provided all the answers, but has forgotten, say, the first and third, we still have six observations $(y_3, u_3), (y_5, u_5), \ldots, (y_9, u_9)$ to which the regression may be applied. Clearly, the amount of information is reduced as the number of answers decreases. More or less arbitrarily, we excluded two-point answers from the sample.

III. Estimation results

Before outlining the main results, we should ask what we have measured. Is it the individual welfare function, or something else? Since the individual welfare function of income is only a theoretical construct, there is no way of demonstrating that what we are measuring *is* the individual welfare function. The only thing we maintain is that the measured relationship comes rather close to our *a priori* concept of an individual welfare function. The concept is actually defined empirically by the measurement method. If the results of repeated sampling and estimation are consistent, the concept is empirically validated. In a similar way, the concept of chronological time acquired significance in the Middle Ages; the concept of temperature was empirically validated in the 18th century; and in our century, the even less tangible concept of I.Q. has become accepted.

Let us now consider the main results. For a more detailed analysis we refer to Van Praag (1971), Van Praag and Kapteyn (1973), Kapteyn and Van Praag (1976), Kapteyn, Van Praag and Van Herwaarden (1976), Van Herwaarden, Kapteyn and Van Praag (1977).

The regression equation

$$\ln y_i = \sigma u_i + \mu + \varepsilon_i$$

has now been estimated for well over 12,000 individuals in the period since 1969. About half the sample refer to Belgians and the other half to Dutchmen. Recently, a few small surveys have been performed in other countries in the European Community. All the results point in the same direction and they are highly consistent. The results may be summarised as follows:

(a) The correlation coefficient R, corresponding to the above regression, is 0.98 on average. The standard errors are almost always very small compared to the regression coefficients. We conclude that the individual welfare function (as defined by our estimation method) may be approximated by a lognormal function $\Lambda(y; \mu, \sigma^2)$.

(b) The *welfare sensitivity* σ varies over individuals. Its average value is 0.50. It cannot be explained by objective individual characteristics, although education seems to have a slight positive influence on σ.

(c) *The natural unit* e^μ varies a great deal. Its variation can be explained in a systematic way.

We estimated the relationship

$$\mu = \beta_0 + \beta_1 \ln(fs) + \beta_2 \ln(y_a) + \varepsilon,$$

where μ is measured per individual income earner, fs is his family size, y_a his actual net income (post-tax) and ε an error term. For a sample of 2,964 observations among members of the Dutch Consumer Union in 1971, we found

$$\mu = 3.02 + 0.13 \ln(fs) + 0.64 \ln(y_a) \qquad (R^2 = 0.60). \tag{3}$$
$$\quad (0.11) \quad (0.01) \qquad\quad (0.01)$$

In other samples we found approximately the same relationship with comparable reliability.

The interpretation is fairly easy. An increase of μ (to $\mu + \Delta\mu$, say) implies a shift of the individual welfare function to the right (see figure 5.3). Hence, the same income is given a lower valuation as μ increases. In fact, a rise in μ may be interpreted as an increase in the real price level. In the same way, (3) indicates that as family size increases, the value attached to any (constant) income level declines. This leads to the construction of family equivalence scales (see Kapteyn and Van Praag (1976)).

The third term indicates that people have bigger needs when they receive more income. Let an individual have income y_a, valued by himself at $N(\ln(y_a) - \mu)/\sigma; 0, 1)$ and let another individual have an income $y_a(1 + \alpha)$. Then, neglecting ε,

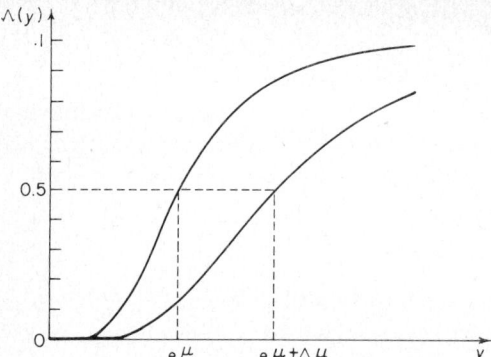

Figure 5.3. A shift of the welfare function caused by an increase in μ.

the second person will value this income, not at $N((\ln(y_a) + \ln(1 + \alpha) - \mu)/\sigma))$, but at $N((\ln(y_a) + (1 - \beta_2)\ln(1 + \alpha) - \mu)/\sigma))$. This means that approximately $\beta_2 \alpha$ of the income difference is absorbed without any impact on perceived welfare. We call this phenomenon *"preference drift"*. If $\beta_2 = 0$, any difference in income is wholly perceived as a difference in welfare. If $\beta_2 = 1$, no change in income is perceived as a change in welfare.

In the Netherlands, and also in Belgium, the preference drift appears to be fairly high. Obviously the parameter values vary somewhat as we consider fairly homogeneous subgroups. Table 5.1 gives the estimates for a number of subgroups. (These figures differ slightly from those in Van Praag and Kapteyn (1973) because some improbable observations, due to misunderstandings by the respondents, have been removed.)

Quite recently, this material was re-examined in an attempt to test the following hypothesis. The assessment of income by an individual depends not only on his family size, the income received and other individual characteristics, but is also influenced by his environment or reference group. More specifically, if somebody's income equals the average income in his reference group, then he will not consider his income to be very small or extremely large. The standard by which an individual measures his income is provided, more or less, by the mean income of the individual's reference group.

Using a slightly reduced sub-sample, we estimated two equations:

$$\mu = 2.56 + 0.13 \ln(fs) + 0.57 \ln(y_a) \qquad (R^2 = 0.634),$$

$$\qquad (0.62) \quad (0.02) \qquad\quad (0.01)$$

$$\mu = 1.92 + 0.13 \ln(fs) + 0.50 \ln(y_a) + 0.30\mu_y \qquad (R^2 = 0.649), \qquad (4)$$

$$\qquad (0.44) \quad (0.02) \qquad\quad (0.01) \qquad\quad (0.05)$$

$$(N = 2{,}774).$$

where μ_y represents the mean log-income for the individual's reference group and where the individual's reference group is empirically determined in such a way that the sum of squared residuals from the estimated equations is minimised.

Table 5.1. Basic parameters for the Netherlands (1971).

	β_0	β_1	β_2	σ_1
Total population	3.02	0.13	0.64	0.54
Occupation				
Skilled labour	5.17	0.10	0.42	0.43
Administrative personnel	5.00	0.18	0.44	0.49
Lower and middle executives	2.36	0.13	0.72	0.48
Non-civilian army and police personnel	1.39	0.09	0.83	0.48
Instructors, teachers	4.33	0.17	0.52	0.53
Professional experts	3.27	0.12	0.63	0.51
The professions	3.30	0.06	0.64	0.58
Commercial professions	3.99	0.07	0.56	0.57
Working environment				
Civil service	2.63	0.11	0.70	0.52
Non-profit organisation	3.77	0.13	0.58	0.50
Private enterprise	3.07	0.13	0.65	0.50
Independent	4.31	0.11	0.52	0.61
Education level				
Primary education	6.09	0.11	0.33	0.44
Extended primary education	2.27	0.14	0.73	0.48
Primary vocational education	4.45	0.10	0.50	0.46
Secondary education	2.66	0.09	0.70	0.52
Secondary vocational education	3.07	0.16	0.65	0.48
Higher vocational education	3.26	0.18	0.62	0.52
University education	3.55	0.17	0.60	0.56

Details of how these reference groups are determined are given in Kapteyn, Van Praag and Van Herwaarden (1976).

The interpretation is straightforward. Suppose the incomes of all those in the reference group rise in the same proportion α. Then the individual's μ rises by 0.30α. If his own income also increases by α, his μ will rise all together by 0.80α, due to the additional preference drift. This phenomenon is well-known in sociology and is recognised in economics (see Duesenberry (1949), Easterlin (1974)). However, to our knowledge, this is the first quantitative estimate of this phenomenon.

It is tempting to assume that $\beta_2 + \beta_3 = 1$, implying that, apart from a number of objective variables, the assessment of income is completely determined by comparison with a reference income distribution. Our analysis, on a cross-section basis, did not confirm this. In a time series analysis, however, it may be true that $\beta_2 + \beta_3 = 1$, where μ_y is the mean log-income for the whole population, rather than the mean for a particular subgroup.

Below, we shall use the specification (3). Although fs and y_a are partially correlated, we neglect $\ln(fs)$ and replace it by its average value $\overline{\ln(fs)}$ $(= 1.1125$ in the Dutch survey). Then (3) simplifies to

$$\mu = 0.64 \ln(y_a) + 3.16. \tag{5}$$

Finally, we note that the log-normal function has a unimodal density function with the mode at $e^{\mu - \sigma^2}$. This corresponds to a welfare value

$$N(\mu - \sigma^2; \mu, \sigma) = N(-\sigma; 0, 1),$$

or about 0.3 on the [0, 1] scale, given the average value of 0.54 for σ. This implies that the individual welfare function is *not* concave at very low income levels (or, using our terminology, when income is "bad"). This non-concavity may offend some welfare theorists, especially in the income distribution field, because it suggests that in certain circumstances egalitarian income transfers may be difficult to justify, since they lead to a reduction in social welfare. However, this non-concavity is frequently recognised when national income is not sufficient to keep everyone above starvation level. In this harsh reality, it seems to be assumed that there is a threshold value below which life no longer has any value. Part of the population is sacrificed to save the others and to guarantee a standard above starvation level to the survivors.

In fact, there are no compelling reasons why an individual welfare function should be concave everywhere, although Gossen's First Law has some appeal. In the theory of decision making under uncertainty, the phenomenon of gambling has to be explained by the convexity of the utility function for small amounts of money. A footnote in Leibenstein (1974) is also of interest:

"The normal assumption of diminishing marginal utility as we consume more is true only if targets are not involved. Where targets are involved, part of the marginal utility curve can rise. For example, Tensing and Hillary obtained much more satisfaction from the last hundred feet in their climb to the summit of Everest than from any previous hundred feet. Consider an antibiotic (or alcoholic drink (BvP)) for which a certain minimum amount, say 20 grams, is certain to stop infection but less will not. Surely, the twentieth gram will be associated with a higher utility than the 19th or 18th. There is no reason why socially determined consumption targets should not operate in a similar fashion. Unfortunately, conventional theory does not take phenomena of this type into account. It is of interest that in a well known article by Friedman and Savage, a segment of their *total* utility-income function implies increasing marginal utility of expenditures. However, they seem to invent their function out of the blue and do not relate it to individual goals or to expenditure components. Their concern was to explain insurance purchases and gambling simultaneously".

From our investigations it appears that almost everybody is to be found in the concave region of *his own* individual welfare function. This implies, that nearly everyone faces decreasing marginal utility of income for small income increments. Since the welfare function and the corresponding marginal utility schedule shift to the left when actual income falls, because of the preference drift, we can have a situation where A, with f 20,000 of income, believes that the turning point is at f 10,000, while B, with f 10,000 of income, believes that the turning point is at f 4,000 (see figure 5.4).

IV. A direct measure of marginal welfare differences

As mentioned in the introduction, the assessment of income inequality is not just a statistical exercise. This becomes evident when we look for a characterisation of income *equality*. Traditionally equality is defined as follows: If there are n

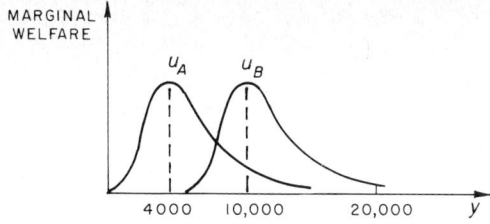

Figure 5.4.

individuals with incomes $y_1, \ldots, y_n$, complete equality is attained if $y_1 = y_2 = \ldots = y_n$. However, if the first person has a family of two and the second a family of four, it is clear that the situation may be called one of equality, but not one of equity. So we have to consider the *distribution of welfare* rather than the distribution of income. This is consistent with Sen's (1973) Weak Equity Axiom.

Let the individuals have welfare functions $U_i(y)$ ($i = 1, \ldots, n$) with corresponding marginal welfare functions $u_i(y)$. We suppose that individuals judge the equity of the income distribution by the extent to which that distribution fails to optimise a democratic social welfare function. Assume that each individual evaluates the income distribution using a social welfare function

$$SW(Y) = W(U_1(y_1), \ldots, U_n(y_n)), \tag{6}$$

which is "democratic", i.e.

$$\frac{dW}{dU_i} = \frac{dW}{dU_j} \quad \text{for } i, j = 1, \ldots, n.$$

In other words, the weighting given to all citizens is the same. If this holds for *all* income distributions, the social welfare function must be of the Bergson-Harsanyi type

$$SW(Y) = SW(y_1, \ldots, y_n) = \sum_{j=1}^{n} U_j(y_j). \tag{7}$$

For the optimal distribution, $SW(y_1, \ldots, y_n)$ is maximised subject to $\sum_{j=1}^{n} y_j = Y$. The first-order conditions are $u_j(y_j) = u_i(y_i)$ for all i, j. This corresponds to income equality when the marginal welfare functions are identical. If this is not the case, equality of marginal welfare implies *in*equality of income.

The consideration of equity problems may involve interpersonal comparisons. Is an individual able to place himself in the position of all his fellow-citizens, and to understand and imagine their welfare functions? And, assuming for the moment that this is possible, is it likely that he will do so? Statements concerning the distribution only make sense if we assume that people know about the income distribution, i.e., the frequencies in different income ranges. However, we do not believe that a person knows how his fellow-citizens in a specific income range evaluate their incomes. Even if that were the case, it is difficult to believe that individual i would regard it ethically just that individual j needs twice as much money to reach the same level of welfare as himself, unless it could be attributed to "objective" differences like children, physical handicaps, etc. Neglecting such differences, we suppose that individual i assumes that *all* other individuals evaluate their income (or ought to evaluate their income) according to his own welfare function $U_i(y)$. Then the social welfare function for individual i becomes

$$SW_i(y_1, \ldots, y_n) = W(U_i(y_1), \ldots, U_i(y_n)). \tag{8}$$

Obviously, this individualisation of the social welfare function ends any pretence that *the* social welfare function should describe *society's* preference ordering over the set of income distributions. The function SW_i describes *only* individual i's preference ordering, where he assumes all fellow-citizens to be like himself. The function SW defined in (6) could be regarded as the SW function used by the authorities. However, such a specification implicitly assumes that the authorities are able to compare the welfare levels of different persons, measured according to their *own* individual scales. If the authorities state at the outset that a family with $f\,10{,}000$ is poor and a family with $f\,100{,}000$ is rich, and by doing so impose their own individual welfare function $U_{\text{auth}}(y)$, they also take recourse in the specification given by (8).

If individual i does not feel that $SW_i(y)$ is optimised, perceived inequality is determined by the dispersion of the $u_i(y_i)$. This leads to the suggestion that inequality, or rather inequity, should be measured by

$$\text{var}\,(u(y)) = \sum_{j=1}^{n} (u_i(y_j) - \bar{u}_i)^2,$$

or

$$\text{var}\,(\ln u(y)) = \sum_{j=1}^{n} (\ln (u_i(y_j)) - \overline{\ln u_i})^2 = \sigma_u^2. \tag{9}$$

On the basis of the Weber–Fechner Law (and also common sense), it seems more attractive to use the latter measure, as we shall do below, although it is true that the first criterion supplies essentially the same information. Moreover, the latter measure is invariant under positive linear transformations.

Let the income distribution be described by its density function $dM(y)$, and let

$$\int_0^\infty y\,dM(y) = m, \qquad \int_0^\infty \ln y\,dM(y) = \mu_2,$$

$$\int_0^\infty (y - m)^2\,dM(y) = s^2, \qquad \int_0^\infty (\ln y - \mu)^2\,dM(y) = \sigma_2^2.$$

Then it is easy to obtain expressions for the inequality measure σ_u^2 corresponding to various forms for the individual welfare function.

(A) If $\ln u(y) = \alpha y + \beta, \qquad U(y) = 1 - C\,e^{-\alpha y}$

and $\displaystyle\int_0^\infty (\ln u(y) - \overline{\ln u})^2\,dM(y) = \alpha^2 \int_0^\infty (y - m)^2\,dM(y) = \alpha^2 s^2$

(B) $\ln u(y) = \alpha \ln y + \beta,\qquad U(y) = Cy^{1+\alpha}$

and $\int_0^\infty (\ln u(y) - \overline{\ln u})^2 \, dM(y) = \alpha^2 \int_0^\infty (\ln y - \mu)^2 \, dM(y) = \alpha^2 \sigma_2^2$

(C) $\ln u(y) = \alpha (\ln y)^2 + \beta \ln y + \gamma,\qquad U(y) \simeq \int_{-\infty}^{\ln y} e^{-(\alpha(\ln \eta)^2 + \beta \ln \eta + \gamma)} \, d\eta$

and $\int_0^\infty (\ln u(y) - \overline{\ln u})^2 \, dM(y) = \int_0^\infty [\alpha (\ln y)^2 + \beta \ln y + \gamma - \alpha(\sigma_2^2 + \mu_2^2)$

$- \beta\mu_2 - \gamma]^2 \, dM(y)$

$= \int_0^\infty [\alpha\{(\ln y)^2 - \sigma_2^2 - \mu_2^2\} + \beta(\ln y - \mu_2)]^2 \, dM(y).$
(10)

The expressions bear a close resemblance to those for the absolute and relative risk aversion functions $(d \ln u(y))/dy$ and $(d \ln u(y))/d \ln y$, respectively. (See Arrow (1965), Pratt (1964).) Notice that example (A) refers to a utility function with constant absolute risk aversion; the second (B) to a utility function with constant relative risk aversion. If an individual evaluates income according to one of these functions, σ_u^2 boils down to either the variance or log-variance of the income distribution. This is certainly an unexpected welfaristic interpretation of these measures. Case (C) corresponds to a utility function with linearly *decreasing* relative risk aversion. The corresponding utility function is always of the lognormal type.

If we require $\int_0^\infty u(y) \, dy = 1$, this imposes an additional constraint on α, β, γ and we have

$$-\frac{1}{2\sigma_1^2}(\ln y - \mu_1)^2 - \ln \sigma_1 - \tfrac{1}{2} \ln (2\pi) \equiv \alpha (\ln y)^2 + \beta \ln y + \gamma. \qquad (11)$$

This identity gives

$$\alpha = -\frac{1}{2\sigma_1^2}, \qquad \beta = \frac{\mu_1}{\sigma_1^2}, \qquad \gamma = -\ln \sigma_1 - \tfrac{1}{2} \ln (2\pi) - \frac{\mu_1^2}{2\sigma_1^2}$$

where μ_1, σ_1 are the parameters of the individual welfare function.

It is obvious that (10) includes moments of $dM(x)$ up to the fourth degree. Although this is no serious problem for the calculations, it makes interpretation difficult. We shall make the simplifying assumption that the income distribution is also lognormal, i.e. $M(y) = \Lambda(y; \mu_2, \sigma_2)$. A little algebra reveals

$$\sigma_u^2 = \frac{\sigma_2^2}{4\sigma_1^4}[\sigma_2^2 + 2(\mu_2 - \mu_1)^2],$$

and

$$\overline{\ln u} = \frac{1}{2\sigma_1^2}[\sigma_2^2 + (\mu_2 - \mu_1)^2] - \ln(\sigma\sqrt{2\pi}), \tag{12}$$

where we use the well-known properties of the normal distribution, $E(\ln y - \mu_2)^3 = 0$ and $E(\ln y - \mu_2)^4 = 3\sigma_2^4$.

It is frequently remarked that the income distribution is not approximately lognormal. If that is the case, we might consider a convex combination of several lognormal distributions, i.e.

$$M(y) = \sum \alpha_i \Lambda(y; \mu_2^{(i)}, \sigma_2^{(i)}).$$

It is no more difficult to calculate (9), since $M(y)$ is only a simple linear mixture; and even an income distribution which is clearly not lognormal (bi-modal perhaps) may be well approximated by a convex combination of several lognormal distributions.

V. Further analysis of the variance of log-marginal welfare differences

In this section we shall assume a lognormal income distribution, although most of the results can be generalised to any arbitrary income distribution. We now want to get a better understanding of the measure by considering various aspects.

V.1. *The sign*

σ_u^2 fulfils the requirement that $\sigma_u^2 > 0$ for all distributions unless all marginal utilities are equal, in which case $\sigma_u^2 = 0$.

V.2. *The Pigou–Dalton condition*

This requires that an income transfer from a richer person to a poorer one always reduces income inequality. It can be shown that σ_u^2 is not reduced by all such transfers. However, this is not very damaging to our measure, which reflects *individual perceptions*. Consider, for example, the income distribution $y_1 = 10,000$, $y_2 = 11,000$, $y_3 = 100,000$ and suppose that I am the first person. Let us make a transfer so that the distribution becomes $y_1 = 10,000$, $y_2 = 31,000$, $y_3 = 80,000$. It is doubtful whether I would view such a transfer as a reduction in inequality. In fact, the universal validity of the Pigou-Dalton principle would, in our opinion, be an undesirable property for σ_u^2.

V.3. *Dependence on the monetary unit*

σ_u^2 does not depend on the unit of account, since it only contains a term $(\mu_2 - \mu_1)$.

V.4. Individualistic character

In what way does σ_u^2 depend on the personal circumstances of the individual observer? This can be answered by substituting the relationship

$$\mu_1 = \beta_0 + \beta_2 \ln y_a,$$

and we obtain

$$\sigma_u^2(y_a) = \frac{\sigma_2^2}{2\sigma_1^4}[\sigma_2^2 + 2(\mu_2 - \beta_2 \ln y_a - \beta_0)^2].$$

This is a quadratic function in $\ln y_a$. Its minimum is $\frac{1}{2}(\sigma_2/\sigma_1)^4$ which is attained at $\ln y_a = (\mu_2 - \beta_0)/\beta_2$. It has been sketched in figure 5.5. Up to a certain income level, the perception of inequality falls as income increases; the turning point is reached at $\mu_2 = \mu_1$, when the observer believes that 50% of the population earns less than an income he evaluates at 0.5 (i.e. "barely sufficient").

When y_a is distributed lognormally, it can be shown that $\sigma_u^2 - \frac{1}{2}(\sigma_2/\sigma_1)^4$ has

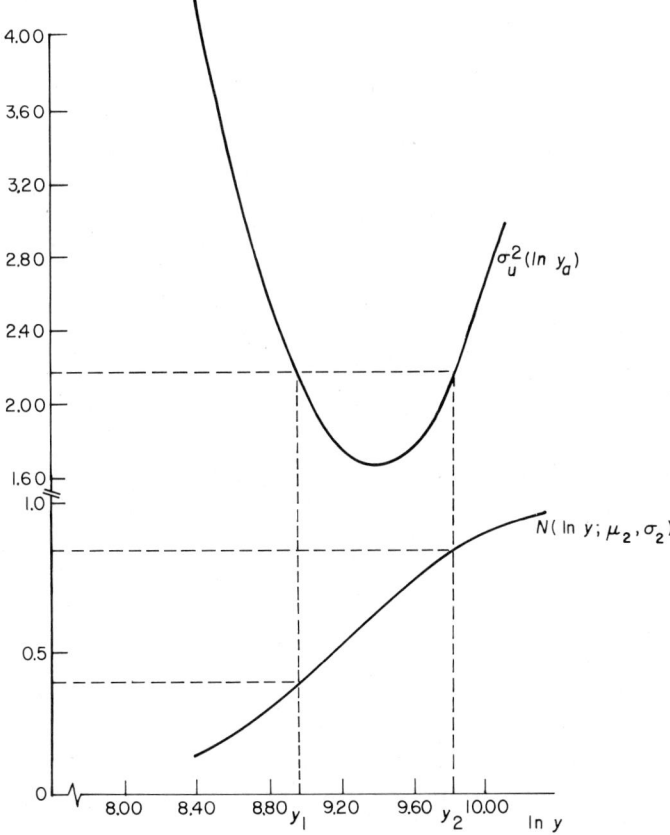

Figure 5.5. σ_u^2 as a function of income.

a non-central chi-square distribution with one degree of freedom. From figure 5.5 it can be seen that a simple way of calculating the distribution is to use the fact that

$$P[\sigma_u^2 \leq \alpha] = P[\ln y_1 \leq \ln y_a \leq \ln y_2]$$

V.5. *An overall change in the income distribution*

In practice, observed changes in the income distribution affect everyone simultaneously (wage-rises, etc.). Both before and after, the distribution is approximately lognormal. If we assume that the ranking of individuals remains the same, this can only occur when the transformation is log-linear

$$\ln \tilde{y}_i = \alpha \ln y_i + \theta,$$

where y_i and $\tilde{y}_i$ are the incomes of individual i before and after the change. Then it can be shown that

$$\tilde{\mu}_2 = \alpha \mu_2 + \theta$$

and

$$\tilde{\sigma}_2^2 = \alpha^2 \sigma_2^2.$$

A redistribution of *constant* national income also requires $\alpha \mu_2 + \theta + \frac{1}{2} \alpha^2 \sigma_2^2 = \mu_2 + \frac{1}{2} \sigma_2^2$, which implies a relationship between α and θ. When $0 < \alpha < 1$, there is a levelling of incomes. When $\alpha = 0$, all incomes are increased or reduced by the factor $e^\theta \simeq 1 + \theta$ (if θ is small). When $\alpha < 1$ and $\theta = 0$, a change will normally decrease σ_u^2, but not always. For if $\mu_1 > \mu_2$, the term $(\alpha \mu_2 - \mu_1)^2$ clearly increases. When μ_1 is significantly greater than the population's μ_2, it may be perceived as an increase in inequality.

The situation when all incomes increase in the same proportion ($\theta > 0$, $\alpha = 0$) is very interesting. The impact on σ_u^2 depends on the term $(\mu_2 + \theta - \mu_1)^2$. When $\mu_2 < \mu_1$, the proportional rise leads to a *reduction* in inequality. When $\mu_2 > \mu_1$, it causes inequality to *increase*. In other words, more affluent people see a proportional rise as reducing inequality, while poorer people see quite the opposite.

This result seems to provide a solution to Kolm's (1976) problem. He argued that, although conventional measures suggest that a proportional increase in all incomes does not change inequality, many people at lower income levels seem to regard a proportional wage rise as an increase in inequality. Instead, they consider that a wage increase of *equal absolute* amounts leaves inequality unchanged. The first (proportionalist) view is ascribed by Kolm to "rightists" and the other (absolutist) view to "leftists".

Kolm solves this problem by constructing *two* inequality measures, one conforming to the views of "rightists" and one to those of "leftists". In our context this problem is solved because the variance of marginal welfare itself changes character gradually from leftist to rightist. We do not have to use two measures; one, which incorporates the different perceptions of individuals, is sufficient. Obviously θ may happen to be negative due, for example, to a price increase arising from a uniform Value Added Tax. This will reverse the argument. The left will hail it as a reduction in inequality and the right will despise it.

V.6. Intertemporal comparisons when individual circumstances change

If each income increases by a factor e^θ, this will trigger the preference drift of our individual observer, since he adjusts his standards over time to his new income. His original μ_1 changes to $(\mu_1 + \beta_2\theta)$, so $(\mu_2 - \mu_1)^2$ changes initially to $(\mu_2 + \theta - \mu_1)^2$ and later returns to an intermediate position $(\mu_2 + \theta - \mu_1 - \beta_2\theta)^2$. Thus the initial *ex ante* change in inequality seems *ex post* to be exaggerated. Recalling the estimated equation (4),

$$\mu_1 = \beta_0 + \beta_1 \ln fs + \beta_2 \ln y_a + \beta_3 \mu_y,$$

it is clear that over a longer period still "the reference group effect" will also come into play. When $(\beta_2 + \beta_3) = 0.8$, or even closer to one as we suppose, a proportional wage rise will *not* lead to any change in inequality in the long run. This seems an important conclusion for economic policy, even if it is not completely true.

V.7. Intertemporal comparisons of different income distributions

Inequality measures are frequently used to compare income distributions over time or for different countries. Consider two moments in time, say past and present. The past distribution is $\Lambda(\mu_{21}, \sigma_{21})$, and the individual parameters are μ_{11}, σ_{11} and y_1. The present distribution is $\Lambda(\mu_{22}, \sigma_{22})$ and the individual parameters are μ_{12}, σ_{12} and y_2. Then we can distinguish *three* ways of evaluating the evolution of income inequality.
(a) We evaluate both distributions at present standards.
(b) We evaluate both distributions at past standards.
(c) We evaluate both distributions by the standards of their own time.

Define

$$\sigma^2_{u,ij} = \frac{\sigma^2_{2i}}{4\sigma^2_{1j}}[\sigma^2_{2i} + 2(\mu_{2i} - \mu_{1j})^2],$$

where $\sigma^2_{u,ij}$ is the inequality at moment i using the standard of time j. The three types of comparisons may yield different outcomes, since μ_1 and σ_1 may have changed over time. In our societies, increases in the education level suggest a slight increase in σ^2_1; on the other hand, there seems to be a small positive relationship between σ_1 and σ_2. On balance σ_1 may be assumed constant over time.

Consider a proportional change in all incomes by a factor θ. Then method (a) would compare $(\mu_{21} - \mu_{12})^2$ and $(\mu_{21} + \theta - \mu_{12})^2$. When $\mu_{21} + \theta < \mu_{12}$ (i.e. for the more affluent), the proportional increase is perceived as inequality-reducing; for poor people the reverse is true. Approach (b) would make a comparison between $(\mu_{21} - \mu_{11})^2$ and $(\mu_{21} + \theta - \mu_{11})^2$. However, it is difficult to believe that many observers are able to remember and apply their own past standards. When interpreted as a comparison of the *present* to the *future*, we see that a future proportional income rise is regarded by poor people as inequality-increasing and by rich people as a fall in inequality. Finally we may compare $\sigma_{u,11}^2$ with $\sigma_{u,22}^2$. Since it is likely that both μ_1 and y_a have increased by the factor θ, we compare $(\mu_{21} - \mu_{11})^2$ with $(\mu_{21} + \theta - \mu_{11} - \theta)^2$. The conclusion is that there is no change in inequality over time whatsoever.

V.8. *Comparisons between countries*

The same analysis may be applied to different countries. Let country 1 be poor and country 2 rich; for example, $\mu_{22} = \mu_{21} + \theta$ and, similarly, $\mu_{12} = \mu_{11} + \theta$. Then the same paradoxes occur if we evaluate the differences at "rich" standards, "poor" standards, or both countries at their own national standards.

V.9. *A collectivist measure*

Finally, we are interested in an aggregate measure, reflecting the average of the individual perceptions. This does not, in fact, require interpersonal *utility* comparisons, since welfare is only compared intra-personally. It does require the assumption that people who give the same number to perceived inequality (about any marginal utility level) feel equally strongly about welfare inequality. Under this assumption it is natural to use the mean value of σ_u^2, averaged over the income distribution, as the aggregate measure. This is denoted by $\bar{\sigma}_u^2$. After some calculation we obtain

$$\bar{\sigma}_u^2 = E_{\ln y}\sigma_u^2(\ln y) = \frac{\sigma_2^4}{\sigma_1^4} + \frac{\sigma_2^2}{2\sigma_1^4} E_{\ln y}[\beta_2(\ln y - \mu_2) + \beta_0 - (1 - \beta_2)\mu_2]^2$$

$$= \frac{\sigma_2^4}{\sigma_1^4} + \tfrac{1}{2}\beta_2^2 \frac{\sigma_2^4}{\sigma_1^4} + \tfrac{1}{2}\frac{\sigma_2^2}{\sigma_1^4}[\beta_0 - (1 - \beta_2)\mu_2]^2.$$

VI. The lognormal specification applied to some conventional measures

Two well-known measures are based on an individual welfare function – those of Dalton and Atkinson. We shall examine these measures using our estimated individual welfare function.

Let us begin with the Dalton (1920) approach. Let $W(U_1(y_1), \ldots, U_n(y_n))$ be a social welfare function which depends only on the distribution of income. Then Dalton assumes that, for a given national income Y, the highest level of social welfare is attained when there is complete equality. (All individuals have the same individual welfare function.) If the corresponding level of social welfare is given by $W_e = W(U(m), \ldots, U(m))$, Dalton's measure D is

$$D = \frac{W(U(y_1), \ldots, U(y_n))}{W_e}.$$

It is difficult to assess the value of D as an inequality measure. To begin with, it is based on the assumption that complete equality is optimal. However, this is guaranteed only when the functions U and W are concave and quasi-concave respectively. This implies, that the measure is less general than has been suggested. If these conditions are not fulfilled, D may be greater than one.

Assuming that W is additive, that U is lognormal $\Lambda(\mu_1, \sigma_1)$ and that the income distribution is also lognormal (say $\Lambda(\mu_2, \sigma_2)$), D may be calculated explicitly.[5] Consider an individual with the individual welfare function (i.w.f.) $\Lambda(\mu_1, \sigma_1^2)$ who is confronted with an income distribution $\Lambda(\mu_2, \sigma_2^2)$. He computes the average individual welfare[6]

$$W = \int_0^\infty \Lambda(y; \mu_1, \sigma_1^2) \, d\Lambda(y; \mu_2, \sigma_2^2)$$

$$= N(0; \mu_1 - \mu_2, \sigma_1^2 + \sigma_2^2).$$

National income per capita is $\bar{y} = e^{\mu_2 + \frac{1}{2}\sigma_2^2}$. Hence the individual welfare corresponding to $\bar{y}$ is $W = N(\mu_2 + \frac{1}{2}\sigma_2^2; \mu_1, \sigma_1^2)$. The Dalton measure is then

$$D = \frac{W}{W_e} = \frac{N((\mu_2 - \mu_1)/\sqrt{(\sigma_2^2 + \sigma_1^2)}; 0, 1)}{N((\mu_2 - \mu_1 + \frac{1}{2}\sigma_2^2)/\sigma_1; 0, 1)}.$$

This is a somewhat difficult expression to analyse, but note that $D = 1$ if $\sigma^2 = 0$,

---

[5] We use a number of formulae without proof (see Aitchison and Brown (1957, ch. 2)):

(a) Moments:
$$\int_0^\infty x^j \, d\Lambda(x; \mu, \sigma^2) = e^{j\mu + \frac{1}{2}j^2\sigma^2},$$

(b) Moment distribution:
$$\frac{\int_0^x \xi^j \, d\Lambda(\xi; \mu, \sigma^2)}{\int_0^\infty \xi^j \, d\Lambda(\xi; \mu, \sigma^2)} = \Lambda(x; \mu + j\sigma^2, \sigma^2),$$

(c) Convolution:
$$\int_0^\infty \Lambda(ax^b; \mu_1, \sigma_1^2) \, d\Lambda(x; \mu_2, \sigma_2^2)$$
$$= \int_0^\infty \Lambda(1; \mu_1 - b \ln x; \mu_1, \sigma_1^2) \, d\Lambda(x; \mu_2, \sigma_2^2)$$
$$= \Lambda(a; \mu_1 - b\mu_2, \sigma_1^2 + b^2\sigma_2^2).$$

[6] Note that the individual is assumed to evaluate the income of others on his *own* welfare scale.

which corresponds to complete income inequality; and D does not depend on the unit of account, since it depends only on $(\mu_2 - \mu_1)$.

Obviously D depends on the individual observer, or rather his income y_a, since $\mu_1 = \beta_2 \ln y_a + \beta_0$. Let us consider the difference

$$\frac{\mu_2 - \mu_1 + \frac{1}{2}\sigma_2^2}{\sigma_1} - \frac{(\mu_2 - \mu_1)}{\sqrt{(\sigma_1^2 + \sigma_2^2)}} = (\mu_2 - \mu_1)\left\{\frac{1}{\sigma_1} - \frac{1}{\sqrt{(\sigma_1^2 + \sigma_2^2)}}\right\} + \frac{1}{2}\frac{\sigma_2^2}{\sigma_1}.$$

Since μ_1 increases when $\ln y_a$ increases, this is a decreasing linear function in $\ln y_a$. It is zero when

$$\mu_2 - \mu_1 = \frac{\frac{1}{2}\sigma_2^2}{1 - \frac{\sigma_1}{\sqrt{(\sigma_1^2 + \sigma_2^2)}}}.$$

This implies

$$\ln y_a = \frac{1}{\beta_2}\left\{-\beta_0 + \mu_2 - \frac{\frac{1}{2}\sigma_2^2}{1 - \frac{\sigma_1}{\sqrt{(\sigma_1^2 + \sigma_2^2)}}}\right\}.$$

At this income level the observer sees the social welfare corresponding to the existing income distribution as equivalent to that associated with an egalitarian distribution of the same total income. If y_a increases, he will even prefer the existing distribution from a social welfare standpoint.

This shows that D is not always less than one. This is due to the initial non-concavity of the i.w.f. It can be shown that this anomalous situation arises only at very high income levels. From numerical calculations, D itself is found to be a non-monotonic function of $\ln y_a$. It decreases at first, and increases again when the middle income range has been passed. When σ_2 increases and total income is fixed, the denominator remains constant, but the numerator of D decreases. This shows that D decreases when σ_2 increases, as it should.

The measure proposed by Atkinson (1970) uses the utility function of income $U(y) = y^{1-\varepsilon}/(1 - \varepsilon)$. Some of Atkinson's ideas can be traced to Kolm (1969). For a lognormal income distribution, aggregate welfare is

$$W = \frac{1}{1 - \varepsilon}\int_0^\infty y^{1-\varepsilon}\,d\Lambda(y; \mu_2, \sigma_2) = \frac{1}{1 - \varepsilon}e^{(1-\varepsilon)\mu_2 + \frac{1}{2}(1-\varepsilon)^2\sigma_2^2}.$$

The income level y_{EDE}, for which $[1/(1 - \varepsilon)]y_{\text{EDE}}^{1-\varepsilon} = W$, is given by

$$y_{\text{EDE}} = \exp\left[\frac{(1 - \varepsilon)\mu_2 + \frac{1}{2}(1 - \varepsilon)^2\sigma_2^2}{1 - \varepsilon}\right],$$

$$A = 1 - \frac{y_{\text{EDE}}}{\bar{y}} = 1 - e^{-\frac{1}{2}\varepsilon\sigma_2^2}.$$

The value of A is less than one when $\varepsilon > 0$. It is zero if $\sigma_2 = 0$.

Now we substitute the lognormal i.w.f. for the Atkinson utility function. We find that aggregate welfare is

$$W = N\left(\frac{\mu_2 - \mu_1}{\sqrt{(\sigma_1^2 + \sigma_2^2)}}; 0, 1\right),$$

and obtain $\ln(y_{EDE})$ from the equation

$$\frac{\ln(y_{EDE}) - \mu_1}{\sigma_1} = \frac{\mu_2 - \mu_1}{\sqrt{(\sigma_1^2 + \sigma_2^2)}},$$

so

$$\ln(y_{EDE}) = \frac{\sigma_1}{\sqrt{(\sigma_1^2 + \sigma_2^2)}}(\mu_2 - \mu_1) + \mu_1.$$

The modified Atkinson measure $\tilde{A}$ is given by

$$\tilde{A} = 1 - \frac{y_{EDE}}{\bar{y}} = 1 - \exp\left\{-\tfrac{1}{2}\sigma_2^2 + (\mu_1 - \mu_2)\left(1 - \frac{\sigma_1}{\sqrt{(\sigma_1^2 + \sigma_2^2)}}\right)\right\}.$$

Notice that $\tilde{A}$ is zero when either $\sigma_2 = 0$ or

$$\mu_1 - \mu_2 = \frac{\tfrac{1}{2}\sigma_2^2}{1 - \dfrac{\sigma_1}{\sqrt{(\sigma_1^2 + \sigma_2^2)}}}.$$

Notice also that both the Dalton and Atkinson measures have their turning point at the same income level. When μ_1 rises as $\ln y_a$ increases, a higher evaluation is given to some specific income distribution when the observer's income increases. At the highest income levels, the actual distribution seems to generate greater social welfare than the egalitarian distribution. The same is true of the Dalton measure.

Atkinson introduces a parameter into inequality measurement which corresponds to variations in the value judgements of individuals. This value ε is known both as the index of relative risk (inequality) aversion and as the elasticity of the marginal utility of income. (See Frisch (1959), Arrow (1965)). If ε changes along with the observer's income, variations in the measure A may correspond to those of $\tilde{A}$.

In Van Praag (1971) an estimate of ε was derived from the lognormal i.w.f. This was given by[7]

$$\varepsilon = -1 - \frac{(\ln y - \mu_1)}{\sigma_1^2}.$$

Substituting our estimate of ε, for an individual with income y_a, into Atkinson's measure, we obtain

$$A_E = 1 - \exp\left[\tfrac{1}{2}\sigma_2^2 - \tfrac{1}{2}\left(\frac{\sigma_2}{\sigma_1}\right)^2(\ln y_a - \mu_1)\right].$$

In this way Atkinson's welfare function is individualised by assigning to each individual an $\varepsilon(y_a)$ which is equal to elasticity of his marginal utility of income.

---

[7] Using the estimated parameter values, ε varies between -1 and -3 for realistic values of y.

On the other hand, when constant relative inequality aversion is assumed, no provision is made for the possibility that $\varepsilon(y)$ is a *de*creasing log-linear function of income.

Using the formula, A_E is seen to increase as the observer's income increases, with an absolute upper bound of one.

We conclude that both the Dalton *and* Atkinson measures derive their attractiveness from two *a priori* assumptions, the first resting on tradition, the second on a value judgement: (a) the individual welfare function is concave everywhere; (b) the egalitarian distribution is not only ethically preferable, but also yields the highest social welfare, when social welfare is measured in the Bergsonian way. If we do not accept these assumptions, the value of either inequality measure seems questionable.

VII. Further discussion and numerical results

The concepts discussed in the previous sections have been applied to the Dutch post-tax income distribution in 1971. Later data on the income distribution *and* the Dutch individual welfare function are not yet available. In 1971 the mean log-income $\mu_2 = 9.19$, the log-variance $\sigma_2 = 0.73$ and mean income was exp (9.45). The average for the logarithm of family size was estimated at $\overline{\ln fs} = 1.1125$.

Data on the individual welfare function are given in Table 5.2. For observers at the nine decile levels we calculated
(i) the social welfare function W,
(ii) welfare under equal distribution W_e,
(iii) the Dalton ratio,
(iv) the elasticity of the marginal utility of income, derived from the lognormal i.w.f.,
(v) the individualised Atkinson measure, where $\varepsilon(y_a)$ has been substituted into the Atkinson utility function $U = y^{1-\varepsilon}$,
(vi) the inequality measure σ_u^2.

Social welfare W is evaluated by poor people at approximately 0.8, but at only about 0.3 by the top decile. Between these two extremes social welfare declines

Table 5.2. Comparisons of some inequality measures for the Dutch income distribution (1971).

	Net income level in guilders	W	W_e	D	$\varepsilon(\ln y)$	A_E	σ_u^2
bottom decile	3,849	0.793	0.969	0.818	−0.339	0.086	5.119
2nd decile	5,307	0.723	0.931	0.776	−0.736	0.178	3.472
3rd decile	6,655	0.667	0.888	0.751	−1.015	0.237	2.630
4th decile	8,164	0.613	0.836	0.734	−1.268	0.287	2.095
5th decile	9,799	0.563	0.776	0.725	−1.493	0.328	1.799
6th decile	11,760	0.512	0.707	0.724	−1.718	0.367	1.674
7th decile	14,428	0.455	0.618	0.735	−1.971	0.409	1.737
8th decile	18,092	0.392	0.513	0.764	−2.250	0.451	2.057
highest decile	24,944	0.309	0.364	0.847	−2.647	0.506	2.963

steadily. This is due to the preference drift. For the same reason, social welfare corresponding to an egalitarian distribution is given a very high valuation (0.97) by poor people and a very low assessment (0.36) by the rich. The variation in the resulting Dalton ratio W/W_e is not spectacular. We notice that the middle classes appear to expect the most from an egalitarian redistribution of national income.

The elasticity of the marginal utility of income is always negative, but varies from -0.33 to -2.65. This reflects the feeling that marginal utility declines slowly for poor people, but the rich derive increasingly less utility from proportional income increases. This leads to a rather puzzling result. When ε is adjusted to individual standards, Atkinson's measure suggests that the poor give a more moderate assessment to income inequality than all other people in society. Clearly, this follows from the fact that we estimated ε to be a declining function of income; however, it is very unlikely that the elasticity increases with income.

The last column gives values for our marginal welfare variance measure, σ_u^2. We see that it starts at about 5.19, decreases to 1.67 in the middle income range and then slowly increases. This is consistent with the notion that income inequality, regarded as high by very poor people, is viewed by the middle classes as moderate. In the top tail of the income distribution, it becomes clear to the rich observer that he earns much more than the majority of the population; in other words, that there is considerable inequality.

The variance measure may be better understood using figure 5.6. Consider a person with income y_a and the marginal welfare density function as sketched. He assumes that average marginal welfare is $\ln u$ and that the average proportional deviation is given by e^{σ_u}. Thus, if $\sigma_u = 1$, the proportional deviation lies between $\bar{u}e^{-1}$ and $\bar{u}e$. In general, the factor will be e^{σ_u}. Our estimates suggest $E(\sigma_u^2(y)) = 1.780$. In other words, people feel that relative marginal welfare differences about the mean are on average $e^{1.334} \simeq 3.797$.

Each individual determines $\sigma_u^2(y)$ with regard to own welfare function. There are no interpersonal welfare comparisons at this stage. Nor does averaging over the individual values of $\sigma_u^2(y)$ imply interpersonal comparison of the welfare or marginal welfare levels of individuals. We conclude that $\bar{\sigma}_u^2$ is a meaningful inequality measure, even if one rejects the possibility of making *inter*personal welfare comparisons.

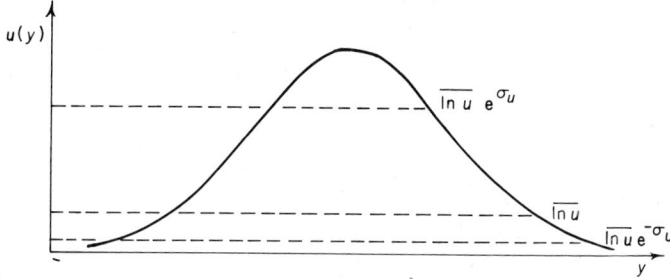

Figure 5.6. The average variation of marginal welfare.

VIII. Conclusions

The approach taken in this paper clearly relies on estimating individual welfare functions. We are aware that this poses some problems. However, our experience in recent years with numerous large-scale surveys suggests that these problems are not insuperable.

The proposed measure does not depend on the specific welfare function chosen. The estimation method outlined in section VI can be used for other functional forms.

The results obtained are intuitively plausible, but it should be remembered that the 1971 sample, on which our calculations are based, is not completely representative of the Dutch population.

References

Aitchison, J. and J.A.C. Brown, *The Lognormal Distribution*, Cambridge University Press (1957).
Arrow, K.J., *Aspects of the Theory of Risk-Bearing*, Helsinki, 1965.
Atkinson, A.B., "On the Measurement of Inequality", *Journal of Economic Theory*, 1970.
Dalton, H., "The Measurement of the Inequality of Income", *Economic Journal*, 1920.
Duesenberry, J.S., *Income, Saving and the Theory of Consumer Behavior*, Harvard University Press, Cambridge (Mass.), 1949.
Easterlin, R.A., "Does Economic Growth Improve the Human Lot? Some Empirical Evidence", in: P.A. David and M.W. Reder (eds.), *Nations and Households in Economic Growth. Essays in Honor of Moses Abramowitz*, Academic Press, New York, 1974.
Friedman, M. and L.J. Savage, "The Utility Analysis of Choices Involving Risk", *The Journal of Political Economy*, 1948.
Frisch, R., "A Complete Scheme for Computing All Direct and Cross Demand Elasticities in a Model with many Sectors", *Econometrica*, 1959.
Van Herwaarden, F., A. Kapteyn and B.M.S. Van Praag, "12,000 Individual Welfare Functions of Income: A Comparison of Six Samples in Belgium and The Netherlands", *European Economic Review* (1977).
Kapteyn, A. and B.M.S. Van Praag, "A New Approach to the Construction of Family Equivalence Scales", *European Economic Review*, 1976.
Kapteyn, A., B.M.S. Van Praag and F. Herwaarden, "Individual Welfare Functions and Social Reference Groups", Report 76.01, Economic Institute of Leyden University, 1976.
Kapteyn, A., *A Theory of Preference Formation*, Ph.D. dissertation, Leyden, 1977.
Kolm, S.C., "The Optimal Production of Social Justice", in: J. Margolis and H. Guitton (eds.), *Public Economics*, McMillan, 1969.
Kolm, S.C., "Unequal Inequalities", *Journal of Economic Theory*, 1976.
Leibenstein, H., "An Interpretation of the Economic Theory of Fertility", *Journal of Economic Literature*, 1974.
Pen, J. and J. Tinbergen, "Hoeveel bedroeg de inkomensegalisatie sinds 1938?", *Economisch-Statistische Berichten*, 1976.
Van Praag, B.M.S., *Individual Welfare Functions and Consumer Behavior*, North-Holland, Amsterdam, 1968.
Van Praag, B.M.S., "The Welfare Function of Income in Belgium: An Empirical Investigation", *European Economic Review*, 1971.
Van Praag, B.M.S. and A. Kapteyn, "Further Evidence on the Individual Welfare Function of Income: an Empirical Investigation in The Netherlands", *European Economic Review*, 1973.
Pratt, J.W., "Risk Aversion in the Small and in the Large", *Econometrica*, 1964.
Sen, A.K., *On Economic Inequality*, Clarendon Press, Oxford, 1973.

5 DISCUSSION

PAPER BY BERNARD VAN PRAAG

Dr. Wagner sympathised with the attempt to estimate empirical welfare functions and to relate the perception of inequality to the position of the individual in the income hierarchy. He commented on three topics: (1) the estimation of empirical welfare functions from interviews; (2) the derivation of a specific measure of income inequality; and (3) differences in the perception of inequality.

It is surprising that the paper indicates a log-normal specification for individual welfare functions with a non-concave portion at the lower end. He suggested that this feature might arise from a measurement error on the part of the individuals being interviewed. Since the non-concavity occurs at income levels substantially below the actual income of the respondent, it is possible that the respondent does not try hard enough to imagine what their life would be like if their income fell substantially below their current level. This lack of imagination leads individuals to say they are indifferent between a low income and one which is even lower. However, a person who is really experiencing a low income may be very sensitive to further reductions. If Professor van Praag corrected for this "measurement error" caused by the lack of imagination on the part of respondents, the welfare function would exhibit concavity over the whole range.

Secondly, he pointed out that the paper uses an unweighted average of individual welfare functions to arrive at a measure indicating the general concern about inequality. From a normative point of view this linear aggregation may be unsatisfactory. It can be argued that someone with a higher income should get a lower weighting in the derivation of the social inequality measure.

He was also concerned with the values of the Dalton indicator D in Table 5.2. These show that the middle-class expect most from an egalitarian redistribution of national income. This seemed counter-intuitive and led him to ask whether this meant that the middle-class should be considered the true revolutionary class.

Professor Wiles argued that the use of the term middle-class here was misleading. The results of table 5.2 seem perfectly reasonable if we remember that the middle part of the distribution, around the fifth and sixth deciles, corresponds to the semi-skilled manual occupations. The first decile contains mainly the young and students, the second pensioners. What are normally called the middle-class are to be found around the 95th percentile. So to a good Marxist the fifth and sixth deciles are the true revolutionary class. Those occupying the low deciles, who either expect high incomes in the future or who may have received high incomes in the past, may be very conservative.

Dr. Wagner continued by pointing out that Professor van Praag's use of the variance of log incomes as an inequality measure loses much of its attraction if welfare functions other than the log-normal are considered. Most measures of inequality will then no longer be monotonic functions of the variance of the logs.

Professor Abele was interested in the connection between the different attitudes of individuals towards inequality and their position in the distribution, or more precisely the individual's parameters in relation to those of the overall distribution. He asked whether we could conclude from the attitude towards inequality of the Dutch participants that they could be found at the extreme ends of the distribution. This relationship between ethical attitudes and the empirical fact of one's position in the income scale, linking the ethical aspects of inequality to the empirical aspects, seemed to be an inference of Professor van Praag's approach as he understood it.

He was also interested in the subjective evaluation of various changes in the distribution other than the simple Pigou–Dalton shift. However he was unable to evaluate all the consequences of these experiments, for example the responses to questions about proportional rises in all incomes, price increases, and uniform VAT changes. These changed not only the overall distribution but also the parameters of the individual welfare functions. It may therefore be very difficult to predict the outcome of such experiments and to judge the sensitivity of the inequality measure on the basis of these exercises.

He was encouraged by the fact that Professor van Praag was able to empirically estimate individual welfare functions even when these depended on the environment or reference group of the individual. However there may be serious difficulties with this approach if the separability assumption is abandoned. He was also concerned with the non-concavity feature of the individual welfare function. He could think of no justification for a point of inflection in the individual welfare function, particularly if income is the argument. It seemed to imply some sort of "relative saturation" with respect to income increases. Finally he commented on two potential weaknesses in the estimation procedure. As was mentioned in a previous discussion, there is a danger that individuals may misrepresent their preferences, and the problem of ignorance of the position at other income levels, on which Dr. Wagner had already remarked.

Professor Krelle drew attention to a crucial assumption in the derivation of the log-normal form for the individual function – the assumption that people have the same utility threshold regardless of their income level. This is explicitly mentioned in Professor van Praag's *European Economic Review* article, but not in the paper under discussion. If it were the case that richer people were more sensitive to changes in welfare than people with low incomes, the utility threshold would decrease with income and the non-concavity may disappear. He suggested that tests might be made to discover whether the sensitivity to welfare changes was indeed independent of income levels.

Mr. Layard suggested a possible explanation for the non-concavity of the welfare function. If these are interpreted as short-run functions, related to short-term changes in income, only the interval around current income is important. A reduction in income may initially cause a significant decline in welfare which in the long run becomes less severe as individuals get used to their lower income level. In the long-run, the sequence of points on short-run welfare functions may quite well generate a concave long-run welfare function.

Professor Adelman supported this view. The measurement difficulties indicated by other speakers could perhaps be overcome if individuals were only asked to comment on incomes in a neighbourhood of their own. A kind of envelope curve could then yield the ultimate welfare function. She believed that the approach adopted in the paper might be very valuable in inter-country comparisons of deprivation, since it fell somewhere between relative and absolute measures of deprivation.

Professor Taubman asked whether it was being argued that the social welfare function should correspond to the individual welfare function being estimated. He also wondered whether there may be some confusion between absolute and relative welfare levels arising from the use of verbal categories in the interviews.

Professor Stiglitz thought that the fact that systematic responses were obtained to the questions asked required explanation, but was not convinced by the explanation being offered. He recalled that, in the psychological literature concerning subjective probabilities, systematic misperceptions are observed. For example, individuals may be asked to draw a number at random from a hat and then answer a question such as "How many ships pass through the Panama Canal each year?". It is found that there is a correlation between the number drawn and the answer given to the question. This has been explained by a phenomenon known as "anchoring" – that people anchor their responses to almost anything they know about. In the context of income distribution, people relate their views to the incomes they know, but the interpretation of that evidence is an open question.

He asked whether some alternative specification might provide a better fit than the log-normal distribution. In other areas doubts have recently been raised about functional forms which have been traditionally used. This issue has some importance because of the welfare implications. If we take the log-normal specification seriously and wish to maximise *ex ante* utility, the optimal distribution would involve a good deal of inequality. Furthermore the assumption of bounded utility is very strict. In the context of risk analysis, a bounded utility function together with constant elasticity curves restricts the set of possible utility functions to just one.

Professor Krupp also questioned whether the log-normal specification was ideal. Numerous studies suggest that the log-normal does not fit the distribution very well in the tails. To overcome this, the paper suggests using a linear combination of a number of log-normal distributions, but this would make the analysis somewhat complicated if the number becomes large. He also wondered whether it was advisable to try to reconcile the subjective and objective elements of income inequality, as the paper attempts to do. He suggested that these should be kept clearly separated, since all the evidence points to the fact that a reconciliation cannot be obtained by a mixture of the two views. Individual evaluations of their own income are not important in the objective description of overall income inequality, although a politician would be unwise to ignore the fact that individuals may be subjectively dissatisfied with their own incomes, even if an assessment of the overall distribution based on social welfare functions is perfectly satisfactory.

Professor Sen felt that the view of welfare based on the comparison of marginal utilities was rather limited, since it is concerned with concepts of optimality rather than inequality. For example, Professor van Praag justifies the Pigou–Dalton criterion of inequality reduction on the basis of the individuals' desires to equalise marginal utilities. But the Pigou–Dalton condition is the most generally acceptable statement of an unambiguous reduction in inequality (a transfer from the rich to the poor) and need not rely on any special assumptions about marginal utilities. He also agreed with other speakers that it is a mistake to confuse the perception of inequality with policy issues. When people differ in their assessment of inequality, it is more likely to be on the question of how to handle inequality than the perception of inequality itself.

On the estimation side he found Professor van Praag's approach very appealing, but felt that it was worth checking how seriously people try to imagine being in other income situations. He also agreed with Professor Krelle that the assumption of equal welfare intervals was arbitrary and suggested that additional questions may give more information about the numerical gaps to be associated with the verbal welfare categories.

Professor van Praag agreed that individuals may misperceive welfare at income levels significantly different from their own, but denied that this needed rectifying. If individuals believe that their welfare would change in a particular way, it is this belief, rather than what would actually happen, which is relevant to policy recommendations which reflect individual desires. Individual desires are based on their perceptions and have to be accepted whether or not they are rational. As people move to different income levels, the preference drift will occur and the individual welfare functions will shift, correcting the non-concavity. Mr. Layard was therefore quite right in viewing the welfare function as a short-run concept. But the short-run takes precedence over any long-run considerations, as far as the policy maker, considering the evaluation of income changes, is concerned.

The overall inequality indicator, calculated as an unweighted average of individual welfare levels, should be seen as a simple statistic indicating the average feeling in society towards inequality and welfare. For other purposes some weighted average may well be preferable.

Several speakers had commented on the use of a lognormal utility function. This might be justified on the basis of a set of theoretical assumptions which generate the lognormal function. Although some of these might be regarded as strange, Professor van Praag did not know of another set of assumptions yielding any other form. Alternatively, use of the lognormal function may be justified on the grounds that it provides an adequate description of the empirical evidence derived from the survey data. Other forms had been tried, but none appeared to be a significant improvement over the lognormal.

6   ON COMPARISONS OF DISTRIBUTION PROCESSES

*MICHAEL WAGNER**

I. Process inequality: An introduction

Economic justice refers to the process of distributing social welfare. This process consists of two components, each of which is important when income inequality is considered:

- First, the *outcome* of the distribution process, i.e. a particular allotment of income among individuals.
- Secondly, the *properties* of the distribution process, i.e. the mechanism by which income is allocated among individuals.

This second component of a distribution process may conveniently be called the "*imputation mechanism*". The term refers to rules of economic interaction, determining what individuals actually receive: individuals get what the mechanism imputes to them. Thus an imputation mechanism models the "distributional side" of economic activities (it is not just a device for calculating "shadow prices")[1].

The two components of a distribution process – the imputation mechanism and the particular distribution of income – have to be discussed to some extent separately if one tries to give a full account of economic inequality.

Restriction of equity considerations to the outcome of a distribution process is bound to miss an important feature of economic justice. This may be illustrated by a simple example. Consider the notion of "discrimination" which is certainly related to economic justice: it is argued that women are discriminated against if, for example, women get lower pay than men even though they have the same productivity and engage in identical occupations. In this situation it is not only inequality due to different earnings of men and women which matters. Moreover, the way in which this inequality is generated is thought to be unjust. Discrimination not only refers to the result of the distribution process, but to some features of the process itself – the "unequal treatment between male and female employees which

---

* I am grateful to Hanns Abele and Tony Atkinson for stimulating suggestions and to Peter Mitter for his permission to use some material from our joint work on "Inequality in a Markovian Framework" and some results of his paper on "Two Stochastic Models of Income Mobility". Remaining errors and shortcomings are solely my responsibility.

[1] Our use of the term "imputation mechanism" is closer to the meaning originally attached by the Viennese School rather than to the current usage in linear programming. Within game theory the original meaning has partly been preserved; cf. Neumann and Morgenstern (1953, esp. § 4).

does not directly result in cost minimisation in monetary terms in relation to labour utilisation".[2]

The example of discrimination illustrates an important aspect of economic justice (which is the conceptual basis of inequality): *People not only care about how much they receive, but also about the way they get their share.*[3] Or, to put it in more general terms, the working properties of an imputation mechanism are themselves of normative interest when inequality is considered. This is due to the fact that there is generally no one-to-one correspondence between the structure of an imputation mechanism and the actual distribution of income. Consider once more the example of discrimination. Let us assume that the same distribution of income has emerged from two different processes. The first process exhibits discrimination against women, whereas in the second process women's productivity is lower, but they are not discriminated against by entrepreneurs. In the second case, it is differences in the acquisition of human capital rather than economic discrimination which causes income inequality.[4] From a normative point of view, people may prefer the distribution process without discrimination, although the resulting distributions of income are identical. This implies, in terms of a social welfare function, that "discrimination" reduces social welfare in addition to the losses caused by the unequal distribution of income. The existence of discrimination relates to a property of the imputation mechanism itself and is not identifiable solely from a given distribution of income. Thus, in addition to the static inequality of a given income distribution, it is necessary to evaluate the inequality inherent in the underlying imputation mechanism.

Any attempt to construct an operationally meaningful measure of process inequality has to cope with two difficulties:

– First, a decision has to be made about which models of the imputation mechanism are to be used in the analysis of process inequality.
– Secondly, it is necessary to state certain principles upon which the identification of process inequality can be based.

We can hardly expect to solve these two problems – of finding a descriptive framework and a normative standard – by discussing them in general terms. Instead it is preferable to consider the difficulties involved in these two decisions by using a particular model of the distribution process. Such a model is proposed in part II of the paper. It should, however, be made clear that the particular model proposed is quite separate from our general concern with the necessity of studying process inequality (as opposed to the static inequality of the income distribution at a particular point in time).

---

[2] Chiplin and Sloane (1976).
[3] Consider a libertarian having the chance to get the same amount of income from the market place and from a social security system. Would he be indifferent?
[4] This systematic difference in acquiring human capital indicates, however, the existence of social discrimination against women.

II. Measuring process inequality: The "chance" model

It is widely held that economic inequality is unjust as far as unequal opportunities are concerned.[5] However, it is by no means clear what an economic or social system offering equal opportunities should look like. As a starting point we may consider the income dimension of unequal opportunities. How are the opportunities to experience an increase (or a decrease) in income distributed? To answer this question we need a model of the imputation mechanism relating a set of input variables to the distribution of income changes. The simplest models of this type available are stochastic models. Stochastic models relate the chances of income change to the actual level of income. The present level of income is used as an input variable to determine the chance of success and failure. Although the income level is a very rough guide to an individual's position, it is by no means far-fetched to use the income level as a criterion to classify a population for the purpose of discussing economic inequality within the distribution process.[6]

II.1. *Stochastic processes as descriptive models*

Stochastic models have been criticised for not providing an explanation for distribution processes in terms of economic variables.[7] Although this criticism is correct, it is not an objection against the use of stochastic processes as descriptive models. We may interpret a stochastic model as a framework for organising data about distribution processes. This particular way of organising the data is of special interest, since it reveals certain implications of a distribution process: how chances of failure and success are related to income levels. It may be difficult to interpret this "income chance" relation as the "structural" form of a causal relationship. However, even if we consider the relation as a quasi "reduced" form (of an unknown "true" model of the imputation mechanism) we gain important information.[8] Since people care about chances and opportunities, we may use stochastic models as a framework to discuss desirable equity properties of an imputation mechanism. For example, certain types of "income chance" relationships may serve as points of reference in discussions concerning the design of economic institutions. An equity-minded economist may inquire about the implications of an observed set of property rights for the distribution of opportunities. One way of tackling this problem is offered by the use of stochastic models. Stochastic models organise the data of income mobility *as if* the imputation mechanism generates income distribution in patterns that observe the rules of stochastic processes. In this case *stochastic processes serve as descriptive models* of the imputation mechanism. Thus we may analyse inherent inequalities within the framework of stochastic processes.

---

[5] See the introductory chapter in Jencks et al. (1972).
[6] At least not in societies influenced by the "spirit of capitalism".
[7] Lydall (1968), is quoted frequently on this subject.
[8] Shorrocks (1975) takes a different line of defence of stochastic models; see also his comments in Atkinson, ed. (1976).

It should be stressed that such an analysis of inbuilt inequality is directly related to the general structure of the stochastic process and not to particular states (of income distribution). The stochastic process used in the following section will be a homogeneous, discrete first-order process.[9] Thus the general structure of the imputation mechanism is modelled by a transition matrix. The discussion of process inequality refers to this transition matrix rather than to any particular state, regardless of whether or not it is an equilibrium.

II.2. Notation

It may be useful to give a list of the symbols used to describe the process before discussing some of its properties.

i, j ... indices for income classes
k ... number of income classes
η ... proportionality factor for grading income
K_i ... income in class i
p_{ij} ... probability of transferring from income class i to income class j
q ... probability of descending from top class
r ... probability of ascending from bottom class
c ... ratio r/q
P ... transition matrix: $P = [p_{ij}]$, $\sum_i p_{ij} = 1$ for all i
$h(t)$ ... distribution vector at time t
$\qquad h(t) = (h_1(t), h_2(t), \ldots h_i(t), \ldots h_k(t))$
g ... vector of the equilibrium distribution
λ ... index of "static" inequality related either to $h(t)$ or g
δ ... index of process inequality related to P

II.3. Basic properties of the CHANCE-model

The CHANCE-model is a special type of stochastic process. The imputation mechanism exhibits the following properties:
(i) The distribution of income is discrete. Income is divided into classes equally spaced on a logarithmic scale.
(ii) The chance of experiencing an increase or decrease in income, or to stay at the same income level, depend only on the current level of income. These probabilities are the same for all individuals within any particular income class.
(iii) In each class there is a positive probability of both staying and moving. Within one time period the change in income is limited to a step into one of the immediately adjacent classes.

The states are defined by incomes

$$K_i = K_1 \eta^{i-1}, \quad 1 \leq i \leq k, \quad \eta > 1. \tag{1}$$

---

[9] Cf. Feller (1968).

The distribution process consists of the transformation of a given distribution at time t:

$$h(t) = (h_1(t), h_2(t), \ldots, h_i(t), \ldots, h_k(t)) \tag{2}$$

into another distribution at time $t + 1$:

$$h(t + 1) = (h_1(t + 1), h_2(t + 1), \ldots, h_i(t + 1), \ldots, h_k(t + 1)) \tag{3}$$

The imputation mechanism is modelled by the transition matrix:

$$P = [p_{ij}] \text{ with } \sum_{j=1}^{k} p_{ij} = 1 \text{ for all } i = 1, \ldots, k. \tag{4}$$

and the transformation process described by:

$$h(t + 1) = P'h(t) \tag{5}$$

Assumption (iii) ensures that P is tri-diagonal:

$$\begin{aligned} p_{ij} = 0 & \quad |i - j| > 1 \\ p_{ij} > 0 & \quad |i - j| \leq 1 \end{aligned} \tag{6}$$

Thus P is *indecomposable* and the *process is ergodic*.
This implies that there exists a distribution g,

$$g = (g_1, g_2, \ldots, g_i, \ldots, g_k) \tag{7}$$

such that

$$g = P'g. \tag{8}$$

This *equilibrium distribution* g depends only on the off-diagonal elements of P:

$$g_i = \frac{p_{12}p_{23} \cdots p_{i-1,i}}{p_{21}p_{32} \cdots p_{i,i-1}} g_1, \quad 1 < i \leq k, \tag{9}$$

where g_1 is chosen such that:

$$\sum_{i=1}^{k} g_i = 1. \tag{10}$$

It may be of interest to note that the assumption about the tri-diagonal structure of the matrix P is not an analytically necessary restriction. Instead it is a convenient technical simplification.[10] The length of the transition period has to be chosen

---

[10] This simplification is necessary to obtain the simple algebraic expression (9) for the equilibrium distribution associated with the transition matrix. The recursive formula (9) for the equilibrium distribution is easily obtained from the set of equations

$$\begin{aligned} g_1 &= p_{11}g_1 + p_{21}g_2, \\ g_2 &= p_{12}g_1 + p_{22}g_2 + p_{32}g_3, \\ &\vdots \\ g_{k-1} &= p_{k-1,k}g_{k-1} + p_{kk}g_k. \end{aligned}$$

This recursive formula is obvious for the first equation. In the second equation g_2 is replaced by the expression obtained from the first equation, and so on. The same procedure can be started from the last equation.

such that it is not too unrealistic to assume that an individual cannot move more than one income bracket within one period. Obviously the length of this time interval is related to the distances between the income classes, i.e. the choice of the grading factor η.

II.4. Dynamic Equity Principle.

Using the transition matrix as a model of the imputation mechanism, we may proceed to the next question: What principles should guide the analysis of process inequality? Such principles should reflect an egalitarian point of view (otherwise the whole attempt to evaluate process inequality will be of little normative interest). Furthermore, it must be possible to classify and order, at least partially, the alternative transition matrices according to the equity principle.[11]

Instead of attempting to define a very general equity principle, we will restrict ourselves to a particular aspect of the equity considerations related to the imputation mechanism. Moreover, these equity considerations will be discussed within a specific formulation related to our previous choice of the CHANCE-model as a model of the imputation mechanism.

Dynamic Equity Principle:

(1) The chance of an increase in income should be negatively correlated with current income.
(2) The chance of a decrease in income should be positively correlated with current income.

Though it may be hard to find a general ethical postulate from which this particular principle could be derived, there are several intuitive ideas about economic justice which are expressed in this principle. First of all, the Dynamic Equity Principle requires a kind of "regression towards the mean" built into the imputation mechanism. This reflects an egalitarian point of view. Another equity argument raised in support of this principle goes as follows: those who are already well off are less deserving of an increase in income than those who are in a worse income position.[12] This point of view brings out the "dynamic" aspect of this principle: that the change of income should be related to the current level of income.[13]

---

[11] The problem of gaining sufficient discriminatory power using relatively weak normative assumptions has attracted interest in the literature on the welfare theoretic background to inequality indices; cf. Atkinson (1970), Dasgupta et al. (1973).

[12] It is interesting to note, that the Dynamic Equity Principle may be related to an implicit postulate of efficiency. Such a postulate would be built upon the following concept: Economic activities are carried out in hierarchical social framework. This hierarchy determines two factors simultaneously: First, the extent to which a decision taken by a person affects the total population (the influence increases from the bottom to the top). Secondly, the income received by a person at a specified level of the hierarchy. The "efficiency" version of the Dynamic Equity Principle asks the following. Those at the top have to make stronger efforts not to fall from their position than those at a lower level in the hierarchy. This is justifiable on efficiency grounds because the relative social impact of decisions taken by a person increases monotonically towards the top.

[13] The Dynamic Equity Principle requires a kind of intertemporal compensation by relating income

The difficulty in finding a coherent normative basis for the Dynamic Equity Principle is partly due to the "reduced form" in which it is expressed. This notion of a (normative) reduced form parallels the econometric concept of a (descriptive) reduced form in which income data are organised by stochastic models. Although a reduced form expresses a relation which is thought to be valid, it is difficult to justify the relation directly with reference either to causality (descriptive model) or to economic justice (normative standard).[14]

II.5. *Reflecting Barriers*

To illustrate some applications of the Dynamic Equity Principle, consider the so called "vicious circle of poverty". The existence of such a vicious circle indicates that the underlying imputation mechanism makes it very difficult for the poor to rise above the poverty line. Under such circumstances there exists a kind of *reflecting barrier* which inhibits upward income mobility for the lower income classes. This obviously violates part (1) of the dynamic equity principle. Another example is provided by bureaucratic systems in which failure is unlikely once you are established at the top. In this case, there are quasi-reflecting barriers with respect to downward mobility.

The concept of quasi-reflecting barriers[15] (i.e. very small non-zero off-diagonal elements in the transition matrix P) fits well into our intuitive notion of process inequality within the dynamics of income distribution. The existence of reflecting barriers is a special case of a violation of the monotonicity property of the Dynamic Equity Principle. We may classify transition matrices according to whether the off-diagonal non-zero elements are monotonic functions of the income level. If the imputation mechanism does not exhibit the monotonicity property, the dynamic equity principle is violated. Whilst it is of interest for empirical research on income inequality[16] to study the existence of reflecting barriers, we have to restrict our theoretical analysis to imputation mechanisms observing the monotonicity property. By this restriction we will gain further analytical results without excluding the imputation mechanisms which underly the standard stochastic models, i.e. the "proportionate effect models".

II.6. *MONOTONE-model*

Consider the class of CHANCE-models exhibiting the monotonicity property: The non-zero off-diagonal elements of the transition matrix P are a monotonic

---

mobility to the current level of income. A notion of compensation is also found in Sen's Weak Equity Axiom; cf. Sen (1973).

[14] The justification of normative standards is a difficult task not only with respect to process inequality. In the field of measuring static inequality similar questions have been raised, e.g. whether from a normative point of view "mean independence" is a desirable property of an inequality measure; cf. Sen (1973), Kolm (1976).

[15] The term "reflecting barrier" is borrowed from the theory of stochastic processes; cf. Feller (1968).

[16] Empirical research does not have to make rather general analyses of imputation mechanisms. Special cases attract interest even though no systematic comparison with other imputation mechanisms can be carried out.

function of the income level. Let us call imputation mechanisms of this type MONOTONE. A simple example of a MONOTONE model is provided by the following transition matrix P.

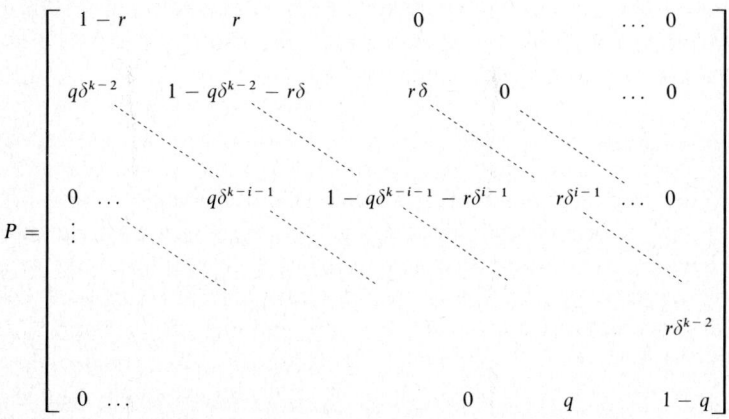

P is characterised by four parameters:

q ... downward mobility in the highest income class
r ... upward mobility in the lowest income class
δ ... the factor by which upward mobility is increased and downward mobility decreased.
k ... number of income classes

These parameters have to observe the following restrictions

$$0 < r\delta^{i-1} < 1, \quad 0 < q\delta^{k-i-1} < 1 \quad \text{where } 1 \leq i \leq k - 1 < \infty$$
$$0 < 1 - r\delta^{i-1} - q\delta^{k-i-1} < 1 \quad \text{where } 2 \leq i \leq k - 1 < \infty \tag{11}$$

The four parameters characterising P can be employed to compare different imputation mechanisms of the MONOTONE type. First we may classify MONOTONE models with respect to the dynamic equity postulate. This can be done by referring to parameter δ. There are three cases:

$\delta > 1$ "amplifier of dynamic inequality" (AMPL)

$\delta = 1$ "proportionate effect" (PROPOR)

$\delta < 1$ "regression towards the mean" (REGRESS)

The AMPL case obviously exhibits a tendency to increase income inequality: The richer you are the less chance there is of failure and greater are the chances of success. The poorer you are, the higher are the chances of failure and lower the chances of experiencing an increase in income.

The PROPOR case is frequently discussed in the literature on stochastic models of income distribution. Those models are built on the assumption that the "law of proportionate effect" holds.[17] This implies that the transition probabilities depend only on the relative size of the change of income. This implies, within the framework of the CHANCE-model, identical non-zero off-diagonal elements of the transition matrix P. Looking at the "proportionate effect" assumption not as a "law", but rather from a normative point of view, we observe that it violates the Dynamic Equity Postulate. Thus we may conclude that the "proportionate effect" is an undesirable property of an imputation mechanism.

Only the "regression towards the mean" (REGRESS) case is compatible with the Dynamic Equity Postulate. Within this class of REGRESS imputation mechanisms the analysis can be carried one step further.

II.7. δ-inequality in REGRESS-models

The class of REGRESS-models is characterised by the range of the four parameters p, q, δ and k:

$$0 < r, q < 1,$$
$$0 < \delta < 1, \quad (12)$$
$$0 < 1 - r\delta^{i-1} - q\delta^{k-i-1} < 1, \quad 2 \leq i \leq k - 1 < \infty.$$

For any given p and q the parameter δ represents the strength of the equalising forces built into the imputation mechanism. The larger δ is, the weaker are the regression towards the mean tendencies. Thus we may use the parameter δ as a measure of process inequality.[18]

The parameter δ has some advantages and some drawbacks. The major advantage of δ is to be found in the possibility of ordering REGRESS-models. The use of a scalar as a dynamic inequality index offers a simple way of ordering. Such an ordering is independent of the levels of q and r, provided the parameter δ is interpreted as the "relative strength" of the regression towards the mean tendency. The value of δ measures the REGRESS property relative to the level of q and r. A slight disadvantage in using δ as an inequality measure arises from the restrictions imposed on it. These restrictions are necessary to preserve the "stochastic" properties of the matrix P. This implies that δ has to be chosen from a set which observes for given q, r and k the restrictions of (12). However, these restrictions do not substantially limit the applicability of the measure δ for two reasons: first, whenever the CHANCE-model is estimated from empirical data, restriction (12) is observed automatically. Secondly, in constructing examples, formulae (12) can always be satisfied *a priori*. There is only one case in which the restriction (12) substantially limits the analysis. This is AMPL-models with $\delta > 1$. However,

---

[17] Cf. Steindl (1965). This principle has played an important part in the derivation of Pareto's Law; see also Champernowne (1973).

[18] It maybe worth while noting that δ is not a measure of the speed of convergence to an equilibrium distribution. Such a measure, e.g. the second largest eigenvalue of the transition matrix, has to be sensitive to the number of income classes. Thus, a measure of convergence does not qualify as a measure of dynamic inequality.

this class of models is not of special interest in the context of income distribution since such a system is only stable when income is concentrated mainly in the top and bottom classes.

From these comments on various CHANCE-models of the imputation mechanism, on the dynamic equity principle and the measure derived from it, we may proceed to the third problem to be discussed: does "process inequality" contain normatively relevant information about income inequality? Or is process inequality fully reflected in the outcome of the distribution process, i.e. in the static inequality exhibited by the distribution of income? These two questions amount to asking whether there exists a monotonic function between the measures of process inequality and static inequality measures related to the distribution of income. The next section will show that there does not generally exist such a function within the framework of REGRESS-models. The two types of inequality measures are in some sense independent of each other.

II.8. *Independence properties of the δ-measure*

An advantage of using stochastic models of the imputation mechanism is the ability to distinguish "short-run" effects from "long-run" effects of process inequality. Within the framework of the CHANCE-model we may call the change in a given distribution of income from one period to the next, the short-run effect of the imputation mechanism P. This change in static inequality may be indicated by some inequality index λ_t.

$$\lambda_t = \lambda(f(t)) \tag{13}$$

where $f(t)$ is the discrete distribution of income at time t. Thus the short-run effect of P on λ is:

$$\begin{aligned}\Delta\lambda_t &= \lambda_t - \lambda_{t+1} \\ &= \lambda(f(t)) - \lambda(f(t+1)) \\ &= \lambda(f(t)) - \lambda(P'f(t))\end{aligned} \tag{14}$$

The *short-run effect of process inequality* is the change in a static inequality index defined on the distribution of income.

The *long-run effect of process inequality* is related to the question of how the distribution of income will look when the imputation mechanism is applied repeatedly to the same population. To this we can give a straightforward answer, since all CHANCE processes are ergodic and have invariant distributions. Thus the long run effect of process inequality can be represented by an inequality index for the equilibrium distribution g:

$$\lambda(g) = \lambda(g(P)) \tag{15}$$

With help of the two concepts – short- and long-run effects – the independence problem can be divided into three questions:

(i) Does the existence of regression towards the mean, i.e. $\delta < 1$, imply a short-run reduction of static inequality?
(ii) Does short-run reduction of static inequality imply that the underlying PMIL-model satisfies the dynamic equity axiom?
(iii) Does lower process inequality, as measured by δ, imply lower static inequality for the corresponding equilibrium distribution?

If the process inequality index is expected to provide information additional to static inequality indices (related to the distribution of income), questions (i)–(iii) have to be answered in the negative. This is indeed the case.

II.8.1. Short-run independence I

Consider a distribution $f(t)$, where

$$f(t) = (0, 0 \ldots, f_i(t), \ldots, 0) \tag{16}$$

All people have the same income at time t. The tri-diagonal P operates such that:

$$f(t+1) = (0, \ldots 0, f_{i-1}(t+1), f_i(t+1), f_{i+1}(t+1), 0 \ldots, 0) \tag{17}$$

where

$$f_{i-1}(t+1), f_i(t+1), f_{i+1}(t+1) > 0$$

This implies

$$\lambda(f(t)) < \lambda(f(t+1)) \tag{18}$$

Thus there is a short-run increase of static inequality, although P exhibits the REGRESS property.

This example not only proves an independence property for the measure δ. It indicates another important feature of process inequality:

Process inequality exists whenever $\delta > 0; 1 > p, q > 0$.

The inequality parameter δ reflects only the relative degree of inequality. Thus it is not counter-intuitive that even a process with comparatively low inherent inequality may transform a situation of equal personal incomes into one for which the index of inequality is larger.

II.8.2. Short-run independence II

Consider the following REGRESS-model in which P is characterised by the properties:

(i) k is an odd number
(ii) $r = q = 0.5$
(iii) $\delta > 0$ \hfill (19)

(iv) $P_{m,m-1} < q\delta^{k-m-1}$

$P_{m,m+1} < r\delta^{m-1}$ when $m = \dfrac{k+1}{2}$

Condition (iv) implies the existence of quasi-reflecting barriers in income class K_m. However, this does not necessarily imply a short run increase in static inequality. Consider the following example. Let any P satisfying (19) operate on a distribution $f(t)$:

$$f(t) = (f_1(t), f_2(t), \ldots f_i(t), \ldots f_k(t)) \qquad (20)$$

where

$$f_1(t) = f_2(t) = \ldots = f_i(t) = \ldots = f_k(t) \qquad (21)$$

When P operates on $f(t)$, then

$$\lambda(f(t)) > \lambda(f(t+1)) \qquad (22)$$

Thus there is a reduction in short run inequality even though the matrix P does not observe the Dynamic Equity Principle.

II.8.3. Long-run independence

Consider the following class of PMIL-models of the imputation mechanism. Income is graded into five classes, starting with $K_1 = 2000$ and a grading factor $\eta = 0.58$. Furthermore $c = r/q = 3.0$. This implies that the probability of ascending from the lowest income class K_1 is three times larger than the chance of falling from the highest income class K_5. What happens to the value of the inequality index for the equilibrium distributions, when the process inequality index varies monotonically?

Index of process inequality δ	Gini-coefficient of the equilibrium distribution corresponding to δ
0.1	0.098
0.3	0.149
0.5	0.189
0.7	0.189
0.9	0.150
1.0	0.128

The discussion of the three questions (i), (ii), and (iii) has proved that the measure δ is essentially independent of traditional measures like the Gini coefficient. This holds for both the short and long run.[19] The measure of process inequality δ

---

[19] The "independence property" refers to a negative result: There does not generally exist a monotonic function relating static inequality indices to the measure of process inequality. However, such

contains information that is not reflected in inequality indices for the current (or equilibrium) distribution of income. However, two questions may arise:

- Do MONOTONE-models resemble any process compatible with empirically observed data?
- Granted that the δ-measure contains information not contained in static measures, is this additional information relevant to a normative evaluation of economic inequality?

The following two sections will be devoted to these problems.

II.9. *England vs Shorrocks' Land*

In a recent paper Shorrocks (1976) presents data on income mobility of English male employees during the period 1963–1969. Income is graded into five classes, but no assumption is made about tri-diagonality. The matrix M is based on direct observations of individual income mobility.

$$M = \begin{bmatrix} 0.64 & 0.29 & 0.04 & 0.03 & 0.00 \\ 0.14 & 0.56 & 0.26 & 0.03 & 0.01 \\ 0.02 & 0.22 & 0.54 & 0.21 & 0.01 \\ 0.01 & 0.04 & 0.27 & 0.54 & 0.14 \\ 0.00 & 0.01 & 0.05 & 0.27 & 0.67 \end{bmatrix}. \qquad (23)$$

The entries of this matrix M reflect the chance of moving from one income class to another within a time period of three years. Assuming that the matrix M represents the results of a Markov process based on year-to-year changes, we may ask the following two questions: What does the equilibrium distribution corresponding to a process characterised by M look like? Secondly, does a process of the MONOTONE type exist which leads to approximately the same equilibrium distribution as the process M?

To answer these questions consider first the equilibrium distribution corresponding to M:

$$g = (0.12, 0.25, 0.29, 0.30, 0.11). \qquad (24)$$

There is an easy way to check whether the equilibrium distribution of (24) can be generated by a MONOTONE process.[20] Consider a MONOTONE-model with

$$c = r/q = 1. \qquad (25)$$

functions do exist in special cases. One example is MONOTONE-models with $c = p/q = 1$ and $0 < \delta < 1$. The equilibrium distributions of such models are symmetrical over the income classes. As δ decreases the equilibrium distribution loses weight symmetrically in its tails. Thus the new equilibrium distribution Lorenz dominates the old one; cf. Rothschild and Stiglitz (1973), Mitter and Wagner (1977).

[20] See Mitter (1977).

For such processes the following holds true:

$$\frac{g_{i+1}}{g_i} = c\delta^{2i-k}. \tag{26}$$

From this we obtain

$$\delta^2 = \frac{g_{i-1} \cdot g_i}{g_{i+1}^2} \tag{27}$$

Making use of (27) we may calculate from the equilibrium distribution (24) three values of δ. Each of these three values is close enough to 0.8 such that we may draw the following conclusion: A MONOTONE-model characterised by

$$\begin{aligned} c &= r/q = 1 \\ \delta &= 0.8 \end{aligned} \tag{28}$$

provides a reasonable explanation for the equilibrium distribution (24) of the process characterised by M, which is based on empirical observations. This is confirmed by the equilibrium distribution (29) corresponding to the MONOTONE-model defined by (28):

$$g = (0.12, 0.23, 0.29, 0.23, 0.12) \tag{29}$$

While Shorrocks infers from his data that the assumption of proportionate effect cannot be rejected, it is fair to argue that quite a different state of affairs is conceivable. Let us turn from England (through Shorrocks' glasses) to Shorrocks' Land (through MONOTONE-glasses): In Shorrocks' Land the poor had enough political power to bargain for a set of property rights which ensure that the imputation mechanism observes the Dynamic Equity Principle.[21] Agreement was reached that the poor in the lowest class should stand the same chance of moving up as the rich in the top class have of moving down thus $c = r/q = 1$. Then the δ-Inequality factor was fixed at $\delta = 0.8$. This was thought to be a victory for the Dynamic Equity Faction in the constitutional committee of Shorrocks' Land. When some critics confronted this faction with the fact that the equilibrium distribution for Shorrocks' Land was nearly the same as in England, the Dynamic Equity Faction took the following view: although in the long run, little is to be gained in static inequality over England, the resulting equilibrium distribution is achieved in Shorrocks' Land by a process to be preferred-one observing the Dynamic Equity Principle (whereas in England this principle is violated).

---

[21] An imputation mechanism is always related to a set of property rights which provides the framework for a penalty-reward structure (Furubotn and Pejovich, 1972). This penalty-reward structure of economic interaction may exhibit considerable asymmetry, favouring some social groups and discriminating against others. Such asymmetry corresponds to the inbuilt inequality of imputation mechanisms. Thus from the point of view of the "contractual theories of distribution" we may consider the degree of process inequality as being part of the contractual agreement reached in a pre-constitutional stage; cf. Buchanan and Bush (1974).

II.10. Normative interrelations

Is the argument of the Dynamic Equity Faction reasonable? Does it not draw too strict a line of demarcation between the "rules of the game" and the resulting outcomes? Though such a distinction is useful for analytical purposes, it can be rather misleading when used in a normative evaluation of alternative distribution processes. One should not infer from the necessity to distinguish in descriptive models between the current distribution of income and the underlying imputation mechanism, that from a normative point of view these two components of the distribution process are to be evaluated separately. Such a separate evaluation could not be done unambiguously, since people frequently let their normative evaluation of a given distribution of income depend on the way it was achieved. People are more willing to accept a given level of static inequality once they have been convinced that it is the outcome of a "fair game" (whatever their criteria of "justice" of "fairness" may be).[22] On the other hand, an imputation mechanism that is thought to be "fair" in principle may drop substantially in normative evaluation when, from a normative point of view, disastrous distributions of income emerge. Even among those who believe that a competitive market imputes "just" rewards to those engaged in economic activities, some may find a pure market imputation system unbearable if it leads to large scale poverty. Thus the losses of welfare implied by static and process inequality are interdependent.

To this interdependence Sen (1973) has referred indirectly when writing: "The relation between inequality and rebellion is indeed a close one, and it runs both ways. That a perceived sense of inequity is a common ingredient of rebellion in societies is clear enough, but it is also important to recognise that the perception of inequity, and indeed the content of that elusive concept, depend substantially on possibilities of actual rebellion." Obviously rebellions and, even more, revolutions try to change the imputation mechanism. Partly because they try to change the distribution of income, partly because they detest the working properties of the old imputation mechanism itself, as was the case in the Russian and Chinese revolutions. This illustrates once more the conclusion to be drawn from the above considerations: *Process and static inequality are normatively interrelated but there is no one-to-one correspondence.* Thus welfare economics should consider process inequality in an adequate analytical framework to gain a fuller understanding of income inequality. Restriction to just the distribution of income will do not.

II.11. The descriptive framework reconsidered

The construction of an analytical framework for studying process inequality is not only impeded by the difficulties of finding an adequate normative standard. Already the choice of the descriptive framework is a more complicated task in the case of process inequality than in the field of static inequality. (There is general

---

[22] For a sample of alternative principles, see Sen (1973).

agreement about using distribution functions as a descriptive framework for measuring static inequality.) Already the choice of the descriptive framework, i.e. a model of the imputation mechanism, is crucial since not all models reveal inbuilt inequality to the same extent. Some models of the imputation mechanism start from assumptions which *a priori* exclude process inequality. Consider as an extreme example a model of a competitive tatonnement process for a pure exchange economy. Such a tatonnement process is always "distributionally neutral". As commodities are exchanged at equilibrium prices, no trader can lose or gain in terms of money income. Even less extreme models, applied in empirical research in the field of income distribution, make assumptions which partly beg the question. For example, in the basic human capital model [23] it is assumed that lifetime income is equalised for the entire population. One does not have to be a radical economist to question this assumption, which makes it rather difficult to find any process inequality in the earnings function. Thus the choice of the descriptive framework already depends on the economist's sensitivity towards process inequality.

This sensitivity towards process inequality is clearly reflected in our choice of the CHANCE-model as a descriptive framework for discussing inherent inequality. However, the CHANCE-model is subject to two substantial limitations. First, it is a reduced form model; and secondly, it only considers the income dimension of social welfare. These shortcomings are partly balanced by the favourable features of the CHANCE-model. Its analytical framework offers the opportunity:

- to systematically organise empirical data on distribution processes;
- to make a clear descriptive distinction between the imputation mechanism and a particular distribution of income;
- to consider changes of the imputation mechanism over time;
- to identify process inequality;
- to analyse the relation between static and process inequality.

With respect to this last item, – the relation between process and static inequality – the paper has by no means made use of all analytical possibilities offered by the CHANCE-model.[24] One aspect of the CHANCE-model in particular needs further consideration: our analysis has proceeded on the assumption of an "eternal population". This is a useful device to bring out some characteristics of the imputation mechanism. In reality, however, we observe an influx and outflow of income units to and from the imputation mechanism. The structure of such a "birth-and-death" process is another important dimension of income inequality.[25] It indicates how unequally distributed starting positions are. An advantage of the CHANCE-model is that it provides an explicit link between the influx of income units into the economic system, the dynamics of the imputation mechanism, and the observed distribution of income.

---

[23] See Mincer (1976).
[24] Stochastic models, e.g. mover-stayer models, can be used to identify discrimination; cf. McCall (1971).
[25] The structure of a "birth and death" process can be used to control the distribution of income; cf. Bartholomew (1973).

III. Conclusions

(1) There are two components to be distinguished in the analysis of distribution processes: the current distribution of income and the imputation mechanism. A comparison of distributional states is usually restricted to the output of a distribution process, i.e. to the distribution of income. This limitation seems to be unsatisfactory once it is recognised that people not only care about how much they get, but about the way they get their share. Thus the imputation mechanism has to be included in the comparison of distribution processes, regardless of whether the comparison is carried out for descriptive or normative purposes.

(2) The construction of an analytical framework for comparisons of imputation mechanisms regarding "process inequality" has to face two difficulties: the choice of a descriptive framework, i.e. a model of the imputation mechanism, and the formulation of a normative standard upon which an operational measure of process inequality may be justified. Different models of the imputation mechanism imply different measures of process inequality. Thus such measures can only be used when comparisons are restricted to the same model of the imputation mechanism.

(3) As a descriptive framework we have chosen a model of the imputation mechanism which refers to the concept of "unequal opportunities". The CHANCE-model relates the opportunities of experiencing an increase (or decrease) in income to the present level of income. The CHANCE-model organises data on income mobility as if the imputation mechanism generates income distributions observing the rules of some particular stochastic process.

(4) As a normative standard for our analysis we have formulated a Dynamic Equity Principle: the chance of experiencing an increase in income should be negatively correlated with the level of income; whereas the chance of experiencing a decrease in income should be positively correlated with the level of income.

(5) Within the framework of CHANCE-models the Dynamic Equity Principle is applicable to two types of analysis. First, we may check whether an imputation mechanism observes the Dynamic Equity Principle. Secondly, we may try to evaluate the degree of inbuilt inequality. Reflecting barriers' are an example of the first type of analysis, whereas the measure δ can be used for a comparative evaluation of imputation mechanisms of the MONOTONE type.

(6) The Measure of process inequality δ contains normatively relevant information *sui generis* which cannot be obtained by considering only the static inequality exhibited by the current (or equilibrium) distribution of income. There does not generally exist a monotonic function relating static inequality indices to the measure of process inequality. This holds for both the short and long run. Whilst there does not exist a one-to-one correspondence between process and static inequality, it is necessary from a normative point of view to evaluate both types of inequality simultaneously.

References

Atkinson, A.B., "On the Measurement of Inequality", *Journal of Economic Theory*, 1970.
Atkinson, A.B., ed., *The Personal Distribution of Incomes*, London; Allen & Unwin, 1976.
Bartholomew, D.J., *Stochastic Models for Social Processes*, London; Wiley, 1973.
Buchanan, J.M. and W.C. Bush, "Political Constraints on Contractual Redistribution", *American Economic Review, Papers & Proc.*, 1974.
Champernowne, D.G., *The Distribution of Income between Persons*, Cambridge: University Press, 1973.
Chiplin, B. and P.J. Sloane, "Personal Characteristics and Sex Differentials in Professional Employment", *Economic Journal*, 1976.
Dasgupta, D., A. Sen and D. Starrett, "Notes on the Measurement of Inequality", *Journal of Economic Theory*, 1973.
Feller, W., *An Introduction to Probability Theory and its Application*, Vol. I, New York, Wiley, 1968.
Furubotn, E.G. and S. Pejovich, "Property Rights and Economic Theory: A Survey of Recent Literature", *Journal of Economic Literature*, 1972.
Jencks, C. et al., *Inequality*, Harmondsworth; Penguin, 1972.
Kolm, S.C., "Unequal Inequalities", *Journal of Economic Theory*, 1976.
Lydall, W., *The Structure of Earnings*, Oxford: Clarendon, 1968.
McCall, J.J., "A Markovian Model of Income Dynamics", *Journal of the American Statistical Association*, 1971.
Mincer, J., "Progress in Human Capital Analyses of the Distribution of Earnings", in: A.B. Atkinson, ed. (1976).
Mitter, P., "Two Stochastic Models of Income Mobility", Discussion Paper 3/77, Economics Department, Institute for Advanced Studies, Vienna, 1977.
Mitter, P. and M. Wagner, "Inequality in a Markovian Framework", Discussion Paper 1/77, Economics Department, Institute for Advanced Studies, Vienna, 1977.
Neumann, J. and O. Morgenstern, *Theory of Games and Economic Behaviour*, Princeton: University Press, 1953.
Rothschild, M. and J.A. Stiglitz, "Some Further Results on the Measurement of Inequality", *Journal of Economic Theory*, 1973.
Sen, A., *On Economic Inequality*, Oxford: Clarendon, 1973.
Shorrocks, A.F., "Income Mobility and the Markov Assumption", *Economic Journal*, 1976.
Shorrocks, A.F., "On Stochastic Models of Size Distributions", *Review of Economic Studies*, 1975.
Steindl, J., *Random Processes and the Growth of Firms*, London; Griffin, 1965.

6 DISCUSSION

PAPER BY MICHAEL WAGNER

Mr. Bartels said that the basic idea of the paper was that we should take into account the process that generates personal incomes when comparing different income distributions. He did not find this particularly attractive. Frequently we are only interested in a descriptive comparison of different distributions and therefore look to an inequality measure defined on individual incomes which indicates explicitly the weights attached to different individuals. Several statistical indicators meet this requirement. More indirect measures of inequality, using individual welfare functions for income or the process generating personal incomes, only served to make the inequality indicator more arbitrary and difficult to interpret. The arbitrariness results from the difficulty of choosing a satisfactory explanatory model from the many alternatives which are available. Interpretation difficulties arise from the indirect definition, as opposed to a direct, explicit statement of the weights used in the inequality measure. He therefore recommended concentrating attention on two separate topics; the comparison of distributions using summary indicators and the explanation of distributions by means of theories with a high empirical power.

He pointed out that the paper deals only with a stochastic approach using a Markov chain model. Other approaches may also have been incorporated, studies like those of Gibrat and Roy, which exploit the distribution and interaction of several independent variables, and perhaps also the maximum entropy approach used by Mogridge. It is not clear why the simple Markovian model has been chosen in preference to these alternatives. Nor did he understand why substantially different approaches, for example the Human Capital model, had not been considered.

The stochastic model is used as a framework to organise data. It is justified by the argument that we can consider the income generating process *as if* it followed a Markov chain. However Mr. Bartels regarded this procedure as rather dangerous in the present context. If implications about equitable income distributions are to be stated, explicit attention should be given to the independent variables that generate income differences. Equity criteria can then be stated in terms of justifiable compensatory differences, which cannot be done in the crude Markov approach. He questioned whether the Dynamic Equity principle, chosen to reflect "intuitive conceptions of economic justice", really achieved its aim. He preferred to call it a "dynamic equality principle".

Mr. Bartels also questioned whether the restrictions placed on the matrices in the examples given were necessary. Use of the tri-diagonal form seems to exclude several groups of income recipients; for example, independent workers, people who start working immediately after receiving a grant for study and people who retire. All these types of individuals may transfer to non-adjacent categories in the income distribution. He asked whether summary indicators of process inequality could be defined for more complicated matrices. Furthermore, he found the hypothetical example used to show that a value of δ smaller than 1 may not imply a reduction in static inequality, rather unrealistic.

Finally he took up Dr. Wagner's suggestion that the Markov model might be regarded as some kind of reduced form of a more complicated model. If this is the case, he was interested in knowing what kind of structural models might generate these reduced forms.

Professor van Meerhaeghe thought that the paper exhibited imagination but doubted whether the concepts had any operational content. He would have liked to see criticism of conventional inequality analysis involving statements like "x per cent of the population have y per cent of income".

Professor Sen said that one way in which the paper departed from traditional approaches was the concern with groups of named individuals rather than groups of income categories. This was the reason why patterns of static inequality cannot be established from the Dynamic Equity principle. There was indeed much to be said for considering named individuals and he gave as an example a society with identical income distributions at two points of time, but where all the rich people had become poor and vice versa. Static inequality remains the same but there has been a radical change in terms of movements. Dynamic Equity seemed a good choice of name to him, capturing both inequality at a point of time and some notion of mobility.

For empirical application, he suggested relating the approach involving transition probabilities to the kind of questions considered in the paper by Professor Taubman. For example, to what extent education differentiates the earning power of individuals from that corresponding to their family background.

Finally he was sympathetic to the general concern with imputation mechanisms mentioned in the first part of the paper. The view that we should look both at the *consequences* on the welfare side as well as the *causes* of inequality in judging a distribution seemed to him to be right.

Professor Adelman referred to similar research on which she was working with Professor Whittle at Cambridge. They had evolved a measure which combines both static and dynamic inequality and applied this to transition matrices for intra and inter-generational transfers. Their transition matrices for the United States and Great Britain differed substantially from the tri-diagonal form used in the paper. She was very much in favour of taking the dynamic aspects into account and felt that the perception of static inequality would depend to a large extent on the degree of mobility over time.

Professor Chiswick rather liked the notion that the process generating the distribution of income is an important dimension of income inequality measures. Although several of the conference participants from the Netherlands had indicated that equality of incomes is an important social objective in their country, she recalled a survey of blue-collar workers in the United States which clearly indicated a desire for equality of opportunity rather than equal incomes *per se*. It is at least plausible that an American policy-maker concerned with reducing welfare inequality might prefer an income distribution with somewhat greater inequality if this were accompanied by more mobility between income classes.

Professor Pen asked whether the present approach could explain changes in inequality over time, such as the sharp decrease in inequality in the Netherlands over the last few decades as measured by the Theil coefficient, for example.

Professor Somermeyer disliked the imputation mechanism based on random influences. Whilst not denying the importance of stochastic or accidental factors (in income distribution), he believed that they apply mainly to entrepreneurs, who are a rapidly vanishing group in the western world: therefore, the stochastic element in income distributions tends to decrease. He would have preferred a synthesis of deterministic and stochastic approaches either by relating the transition probabilities to supply and demand, or by superimposing a stochastic process on a deterministic model.

Dr. Shorrocks said that criticisms that the paper concentrated on random or chance factors were completely misplaced. The Markov chain approach adopted in the paper was usually called "stochastic" and interpreted in terms of probabilities of movements between various income classes. But there was an alternative deterministic interpretation, where the elements of the transition matrix are regarded as the proportions of individuals moving from one class to another. In fact the matrix elements are normally computed from observations of such transition *proportions*.

The Dynamic Equity principle in the paper corresponds to "regression towards the mean": that expected income growth declines with income. However if the process is non-Markovian, so previous history has to be taken into account, the simple relationship between Dynamic Equity and regression towards the mean vanishes. Suppose, for example, one individual (usually rich) is temporarily poor and one normally poor person is temporarily well off. If there is regression towards the mean during the next period, the normally rich person will experience an increase in income. In these circumstances it is doubtful whether we would say that this last change has increased equity. Exactly how the Dynamic Equity principle might be extended to cover non-Markovian processes is open to question.

The process could satisfy the Markov assumption if sufficiently long time periods are chosen. This reduces the importance of transitory income, which is one major reason why the Markov assumption may be violated. However increasing the time period means that it is more likely that transitions between non-adjacent categories will occur, so the tri-diagonal form considered in the paper becomes less realistic.

Finally he pointed out that the extreme groups are frequently aggregated to get reasonable sample sizes. This tends to inflate the proportion of those remaining in the lowest (and highest) class. The paper suggests that this may be taken as evidence of a poverty trap, but this interpretation may be quite inappropriate when classes have been grouped together.

Professor van Praag thought that stochastic models provided good descriptions of the genesis of income distributions. He pointed out that the crucial parameter δ is restricted by the fact that the rows of the matrix sum to one, so the upper bound on δ depends on the number of classes actually distinguished, and falls towards one as the number of classes tends to infinity. He also felt it would be interesting to study the relationship between the value of δ and static inequality corresponding to the stationary state distribution, for example. The parameter δ might also be linked with the entropy measure defined for a Markov chain process.

Dr. Mustert believed that severe problems arise from having only a finite number of states and recommended that the model should be modified to allow for an infinite number of states.

Professor Stiglitz approved of using matrices to examine inequality and felt that some of the statistical literature on ranking transition matrices might be relevant. However a different normalisation may be necessary, since, in the example given in the paper, the mean of the distribution changes as δ is varied. He also believed that the potential applications would be rather limited unless it was based on a structural model with the economic considerations clearly specified.

Dr. Kuipers agreed with the distinction between equity of income and equity of the distributional process but wondered whether Markov models provided the most appropriate framework. Sociological studies of actual distribution processes might be more useful.

Secondly, the equity principles described by the author refer primarily to the outcome of the distributional process, which means they are actually defined in terms of the static income distribution.

Finally, he would define process equality to be the situation in which everybody has the same chance of receiving a higher or lower income (in terms of the model, $\delta = 1$).

Professor Krelle thought the contribution of the paper was to describe the development of income distribution and to hint at some explanation. The process was summarised by the parameter δ and it is therefore necessary to indicate how this parameter is determined. He suggested distinguishing between property and labour income, with random rates of return, as a possible way of identifying the economic influences on δ. These influences are not the same for both kinds of income.

Dr. Wagner had the impression that some discussants thought that process inequality does matter. However, he was willing to accept that others, like Professor van Meerhaeghe and Mr. Bartels, do not care about inequality built into the imputation mechanism. He did not take this to imply that the search for an analytical framework applicable to the study of process inequality is useless.

On the use of a "reduced form model" as a descriptive framework, he stressed that the CHANCE-model was just a starting point. He agreed with Professors Krelle and Stiglitz that an additional model determining the structure of the transition matrix would prove useful. However, some of the discussants seemed to have underestimated the analytical possibilities offered by a reduced form model. The first order Markov process does not describe a gambling mechanism. Nor is the past history of an individual necessarily neglected – it depends on the definition of the state space whether past levels of income are taken into account.

As to Mr. Bartels' remark that stochastic models are not suitable for organising data, he pointed out that these models were introduced into economics specifically for the purpose of modelling "unexplained" regularities in data, such as Pareto's law.

He then turned to the structure of the transition matrix. He agreed that choosing a long time period for the transitions would lead to a violation of the tri-diagonality assumption. Furthermore, as Dr. Mustert had observed, the restriction to a finite number of income classes may lead to a bias in the empirical estimation of the coefficients for the top income class. However, these restrictions were chosen deliberately so that a simple mathematical framework would suffice to carry out the analysis. A general approach to the measurement of dynamic inequality using Markov processes requires neither tri-diagonality nor a finite number of income classes.

As Professor van Praag had observed, one of the advantages of the model is the opportunity offered to analyse the relationship between "static" and "dynamic" inequality. One of the major results of the paper had been to show that there does not exist a one-to-one relationship between δ and the standard measures of inequality. This can be proved even though mean income changes when δ varies, as Professor Stiglitz had pointed out.

Finally Dr. Wagner mentioned possible further extensions of his analysis, in particular the formulation of a structural model determining δ, the inclusion of birth-and-death processes and the use of the concept of reflecting barriers in empirical studies.

PART III

DATA ON INCOME DISTRIBUTION

7 OUR SHAKY DATA BASE

PETER WILES[1]

I. Introduction

This contribution is the purest vulgar factology. It shows:

(1) How to "percapitalise" a per-household income distribution (section II);
(2) That North American incomes are much unequally distributed than West European, contrary to much accepted doctrine (section III);
(3) The fatal consequences of section III for the notion that high development goes with equality (section IV);
(4) The extreme importance of the new household problem (section V);
(5) The technique of certain simple ratios, which could perhaps after development be used to check bad distribution data against good ones (section VI);
(6) Some recommendations as to data reporting, which this conference should adopt (section VII);[2]
(7) My amended general international comparison up to date (section VIII).

It will also indicate the various tricks of interpolation rendered necessary by the inconvenient and incomparable way in which data are always published; and the extremely bad state of all our basic data, and our inexcusable carelessness about this fundamental fact.

It seems to me that the first task of the student of this subject, especially, but not only, if he is in government service, is to improve the accuracy and comprehensiveness of the data, and to present them in a more intelligible way. It is true that there is slow improvement: the Polish and British governments, for instance, have recently begun to present more distributions in deciles; and micro-data, from which anyone may draw his own concept, are available in the F.R.G. However the present faults will not soon be eradicated, and it is eminently worthwhile to develop techniques for dealing with them, even in the certain knowledge that they will one day be obsolete. First we must know the general shape of our universe (cf. section III); we can be clever theorists later. Before there is algebra, there must be a very great deal of arithmetic. Sufficient unto the decade are the problems thereof. Euclid built upon a great deal of Greek field surveying: he had *something to axiomatise*, while our axioms simply float on air.

---

[1] I am extremely grateful to Mr. Michael O'Higgins for a number of calculations and corrections.
[2] It did not adopt them! – to some extent because there was no time for discussion.

I shall not repeat here the arguments for using extreme quantile ratios, instead of magical single formulae like the Gini coefficient, as *descriptive* measures of inequality. They are adequately set out in Wiles (1974) and Wiles (1975). History seems in this matter to be on my side: quantile ratios are gaining everywhere on magical formulae. But note that, of my three preferred ratios, the decile is perforce gaining ground. The quartile is uninteresting, since it is almost always (for per capita income) between 1.8 and 2.5. And the lower semi-decile has been plunged into doubt by the recent discoveries of section V – though P_{95}/P_{10} is still a good measure. For the irrelevance of welfare to description, see Sen's paper in this volume and the discussion theoreon.

II. Percapitalisation

Since it is human beings not hh^3 that have stomachs and feel the cold, for all welfare and fiscal purposes we need to use the distribution of per capita income *only*. There is an immortal conversation from a goodish play that bears on this (the female is trying to hold the male to his promise of marriage):

Catherine: I've heard it said that two can live as cheaply as one.
John: Don't you believe it. Two can live as cheaply as two, and that's all there is to it.
Catherine: Yes, I see. I didn't know.
John: Unlike you I have a practical mind, Kate.
– Terence Rattigan, *The Winslow Boy*, Act III.

In this matter academic statisticians are Catherines, but governments, in fixing their tax and social-service scales, are Johns. They are so for a very good reason: they would not long survive the wrath of their electorates if they neglected *hh* size. Per *hh* income is of econometric value only (the *hh* is the decision-making unit). It is of no relevance at all for social justice: nor is it relevant for international comparisons of inequality, since it assumes a demographic and sociological uniformity quite absent from international cross-sections of the real world (Table 7.16). Furthermore, it tells us nothing about scarcity or incentives in the labour-market, for which the distribution of earnings per earner is the appropriate concept.[4] It owes its persistence, I think, to mere conservatism, though a certain stability of *hh* size by income quantile may be assumed for shortish inter-temporal comparisons within one country. It would be still better to use adult equivalents and to take account of the economies of *hh* scale – a limited concession to Catherine's position – but we very seldom have data for the age-composition of *hh* broken down by income.

We begin with the basic US data for 1974 (table 7.1), and show the method of

---

[3] Note a common abbreviation: *hh* = household.
[4] But welfare services, even though based on per capita income, certainly affect incentives and sometimes even wages; and income tax must be deducted from earnings to obtain the "incentive", though not the "scarcity", distribution, for which purpose the tax has to be based on the average family responsibility of the earnings bracket.

Table 7.1. Percentage distribution of total household money income by household size, USA, 1974.

Household size	All households (thousands)	Total household income ($)										
		<1000	1000–1499	1500–1999	2000–2499	2500–2999	3000–3499	3500–3999	4000–4999	5000–5999	6000–6999	7000–7999	8000–8999	9000–9999	10000–11999
1	13 939	4.0	3.7	8.0	9.8	8.9	7.5	4.4	8.3	6.8	6.2	5.4	4.7	3.8	6.6
2	21 753	1.4	0.9	1.0	1.5	2.4	2.8	2.9	6.2	6.6	6.2	5.8	5.5	5.4	10.2
3	12 384	1.3	0.7	0.8	1.1	1.1	1.4	1.5	3.6	3.7	3.8	4.5	4.8	5.1	11.3
4	11 103	1.0	0.4	0.4	0.7	0.7	1.0	1.2	2.2	2.8	2.9	3.3	3.8	4.6	10.4
5	6 399	0.9	0.2	0.5	0.7	0.5	1.3	1.0	2.5	2.7	2.5	3.3	3.5	3.6	9.4
6	3 059	0.7	0.2	0.4	1.4	0.8	0.9	0.6	3.4	2.7	3.5	3.4	3.6	3.7	9.8
7 or more	2 484	1.2	0.7	0.5	0.8	1.6	0.9	1.0	3.1	3.4	5.0	3.8	4.2	3.6	7.8
Total	71 120	1.8	1.2	2.2	2.8	2.9	2.9	2.3	5.0	4.9	4.8	4.7	4.6	4.6	9.5

Household size	All households (thousands)	Total household income ($)					Median income ($)	Mean income ($)
		12000–14999	15000–24999	25000–49999	50000 and over	Total		
1	13 939	5.7	5.0	0.9	0.2	100.0	4 430	6 169
2	21 753	12.4	21.3	6.8	0.8	100.0	10 308	12 299
3	12 384	15.3	28.8	10.1	1.0	100.0	13 013	14 577
4	11 103	16.0	34.3	13.2	1.2	100.0	14 758	16 289
5	6 399	15.7	35.8	14.4	1.7	100.0	15 504	17 031
6	3 059	14.5	33.2	15.5	1.8	100.0	15 140	16 840
7 or more	2 484	12.6	33.1	14.8	1.8	100.0	14 952	16 748
Total	71 120	12.5	23.7	8.6	0.9	100.0	11 101	12 893

Interpolations[a]

	15000–18399	18400–24999	25000–30299	30300–49999
1	3.5	1.5	0.5	0.4
2	11.8	9.5	3.5	3.3
3	16.1	12.7	5.3	4.8
4	19.2	15.1	7.0	6.2
5	19.0	16.8	7.4	7.0
6	17.2	16.0	7.9	7.6
7 or more	17.1	16.0	7.5	7.3
Total	13.2	10.5	4.5	4.1

Source: U.S. Bureau of Census, Current Population Reports, Series P-60 no. 100, 1975, p. 9. Excludes inmates of institutions. Includes 1,064,000 members of the Armed Forces in the United States living off post or with their families on post but excludes all other members of the Armed Forces. Households as of March 1975.

Notes: Average hh size = 2.94 persons (page 5). $P_5 = \$1960$, $P_{10} = \$2830$, $P_{50} = \$11,080$, $P_{90} = \$24,574$, $P_{95} = \$30,300$. So the decile ratio of gross money income by households is 8.67. The Gini coefficient is 0.392.

[a] The following data are given for all households: $P_{20} = \$4700$, $P_{40} = \$9000$, $P_{60} = \$13,200$, $P_{80} = \$18,400$, $P_{95} = \$30,000$. The interpolations for each hh size are mine. Their weighted averages correspond to the numbers in the "Total" row.

Table 7.2. Table 7.1 per capita.

Size of family	Income ranges $p.a.	<500	500–999	1,000–1,499	1,500–1,999	2,000–2,499	2,500–2,999	3,000–3,999
1	% hh	1.0	3.0	3.7	8.0	9.8	8.9	11.9
	no. of persons	139.4	418.2	515.7	1115.1	1366.0	1240.6	1658.7
2	% hh	1.4	1.9	3.9	5.7	6.2	6.6	12.0
	no. of persons	609.1	826.6	1696.7	2479.8	2697.3	2871.4	5220.7
3	% hh	2.0	3.0	2.9+1.8	1.8+3.7	3.8+2.2	2.3+4.8	16.4
	no. of persons	743.0	1114.6	1746.1	2043.4	2229.1	2637.8	6092.9
4	% hh	1.8	3.6	5.0	6.2	8.4	10.4	16.0+6.0
	no. of persons	799.4	1598.8	2220.6	2753.5	3730.6	4618.8	9770.6
5	% hh	2.3	5.3	5.2+1.5	1.8+6.1	9.4+3.0	12.7	19.0+4.5
	no. of persons	735.9	1695.7	2143.7	2847.6	3967.4	4063.4	7518.8
6	% hh	3.5	7.6	10.5	13.5	14.5	16.2	1.0+14.5
	no. of persons	642.4	1394.9	1927.2	2477.8	2661.3	2973.3	2844.9
	exact hh size[c]	8.07	8.07	8.01	7.94	7.87	7.83	7.83
7+	% hh	6.7	11.5+3.4	0.2+7.8 +7.4	+6.0 0.4+12.6	11.1+5.0	10.5	0.7+7.5 +1.0
	no. of persons	1345	3011	3084	3747	3147	2002	1792
Total no. of persons		5013	10061	13335	17465	19798	20407	34900

Notes: $P_5 = \$790$, $P_{10} = \$1235$, $P_{25} = \$2167$, $P_{50} = \$3530$, $P_{75} = \$5500$, $P_{90} = \$8340$, $P_{95} = \$10650$. Decile ratio of gross money income per capita = 6.75; Gini = 0.385.

[a] This is 71120 × 2.94. The sum of the rows and columns is 209191, each row being the sum of the figures in it.
[b] This is the sum of the row. The residual from table 7.1 is 19735.
[c] While the average for the row is deduced, the individual items are guessed: see text above.

"percapitalisation" in table 7.2. We need these data for section III. We then present the Canadian data (also needed later), and are able in this case even to provide a check on our workings. Our US source is the regular official source, the P-60 series of the Bureau of Census. It is one of the most detailed in the world for our purposes. It has come out annually since 1947 and shown great consistency (namely, a slight trend towards equality). It is based on a large sample taken by highly qualified people. It is, however, in rather sharp contradiction with the other official source: that of the Office of Business Economics (OBE). We have little space to judge between these sources (section III).

Table 7.1 gives the data that are basic for our purposes. We note that the authors have, like so many of their colleagues, retained traditional income intervals in a period of inflation and real growth, so that the right-hand part of the table is very crowded and needs disaggregating. Happily, as so often happens in these documents, this is possible from other data provided: we show our interpolation on the right. These other data would have been perfect for our purposes, were they not mostly in quintiles. But a quintile is a very gross measure indeed, at both

4,000–4,999	5,000–5,999	6,000–6,999	7,000–7,999	8,000–8,999	9,000–9,999	10,000–11,999	12,000+	Total
8.3	6.8	6.2	5.4	4.7	3.8	6.6	11.8	(100)
1156.1	947.2	864.2	752.7	655.1	529.7	920.0	1644.8	13924
10.9	10.2	8.5	3.9+3.6	7.4	0.8+4.2	5.0	0.3+7.6	(100)
4742.2	4437.6	3698.0	3263.0	3219.4	2175.3	2175.3	3437.0	43549
15.3	15.1	1.0+6.5	5.5	0.7+3.0	2.2	0.1+2.0	2.8+1.0	(100)
5684.3	5610.0	2786.4	2043.4	1374.6	817.3	780.2	1911.8	37115
13.2+4.0	9.5	1.6+4.0	3.0+1.5	2.1	1.2	1.3	0.1+1.2	(100)
7638.9	4219.1	2487.1	1998.5	932.7	532.9	577.4	577.4	44456
12.3	7.1	0.3+3.0	2.0	1.2	0.8	1.0	0.7	(100)
3935.4	2271.6	1055.8	639.9	383.9	256.0	320.0	224.0	32059
1.5+7.5	0.4+2.8	2.6	2.1	0.1+0.4	0.4	0.6	0.4	(100)
1651.9	587.3	477.2	385.4	91.8	73.4	110.1	73.4	18372
7.83	7.83	7.83	7.83	7.83	7.83	7.83	7.83	(7.945)
								(100)
4.0	2.1	0.2+0.5	0.4	0.3	0.2	0.2	0.2	
780	409	138	80	60	40	40	40	19715[b]
5589	18483	11506	9163	6718	4424	4922	7408	209093[a]

extremes. Thus, the fact that P_{20} is $4700 tells us nothing at all about P_{10}, which turns out to be $2830.

Tables such as table 7.1 are commonly, but not universally, produced by the statisticians responsible for income distribution. Per capita income distributions are given as such by East European countries, the USSR and occasionally India. (Communist countries do not publish per household data, and this is the origin of my personal interest in capitalist per capita data). Where they are not given, we can either apply for them as a favour, from the statistical office responsible, or interpolate. Interpolation is less accurate, much quicker, much more illuminating – and most often our only course of action, since non-Communist public bodies simply do not have per capita data, do not keep their files well enough to extract them, and are unwilling to release their files for others to work on.

In table 7.2 the incomes of table 7.1 are divided by the *hh* size, and the *hh* are rearranged accordingly. Where a single number in table 7.1 must be divided among many columns in table 7.2, its component parts receive a common underlining, to assist the eye. A good deal of extrapolation will be noted in the left-hand top

Table 7.3. Canada: Percentage Distribution of Family Pre-Tax Income Groups by Family Unit Size, 1973.

Family income	Family size 1	2	3	4	5+	Assumed size of 5+ hh
under $2000	24.2	3.5	2.8	1.4	1.3	6.14
2000– 2999	18.0	5.7	2.0	1.2	1.0	,,
3000– 3999	8.4	7.6	2.9	2.2	1.6	,,
4000– 4999	8.8	8.5	3.7	2.8	3.2	,,
5000– 5999	8.2	6.5	4.3	3.1	3.7	,,
6000– 6999	6.1	5.3	5.6	3.4	3.9	,,
7000– 7999	5.9	5.8	5.9	4.6	4.7	6.04
8000– 8999	4.9	6.3	6.5	5.7	5.3	,,
9000– 9999	3.1	5.3	6.8	6.3	5.9	,,
10000–10999	} 5.2	6.0	7.3	6.8	6.3	,,
11000–11999		5.5	6.4	6.9	5.6	5.93
12000–12999		5.1	6.7	7.1	6.6	,,
13000–13999	} 3.6	4.2	5.8	6.0	5.6	,,
14000–14999		4.4	4.4	6.9	5.2	,,
15000–16999		6.6	8.2	9.6	9.3	5.83
17000–19999	} 3.6	6.2	8.7	10.5	11.6	,,
20000–24999		4.6	7.0	8.7	9.5	5.73
over 25000		2.9	5.0	6.8	9.7	,,
Total	100.0	100.0	100.0	100.0	100.0	(5.93)

Families by per capita income	Family size 1	2	3	4		5+
under $500	0.5	0.4	} 2.8	1.4	under $354	1.3
500– 666	} 2.0	1.0		} 1.2	354– 499	0.8
667– 749			0.5		500– 531	0.2
750– 999	3.5	2.1	1.5	2.2	532– 707	1.6
1000– 1249	4.0	2.6	2.1	2.8	708– 749	0.7
1250– 1333	} 4.5	3.1	0.8	} 3.1	750– 884	2.5
1334– 1499			1.7		885– 999	1.9
1500– 1666	} 4.9	3.6	2.0	} 3.4	1000–1061	1.8
1667– 1749			1.0		1062–1238	3.9
1750– 1999	4.8	4.0	3.3	4.6	1239–1249	0.2
					1250–1415	4.5
					1416–1499	2.7
5000– 5666	–	–	8.2	} 7.7	1500–1565	2.6
5667– 5999	–	–	3.5		1566–1912	12.2
6000– 6249	–	} 5.1	} 5.2	1.0	1913–2184	12.2
6250– 6499	–			0.7	2185–2479	10.8
6500– 6666	–	} 4.2		} 1.2	2480–3251	20.9
6667– 6999	–		1.9		3252–3999	9.5
7000– 7499	–	4.4	} 4.3	1.0	4000–4999	4.8
7500– 7999	–	3.6		0.8	5000–5999	2.5
8000– 8333	–	} 3.0	0.8	} 0.6	6000–6999	1.3
8334– 8499	–		} 1.2		7000–7999	0.7
8500– 8999	–	2.4		0.5	8000–8999	0.3
9000– 9999	–	3.8	1.0	0.6	9000–9999	0.1
over 10000	–	8.5	2.8	1.4	over 10000	0.

Table 7.4. Table 7.3 per capita.

Household size	Income per capita <500	500–749	750–999	1000–1249	1250–1499	1500–1749	1750–1999	2000–2499	2500–4999	5000–5999	6000–6999	7000–7999	8000–8999	9000–9999	10000+	Total
1 % of households	0.5	2.0	3.5	4.0	4.5	5.0	4.7	10.0	25.2	8.2	6.1	5.9	4.9	3.1	12.4	100.0
no. of persons	9531	38126	66721	76252	85783	95313	89594	190626	480378	156313	116282	112469	93407	59094	236376	1906260
2 % of households	0.4	1.0	2.1	2.6	3.1	3.6	4.0	8.5	29.2	11.5	9.3	8.0	5.2	4.0	7.5	100.0
no. of persons	13429	33573	70503	87289	104076	120862	134291	285369	980326	386087	312227	268582	174579	134291	251796	3357280
3 % of households	1.9	1.4	1.5	2.1	2.5	3.0	3.2	8.0	47.4	11.7	7.1	4.3	2.0	1.0	2.8	100.0
no. of persons	60284	44420	47592	66629	79321	95185	104703	253826	1503921	371221	225271	136432	63457	31728	88839	3172830
4 % of households	1.4	1.2	2.2	2.8	3.1	3.4	4.6	12.0	53.8	7.7	2.9	1.8	1.1	0.8	1.4	100.0
no. of persons	64128	54967	100772	128256	141997	155739	210706	349667	2464341	352703	132836	82450	50386	27483	64128	4580560
5+ % of households	2.1	2.5	4.4	5.9	7.2	8.7	10.1	13.0	41.2	2.5	1.3	0.7	0.3	0.1	0	100.0
no. of persons	173730	206821	364005	488098	586626	708033	821970	1052918	3209131	193249	100489	54110	23190	7730	0	7990100
Total no. of persons	321102	377907	649593	846524	997803	1175132	1361264	2331776	8638097	1459573	887105	654043	405019	260326	641139	21007030
% of total persons[a]	(1.8)	(2.2)	(3.2)	(4.0)	(4.9)	(5.5)	(5.6)	(12.6)	(38.5)	(7.1)	(4.5)	(3.2)	(2.4)	(1.7)	(2.8)	100.0
	1.5	1.8	3.1	4.0	4.7	5.6	6.5	11.1	41.1	6.9	4.2	3.1	1.9	1.2	3.0	

Notes: $P_5 = (823); 890$ $P_{10} = (1148); 1227$ $P_{25} = (1904); 1950$ $P_{50} = (2840); 3170$ $P_{75} = (4712); 4437$ $P_{90} = (7000); 6784$ $P_{95} = (8759); 8484$

Therefore, the semi-decile ratio = (10.6) 9.0; the decile ratio = (6.1) 5.5; and the quartile ratio = (2.5) 2.3.

[a] Figures in brackets are the result of an earlier interpolation by Mr. Hal Berndt of the Canadian Dept. of Finance: see text below.

and right-hand bottom corners. But the effect on the values of P_{10} and P_{90}, even of P_5, is very small indeed, since the numbers involved are very small. Indeed it would be impossible to propose a plausible change in the interpolations or the extrapolations that would have a serious effect.

The largest (open-ended) *hh* size is always a special problem. Its average value is seldom given in the original publication, but it is usually easy to deduce. But the size can, and presumably does, also vary slightly with income, and here we are reduced to guesswork. My assumption is that per capita income decreases with *hh* size within this group, as within the population at large, i.e. that *hh* of exactly 7 have a more "pro-poor" distribution than *hh* of 6, but less so than *hh* of 8 etc. The matter is important because of the great weight of these *hh* at the lower extreme (in table 7.2, more than a quarter of all people at the fifth percentile come from *hh* with seven or more members).

Note the enormous number of people who are moved about between tables 7.1 and 7.2. About one third of the *hh* in the top decile of the *hh* distribution contain people found below the median in the per capita distribution.

Table 7.3 is from the annual survey by Statistics Canada. Statistics Canada has a deservedly high reputation in all fields. We percapitalise table 7.3 in the same way (table 7.4). But this time we have a check: Statistics Canada *can* pull per capita figures out of their files! The experience has been a rude shock to me: I am certainly a sensitive, experienced and devoted interpolator, expending tender loving care upon *each number*, but I do not appear to be a very good one from the evidence presented in table 7.5.

Berndt and I worked as described in Wiles (1974, appendix III). O'Higgins cumulated the data and used a Paretian formula for interpolation:

$$\frac{\ln(X/L_1)}{\ln(L_2/L_1)} = \frac{\ln(S/N_1)}{\ln(N_2/N_1)},$$

where L_i are income interval limits, and $L_2 > X > L_1$; and N_i are populations cumulated from the rich end, with $N_2 < S < N_1$. Pareto's α is thus $\ln(N_2/N_1)/\ln(L_1/L_2)$ (cf. Sawyer (1976)). At the top and bottom, α was taken from the adjacent income class. I alone of the three of us have (arbitrarily) varied the size of the $5 + hh$ (for which Statistics Canada were able to pull the average of 5.93 out of their files). I have evidently overdone it, unless Statistics Canada themselves used a constant size. But it seems fairly clear that the average size of the $5 + hh$ increases as per capita income falls, as in the US. For the error at P_5, see section IV.

III. North American inequality

The impression that US income distribution is rather equal comes, with most authority, from Kuznets (1963). He refers the reader back to these calculations himself, in Kuznets (1966), when he requires distribution statistics. Kuznets (1963) gives us the following "shares of ordinal groups", and it is upon these data that the whole claim seems to rest. In tables 7.6, 7.7 and 7.8, I present most of his data verbatim and add his UK comparisons.

Table 7.5. Canada 1973: Interpolation versus reality.

	Statistics Canada (from their data files)	Berndt	Wiles	O'Higgins
P_5	776	832	890	827
P_{10}	1120	1181	1227	1138
P_{50}	2960	2840	3170	2924
P_{90}	6802	7000	6784	6880
P_{95}	8681	8759	8484	8704

Table 7.6. USA: Sundry Verbatim Extracts from Kuznets (1963).

Page in Kuznets (1963)	Concept	Unit	Date	0–20%	21–40%	41–60%	61–80%	81–90%	91–95%	96–100%	Gini
13	Gross personal income[a]	Consuming units	1950	4.8	11.0	16.2	22.3	15.4	9.9	20.4	0.35
28	Ditto, less federal income tax[a]			(5.2)	(11.5)	(16.9)	22.9	15.7	9.8	18.0	–
32	Gross money income[b]	Consuming units	1952	–	31.0	–	23.8	15.8	10.4	19.0	0.35

[a] US Dept. of Commerce, *Income Distribution in the United States,* (Washington, 1953), p. 85 (supplement to the Survey of Current Business). [I have restored the figures in brackets from the original source.]

[b] US Bureau of Census, *Current Population Reports: Consumer Income,* Series P-60 no. 15, Washington, April 1954, p. 10. "The median size of family shown for each income bracket was raised a tenth to approximate the arithmetic mean."

All these figures, as presented by Kuznets (1963), only yield one decile ratio, and it is in no way clear how Kuznets derives Gini coefficients from the other rows quoted, which combine the bottom six deciles into one figure. From row 1 of table 7.6, we find by interpolation that the income shares of the centiles P_{10} and P_{90} were 0.23 and 1.78, so the decile ratio of family income was about 7.7. But if we go back to the raw data (table 7.11), we find it to be more like 6.6.

However, that row is from the Survey of Current Business, which by no means agrees with the P-60 Series (third row). It used the data of the Office of Business Economics, which were based mainly on the Federal income tax, and used the Census sample only as a supplement. We have little space here for the pros and cons of each source, but we note that the OBE series, announced in 1953 as a major new one, was discontinued in 1964.[5] It is used to be published in each April issue of the Survey of Current Business, but, in April 1964, Fitzwilliams presented the 1963 data with an apparently valedictory text. Nothing more appeared in this

[5] Cf., for an account of the differences, Miller (1964).

Table 7.7. Effects of Redistribution through Taxes and Benefits on Shares of Ordinal Groups in Total Personal Income, Selected Countries, Late 1940s or 1950 (Verbatim Extract from Kuznets (1963, p. 26)).

	Shares of ordinal groups					Gini
	0–60%	61–80%	81–90%	91–95%	Top 5%	
Great Britain, Consuming Units, 1948/49						
7. Personal factor income	33.3	20.0	12.9	9.4	24.4	0.35
8. Total personal income	36.6	19.6	12.2	8.9	22.7	0.31
9. Line 8, excl. taxes	39.3	21.0	12.9	9.0	17.8	0.26
10. Line 9, incl. benefits	40.1	20.8	12.5	8.3	18.3	0.25
United States, Consuming Units, 1949/50						
14. Personal factor income	31.5	20.4	14.5	8.5	25.1	0.37
15. Total personal income	33.8	20.2	14.0	8.0	24.0	0.34
16. Line 15, excl. taxes	35.4	20.0	13.9	8.1	22.6	0.32
17. Line 16, incl. benefits	35.9	20.1	14.0	8.1	21.9	0.31

Sources:
Lines 7–10: Based on Cartter (1955) Personal income (i.e., personal factor income adjusted for transfers) is taken from Table 3, p. 32, and the number of units from Table 1, col. 1, p. 27. Direct taxes on personal income (from Table 7, p. 39) and indirect taxes (from Table 11, p. 43), but not death duties or profits and income taxes on non-personal income, are subtracted in deriving the shares in line 9. Benefits are derived by averaging estimates based on three assumptions: that indivisible expenditures (i.e., general government operations, defence, and the like) are equal per capita, proportional to net private income, or proportional to taxes. The resulting average is close to proportionality to income (see Table 16, p. 52). Cartter's estimates take into account taxes and benefits of the central government alone.

Lines 14–18: Based on Conrad (1954). Benefits not directly allocable are an average of estimates based on the assumptions of equal per capita distribution and of proportionality to the tax burden (see Redistribution Table IV, p. 201). Thus the assumption is fairly similar to those underlying lines 3a, 6 and 10. We exclude from benefits, items considered as transfer incomes (interest on government debt, veterans' services and benefits, and social security and relief payments, as given in Table III, p. 214) and add them to income (as in Redistribution Table I, p. 197), since the latter presumably excluded transfers. We also limit taxes to those bearing upon consumer income alone, excluding corporation income taxes and death and gift duties (for the latter, see Redistribution Table II, p. 204). [Note: The reader interested in checking Kuznets' work should know that row 14 appears to be an interpolation from Conrad's Table I line (5), p. 203. It is in my opinion a correct interpolation. The period concerned is the fiscal year 1950].

series until 1974 when, in the October issue, Radner and Hinrichs restarted the series, beginning with 1964. They give a full explanation there, and it is enough for me to say that their decile ratio of "total money income" by *hh* in 1971 is 8.1 before tax; while the Bureau of Census gives us 8.8 in 1968 after tax (table 7.15 here), and 8.7 in 1974 before tax (table 7.1). In view of the lightness of the income tax, we are clearly now "all in the same ball-park".[6]

However, in 1950, with the OBE's old series, we were not in the same ball-park. I append in tables 7.9–7.11 the 1950 data from both sources in full: the Census yields a per family decile ratio of about 12 as opposed to the 6.6 implied by the OBE.

It is not clear to what extent either set of data was based on the "rule of zero"

---

[6] Radner and Hinrichs also yield a decile ratio of "family personal income" of 6.8 (by *hh*, 1971, before tax). This concept includes many sorts of income in kind, especially from social services. They also confirm the marked trend to equality that emerges from the Bureau of Census data.

Table 7.8. Effects on the Shares of Ordinal Groups of the Allowance for Direct Taxes and of the Shift to the Distribution of Consumption Expenditures, Family or Consumer Units, Selected Countries, Late 1940s and Early 1950s (verbatim extract from Kuznets (1963), p. 28).

	Shares of ordinal groups					Gini
	0–60%	61–80%	81–90%	91–95%	Top 5%	
Great Britain, 1951/52						
7. Total income	33.4	22.4	14.3	9.0	20.9	0.33
8. Line 7 excl. direct taxes	36.0	23.9	14.8	9.2	16.1	0.29
9. Consumption expenditure	38.0	24.2	15.1	8.9	13.8	0.26
United States, 1950						
10. All consuming units, total income	32.0	22.3	15.4	9.9	20.4	0.35
11. Line 10, excl. federal income tax liability	33.6	22.9	15.7	9.8	18.0	0.32
12. Urban families, income after taxes	40.2	22.4	14.1	8.5	14.8	0.24
13. Urban families, consumption expenditure	44.7	22.8	13.6	7.8	11.1	0.18

Sources:

Lines 7–9: Based on Lydall (1955), Table 9, p. 24, for income including taxes (designated "gross" in the source); Table 24, p. 51, for income excluding direct taxes (designated "net" in the source); and Table 68, p. 138, for consumption expenditures.

Lines 10–11: Based on US Dept. of Commerce, *Income Distribution in the United States*, 1953, Tables 19–22, p. 85.

Lines 12–13: Based on US Bureau of the Census, *Historical Statistics of the United States* (Washington, 1960), Series G-353 through G-372, p. 182. The underlying data refer to income after taxes and current consumption expenditures of all families of two or more persons in cities of 2,500 and over.

(section IV below). How much difference does the "rule of zero" make to international comparisons? My answer is, not much to P_{90}/P_{10}. To be precise, rather extreme assumptions, applied to the quite detailed Canadian data, raise P_{10} by 14% and P_{90} by 2%.[7] A 12% fall in the decile ratio still leaves North America far more unequal than Protestant Europe.

Within one country, if we ask whether equality has fallen or risen over time, the "rule of zero" is clearly a far smaller source of inaccuracy. Note then the very great contrast between 1950 and 1974 (table 7.17). After the USSR, the USA is the country with the most successful current equalisation drive known to me.

I conclude that Kuznets differs from me because:
(i) he has not brought his data up to date;
(ii) he is unconscious of the need to disaggregate at the bottom, and has actually amalgamated the bottom 60% into one figure, except in one case (1950, gross), and even there he only gives a quintile;
(iii) he used OBE, not Census, data in that one case;
(iv) when he used the Census data, he obscured them as in (ii).

[7] Calculations available from the author on request.

Table 7.9. Distribution of Families and Unrelated Individuals by Total Money Income and Major Source of Earnings, by Size of Family, for the United States: 1950 (Census).

Brackets	Total		Unrelated individuals		All families		Families of specified number of related persons					
							2	3	4	5	6	7 or more
thousands	49,016		9,194		39,822		13,084	9,984	8,228	4,434	2,136	1,956
percent	100.0		100.0		100.0		100.0	100.0	100.0	100.0	100.0	100.0
Averages												
Under $500	9.8		27.8		5.8		9.2	4.3	3.6	3.1	4.7	7.0
$500 to $999	8.6		21.3		5.7		9.2	4.6	3.1	3.5	5.3	5.1
$1000 to $1499	7.0		10.4		6.2		8.6	5.3	3.8	5.6	4.8	8.6
$1500 to $1999	7.2		8.4		7.0		8.1	7.2	5.4	6.0	6.1	8.4
$2000 to $2499	9.0		9.3		8.9		9.8	8.9	8.1	8.0	9.5	8.9
$2500 to $2999	8.5		7.1		8.9		8.6	9.3	9.4	8.5	9.0	7.2
$3000 to $3499	10.7		6.4		11.7		10.8	12.0	13.2	11.6	9.8	11.4
$3500 to $3999	8.1		3.8		9.0		7.6	9.8	10.0	9.7	9.0	8.2
$4000 to $4499	6.8		1.9		7.9		6.2	8.8	9.0	8.7	8.5	6.4
$4500 to $4999	4.9		1.2		5.7		4.3	6.6	6.7	6.0	6.9	4.4
$5000 to $5999	7.5		1.2		9.0		7.2	9.7	10.7	10.7	7.9	7.0
$6000 to $6999	4.3		0.4		5.2		4.3	5.2	5.7	6.1	6.8	5.4
$7000 to $9999	4.8		0.6		5.8		3.6	5.1	7.4	8.6	7.0	8.4
$10000 and over	2.7		0.4		3.3		2.5	3.1	4.0	3.8	4.6	3.7

Source: as for Table 7.1, P-60 no. 9, 1952, p. 24.

Notes: $P_{10} = \$510$, $P_{50} = \$2990$, $P_{90} = \$6500$; the decile ratio is 12.7 and the Gini coefficient 0.395. The "bracket averages" are those used in calculating the Gini coefficient. P-60 no. 41, Oct. 1963, p. 35, quotes very slightly different figures for 1950. The average size of families of 7+ is not deducible from the document. But the average size of the *hh* was 3.42 in the 1950 Census, where "*hh*" includes unrelated individuals.

Table 7.10. Table 7.9 per capita.

Size of family	$p.a.	<124	125–249	250–374	375–499	500–749	750–999	1000–1499	1500–1999	2000–2999	3000–3999	4000–4999	5000–5999	over 6000	Total[c]
1	% hh	3.0	7.8	10.0	7.0	10.8	10.5	10.4	8.4	16.4	10.2	3.1	1.2	1.4	(100)
	no. of persons	276	717	919	644	993	965	956	772	1508	938	285	110	129	9194
2	% families	3.2	6.0	4.7	4.5	8.6	8.1	18.4	18.4	17.7	4.3+1.8	1.8	2.5		(100)
	no. of persons	837	1570	1230	1178	2250	2120	4815	4815	4632	1596	471	654		26168
3	% families	3.3	1.0+2.3	2.3+1.0	4.3	7.2+4.0	4.9+9.3	30.6	16.3	5.2+3.8	1.3+1.5		1.6		(100)
	no. of persons	938	988	988	1288	3355	4253	9165	4882	2696	839		479		29952
4	% families	3.6	3.1	3.8	5.4	17.5	23.2	26.4	5.7+3.7	3.7+1.7		2.3			(100)
	no. of persons	1185	1020	1251	1777	5760	7636	8689	3094	1777		757			32912
5	% families	3.1+0.8	2.7+2.8	2.8+4.5	1.5+8.0	20.1+5.0	4.7+14.7	16.8+2.0	6.6	3.0		0.8			(100)
	no. of persons	865	1219	1618	2106	5565	4302	4168	1463	665		177			22170
6	% families	4.7+2.6	2.7+4.8	6.1+4.5	5.0+9.0	27.3	14.8	13.8	3.0	1.3		0.3			(100)
	no. of persons	936	961	1358	1794	3499	1897	1769	384	167		38			12816
7+	exact family size[a]	8.11	8.11	8.00	8.00	7.91	7.87	7.87	7.87	7.87	7.87	7.87			(8.0)[a]
	% families	12.1	17.0	16.1	19.6	17.8	5.4+4.2	4.2+1.7	1.5	0.4		0.1			(100)
	no. of persons	1919	2695	2519	3067	2753	1478	909	237	61		16			15648
Total no. of persons		7006	9170	9883	11854	24175	22650	30471	15647	11506	(4361)	(1235)	(764)	(129)	148860[b]
												6489			

Notes: $P_5 = \$130$; $P_{10} = \$233$; $P_{25} = \$494$; $P_{50} = \$880$; $P_{75} = \$1430$; $P_{90} = \$2143$; $P_{95} = \$2894$. Therefore the decile ratio is 9.20. The Gini coefficient is 0.404.

[a] See text.
[b] The sum of the above items; the row total is 148856.
[c] These numbers are derived from Table 19 up to 6 member families; they are not the sum of the rows as in Table 7.2.

Table 7.11. Basic U.S. data for 1950, OBE. Distribution of consumer units, family personal income, and Federal individual income tax liability, by family personal income level, 1950.

Family personal income (before income taxes)	Number of families and unattached individuals (thousands)	Family personal income Aggregate (millions of dollars)	Family personal income Average (dollars)	Federal individual income tax liability Aggregate (millions of dollars)	Federal individual income tax liability Average (dollars)	Tax rate (per cent)	Percent distribution Number	Percent distribution Income	Percent distribution Tax liability
<$1000	3,704	1,854	501	1[1]	29	[2]	7.6	0.9	[2]
$1000–$1999	7,328	11,170	1,524	216	29	1.9	15.1	5.1	1.2
$2000–$2999	8,044	20,144	2,504	709	88	3.5	16.5	9.3	3.9
$3000–$3999	8,463	29,569	3,494	1,353	160	4.6	17.4	13.6	7.4
$4000–$4999	6,980	31,215	4,472	1,626	233	5.2	14.4	14.4	8.9
$5000–$7499	8,484	51,200	6,035	3,525	415	6.9	17.5	23.6	19.4
$7500–$9999	2,860	24,218	8,468	1,960	685	8.1	5.9	11.2	10.8
$10000 and over	2,727	47,388	17,377	8,810	3,231	18.6	5.6	21.9	48.4
Total	48,590	216,758	4,461	18,200	375	8.4	100.0	100.0	100.0

[1] Less than 50 cents.
[2] Less than 0.05 percent.

Distribution of family personal income and Federal individual income tax liability among quintiles and top 5 per cent of consumer units ranked by size of family personal income, 1950.

Quintile	Range of family personal income[1] (before income taxes)	Average (dollars) Family personal income	Tax liability	Tax rate (per cent)	Percent distribution Income (before taxes)	Percent distribution Tax liability
Lowest	Under $1,840	1,080	15	1.4	4.8	0.8
2	$1,840–$3,040	2,444	85	3.5	11.0	4.5
3	$3,040–$4,200	3,612	169	4.7	16.2	9.0
4	$4,200–$5,960	4,971	289	5.8	22.3	15.4
Highest	$5,960 and over	10,197	1,316	12.9	45.7	70.3
Total		4,461	375	8.4	100.0	100.0
Top 5 per cent	$10,500 and over	18,250	3,518	19.3	20.4	47.0

[1] Rounded to nearest $10.

Source: U.S. Dept. of Commerce, *Income Distribution in the United States*, p. 85. (Supplement to the Survey of Current Business.) No date, but clearly 1953.

While we can make no judgement on (iii), we are bound to regret that the accepted distribution in so important a country, used for international comparisons, should rest on so slender a basis. We here accept the usual current practice, unfounded as it probably is, that the Census P-60 must be the basis for international comparison. It indicates for 1950 a decile ratio 80% higher than that given by Kuznets and so puts a wholly different complexion on the relationship between development and distribution throughout the world. It also brings US inequality above Canadian, where it surely should be.[8]

In the 1950 data given in tables 7.9 and 7.10, it has not proved possible to deduce the average size of the 7+ family from any of the data published about the sample. Indirect calculations prove very unsatisfactory.[9] I have accordingly raised my 1974 estimates to average 8.0.

Combining the two sets of OBE data given in table 7.11, we arrive at the following reconstruction

Income ($)	Families (%)	
0– 999	7.6	
1000–1499	7.0	
1500–1839	5.4	15.1
1840–1999	2.7	
2000–2499	8.1	16.5
2500–2999	8.4	
3000–3039	0.8	
3040–3499	8.2	17.4
3500–3999	8.4	
4000–4199	3.4	
4200–4499	4.4	14.4
4500–4999	6.6	
5000–5959	9.0	
5960–6999	6.1	17.5
7000–7499	2.4	
7500–7999	2.0	
8000–8999	2.4	5.9
9000–9999	1.5	
10000–12499	2.6	5.6
12500 +	3.0	

The quintile limits are underlined. P_{10} is about \$1180, P_{50} about \$3600, P_{90} about \$7800. The decile ratio = 6.6, Gini coefficient 0.398.

It will be observed that the Census has far better coverage of the poor, the OBE of the rich. If both are more correct at "their" extreme, inequality is understated by both.

---

[8] In more modern times, however, the USA has moved far more quickly towards equality than Canada, and may have overtaken her. Kuznets (1976) has returned to the subject of US income distribution. Basing himself on the Bureau of Census for 1969 (P-60, no. 75), he derives gross money income per head by a technique evidently very similar to mine (pp. 33–4). I have some doubts about the details, but am able to derive P_{10} = \$850 p.a., P_{90} = \$6600 p.a., decile ratio = 7.76 (calculations available on request). This compares well with Table 7.2 here, though Kuznets attempts neither intertemporal nor international comparisons on this occasion. Above all he does not ask himself how this fits in with his previous work.

[9] Available from the author on request.

Kuznets also quoted the British data as shown above. We must reexamine them too. In Lydall (1955) the decile ratio presents no problem. He works it out himself on page 25. In his top line $P_{10} = £110$, $P_{90} = £700$. So the ratio is 6.36, equal to the OBE's ratio for the USA, but 55% of the Census estimate.

Cartter's decile ratio is a far more complicated question, and one well worth our prolonged attention, since it involves most of the techniques of interpolation, other than those illustrated in tables 7.1 and 7.2, which concern this contribution. He gives us the data reproduced here in table 7.12.

Table 7.12. UK 1950: Cartter's basic data.

(1) "Taxable" income[a] (£p.a.)	(2) Number of income units[a] (thousands)	(3) Personal income shares enjoyed by column (2)[b]	(4) Medians in (1)[c]	(5) Averages in (3)[d]
0–135	2793	493.7	–	177
135–250	8943	2239.6	192	250
250–500	8417	3390.6	325	403
500–750	1658	1134.3	580	684
750–1000	583.0	571.8	830	981
1000–2000	532.0	787.0	1370	1479
2000–3000	110.7	297.2	2400	2685
3000–5000	63.5	266.3	3750	4193
5000–10,000	30.1	216.8	?7125	7202
10,000–20,000	8.4	121.8	–	14500
20,000 +	2.3	88.1	–	38304
Total	23141.0			

[a] Cartter (1955, p. 27); [b] Cartter, p. 32; [c] from Fig. 1 below; [d] (3) ÷ (2).

He has committed the alas characteristic fault of having very large brackets towards the extremes (cf. table 7.1). Just how many pounds below the 2793rd unit the 2314th came would appear to be anyone's guess, but the range can be shown to be extremely narrow. Figure 7.1, the histogram for "taxable" income, is a multi-purpose figure, and we concentrate first on the two poorest columns.

In the first trial we take the very low minimum income of £50 (the left-hand side of the rectangle vz). But we allow rather few people at this income (u) and interpolate the true frequency curve of income distribution as the straight line uw, giving us two equal triangles uvt, wyt. The triangles must of course be of equal area because the area of the rectangle vz is given. Straight-line interpolation is evidently permissible where the slope is so steep. The area below ux is found to contain 28.9 squares, or the required 2314 people, and income at x is about £127.5 (the slope at x is 14.5 to 1 and its horizontal distance from u is 1.55 squares). In the second trial we put £85 as the minimum income (the rectangle v'z). But we feel compelled to put rather many people at this income (u'), and this offsets the other change. The line u'w' is not actually drawn. The result is that income at x', calculated as above, is £127.0 (x' is not shown in the figure: the slope at x' is 12 to 1 and its horizontal distance from u' is 0.84 squares). P_{10} is therefore about £127.

For P_{90} we require far less interpolation, but this is a good opportunity to show the method to the right of the mode. The true frequency curve must now show

Our shaky data base 183

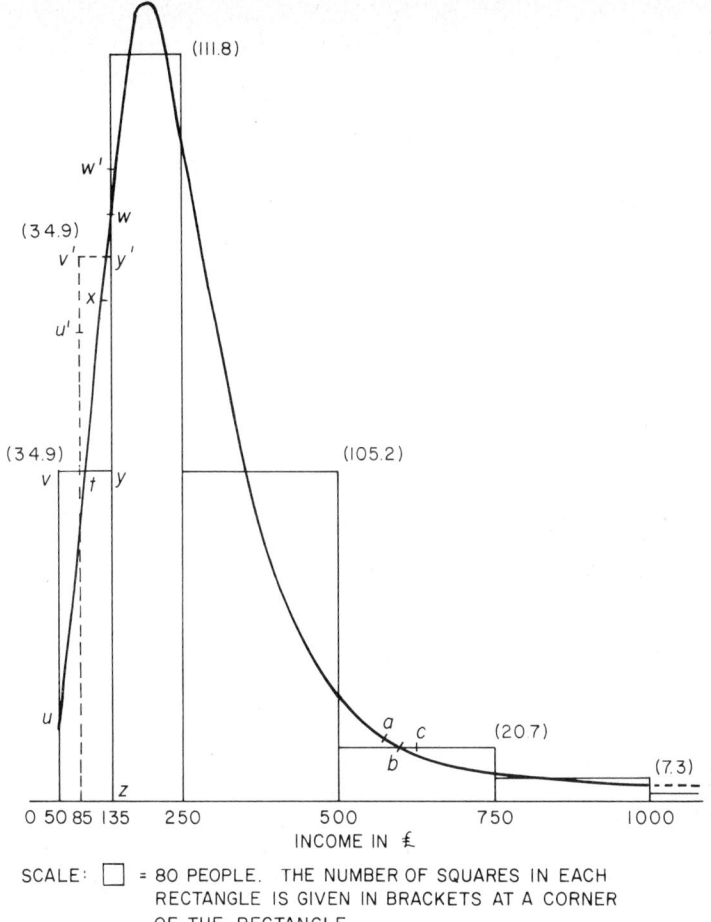

SCALE: ☐ = 80 PEOPLE. THE NUMBER OF SQUARES IN EACH RECTANGLE IS GIVEN IN BRACKETS AT A CORNER OF THE RECTANGLE.

Figure 7.1. The histogram of Cartter's taxable income.

curvature, but the areas it cuts out of each histogram panel must still equal those it adds, and this is a powerful constraint upon interpolative choice.[10] It follows from this constraint, and the fact that the curvature is convex to the origin, that the point b, where the true frequency cuts the top of the histogram panel, must always lie to the left of c, the mid-point of the histogram range. The median a is shown to the left of b, but this might not be so:

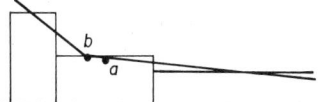

The point b seems to have no economic significance. The mean income within the bracket can only be obtained by multiplying each frequency by each income

[10] And one disgracefully not made explicit in Wiles (1974), appendix III.

underneath the true curve, and is clearly always smaller (this side of the mode) than the midpoint multiplied by the total frequency. It is this tedious little circumstance that confirms the writer in his preference for quantile boundary ratios over quantile share ratios.

Anyway we seek, to complete the tenth decile, the top 984 units in the bracket £500–750, or 12.3 squares. This is about £570. So the decile ratio of taxable income is 4.49.

It would be difficult at this late date to discover how Cartter derived the "Personal Income" *shares* in table 7.12. It is not surprising that, at the very bottom, average personal income greatly exceeds the bracket median, indeed the bracket upper limit, of taxable income. But the precise units who were in the lowest taxable brackets were not the same as those in the lowest personal income bracket. Some were promoted out of the lowest 2793 units by the redistributive process, and some fell down into it. We have no guarantee that these flows were of the same size, and we are only told that the lowest 2793 "taxable" units got such and such a personal income. We do not know how much "personal" income went to the lowest 2793 in the "personal" income distribution. Thus Kuznets has illegitimately merged two sets of Cartter's data, and we do not know how serious the error is.[11]

Moving down column (5), the migration between quantiles that probably took place at the bottom is now unlikely: the main redistributor is now the progressive income tax, which cannot have this effect. It is, however, evident that the distribution of personal income is far more equal than that of taxable income. Therefore the decile ratio is even lower. Therefore Cartter's data make the UK incomparably more equal than the USA.

To conclude section III, we have the indices of inequality of gross income shown in table 7.13.

Table 7.13. USA and UK, inequality indices.

	Original Source	Gini in Kuznets	Gini re-estimated by Mr. O'Higgins	Decile ratio
USA, hh				
1949/50	Conrad	0.37	0.412	–[c]
1950	OBE	0.35	0.398	6.6
1950	Census	–	0.395	12.7
1952	”	0.35	–	10.5[a]
1962	”	–	–	10.5[b]
1974	”	–	0.392	8.7
UK, hh				
1948/9	Cartter	0.35	0.333	4.5
1951/2	Lydall	0.33	0.386	6.4

[a] Derived by me directly from P-60 no. 15, April 1954, p. 10.
[b] Derived by me directly from P-60 no. 41, Oct. 1963, pp. 26, 27.
[c] This table includes almost self-contradictory items and is highly suspect. I do not think it worthwhile to estimate a decile ratio.

[11] A shift in this kind can be very clearly seen in the Swedish data: the third per *hh* decile in order of distributed factor income has a lower average per capita disposable income than the second decile. Source as in Table 7.17, footnote j.

The Gini coefficient is in fact grossly insensitive to movements at the extremes, as I have very simply shown by semi-arbitrary examples (Wiles (1974), pp. 7–12). This may not be, however, the only reason for the terrible débâcle shown above; for we are not provided with the basic data for the calculation of the coefficient, and we do not know on what interpolations and extrapolations the calculation rested.

When we take into account the far higher weight and progressivity of British income tax at the top, nothing at all is left of Kuznet's strange notion that UK and USA were in the same ball-park in 1948-52 (Lydall's net income figures are: Gini re-estimated 0.341, decile ratio 5.6).

IV. Development and equality

I dot not wish here to get too far away from mere data-mongering. But the consequence of section III, and of all my work on Communism (Wiles, 1974; 1975), is that inequality is *not* a cross-sectional function of development. Canada – and no doubt the Caribbean except Cuba – are unequal because of the pull of the US labour market at the top: migration is the main influence. The USA is not only rich, so that it has that kind of pull, but also unequal for various reasons. Protestant Europe is much more equal than the USA, though less rich. Catholic Europe is unequal, but the figures are very bad.[12]

It is still, however, possible to maintain that every non-Communist country pursues a historical course, peculiar to itself, from the equality-in-poverty of the bottom nine deciles, through an industrialising period of greater inequality between all deciles, into an affluent welfare-state period of greater equality; but all by its own historic standards. In the early period, distribution above P_{90}, or possibly above P_{97}, is a function of the particular social system. As always, we must avoid magical formulae and say *which* quantile our theory is comparing with which other one. Such a historically particularist theory (or, better, generalisation) is very tempting, but it rests upon essentially no data, with the possible exception of the USA in the 1860's. It is for instance quite impossible to say which British quantile ratios behaved in which way until 1913; and really serious figures begin in 1953.

In such a theory the welfare state is a politically determined affair, spreading within one country by Parkinson's Law and between countries by cultural diffusion. Its main connection with economics is that there is an economic constraint: the country must be rich enough and have enough competent clerks. Thus these arrangements need not, and in fact did not, begin in the richest country, but in Bismarck's Germany.

---

[12] France is flatly unknown, Spain may have adopted the rule of zero in a one-off survey. Italy is perhaps an exception: her 1974 figures are a great improvement on her 1969 figures quoted in Table 7.17, but yield the same result. Portugese and Austrian (also Greek) figures barely exist. My suggestion that the distinction is religious is semi-serious. First, it conforms to such facts as are known. Secondly it is *a priori* probable that a society which holds itself unequal before God, at any rate on this earth, will more easily accept, even after the Death of God, that it is unequal before the tax collector.

A purely economic theory would deal better with factor incomes gross of tax. But in fact everything said above still applies though in lesser degree.

Communism is a distributive system on its own. Poland, Czechoslovakia, Hungary and Bulgaria are very equal by the standards of Protestant Europe, and the first three have shown little change since 1955-60 (Wiles, 1975). The USSR has shown very great changes since October 1917, all apparently unconnected with the level or rate of growth, and solely due to the Politburo's ideas about those and other matters. At present the USSR has at last achieved the equality of her four smaller allies named. We have no figures for other Communist countries, though the GDR has at last put a toe into the hot bath by producing a partial per-*hh* distribution.[13]

V. The problem of new households

North American statistics present another problem: the "rule of zero" for new *hh*. According to this methodology, a random sample of *hh* is picked and interviewed in year t about their income in year $t - 1$. Mostly the interviews take place in the spring of t, which is a calendar year – a very important point, since the lag determines how many new *hh* there are. When the surveyor finds he has a new *hh*, he asks *each member* what his/her *personal* income was last year in the old *hh*, sums these figures and writes down the total as if it were the income of the new *hh* in $t - 1$.

The trouble with this is that *hh* size, and even *hh* existence, vary from $t - 1$ to t, and in a highly biased manner. In the USA the percentage of new *hh* formed every year is about 6. The majority of the members of these *hh* had no income last year, or only a small part-time juvenile wage and maybe a little savings account interest. This majority consists of two groups: the young entering the labour market at the same time as they set up a *hh*, and widows (who are heads of *hh*, but the *hh* are counted as new). The result is that the bottom Canadian centile has always zero income! And improbably low mini-incomes (disposable incomes), which would kill even a single-person *hh* during the North American winter, influence even the fourth centile.

This method seems to have originated in Canada or the USA. First and foremost we note that it unequivocally entails the publication of falsehoods: there were no such *hh* as these artificial constructs in $t - 1$. The procedure has been defended to me on the following grounds:

(a) bankrupt businessmen pull down the first centile; yet they usually consume an adequate amount out of capital. This I admit, but they and their *hh* are a very small fraction of the first centile.[14]
(b) other poor *hh* borrow all their money for consumption. I know of no data for this in North America, but must point out that even in India, poor *hh* only borrow 21% of their consumption.[15]

---

[13] See the contribution of Michal in this volume.
[14] Statistics Canada, privately communicated.
[15] This is the bottom 42.5% in towns, however: Mueller and Sarma (1965).

(c) other ways of conducting the survey are also objectionable. In particular the British way, of collecting figures for income accruing *after* the first visit of the surveyor, leads to greater non-response and deterioration of data quality. But surely these would at least be unbiased? We note, en passant, that a simple survey of last year's tax returns solves at least this problem altogether.

However none of these arguments tries to answer the basic point: it is *false* that the members of new *hh*, who have just entered the labour force, constituted zero-income *hh* last year. If it were true, they would be dead. Falsehoods should be corrected even if trivial. The proportion of these to other very-low-income *hh* is admittedly unknown, but it would seem to me that in countries with quite generous and fairly comprehensive welfare services that easily lift their recipients out of this range, the victims of the "rule of zero" must be the majority of the first two or three centiles. I regard the early correction of this falsehood as an urgent task. Until it is done the whole question of poverty, as well as that of distribution, remains up in the air.

I suggest the following new rules:

(i) When a widow takes over from her husband the *hh* is defined as old, not new, and its total income last year is recorded.
(ii) New *hh* formed by young entrants to the labour market shall be disregarded if they were formed in year t. If they were formed during $t - 1$ their income after formation will be multiplied by $365/X$ where X is the number of days for which they existed.
(iii) Other new *hh* shall be excluded, but reported on in detail in an appendix.

Numerologists – I cannot call them statisticians – will be impressed by the further argument that North American income distributions are not lognormal: $P_{50}/P_5 > P_{95}/P_5$. Since there is no reason why any income distribution should be lognormal, I merely report this fact.

VI. Useful empirical ratios

So our data are still very bad indeed. Perhaps, however, there exist empirical constants, as inexplicable as Pareto's, which will at least bolster our confidence in the estimates that conform to them? Like the primacy of per capita data, I owe also this idea to the Russians, and specifically to Rabkina and Rimashevskaya (1972). These few figures only begin the subject in respect of other countries.

The distribution of gross earnings per earner is much more accurately known than that of disposable income per *hh* or per capita. It comes from employers, who keep far better records, and it presents fewer problems of definition. For instance the centile/median ratio (P_{99}/P_{50}) of British earnings is a well-behaved ratio (Wiles (1975, p. 58)), while one hesitates to use P_{95}/P_{50} of disposable income. So, if in the countries with the best information on disposable income the ratios of, say, E_{90}/C_{90} and E_{10}/C_{10} (E = earnings per earner, C = disposable income per capita) are well-behaved, we can perhaps reason towards the C's of a country where they are less firmly based, from the E's of that country. Needless to say

E_i/C_i is the product of a whole waste-paper basket of causes: social legislation, fiscal burden, demographic habits etc. But the idea appears to be worth trying. Table 7.14 gives some results.

Table 7.14. E_i/C_i for certain countries.

	E_{10}	C_{10}	E_{10}/C_{10}	E_{90}	C_{90}	E_{90}/C_{90}
USSR 1958[c], excl. Kolkhozniki	–	–	2.09	–	–	1.85
Ditto 1967[c]	–	–	1.88	–	–	1.63
Austria 1964/5 Schilling p.m.	836[f]	700[d]	1.19	4750[f]	3480[d]	1.36
UK 1968/9, £p.a.	468.4[a]	237.6[b]	1.97	1745.4[a]	807.2[b]	2.16
Poland, state sector 1967, Zloty p.m.	1140[e]	650[i]	1.75	3653[e]	1723[i]	2.12
Canada 1971, $p.a.	3167[g] 500[h]	790[j]	4.01 0.63	c. 13000[g] c. 12500[h]	5568[j]	2.33 2.24
Bulgaria, 1965, levas p.a.	724[l]	331[k]	2.19	1710[l]	1000[k]	1.71

Notes
General: E is always gross of tax, C is always disposable income. C is mostly my own work and its constancy of definition can be guaranteed within reason. But the inclusion of apprentices and part-time workers in E is spotty and unreliable.

[a] Royal Commission (1975), p. 55: men and women over 17 in full or part-time employment throughout the year.
[b] Wiles (1974), p. 46.
[c] Rabkina and Rimashevskaya (1972), p. 215.
[d] Own workings from Der Verbrauch der Städtischen und Bäuerlichen Bevölkerung Oesterreichs, Oe. Stat. Zent. Amt, Vienna, 1966, pp. 14, 32.
[e] R.S., 1968, pp. 528 sqq., p. 548; R.S., 1971, p. 309; R.S. Pracy, 1971, p. 309; Kordas and Stroinska (1971), p. 11. Refers to full-time workers in September, excl. apprentices: see the definitions in R.S. Pracy, 1945–68, p. XXII/4–6.
[f] Dr. Friedrich Levcik, personal letter, July 1976.
[g] Full-time: Statistics Canada, many publications.
[h] All: derived from Love and Wolfson (1976), p. 91.
[i] Wiles and Markowski (1971); omits hh headed by state pensioners.
[j] Statistics Canada, privately communicated; taken from the original data.
[k] Statisticheski Godishnik 1971, p. 407.
[l] Provided by Mr. Paul Wiedemann.

It is clear that work on these ratios has a long way to go before we can be sure of much. We note in particular the usual instability of numbers concerning the poor. At P_{90} I am inclined to accept that (a) ratios should vary between 1.8 and 2.4; (b) E_{90} is by its nature rather accurate. Therefore my Austrian C_{90} is wrong. The Soviet source is good, though it is surprising to see the ratios fall instead of rising. However Bulgaria follows USSR in this as in other matters.

In capitalist countries, where ratios for hh income (H) are far more commonly available than for C, it is also convenient to compare these two concepts, as is done in table 7.15.

Table 7.15. H/C in certain countries.

	H_{10}	C_{10}	H_{10}/C_{10}	H_{90}	C_{90}	H_{90}/C_{90}
UK 1969 £p.a.	485.2[b]	237.6[a]	2.04	2538[b]	807[a]	3.14
USA 1968 $p.a.	1615[d]	794[c]	2.03	14200[d]	5460[c]	2.60
Italy 1969[f] thousand lire p.a.	500	157	3.18	3390	920	3.68
Sweden 1972[e] Kroner p.a.	c. 8598	5152	1.67	c. 44127	18506	2.38

[a] Source as in table 7.17.
[b] Family Expenditure Survey for 1969, p. 80. I have deducted income tax as follows: P_{10} zero, P_{90} 15% (derived from Wiles (1974), pp. 42–5).
[c] Wiles and Markowski (1971), p. 507.
[d] As in Wiles and Markowski (1971), table 8 (calculations available on request). I have deducted 10% for income tax at P_{90}.
[e] Swedish Survey on Relative Income Differences 1972, Central Statistical Bureau, 1974, pp. 22, 35 (our interpolations available on request).
[f] From materials provided by the Banca d'Italia. Note that my previous statement on these ratios (Wiles (1974), p. 3) was simply an error.

Table 7.16 reflects the "cross-migration" between a per-*hh* and a per-capita distribution referred to in section I. Some of the nearly-poorest individuals in the largest *hh* are in the top decile by *hh* income, and some not very-poor individuals in the smallest *hh* are in the bottom one.

Table 7.16. *hh* sizes at certain quantiles.

	C_{10}	C_{90}	H_{10}	H_{90}
USA 1974[a]	3.65	2.19	1.68	3.74
UK 1969[b]	3.45	2.15	2.78	3.85
Austria 1964[c]	3.9	2.1	1.7	3.2
Italy 1969[d]	4.25	2.90	2.9	4.1
Sweden 1972[d]	3.0	1.5	1.4	3.1

Notes:
[a] Tables 7.1 and 7.2 above. Disposable income plus income tax.
[b] Wiles (1974), Lecture II, Tables II and IV.
[c] Own workings as in Table 7.14, note d.
[d] As above. H_{10} and H_{90} are approximate, since they derive from an ordering of *hh* by factor, not disposable, income.

VII. Recommendations for data reporting

In conclusion I feel we are still at the stage of alchemy: we have no solid data. We are better than alchemists only because most of us have the decency to have no theory either! Whenever we want to study an official distribution seriously we are forced into dangerous interpolation. Perhaps, however, the conference could agree to ask that official statistics always include:

(i) Disposable income per *hh*, ranked by *hhs*.
(ii) Disposable income per capita (i.e. *hh* income divided by members), ranked by capita.

(iii) In all serious tables for the distribution of anything, the absolute levels of the upper boundaries of the following quantiles: $P_1, P_2, P_3, P_4, P_5, P_7, P_{10}, P_{20}, P_{25}, P_{30}, P_{40}, P_{50}, P_{60}, P_{70}, P_{75}, P_{80}, P_{90}, P_{95}, P_{96}, P_{97}, P_{98}, P_{99}$ [I choose these quantiles because some are traditional (the quartiles). some are simply deciles which everybody needs, and some are the interesting and important extremes]. Against more detail in terms of quantiles, we could do without tables that compare different years in current prices and use constant nominal brackets.

(iv) The income shares instead of the income upper boundaries of these quantiles would be an acceptable alternative (and interpolation could easily convert one into the other) but for three points:
   a. the upper boundary of P_{50} is the median, upon which much hangs;
   b. the Communist countries have standardised upon the upper boundaries;
   c. belief in the value of *any* quantile's income share depends by logical necessity on belief that we know the total income – which entails that we know the extreme quantiles' income shares. But we do not. The beauty of upper quantile boundaries is their modesty: they do not tell us what we do not know.

(v) There is little harm in demanding also a few "magical formulae": say Gini, Theil and the variance of the logs. Note that these formulae are without exception open to the objection in (iv.c).

We should also demand that the treatment of new *hh* be described at length. This applies even to the British Family Expenditure Survey, which uses last year's income where the head of *hh* is self-employed.

VIII. An international comparison

My *final results*, as far as they go, for all the countries that make me feel in any way confident, are in table 7.17. The main object of this unreliable table, wholly dependent on others' work, is to provoke others into better work, as it expands from publication to publication. Note that the data presentation has been standardised on the practice of Vielrose and Michal in this volume, which is surely better than my previous method. The relation of every other quantile to the median, which itself is given as an absolute number, enables other researchers quickly to derive all the absolute values, and to judge skewness.

References

Cartter, A.M., *The Redistribution of Income in Postwar Britain*. New Haven: Yale University Press, 1955.

Conrad, A.H., "Redistribution through Government Budgets in the United States, 1950", in: A.T. Peacock (ed.), *Income Redistribution and Social Policy*, London, 1954.

Kordas, J. and Z. Stroinska, *Statystyczne Metody Analizy Rozkladu Plac i Dochodów Ludnosci*. Warsaw, 1971.

Our shaky data base

Table 7.17. Our grand results (per capita income).[i]

		U.K.[m]		Italy[g]	Hungary		Poland[d]	Czecho-slovakia[d]	Bulgaria[f,e]	USSR[b,e]		Sweden		Canada[k]	USA[a]		FRG[o]
		1953–4	1969	1969	1967[h]	1972[n]	1971	1965	1965	1958	1967	1967[c]	1971[j]	1971	1950	1974	1969
P_{95}/P_{50}	%	251.1	251.4	331	?201	?206.5	na	190	174.5	na	na	231.1	226.0	300.0	315.6	289.8	2.66
P_{90}/P_{50}	%	194.5	204.4	234	171.5	173.3	167	167	152.2	190.6	179.4	197.0	182.5	226.7	200.0	229.4	2.09
P_{75}/P_{50}	%	143.2	149.2	154.7	134.2	140.8	130	133	127.1	137.5	128.3	148.1	138.1	153.7	160.0	153.0	1.46
P_{25}/P_{50}	%	73.3	71.2	61.5	75.3	76.7	74	72	77.6	68.1	76.6	71.7	74.5	64.8	58.0	63.5	0.712
P_{10}/P_{50}	%	52.9	52.0	39.9	57.3	57.0	58	53	58.0	46.7	57.7	53.7	51.0	38.4	28.1	36.7	0.545
P_{5}/P_{50}	%	43.5	42.5	29.5	?50	?48.4	51	42	47.8	na	na	35.8	25.3	?25.0	?15.7	?23.9	0.470
P_{50} in local money		3.29	9.05	394,000	1080	1403	18700	8400	624	39.2	56.3	7140	10131	2002	826	3311	5464.60
(period)		(week)	(week)	(year)	(month)	(month)	(year)	(year)	(year)	(month)		(year)		(year)	(year)		(year)

[a] From the P-60 series for the relevant years, i.e. tables 7.2 and 7.10 above. The rates of federal and state income taxes combined are put thus: P_{95} 11.0%, P_{90} 9.8%, P_{75} 8.5%, P_{50} 6.6%, P_{25} 3.1%, P_{10} 1.5%, P_{5} 0% (for 1966). Cf. Pechman and Okner (1976, table 4-7). These rates are for tax units, not individuals. I have made no correction for the "rule of zero".

[b] Macauley (1977) excludes *hh* headed by pensioners and students, and state and collective farmers.

[c] By courtesy of Dr. Roland Spånt, Stockholm University. Taken directly from the basic data in Söderstrom (1971).

[d] Michal in this volume, tables 8.3 and 8.5.

[e] Deducting 5% arbitrarily to allow for the income tax on P_{95} and P_{90}, 2% on P_{75}. For the probable actual impact of Polish income tax cf. Wiles and Markowski (1971), pp. 361, 364. Communist figures always treat the income-tax as an expenditure out of income.

[f] Statisticheski Godishnik, 1973.

[g] From data supplied by the Banca d'Italia. Omits auto-consumption, interest and dividends. Consists mainly of employment and social service incomes net of such income tax as is deducted at source. Calculations available on request.

[h] Statistical Yearbook 1968, p. 326; Matyás Timár in: Népszabadság, 19 Dec. 1970: private information on "grey" incomes (which are here included alone among all countries). Hungary has the smallest of all Communist incomes taxes, so I have deducted 5% from P_{95} alone, to allow for its impact on private incomes. The reforms were in 1968. They certainly redistributed income: from workers and bureaucrats to managers and peasants. Calculations available on request.

[i] All sources except U.K. omit imputed owner-occupiers' rents. All figures are net of income tax and national insurance unless otherwise stated.

[j] Swedish Survey on Relative Income Differences 1972, p. 22 (Statistiska Centralbyrån, 1974), as re-worked by me. The two Swedish estimates are not in continuity with each other. They rely heavily on income-tax data, though there was in each case a survey and interviews.

[k] Privately communicated by Statistics Canada. I have made no correction for the "rule of zero".

[m] Wiles (1974), Lecture II: from Family Expenditure Surveys of relevant years.

[n] No allowance this time for black income, though it must have been greater. Own calculations (available on request) from A Családi Jövedelmek Szinorala és Szóródása 1972-ben (Központi Statisztikai Hivatal, 1975).

[o] From the Micro Data Files IMDAF which belongs to SPES (Sozialpolitisches Entscheidungs- und Indikatorensystem für die BRD).

Kuznets, S., "Quantitative Aspects of the Economic Growth of Nations", *Economic Development and Cultural Change*, 1963.
Kuznets, S., *Modern Economic Growth*. New Haven, 1966.
Kuznets, S., "Demographic Aspects of the Size Distribution of Income: An Exploratory Essay", *Economic Development and Cultural Change*, 1976.
Love, R. and M.C. Wolfson, *Income Inequality: Statistical Methodology and Canadian Illustrations*. Statistics Canada, 1976.
Lydall, H., *British Incomes and Savings*. Oxford, 1955.
McAuley, A., "The Distribution of Earnings and Incomes in the Soviet Union", *Soviet Studies*, 1977.
Miller, H.P., *Rich Man, Poor Man*. New York, 1964.
Mueller, E. and I.R.K. Sarma, "Pattern of Income Distribution in an Underdeveloped Economy: A Case Study of India: Comment", *American Economic Review*, 1965.
Pechman, J.A. and B.A. Okner, *Who Bears the Tax Burden?*, Washington, 1976.
Rabkina, N. and N.M. Rimashevskaya, *Osnovy Differentsiatsii Zarabotnoi Plati i Dokhodov Naseleniya*. Moscow, 1972.
Royal Commission on the Distribution of Income and Wealth, *Report No. 1*, HMSO, 1975.
Sawyer, M., "Income in OECD Countries", OECD Occasional Studies, Paris, July 1976.
Söderström, L., "Den Svenska Köpkraftsfördelningen 1967", Inrikesdepartamentet (Låginkomst utredningen), Stockholm, 1971.
Wiles, P.J.D., *The Distribution of Income, East and West*. Amsterdam, 1974.
Wiles, P.J.D., "Stalin and British Top Salaries", in: A.B. Atkinson (ed.), *The Personal Distribution of Incomes*. London, 1975.
Wiles, P.J.D. and S. Markowski, "Income Distribution under Communism and Capitalism. Some Facts about Poland, the UK, the USA and the USSR", *Soviet Studies*, 1971.

7 DISCUSSION

PAPER BY PETER WILES

Professor Michal intended to concentrate on table 7.17, containing the inequality coefficients of percapitalised money incomes of households in eleven countries. He agreed with the argument that summary measures of income dispersion, for example the Gini coefficient, do not do justice to complex concepts such as income inequality. However he pointed out that the semi-decile, decile and quartile ratios used in the paper are themselves single number inequality coefficients and therefore suffer from the same shortcomings. Only when all three ratios are used in combination, together with additional income ratios for the extreme top and bottom of the distribution, can the shape of the distributions under study be satisfactorily understood. Professor Wiles provided this information for at least some of the countries under consideration.

Household incomes are percapitalised to compensate for differences in household size. This method of standardisation, used officially in some socialist countries (excluding the GDR), has its advantages. However, as the paper points out, it does not allow for the non-equivalence of household members of different ages and for economies of scale in consumption of large households.

He said that a valiant effort had been made to adjust for the incidence of income tax, and various footnotes indicated the problems of comparability imposed by the available data. For example, UK figures include some non-monetary income such as imputed rent and the Italian figures exclude interest and dividend income.

For the chosen inequality measures and income definitions, Professor Wiles finds that, during the period considered, the USA and Canada had the most unequal distribution, followed by Italy (an example of "Catholic Europe"), Sweden and the UK (examples of "Protestant Europe"), with the socialist countries displaying the lowest inequality of this kind. Of the many problems associated with inter-country comparisons, Professor Michal focused on the inter-regional differentials within countries as being one which might explain some of the differences. Within the US, for example, prices are higher in Alaska than in the South and the cost of living in Alaska is further increased by the additional consumption of fuel, clothing etc., necessary to maintain a comparable standard of living. The disutility of work is also higher in Alaska. All these factors are reflected in higher money earnings. He suggested that inter-regional differences may explain why the largest non-socialist countries, the US and Canada, showed the highest inequality coefficients and why, amongst the socialist countries, the largest one (the USSR), also appears to be more unequal than the smallest country (Bulgaria).

A substantial part of the paper disputes Kuznets' claim that, in the period 1948–1952, inequality of money incomes in the US was not significantly higher than in the UK. He found this critique to be plausible and supported by other recent evidence, for example the OECD study of June 1976 by Sawyer.

His last point concerned the suggestion that Gini ratio is insensitive to movements at the extremes of the income distribution. When adjusting incomes by fixed absolute amounts, the sensitivity of the Gini coefficient depends simply on the frequency of recipients in the income class considered. It is therefore low for the extreme income classes. However, if proportional income adjustments are made, the Gini coefficient becomes very sensitive at the top end of the distribution. In the OECD study mentioned above, Sawyer shows that the Gini ratio is much more sensitive to a one per cent income increase in the top decile than most other summary measures of inequality, such as the Theil index or the variance of logarithms. This will always be the case unless the distribution has an extremely thin upper tail with frequencies close to zero in the highest income classes.

Professor Lecaillon said the paper made an important contribution to accurate inequality comparisons for the US and Western Europe. Whilst he agreed that North American incomes are more unequally distributed than in England or Scandinavia, he did not feel the findings were sufficient to refute Kuznets' theory that a high degree of development was associated with more equality. He supported Professor Michal's suggestion that the size of the countries should be taken into account and wondered if the comparison between the US and Western Europe would change if US income inequality was compared with the whole Common Market area.

Professor Tinbergen agreed with the use of percapitalised income when making social comparisons of inequality but pointed out that the appropriate income concept depends on the problem under consideration. If the problem concerns the determinants of earnings inequality, then the individual earner is the natural choice of unit. He emphasised the need to discover the determinants of high and low incomes, and pointed out that in Holland large families now comprise a much smaller proportion of high income families than, say, thirty years ago. He also suggested that the 1954 figure for inequality in Holland was an underestimate, since the figures were derived from data on *taxable* incomes and many people in earlier years were below the tax limit. The reduction in inequality since 1954 was therefore greater than had been indicated.

Professor Pen pointed out that the reduction in Dutch inequality from 7.33 to 5.73 during the period 1956–1967, representing a fall of some twenty-five per cent, substantially underestimated the reduction which would have been observed had the data been constructed on a percapitalised basis as Professor Wiles recommends.

Professor Taubman mentioned there was another US data source which he thought preferable for these kinds of comparisons. The Office of Business Economics now supplies estimates of the size distribution of income, and includes food stamp programmes and medicare payments, which were large even in 1971. As he recalled the figures, the share of the bottom twenty per cent is increased by about one-fifth and the share of the top twenty per cent falls by about five per cent.

It is also true in the US, that problems of comparability over time arise from changes in the age structure and the relationship between earnings and age. Recent studies by Paglin, and Smith and Welch show that in the post-war period a major equalisation trend has been disguised by a shift in the age distribution. Such changes in the age structure may make comparisons between countries more difficult. Furthermore, inequality calculations based on households are affected by changes in the structure of the households over time. Nowadays a much larger proportion of the elderly live on their own and a higher proportion of children live away from their parents. Both of these groups tend to have small incomes, but nevertheless choose to live away from the main family and therefore are presumably better off.

He also pointed out that the data available rarely include fringe benefits. In the US there has been a trend amongst the top businessmen to take income in a tax-preferred form. A study by Lewellyn suggested that in 1963 roughly half the income of the top executives in large companies fell into this category and that, had all their income been taxable, they would have required something around ten times their current income to be equally well off. Finally, while he tended to agree with Professor Wiles on the magnitude of the incentive effects, evidence suggests that the labour supply of women is fairly elastic.

Professor Krupp thought that international comparisons should be treated with caution until the conceptual problems within countries had been solved. Just considering changes in the population base – for example, deciding whether to include migrant workers, or whether to treat unrelated individuals living with a family as part of the household – may be sufficient to produce the range of values found over different countries.

Dr. Wagner said that the 1964–65 household survey data was perhaps the worst data on income distribution available for Austria. He believed that more reliable estimates for Austria would have significantly changed its position relative to other countries.

Professor Adelman wondered whether the exclusion of the non-socialist sector in the USSR may have affected the relationship between development and inequality. It was her belief that the non-socialist sector was decreasing in importance over time and the fact that this was not reflected in the data may have had some effect.

Professor Bentzel said the international comparison of inequality reminded him of another conference in which a similar table had been produced. The German representative thought the table enormously interesting but pointed out that the German figures were incorrect. The English representative also thought the figures interesting, apart from the data for England which were wrong. Similar remarks were made by all the participants until there was nothing left. The calculations provided by Professor Wiles for Sweden were based on survey data with a small sample and concentrated on low income groups. He did not feel this was a reliable guide to income inequality in Sweden.

Professor Somermeyer disagreed with the suggestion that data collection should precede theorising. If data were collected without some theory in mind, it may have very limited value for practical and analytic purposes. However, he was in agreement with the preference for percapitalised rather than household income.

He also pointed out that if inequality were computed for all individuals, including those who had zero earnings, inequality in the Netherlands would be very high since the labour participation rate of women was less than one third. He felt that the contribution of inter-regional variations to national income inequality may be small, since the contribution of between-group differences to the total variance is often swamped by the within-group differences. Finally he wondered about the effect of religion on income (distribution), particularly with regard to Max Weber's views on the effect of Protestantism on Capitalism.

Mr. Layard pointed out that efficiency problems arise even when labour supply curves are backward bending, since there is still substitution between leisure and goods. He was very much in favour of attempting to standardise income definitions for the purposes of international comparisons and hoped the conference might be able to suggest a universally acceptable definition. He emphasised the importance of imputing values for owner occupied housing and felt it essential that this should be included.

In reply *Professor Wiles* expressed his sympathy for attempts to adjust for regional differences, particularly if the regions contained a significant proportion of the total population. However he doubted, for example, whether the whole northern part of Canada had anything like the statistical weight of Prince Edward Island, which is very poor. He also agreed that climatic differences in consumption requirements made a poor person in a hot climate much better off than a person with similar purchasing power in a cold climate. But he doubted whether the extent of regional variations bore much relation to geographical size. Variations between political regions in Yugoslavia were roughly fourfold, whilst in Italy the corresponding figure was about three and for Canada, the USA and the Soviet Union, roughly two. Regional variations were more likely due to historical circumstances than geographical size. Deflation by inter-regional (i.e. instead of intertemporal) cost of living indices is urgently required, but there is no north-south one for Canada or the USA.

Similar problems to those due to aggregation over regions within a country arise from the inclusion of the non-socialist sector in the Soviet data. Bringing in the Kolkhozniks was like bringing in a poor region. His own attempts to include them produced the startling result of virtually no change in inequality. The reason seems to be the long upper tail of the non-kolkhoznik distribution: for example P_{90} is reduced by a substantial amount when these millions of poor people, who are however not much poorer than the old poor, are added at the other end. Thus if kolkhozniks are 1/3 of the whole population, and all come below P_{80}, the new P_{90} equals the old P_{85}, and that is a considerable drop. But P_{10} hardly moves. There is greater "equality in poverty".

On the connection between growth and income distribution he could only repeat his belief that each country goes through a period of maximum inequality during industrialisation and then falls back, principally because it becomes able to afford a welfare state. He agreed with the point of Professor Taubman regarding food stamps and noted that, even without this additional equalising factor, the reduction in US inequality has been fairly substantial. However he did not feel that the expansion of the number of small young and old households would have a significant impact on the distribution of *per capitalised* household income.

Finally, in reply to Mr. Layard, he said that the efficiency problem is less severe if labour supply is inelastic. He could not accept that the pursuit of more equality could have serious disincentive effects in the face of the obviously very low elasticity of labour supply, except for emigration at the top and unemployment pay at the bottom.

8 SIZE-DISTRIBUTION OF HOUSEHOLD INCOMES AND EARNINGS IN DEVELOPED SOCIALIST COUNTRIES; WITH A PROPOSED MARGINAL-UTILITY-WEIGHTED GINI COEFFICIENT

*JAN M. MICHAL**

I. Introduction

This study inquires into the relative dispersion (inequality) of post-transfer money incomes of households (after some standardization for household size) in Czechoslovakia, the German Democratic Republic, Hungary and Poland, and of individual labour incomes (earnings) in Czechoslovakia, Hungary and Poland.[1] It covers selected years in the nineteen-sixties and seventies. This is a period when, after the dismantling of most physical rationing and after some price reforms, the distribution of money incomes had become economically more meaningful than it was under the rigid administrative planning of the fifties; and the East European Communist Parties and Governments displayed much interest, not only in the distribution of income among broad social classes, but also in the size-distribution (personal distribution) of incomes.

Like all empirical studies of income dispersion, this one faces four basic methodological problems: a meaningful construct of inequality coefficients, and appropriate definitions of income, the recipient unit, and the period over which income is accounted. The applied methodology is discussed in section II; the construction of a hitherto unpublished marginal-utility-weighted Gini coefficient, which I shall use as one of my measures of income dispersion, is presented in Appendix A.

The observed inequality coefficients and other statistical results will be found in section III; the discussion of some peculiarities of the underlying East European raw data has been relegated to Appendix B.

Dispersion of socialist incomes is largely the result of strong normative elements. It would, therefore, be difficult to set up a formal model explaining socialist income distributions in a deterministic way. Furthermore, the available statistics are seldom disaggregated by age and sex of income recipients, and almost never by fairly homogeneous occupational groups, the level of educational achievement,

---

* I gratefully acknowledge Professor Ronald Britto's contribution on the construction of the modified Gini coefficient. Mr. Fenwick Yu provided valuable computational assistance. Any errors in this paper are my responsibility.

[1] Statistics of the size-distribution of earnings are not available in the statistical yearbooks of the German Democratic Republic.

the age, the area of residence, and other important characteristics of recipients, whose interrelationships affects the observed inequality of incomes. An explanatory model, therefore, could not be statistically tested. In section IV, I shall, however, try to trace informally the main factors which have contributed to what appears, in historical perspective, to be a significant equalization of incomes under socialism, and shall outline some recent trends in distributional policies in Eastern Europe.

II. Measures of inequality and other methodological problems

The distributions under study are all positively skewed (with the mean invariably exceeding the median), have a relatively short upper tail, and their overall inequality does not vary dramatically. This is due, *inter alia*, to similarity of economic systems and of the level of economic development, to the small geographic size of the four socialist countries, and the short period covered by this study. Yet, the distributions do display a variety of actual shapes, especially in cross-section comparisons; no single-number coefficient could serve as a fully satisfactory comparative measure of inequality. My first measure is, therefore, a set of ratios of income at selected cumulative frequencies (centiles of recipients to the median, $P_i = y_i/y_{50}$, where y_i is income at the ith cumulative frequency of recipients. The P_i's are related to the median rather than to the mean because of the statistical difficulty of finding the true mean for most distributions.[2]

The more unequal the distribution in the lower half, the more the value of P_i falls below 1 for $i < 50$. The more unequal the distribution in the upper half, the more P_i exceeds 1 for $i > 50$.

The P_i's provide a convenient check of whether the pertinent Lorenz curves intersect within the known part of the distribution. If $P_i^A > P_i^B$ for all $i < 50$, and $P_i^A < P_i^B$ for all $i > 50$, the Lorenz curve A is inside of Lorenz curve B between the lowest and the highest known i.

The P_i's are, of course, partial coefficients of inequality at selected points of the distribution. One would like to generate an overall (aggregate) measure of inequality. Such a summary measure of inequality is the Gini ratio of concentration. It satisfies the six basic criteria for an income inequality index suggested by Champernowne (1974),[3] but has been rightly criticized for not ranking the income distributions according to strictly concave social utility functions (Atkinson, 1970, 1975) and for being insensitive to changes in low incomes. This weakness of the Gini coefficient stems from its failure to allow for the diminishing marginal utility of income, a property immediately apparent from the standard formula:

---

[2] Estimation of the mean is extremely difficult if available distribution statistics use open-ended income classes, and/or broad class intervals. But even when a fine classification of income intervals or actual means in each income class are available in some socialist statistics, the quality of data at the tails is dubious. This not so much because of under-reporting (which may be more typical of capitalist distributional statistics), but because the frequency of recipients in the extreme income classes of some household samples is low.

[3] However, Champernowne's criterion 1 (convenience for computation from statistics in a readily available form) and 6 (range of value from zero to one) are not fully satisfied if the Gini coefficient is computed from grouped income data, or if negative incomes are present.

$$G = \frac{\sum_{j=1}^{n}\sum_{k=1}^{n}|y_j - y_k| f_j f_k}{2n^2 \bar{y}},$$

where y_j is the mean income of the jth income class, f_j the relative frequency of recipients in the jth income class, $\bar{y}$ is the mean income of the population, and n is the number of observations.

If $f_j = f_k$ for all j, k, a given *absolute* difference between incomes y_j and y_k has the same effect on G regardless of whether the pair of incomes y_j, y_k is at the low end, in the middle, or at the top of the distribution. As a consequence, the Gini coefficient is insensitive to changes at the low tail of the distribution which, although high as *proportion* of low incomes, are small relative to the mean; and it is very sensitive even to small *proportional* changes in high incomes.[4]

The relative insensitivity of the Gini coefficient to changes of low incomes can be remedied easily by modifying the standard formula into

$$G_{mu} = \frac{\sum_{j=1}^{n}\sum_{k=1}^{n}|y_k y_k^{\alpha-1} - y_j y_j^{\alpha-1}| f_j f_k}{2n^2 \dfrac{\sum_{j=1}^{n}|y_j y_j^{\alpha-1} f_j|}{\sum_{j=1}^{n} f_j}}$$

where the exponent $\alpha - 1$ is the constant elasticity of marginal utility with respect to income. This marginal-utility-weighted Gini is derived in Appendix A from a simple social utility function (without any claim of separability into individual welfare functions).

Inasmuch as G_{mu} attaches more importance to the position of low income groups, it resembles the Atkinson index. Yet there are noteworthy differences between the two measures. Atkinson (1970, 1975) uses perfect equality of incomes as the benchmark[5] and views his index as a *cardinal* measure of the distance between the level of *social welfare* under a given distribution of incomes and the welfare level which could be achieved with the same total income if incomes were perfectly equally distributed.[6]

The G_{mu} is not intended as a cardinal measure of the distance separating the income distributions under study from a state of perfect equality. Technically, it does take the value 0 if, under *given* definitions of income, recipient unit and accounting period, all incomes are equal. But it should be recognized that a meaningful concept of "perfect equality" of income is elusive: equality of individual (personal) incomes conflicts with equality of household incomes because of the

---

[4] Hence the great sensitivity of the Gini coefficient to errors in estimating the mean in the highest open-ended income class. It has been pointed out that the Gini coefficient is very sensitive to income changes in the middle of the distribution. That does not contradict the above argument.

[5] The Atkinson coefficient is defined as:

$$A = 1 - \left[\sum_{i=1}^{n} \frac{y_i}{\bar{y}}^{1-\varepsilon} f_i\right]^{\frac{1}{1-\varepsilon}}$$

The term in squared brackets is an equality index: if $y_i = \bar{y}$ for all i's, the term takes the value of 1 and A the value of zero, irrespective of the value of the distributional parameter ε.

[6] Atkinson (1975) gives the following example: a value of $A = 0.12$ (equality index in squared brackets $= 0.88$) means that we could reach the same level of social welfare with only 88% of the present total income if incomes were equally distributed.

varying number of earners within households; equality of total household incomes conflicts with equality of incomes per household member because of the varying number of dependents; equality of shorter-period incomes conflicts with equality of life-time incomes because of the varying age profile of incomes and the varying span of earning years between occupations. And even if a consensus were reached on the appropriate definition of the recipient unit and accounting period, equality of undeflated incomes would still conflict with equality of incomes deflated for regional cost-of-living differentials, etc. Part III of this paper will provide some examples of the existence of such conflicts of "equality" in Eastern Europe.

The G_{mu} should, therefore, be viewed only as an *ordinal* measure of income inequality.[7] And for reasons explained in Appendix A, it is being used in this study only as a *descriptive* measure, with no implications for social welfare.

The distributional parameters of G_{mu} and the Atkinson measure are also different. Whereas Atkinson's ε ("inequality aversion") is a pure value judgment, $\alpha - 1$ (the rate at which the marginal utility of income falls with rising income) can be based, hopefully with a degree of "paternalistic" objectivity, on empirical studies of social utility functions. For example, in the United States, Fellner (1967), Powell and Hoa (1968) and Mera (1969) arrived independently at an estimate of the constant elasticity of social utility with respect to income, $\alpha - 1 = -1.5$, implying the value $\alpha = -0.5$.

Unfortunately, no similar estimates are available for the countries studied here. On the one hand, one can argue that the marginal utility of socialist income declines faster with rising income, as high incomes probably do not provide the recipient unit with more political power, better social standing, a necessary hedge against costly illness, a source of funding better education for their children, etc., to the extent they probably do in some capitalist countries. On the other hand, socialist price structures must also be considered. The governments in the countries studied here tend to subsidize the prices of what they consider to be necessities, and impose very heavy excise ("turnover") taxes on what they consider to be luxuries. Consumer expenditure tends to decrease as a proportion of rising income only up to the brackets near the highest income, then it increases, and occasionally falls again in the very highest income class, as shown by the following example:

Net annual income per household member in Poland, 1973, in Zlotys	up to 9600	9601–12000	12001–15000	15001–18000	18001–24000	24001–30000	30001–36000	Over 36000
Expenditures per household member (percentage of net income)								
All consumer expenditure	94.2	94.3	93.7	93.6	93.6	94.0	92.7	92.1
Purchases of consumer goods and services	90.7	89.5	87.5	85.7	83.9	82.4	79.4	74.5

Source: *Rocznik Statystyczny*, 1974, p. 151.

---

[7] In contrast to "perfect equality," "complete inequality" does not depend heavily on the choice of definitions of recipient unit and income. It can be conceptualized as a situation when one single recipient (and thus one single composite unit of recipients) receives all (undeflated and deflated) income.

Socialist countries

An even more pronounced increase in the propensity to consume near the highest income emerges from the Czechoslovak data in table 8.2.

One could argue that the marginal utility of consumer expenditure (and thus of current income which, under socialism, is the main source of funding consumer expenditure) does not fall monotonically with rising income; if so, another form of utility function is called for in socialist economies.

In the absence of available empirical studies, I have assumed a constant elasticity of utility with respect to socialist incomes, with $\alpha = -0.5$. However, in Appendix A examples are given of G_{mu} coefficients assuming a faster falling and a more slowly falling marginal utility of income, with different (negative and positive) α values.

It is worth mentioning that G_{mu} gives a more satisfactory ranking of distributions when their Lorenz curves intersect. This is illustrated by Figures 8.1 and 8.2 below:

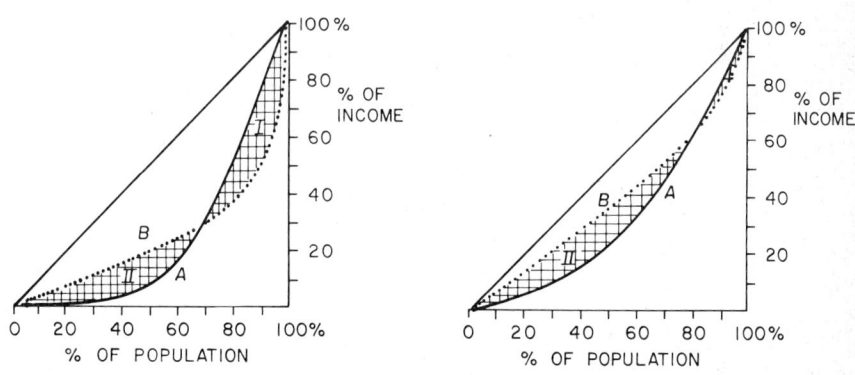

Figure 8.1   Figure 8.2

The solid Lorenz curve A indicates widespread "relative poverty" with relatively unimportant "super incomes" whereas the opposite is true for distribution B (dotted Lorenz curve). Yet the standard Gini coefficient will have the same numerical value for both distributions, since the shaded area I equals the shaded area II in figure 8.1. If we allow for the falling marginal utility of income in figure 8.2 (assuming $\alpha = -0.5$), area II becomes larger relative to area I, showing that G_{mu} regards distributions A as more unequal than distribution B.

The answer to other basic methodological questions – definitions of income, recipient unit and accounting period – are necessarily given by the nature of available official statistics. There are two main sources of data on socialist income dispersion:

(a) Frequency of households by "*net*" *annual money income per household member* in Czechoslovakia, Hungary, and Poland, and frequency of households by net *monthly* money income *per household* in the German Democratic Republic. Information on the dispersion of personal incomes in kind, and of the rather important social benefits in kind, is scarce; however, inequality coefficients have been adjusted for such non-monetary incomes when data are available.

(b) Frequency of *civilian full-time* wage and salary earners by *monthly earnings* in the socialized sector in Czechoslovakia, Hungary and Poland.

III. Observed size-distributions

III.1. *Distribution of household incomes after transfers*

Table 8.1 shows the composition of what is called, in East European statistics, "net money income" (or "net revenue")[8] of households; within the limits of data availability, the structure of income is given for the whole household population and is also broken down by the main socio-economic groups of households and by extreme classes of income per household member. Incomes from employment (wages, salaries and other cash compensation) appear to be the most important income source (except in agricultural and pensioner households), followed by cash transfers (social benefits in cash) and incomes from agriculture. Income from other sources, e.g. from limited non-agricultural private enterprise, interest earned on savings deposits, winnings in the State lottery, etc., is rather unimportant, especially in Czechoslovakia in recent years. The high proportion of transfers in the lowest income class of all households indicates not only the progressive nature of transfers, but also the high concentration of pensioner households in that income class.

The definition of "net income" or "net revenue", as given in official statistical yearbooks, is not very detailed, and differs slightly between countries and between years. A sharp distinction between income and loans granted by the Government (State banks) is not possible, as repayment of some loans is frequently waived (e.g. family loans when children are born). The dividing line between direct taxes and some other household payments to the State agencies is also vague.

"Net income" depends on the method of balancing gross money revenue of households (including "income" shown in table 8.1; all loans received; and savings withdrawals) against gross money expenditure (including consumer spending on goods and services; "payments" such as direct taxes, duties and fees; repayment of loans; other "expenditures", like the down-payment on cooperative housing, cars to be delivered at some future date; and gross saving deposits). The only published statistics I could find of gross revenue and gross expenditure items, with a sufficiently fine classification of income, are those for Czechoslovakia. I used them to compute "net money revenue" and "disposable money income" for wage earners' households in table 8.2. But my estimate of "net revenue" in some instances slightly exceeds the corresponding "net income" upper class limit, and my estimate of "disposable income" occasionally falls below the corresponding lower class limit of "net income".

Table 8.2 also provides my estimates of propensities to consume and save by income classes; these may be of interest as they bear upon the shape of socialist utility functions. Consumption in kind (not to be confused with social benefits in kind, as described below) is also given. Finally, table 8.2 shows that the average number of dependent children falls monotonically from 4.14 in the lowest income class to 0.3 in the highest. Low income per household member appears to be

---

[8] The Czech term "příjmy" and the Polish term "przychody", can be translated either as "revenue" or "income".

closely related to a high number of children per household, despite transfer payments which are even greater in Czechoslovakia than in other East European countries, as indicated in table 8.1.

Czechoslovak, Hungarian and Polish distributional statistics rank households according to income per household member. This has some merits; for instance, in contrast to personal income distribution, the distribution of percapitalized household incomes allows for zero incomes (of dependents). But it does not allow for differences in consumption by people of different ages and for economies of scale within households. The need for a more sophisticated standardization of household incomes has been recognized explicitly in recent Polish statistical yearbooks; they indicate the average number of "consumer units" within households, e.g. in 1974:

Upper class limit of income per household member in 1000 Zlotys:	12	15	18	24	30	36	Over 36
Average number of members per household	4.34	3.75	3.62	3.45	3.14	2.83	2.31
Average number of consumer units per household	3.39	2.99	2.95	2.84	2.64	2.42	2.02

If the number of consumer units varies less between low and high income classes than the number of household members, the inequality of income per consumer unit is smaller than the inequality of income per capita. Other East European statistics do not provide systematic data on the income distribution among standardized consumer units, and the inequality coefficients in this study refer, therefore, to the distribution of household incomes per capita, without adjustment for the non-equivalence of household members.

Furthermore, most inequality coefficients in this study disregard the distribution of social benefits *in kind*, such as medical treatment, medicines, cultural services, and other goods and services received by households without payment, or at a heavily subsidized price. Estimated from official macroeconomic data, these transfers in kind amounted in Czechoslovakia to 12% of personal money income of the whole population in 1965, and 14.1% in 1975; in Hungary, they were 14.0% in 1965 and 14.5% in 1974. In the GDR, according to budget statistics for households of wage and salary earners, such transfers were 22.2% of net money incomes in August 1965, 30.4% in August 1975. In Poland, benefits in kind increased from 12.3% of paid-for *consumption* of the whole population in 1970 to 13.1% in 1973.[9] It is extremely difficult to allocate these transfers in kind among households by classes of money incomes. Yet, Ferge (1975) did so for Hungarian incomes per household member in 1967; I used her estimates to examine the effect of transfers in kind on the Hungarian inequality coefficients.

[9] Estimated from data in *Statistická ročenka ČSSR 1975*, pp. 484, 487. *Statistical Yearbook* (English-Russian edition) 1974, Budapest, 1976, p. 359; *Statistisches Jahrbuch 1975 der DDR*, p. 318; *Concise Statistical Yearbook of Poland*, 1974, p. 65.

Table 8.1. Structure of "net money income" of households by socio-economic groups.
A – average of all households; L – households in the lowest available income class; H – households in the highest available income class.

Czechoslovakia (income per household member)

		All households 1965						Households of																		All households 1973		
								Wage earners 1965				Salary earners 1965				Cooperative farmers 1965				Pensioners 1965								
		A	L	H				A	L	H		A	L	H		A	L	H		A	L	H				A	L	H
Kčs		8467	<2400	24000+				8479	<2400	24000+		10013	<2400	24000+		8118	<2400	24000+		6993	<2400	24000+				13705	<7500	21000+

As a percentage of total income

	A	L	H				A	L	H		A	L	H		A	L	H		A	L	H				A	L	H
Employment (wages, salaries, etc.)	70.3	6.7	68.1				84.5	61.6	85.3		88.0	69.4	86.6		17.4	...	5.2		25.3	0.5	42.6				68.0	27.1	75.7
Agriculture	8.2	23.9	11.8				0.6	1.2	0		0.2	0.2	0		68.0	66.5	92.5		5.3	5.0	0				7.8	3.9	11.5
Transfers	19.7	59.5	8.0				13.8	34.4	10.5		10.8	28.1	6.5		13.4	31.2	2.2		67.0	92.2	45.9				22.2	62.4	11.0
Other	1.8	9.9	12.1				1.1	3.1	4.1		1.1	2.3	6.8		1.2	2.0	0.1		2.4	2.3	11.5				2.0	6.6	1.8

Poland (income per household member)

	All households 1971			Households of												Wage and salary earners 1974		
				Wage and salary earners 1974			Worker-peasants[1] 1974			Peasants[2] 1974			Pensioners 1974					
	A	L	H	A	L	H	A	L	H	A	L	H	A	L	H		A	L	H
Zlotys	18292	<9600	30000+	22771	<12000	36000+	18136	<12000	24000+	18758	<12000	36000+	17661	<12000	36000+		22771	<12000	36000+

As a percentage of total income

	A	L	H	A	L	H	A	L	H	A	L	H	A	L	H
Employment	87.6	74.1	92.2	90.1	70.7	43.8	54.8	58.4		4.7	8.7	1.4	11.7	6.2	19.6
Transfers	8.7	15.8	5.2	4.6	16.7	3.0	6.6	11.2		3.9	6.3	0.9	76.8	73.3	62.8
Agriculture	3.7	10.0	2.6	5.3	12.6	51.2	36.8	25.1		88.9	75.3	96.5	11.5	20.4	17.5
Other						2.0	1.6	5.3		2.4	9.7	1.1			

Socialist countries

Hungary (income per household member)

	Households of		
	Wage earners 1968	Salary earners 1968	Peasants and worker-peasants 1968
	A	A	A
Forints	13332	18284	11163
As a percentage of total income			
Employment	78.6	80.2	0.4
Transfers	9.2	7.9	8.5
All other income	12.2	11.9	91.1

German Democratic Republic (income per household)

	Households of wage and salary earners	
	1960	1974
	A	A
Marks	843	1253
As a percentage of total income		
Employment	94.9	90.3
Transfers	4.6	7.7
All other income	0.5	2.0

General note:

The definition of "net income" varies between countries and between time periods; inter-temporal and inter-country comparisons should be made with caution.
The socio-economic group of each household is determined by the main occupation of the household head.
Transfers include all social benefits in cash such as sickness, maternity and old age payments, child allowances, etc.
[1] In Polish: Gospodarstwa robotniczo-chłopskie.
[2] In Polish: Gospodarstwa chłopskie (small private farms).
The percentage distribution of income by source has been estimated from incomes reported in the following sources:
    Statistická ročenka ČSSR, 1967, pp. 461–463; 1975, p. 478.
    Rocznik statystyczny 1973, p. 554; 1975, p. 94.
    Statistical yearbook (English-Russian edition of the Hungarian statistical yearbook) 1968, Budapest, 1970.
    Statistisches Jahrbuch 1975 der Deutschen Demokratischen Republik, p. 317.

Table 8.2. Gross revenue, direct tax payments, net revenue, disposable income, consumption expenditure, saving, consumption in kind and some demographic characteristics of households of wage earners in Czechoslovakia, 1968, by net revenue classes.
Unless stated otherwise, all figures are in Czechoslovak koruny per household member.

Figures in brackets refer to lines; e.g. (1–2), reads line 1 minus line 2	Average	"Net revenue" class intervals											
		Up to 4800	4801–6000	6001–7200	7201–8400	8401–9600	9601–10800	10801–12000	12001–13200	13201–14400	14401–14500	15601–16800	16801 & over
1. Gross money revenue	13061	4847	6260	7944	9297	10980	12475	14263	16008	18407	19805	20157	25364
2. All direct taxes & duties	1354	209	407	563	770	1019	1253	1456	1806	2169	2525	2528	3390
3. Net cash revenue (1–2)	11707	4638	5853	7381	8527	9961	11222	12807	14202	16238	17280	17629	21978
4. Tax and duty payments as % of gross money revenue (2 as % of 1)	10.4	4.3	6.5	7.1	8.3	9.3	10.0	10.2	11.3	11.8	12.7	12.5	13.4
5. Savings withdrawals	914	178	248	495	460	682	740	1037	1169	1809	1263	1771	2550
6. Loans received and returned down-payments	403	0	72	234	282	292	348	501	576	764	547	975	638
7. "Disposable cash income" (3–5–6)	10390	4460	5533	6652	7785	8987	10134	11269	12457	13665	15470	14883	18790
8. Consumer expenditure	9771	4319	5150	6360	7363	8478	9379	10688	11726	13323	14296	14144	17748
9. Consumer expenditure as % of net revenue (8 as % of 3)	83.5	93.1	88.0	86.2	86.3	85.1	83.6	83.5	82.6	82.0	82.7	80.2	80.8
10. Consumer expenditure as % of "disposable income" (8 as % of 7)	94.0	96.8	93.1	95.6	94.6	94.3	82.7	94.8	94.1	97.5	92.4	95.0	94.5

Socialist countries

11. Savings deposits, gross	1001	206	303	476	541	759	950	1087	1372	1458	1665	1416	2770
12. Deposits net of withdrawals (11–5)	87	28	55	19	81	77	210	50	203	−351	402	−355	220
13. Net savings deposits as % of net revenue (12 as % of 3)	0.74	0.60	0.94	0.26	0.95	0.77	1.87	0.39	1.43	−2.16	2.33	2.01	1.00
14. Net savings deposits as % of "disposable income" (12 as % of 7)	0.84	0.63	0.99	0.29	1.04	0.86	2.07	0.44	1.63	−2.57	2.60	−2.39	1.17
15. Consumption in kind	377	0	492	422	294	378	362	348	392	289	540	362	417
16. Net total revenue (in cash and in kind, 3 + 15)	12084	4638	6345	7803	8821	10339	11584	13155	14594	16527	17820	17991	22395
17. Sample size (no. of households)	1305	5	35	91	168	189	203	149	150	79	69	46	121
18. Average number of household numbers	3.71	6.40	5.73	4.87	4.56	4.19	3.91	3.57	3.14	2.99	2.61	2.55	2.28
19. Average number of dependent children	1.51	4.14	3.41	2.66	2.34	2.01	1.62	1.32	0.99	0.80	0.57	0.23	0.26

Note: Consumption expenditure and net saving do not add up exactly to "net disposable income" because of (very small) inter-household loans and transfers not recorded in this table. Loans received (from state banks) include small amounts of down-payments returned by State trading organizations. Consumption in kind (such as fuel, food, service apartments, etc., provided by employing firms) does not include social benefits in kind (such as free medical services).

Source: Ceskoslovenská Statistika, Skupina B, Statistika životní úrovně domácností, 2. díl, 1. část, *Příjmy, vydání, spotřeba* – Stálý soubor v letech 1966, 1967 a 1968. Prague, 1970. Cena Kčs 25.05.

In addition to the data for households of wage earners, this source also provides data for households of salary earners and for households of members of agricultural cooperatives. They are available from this author on request.

Needless to say, illegal incomes (from the black-market, unauthorized moonlighting, etc.) are not captured by official distributional statistics and by the inequality coefficients in this study. Their effect is probably not greater than the effect of unreported capital incomes in capitalist countries.

Inequality coefficients of percapitalized household incomes in Czechoslovakia, Hungary, and Poland may be found in tables 8.3 to 8.5 respectively. They should not be confused with inequality of incomes per household member (which may be obtained by applying estimated frequencies of household *members* (rather than frequencies of households) to class means of income per household member; the difference between $G_{mu}(G)$ for percapitalized household incomes and $G_{mu}(G)$ for incomes per household member is not very great,[10] but the overall means of percapitalized household income exceed the means of income per household member, as explained in Appendix B.

The shapes of the distributions of percapitalized household incomes in Czechoslovakia, Poland and Hungary are fairly similar: incomes at the 10th centile range from 50 to 60 per cent of the median, incomes at the 90th centile range from 163 to 181 percent of the median. But the time trend differs between countries: in Czechoslovakia, inequality was reduced between 1965 and 1970 as well as between 1970 and 1973, while in Poland, inequality increased between 1971 and 1973. In Hungary, after some equalization between 1962 and 1967, the G_{mu} coefficient increased slightly from 1967 to 1969 (the last year for which income distribution data are available), while the standard Gini coefficient remained practically unchanged.[11]

Some distribution coefficients are also available disaggregated by socio-economic groups. For the households of collective farmers and pensioners in Czechoslovakia in 1965, the average money income per household member was lower, and the inequality of percapitalized household incomes was greater than for households of wage and salary earners. Since 1965, the lowest pensions have been increased substantially, reducing somewhat the dispersion of percapitalized incomes in pensioner households, and bringing the mean closer to the mean income of other groups. This helps to explain why the inequality of percapitalized income of the whole household population in Czechoslovakia has fallen, in spite of the increasing proportion of pensioner households. Incomes of members of

---

[10] For instance, the $G_{mu}(G)$ coefficients for the Polish household groups in 1975 are as follows:

	Wage and salary earners	Households of workers-peasants	Peasants	Pensioners
Percapitalized household incomes	0.104 (0.204)	0.116 (0.233)	0.128 (0.265)	0.088 (0.187)
Incomes per household member	0.103 (0.203)	0.113 (0.231)	0.131 (0.285)	0.089 (0.188)

[11] The time trend refers to the distribution of undeflated incomes. It is being recognized that the cost of living does not move in a parallel way for all income classes and all socio-economic groups of households. Statisticians in some socialist countries have disaggregated the cost of living indices accordingly (see, e.g., J. Mach, "Revize indexu životních nákladů", *Statistika* 11/12, 1969, p. 516), but disaggregated indices have not been published regularly.

Table 8.3. Distribution of net annual percapitalized income of households in Czechoslovakia.

	All households			Wage earners	Salary earners	Members of agricultural cooperatives	Pensioners
	1965	1970	1973	1965	1965	1965	1965
P_5	0.42	(0.42)	(0.48)	0.50	0.55	0.46	0.39
P_{10}	0.53	0.53	0.56	0.59	0.63	0.60	0.52
P_{25}	0.72	0.74	0.72	0.76	0.80	0.75	0.73
P_{75}	1.33	1.32	1.33	1.30	1.14	1.32	1.37
P_{90}	1.67	1.68	(1.67)	1.63	1.56	1.70	1.73
P_{95}	1.90	(1.98)	....	1.81	1.75	1.91	2.02
P_{98}	2.19	....	....	2.06	2.00	2.22	2.32
Median (estimated) in Kčs	8,400	11,850	13,280	8,810	10,045	8,090	6,245
G	0.240	0.236	0.207	0.212	0.194	0.232	0.249
$G_{mu}(\alpha = -0.5)$	0.134	0.126	0.107	0.109	0.098	0.123	0.135
Inequality index (1965 = 100)							
G	100	98.4	86.4	–	–	–	–
G_{mu}	100	93.7	79.7	–	–	–	–
Mean (estimated) in Kčs	8873	12666	13706	9348	10855	8720	6804
Mean (reported) in Kčs	8467[1]	12231[1]	13705	8479[1]	10013[1]	8118[1]	6993[1]
Number of classes	20	13	13	20	20	20	20
Sample size (number of households)	39275	(very large, from micro-census)		15039	8563	3189	9911

General note and explanation of signs:
 ... Raw data not available, or not sufficiently detailed.
( ) Estimate subject to large computational error.
Estimates of the median obtained by intrapolating nearest available points on the graduation curve.
Number of classes is the number of income (net revenue) brackets in available official statistics.
[1] Mean income per household member (see Appendix B).
Source: Statistická ročenka CSSR, 1967, pp. 461–3; 1972, p. 474; 1975, p. 478.

agricultural collectives have also increased faster than the average of all household incomes; if incomes in kind are included, by 1968 they had even surpassed average income per household member in wage earners' households (Michal (1973, p. 421)).

In Poland (table 8.5) percapitalized money· incomes of (non-collectivized) peasant households has remained, on the average, lower and more dispersed than income in households of wage and salary earners. Incomes per household member

Table 8.4. Distribution of net monthly percapitalized income of households in Hungary.

	Money incomes (after social benefits in cash)			Incomes including social benefits in cash and imputed social benefits in kind	Incomes excluding all social benefits
	1962	1967	1969	1967	1967
P_5	....	....	....	....	....
P_{10}	....	0.58	0.58	0.58	0.52
P_{25}	....	0.76	0.74	0.78	0.77
P_{75}	1.37	1.31	1.30	1.25	1.37
P_{90}	1.76	1.63	1.64	1.49	1.78
P_{95}	2.11	1.78	1.82	1.70	2.06
Median (estimated) in forints	750	1065	1210	1240	925
G	(0.269)	0.235	0.236	0.211	0.274
$G_{mu}(\alpha = -0.5)$	(0.130)	0.118	0.121	0.102	0.144
	Inequality index (1967 = 100)			Inequality index (column 2 = 100)	
G	(115)	100	100.4	89.8	116.6
G_{mu}	(100)	100	102	86.4	122.0
Mean (estimated) in forints	....	1156	1316	1330	1030
Number of income classes	9	9	9	9	9

Sources: Columns 1 to 3: Eltétö and Lang (1971, p. 216).
Columns 4–5: Estimate on the basis of Ferge (1975), pp. 67, 73.

in pensioner households are, on the average, much lower and less dispersed than incomes in other groups of households.

Turning now to the effect of social benefits *in kind*, we find, from the Hungarian example in table 8.4, that they equalize percapitalized household incomes mainly near the middle of the distribution (they do not increase the P_i's at the low tail and reduce the G_{mu} slightly more than the standard Gini coefficient). Using Ferge's previously cited estimates, I took social benefits *in cash* out of net money incomes, which increased the G_{mu} coefficient by a full 22% and the standard G by 16.6%. The result confirms that the equalizing effect of benefits in cash is greater than the equalizing effect of benefits in kind, especially at the low tail of income distribution.

In the German Democratic Republic, the official distributional statistics are available only for households whose head is a wage or salary earner. They use only one month (August) as the income accounting period, and households rather than household members as the recipient unit, but the household population data are disaggregated into cohorts of households according to the number of household members. The corresponding inequality coefficients can be found in table 8.6. Between 1965 and 1974, the G and G_{mu} coefficients decreased in an almost parallel way (indicating equalization of the income distribution at both tails) except for the largest households of 5 or more members, for which G_{mu} decreased while the

Table 8.5. Distribution of net annual percapitalized household income in Poland.

	Households of wage and salary earners					All households			Worker-peasant households				Peasant households				Households of pensioners		
	1971	1973[2]	1974[2]	1975[2]		1973	1974		1973	1974	1975		1973	1974	1975		1973	1974	1975
P_5	0.51	0.49	...	0.50		...	...		...	...	...		...	...	...		...	...	...
P_{10}	0.58	0.58	0.58	0.57		0.60	...		...	...	...		...	...	...		0.66	...	...
P_{25}	0.74	0.76	0.76	0.75		0.74	0.68		0.77	0.75	0.73		0.69	0.70	0.71		0.80	0.81	0.79
P_{75}	1.30	1.31	1.31	1.27		1.40	1.32		1.35	1.38	1.31		1.42	1.45	1.47		1.28	1.28	1.29
P_{90}	1.67	1.71	...	...		1.81	1.75		1.69	1.74	1.72		2.04	2.01	...		1.61	1.62	1.63
P_{95}	...	...	...	...		2.09	...		2.04	2.00	...		...	...	...		1.86	1.89	1.91
Median (estimated) in Zlotys	18700	20000	22900	25600		17900	20300		15850	17950	20300		15900	17200	18500		14800	16100	17800
G	0.203	0.219	0.210	0.204		0.240	0.238		0.225	0.231	0.233		(0.275)	0.284	0.265		0.181	0.182	0.187
$G_{mu}(\alpha = -0.5)$	0.102	0.110	0.106	0.104		0.117	0.118		0.111	0.113	0.116		(0.127)	0.133	0.128		0.088	0.086	0.088
Inequality index (1st reported year = 100)																			
G	100	(107.9)	(103.4)	(100.4)		118.2	117.2		100	102.7	103.6		100	(103)	(96)		100	100.6	103.3
G_{mu}	100	(107.8)	(103.9)	(102.0)		114.7	115.7		100	101.8	104.5		100	(105)	(101)		100	102.3	100.0
Mean (estimated) in Zlotys	20276	21997	24745	27368		20304	22348		17473	19747	21905		(19023)	20304	21366		16813	18320	20222
Mean[1] (reported) in Zlotys	18292	19950	22271	25128		18476	20697		16142	18136	20151		17277	18758	20721		16024	17661	19450
Number of classes	7	8	7	7		8	7		8	7	7		8	7	7		8	7	7
Sample size (number of households)	3453	5489	5438	5398		9898	9901		1456	1470	1484		1616	1607	1594		1337	1386	1436

General note: See Table 8.3.
[1] Income per household member (see Appendix B).
[2] Not quite comparable with 1971 because of changed data base.

Sources: *Rocznik Statystyczny*, 1973, pp. 553–4; 1975, pp. 93–4; 1976, pp. 88–9.

Table 8.6. Distribution of net incomes per household of wage and salary earners in the German Democratic Republic (August).

	Households of wage and salary earners				1-person households		2-person households		3-person households		4-person households		Households of 2 adults and 2 children		Households of 5 or more persons		Households of 3 children and 2 adults	
	1965	1970	1972	1974	1965	1974	1965	1974	1965	1974	1965	1974	1965	1974	1965	1974	1965	1974
P_5	...	...	...	0.53	...	...	...	...	...	0.67	...	0.62	...	0.64	...	0.61	...	0.65
P_{10}	...	...	(0.51)	0.75	...	...	...	0.60	...	0.79	0.67	0.70	0.68	0.74	0.66	0.70	0.68	0.72
P_{25}	0.73	0.74	0.74	1.22	...	...	...	0.77	0.81	0.98	0.82	0.84	0.82	0.85	0.81	0.84	0.79	0.88
P_{75}	1.24	1.23	1.20	1.47	...	1.17	1.27	1.21	1.18	1.39	1.20	1.19	1.20	1.15	1.23	1.21	1.30	1.17
P_{90}	1.54	1.50	1.46	(1.66)	...	1.54	1.46	1.41	1.41	1.66	1.46	1.40	1.43	1.34	1.50	...	1.38	1.40
P_{95}	1.70	1.69	1.64		...	1.75	1.64	1.55	1.57	1.79	1.66	...	1.58	1.48	1.75	...	1.56	(1.63)
Median (estimated) in marks	824	1012	1118	1236	...	610	755	1110	910	1105	960	1390	900	1330	985	1510	909	1408
G	0.237	0.210	0.200	0.207	...	(0.207)	(0.208)	0.178	0.174	0.158	0.181	0.159	0.166	0.121	0.171	(0.175)	(0.158)	(0.117)
$G_{mu}(\alpha = -0.5)$	0.131	0.112	0.108	0.114	...	(0.172)	(0.107)	0.095	0.096	0.083	0.096	0.081	0.085	0.065	0.092	(0.087)	(0.082)	(0.062)
Inequality index (1963 = 100)																		
G	100	88.8	84.6	87.5	...	...	100	(86.2)	100	90.8	100	87.8	100	72.9	100	(102.3)	100	(74.1)
G_{mu}	100	85.0	82.4	87.0	...	...	100	88.7	100	86.5	100	84.3	100	76.5	100	(95.2)	100	(75.6)
Mean (estimated) in marks	(830)	1034	1126	1254	...	...	(760)	1115	921	1337	995	1446	932	(1310)	1019	(1606)	...	(1420)
Mean (reported) in marks	843	1031	1126	1253	451	655	765	1118	929	1339	1000	1440	...	...	1037	1583	...	...
Number of income classes	9	9	9	9	9	9	9	9	9	9	9	9	9	9	9	9	9	9

* Size of sample: approximately 30,000 households. The inequality index has been calculated from four-digit G_{mu}, and G coefficients.

Source: *Statistisches Jahrbuch 1975 der Deutschen Demokratischen Republik*, pp. 316–317.

Table 8.7. Distribution of full-time civilian earnings in the socialized sector in Czechoslovakia and Poland.

	Czechoslovakia, May					Poland, September				
	1959	1968	1970	1973	1975	1960	1968	1970	1972	1973
P_2	0.48	0.49	0.48	0.49	0.50	....	....	....	....	0.44
P_5	0.55	0.57	0.57	0.56	0.57	(0.50)	(0.44)	....	0.51	0.52
P_{10}	0.63	0.64	0.64	0.64	0.64	0.57	(0.55)	0.59	0.60	0.60
P_{25}	0.78	0.80	0.78	0.79	0.79	0.75	(0.74)	0.76	0.76	0.79
P_{75}	1.25	1.25	1.26	1.26	1.25	1.34	(1.35)	1.30	1.30	1.31
P_{90}	1.52	1.53	1.56	1.56	1.54	1.74	(1.74)	1.67	1.69	1.71
P_{95}	1.81	1.75	1.79	1.77	1.76	2.09	(1.92)	1.99	2.00	2.07
P_{98}	2.10	2.04	2.08	2.11	2.07	2.45	....	2.45	2.47	2.49
Median (estimated) in national currencies	1345	1720	1890	2120	2260	(1550)	(1900)	2085	2375	2710
Mean (estimated) in national currencies	1405	1816	2017	2272	2392	(1570)	(1920)	(2289)	(2650)	3017
G	0.196	0.195	0.199	0.199	0.197	0.197	0.202	0.232	0.226	0.232
$G_{mu}(\alpha = -0.5)$	0.100	0.097	0.099	0.099	0.098	0.098	0.100	0.144	0.110	0.113
Inequality index (first reported year = 100)										
G	100	99.2	101.6	101.3	100.4	100	102.5	117.6	114.8	117.9
$G_{mu}(\alpha = -0.5)$	100	97.1	99.4	99.0	98.2	100	102.5	117.1	112.7	116.1
Number of income classes	13	21	21	21	21	10	10	10	10	10

In Czechoslovakia, the reported earnings are *gross of wage tax;* in Poland, they are *net* of payroll taxes. For incidence of taxes in wage earners households in Czechoslovakia (most of which are wage taxes), see Table 8.2.

Definition of "*full-time*" varies from approximately 140 to 180 hours worked per month, depending on country, year, and industry; it is shorter in the mining industry.

The socialist sector (i.e., State sector and cooperative sector combined) employed in Czechoslovakia over 99.8% of all civilian earners throughout the period covered by this table. In Poland, 95.4% in 1960, 96.1% in 1970 and 1973. *Earnings of the armed forces, police, foreign service and some other Government officials, apprentices and prisoners are excluded.*

See Table 8.3 for explanation of signs.

Sources: *Statistická ročenka* CSSR 1967, 1971, 1975.
Rocznik Statystyczny 1975, and previous editions.

standard G increased (indicating an equalization at the low tail accompanied by a disequalization at the high tail of the distribution).

III.2. Distribution of earnings (individual labor incomes)

The official Czechoslovak, Hungarian, and Polish distributional statistics cover only full-time earnings, as specified in tables 8.7 and 8.8. Part-time employment in Eastern Europe is, however, rather limited, typically around 5% of total employ-

Table 8.8. Distribution of full-time civilian earnings in the socialized sector and the State sector in Hungary.

	Socialized sector, September			State sector, September			
	1970	1972	1974	1960	1968	1970	1974
P_2	....	0.44	0.40	....	....	....	0.40
P_5	0.52	0.47	0.46	0.56	0.55	0.50	0.47
P_{10}	0.58	0.54	0.55	0.62	0.61	0.60	0.57
P_{25}	0.74	0.76	0.76	0.77	0.78	0.76	0.77
P_{75}	1.30	1.29	1.26	1.30	1.30	1.31	1.27
P_{90}	1.60	1.62	1.88	1.62	1.61	1.62	1.61
P_{95}	1.84	1.91	1.90	1.88	....	1.97	1.93
P_{98}	2.33	2.46	....	2.08	....	2.34	(2.36)
Median (estimated) in forints	2060	2350	2750	1460	1780	2180	2750
Mean (estimated) in forints	(2200)	2529	(2912)	(1562)	(1909)	(2382)	(2939)
G	0.208	0.221	0.223	0.197	0.202	0.220	0.221
G_{mu}	0.101	0.108	0.112	0.098	0.100	0.106	0.111
Inequality index (first reported year = 100)							
G	100	106.3	107.2	100	102.5	111.7	112.2
G_{mu}	100	106.0	110.9	100	102.0	108.2	113.3
Number of classes	7	7	7	7	7	7	7

For explanation of signs, see table 8.3.
For general note, see table 8.7.
Socialized sector in Hungary employed 98.8% of all wage and salary earners in 1975; the State sector employed 57.5% in 1960, 66.6% in 1968, 67.7% in 1970.

Source: Statisztikai Evkönyv 1975, p. 101, and previous years.

ment.[12] There exists the right, as well as the duty, of adults to work full-time (except for mothers with very young children, sick persons and people of retirement age, generally 60 for men and less for women).

The coefficients of dispersion of full-time earnings in Czechoslovakia and Poland can be found in table 8.7.[13] The Czechoslovak earnings are reported gross of wage tax.[14] Yet they are less dispersed than the Polish earnings after deduction of payroll tax. They are also less dispersed than earnings in Hungary (table 8.8). The different time trend is also interesting. In the socialist sector in Czechoslovakia

---

[12] E.g. in Poland in 1973 there were 10,882,000 full-time earners and only 595,000 part-timers. For definition of "full-time", see table 8.7.

[13] Earnings statistics in Czechoslovakia and Poland, as well as in Hungary, are available only for one calendar month and are not adjusted for seasonal fluctuations. Seasonal fluctuations in employment are relatively small under socialism, but payments of bonuses, etc., do fluctuate.

[14] Marginal wage tax rates in Czechoslovakia are mildly progressive. For a household with 2 dependents, they increase from 4% to 20%. As the incidence depends on household status and other characteristics of earners, available earning statistics cannot generally be adjusted for actual wage-tax payments.

(which is practically the only employer of wage and salary earners), dispersion of earnings did not change significantly between 1959 and 1975. In Hungary and Poland, both tails of the distribution of earnings in the socialist sector have significantly widened (with G and G_{mu} coefficients[15] rising in an almost parallel way).

The main factors contributing to the equalization of socialist earnings, particularly in Czechoslovakia in the 1960s and early 1970s, were a very flat age profile of earnings, and relatively small inter-regional differentials, while significant earnings differentials between sexes and among industries continued to exist (Michal (1973, p. 414)). This seems to be true in the mid-seventies as well.

Estimates of mean and median full-time earnings for men and women, and the corresponding coefficients of dispersion in more recent years, can be found in table 8.9. The mean and median of women's earnings have come slightly closer to those of men, but there is still a sizeable difference. The principle of "equal pay for equal work" is officially applied in Eastern Europe; differences between earnings of men and women apparently originate in the high proportion of women in economic sectors with below average earnings,[16] and in the different occupational pattern of women's employment. It is interesting to note in table 8.9 that women's earnings show less dispersion than those of men (in contrast to the usual pattern in capitalist countries).

Differences in average socialist wages (earnings) between economic sectors in Czechoslovakia and Poland are shown in table 8.10. In Hungary, differences in average earnings by economic sectors are also important, but the Hungarian published data are not quite comparable. If earnings are further disaggregated by individual industries, the difference appears even greater. Variation of average earnings between sectors and industries reflects, *inter alia*, the varying composition of employment by occupational groups, sex and age of earners, within each sector and industry. The available earnings data are not disaggregated enough to allow separation of pure inter-sector differentials from inter-occupational, inter-sex and inter-age differentials.

Inter-occupational differentials in socialist earnings would be of great interest. Unfortunately, official data, published in the 1960s, used only very broad, non-homogeneous occupational categories: "Manual workers," "engineers and technical staff" and "administrative staff" (office workers); and publication of these data has been discontinued in recent years. Inequality coefficients for earnings within these broad occupational categories appeared only slightly lower than the inequality coefficients for all full-time earners (Michal (1971, pp. 24, 56)).

[15] The G_{mu} coefficients for full-time earnings have been computed assuming $\alpha = -0.5$, i.e. the same concavity of the utility functions as for percapitalized net household incomes. Utility of earnings should not be considered outside the context of household incomes, and the very name "marginal-utility-weighted Gini coefficient" is here a misnomer. The G_{mu} coefficients in Tables 8.7 to 8.9 should be viewed simply as Gini coefficients with an (arbitrarily) increased sensitivity to changes of earnings at the low tail of the distributions.

[16] In Czechoslovakia in 1975, the proportion of women in total employment in sectors with the highest average wage (transport and constructions, see Table 8.10) was 24% and 17%, respectively; in sectors with below-average wages (for example, trade & catering, and education & culture) it was 76% and 68%, respectively (*Statistická ročenka CSSR, 1975*, p. 113). A similar pattern of employment of women can be observed in Poland (*Rocznik Statystyczny 1976*, pp. 58, 60).

Table 8.9. Distribution of full-time earnings of men and women in the socialized sector in Czechoslovakia, Hungary and Poland.

	Czecho-slovakia, May 1970		Hungary, Sept. 1974		Poland, September			
					1972		1973	
	M	F	M	F	M	F	M	F
P_2	0.51	....	0.43	0.46	....	....	0.45	....
P_5	0.61	0.64	0.50	0.51	0.55	....	0.55	0.58
P_{10}	0.70	0.72	0.64	0.58	0.63	0.63	0.64	0.66
P_{25}	0.84	0.84	0.82	0.77	0.80	0.80	0.80	0.84
P_{75}	1.21	1.19	1.22	1.22	1.29	1.24	1.24	1.24
P_{90}	1.46	1.43	1.54	1.50	1.68	1.49	1.59	1.47
P_{95}	1.65	1.61	1.76	1.72	1.96	1.67	1.90	1.70
P_{98}	1.98	1.85	....	2.18	2.38	1.99	2.36	2.06
Median (estimated) in national currencies	2227	1495	3200	2200	2725	1935	3180	2200
Mean (estimated) in national currencies	(2345)	1565	(3383)	(2315)	(3050)	(2072)	(3516)	(2349)
G_u	0.1690	0.1578	0.200	0.191	0.213	0.183	0.2157	0.1865
$G_{mu}(\alpha = -0.5)$	0.0842	0.0776	0.101	0.095	0.103	0.097	0.1061	0.0942
Women as % of men:								
Median	100	67.1	100	68.8	100	71.0	100	69.2
Mean	100	(66.7)	100	(68.4)	100	(67.9)	100	(66.8)
G_u	100	93.4	100	95.5	100	85.9	100	86.5
G_{mu}	100	92.2	100	94.1	100	94.2	100	88.8

Earnings in Czechoslovakia are before wage tax.
Other notes and sources: see tables 8.7, 8.8.

Comprehensive earnings data with more disaggregated occupational groups are not available; inter-occupational differentials in earnings, seem to be small, however, especially in Czechoslovakia.[17]

An estimate of differences in lifetime earnings by occupation in the Czechoslovak engineering industry (Tomášek (1967), quoted by Michal (1973, p. 424)) is interesting as an example where equalization of short-period earnings conflicts with equality of life-time earnings. Although not discounted to a common time base, cumulative earnings of a designer (konstruktér) up to the normal retirement age of 60 years appear to be only 88 %, and those of a lawyer only 79 %, of the cumulative earnings

---

[17] An index based on mean earnings of wage earners of all skills below foreman (= 100) by Gerloch (1962) suggests moderate inter-occupational differentials within the same industry, and pronounced inter-industry differentials for most occupational groups, as illustrated below:

	Foreman	Bookkeeper	Manager of a production unit	Technical manager of a large-scale enterprise	Director
Fuel industry	159	67	193	300	343
Chemical industry	139	94	206	174	257
Food processing	129	102	163	136	228

Table 8.10. Average monthly wages by economic sector in the socialist sector in Czechoslovakia and Poland. In national currency units and as % of the average of the whole socialist sector.

	Czechoslovakia, in Korunas (Kčs)						Poland, in Zlotys				
	1960	%	1974	%	1975	%		1960	%	1974	%
Industry	1442	105.6	2257	101.1	2340	100.6	Industry	1708	109.3	3283	103.4
Construction	1521	111.4	2513	112.6	2589	111.3	Construction	1786	114.3	3876	122.0
Agriculture	1113	81.5	2155	96.6	2217	95.3	Agriculture	1267	81.1	2806	88.4
Forestry	1265	92.7	2227	99.8	2322	99.8	Forestry	1125	72.0	2727	85.9
Transport[1]	1475	108.1	2569	115.1	2663	114.4	Transport & communication	1521	97.3	3332	104.9
Communications[1]	1205	88.3	1994	89.3	2035	87.5					
Material procurement	1303	95.5	2137	95.7	2209	94.9	Internal trade	1318	84.3	2711	85.4
Trade & catering	1103	80.8	1912	85.7	1950	83.8	External trade	1884	120.5	3503	110.3
Farm produce procurement	1284	94.1	2119	94.9	2227	95.7					
Transport[2]	1439	105.4	2485	111.3	2586	111.1					
Communications[2]	1205	88.3	1994	89.3	2035	87.5					
Science & research	1545	113.2	2524	113.1	2605	111.9	Science	1846	118.1	3714	116.9
Communal services	1053	77.1	1726	77.3	1779	76.5	Community services & housing	1473	94.2	3010	94.8
Housing	772	56.6	1539	69.0	1600	68.8					
Health & welfare	1183	86.7	2174	97.4	2225	95.6	Health & welfare	1239	79.3	2666	83.9
Education, culture	1293	94.7	2124	95.2	2182	93.8	Education	1376	88.0	2774	87.3
							Cultural services	1447	92.6	2687	84.6
Public administration, justice	1388	101.7	2344	105.0	2446	105.1	Public administration, justice	1458	93.3	3420	107.7
Banking, insurance	1323	96.9	2335	104.6	2404	103.3	Finance, insurance	1471	94.1	2825	88.9
Standard deviation	191	–	276	–	290	–	Standard deviation	234	–	417	–
Overall average	1365	100	2232	100	2327	100	Overall average	1563	100	3176	100

Data exclude apprentices and employees of agriculture cooperatives (they include employees of state farms). Workers with "very small obligation" are excluded in Czechoslovakia. Wages before tax in Czechoslovakia; after payroll tax in Poland. In Poland, average monthly wages of part-time workers have been computed in full-time equivalents.

[1] Within the "material sphere of production".
[2] Within the non-material sphere.

Source: *Statistická Ročenka CSSR* 1976, p. 122; 1971, p. 135.
Concise statistical yearbook of Poland, 1975, p. 54.

of a fitter (who starts to earn in the age-group 16 to 20, whereas lawyers and designers start to earn in the age-group 21 to 25 years).

IV. Some concluding remarks on socialist distributions

In the preceding section, we observed a continued, very narrow dispersion of earnings in Czechoslovakia,[18] and recently increased dispersion of earnings in Poland and Hungary, where a new system of economic management and material incentives is being applied. In historical perspective, the inequality of socialist earnings is generally small. Fully comparable data for the pre-socialist period do not exist, but a rough comparison suggests that in Czechoslovakia between 1947 (the last year of the mixed system) and the 1960s, the standard Gini coefficient for earnings was reduced by approximately one-third (Michal (1971, p. 17)). The advent of socialist systems in other East European countries probably had an even stronger equalizing effect than in traditionally egalitarian Czechoslovakia.

In international comparisons of earnings, dispersion in Eastern Europe also appears to be small (cf. Lydall (1968); he measured inequality of earnings in terms of P_i coefficients).

The narrow dispersion in individual earnings affects the distribution of percapitalized household income in a complex way. In Czechoslovakia in 1965, inequality of individual pre-tax *earnings* was smaller (in terms of the G, G_{mu} and most P_i coefficients) than the inequality of post-tax, post-transfer *incomes* per capita in wage earners' households (see tables 8.3 and 8.7), despite very high social benefits for low income households. Significant equalization of individual earnings conflicts with equality of percapitalized household incomes, as the varying ratio of earners to dependents becomes the dominant factor in the distribution of household income per capita.

Policy pronouncements in Eastern Europe envisage increased dispersion in labor earnings, accompanied by a policy of continued low inequality of standardized household incomes after transfers. If increased earnings dispersion arises mainly from a greater age differential (possibly linked with higher rewards for seniority), this may, indeed, enhance rather than reduce the equalization of percapitalized household incomes.[19]

But the aim of the proposed earnings differentials, especially in Hungary, is to bring individual labor rewards more into line with the general economic performance of workers, as well as with the performance of production units to which they belong. The new method of determining earnings may then tend to disequalize percapitalized household incomes; an attempt to compensate for such disequaliza-

---

[18] Although the "levelling of wages" has been frequently criticized by communist officials and economists in Czechoslovakia as contrary to the principle of rewarding labor according to the "quantity, quality, and social usefulness of work".

[19] If earnings data are disaggregated by industries, the age profile appears to be extremely flat. For example, in Czechoslovakia's construction industry in 1967, earnings in the 31–40 years of age groups were only 1/5 higher than in the age group below 20 (cf. Michal (1971, p. 57)). Increased earnings of age groups normally supporting dependents, relative to earnings of non-supporting age groups, would obviously tend to equalize household incomes per capita.

tion by increased transfers may conflict with the objective of strengthening material incentives to produce (unless individual earners regard their earnings more as a status symbol than as a contribution to the utility of their households).

The delicate balance between the goal of increased material incentives and the goal of low inequality of percapitalized household incomes seems to incline somewhat toward the former. Yet percapitalized (or otherwise standardized) household incomes after transfers in Eastern Europe will probably continue to be quite equally distributed in comparison to the period before the introduction of socialist systems and to contemporary mixed capitalist economies.

Rigorous inter-country comparisons are, however, extremely difficult because of differences in definitions of income and the recipient unit, interlocational cost-of-living differentials, demographic structures, convertibility of money incomes into goods and services, stability of income over time, and so on. A meaningful comparison of income inequality between countries goes much beyond the scope of this study. Regretfully, I must conclude with a caveat that the statistical results of my investigation should not be used for international comparisons without qualification.

Appendix A: Derivation of, and some comments on, a marginal-utility-weighted Gini coefficient of income inequnlity

Assume a non-subjective utility function with constant elasticity of utility with respect to income

$$U_i = \beta y_i^\alpha, \tag{1}$$

and thus marginal utility

$$\frac{dU_i}{dy_i} = \alpha\beta y_i^{\alpha-1}. \tag{2}$$

Weighting income by marginal utility of income in the standard Gini formula, we obtain

$$G_{mu} = \frac{\sum_{j=1}^{n} \sum_{k=1}^{n} |y_k \alpha\beta y_k^{\alpha-1} - y_j \alpha\beta y_j^{\alpha-1}| f_j f_k}{2n^2 \frac{|\sum_{j=1}^{n} y_j \alpha\beta y_j^{\alpha-1} f_j|}{\sum_{j=1}^{n} f_j}} = \frac{\sum_{j=1}^{n} \sum_{k=1}^{n} |y_k y_k^{\alpha-1} - y_j y_j^{\alpha-1}| f_j f_k}{2n^2 \frac{\sum_{j=1}^{n} y_j y_j^{\alpha-1}}{\sum_{j=1}^{n} f_j}}, \tag{3}$$

where y_j is the mean income of the jth income class, f_j is the frequency of recipients in the jth income class, n is the number of observations, and $\alpha - 1$ is the constant elasticity of utility with respect to income.

As β disappears in the final form of (3), the marginal-utility weighted Gini coefficient G_{mu} can be computed if we have just an estimate of the $\alpha - 1$ parameter.

With the form of utility function (1), formula (3) is actually equivalent to the Gini coefficient for the distribution of utility.

$$G_u = \frac{\sum_{j=1}^{n} \sum_{k=1}^{n} |\beta y_k^\alpha - \beta y_j^\alpha| f_j f_k}{2n^2 \frac{\sum_{j=1}^{n} \beta y_j^\alpha f_j}{\sum_{j=1}^{n} f_j}} = \frac{\sum_{j=1}^{n} \sum_{k=1}^{n} |y_k^\alpha - y_j^\alpha| f_j f_k}{2n^2 \frac{\sum_{j=1}^{n} y_j^\alpha f_j}{\sum_{j=1}^{n} f_j}} \quad (4)$$

(4) is equivalent to (3) since $y_j^\alpha = y_j y_j^{\alpha-1}$. However, with another form of utility function, e.g. with $U_j = k + \beta y_j^\alpha$, $G_{mu} \neq G_u$. If $\alpha = 1$, both G_{mu} (3) and G_u (4) collapse into the standard Gini coefficient.

The lower limit of G_{mu} and of G_u, like the lower limit of the standard Gini coefficient, is zero for technical equality when (under given definitions of income, recipient unit and accounting period) $y_k = y_j$ for all k, j, so that the numerator of (3) and (4) is zero, irrespective of the value of α.

Even with $y_k \neq y_j$, the $G_{mu}(G_u)$ still takes the value of zero if $\alpha = 0$, since $y_k y_k^{-1} = y_j y_j^{-1} = y_k^0 = y_j^0 = 1$ and the numerator of (3) and (4) takes the value of zero. This is a case when the distribution of utility is assumed to be totally unresponsive to the distribution of income. A realistic assumption is therefore that $\alpha \neq 0$.

With $\alpha \neq 0$, the upper limit of G_{mu} (like the upper limit of the standard Gini coefficient) is 1 (assuming no negative incomes).

The negative value of alpha, as estimated by Fellner and others and used in this study, means that the utility function is plotted in the fourth quadrant; utility is negative and the utility curve asymptotic to the vertical axis. With a positive α, we plot the utility function in the first quadrant, as a curve going through the origin, and concave to the income axis if $0 < \alpha < 1$. The standard Gini coefficient assumes a utility function that can be drawn as a straight line going through the origin.

A positive or negative α can be used in the $G_{mu}(G_u)$ formula. With a falling *negative* value of α, the $G_{mu}(G_u)$ coefficient attaches increasing weight to inequality at the low tail of the distribution; as α rises closer to zero, $G_{mu}(G_u)$ ranks the distributions in a way more like the standard G. However, the value of $G_{mu}(G_u)$ falls as α rises closer to zero. As long as we use $G_{mu}(G_u)$ only as an ordinal measure, the absolute value of $G_{mu}(G_u)$ is unimportant.

With $0 < \alpha < 1$, the $G_{mu}(G_u)$ coefficient again attaches increasing weight to inequality at the low tail as the value of α falls, and it ranks the distributions in a way more like the standard G as the value of α rises (closer to 1). With a *positive* α, the value of G_{mu} rises with an increasing value of α.

These are some illustrations of $G_{mu}(G_u)$ with different negative and positive α values:

	$\alpha=-0.75$	$\alpha=-0.5$	$\alpha=-0.25$	$\alpha=1$ (Standard Gini)	$\alpha=0.75$	$\alpha=0.50$	$\alpha=0.25$
Czechoslovakia, net annual income per household member:							
1965	0.2046	0.1342	0.0659	0.2400	0.1836	0.1248	0.0636
1973	0.1759	0.1176	0.0588	0.2249	0.1711	0.1154	0.0582
Index, 1965 = 100	86.0	87.6	89.2	93.7	93.2	92.4	91.7

	$\alpha=-0.75$	$\alpha=-0.5$	$\alpha=-0.25$	$\alpha=1$ (Standard Gini)	$\alpha=0.75$	$\alpha=0.50$	$\alpha=0.25$
Hungary, net annual income per household member, 1967							
A. excluding all social benefits	0.2156	0.1441	0.0720	0.2739	0.2085	0.1408	0.0711
B. including all social benefits in cash and in kind	0.1514	0.1019	0.0514	0.2106	0.1575	0.1046	0.0520
Index, A = 100	142.4	141.4	140.0	130.0	132.4	134.6	136.7

Sources of data: as in tables 8.3, 8.4.

In this study, most G_{mu} coefficients move in the same direction as the G coefficients, as the pertinent Lorenz curves do not intersect. This is an example of intersecting Lorenz curves from the United States (based on Bureau of the Census data, *Current Population Reports*, P-60 Series):

	Income per family member		Income per family	
	1968	1972	1968	1972
G	0.311	0.319	0.340	0.351
$G_{mu}(\alpha=-0.5)$	0.242	0.216	0.269	0.252

This example indicates that, between 1968 and 1972, inequality decreased in the lower part (reflected in a falling G_{mu}), but increased in the upper part of the distribution (reflected in a rising G).

The observed G_{mu} values for socialist distributions in this study should not be viewed as G_u equivalents for two basic reasons:
(a) The available data covers only dispersion of money incomes (seldom also incomes in kind). Money incomes have not been deflated for regional differentials in the cost of living. Above all, the available data completely disregard the dispersion of non-income components of social welfare, such as leisure, etc. The available data base is, therefore, not suitable for measuring dispersion of social welfare in a meaningful fashion.
(b) The utility functions in the socialist countries have not been empirically examined. Their form may be different from the constant-elasticity form assumed in (1) so that the equivalence of G_{mu} (3) and G_u (4) may not obtain.

However, with an appropriate data base and an appropriate social utility function, the modified Gini coefficient (G_u) could be used as a suitable measure for the distribution of social welfare. Since α can easily be made a function of the income level or other variables, the concept of G_u is compatible even with individualistic utility functions (as proposed, for example, by van Praag in his contribution to this volume).

Appendix B: Some statistical problems

(1) Official Czechoslovak and Polish household budget statistics report frequencies of households by income per household member, class means, and overall mean income "per 1 person". Weighting the reported class means by the reported frequencies of households in Czechoslovakia in 1973, I obtained an estimate of the overall mean which equals exactly the reported mean income (see table 8.3).

However, analogous estimates of the overall mean income in Poland, and in Czechoslovakia prior to 1973, consistently exceed the reported mean income. This is so because the reported mean "income per 1 person" is the mean income per household member and not the mean percapitalized household income. Mean income per household member can be approximated from the published data by weighting the published income class means by the frequency of households *multiplied* by the reported (rounded) average number of members per household in each income class.

Below is a comparison of the reported and estimated mean incomes per household member with the estimated mean percapitalized household income in Poland, 1975 (in Zlotys):

Households of:	Mean income per household member		Mean percapitalized household income
	Reported	Estimated	
Wage & salary earners	25128	25326	27368
Workers-peasants	20151	20213	21905
Peasants	20721	21030	21366
Pensioners	19450	19687	20222

Data source: *Rocznyk statystyczny 1976*, pp. 88–9. I am grateful to the Polish People's Republic Central Statistical Office for helping me to understand the reported mean "per 1 household member".

(2) The GDR statistics provide the frequencies of households by income per household and the overall mean income per household, but not the class means. I had to estimate these (with the help of Pareto's alpha). Surprisingly, the weighted average of class means comes very closely to the reported mean for the whole household population (see table 8.6).

(3) The Hungarian statistics provide the frequencies of households by income per household member and the overall means, but not the class means. Again, I had to estimate these. Weighting the estimated class means by household frequencies, I obtained the overall mean percapitalized household income of 1156 Forints in 1967, whereas the reported "overall mean" is 1184 Forints.

References

Atkinson, A.B., "On the Measurement of Inequality", *Journal of Economic Theory*, Vol. 2, 1970.
Atkinson, A.B., *The Economics of Inequality*. Clarendon Press, Oxford, 1975.

Champernowne, D.G., "A Comparison of Measures of Inequality for Income Distribution", *Economic Journal*, Vol. 84, 1974.
Concise Statistical Yearbook of Poland. Central Statistical Office, Warszava annual editions.
Eltétö Ö. and Gy. Láng, "Income Level – Income Stratification in Hungary", *Acta Oeconomica*, Vol. 7, 1971.
Fellner, William, "Operational Utility: The Theoretical Background and a Measurement", in: W. Fellner et al., *Ten Economic Studies in the Tradition of Irving Fisher*, New York, 1967.
Ferge, Zs., "Social Policy and Centralized Redistribution", *Acta Oeconomica*, Vol. 15, 1975.
Gerloch, Vladimír, *Mzda a její význam za socialismu*. Prague, 1962.
Lydall, H., *Structure of Earnings*. Clarendon Press, Oxford, 1968.
Mera, Koichi, "Experimental Derivation of Relative Marginal Utilities", *The Quarterly Journal of Economics*, Vol. LXXXII, 1969.
Michal, J.M., "Size Distribution of Incomes Under Socialism in Czechoslovakia", Institute for Advanced Studies, Vienna, Research Memorandum No. 57, 1971.
Michal, J.M., "Distribution of Earnings and Household Incomes in Small Socialist Countries", *Review of Income and Wealth*, December 1973.
Michal, J.M., "An Alternative Approach to Measuring Income Inequality", in Z. Fallenbuchl, ed., *Economic Development in the USSR and Eastern Europe*. Praeger, New York, 1975.
Powell, Alan A. and Tran Van Hoa, "A Multi-sectoral Analysis of Consumer Demand in the Post-War Period", *Southern Economic Journal*, vol. 35, 1968.
Rocznik Statystynczny. Glówny urzad statystyczny, Warszawa, annual editions.
Statistical Yearbook. Hungarian Statistical Office, Budapest, annual edition.
Statistická ročenka CSSR. Federální statistický úrad, Praha, annual editions.
Statistisches Jahrbuch der Deutschen Demokratischen Republik. Staatliche Zentralverwaltung für Statistik, Berlin, annual editions.
Statisztikai Évkönyv. Hungarian Statistical Office, Budapest. Annual.

8 DISCUSSION

PAPER BY JAN M. MICHAL

Professor Vielrose found the G_{mu} coefficient a useful device. He approved of the fact that it was less sensitive to high incomes than the Gini coefficient, but was concerned about the accuracy of the computed values. Ideally the G_{mu} coefficient required information about the incomes of all individual units. With grouped data and open-ended intervals, errors are inevitable and he felt that computation of G_{mu} to three significant figures gave a spurious impression of accuracy. Probably only two digits are significant. If the magnitude of the grouping error is unknown, comparisons of the G_{mu} coefficient between countries and over time should be approached with caution. With a time series of sufficient length it may be possible to distinguish a trend, but if the values of G_{mu} fluctuate, any potential trend must be in doubt.

He remarked that the G_{mu} coefficient is very sensitive to changes in the value of the income elasticity of utility. Thus observed differences in the values of G_{mu} may be due to differences in the pattern of distribution and to differences in income elasticities. To apply the index consistently, different values of the elasticity parameter may be needed for the various population sub-groups, for example educational and professional status categories. Professor Michal uses a standard utility function and so eliminates the first source of differences which make the values of G_{mu} directly comparable.

Referring to the evidence that in Poland and other socialist countries the proportion of income spent on consumption falls with income only up to the brackets near the highest incomes, and then increases, Professor Vielrose said he had tried to repeat the calculations for more homogeneous groups. For example he had taken households of a specific size. In some cases such a disaggregation eliminated this increase at high income levels. Finally, he agreed that the evidence suggesting increasing income dispersion in Poland was correct, but did not believe that this was a long term trend. It may have arisen from a short term shortage of particular types of labour, with high incomes being used as incentives in certain occupations.

Mr. Bartels approved of the introduction of weights in the G_{mu} coefficient, but asked what values were being assumed for β. It appeared that β must be negative, in which case G_{mu} would also be negative. He suggested another modification of the Gini index

$$C \sum_{jk} |y_j - y_k|^\alpha f_j f_k w(j, k)$$

where C is an appropriate normalisation and $w(j, k)$ are weights determined by the classes being compared.

Professor Sen wanted to make one clarificatory remark with regard to the G_{mu} coefficient. It is easy to show that, if incomes are ordered so that $y_1 \geq y_2 \geq \ldots \geq y_n$, then $1 - G = A + B \sum_i i y_i$, where G is the Gini coefficient. The S-concavity of the Gini coefficient follows from the fact that for lower and lower incomes the weights become higher and higher. However it is not a separable function and utility cannot be regarded as a function of income in this context. Professor Michal had effectively increased the degree of equality preference compared with the simple Gini coefficient. His formulation might be written

$$1 - G_{mu} = A^* + B^* \sum_i i^* u'_i y_i$$

where i^* denotes the ranking by people's income *times* their marginal utilities, as opposed to just incomes alone. This can sometimes give perverse results though, since marginal utility may decline more than proportionately than the rise in income.

Professor Taubman said that it had been suggested many years ago that inequality measures might weight the area under the Lorenz curve differently for different income levels, in contrast to the equal weights used in the Gini coefficient. He questioned whether information on the relationship between utility and income could ever be derived from tax data. Even if it is assumed that the government sets tax rates rationally, they are not based on pure "ability to pay" criteria but also involve a trade-off between equality and efficiency. He was also unsure of the value of spending a great deal of time collecting this data to make cross country comparisons, since a good deal of welfare differences arise because of the provision of government services.

Professor van Praag pointed out that the value of -0.5 chosen for α differed from the Dutch estimate of $\alpha = -2$ made by Theil and Barten, and by himself.

Professor Pen felt that the techniques were too sophisticated for the purposes in hand. He suggested that we should consider socialist countries in the same way as military organisations or bureaucracies, and stick to simple comparisons.

Professor Bentzel suggested that the high degree of earnings equality was largely attributable to the flat age profile. He would have liked to see the earnings distribution disaggregated by age groups.

Dr. Thomas referred to the age profiles and asked whether the age data had been correctly recorded. He believed that regression analysis using a number of variables would provide a useful guide to the earnings pattern.

Professor Tinbergen asked how much of the Hungarian economy was covered by the socialist sector.

Professor Krelle was interested in how the results might change if income in kind, such as holidays abroad, were taken into account. He also wondered whether the continual egalitarian trend in Czechoslovakia, which contrasted with the experience in the other socialist countries, reflected the different policies being followed, or was merely spurious.

Professor van Meerhaeghe doubted whether comparisons could be made for earnings and consumption, since the opportunities for acquiring consumption goods were substantially different at different income levels. Echoing the remarks of Professor Krelle, he suggested that increases in non-pecuniary benefits may have offset the tendency towards equality.

Professor Morrisson said that second, unofficial jobs seemed to be common practice in some socialist countries and he wondered whether they had been taken into account.

Dr. Wagner was concerned with the substantial differences between countries in the proportion of income received as transfers. He asked whether there was any explanation for (1) the increasing share of transfer income; (2) differences between countries in the level of total transfers; and (3) the extremely low ranking of Polish peasants with respect to the amount of transfers received.

Professor Michal had no quarrel with the remarks of Professor Vielrose or those of Professor Sen. He wished only to add that his G_{mu} coefficient is not very sensitive to moderate changes in the elasticity of utility of income, as illustrated in Appendix A of the paper, and that the "perverse" result described by Professor Sen is unlikely to occur if a realistic utility function is used. Responding to the remarks of Mr. Bartels, he said that β disappears in the final G_{mu} formula, and G_{mu} is not negative; yet even a negative G_{mu} could serve as an ordinal measure of inequality. With reference to Professor Pen's criticism of the G_{mu} coefficient, he pointed out that every overall measure of inequality implies some judgement about the shape of the welfare function; those who prefer purely descriptive partial coefficients of inequality might use his P_i's.

To Professor Tinbergen he replied that in Hungary and Poland slightly less than 5% of salaried employment was still in the non-socialist sector. He did not have comprehensive data on entrepreneurial incomes outside of the socialised sector, but these were important under the new economic system in Hungary. Socialist incomes in kind, mentioned by Professor Krelle and others, were even more important, and he had attempted to make adjustments for social benefits in kind in Hungary. The problem of income in kind is similar to the problem of taking fringe benefits into account in Western countries. There is also the moonlighting problem mentioned by Professor Morrisson, but this, too, occurs everywhere; it may be more important in the Socialist countries, but even in the West it escapes statistical quantification.

9 PATTERNS OF THE DISTRIBUTION OF EARNINGS IN POLAND

EGON VIELROSE

I. Introduction

Information on the distribution of earnings in Poland has been collected and published since 1955. Its coverage, however, is restricted to full time employment in the socialized sector of the economy. Earnings of individual farmers, craftsmen and others working for themselves are not included. Nor are the Army, Police and some minor groups.

The published figures refer to monthly earnings during September of each year. Over time, changes have occurred in the income classes used (see Appendix table A) as well as the breakdown by sector in the national economy. Separate figures are usually reported for wage and salary earners, and sometimes a classification by sex is also given. One major change has been the substitution of net earnings (after income tax) for the gross earnings recorded until 1970. This makes it difficult to compare distributions for the periods before and after 1970.

Additional data was collected in 1964 and 1968 on the gross earnings of people with university education and secondary professional education, subdivided into professional groups. Another useful source is a sample survey taken in October 1973 covering aspects of the earnings distribution not considered elsewhere. The aim here is to present all this information in such a way that comparisons may be possible between different groups of workers and between different points of time.

As net earnings are certainly more suitable for analysis than gross earnings, we shall concentrate on the period after 1970. Particular attention will be paid to the detailed breakdowns available for 1972, with other aspects analysed on the basis of the 1968 and 1973 surveys. Only a few figures will be given for 1976, since the information available is not sufficiently detailed to allow a thorough analysis.

II. Earnings by year, status and sex

As the lowest and highest class intervals in the earnings distribution are open-ended, and the remaining intervals are usually unequal, it is not advisable to use arithmetic means and related statistics. Quantile statistics are much more satisfactory. Although quantiles are not comparable over time or for different groups of workers, relative magnitudes, such as ratios of quantiles to the median, can be compared. Here distributions will be characterised by the median (giving the overall level of earnings) and the ratio of each decile to the median.

Table 9.1 provides details of the earnings distribution of all full time workers in the socialized sector of the economy for selected years. There were only minor and rather irregular changes in the pattern of the earnings distribution, indicating that all incomes changed more or less in the same proportion.[1] The pattern of net earnings is significantly different from that of gross earnings.

These findings are confirmed by a crude, but simple, measure of dispersion, obtained by subtracting the sum of the four lowest relative deciles from the sum of the four highest. Since this statistic is based on relative values, it is comparable between different groups of workers and also over time. The values of this measure of dispersion are as follows:

	Gross earnings	Net earnings
1955	2.773	–
1960	2.651	–
1965	2.899	–
1970	2.649	2.313
1972	–	2.327
1976	–	2.620

For 1972 a breakdown by status and sex is given in table 9.2. The range of relative deciles for females is markedly narrower than for males of the same status, reflecting the smaller dispersion in female earnings. This is again confirmed by the measure of dispersion:

	Wage earners	Salary earners
Males	2.087	2.191
Females	2.009	1.664
Total	2.371	2.332

There is no significant difference in dispersion between wage and salary earners.

III. Low and high earnings

The data allow the numbers and proportions of low and high earnings to be calculated, providing another indicator of the dispersion of earnings. Throughout this paper "low" earnings are taken to be those less than half the median value, whilst "high" earnings are those at least twice the median. In 1972, median income was 2380 złotys, giving 1190 złotys as the upper limit for low earnings and 4760 złotys as the lower limit for high earnings. These limits apply to all groups of

---

[1] The number of employees was increasing steadily over the whole period.

Distribution of earnings in Poland

Table 9.1. Relative deciles and medians, all employees.

Year	Relative deciles									Median (in zlotys)
	1	2	3	4	5	6	7	8	9	
Gross earnings										
1955	0.540	0.677	0.784	0.889	1.00	1.082	1.277	1.490	1.814	956
1960	0.548	0.682	0.790	0.890	1.00	1.127	1.254	1.441	1.739	1248
1965	0.560	0.693	0.792	0.895	1.00	1.131	1.279	1.480	1.949	1861
1970	0.557	0.670	0.776	0.894	1.00	1.122	1.270	1.451	1.703	2360
Net earnings										
1970	0.582	0.704	0.807	0.904	1.00	1.106	1.217	1.375	1.612	2104
1972	0.611	0.732	0.825	0.911	1.00	1.098	1.228	1.399	1.681	2380
1976	0.573	0.704	0.797	0.893	1.00	1.133	1.248	1.423	1.783	3675

Table 9.2. Relative deciles by status and sex, 1972.

Status and sex group	Relative deciles									Median (in zlotys)
	1	2	3	4	5	6	7	8	9	
Wage earners										
Males	0.625	0.754	0.837	0.923	1.00	1.082	1.200	1.348	1.596	2619
Females	0.608	0.716	0.817	0.909	1.00	1.094	1.196	1.316	1.453	1720
Total	0.569	0.701	0.809	0.906	1.00	1.099	1.219	1.383	1.655	2305
Salary earners										
Males	0.641	0.745	0.832	0.914	1.00	1.099	1.215	1.366	1.643	3107
Females	0.790	0.782	0.857	0.927	1.00	1.079	1.166	1.295	1.480	2126
Total	0.639	0.740	0.827	0.912	1.00	1.103	1.230	1.415	1.702	2464

workers, so the proportions of low and high earnings are comparable between groups.

Table 9.3. Low and high earnings by status and sex, 1972.

Status and sex group	Absolute numbers (thousands) and percentage of each group	
	Low earnings	High earnings
Wage earners		
Males	89.5 (2.0%)	270.9 (6.1%)
Females	391.6 (17.9%)	15.6 (0.7%)
Total	481.1 (7.3%)	286.5 (4.3%)
Salary earners		
Males	6.3 (0.4%)	216.4 (13.8%)
Females	36.4 (1.8%)	17.7 (0.9%)
Total	42.7 (1.2%)	234.1 (6.5%)
All employees	523.8 (5.1%)	520.6 (5.1%)

For all males (wage and salary earners together) the proportions of low and high earnings are 1.6% and 8.1% respectively, compared with 10.1% and 0.8% for females. Thus there is a much higher proportion of females with low earnings and of males with high earnings. Low earnings are concentrated in the group of female wage earners whilst high earnings are to be found most frequently among male salaried employees.

The numbers and proportions of low and high earnings were also obtained for particular sectors of the national economy and are given below in table 9.4.

Table 9.4. Low and high earnings by status and sector, 1972.

Sector	Absolute numbers (thousands) and percentage of each group			
	Wage earners		Salary earners	
	Low	High	Low	High
Industry	71.7 (2.0%)	172.0 (4.8%)	2.5 (0.3%)	85.6 (10.5%)
Construction	28.9 (3.6%)	65.7 (8.2%)	1.8 (0.6%)	56.1 (18.5%)
Agriculture	26.6 (7.3%)	1.8 (0.5%)	1.6 (1.0%)	7.0 (4.4%)
Forestry	5.3 (7.1%)	1.0 (1.4%)	1.0 (2.4%)	0.6 (1.4%)
Transport and communication	16.1 (2.4%)	17.4 (2.6%)	1.2 (0.4%)	15.2 (5.0%)
Trade	39.7 (13.3%)	1.2 (0.4%)	8.5 (1.4%)	6.7 (1.1%)
Community services and housing	12.3 (4.6%)	6.7 (2.5%)	0.6 (0.6%)	4.8 (4.5%)
Science	2.0 (6.3%)	0.4 (1.2%)	0.2 (0.2%)	11.2 (13.7%)
Education	101.8 (62.4%)	0.1 (0.0%)	4.3 (0.4%)	18.2 (3.8%)
Cultural services	6.5 (26.2%)	0.0 (0.1%)	1.3 (2.0%)	2.5 (4.0%)
Health services	78.4 (41.3%)	0.1 (0.0%)	11.9 (3.8%)	7.5 (2.4%)

Within the group of wage earners, the proportion of low earnings is smallest in the Industry sector and greatest in Education. The Construction sector comes top in the proportion of high earnings, with Industry next. Education and Health Services contain almost no workers with high earnings.

For salaried employees the ranking is somewhat different. There is a relatively large number with low earnings in Health Services, followed by Forestry. Science and Industry have relatively few salaried workers with low earnings. Construction ranks first in the proportion of salaried employees with high earnings, while Trade and Forestry come last.

IV. Educational background

The 1973 survey allows a similar analysis by educational level,[2] but without any further breakdown. The results are given in table 9.5.

Median earnings are highest for university graduates and lowest for those who did not complete secondary education. Workers with primary education or below have a higher median than those with completed or uncompleted secondary general education. The median earnings corresponding to basic professional education is only slightly less than for secondary professional education.

The measure of dispersion, calculated as before, is

University	2.375
Secondary Professional	2.024
Secondary General – completed	1.875
– uncompleted	1.843
Basic Professional	2.288
Primary or Below	2.267
All Groups	2.323

University graduates show the widest dispersion of earnings, closely followed by those with basic professional and primary (or below primary) education. Workers with secondary education of various kinds have a markedly lower dispersion in earnings. Thus earnings dispersion is greatest within the highest and lowest educational groups, with differences in earnings reduced significantly at the intermediate educational levels. It appears that higher earnings dispersion is associated with higher levels of earnings, although workers with secondary professional education violate this general rule, ranking second in median earnings but fourth in dispersion.

Proportions of low and high earnings were also calculated. As the overall median is 2713 złotys, the upper limit for low earnings is 1356 złotys and the lower limit for high earnings 5426 złotys. The results are given in table 9.6.

---

[2] The duration of schooling at different levels is as follows:

primary	8 years
basic professional	3 years (after completion of primary education)
secondary general	4 years
secondary general	2–6 years (average 4 years)
university	3–6 years (average 5 years)

Table 9.5. Relative deciles and medians by educational level, 1973.

Educational level	Relative deciles									Median (in zlotys)
	1	2	3	4	5	6	7	8	9	
University	0.621	0.727	0.823	0.910	1.00	1.105	1.237	1.429	1.685	4249
Secondary professional	0.624	0.781	0.852	0.920	1.00	1.081	1.187	1.353	1.580	2886
Secondary general										
– completed	0.683	0.788	0.851	0.922	1.00	1.086	1.185	1.313	1.535	2516
– uncompleted	0.674	0.774	0.857	0.932	1.00	1.084	1.180	1.303	1.513	2485
Basic professional	0.616	0.726	0.822	0.906	1.00	1.100	1.224	1.387	1.647	2750
Primary or below	0.597	0.722	0.822	0.913	1.00	1.094	1.211	1.367	1.649	2583
All groups	0.605	0.730	0.826	0.907	1.00	1.098	1.221	1.401	1.671	2713

Table 9.6. Low and high earnings by educational level, 1973.

Educational level	Absolute numbers (thousands) and percentage of each group	
	Low earnings	High earnings
University	0.0 (0.0%)	148.6 (24.1%)
Secondary professional	9.8 (0.6%)	81.6 (5.0%)
Secondary general		
– completed	7.2 (1.8%)	37.6 (9.4%)
– uncompleted	5.4 (2.5%)	4.3 (2.0%)
Basic professional	65.4 (3.1%)	120.3 (5.7%)
Primary or below	323.3 (5.7%)	255.2 (4.5%)
All groups	411.1 (3.8%)	647.6 (6.1%)

The proportion of low earnings in each category is directly related to the level of education: as the level increases, the proportion of low earnings declines. There are virtually no low income earners among university graduates, while the proportion among those with primary education is 5.7%. The opposite relationship might be expected for high earnings, but this is not confirmed by the results. Although university graduates rank first, as anticipated, workers with uncompleted secondary education occupy the last place rather than those with only primary education. In addition, high earnings are slightly more frequent among people with basic professional education than among those with secondary professional education.

For workers with university education and secondary professional education, subdivided into professional groups,[3] relative deciles for gross earnings in January 1968 are also available. These are not comparable with the figures in the earlier tables 9.2 and 9.5.

The measures of dispersion for each professional group and education level are

	University education	Secondary professional education
Technicians	2.425	2.273
Agricultural workers	1.977	2.040
Economists	1.985	2.140
Specialists in		
– Health services	1.955	1.076
– Exact sciences	2.073	–
– Humanities	2.339	–
Teachers	–	1.497
All groups	2.394	2.523

At both levels of education, technicians show the greatest dispersion in earnings and health service specialists the smallest.

---

[3] The Economist category includes statisticians, planners etc.

Table 9.7. Relative deciles and medians by professional groups, 1968.

	Relative deciles									Median (in zlotys)
	1	2	3	4	5	6	7	8	9	
University education										
Technicians	0.618	0.738	0.827	0.906	1.00	1.103	1.234	1.420	1.757	4279
Agricultural workers	0.640	0.760	0.832	0.931	1.00	1.081	1.183	1.328	1.548	3193
Economists	0.653	0.762	0.849	0.923	1.00	1.079	1.196	1.326	1.571	3641
Specialists in										
– Health services	0.649	0.773	0.848	0.920	1.00	1.083	1.189	1.338	1.535	3196
– Exact sciences	0.661	0.749	0.838	0.920	1.00	1.098	1.207	1.336	1.600	2909
– Humanities	0.630	0.725	0.820	0.910	1.00	1.111	1.242	1.423	1.648	3013
All groups	0.602	0.729	0.821	0.917	1.00	1.102	1.239	1.401	1.721	3501
Secondary professional education										
Technicians	0.588	0.728	0.834	0.918	1.00	1.094	1.206	1.361	1.680	2887
Agricultural workers	0.612	0.740	0.841	0.925	1.00	1.091	1.198	1.331	1.538	2005
Economists	0.612	0.742	0.828	0.914	1.00	1.097	1.210	1.352	1.577	2204
Specialists in health services	0.769	0.838	0.900	0.953	1.00	1.051	1.097	1.152	1.236	1721
Teachers	0.747	0.819	0.884	0.944	1.00	1.053	1.152	1.268	1.418	1826
All groups	0.619	0.734	0.814	0.894	1.00	1.111	1.280	1.464	1.729	2207

Table 9.A. Frequencies of monthly earnings (September).

Year	Income classes (in zlotys)															Total
	<400	401–500	501–600	601–700	701–800	801–1000	1001–1200	1201–1400	1401–2000	2001–2500	2501–3000	3001–4000	4001–5000	5001–7000	7000+	
Gross earnings																
1955	3.5	5.4	6.6	9.0	10.5	18.8	14.8	14.2	10.8[b]	3.8	1.5	{1.0		0.1}		100.0
1960	–	–	3.1	2.1	2.6	8.3	11.6	19.0[a]	25.2[b]	14.1	7.0	{6.2		0.8}		100.0
1965	–	–	–	–	{8.5	}	7.3	9.4	31.1	18.3	11.2	12.5	{1.7		}	100.0
1970	–	–	–	–	{4.2	}	4.5	6.1	25.4	19.7	14.5	21.4	{4.2		}	100.0
Net earnings																
1970	{9.2						}	7.3	29.2	22.2	14.7	11.7	3.5	1.9	0.3	100.0
1972	{4.8						}	4.4	23.7	23.0	17.2	16.8	6.0	3.3	0.8	100.0
1976	{7.4								}	{24.4	}	27.6	18.2	15.4	7.0	100.0

[a] The class interval is 1201–1500.
[b] The class interval is 1501–2000.

Table 9.B. Frequencies of monthly earnings, September 1972, 1976.

	Income classes (in złotys)									
	<1200	1201–1400	1401–2000	2001–2500	2501–3000	3001–4000	4001–5000	5001–7000	7000+	Total
1972 Wage earners										
– male	2.1	2.6	16.8	22.6	21.3	22.1	7.7		4.8	100.0
– female	18.3	11.3	37.5	22.9	7.8	2.1	0.1		0.0	100.0
– total	7.2	5.3	23.4	22.8	17.1	15.7	5.3		3.2	100.0
Salary earners										
– male	0.4	0.8	9.0	16.5	19.5	29.1	13.2		11.5	100.0
– female	1.9	4.8	35.5	28.6	15.9	10.4	2.2		0.7	100.0
– total	1.2	3.0	24.1	23.4	17.5	18.6	7.0		5.2	100.0
1976 Wage earners		9.3		24.9		26.8	17.9	14.6	6.5	100.0
Salary earners		3.7		24.9		29.0	18.9	17.1	7.9	100.0

Table 9.C. Frequencies of monthly earnings by educational level, Lctober 1973.

	Income classes (in złotys)									
	<1200	1201–1400	1401–2000	2001–2500	2501–3000	3001–4000	4001–5000	5001–7000	7001–10000	10000+	Total
University	0.0	0.0	1.3	6.4	10.7	26.1	22.2	22.3	8.8	2.2	100.0
Secondary professional	0.3	0.6	11.9	24.0	22.3	25.0	9.7	4.9	1.2	0.1	100.0
Secondary general											
– completed	0.7	1.7	19.3	27.6	21.5	20.3	5.9	2.5	0.5	0.0	100.0
– uncompleted	1.1	2.1	20.6	27.0	21.7	19.2	5.8	2.2	0.3	0.0	100.0
Basic professional	1.5	2.3	16.5	20.3	18.7	23.8	9.9	6.0	0.9	0.1	100.0
Primary or below	3.1	3.6	18.6	21.5	19.3	20.7	7.7	4.5	0.9	0.1	100.0
All groups	2.0	2.6	16.2	21.0	19.3	22.3	9.2	5.8	1.4	0.2	100.0

9 DISCUSSION

PAPER BY EGON VIELROSE

Professor Adelman thought the paper provided the kind of information essential to understanding historical trends in the distribution of income. The data covered only earnings of those paid wages and salaries, therefore excluding the subsidised portion of consumption and transfers in the form of health and education expenditure. Taking these into account the pattern of dispersion is similar to that found in non-socialist countries. It would be a mistake to imagine that the income distribution in Poland was markedly less unequal than that found in many developing and developed countries. She also felt that the smaller dispersion in female earnings compared to male earnings was due to a narrower range of occupational choice.

Professor Michal was happy to see that the decile estimates were almost identical to his own calculations, which required interpolation. He wondered why household income after transfers had not been considered, since some data on this was available. He also knew that some evidence on the incomes of individual farmers and peasants was available in Polish publications. He thought it very valuable to have the decile limits for age and occupational groups, since this data is very scarce for socialist countries.

Professor Wiles suggested that the increase in the dispersion of wages in Poland did not mean an increase in the dispersion of incomes, as others had argued. He believe there had been a movement of people from the peasant class, predominantly the young and poor, into the urban working class. Precisely this kind of equalising tendency within the national income distribution may appear to cause more inequality in the earnings distribution. It was a perfect illustration of the importance of considering particular quantiles and avoiding magical single-number formulae. He also noted that socialist countries like Czechoslovakia and, to a lesser extent, Poland continued to function despite a significant compression of the wage scale compared with non-socialist countries. Perhaps this implied that the rich were overpaid under capitalism and it was incorrect to argue that the market determined a degree of inequality which could not be tampered with.

Dr. Kuipers was puzzled by the large percentage of low earners to be found in the education, cultural services and health sectors compared with, say, community services and housing. He asked if there was any explanation for this difference.

Professor Pen said that the paper contained useful information on employees but he wanted to know more about those who did not want to work. Were these supported by the state in any way?

Professor Vielrose responded first to Professor Adelman's remark that the pattern of income dispersion in socialist and non-socialist countries is fairly similar. He said that detailed analysis was required before coming to any clear conclusion, but it does appear that very high incomes are much less frequent in socialist countries than in non-socialist countries. Whilst Professor Michal was quite right to state that data on household incomes by size were available for Poland, they do not contain benefits in kind and are not comparable over as long a period as the earnings data. Moreover, data for individual households of farmers suggest an average land significantly above the overall average and require appropriate adjustments. There is no information on income distribution in the private sector. So he decided to limit his investigation to earnings distributions only. He thought that Professor Wiles was quite right to suggest there was no disequalisation but rather a trend towards equalisation, if we also take private agriculture into account.

Replying to Professor Kuipers he said that the large percentage of low income earners in education, cultural services and health services was due to the high proportion of auxiliary unskilled personnel in these sectors. There is also a higher proportion of females who tend to be paid considerably less. In contrast, the community services and housing sector contains few auxiliary personnel.

To Professor Pen he said work was regarded as a duty. If people did not want to work, they received no payment from the state and would have to rely on their friends and family. The incentive to take work was therefore strong, as soon as the period of formal education had been completed.

10 INCOME DISTRIBUTION IN LESS DEVELOPED COUNTRIES: METHODOLOGICAL PROBLEMS

CHRISTIAN MORRISSON

Income distribution analysts have recently paid particular attention to methodological problems arising in the comparison of distributional statistics based on widely different sources (fiscal data, household surveys, surveys of the working population, disaggregated national accounts, etc.) and referring to different units (family, household, individual, income earner, etc.). These comparisons have appeared less and less worthwhile as research on the biases peculiar to each source or unit has progressed. This difficulty is even more acute in less developed countries where the sources are less reliable and there is a wider margin of error in every estimate. Even if one author is quite aware of the tentative nature of his estimates, once published they are liable to be used by other economists in international comparisons (including comparisons with developed countries) or even for testing models. It is therefore essential to analyse the several types of biases associated with any estimate for less developed countries, so that meaningful international comparisons can be made using data adjusted for these biases.

I. Family income distribution and personal income distribution

The interest of this point is limited, due to the nature of available statistics. If, for each country, we could provide estimates based on different units (such as income earner, family, individual, consumer), an international comparison could clearly use the one most suitable; but, as everyone of us knows from experience, we have to deal with unreliable and incomplete data. In one country, the only reliable estimate will be the population census; in another, the only source covering incomes will be a household survey. In such circumstances, any international comparison is an extremely dangerous exercise. There are two reasons for this: the data are both unreliable and non-comparable. In the same country, using the same sources, distributions vary appreciably according to the unit chosen. Moreover, variations may be in the opposite direction in another country, so it is impossible to make a correction on the basis of experience elsewhere. For instance, if, in North America, personal income inequality is observed to be 15% higher than the corresponding figure for families, one cannot infer that the same is true in South America.

Household surveys provide the most common data source in less developed countries, and are often the only one available. From experience in developed countries, we know that the relationship between the family distribution and other distributions varies. If the family distribution exhibits less inequality than the personal distribution or the distribution over consumer units, it is necessary to analyse the relationship between these different distributions, in order to avoid any bias in an international comparison based on family units.

The only satisfactory method of moving from household to personal income distribution, requires a breakdown of the household distribution by size and income, from which the income per person living in family units, can be inferred. The personal distribution is then obtained by classifying individuals and grouping them according to their income.

Such a breakdown is available for Hong Kong and Trinidad-Tobago,[1] so I have been able to calculate the personal income distribution and compare it with the household distribution. In Hong Kong, the Gini ratio is higher for personal incomes (0.467 versus; 0.417); in Trinidad-Tobago the ratios are identical, but the decile shares vary according to the unit chosen. The share of the first five deciles is higher in the personal distribution (17.7% compared with 16.5%) and the same is true for the share of the top decile (36.1% instead of 33.9%). Thus the household distribution underestimates the shares of the highest and lowest income holders in the personal distribution.

These results confirm Kuznets' (1976) figures for Taiwan and the Philippines. In both countries, personal and household income inequality are nearly the same: the TDM^2 is 41.6 and 42.2, respectively, in Taiwan, 70.4 and 69.2 in the Philippines. But in developed countries the household distribution appears to be more concentrated than the personal distribution. According to Kuznets, in West Germany the TDM is 56.2 for household and 47.4 for personal income, whereas in the United States comparable figures are 56.2 and 55.4, respectively. The figures for four less developed countries (Taiwan, the Philippines, Hong Kong, Trinidad-Tobago) are broadly consistent and allow us to draw two conclusions: the Gini ratio for personal incomes in a less developed country may be compared with the Gini ratio for household income in another less developed country; but one must be very cautious when introducing developed countries into the comparison. Since the Gini ratio for household incomes probably exaggerates the real inequality between individuals in developed countries, we are likely to underestimate the difference in income inequality between Third World and developed countries, whenever household incomes are used for the latter.

An examination of household income distributions for Hong-Kong and Trinidad-Tobago, disaggregated by household size, is consistent with Kuznets' analysis for Taiwan and the Philippines. In Trinidad-Tobago, the average number of persons per household rises from 2.42 to 4.84 between the lowest and the highest income class (>1000), while the maximum average household size (5.45) occurs in the income interval 600 to 799. As a result the distribution of per capita family

---

[1] Henry (1975), Hsia and Chau (1975).
[2] TDM is the Total disparity measure, defined as the sum of the absolute differences (disregarding the sign) between the percentage of the population and the percentage share of income in each income class. The summation is taken over all the income classes distinguished.

income[3] is less concentrated: the TDM is only 58.8 compared with 70.2 for the personal distribution. In Hong Kong, on the other hand, the number of persons per household is much the same in all income classes except the lowest, and the TDM is almost identical for both distributions (61.4 and 59.8). On the basis of these figures, Hong Kong is in marked contrast to developed countries. According to Kuznets (1976), the average size of households increases in proportion to household income in Germany, and the TDM is reduced by a half when individuals, rather than households, are considered (33.4 instead of 56.2). In Taiwan and the Philippines, the increase in the size of households is less noticeable, and the same is true of the change in the TDM: 42.2 and 30.6 in Taiwan; 69.1 and 62 in the Philippines. Thus the size of low income families in rich countries tend to be significantly below average, whereas, in less developed countries, they tend to be only slightly smaller.

The distribution of households by size in less developed countries differs considerably from the pattern found in developed countries. For instance, 50.4% of households in Germany contain one or two persons, while the proportion is 7.4% in Taiwan, 9.7% in the Philippines,[4] 28% in Trinidad-Tobago, 27.9% in Hong Kong and 19% in Malaysia.[5] Households of 6 or more persons constitute 4.8% of households in Germany compared to 48.3%, 50.2%, 35.3%, 34.6% and 44.1% in these other countries, respectively. In Germany, relative household income increases considerably with household size (0.51 with 1 person to 1.57 with 5 persons), but the relationship is less pronounced in Third World countries: 0.42 to 0.99 in Taiwan; 0.61 to 0.95 in the Philippines; 0.47 to 1.14 in Trinidad-Tobago, where it shows little increase when household size exceeds 5; 0.58 to 1.10 in Hong Kong, where it is constant for households numbering 6 to 9 persons. As a result, there is a great difference between Germany, or the United States, and less developed countries. When you move from the household distribution to the distribution of family income per person, the TDM decreases from 32 to 13 in Germany, while it increases in all the less developed countries mentioned above: from 12.8 to 18.4 in Taiwan; from 16.2 to 20.6 in the Philippines; from 20.4 to 31.4 in Trinidad-Tobago; from 13.7 to 38.6 in Hong Kong. The last country provides the strongest contrast to Germany, showing a very wide shift in the opposite direction. A significant point about this country is the fairly constant household income for households with between 3 and 9 persons. This example, and also Trinidad-Tobago, challenge one of Kuznets' (1976) conclusions – that household income increases with household size. Although this feature is apparent in developed countries, incomes in less developed nations may increase very little, or even remain stable, as we move from smaller to larger households. Thus the relative income per person in larger households is much smaller in less developed countries. This partly accounts for the impact of rapid demographic growth on income distribution.

[3] This distribution must not be confused with the income distribution per person, which is the only one of significance for the inequality between individuals. The distribution of family income per person is calculated using the *average* number of persons per household within each household income range. But the number varies widely amongst households in the same income range.

[4] Kuznets (1976).

[5] Anand (1973).

II. Income distribution and age

Paglin (1975) and Stoikov (1973) have already stressed the influence of age on income inequality. From another viewpoint, Kuznets (1976) has shown that the inequality attributable to age differences is much less in the Philippines and Taiwan than it is in developed countries. Two points should be mentioned. The inequality measures chosen (the Gini ratio, G, and the total disparity measure, TDM) have one major disadvantage – they cannot be disaggregated. Secondly, the comparison must be extended to other underdeveloped countries, to check the validity of Kuznets' conclusions.

Any comparison between G or TDM for the overall income distribution and the corresponding values for the income distribution over age groups, G_a or TDM_a (assuming income equality within each age group), does not allow us to impute a given percentage of total inequality to differences in age. One can only say that $G - G_a$ represents the distance between the observed distribution and the hypothetical distribution which would arise if age was the only factor causing inequality. An index which can be disaggregated, like the Theil coefficient $T = \sum y_i \log(y_i/x_i)$ (where y_i is the share of class i in total income and x_i is the proportion of the total population in class (i) allows us to estimate the percentage of total inequality which can be imputed to the age structure.[6] T is known for the overall distribution as well as for the distribution over age groups, T_a (assuming equality within each age group). The ratio T_a/T gives the percentage of total inequality attributable to differences in income due to age.

Data used by Paglin for the United States and by Kuznets for Taiwan and the Philippines (in 1968), have been supplemented here by data from Mexico, Brazil, Malaysia and the Philippines (in 1970–71). These are given in table 10.1. The Malaysian statistics are particularly interesting since they give figures for both the total population and ethnic sub-groups – Malays, Chinese etc. In addition, division into 10 age groups indicates the impact of further disaggregation. Tables 10.1 and 10.2 show the data I have used to compute the total inequality and the inequality over age groups. The Gini ratios, G and G_a, and the Theil coefficients, T and T_a, presented in table 10.3, were estimated from these data. Looking at these results, and especially at Brazil, it appears that Kuznets' conclusions are unwarranted. The ratios G_a/G and T_a/T seem to be the same in Brazil and the United States. In fact they are not comparable, because the figures for Brazil, as well as Malaysia, refer to the income distribution for *income earners* rather than *families*. Consequently, many young people with low incomes (who are not heads of families) are included in one case and excluded in the other. The percentage of family heads under 25 (3–8% in Brazil and Malaysia) is quite different from the percentage of income earners under 25 (28–30%). When only distributions for families are compared, the G_a/G and T_a/T ratios are much higher in the United States than in the other countries considered. For example, T_a/T is 0.113 compared to 0.007 to 0.027 in four other cases (Mexico, Taiwan, the Philippines in two different years). When income earners are taken as the unit, it is clear that these ratios increase

---
[6] See, for example, van Ginneken (1975).

Table 10.1. Income distributions by age groups.

	Philippines 1968		Philippines 1970–71	
Age of head of household	Share of income (%)	Percentage of households	Share of income (%)	Percentage of households
<25	2.2	3.0	3.1	5.0
25–34	24.8	25.8	20.6	24.6
35–44	33.5	31.6	26.1	26.9
45–54	22.9	22.3	24.6	21.0
55–64	13.3	13.0	17.6	14.5
65+	3.3	4.3	8.0	7.8

Malaysia						
	All		Malays		Chinese	
Age of income earner	Share of income (%)	Percentage of earners	Share of income (%)	Percentage of earners	Share of income (%)	Percentage of earners
<25	18.21	27.83	18.74	24.80	17.20	32.19
25–34	25.80	24.41	28.43	24.27	28.83	24.96
35–44	24.07	18.72	23.55	19.50	22.29	16.85
45–54	17.93	14.45	17.46	16.06	16.12	11.46
55–64	10.23	9.72	8.22	9.90	11.66	9.93
65+	3.76	4.79	3.60	5.46	3.90	4.61

Mexico			Taiwan		
Age of head of household	Share of income (%)	Percentage of households	Age of head of household	Share of income (%)	Percentage of households
<30	9.5	13.5	<25	2.0	2.8
30–39	24.5	26.9	25–34	22.9	25.2
40–49	29.4	26.5	35–44	33.1	34.1
50–59	19.9	16.2	45–54	28.0	25.5
60+	16.7	16.9	55–59	7.5	6.4
			65+	6.5	6.0

Brazil			United States		
Age of income earner	Share of income (%)	Percentage of earners	Age of head of household	Share of income (%)	Percentage of households
<20	5.1	14.3	<25	4.8	7.7
20–24	11.1	15.8	25–34	20.0	22.0
25–29	13.6	13.7	35–44	22.5	19.7
30–39	27.9	23.1	45–54	25.7	20.7
40–49	23.5	17.2	55–64	17.7	16.0
50–59	12.7	10.1	65+	9.3	13.9
60–69	5.0	4.5			
70+	1.1	1.3			

Sources: Anand (1973), Encarnacion (1974), van Ginneken (1975), Kuznets (1976), Langoni (1973), Paglin (1975).

Table 10.2. Decile shares for households or income earners.

Decile	Brazil	Philippines, 1968	Taiwan	Mexico	United States
1	1	2	3.0	2	2.4
2	1.5	2	4.7	2.5	3.0
3	2	3	5.6	3.5	5.2
4	3	5	7.0	4.5	6.7
5	5	6	7.8	5	8.0
6	6.5	7	8.8	5.5	9.5
7	8	8	10.0	7	11.0
8	13	12	12.1	9	12.9
9	16	15	14.8	13	14.9
10 {90–95%	13	15	10.0	15	10.5
10 {top 5%	31	25	16.2	33	16.5

	Malaysia			Philippines 1970–71	
Deciles	All	Malays	Chinese	Percentage of households	Share of income (%)
1	1.5	1.4	1.8	17.3	2.9
2	2.0	1.9	2.2	23.9	9.6
3	3.0	4.0	3.6	17.7	11.8
4	4.8	5.5	5	20.0	20.4
5	6.5	6.8	6.3	11.4	19.1
6	7.5	8.0	7.5	7.3	20.3
7	8.7	9.0	8.5	2.4	15.9
8	11.0	11.5	10.5		
9	15.0	16.0	15.0		
10 {90–95%	11.5	12.4	12.1		
10 {top 5%	28.5	23.5	27.5		

Sources: as in table 10.1.

substantially. Another source, Lean (1974), tells us that 7% of Malaysian households are headed by someone under 25, while 28% of all income earners are included in this age group. Of the income earners under 25, it is likely that those who are already heads of households tend to have higher incomes. This suggests that the T_a/T ratios in Brazil and Malaysia would be reduced by roughly a half (i.e. to 0.06 and 0.04), if they were computed for families.

Kuznets' conclusions is, in fact, confirmed: age has much less impact on inequality in Third World countries than in the United States. But there is some variation within Third World countries and the impact of age is more significant in Brazil, for instance, than in Taiwan and the Philippines.

Considering changes in the Theil coefficient, which is the only one of significance,[7] age (on its own, neglecting interactions with other variables) accounts for more than 11% of inequality in the United States, compared to 3 or 4% in Third World countries. Consequently, international comparisons between observed distributions in a given year, do not enable conclusions to be drawn for the distributions of lifetime incomes for the same countries. "Lifetime income" distribution, which

---

[7] The ratio G_a/G is of no particular significance. Only the difference G-G_a between the observed and hypothetical distributions is important, as already noted.

Table 10.3. Gini ratios and Theil coefficients for overall distributions and distributions by age.

Country	Number of age classes	Year	Units	Distribution over age groups		Overall distribution	
				C_a	T_a	C	T
Mexico	5	1968	Head of household	0.088	0.0132	0.532	0.5798
Taiwan	6	1966	Head of household	0.052	0.0048	0.323	0.1793
Brazil	8	1970	Income earners	0.183	0.0658	0.569	0.5983
Philippines	6	1968	Head of household	0.036	0.0033	0.493	0.4412
		1970–71		0.091	0.0141	0.476	0.4237
Malaysia							
All	6			0.133	0.0316	0.498	0.4691
	10			0.143	0.0355		
Malays	6	1968	Income earners	0.109	0.0211	0.463	0.3850
	10			0.112	0.0222		
Chinese	6			0.183	0.0633	0.483	0.4414
	10			0.188	0.0643		
United States	6	1972	Head of household	0.112	0.0243	0.358	0.2159

is perhaps more important than annual income distribution as a reflection of inequality, is much less concentrated in developed countries; in underdeveloped countries the lifetime income distribution is almost as unequal as the observed annual distribution. To illustrate the significance of this point, assume an observed Gini ratio of 0.50 in underdeveloped countries and 0.35 in developed countries, a difference of 43%. The lifetime income Gini ratio would be 0.48 in the first case and 0.31 in the other, so the difference increases to 55%.

Table 10.1 suggests that these differences can be partly explained by the number and incomes of aged families or income earners. Firstly, the percentage of old people is higher in the United States (13.9% over 65) than in Malaysia, the Philippines, Taiwan and Brazil (3% to 8%), and even Mexico (9%).[8] Secondly, the average income of these family heads (or income earners) is very close to the national average in Taiwan, Brazil, Mexico and the Philippines (1971), whereas it falls to only two-thirds of the national average income in the United States. In Malaysia and the Philippines (1968), it is 20% below the national average.

The proportion of young people may also help to explain these differences, as it is higher in the United States (7.7%) than in Taiwan, the Philippines and, to a lesser extent, in Mexico. These young people have an income much below average, so the fact that they are under-represented in less developed countries reduces the disparity due to age.

The higher percentage of young income earners in Brazil and Malaysia, demonstrates that the reasons for this under-representation are not the same as those for old people. The earnings of these young people tend to be quite low and they cannot get married, whereas, in the United States, young working people receive a relatively high income in terms of dollars, even if it is well below the national average. Consequently, it is easier for them take on family responsibilities. As regards the small percentages of aged people, this is primarily a result of the demographic structure of each country, as Kuznets has noted. In developing countries, relative incomes decline more slowly with age for a number of reasons; the proportion of self-employed is much higher than in the United States due to the importance of agriculture, and the majority of those in agriculture continue working after the age of 65; the share of property income in household income is often higher; and the incomes of young working people still living with their families, are added to those of the family head.

The statistics for Malaysia have the special feature of being disaggregated according to ethnic origin.[9] The two inequality measures reveal considerable differences between Malays and Chinese. The values for G_a are 0.109 and 0.183, respectively, and for T_a they are 0.021 and 0.63. The average Chinese income earner received nearly double that of Malays, and the percentage of income earners with no education is 32.5% among Malays compared to 22% among Chinese. The percentage of income earners with secondary or university education is also higher for the Chinese (26% compared to 13%). Furthermore, the distribution of

---

[8] Assuming the same distribution within the 60–65 and over 65 age groups in Mexico and Malaysia.

[9] They also show that a more refined disaggregation by age barely changes the results: G_a only increases from 0.133 to 0.143 and T_a from 0.0316 to 0.0355. Variations are even less marked within each of the ethnic groups.

the active population shows Malays to be relatively more numerous in agriculture than the Chinese. All the data point in the same direction: the share of inequality due to age increases as the rate of higher or secondary education increases; when average income increases; or when the percentage employed in agriculture decreases. This analysis for ethnic groups confirms the conclusions suggested by an international comparison.

III. Income distribution and the life-cycle: The distribution of expected future incomes

The analysis of lifetime incomes for developed countries should not be applied without modification to developing countries since both life expectancy and the relationship between the level and variance of income are different in less developed countries. For both of these reasons, the income distribution observed at a point in time may differ, other things being equal, from that of total future income expected at the beginning of active life.

In developed countries, life expectancy varies with income. In the absence of statistics relating mortality to income, we have to rely on those based on socio-economic categories. We know that all unskilled workers are to be found in the first two quintiles of the earnings distribution, while the majority of executives, who have worked the whole year, are in the fifth quintile. Life expectancy for unskilled workers corresponds roughly with the retirement age, whereas for executives it is some years longer.[10] But these differences have no impact on the incomes received during working life, because life expectancy coincides with retirement for lower income earners.[11]

The situation is quite different in developing countries, where the life expectancy of low income earners is considerably below 65 years. In these countries, the total future income expected at the age of eighteen (that is, the total income anticipated by one category of earners over the period corresponding to their life expectancy) is related to both their earnings profile and life expectancy. For instance, unskilled workers (a) and executives (b) might have the following earnings profiles and life expectancy:

Age	18–23	24–33	34–43	44–53	54–63
Income (a)	75	80	90	100	90
Income (b)	0	400	600	800	750
Life expectancy: (a) 48 years, (b) 68 years					

Suppose that the population and age structure of these two groups of workers remain the same over time, that deaths for group (a) are uniformly distributed over

---

[10] In France, for instance, life expectancy at the age of 30 for an unskilled worker is 34 years, compared to 40 years for an executive, which implies death at ages 64 and 70, respectively.

[11] On the other hand, if one takes a utility function defined over incomes received during the whole lifespan, this difference in life expectancy must be taken into account.

the age range 44–52 (with an average of 48 years) and that deaths for group (b) are uniformly distributed over the age range 64–72 years. Then the average annual incomes for the groups will be $y(a) = 2{,}550/30 = 85$ and $y(b) = 25{,}500/45 = 567$. In this example, expected income at the age of 18 is given by

(a): $(75 \times 6) + (80 \times 10) + (90 \times 10) + (100 \times 4) = 2{,}550$

(b): $(400 \times 10) + (600 \times 10) + (800 \times 10) + (750 \times 10) = 25{,}550$

The ratio of lifetime incomes is 1 : 10, which would be substantially underestimated if differences in life expectancy were neglected (85 : 567 or 1 : 6.7).

A rough estimate of income differences between socio-economic groups indicates the potential bias. Taking a population with 10% executives and 90% unskilled earners, the overall average income is

$$\bar{y} = (0.1 \times 567) + (0.9 \times 85) = 56.7 + 76.5 = 133.2$$

Thus 10% of earners receive 42.6% of total income (i.e. 4.26 times the average income $\bar{y}$) and 90% receive 57.5% (or $0.64\bar{y}$). On average, executives receive 6.7 times the income of unskilled workers. In fact, total lifetime income is ten times higher for executives. Of the total future income expected at the age of 18 by these earners (10% of them executives and 90% unskilled) 52.7% is allocated to executives and 47.3% to the unskilled. The observed distribution may be adjusted simply by reducing the observed share of unskilled workers by 33%, which is the factor by which the length of their working life is smaller than that of executives. We obtain

$$56.7 + (76.5 \times 0.666) = 56.7 + 51 = 107.7,$$

with

$$\frac{56.7}{107.7} = 52.7\%, \quad \frac{51}{107.7} = 47.3\%.$$

Statistics on the relationship between mortality rates or life expectancy and income do not, apparently, exist in the countries we are studying. But there is information on mortality according to ethnic origin, socio-economic groups, education level and location.[12] These variables are closely related to income levels, and substantial differences in life expectancy are found between races and geographical regions. The extreme case is that of Rhodesia, where the life expectancy of black Africans is as low as 37.5 years compared to 70 for whites. The gap is still wide in South Africa with 46.5 years for blacks, 55.5 for Indians and 67.5 for whites. Since the average annual income of black African earners in Rhodesia is \$193 compared to \$3,150 for the whites, it may be inferred that differences between ethnic groups correspond to those arising from income. In Algeria and Argentina there are only regional statistics: life expectancy in Algeria varies from 50.8 years

---

[12] Congrès International de la Population, 1969, volume 2, p. 887.
Population, 1975, no. 6, pp. 1041–1044.
Desarrollo Economico, Revista de Ciencias Sociales, 1973, volume 12, p. 822.
Bulletin économique et social de la Tunisie, 1951, pp. 43–58.
Recensement et enquête demographiques 1960–61 – Ensemble du Gabon, Paris 1965.

in rural districts (mostly inhabited by peasants in the lower income deciles) up to 62.8 years in Algiers, where a great majority of the employees work in the modern sector. In Argentina, there is a similar gap between the poorest districts (Tucuman, Salta, Juguy) and Buenos-Aires (57.7 to 68.1 years).

Mortality appears to be inversely related to income. In Algeria it is as high as 17.4% for uneducated people (mainly peasants, unskilled workers, self-employed people in the traditional sector; that is, earners who, with few exceptions, never reach the top income decile. And it is as low as 8.1‰ for educated people (either secondary or university level) who generally belong to the highest income decile. In colonised Tunisia in 1947–50, the gap between Europeans and Moslems was equally wide (9.9% for the former against 20.2% for the latter) at a time when most of the European population were in the top quintile of the income distribution. In Gabon, similar differences in mortality are found between socio-economic groups: the rate is only 15–21% for administrative and technical executives, the liberal professions and clerks, and as high as 35% for traditional farmers, unskilled workers, workers employed in agriculture or forestry, and servants. Monthly earnings in the latter group ranged from 7 to 13,000 CFA Francs compared to 30 to 40,000 for clerks and 40 to 120,000 for executives.[13]

Where income inequality is greatest, differences in life expectancy also tend to be large. Under a variety of criteria, the difference in life expectancy between individuals is higher in Rhodesia than in South Africa, and higher in South Africa than in Argentina. The Gini ratios in these three countries (0.635, 0.573, 0.43) are ranked in the same order. This relationship comes as no surprise, since life expectancy depends partly on the standard of living: the quality and quantity of food consumption, housing conditions, health expenditure. Thus, when income inequality is greater, so too is the bias arising from differences in life expectancy, and it becomes even more important to use estimates of the inequality in expected incomes rather than observed incomes.

Since differences in life expectancy are necessarily greater at birth than at age 18, due to the variation in mortality rates with income, the two models below tend to underestimate the differences in life expectancy. The first model assumes *very high* inequality (which applies to Rhodesia or South Africa), the other *high* inequality (applying to countries with a Gini ratio less than 0.55). Assuming that life expectancy increases with income, we may have the following pattern.

Decile	Life expectancy (years)	
	Very high inequality	High inequality
1–4	45 (0.60)	50 (0.71)
5–6	50 (0.71)	55 (0.87)
7–8	55 (0.87)	60 (0.92)
9	60 (0.93)	63 (1.00)
10	63 (1.00)	63 (1.00)

[13] Essai de diagnostic industriel au Gabon. Rapport final de mission, 1970. O.N.U.D.I., p. 97.

The coefficients in parentheses give the working period of the income deciles expressed as a proportion of the maximum working period (18 to 63 years). For the tenth decile we used two coefficients: 1.00 for the whole decile or 1 for the penultimate 5% and 0.89 for the top 5%. The latter figure reflects the fact that executives do not usually earn anything under the age of 23. It overestimates the correct adjustment, however, since some of those in the top 5% are self-employed persons who could have been working from the age of 18.

Any analysis of the distribution of total income expected at the start of working life, must also take into account other phenomena peculiar to Third World countries. Let us consider a country where the first five deciles contain only peasants, and the top decile only civil servants or wage earners in the modern sector. This example is not very far from reality in some countries. Two factors may lead to a bias in the calculation of income inequality.

To begin with, the year chosen for the investigation may be abnormal. If the survey was undertaken in a year of bad crops, the income of peasants may have been 20% to 50% lower than usual. But the earnings of civil servants, or those employed in the modern sector, usually remain stable on such occasions. Thus, much higher inequality occurs in periods when agricultural conditions are poor. There is a risk of bias in the estimation, therefore, arising from the year chosen for the study.

Secondly, in most countries, the first five deciles are composed of farmers and agricultural labourers, and, in urban areas, unemployed or self-employed workers in the traditional sector – all of whom have very variable earnings. The aggregate income share of the first five deciles is more or less constant from one year to the next. In each year, the first decile contains the poorest income recipients, whose "permanent" income is higher than the average income of the first decile. But if the share of the first five deciles is constant, there still remains a source of hidden inequality between these earners and those in the highest decile. Transitory income is important for the former, negligible for others, and even non-existent for civil-servants. A distribution which shows the average income in the tenth decile to be ten times higher than average income in the bottom five deciles, does not take into account annual variations in income. Clearly, the utility attached to a permanent annual income of 100 is higher than that of an average income of 100, which varies between 10 and 150 over the years. This is even more obvious for a poor group, whose average annual income (100) is barely subsistence level. This income has a very high variance when calculated over the whole lifespan. It should be converted into a permanent lifetime income. Any coefficient tends to be arbitrary, but it is not unreasonable to take 0.8 or 0.9. In the calculations presented in table 10.4, we have reduced income in the first six deciles by a factor of 0.9.

In developed countries, on the other hand, annual variations in income are more or less independent of the income level. Incomes in all deciles show comparable fluctuations. There is no need, therefore, to adjust the estimates of inequality. It is the scarcity of human and material capital which results in the privileged position of high-income earners in Third World countries. Managers of modern firms, civil servants, technicians and executives receive fairly constant incomes, whereas unskilled workers, peasants and those self-employed in the

Table 10.4. Gini coefficients and income shares of the bottom 40% for the distributions of annual income and expected lifetime income.

	Rhodesia 1969	South Africa 1965	Tunisia 1970	Ivory Coast 1970
Annual distribution				
G	0.633	0.571	0.497	0.523
Share of bottom 40%	8.2%	6.2%	11.4%	10.4%
Distribution of expected income Assumption A_1				
G	0.697	0.623	0.542	0.567
Share of bottom 40%	5.3%	4.1%	8.7%	7.9%
Distribution of expected income Assumption A_2				
G	0.681	0.612	0.531	0.553
Share of bottom 40%	5.7%	4.2%	8.9%	8.2%
Distribution of expected income Assumption B_1				
G	0.708	0.433	0.557	0.583
Share of bottom 40%	4.9%	3.7%	8%	7.2%
Distribution of expected income Assumption B_2				
G	0.692	0.623	0.546	0.569
Share of bottom 40%	5.2%	3.8%	8.2%	7.5%

Source: Morrisson (1976).

traditional sector, have variable incomes caused by unemployment, fluctuations in agricultural production, weak and variable demand, and chronic under-employment of small shopkeepers and craftsmen.

Table 10.4 presents results for the distribution of expected income, based on four different sets of assumptions: A_1 (estimates based on life expectancy with no adjustment made for the later entry into the labour force of the top 5%); A_2 (the same estimates, with an adjustment for the latter factor); B_1 (estimates based on life expectancy and the income variability of the lowest deciles, with no adjustment made for the age of entry into the labour force of the top 5%); B_2 (the same estimates with an adjustment for the latter factor). The most acceptable figures correspond to assumption B_2, and are given for four countries. In Rhodesia and South Africa, the Gini coefficient for the distribution of expected incomes under assumption B_2, is 0.059 and 0.052, respectively, above the corresponding value of G observed in a single year (i.e. an increase of 10%). The share of the first two quintiles is reduced by nearly a half: 5.2% instead of 8.2%, and 3.8% compared to 6.2%, respectively. Even in Tunisia and the Ivory Coast, where differences in life expectancy are less pronounced, the Gini coefficient increases by 0.049 and 0.046 respectively, i.e. by 9%, and the share of the first two quintiles is appreciably reduced: 8.2% and 7.5% instead of 11.4% and 10.4%, respectively. Comparing Rhodesia and South Africa with Tunisia and the Ivory Coast, shows that the observed income distribution is more unequal when the gap increases between observed inequality and that corresponding to expected income. This is clearly a consequence of the correlation between the different aspects of inequality. As income inequality increases, the associated differences in living conditions and health also increase, and a greater variation is found in the inequality related to the length of working life and expected income. This observation would be confirmed if the comparison were extended to developed countries.

The change in the Gini coefficient under each of the different sets of assumptions indicates the effect of each factor. Two of them, the reduced working period for people in the highest 5% and income variability in the lowest deciles, have a very small impact. Other things being equal, they reduce or increase the Gini coefficient by no more than 0.02. So, it is differences in life expectancy that appears to be the crucial determinant.

Whatever objections are raised against the method proposed here, one essential difference between developed and underdeveloped countries remains: differences in life expectancy are much greater in the latter countries. Inequality in the distribution of total income anticipated at the beginning of active-life corresponds roughly to the figures presented in table 10.4, while the same analysis applied to developed countries would not reveal any comparable gap between the inequality observed in a given year and that for total expected income. Thus, it is absolutely certain that differences between developed and underdeveloped countries are greater if we consider inequality over the lifetime instead of that observed in a particular year.

IV. Retained profits and relative prices

In the course of industrialisation, as the modern sector expands, the share of company profits in total value-added rapidly increases. Such a phenomenon is characteristic of early growth, for instance when GNP per capita is $100 to $500. Such growth later slows down and finally comes to a standstill. Profits still increase, but their share in the value-added by firms may decrease. The evolution of the share of profits in several Western European countries since 1900 confirms this trend. Consequently, there is a potential bias in inequality comparisons with underdeveloped economies. In such economies, 60–80% of total production comes from the traditional sector, and company profits amount to very little. The bias results from neglecting *retained* profits in estimates of income concentration (all *distributed* profits are normally imputed) and is therefore negligible in an underdeveloped economy. In a developing economy, however, retained profits may reach a figure comparable to that in developed countries. In the United States, they amount to 4% of household income in 1966.[14] Such a percentage is close to the maximum, since corresponding figures for Great Britain, France and Italy are certainly less. We can therefore take retained profits to vary between 2 and 5% of household income in developed countries.

In developing countries it is slightly less. In Malaysia, Lean (1974) corrected each distribution to take this income into account. He estimated it to be 2.2% of household income in 1967–1968 and allocated it completely to the tenth decile, whose share was thus increased from 43.1% to 44.2%. In Columbia, non-distributed profits amount to 3.3% of household income, and the growth model which has been

[14] Pechman and Okner (1974).

proposed predicts an appreciable increase in that figure.[15] Even if it is slightly less than in developed countries, its impact on inequality is similar, because the ownership of company stocks is always more concentrated in developing countries. This bias may therefore be neglected when comparing developing economies ($500 to $1500 per capita) with rich countries. But it overestimates concentration in underdeveloped economies (less than $200) compared to other countries. Pyatt (1976) rightly stresses the difficulties involved in making an appropriate allocation: part of the retained profits may be invested abroad to the benefit of the firms' owners. In addition, when companies are state-owned, they may make no profit or even incur deficits, written off with government funds, while their managers give themselves important fringe benefits. Some of the undistributed profit is also taken by the managers. The first situation occurs in capitalist economies, the second one mainly in socialist economies. In both cases, concentration is underestimated; but the bias cannot be calculated, since the people who benefit usually prevent these advantages from being measured.

Even in a developed economy, there are regional variations in prices. However, their impact on income distribution is negligible, for two reasons: they are quite small, and average income is similar in different areas. In less developed countries, such differences are greater and they have a positive – or negative – effect on the income level of particular groups, whose members are mainly found in some specific income bracket. They may therefore have an impact on income distribution.

Two examples will show the extent of these variations. In Ghana, a study[16] comparing the cost of living in urban and rural areas showed the former to be higher by a factor of 1.14, when goods are weighted according to consumption pattern in rural areas, or by 1.04, when the urban expenditure pattern is used. Urban households tend to buy more of those goods which are relatively cheaper for them. The goods which are less expensive in towns include imported food and transportation. In rural areas all products of local origin are cheaper than in towns, regardless of whether they are agricultural products, clothes or furniture. In Indonesia,[17] a price index covering 62 goods varies from 100 (Jakarta) to 155 (East Kalimantan) and 79 (West Nusaenggara). If only Java is considered, variations are reduced to a maximum of 100 (in the capital) and a minimum of 87 (in Yogyakarta). Thus differences of around 5 to 10% seem usual between the capital, or most important cities, and the country. As the majority of households in the first deciles live in rural areas, estimates of the distribution probably understate the share of the first two or three quintiles. If their share is 20%, for instance, a 10% correction raises it to 21.6%. This effect, though small, probably exists in most less developed countries and should be taken into account in any comparison with developed countries.

It can be argued that rural households derive far less benefit from public facilities than urban dwellers. This point, however, is related to redistribution through public expenditure.

---

[15] Bourguignon (1977).
[16] Knight (1972).
[17] Lydall (1977).

V. Income distribution and socio-economic groups

As Kuznets (1976) has noted, estimates of the distribution within socio-economic groups are of great interest: they enable us to avoid several biasses and may be linked more easily with macro-economic data. Within each group, income earners have a variety of ages, families differ in size, and the relative importance of transitory and permanent income vary among income earners. Most of these differences cancel out when the group as a whole is examined; one must allow for intergroup differences in such things as the average size of families or the average age of income earners, but such variations between groups are much smaller than they are between individuals. Moreover, in some countries, it is known how the values of some statistics vary among the groups, and group distributions may therefore be corrected.

I have estimated group distributions in six less developed countries (Columbia, the Ivory Coast, Kenya, Malaysia, Rhodesia and Senegal) and in France. As far as possible, I have tried to allocate income earners or heads of households among three occupational classes: salaried workers, agricultural self-employed and non-agricultural self-employed. The first category is easily sub-divided into three groups: unskilled or poorly skilled salaried workers, which includes all agricultural and domestic workers; skilled workers; and technicians or executives. This classification was applied to each country. But for agriculture it proved impossible to use a single method of classification. Depending on the data source, groups were classified according to income structure (food crops for home consumption or sale being the main item), or to the peasant's status (whether they work alone, or hire one or more people), or to the amount of land. Since income levels are closely related to each of these aspects, the groups thus defined are rather homogeneous. Finally, self-employed workers in the secondary and service sectors, were classified according to whether they belong to the traditional or modern sector, and to the size of the firm (or, if this were not known, to the number of employees).

In each country, these groups were arranged in the order of their average income. G and T (the Theil index) were computed for each distribution, assuming a perfectly equalitarian distribution within each group. As data on the distribution of income by size are available for these countries, comparison between the two estimates is of great interest.[18] The ratio G_1/G_2 compares two numbers, but does not represent that portion of inequality explained by the socio-economic classification. $G_2 - G_1$ corresponds to the distance between the observed distribution and the hypothetical distribution which assumes constant income within each class. On the other hand, T_1/T_2 gives the proportion[19] of inequality which may be explained by inter-group differences in average incomes. The values T_1/T_2 given in table 10.5 are of great

---

[18] Therefore, the values of T given below understate the exact value by 15–20%, in the case of France and Malaysia, and by 10–15% in the other cases. The exact value is determined from the distribution of individual incomes, rather than the distribution over deciles or centiles, when identical incomes are assumed within each decile or centile. The exact value has been computed for $N \to \infty$, and a Pareto distribution over the highest decile with exponent $\alpha = 1.7$.

[19] This proportion is overestimated by 10%, since T_2 is under-estimated by 15%, as explained in footnote 18.

Table 10.5. Gini and Theil coefficients for the aggregate distribution and the distribution over socio-economic sub-groups.

Country	Year	Units	Assumption	Classes	Gini coefficients			Theil coefficients		
					Socio-economic groups G_1	Aggregate distribution G_2	G_1/G_2	Socio-economic groups T_1	Aggregate distribution T_2	T_1/T_2
France	1970	Households	Non-active excluded	8	30.0			0.208		
			Non-active included	9	31.5	43.1	0.73	0.184	0.315	0.58
		Individuals	Non-active excluded	8	30.3			0.152		
			Non-active included	9	37.2			0.177		
Malaysia	1968	Households		5	33.2	49.2	0.68	0.210	0.438	0.48
Ivory Coast	1970	Income earners	High G_2	8	47.0	52.0	0.90	0.533	0.590	0.90
			Low G_2	8	46.8			0.525		
Rhodesia	1969	Income earners	Property income excluded	7	58.4			0.946		
			Property income included	7	60.0	63.5	0.94	—	0.986	0.96
		Individuals	Property income excluded	7	64.0			1.115		
			Property income included	7	65.5			—		
Senegal	1970	Income earners	High G_2	8	52.4	52.6	0.93	0.800	0.750	0.91
			Low G_2	8	49.1			0.686		
Kenya	1969	Income earners	High G_2	9	50.6	61.0	0.83	0.642	0.910	0.71
			Low G_2	9	49.6			0.680		
Columbia	1972	Income earners		7	51.7	57.2	0.90	0.635	0.665	0.95

significance: in all less developed countries, it is much higher than in France, 0.8 or 0.9 compared to 0.6. The only exception is Malaysia, where only 5 groups can be distinguished and this sometimes places salaried workers in the same category as the self-employed in the non-agricultural sector. This anomaly is therefore probably due to the lack of information.

A comparison between France and the other countries, shows that the proportion of total inequality due to age differences, and transitory and permanent income variations within sub-groups, is much lower in less developed countries. Moreover, if demographic data are available for each of the groups, as in France and Rhodesia, both the distribution per family-head and per person may be estimated.[20] Thus another cause of income variations between households is excluded, namely their size. Differences in T_1 or G_1 between countries are, in a way, more significant than differences in T_2 or G_2, because the former excludes those differences in annual incomes which disappear when lifetime incomes are compared. Differences in T_1 and G_1 suggest the following conclusion: we usually under-estimate differences in real inequality (that is, differences among individuals in incomes over a period of several years) between developed and less developed countries.

The distribution over socio-economic groups also enables us to adjust the estimates, to allow for the effect of relative prices, or the retained profits of companies. For instance, cheaper prices in rural areas benefit only certain groups, such as farmers in the traditional sector. Such adjustments to the data in underdeveloped countries, where retained company profits are negligible, tend to reduce the difference in inequality between developed and under-developed countries. On the other hand, they would probably have a small impact in developing countries (those, for instance, where GNP per capita is over $400 or $600). Taking all the necessary corrections into account, the difference in *real* inequality between developend and developing countries is certainly under-estimated.

The analysis of socio-economic groups is also a reliable method of interpreting income distributions and proposing redistributive policies. The income of each group depends on the distribution of productive factors (land, capital, etc.) and on prices of factors and goods. These incomes may be compared directly with national accounts. Consequently the changes resulting from growth, and variations in demand and relative prices, can be investigated.[21] When the groups defined above are examined, it is clear that they may be classified according to the amount of either material or human capital at the income earners' disposal: peasants and unskilled workers have almost none, whilst executives and managers of modern firms, whether medium or large in size, have a great deal. So, this grouping conforms to the distribution of capital, whether material or human. Another conclusion is that such groups may provide a suitable basis for redistributive policies, since they correspond so closely to groups defined by income level. Because their income depends on known variables, it may well lead to a more efficient policy. Needless to say, we are only hinting here at the double prospect which the socio-economic grouping suggests: the subject deserves another paper.

[20] In Rhodesia, for instance, the Gini ratio is much higher for the distribution per person than for the distribution over income earners.
[21] Maton, Paukert and Skolka (1974).

References

Anand, S., *The Size Distribution of Income in Malaysia, Part I and Part II*, Development Research Center, I.B.R.D., Washington, 1973.
Blaug, M., "An Economic Analysis of Personal Earnings in Thailand", *Economic Development and Cultural Change*, 1974.
Bourguignon, F., "Effects of Rural Development, Wage and Income Policies on the Distribution of Incomes in Colombia", I.L.O., Geneva, 1977.
Carnoy, M., "Earnings and Schooling in Mexico", *Economic Development and Cultural Change*, 1967.
Encarnacion, J. "Income Distribution in the Philippines: the Employed and the Self-employed". World Employment Research Programme, Working paper 8, I.L.O., Geneva, 1974.
van Ginneken, W., "Mexican Income Distribution Within and Between Rural and Urban Areas". World Employment Research Programme, Working paper 5, I.L.O., Geneva, 1974.
van Ginneken, W., "Characteristics of the Head of Household and Income Inequality in Mexico". World Employment Research Programme, Working paper 16, I.L.O., Geneva, 1975.
Hanoch, G., "An Economic Analysis of Earnings and Schooling". *Journal of Human Resources*, 1967.
Henry, R., "A Note on Income Distribution and Poverty in Trinidad and Tobago". World Employment Research Programme, Working paper 29, I.L.O., Geneva, 1975.
Hsia, R. and L. Chau, "Income Distribution and Employment Characteristics: Hong Kong 1971". World Employment Research Programme, Working paper 15, I.L.O., Geneva, 1975.
Knight, J., "Rural-Urban Income Comparisons and Migration in Ghana", *Bulletin of the Oxford Institute of Economics and Statistics*, 1972.
Kuznets, S., "Demographic Components in Size-distribution of Income" – *Income Distribution Employment and Economic Development in Southeast and East Asia*, vol. II, 1975.
Kuznets, S., "Demographic Aspects of the Size Distribution of Income: an Exploratory Essay", *Economic Development and Cultural Change*, 1976.
Langoni, C., "Income Distribution and Economic Development in Brazil", *Conjunctura Economica*, 1973.
Lean, L., "The Pattern of Income Distribution in West Malaysia 1957–1970". World Employment Research Programme, Working paper 6, I.L.O., Geneva, 1974.
Lean, L., "Employment and Income Distribution in West Malaysia". World Employment Research Programme, Working paper 24, I.L.O., Geneva, 1975.
Lydall, H., "Employment and Income Distribution in Developing Countries with Special Reference to Indonesia and Sri Lanka", I.L.O., Geneva, 1977.
Maton, J., F. Paukert and J. Skolka, "Redistribution of Income, Patterns of Consumption and Employment. A Case Study for the Philippines". World Employment Research Programme, Working paper 3, I.L.O., Geneva, 1974.
Morgan, J., and M. David, "Education and Income". *The Quarterly Journal of Economics*, 1963.
Morrisson, C., Papers prepared for the Development Research Center, I.B.R.D., Washington, 1972–1974.
Morrisson, C., "La repartition des revenus dans les pays du Tiers-Monde: Un état de la recherche". *Mondes en Développement*, 1976.
Paglin, M., "The Measurement and Trend of Inequality" a "Basic Revision", *American Economic Review*, 1975.
Pechman. J., and B. Okner, *Who bears the tax burden?*, The Brookings Institution, 1974.
Pyatt, G., "On International Comparisons of Inequality", Paper presented at the American Economic Association Meetings, 1976.
Stoikov, V., "How Misleading are Income Distributions?", Mimeographed, Ithaca, 1973.
Thias, H., and M. Carnoy, "Cost-Benefit Analysis in Education. A Case Study on Kenya", I.B.R.D., Washington, 1969.
Velloso, J., "Human Capital, Segmented Markets and the Distribution of Earnings in Brazil." Mimeographed, Stanford University, 1974.

10a DISCUSSION

PAPER BY CHRISTIAN MORRISSON

Professor Adelman congratulated the author on a fine piece of work. The paper not only attempted to explain and unify conceptual differences but also used all the available data to estimate the direction and magnitude of the biases arising from these differences. This enabled their importance to be judged, a sensible approach which she recommended to other economists.

The paper clearly indicates the importance of understanding and allowing for the institutional setting of particular measurements. Time and again these are neither negligible nor trivial. For example, Professor von Weizsäcker in his paper had suggested that self-employment in developed countries could be viewed as a choice by individuals between an income stream with a high average value and high risk, and another with a lower mean and lower risk. In developing countries, groups of self-employed, for instance farmers and agricultural workers, have both low and variable income. For these groups there is no risk premium for self-employment. In fact, the income distribution for the self-employed is bi-modal, with the professional groups at the top.

In the comparison of distributions of lifetime earnings, she drew attention to the age profiles of the labour force participation rates. In developing countries these were very flat, which was not the case in developed countries. She also emphasised the relationship between life expectancy and income. In developing countries life expectancy will be low when income is low. This will not necessarily be true in developed countries since certain groups such as air-line pilots and miners may choose high incomes whilst accepting a higher risk of mortality.

As the paper pointed out, there were significant differences in the institutional setting among developing countries themselves. She was particularly concerned with the differences arising from alternative concepts of income and inequality, which turn out to be large compared with differences attributable to reasonable policy changes. She had recently examined this problem in the context of a simulation study. A change of 0.01 in the Gini coefficient may appear rather small, but it corresponds to what might be achieved with a major public works programme costing 30% of the annual government budget. A 5–10% change in the Gini coefficient, which is within the range of some of the differences reported in the paper, corresponds to what might be achieved by a complete change in the economy from a socialist to a capitalist mode of production or vice versa.

She suggested that an appropriate choice of statistical techniques may compensate to some extent for poor quality data. She personally favoured using statistical techniques which are more robust to measurement errors. For example, using non-parametric tests in preference to parametric methods, techniques developed for use with ordinal data rather than cardinal data, and various analysis of variance techniques. On the whole she did not feel that income distribution data was good enough for regression-type analysis.

Professor Gollas approved of the fact that data limitations were clearly spelt out. He felt that bad information was often more damaging than having no data at all. One important point in the paper was the argument that the distribution of personal incomes was more unequal than the distribution of household incomes. This is not surprising since the personal distribution contains many more observations and a considerable proportion of women and children. However, it is not always the case that the personal distribution is the more unequal and he cited an example for India for the year 1964–65. In this instance average family size increased with average income, resulting in a reduction in inequality when the basis shifted from households to individuals. He would have liked to see, therefore, a discussion of the relationship between household and personal income distribution, and rules proposed for matching individuals and households in a systematic way.

He was not convinced that inequality induced by age was unimportant. A study for Colombia found that, for all educational levels, income increases continually up to age fifty and then begins to decline, particularly in the uneducated group. It is also true that incomes of young people have the greatest variance, so that countries with a high proportion of young people tend to show greater inequality. A similar argument applies to women, who enter the labour force at lower income levels. Inequality is therefore expected to rise when women constitute a high proportion of the workforce. This suggests that the sex composition, as well as the age structure, may be significant.

The argument that age is not important seemed to be inconsistent with the adjustments made later for future expected income, where age is an important factor.

He emphasised the significance of home produced consumption and income in kind, both of which have a substantial impact in developing countries. Another consideration was that income distribution data frequently come from expenditure surveys and this raises the question of how the consumption distribution can be translated into the income distribution. Finally, he mentioned the effects of price changes on inequality, which have to be taken into account when making comparisons over time. Also, the time of year at which the data are collected; in a study for Korea it was found that rural inequality was higher than that for urban areas, contrary to all theories of development, but this could be explained by the fact that the survey was taken during the off season.

Professor Chiswick said a distinction should be made between the question of whether age differences have a substantial impact on the value of an aggregate indicator, such as the Gini coefficient, and whether they alter the importance or interpretation placed on income inequality. For example, if incomes are standardised for age differences, the composition of the top and bottom groups in the income distribution may be affected even though the Gini coefficient is not. When no adjustments are made for age, some of those in the poverty group appear there for reasons not associated with poverty as it is usually understood.

Professor Robinson said that in the national income accounts he had helped to set up in developing countries, self-subsistence income comprised something like 60–80% of national income. These calculations required values to be imputed for a variety of commodities and the eventual figures varied considerably with the method of imputation followed. It is frequently the case that countries use different traditional methods of imputation, totally disregarding attempts to secure international standardisation, and it may be necessary to adjust for these different methods in order to make inequality comparisons between countries.

Professor Krelle said that developing countries may be regarded as being 100 to 150 years behind the developed nations. He therefore thought that it would be interesting to compare current inequality in developing countries with data from Germany, the U.K. or Sweden for the middle of the nineteenth century. He imagined they would be rather similar since the Lorenz curve for Germany had shifted substantially over the past century.

Professor Morrisson suggested that the relatively flat age profiles were probably due to the high proportion of self-employed, for whom income depends very little on age. With employees, differences in income with age are much more substantial. Pronounced age profiles are to be expected when income data are based on surveys of wages for the head of the household, rather than household income for the whole population, on which he had concentrated. In developing countries, very few individuals leave the family while they are still young, and this also contributes to the insignificance of the age factor.

That the income-age profiles for the majority of individuals are flatter than in developed countries, does not mean there are no differences in future expected earnings between socio-economic groups. For example, consider two groups – unskilled workers and professionals – whose respective incomes remain constant over the age range 25 to 65. Assume also that average life expectancy is only 55 for the first group and 70 for the latter. Then variations in age profiles do not explain differences in personal income, but observed inequality is less than that of future expected earnings.

Professor Gollas had indicated how complex the relationship is between the household distribution and the personal income distribution, and how one should approach this subject with caution. However, available data enable two general conclusions to be drawn: in developed countries, the personal income distribution is always significantly more unequal than the household income distribution; and, in less developed countries, the household distribution may sometimes be as unequal as the personal distribution.

On the estimation of the income distribution from expenditure surveys, Professor Morrisson said that the figures can be checked against the national income accounts and corrections made, where necessary, on the basis of other sources. On their own, expenditure surveys were unacceptable.

In reply to Professor Krelle, he pointed out that a comparison between current statistics for developing countries and those for developed countries a hundred years ago, may not be appropriate. For instance, civil servants are much more numerous now in developing nations than they were one hundred years ago in the developed countries. Other aspects of social structure were also quite different. Marx did not discuss income inequality because the division into two social groups was all he felt was necessary to enable him to analyse the problems of interest.

10b DISCUSSION

LONGEVITY AND INCOME DISTRIBUTION

During the discussion of several papers, particularly those of Professor von Weizsäcker and Professor Morrisson, certain problems arose regarding the appropriate treatment of the length of life when welfare comparisons are made. It was suggested that a short discussion should be organised on this particular topic. This was introduced by Professor Wiles.

Professor Wiles said his remarks were in the nature of questions to be answered rather than theses to be defended. Death poses many philosophical perplexities to lawyers, doctors, priests and moralists, but it seems to pose no fewer to economists, who have hardly taken up the challenge.

To begin with, longevity itself has a distribution and measures of dispersion, such as quantile ratios and Gini coefficients, can be computed. By comparison, income is an extremely difficult figure both to define and collect. The distribution indices of age at death are themselves a description of the inequality in a society. If the longevity distribution shows substantial inequality along social or economic lines, the society is very unequal in an important sense.

Secondly, longevity is a rather good proxy for welfare and even perhaps for income. However, several possible exceptions should be mentioned. In the Roman Empire the rich used lead piping which the poor could not afford. In medically unsophisticated countries, therefore, the rich can kill themselves inadvertently and, within certain quantiles, income may be inversely related to age at death. Military castes provide another example, since they are rich, yet the men die young.

He went on to raise a number of questions concerned with lifetime income. He asked whether a long life is preferable to a short one, given constant annual income. The answer is pre-empted by the assumption that longevity is a good proxy for welfare, but on further investigation it is not true that life should be as long possible. Old age reduces the capacity to enjoy and achieve, and minor ailments bulk larger and larger. All this he called *increasing taedium vitae*, or the diminishing marginal utility with age of a constant income. Moreover, medical and heating costs rise (DC' in the figure), so enjoyable income is reduced both from above and from below, until it reaches zero at the individual's optimum age of death. There is, of course, no reason why anyone should actually die at this age.

The optimal length of life can also be considered when the assumption of constant annual income is replaced by constant total lifetime income. This question is less important since so few people face such a choice, but it affects the distribution of income in an obvious way.

Discussion

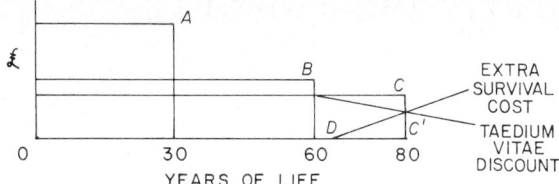

Suppose that the rectangles *A*, *B* and *C* represent the same amount of money (net of tax, at constant prices etc.) spread over different lifetimes. Whilst it may at first appear that we are indifferent between the extremely different experiences *A* and *B*, this neglects the diminishing marginal utility of money, which is taken to cover a certain period only. There is no "myopia" about these periods, i.e. no futurity discount; so *B* is preferred to *A*.

This theory also encompasses the rational spendthrift, who believes that life is not worth living without a high level of consumption (he may also be "myopic", but that is not strictly speaking rational). For him the taedium vitae line is exceptionally steep, beginning whenever his annual income falls below his minimum acceptable level and allowing him only time to drink himself to death on money borrowed from his erstwhile friends. Somewhat similar to the spendthrift, and far more common, is the athlete or beautiful woman (perhaps even pop and film stars) who may think there is no life after thirty, because they are highly sensitive to bodily changes. These have an early taedium vitae line which sets in about age thirty and declines rapidly at first, but flattens out and may increase again as the subject adjusts to middle age.

Professor Hogan disagreed strongly with the use of data on age at death to measure welfare, as Professor Wiles had proposed. The argument that the data were more reliable is untenable. The very societies in which there are severe handicaps to the collection of adequate data on income and income distribution are those where records of ages, and ages at death, are also very poor or worse. Census data can be notorious for the under-enumeration of population and the unreliability of age group estimates. Misgivings about one set of data is no basis for seeking refuge in some other series without equally careful scrutiny.

Professor Sen felt that two quite separate issues should be distinguished. There was the problem considered in Professor von Weizsäcker's paper; how inequality is affected if lifetime rather than annual income is taken as the basis for measurement. A different question concerns whether, given a certain income, longer life is desirable in itself. Then longevity becomes a good thing just like income and we may examine its average value, distribution and so on. He believed this latter problem to be relevant in this discussion.

He pointed out that differences in longevity are not reflected in the usual published statistics relating to welfare. To illustrate his argument he supposed there were two societies with identical time series for GNP and population, and also identical distributions at each point of time. In society 1, however, people died at age twenty-five whilst in society 2 death occurs at age eighty-five. We may well prefer to be born into society 2, but its relative attractiveness will not be indicated by the total GNP, the GNP per capita or the distribution. Something was clearly missing and this led him to suggest that lonevity had to be taken into account directly in determining the overall social welfare level. It also must be considered in the context of distributional equity.

He was delighted that Professor Morrisson had raised the issue in a specific empirical context and shown that income inequality comparisons are reinforced by the longevity of the groups involved. Professor Sen had himself once looked at Indian data to see the extent to which differences in standard of living between states were affected by introducing longevity. It turned out to have a significant impact. For example Kerala, one of the poorest states, has a relatively low mortality rate and a high expectation of life.

He had doubts about the optimal length of life calculations made by Professor Wiles but, assuming they could be done, he pointed out that any welfaristic approach would support execution after the optimal point had been reached. This illustrated very forceably the limitations of welfarism in neglecting questions of individual rights.

Professor Adelman said there was a trade-off between the interests of those already born and the interests of the would-be born. Professor Sen had suggested comparing a society in which people live for twenty-five years with one in which death occurs at age eighty-five. She believed the correct comparison should be between a society with a shorter lifetime and more births, and another with longer life but fewer births.

Professor Sen said he was only suggesting that the society with the longer life had a higher standard of living. The question raised by Professor Adelman was which alternative is socially optimal, an entirely different issue.

Professor Chiswick said there was some confusion as to whether lifetime income was a simple average or a present value concept. She felt strongly that some kind of discounting is needed to assess the relative desirability of different age-income profiles.

Professor Wiles and *Professor Sen* both questioned whether discounting was necessary.

Professor von Weizsäcker said that Professor Wiles had essentially reduced total utility to a function homogeneous of degree one in two arguments, the average utility of annual income through life and the length of life itself. With discounting the function would probably be of degree less than one.

Professor Robinson wondered whether the whole problem was being considered. There was one question of whether we go on enjoying life in old age and another concerned with making provision for the period of retirement. In some occupations, people save from high incomes during their working life and subsequently disinvest, whilst people in other occupations rely heavily on pension rights which do not appear in the income figures. The pre-retirement distribution of income may then be a poor reflection of the true welfare patterns.

Mr. Layard said that, since we are trying to compare welfare levels in different societies, the appropriate welfare function has to be specified. It should be a function of utilities rather than income. The fundamental question is then whether there is any increase in the length of life which would compensate for a reduction in the utility level of lives being lived. Whilst some people would say yes to this question, he was not one of them. But clearly the utility experienced by people while alive is affected by their own prospects of survival and by the actual survival of those they love.

Dr. Wagner felt the discussion was tending to be rather abstract. Attention should be paid to the fact that the utility function changes substantially over time. In particular, the relative disutility of death increases as the individual advances in age. Secondly, it may be misleading to consider the question of lifetime income in a decision-theoretic framework, since individuals are not in a position to decide whether or not they are born.

Professor Bentzel said that old people feared to die too late rather than too early, so it cannot be assumed that, past a certain age, longer life is more desirable.

Professor Krelle said that some discussants had treated the length of life as if it were an individual decision variable. This is rarely the case, except in societies where suicide was acceptable. On the other hand, the length of life can be regarded as a social decision, so it is possible to consider the optimality of different societies. This would take into account the natural endowments of the population, the optimal timing of periods of education and the appropriate division between working life and retirement.

Professor Taubman emphasised the interdependency between the length of life chosen and the income stream associated with it. Thaler and Rosen, for instance, had studied compensatory variations in wage rates for jobs involving a risk of death. This interdependence is also seen in other ways. When life expectancy is short, people may not invest in education and this in turn influences the distribution of annual incomes.

Dr. Shorrocks said the discussion had been mainly concerned with comparisons between different societies. He wished to focus instead on individual lifetime differences within a single society.

Suppose two people had the same constant annual income and the same probability of death, which is unaffected by individual decisions. Then it is reasonable to conclude that they have the same welfare regardless of how long they actually live. If one happened to live twice as long as the other, he would resist the suggestion that that person was twice as well off.

The problem becomes more complicated when account is taken of individual decisions which influence the date of death. Individuals may choose a high risk occupation (deep-sea divers, racing drivers etc.), with full knowledge of the higher mortality, in return for an income premium. Here the risk of death can be regarded as another characteristic of the occupation and treated in the same way as any other characteristic giving rise to disutility. Studies like that to which Professor Taubman referred, may provide evidence on the value which individuals attach to length of life. However, differences between occupational mortality rates may be relatively small compared with the overall variation in lifetimes.

Individuals may also influence the length of life through their consumption patterns. This suggests that low mortality can be treated as a normal good, possibly a luxury good. Empirically it may be difficult to identify the components of consumption directed towards this goal, but expenditure on medical services may provide a reasonable guide. If low mortality is a luxury good, one potentially testable conclusion follows. Those with higher incomes are less homogeneous with respect to mortality since the group contains some who have accepted higher incomes in return for an increased mortality risk, together with those who allocate part of their expenditure, consciously or unconsciously, to lowering the risk of death. The average lifetime of those with higher incomes is likely to be greater as the second factor probably dominates. But the dispersion of length of life is also likely to be greater for the reasons given.

Finally Dr. Shorrocks mentioned that the relationship between wealth and mortality had been studied in some depth in the context of obtaining wealth distribution estimates from the Estate Duty Statistics. There, data on social class mortality rates and on the mortality of those holding life assurance policies had been used as a proxy for the wealth-mortality relationship. Whilst mortality for the top social classes was only about 10% less than the overall mortality rate, and may therefore seem relatively unimportant, it has a significant impact on the composition of the retirement group since a much higher proportion of the wealthy seem to survive to old age.

PART IV

THEORIES OF PERSONAL INCOME DISTRIBUTION

11 EQUALITY, TAXATION AND INHERITANCE

JOSEPH E. STIGLITZ[1]

I. Introduction

This paper is concerned with the determinants of the distribution of income, wealth, and consumption,[2] and the effect of taxation on these distributions. The paper has a simple message: these distributions are *endogenous*, and are critically affected by taxation, but not always in the ways expected. As a result, many of the policies aimed at reducing inequality may, in the end, lead to an increase in inequality. For instance, inheritance taxes and interest income taxes may increase the inequality of wealth.[3]

The error in the conventional reasoning concerning inheritance taxes is simple: it focusses on the direct effect – the heirs inherit less and, to the extent that wealth inequality is due to inheritance, wealth inequality is reduced. Our argument is that the before tax distribution of wealth may change, and it may change so much as to actually increase the after tax degree of inequality.

We are used to finding, in other areas of economic analysis, that such partial equilibrium analyses may be misleading. But generally, the general equilibrium effects, though reducing the magnitude of the direct effects, do not reverse the direction. But in the case of inheritance or capital taxation, the effects on inequality may, under quite plausible conditions, be reversed. This result is perhaps not intuitively obvious, and most of the paper is devoted to explaining it.

Our basic strategy in formulating a theory of the income distribution is to first identify the *exogenous* variables which determine or define how individuals differ from one another. Individuals differ in three important respects:

(i) Endowments: different individuals inherit from their parents different amounts of capital, different abilities and different amounts of human capital; these

---

[1] The author is indebted to innumerable conversations on the topics of this paper with David Bevan. His study on closely related questions has greatly influenced my thinking about these questions. I am also indebted to John Flemming and Jim Mirrlees for discussions on these questions over the years. Financial support from the National Science Foundation is gratefully acknowledged.

[2] We are concerned here with the personal distribution of income and wealth, not the distribution of factor shares.

[3] There is a long discussion of the appropriate measurement of wealth inequality (see, e.g. Atkinson (1970) or Rothschild and Stiglitz (1973)) for a discussion of the measurement of income inequality; some additional complications are involved in developing measures of wealth inequality. For our purposes, however, we need not be particularly precise about what measure we use. In Part B of this paper we employ three measures: the coefficient of variation, the variance, and the Pareto coefficient of the tail of the distribution.

endowments are added to or subtracted from by the state, or by gifts from relatives and friends.

(ii) Tastes: individuals differ in a number of ways which affect not only the temporal pattern and the probability distribution of their own income, but also affect the income and wealth of their children. Among the components of "tastes" which are important in determining the distribution of income are (a) attitudes towards work, leisure, and consumption; this clearly affects the income earned by different individuals with the same endowment; (b) attitudes towards risks; this affects decisions concerning job choices and portfolio allocation, and hence clearly affects the probability distribution of future income; (c) attitudes concerning consumption today versus consumption tomorrow; this affects the savings rate, lifetime consumption patterns, lifetime earnings patterns, and investments in human capital; (d) attitudes towards children, which affects the number of children, the size of bequests, and the form of bequest (human versus physical capital).

(iii) Luck: given a particular set of endowments and particular set of tastes, individuals may still differ, since the outcome of their decisions may well be random. Among the major stochastic elements involved in the distribution of the income and wealth are (a) "occupational luck": being a lawyer may be a risky occupation; some are lucky and make it, some are unlucky and don't; (b) "investment luck": some invest in risk securities and are lucky, others are not; (c) accidents and illnesses, which obviously affect the income and savings of individuals (although in a sense these can be incorporated into a comprehensive definition of endowments.)

The endowments of one generation are related to the endowments, tastes, and luck of the previous generation; the relationship between the two involves both systematic and random components. Parents may differ in their attitudes about the number of children, and about the amount of human and non-human capital to transfer to their children; some, for instance, may wish to leave everything to the eldest son (primogeniture) while others may divide the inheritance equally among their heirs. Some may give a child of mediocre ability more than his brighter brother, to compensate for his poorer endowment, and some give him less, feeling that he can use it less well.

There are at least four important sources of randomness in the interaction of successive generations: (i) the ability of the child is not perfectly correlated with that of his parents; (ii) marriage: the ability of a child is related to that of both of his parents, but mating is, to some extent at least, random; (iii) births: the number of children is, to some extent at least, random; this affects the per capita inheritances of children of parents with a given wealth; (iv) death: so long as there are not perfect annuity markets[4] some individuals will have a positive net worth when they die; the exact amount depends on the date of death, which is random, and hence the amount inherited is random.

---

[4] And the kinds of considerations discussed in Rothschild and Stiglitz (1976) suggest that so long as information is costly, there never will be.

Of the variables listed, many have the property that they are exogenous in the short run, but endogenous in the long; for instance, the endowments of physical and human capital may be given in the short run, but in the long run, they are endogenous. Wage rates may be given in the short run, but in the long run, they depend on the level of capital accumulation, which depends on taxation. Moreover, the magnitude of the stochastic elements themselves are, to some extent, endogenous. The distribution of returns to a particular risky asset may be exogenous, but, since the portfolio allocation is itself endogenous, the distribution of returns to investment as a whole is endogenous.

The theory of the distribution of income and wealth is concerned with how differences in endowments, tastes, and luck[5] become translated into an income and wealth distribution. For instance, if all individuals had the same endowments, if there were no random components in income determination, and if individuals differed only in their attitudes towards work and leisure, then the degree of inequality will depend simply on the distribution of those attitudes; and the effect of a change in the income tax rate on the distribution of income will depend simply on whether those who work more have a lower elasticity of labor with respect to the wage; in figure 11.1, we have depicted a case where they do. The result that the income tax *increases* the degree of income inequality is immediate.

A full model, taking into account individual differences in tastes, endowments, and luck, seems intractable, and if we are to get anywhere we must simplify.

In this paper, we focus on the distribution of lifetime income and wealth; as a consequence, we shall not be concerned with details concerning the lifetime pattern of income, including life-cycle savings. This simplifies matters considerably, but still leaves much to be done.

The basic model underlying our analysis is simple: we postulate that the ability

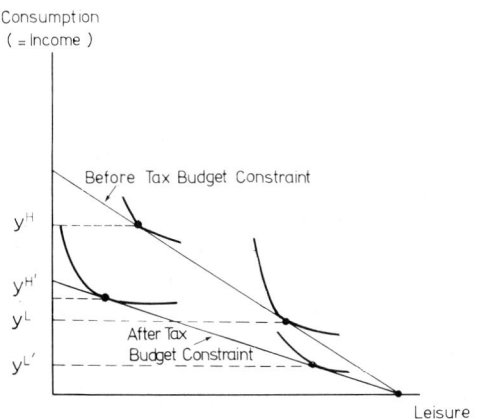

Figure 11.1

[5] Monopoly power (including discrimination) and gifts from the government are sometimes suggested as further determinants of the distribution of income. We will not deal with these explicitly here, although formally, they perhaps should be included in the category of "endowments".

of an individual is a stochastic function of the ability of his parents. The *wage* of an individual is a function of his ability, his human capital, the information about his ability which is available, and certain market aggregates (e.g. the aggregate capital labor ratio). All of these except ability are endogenous variables, affected by government policy.

Similarly, the wealth of an individual is a function of his inheritance and his lifetime savings; the latter depends on his income, including the return he has earned on his capital and his wages. His inheritance is a function of his parents income which depends on their inheritances, the return on their capital, and the tax rates on inheritance. The return he has earned on his capital depends on his portfolio allocation, which in turn depends on tax rates.

The distribution of lifetime income and wealth thus depends on certain underlying sources of randomness – in the above model, on the randomness associated with inherited ability and on the randomness associated with the returns to a particular security; – but these underlying sources of randomness are translated into income and wealth inequality in a most complicated way, and are affected by the decisions of individuals with respect to savings, portfolio allocation, investment in human capital, the amount of screening, etc. Any change in the tax structure changes all of these decisions and hence changes the underlying distribution of income and wealth.

Note that even this model represents a considerable simplification, e.g. we have omitted several of the sources of randomness mentioned earlier.

There have, of course, been earlier stochastic models of income determination (see, for instance, Champernowne (1953) and Mandelbrot (1961)); but these stochastic models have not been structural models; i.e. they have not identified the determinants of the stochastic process describing income determination. There have also been earlier dynamic models of income determination (see, in particular, Stiglitz (1969a)), but these dynamic models, though focussing in an important way on the role of savings behavior, reproductive behavior, inheritance policy, (e.g. primogeniture versus equal division among heirs), and ability differences in the determination of the income distribution, have not, for the most part, been stochastic,[6] and have had only limited scope for the adjustment of individual behavior to, say, changes in tax policy.

Our objective here is to formulate a dynamic, stochastic model in which the behavior of individuals is responsive to tax policy. We have attained only limited success in our objective. A number of "special models" which capture one or another aspect of the income determination process are formulated in the paper. But even the most general model treated does not capture as many of the important aspects as one would like. Hence, this paper should be viewed as a preliminary exploration in an area which has been subjected to too little theoretical investigation. These preliminary results cast coubt on the efficacy and desirability of various government policies designed at redistributing income and wealth.

The paper consists of two parts. Part A presents in a verbal and heuristic manner the argument that capital taxation may increase the degree of inequality. Part B

---

[6] See, however, the brief discussion in Stiglitz (1969a).

presents a sequence of models designed to justify some of the assertions made in Part A.

PART A: Why might capital taxation increase inequality?

We present three sets of arguments for why capital taxation may increase inequality:

(i) Even if factor prices do not change, capital taxation may lead to individuals changing their behavior with respect to investment in human capital, screening and portfolio allocation in such a way as to increase inequality.
(ii) Capital taxation may change the capital–labor ratio (it is likely to lower it); this changes factor prices, which may lead to an adverse change in the distribution of income and wealth.
(iii) The inequality that we should be concerned with is inequality of consumption; and, in general, inheritances serve to decrease inequality[7] of consumption among the members of a single family.

II. Effects with fixed factor prices

In this section, we consider the effect capital taxation has on the degree of observed inequality[8] in the economy when factor prices are fixed. The tax has a number of effects, on labor supply, human capital accumulation, screening, life-cycle accumulation, risk taking, etc. Most of these *may* lead to an increase in inequality of income and/or wealth. Some of them would in fact normally be expected to. Other effects would normally be expected to reduce inequality. Our approach is basically taxonomic, i.e. we list the various effects and trace out their implications. We are not able to construct a single, comprehensive model, and hence we are unable at this stage to make any judgement about whether "normally" one would expect the tax structure to increase or decrease inequality. Our purpose, as we noted earlier, is to show that there is a real possibility that inheritance and other capital taxes might increase inequality; by examining the particular mechanisms by which that is done, it may be possible to design the tax structure so as to reduce the likelihood of undesired consequences of the tax policy.

Of the arguments we present in this section, four relate to the effect of taxation on the distribution of lifetime wage income (two concern the level of wages (human capital, screening), one concerns the effect on the distribution of wage *income* through the effect on labor supply, and the fourth concerns the effect on the distribution of lifetime incomes). The remaining three arguments relate to the effect of taxation on the distribution of inheritances.

---

[7] Obviously, primogeniture may serve to increase inequality. Throughout this paper, we focus on "equal sharing" inheritance policies.

[8] By "observed inequality" we mean inequality in measured income, since differences in effort, leisure, etc. are difficult to observe. "Observed income" inequality and "real income" inequality may be markedly different.

II.1. *Human capital*

Capital taxes may increase investment in human capital. Since "abilities" are unequally distributed, an increase in human capital expenditures may increase inequality of wage income. The simplest way to see this is to assume that the individual's wage is a function of his ability, A, and his human capital, c_h:

$$w = G(A, c_h). \tag{1}$$

The individual invests in human capital (assuming a perfect capital market) to the point where the return is equal to the after tax market rate of interest, $\hat{r}$; that is, individuals maximize their net income, y, where y is equal to wage income plus capital income[9]

$$y = w + \hat{r}(c - c_h), \tag{2}$$

where c is total capital. Hence $c - c_h$ is non-human capital. Hence

$$G_{c_h} = \hat{r}. \tag{3}$$

Lowering the after tax return on physical capital will, with diminishing returns, lead to an increase in c_h.

If everyone had equal total capital, but unequal abilities, this would tend to increase income inequality. Assume, for instance, that G had constant returns to scale; then we can write

$$w = Ag(c_h/A) \tag{4}$$

so (3) becomes

$$g'\left(\frac{c_h}{A}\right) = \hat{r} \tag{5}$$

or

$$c_h/A = g'^{-1}(\hat{r}).$$

For all individuals, human capital is proportional to ability. This means that the variance of y, σ_y^2, can be simply related to the variance of A

$$\sigma_y = \sigma_A\left[g - \frac{c_h}{A}\hat{r}\right],$$

and similarly, the coefficient of variation of y, which we denote as

$$\hat{\sigma}_y \equiv \sigma_y/\bar{y}$$

---

[9] Alternatively, we might have assumed they maximized

$$w + (1 + \hat{r})(c - c_h)$$

which would have yielded

$$G_{c_h} = 1 + \hat{r}.$$

The analysis is identical with this formulation.

where $\bar{y}$ is the mean of y, can be written as

$$\hat{\sigma}_y = \frac{\hat{\sigma}_A\left[g - \frac{c_h}{A}\hat{r}\right]}{g - \hat{r}\frac{c_h}{A} + \hat{r}\frac{c}{A}} = \frac{\hat{\sigma}_A}{1+\gamma},$$

where γ is just the ratio of the income from capital ($\hat{r}c$) to (net) income from wages (net of the human capital), and where $\hat{\sigma}_A$ is the coefficient of variation of A. Hence

$$\frac{d \ln \hat{\sigma}_y}{d \ln \hat{r}} = -\frac{\gamma}{1+\gamma}\frac{g}{g - \hat{r}c_h/A} < 0.$$

Diagrammatically, the result can be seen in figure 11.2. The equilibrium level of human capital is given by the point on the wage curve where the slope is equal to the after tax rate of interest. Total income is also represented in the diagram. Clearly, if there were no investment in human capital, there would be complete equality. If the wage function had no asymptote, then, as human capital increases, the coefficient of variation approaches that of ability.

Thus, if the tax structure encourages human capital accumulation it is likely to lead to greater inequality.[10]

The critical question is whether, on the whole, the tax structure encourages human capital. The inheritance tax undoubtedly does, since gifts of human capital are exempt from the estate and gifts tax. On the other hand, a uniform wage and capital tax would reduce the return to human capital and its opportunity cost proportionately, so that there would be no effect on investment in human capital.

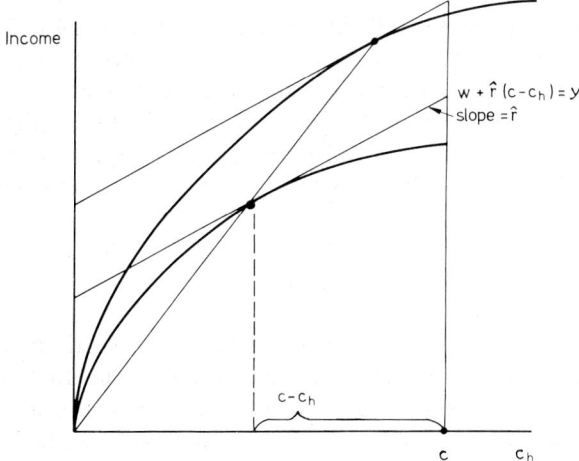

Figure 11.2

[10] This ignores the direct redistribution effects of the tax. A highly progressive inheritance tax will lead to little revenue from redistribution but has a strong incentive effect in encouraging investment in human capital.

To the extent that, as a result of special provisions pertaining to capital (such as the special provisions for capital gains), capital is in fact taxed at an effective rate lower than wages, the tax structure may actually discourage human capital accumulation.

On the other hand, since higher education gives access to jobs with more non-pecuniary benefits, which are not taxed, it may be that, at the margin, the effective tax rate on the return to human capital is lower than that on physical capital.

This is still a partial analysis, for differences in capital are related to differences in parental income; thus, the increased inequality of wage income might lead to an increase in inequality of inherited income, and thus the total degree of inequality is magnified.

We postpone until Part B a detailed description of a dynamic model with human capital accumulation.

II.2. *Screening*

The above analysis assumed that education increased individuals' productivities. But the analysis only required that there be a *private* return to education – the return could be from screening; education provides information concerning individuals' relative abilities. Lowering the opportunity cost of capital encourages individuals to invest in more screening. By its very nature, screening increases inequality (see Stiglitz (1975)).

II.3. *Labor supply*

The labor supply elasticities of different incomes may be different; if the tax reduces the supply of labor less for high income individuals than low income individuals, it will increase observed income inequality. Here we are concerned with capital taxes, so that the supply elasticity we are concerned with is the response of labor to a change in the after tax rate of interest. If higher income individuals retire at a later age, the rate of interest may play a smaller role in labor supply decisions. This effect is likely, however, to be weak, and we only mention it as a possibility.

II.4. *Distribution of life time incomes*

Individuals' wages differ from year to year, in a somewhat stochastic manner. In the long run, many of these stochastic elements even out, some individuals being lucky this year, others lucky next. When the after tax rate of interest is low, the sequence of incomes, i.e. whether one first has a good year followed by a bad year, or a bad year followed by a good year, makes no difference; but if the interest rate is high, the sequence is important. Thus, an interest income tax which lowers the after tax rate of interest reduces the degree of inequality in the present discounted value of wage income. Consider a simple model in which the probability that an individual with income w_i has an income w_j next period is a_{ij}. Assume the matrix

$A = \{a_{ij}\}$ in indecomposable. Then in the limit, at a zero interest rate with infinite lived individuals, average income is independent of initial income; there is complete equality. On the other hand, with an infinite rate of interest, in the steady state, the distribution of lifetime incomes is just equal to the eigenvector of A, i.e. it is given by the vector w^*, where

$$w^* A = w^*.$$

The next three effects are directly concerned with the distribution of inheritances. In this sub-section, we discuss a non-stochastic dynamic model, while in the next two we formulate stochastic models.

II.5. Dependence of inheritances on wage income

If individuals bequeath to their children an amount which is a function of their own income, and if children's wages are perfectly correlated with parental wages, then it can easily be shown that the distribution of inherited wealth will be simply related to the distribution of wage income (including any governmental transfers). The greater the inequality of wage income, the greater the inequality of inherited wealth. Since redistributive capital taxes increase the equality of wage income (after taxes and transfers), they will increase the degree of equality of inheritances. This effect may be the most significant effect of those discussed. On the other hand, to the extent that the first three arguments presented above are applicable (concerning human capital accumulation, screening, and labor supply decision), so that wage income inequality is increased, there will be a "magnification effect", i.e. capital income inequality will thereby also be increased.

II.6. Life-cycle accumulation and unanticipated deaths

This and the next argument are concerned with stochastic, dynamic models giving rise to inequality. The date of death of an individual is stochastic, and individuals cannot obtain complete life insurance (i.e. buy annuities which are actuarially fair). This is partly due to the fact that individuals are better informed concerning their health prospects than are firms, and hence there is a process of adverse selection at work: those who are the worst risk have the strongest incentive to purchase insurance (see Stiglitz, forthcoming). The absence of perfect annuity markets means that individuals will normally have some wealth at the time of their death. The amount of wealth they have to leave to their heirs depends on how soon after retirement they die. Lowering the rate of interest implies that individuals have to save more to provide for an adequate income in their retirement. Thus, at the date of retirement, they *may* have more capital. This means that the degree of inequality of inherited wealth may be increased.

On the other hand, the lower after tax rate of interest discourages lifetime saving, and if this effect dominates the degree of inequality will be reduced.

II.7. *Risk taking*

The final important way that capital taxation changes the distribution of wealth in the long run is through its effect on risk taking. Elsewhere in the literature, there has been an extensive discussion of the effect of taxation on risk taking. In Part B we present a further analysis of this problem. The major conclusion of these studies is that, under not unreasonable conditions, the tax structure may lead to increased risk taking, and indeed to an increased (or unchanged) variance in *after tax* income: to the extent that this is the case, inequality will be increased (or unchanged), not only directly, through its effect on the distribution of incomes, with given capital, but indirectly, through its effect on the inheritances of different individuals (this is analogous to the magnification effect discussed in connection with wage inequality in sub-section II.5 above).

III. The effect of taxation on factors prices and the effect of changes in factor prices on the distribution of income

We wish to show here that:
(i) taxation may have an important effect on changes in factor supplies, and
(ii) the changes in factor supplies may, in turn, have a deleterious effect on the distribution of income and wealth.

There are two types of effects; one operating through the aggregate supply of factors, the other through the allocation of the factors.

III.1. *Aggregate factor supplies*

The argument here consists of three steps:
(i) The tax structure affects the aggregate supply of labor and capital. Here we focus entirely on the latter.
(ii) The changes in the aggregate capital labor ratio changes the factor distribution of income.
(iii) The changes in the factor distribution of income in turn results in a change in the personal distribution of wealth.

We present three arguments for why capital and inheritance taxation may lower the supply of savings.

(a) The first, and perhaps most widely discussed effect arises from the differences in savings propensities of those who are taxed (the wealthy) and those who, in effect, receive the benefits of the tax (the poor). The magnitude of this depends on the magnitude of the differences in savings propensities.

(b) The second effect is the "incentive" effect; conventionally, it has been argued that its effects are ambiguous, with the substitution effect leading to less wealth left to one's heirs; but to leave that amount to one's heirs, one has to save more, so that if the elasticity of supply of *net* inheritances is less than unity, savings are actually increased.

Equality, taxation and inheritance

But this analysis ignores the redistributive nature of the tax. It is simplest to analyze the net effect of the tax if we assume all individuals have identical, homothetic indifference maps between their consumption and the consumption of their heirs. (Then the marginal propensities to save are identical, and, in the traditional discussions, focussing only on differences in savings propensities, there would accordingly be no effect on savings.) This assumption means that we can focus completely on a representative individual, ignoring – for the purpose of calculating the effect on savings – the distribution of wealth. We assume that the inheritance tax is levied at the end of the individual's life, and the proceeds are distributed uniformly in the population.

The before tax equilibrium (at fixed interest rate) can now be represented diagrammatically as in figure 11.3. w_t is the wage, b_t is the bequest he receives, while b_{t+1} is the bequest he gives, $w_t + b_t$ is the lifetime "wealth" of the individual. His budget constraint is given by

$$C_t + \frac{b_{t+1}}{1 + r_t} = w_t + b_t. \tag{6}$$

where, for simplicity, we have assumed a zero rate of population growth (so all variables are per capita), and where r_t is the rate of interest, and C is his consumption. The budget constraint is given by the line BB in figure 11.3.

By the homotheticity assumption we have

$$b_{t+1} = s(w_t + b_t)(1 + r_t), \tag{7}$$

where $s = s(1 + r_t)$ is the "savings" rate (or perhaps better, bequest rate), a function of r_t. Hence, in steady state,

$$b^* = \frac{sw(1 + r)}{1 - s(1 + r)}. \tag{8}$$

b is just the capital stock per capita. Hence, if $f(b)$ is output per man as a function of capital per man (assuming a constant return to scale technology), and if factors get paid their marginal product, we can rewrite (7) to read

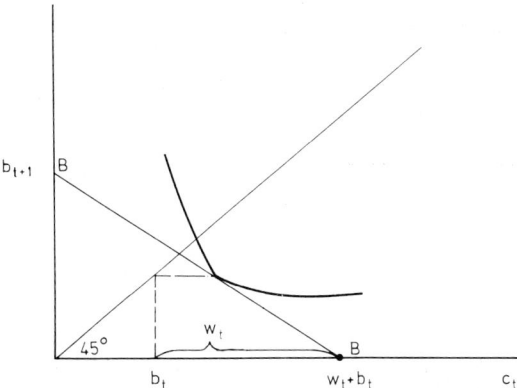

Figure 11.3

$$b_{t+1} = (f(b_t) - b_t f'(b_t) + b_t)s(1 + f'(b_t))(1 + f') \equiv \varphi(b_t). \tag{9}$$

The equilibrium is depicted in figure 11.4.[11]

The imposition of an inheritance tax changes the dynamic equation to read

$$b_{t+1} = [f(b_t) - b_t f'(b_t) + b_t]s((1 + f'(b_t))(1 - \tau))(1 + f') = \hat{\varphi}(b_t). \tag{10}$$

It is immediate that b^* is lowered; the steady state capital stock is lowered and the rate of interest increased. A redistributive inheritance tax lowers savings when there are no differences in marginal propensities to save. The intuitive reason for this result is that, with redistribution, the income effects (at any level of wealth) cancel, and one is left solely with the substitution effect.

(c) The third way capital taxation may lower the rate of savings is through its effect on life cycle savings; and because death is stochastic, different patterns of life cycle savings will result in different levels of inherited wealth as we argued above (II.6).

III.2. *Implications of reduced savings for the distribution of income and wealth*

If the tax structure leads to a reduced level of savings, capital's share in output will increase when the elasticity of substitution between capital and labor is less than unity. And since wealth is generally more unequally distributed than labor, this will increase the degree of inequality of income.

In the long run, the distribution of wealth is itself an endogenous variable; but even when endogeneity of the wealth distribution is taken into account, the

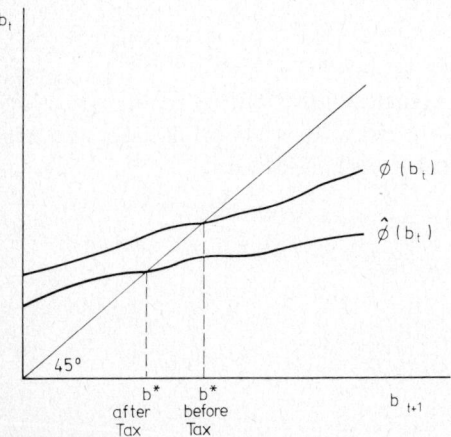

Figure 11.4

[11] We assume the stability condition,

$$\varphi' = (1 - bf'')(1 + r)s + \left(\frac{s'}{s} + \frac{1}{1+r}\right)f''\varphi < 1,$$

is satisfied.

income distribution may become more unequal. The practical importance of this depends critically on the extent to which actions, such as monetary and debt policy, can neutralize the effects of the reduced private savings (see Stiglitz (1978)).

III.3. *Effects of taxation on the allocation of capital and the implications for wealth and income distribution*

In addition to affecting the aggregate level of capital accumulation, capital taxes may affect the allocation of that capital, and this may have a deleterious effect on the distribution of income. There are two mechanisms to which we wish to draw attention.

The first we have already discussed: the inheritance tax may lead to the substitution of human for physical capital; this substitution will lead to a reduction in the total supply of physical capital, and this in turn may lead to a general lowering of wages particularly of those types of labor which are strongly complementary with capital.

The second is a consequence of imperfections in the capital markets and of imperfect information concerning the productivities of different investments. Managers and owners of firms have more information concerning their own firm than do outsiders. Consider the limiting case where the market treats all firms as identical. If there were total reliance on "outside" funding, there would be too little investment in good firms, too much in bad firms. If on average past productivity is positively correlated with current productivity, allowing firms to reinvest their own retained earnings would provide a better allocation of investment.[12] Capital taxes generally have the effect of requiring the firm to rely more heavily on outside financing, and hence lead to a less efficient allocation of capital. But since the demand for labor is a function of the efficiency with which capital is utilized, the demand for labor will be reduced, and hence so will be the equilibrium wage.

IV. **The distribution of consumption**

The variable whose distribution we should probably be most interested in is consumption; lifetime consumption differs from lifetime income by net bequests (differences between inheritances received and inheritances given). Since there is some presumption that individuals leave money to others primarily because they believe that the recipients would otherwise be (or are) worse off than the benefactor, it would seem clear that inheritances are unambiguously equality increasing. They constitute (generally) a particular class of gift, i.e. gifts within a family, but the basic principle, that the recipients are, on average, less well off than the giver, remains

---

[12] If taxes paid and retained earnings were easily and accurately observable, then clearly the market could extract all the information contained in that data, and allocate investment at least as efficiently as it is done by allowing firms to invest up to their retained earnings without having recourse to the market.

valid. Thus restricting this particular class of gifts would, presumably, increase the degree of inequality of consumption. In Part B, section VII we consider a special case of this; there, inheritance is a method by which families redistribute income (within the family) from the more fortunate to the less fortunate: with regression towards the mean, the more able will, on average, have less able heirs. Thus inheritance acts to increase the degree of equality in *consumption*. In Stiglitz (1978) it was shown that if the interest rate were zero, the outright forbidding of inheritance would unambiguously lead to an increase in the long run level of consumption inequality. In section VII, we consider the more general case of a positive interest rate and a partial reduction in inheritance. It is shown that provided the interest rate or the inheritance rate is not too high, an increase in the fraction of income left to one's heirs increases equality of consumption.

In part B we present some simple models showing explicitly the effect of taxation on the distribution of income and wealth. Section V presents the basic dynamic model; sections VI and VII extend the basic model to include random interest income and random wages. Section VIII considers the effect of taxation on the allocation of investment between human and physical capital. Section IX extends the analysis to screening. Section X analyzes the effect of the uncertain timing of death. Finally, section XI presents a general argument that with interest deductibility, a redistributive capital tax will have no affect on risk taking.

PART B: Models of wealth and income distribution

V. **The basic model**

The basic dynamic model, relating the distribution of wealth to the distribution of wages, was presented in Stiglitz (1969a). Since most of the remaining analysis can be viewed as extensions of this basic model, we briefly review it here.

Individuals leave to their heirs what they inherited, plus a constant fraction of their lifetime income; if c is per capita inherited wealth, in discrete time

$$c_{t+1} = \frac{sy_t + c_t}{1 + n}, \tag{11}$$

where s is the fraction of (lifetime) income, y_t, given to one's heirs, and n is the rate of growth of population. Income consists of wage income plus return on (inherited) capital

$$y_t = w_t + rc_t. \tag{12}$$

Thus, we obtain a simple difference equation relating c_{t+1} to c_t:

$$c_{t+1} = \frac{sw_t + src_t + c_t}{1 + n}, \tag{13}$$

or, in continuous time,

$$\dot{c} = sw + (sr - n)c, \tag{14}$$

yielding a steady state distribution of inherited wealth

$$c^* = \frac{sw^*}{n - sr}, \tag{15}$$

which is a simple transform of the wage distribution. Implicitly, we have assumed that the child's wage is perfectly correlated with the parent's wage. Later, we shall show how this assumption affects the analysis.

An immediate implication of (15) is that the coefficient of variation of per capita wealth is just equal to the coefficient of variation of w. Notice that one of the strong implications of this model is that if wages were equal, wealth would eventually be equalized. The fact that the rate of growth of population exceeds net savings out of interest income, sr, means that there is a strong equalizing force resulting from dividing one's wealth equally among one's heirs.

If individuals differ from one another in a pure labor augmenting way, (i.e. one able individual is equivalent to λ less able individuals, where λ is independent of the capital labor ratio) then the coefficient of variation of before tax wages is a constant. Hence, the coefficient of variation of the distribution of wealth is reduced by any linear tax structure, i.e. by any tax structure which imposes a tax which is a linear function of wage and interest income.[13]

The aggregate capital labor ratio is simply the average per capita capital stock of the entire population, i.e.

$$k \equiv Ec = \frac{sEw}{sr - n} = \frac{s\bar{w}}{sr - n}$$

where a bar over a variable represents its average value and E is the expectations operator.

In subsequent sections we shall modify and extend the model by allowing for (a) random return on capital; (b) random wage rates; (c) human capital accumulation.

VI. Random return on capital

If we assume that the return on capital is random, then asymptotically, wealth will not be evenly distributed. Let $\rho(c)$ be the random distribution of returns; we assume that it may depend on c, perhaps because of the portfolio allocation decisions. Let

$$u = \ln c$$

so

$$e^u = c. \tag{16}$$

---

[13] If there is a positive intercept of the consumption function, then the coefficient of variation of capital exceeds that of wages. The imposition of capital taxation may increase inequality. (see Stiglitz (1978)).

Then, assuming returns are described by a simple diffusion process, we have (in the absence of taxation) the stochastic differential equation describing capital accumulation

$$du = \{sw\,e^u + (s\bar{\rho} - n)\}\,dt + \sqrt{(\alpha(c))}\sqrt{(dt)} \tag{17}$$

where $\alpha(c)$ is the instantaneous variance of the rate of return, ρ, on wealth. Thus, if $a(c)$ is the proportion of wealth invested in a risky asset whose return is e, and if the safe return is r,

$$\rho \equiv a(c)(e - r) + r \tag{18a}$$
$$\bar{\rho} = a(c)(\bar{e} - r) + r \tag{18b}$$

then

$$\alpha(c) = a^2 \sigma_e^2 s^2 \tag{19}$$

where σ_e^2 is the variance of e. The asymptotic wealth distribution $h(c)$ satisfies the differential equation[14]

$$\tfrac{1}{2}\alpha h'' + [\alpha' - (sw\,e^{-u} + s\bar{\rho} - n)]h' + [\tfrac{1}{2}\alpha'' + sw\,e^{-u} - s\bar{\rho}']h = 0. \tag{20}$$

In particular, if

$$a \to a^* \quad \text{as} \quad u \to \infty$$
$$a' \to 0 \quad \text{as} \quad u \to \infty$$

then for large u

$$\frac{h''}{h'} \to \frac{2(s\bar{\rho} - n)}{a^2 \sigma_e^2 s^2}. \tag{21}$$

Now the coefficient of variation of y,

$$\hat{\sigma}_y = \sqrt{\left(\frac{a^2 \sigma_e^2 k^2}{\bar{y}^2}\right)}$$

and

$$s\bar{w} = -s\bar{\rho}k + nk.$$

Hence

$$-\frac{h''}{n'} = \frac{2\bar{w}}{\bar{y}}\frac{k}{s\bar{y}}\frac{1}{\hat{\sigma}_y^2} = \frac{2\bar{w}}{n\bar{y}}\frac{1}{\hat{\sigma}_y^2}.$$

---

[14] The distribution of u is given by the solution to the Kolmogorov equation

$$\tfrac{1}{2}\alpha f'' + (\alpha' - \beta)f' - (\tfrac{1}{2}\alpha'' - \beta')f = \frac{df}{dt}.$$

Asympototically, $\dfrac{df}{dt} = 0$.

In this problem $\beta = sw e^u + (s\bar{\rho} - n)$ and $\beta' = sw e^u$.

If for instance, the share of labor is between 0.7 and 0.8 and we take as our time unit a generation, so $n = 2$, and $\hat{\sigma}_y^2$ is between 0.2 and 0.4, then the asymptotic value of $-h''/h'$ is between 2 and 4.

With redistributive taxation, the asymptotic degree of inequality will be affected through the effect on s, $\bar{p}$ and $a\sigma_e$. For instance, later we show that a redistributive capital tax with full interest deductability leaves the after tax variance of return unchanged, and hence inequality is unchanged. If, on the other hand, risk taking increases so much that the after tax return has a higher variance (which can occur if individuals have increasing relative risk aversion, since the tax makes people on average poorer) then inequality may be increased.

VII. A stochastic model of wage and capital accumulation

In the models formulated thus far, the productivity of the child is identical to the productivity of the parent. This is inconsistent with the widely noted phenomenon of rags to riches in three generations. A more realistic model would involve the famous law of regression towards the mean; the purpose of this section is to formulate such a model. To obtain simple analytical results, we again shall use a diffusion model.

We define

$$A = \ln w \qquad (22)$$

(where w is the wage). A is the "ability" of the individual. Without loss of generality, let $EA = 0$. We assume that the average ability of the immediate heirs lies between the ability of the parent and the average ability in the population. On the other hand, there is considerable randomness in inheritance; some children are brighter than their parents (even if their parents are above average). Let $\alpha(A)$ be the instantaneous variance of inheritance, and $\beta(A)$ be the average rate of regression towards the mean; then

$$dA = \beta(A)(A - EA)\,dt + \alpha(A)\sqrt{(dt)}. \qquad (23)$$

The functions β and α completely determine the asymptotic distribution of income. In particular, if we assume that the instantaneous variance of A is constant (since A is the logarithm of wages, this is equivalent to a constant instantaneous coefficient of variation in w) and β is also constant (the average child's ability lies a constant fraction of the way between the parents ability and the mean ability) then the asymptotic ability distribution is the normal distribution with variance equal to[15]

$$\sigma_A^2 = \frac{\alpha}{2\beta}. \qquad (24)$$

---

[15] The Kolmogorov equation (fn. 14, above) becomes

$$\tfrac{1}{2}\alpha f'' + \beta A f' + \beta f = 0.$$

For the normal distribution

Note that since ability is the logarithm of wages, wages are lognormally distributed.

The effect of taxation on the asymptotic distribution of wages can easily be ascertained in terms of their effects on the functions α and β.

For instance, let us divide ability into natural ability ("nature") and "environmental" ability ("nurture").

$$A = A^n + A^e$$

where environmental ability is a function of human capital,

$$A^e = A^n v(c_w).$$

Then

$$A = \frac{A^n}{1 - v}. \tag{25}$$

Hence increasing v – which an inheritance tax would do by encouraging human capital transfers – increases all positive values of A (all A above average) and decreases all negative A (A below average), *thus increasing inequality of wage income.*

Regression towards the mean provides an explanation of why parents with above average abilities leave money to their children; on average, their descendants will be less able than they are. If the parent's utility function includes descendants' utility functions with a discount factor, and children's utility functions are identical to those of parents, then the problem of deciding on the amount to leave to one's children is formally equivalent to the problem of determining the optimal savings rate with a stochastic wage described by a diffusion process with a drift. We shall not address ourselves to that question, but will limit ourselves to the simpler one of describing the consequences of parents following certain simple rules of inheritance.

The natural extension of (14) would be to write

$$dc = [s(w + \hat{r}c) - nc]\,dt \tag{26}$$

(where r is the after tax return on capital) or, letting

$$f = \frac{1}{2\pi\sigma_A} \exp\left(-\frac{A^2}{2\sigma_A^2}\right), \quad \text{when } EA = 0.$$

Hence

$$f' = -f\frac{A}{\sigma_A^2},$$

$$f'' = \frac{fA^2}{\sigma_A^4} - \frac{f}{\sigma_A^2}.$$

Thus we require

$$\tfrac{1}{2}\alpha\left(\frac{A^2}{\sigma_A^4} - \frac{1}{\sigma_A^2}\right) - \beta\frac{A^2}{\sigma_A^2} + \beta = 0,$$

i.e.

$$\frac{\alpha}{2\sigma_A^2} = \beta \text{ or } \sigma_A^2 = \frac{\alpha}{2\beta}.$$

$u = \ln c$,

and recalling that

$A = \ln w$,

$$du = [(s\hat{r} - n) + s e^{A-u}] dt. \tag{27}$$

It is simpler, however, if we take a linearization of (27)

$$du = (s\hat{r} - n) + s(1 + A - u) dt \tag{28}$$

or slightly more generally, we analyze the equation

$$du = [s_2 + s_1 A - s_0 u] dt. \tag{29}$$

To do this, we introduce another change of variable

$$z \equiv \frac{\beta - s_0}{s_1} u + A \equiv vu + A. \tag{30}$$

Then

$$dz = (vs_2 - s_0 z) dt + \sqrt{(\alpha)}\sqrt{(dt)}. \tag{31}$$

Thus z is normally distributed with asymptotic variance given by

$$\frac{\alpha}{2s_0}.$$

Hence

$$u = \frac{z - A}{v}$$

is normally distributed, with variance

$$\frac{1}{v^2}\left[\frac{\alpha}{2s_0} + \frac{\alpha}{2\beta}\right] = \frac{\alpha}{2}\frac{s_1^2}{s_0\beta}\frac{\beta + s_0}{(\beta - s_0)^2} \tag{32}$$

and mean s_2. If $s = s_0 = s_1$, this reduces to

$$\sigma_{\ln c}^2 = \sigma_A^2 \frac{\beta/s + 1}{(\beta/s - 1)^2} \tag{33}$$

β is the force "restoring" wages to the mean; it is the equalizing force in the economy. s is the force leading to greater inequality. Thus, letting $\Omega = \beta/s$

$$\frac{d\sigma_{\ln c}^2}{d \ln \Omega} = \sigma_{\ln c}^2 \left[\frac{\Omega}{\Omega + 1} - \frac{2\Omega}{\Omega - 1}\right]$$

$$= \frac{2\sigma_{\ln c}^2 \Omega(3 + \Omega)}{(1 - \Omega^2)} \gtrless 0, \quad \text{as } \Omega \lessgtr 1. \tag{34}$$

We assume $\Omega > 1$, i.e. the equalizing force, β, exceeds the "unequalizing force", the savings rate.

But perhaps more important than the inequality in w and c is that in consumption (or income). Letting C = consumption

$$C = (1 - s)(w + \hat{r}c)$$

we obtain

$$\sigma_C^2 = (1 - s)^2(\sigma_w^2 + \hat{r}^2\sigma_C^2 + 2\hat{r}E\{(w - \bar{w})(C - \bar{C})\}). \tag{35}$$

Note that with $r = 0$, inheritance unambiguously reduces consumption inequality. More generally, taking a Taylor series expansion for w and c, we have

$$E(e^A - E\,e^A)(e^u - E\,e^u) \approx E\,e^A E\,e^u E(A - \bar{A})(u - \bar{u})$$

$$= \frac{E\,e^A E\,e^u}{v} \sigma_A^2 = \frac{\bar{w}\bar{C}s_1}{\beta - s_0} \sigma_A^2. \tag{36}$$

Hence the coefficient of variation (squared) of consumption is, if $s = s_0 = s_1$,

$$\sigma_c^2 \equiv \frac{\sigma_C^2}{\bar{C}^2} = \alpha^2 \sigma_w^2 + (1 - \alpha)^2 \sigma_c^2 + 2\alpha(1 - \alpha)\frac{s_1}{\beta - s_0}\sigma_A^2$$

$$= \left[\alpha^2 + (1 - \alpha)^2 e^{-2s_2}\frac{\Omega + 1}{(\Omega - 1)^2} + \frac{2\alpha(1 - \alpha)}{\Omega - 1}\right]\sigma_A^2. \tag{37}$$

The net effect of inheritance of consumption inequality is determined by the magnitude of the bracketed term, i.e. whether it is greater or less than unity. If s is small, the bracketed term can be approximated by

$$\alpha^2 + \frac{s}{\beta}(1 - \alpha)^2 e^{-2s_2} + \frac{2\alpha(1 - \alpha)s}{\beta} \lessgtr 1$$

as

$$\Omega \equiv \frac{\beta}{s} \gtrless (1 + \alpha)/[(1 - \alpha) e^{-2s_2} + 2\alpha]. \tag{38}$$

Clearly, if s is small and β is large then the effect of inheritances is to reduce consumption inequality; in other words, provided that there is sufficient regression towards the mean and provided inheritances are not excessively large, then the net effect of inheritances is to reduce consumption inequality.

Heuristically, when the forces of regression towards the mean are working strongly, there is a strong redistribution element in inheritance. The children of the able are, on average, much less able than their parents, hence the gifts from the parent to the child spread wealth more equally. If the forces of regression towards the mean are working slowly, then we obtain the *magnification* effect described earlier: the more able families will accumulate more capital, and the interest income on this capital will enable them to consume more.

Of course, if one wished to minimize the coefficient of variation, there is an optimal s, which though greater than zero, may well be less than that found in the market in the absence of taxes. The optimal s is found by solving (39)

$$\frac{1}{\hat{\sigma}_A^2}\frac{d\hat{\sigma}_C^2}{ds} = -\left[1 + \hat{r} + \frac{s\,d\hat{r}}{ds}\right](1+\alpha)^2 e^{-2s_2}\frac{\Omega+1}{(\Omega-1)^2}$$
$$+\left\{(1-\alpha)^2 e^{-2s_2}\frac{(\Omega^2+2\Omega-3)}{(\Omega-1)^3} + \frac{2\alpha(1-\alpha)}{(\Omega-1)^2}\right\}\frac{\beta}{s^2} = 0. \tag{39}$$

Tax policy may be able to affect s and hence the degree of inequality. Clearly though, abolition of inheritances is not optimal.

VIII. Effect of redistributive taxes on allocation between human and physical capital

One of the features of most inheritance taxation is that the transfer of human capital is untaxed. Thus, raising inheritance taxes encourages individuals to transfer wealth in this form to their heirs. But different individuals have different capacities for using human capital productively (unlike physical capital, for which there is a fairly good market, so that returns to individuals are not likely to differ very much). This, in turn, implies that *inheritance taxation may again actually cause an increase in inequality of wealth.*

In this section of the paper, we provide a simple extension of our basic dynamic model establishing this result. We use the model of section II.1, but this time we consider two different specifications of the production function; in addition to our earlier formulation

$$w = ag(c_w/A) \tag{40a}$$

we consider

$$w = \tilde{g}(Ac_w). \tag{40b}$$

Greater ability means a greater ability to transform human capital into productivity. c_w is a function of the after tax rate of interest; for the two specifications we obtain (using (3)) for (40a)

$$\frac{d\ln c_w}{d\ln r} = \frac{g'}{g''C_w/A} = -\frac{1}{\xi}, \tag{41a}$$

while for (40b) we have

$$\frac{d\ln c_w}{d\ln r} = \frac{\tilde{g}'}{\tilde{g}''Ac_w} \equiv -\frac{1}{\xi}, \tag{41b}$$

where $1/\xi$ is the elasticity of the marginal productivity of human capital.

Thus the effect of an increase in r on wages is, for (40a)

$$\frac{d\ln w}{d\ln \hat{r}} = \frac{d\ln w}{d\ln c_w}\frac{d\ln c_w}{d\ln \hat{r}} = -\frac{g'c_w/A}{g\xi} = -\frac{\eta}{\xi} < 0, \tag{42a}$$

while for (40b),

$$\frac{d\ln w}{d\ln \hat{r}} = \frac{d\ln w}{d\ln c_w}\frac{d\ln c_w}{d\ln \hat{r}} = \frac{h'\theta c_w}{h}\left(-\frac{1}{\xi}\right) \equiv -\frac{\eta}{\xi} < 0, \tag{42b}$$

where η is the elasticity of wages with respect to human capital.

Consider now the asymptotic distribution of physical capital. Assume as before, that each generation leaves a constant fraction of its (lifetime) wealth to its children. We assume that this fraction is unaffected by inheritance taxation (although, of course, it may well be). Then, we now have

$$c_k = s(w + rc_k) - nc_w - nc_k. \tag{43}$$

Thus, in the steady state

$$c_k = \frac{sw - c_w n}{n - s\hat{r}}. \tag{44}$$

With taxation, this needs to be modified to read

$$c_k = \frac{s(w + T) - c_w n}{n - s\hat{r}} \tag{45}$$

where T is the per capita transfer payment,

$$T = \tau rk, \tag{46}$$

and where k is aggregate per capita physical capital

$$k = Ec_k = \frac{sEw - nEc_w}{n - s\hat{r}}. \tag{47}$$

The effect of a tax on the inequality of human capital, physical capital and income will now be examined:

$$\frac{d \ln c_w}{d \ln A} = \begin{cases} 1 & \text{for (40a),} \\ \dfrac{1 - \xi}{\xi} & \text{for (40b),} \end{cases}$$

$$\frac{d \ln c_w}{d \ln A} = \frac{Asg - nc_w}{Asg - nc_w + \tau srk} \quad \text{for (40a),}$$

$$\frac{d \ln c_w}{d \ln A} = \frac{(s\hat{r} - n) - (1 - \xi)n}{\xi[s(g + \tau rk) - c_w n]} \quad \text{for (40b).}$$

It is immediately clear that (if ξ is constant) the tax leaves the coefficient of variation of human capital unchanged; the coefficient of variation of physical capital is reduced, but beyond some point, further increases in τ may increase the coefficient of variation of c_w. Finally, writing

$$y = w + T + rc_k = \frac{n(w + \tau rk - (1 - \tau)rc_w)}{n - sr(1 - \tau)},$$

$$\frac{d \ln y}{d \ln A} = \begin{cases} \dfrac{w - (1 - \tau)rc_w}{w + \tau rk - (1 - \tau)rc_w} = 1 - \dfrac{\tau rk}{w + \tau rk - (1 - \tau)rc_w} & \text{for (40a),} \\ \dfrac{\hat{r}c_w}{w + \tau tk - (1 - \tau)c_w} & \text{for (40b).} \end{cases}$$

For (40a), income inequality is reduced (although beyond a part, further increases in the tax rate may increase inequality). For (40b) if ξ is small, lowering $\hat{r}$ increases the coefficient of variation of income.

IX. Screening and education

The private returns to education consist not only of the increased productivity, but also in the screening of individuals according to ability. It has been shown that this screening may have an important effect on the inequality of income (see Stiglitz (1975)). Capital taxation, by lowering the after tax rate of return, may have a significant effect on the degree of inequality by encouraging more screening.

Consider the following slight modification of the model of the previous section. Let there be two groups in the population, (A_1, A_2) with $A_1 > A_2$. Assume productivity (and A) are not easily observable, so firms use the education level as a screening device. Assume, moreover, that the cost of education, of staying in school (passing exams) through a particular education level is inversely proportional to A.[16] We let E be the education level, $w = w(A, E)$, and c_w, the expenditure on education (in the previous example we did not distinguish between E and c_w) is $c_w = E/m(A)$ where $m' > 0$.

The productivity curves for the two groups are depicted in figure 11.5. With perfect information, each group would purchase education to the point where

$$\frac{dw}{dE} = \hat{r}m(A). \tag{48}$$

With imperfect information, if there is an equilibrium, it is one in which the more able purchase enough education to separate themselves off from the less able,

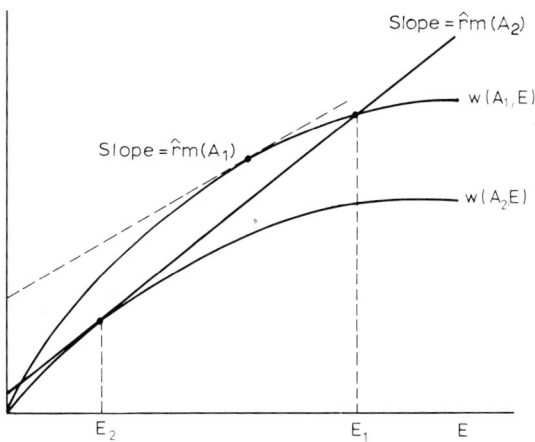

Figure 11.5

---

[16] We assume that the time and effort required by the more able is so much less than that required by the less able that it offsets the fact that the opportunity cost of time of the more able exceeds that of the less able.

i.e. they purchase a sufficiently large amount that the less able (lower A) decide not to try to become identified with the more able. The equilibrium is depicted in figure 11.5 and is described analytically[17] by

$$w(A_2, E_2) + m(A_2)\hat{r}(E_1 - E_2) = w(A_1, E_1). \tag{49}$$

where

$$\frac{dw}{dE_2} = \hat{r}m(A_2). \tag{50}$$

The effect of a lowering of the after tax return on physical capital may now be easily ascertained. Let $w(A, E)$ take on the special form

$$w = Ag(E). \tag{51}$$

Then

$$\frac{d \ln E_2}{d \ln \hat{r}} = \frac{1}{g'' E_2/g'} = -\frac{1}{\xi_2} \tag{52}$$

$$\frac{d \ln E_1}{d \ln \hat{r}} = \frac{m(A_2)r(E_1 - E_2)}{(A_1 g' - m(A_2))E_1} \tag{53}$$

$$= \frac{w_2 \eta_2 (E_1 - E_2)}{w_1 \eta_1 E_2 - \eta_2 w_2 E_1}, \tag{54}$$

where

$$\eta_i = \frac{g'(E_i) E_i}{g(E_i)}.$$

Wages inequality can be measured in this case simply by w_1/w_2,

$$\frac{d \ln w_1/w_2}{d \ln \hat{r}} = \frac{g' E_1}{g} \frac{d \ln E_1}{d \ln \hat{r}} - \frac{g' E_2}{g} \frac{d \ln E_2}{d \ln \hat{r}}. \tag{55}$$

Substituting, we obtain

$$\frac{1}{\eta_2} \frac{d \ln w_1/w_2}{d \ln r} = \frac{1}{\xi_2} - \frac{\eta_1 w_2 (E_1 - E_2)}{\eta_2 w_2 E_1 - \eta_1 w_1 E_2}.$$

Clearly, if ξ_2 is large, this may be negative. In this case lowering the after tax return to capital increases inequality (and conversely for small ξ_2.) There seems no clear presumption either way. Figure 11.6 illustrates a case where inequality is increased.

---

[17] That is, the net wage of the less able if they stay with their own group, $w(A_2, E_2) - \hat{r}m(A_2)E_2$, is exactly the same as if they attempt to pretend to be one of the more able,

$$w(A_1, E_1) - \hat{r}m(A_2)E_1.$$

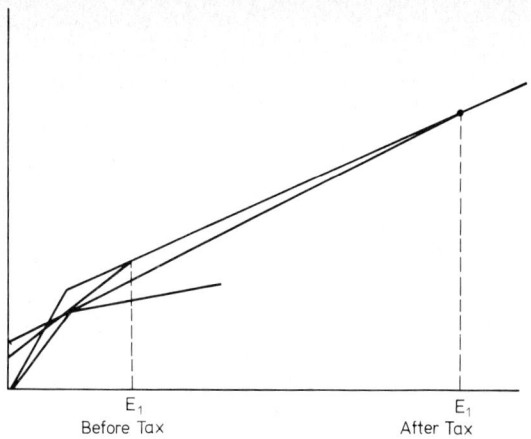

Figure 11.6

X. Stochastic death and imperfect annuity markets

We suggested earlier that an important source of inequality of inheritance is the stochastic nature of death; this means, if there are imperfect annuity markets, that the amount inherited depends on the "luck" of the timing of the death of one's parents; if it is shortly after retirement, one will inherit a considerable amount; if later, one will inherit much less.

The full formalization of this is quite complicated, and ought to take into account parental concern for the welfare of their heirs. The following seems the simplest model which captures the effect. Assume individuals live for at most three periods. They work in the first for a wage w_0, and inherit capital, K_0, but choose a consumption rate to spread their consumption C evenly over their maximum life, i.e. if r is the rate of interest

$$C\left(1 + \frac{1}{1+r} + \left(\frac{1}{1+r}\right)^2\right) = w_0 + K_0 \tag{56}$$

or, letting $\lambda = 1/(1 + r)$,

$$C = \frac{(w_0 + K_0)}{1 + \lambda + \lambda^2}. \tag{57}$$

Their savings for retirement are thus

$$w_0 + K_0 - C_0 = \frac{\lambda + \lambda^2}{1 + \lambda + \lambda^2}(w_0 + K_0), \tag{58}$$

$$\frac{\hat{s}}{1+r}(w_0 + K_0). \tag{59}$$

If a fraction $\frac{1}{2}$ of the individuals died at the beginning of their retirement (the rest living out the full three periods), then $\frac{1}{2}$ of the individuals will have inherited zero wealth; of the remainder, $\frac{1}{2}$ will have parents who have inherited nothing, and so their inheritance is just $\hat{s}w_0$; of the remainder, $\frac{1}{2}$ will have grandparents who have inherited nothing, and so their inheritance is just $(w_0 s + w_0)\hat{s} = (\hat{s} + \hat{s}^2)w_0$. More generally,

$(\frac{1}{2})^n$ of the population will inherit a wealth of

$$\frac{s - \hat{s}^n}{1 - s} w_0.$$

This generates for large n a Pareto distribution with slope

$$\frac{d \ln (1 - H)}{d \ln c} \approx -\frac{\ln 2}{\ln s}$$

where H is the wealth distribution function and c is the (per capita) inheritance.[18]

What concerns us here is the effect of a change in the tax rate on inheritances on the wealth distribution. With interest income taxes at the rate t,

$$\hat{s} \equiv \frac{2 + r(1 - t)}{3 + 3r(1 - t) + r(1 - t)^2}$$

$$\frac{d\hat{s}}{dt} = \frac{r(3 + 4r(1 - t) + (r(1 - t))^2)}{(3 + 3\hat{r} + \hat{r}^2)^2} > 0.$$

The interest income tax increases the savings required to sustain consumption in retirement, and hence increases the inequality of inherited wealth.

XI. Effect of redistributive inheritance and capital taxation on risk taking

It has long been recognized (Domar and Musgrave (1944), Stiglitz (1969b), Mossin (1968)) that, a proportional tax with full loss offset provisions would increase risk taking, because the government acts as a partner in losses as well as gains, effectively sharing risk. These studies, however, ignored the effects of the proceeds of the tax. When these are taken into account, if interest is deductible, aggregate risk taking is completely unaffected, but there is complete shifting of the tax.

Let $H(W_0)$ denote a distribution function of initial wealth, W_0; $a(W_0)$ be the proportion allocated to the risky investment, which yields a return of e; r, the safe return; and t, the proportional tax rate. We assume full loss offset and interest deductibility.

Let U be the utility function and we assume that the risk-averse individual

$$\max_{\{a\}} EU(W)$$

where W is (terminal) wealth, and $U'' < 0$. Then the first order condition for portfolio allocation is

---

[18] The formal similarity between this model and Stiglitz's earlier model of primogeniture should be noted.

$$EU'\{W_0(a(e-r)(1-t)+r) + \overline{aW}(e-r)t\}(e-r) = 0 \tag{60}$$

where

$$\overline{aW} = EaW_0,$$

aggregate expenditure on risk taking, the expectation being taken on the entire population.

We need to calculate

$$\frac{da}{dt} = \frac{E[U''(\overline{aW} - aW_0)(e-r)^2]}{E[U''(e-r)^2(1-t)W_0]} \tag{61}$$

$$= \frac{\overline{aW} - aW_0}{(1-t)W_0}.$$

Hence the change in aggregate risk taking is

$$\int W_0 \frac{da}{dt} dH(W_0) = \frac{1}{1-t} \int (\overline{aW} - aW_0) dH(W_0) = 0. \tag{62}$$

A capital tax with interest deductibility has absolutely no effect at all on aggregate risk taking. Indeed, letting W be terminal wealth, with

$$W \equiv W_0[a(e-r)(1-t) + r] + \overline{aW}(e-r)t \tag{63}$$

and differentiating with respect to t, using (61), we immediately observe that *proportional taxation with interest deductibility has no effect on the distribution of income.* The redistributive effects of the tax are precisely offset by changes in the portfolio composition.

However, if there is not an interest deductibility provision, then the capital tax may either cause aggregate risk bearing to increase or decrease:

$$\frac{da}{dt} = -\frac{\overline{aW} - aW_0}{(1-t)W_0} - \frac{r(\overline{W} - W_0)}{(1-t)W_0} \frac{EU''(e-r)}{EU''(e-r)^2} \tag{64}$$

so

$$EW_0 \frac{da}{dt} = -\frac{1}{(1-t)} E\left\{(\overline{W} - W_0) \frac{EU''(e-r)}{EU''(e-r)^2}\right\}. \tag{65}$$

What is important for the results of section VI is the effect on large wealth holders:

$$\frac{da(1-t)}{dt} = -a + (1-t)\frac{da}{dt}$$

$$= r \frac{EU''(e-r)}{EU''(e-r)^2}$$

$$= r \frac{EAU'(e-r)}{EU''(e-r)^2} \gtreqless 0 \quad \text{as} \quad A' \lesseqgtr 0,$$

where $A = -U''/U'$, the measure of absolute risk aversion. Hence with the normal presumption that absolute risk aversion is decreasing, large wealth holders have an increased after tax variance in wealth.

XII. Concluding remarks

This paper has argued that inheritance and capital taxation are probably less efficacious in leading to greater long-run equality than is widely believed; indeed, inequality may actually be increased. In several of the models examined, although inequality was reduced for low tax rates, beyond a point further increases in taxes increased inequality.

Two limitations of the study should be noted. First, we have focussed on proportional taxation. The distortionary affects of progressive taxation are likely to be larger in some areas – such as risk taking – but smaller in others (such as the allocative effects on human capital, since markedly diminishing returns are likely to set in for investments in human capital beyond some point). The redistributive effects are likely to be larger.

Secondly, we have not engaged in any explicit welfare analysis; we have focussed entirely on the "positive" analysis of taxation on the distribution of income and wealth. There is some question about what the appropriate normative framework ought to be. For instance, if individuals were given a choice of having their parents live through retirement or dying at the beginning of retirement, then most would probably prefer the former; thus inheritances generated by uncertain lifetime of parents can be treated as partial compensation for the untimely death of one's parents.

With a utilitarian framework, there is a presumption that bequests are "good" things, since both the giver and the receiver derive utility from them. Hence, if the elasticities of supply of bequests is of the same size as say the elasticity of supply of savings for retirement, bequests should be taxed at a lower rate than savings for own-consumption.

Neither of these arguments take into account two important issues which seem to be the subject of much popular discussion: (i) political power: excessive concentration of wealth often, it is argued, leads to accumulation of political power, and this may affect the nature of our political processes; (ii) mobility and equal opportunity: we have focussed on steady state distributions, not on differences in life chances of individuals born of different parents; much of the recent concern with income distribution has been concerned more with equalizing opportunity than with equalizing the distribution of income itself.

Though the models used are highly idealized, the kinds of considerations raised are nonetheless of some relevance in assessing the desirability of inheritance and capital taxation.

References

Atkinson, A.B., "On the Measurement of Inequality", *Journal of Economic Theory*, Sept. 1970.
Champernowne, D.G., "A Model of Income Distributions", *Economic Journal*, 1953.
Domar, E. and R. Musgrave, "Proportional Income Taxation and Risk-Taking", *Quarterly Journal of Economics*, May 1944.
Mandelbrot, B., "Stable Paretian Random Functions and the Multiplicative Variation of Income", *Econometrica*, October 1961.
Mossin, J., "Taxation and Risk-Taking, An Expected Utility Approach", *Economica*, February 1968.
Rothschild, M. and J. Stiglitz, "Some Further Results on the Measurement of Inequality", *Journal of Economic Theory*, April 1973.
Rothschild, M. and J. Stiglitz, "Equilibrium in Competitive Insurance Markets: An Essay on the Economics of Imperfect Information", *Quarterly Journal of Economics*, November 1976.
Stiglitz, J. "Distribution of Income and Wealth Among Individuals", *Econometrica*, July 1969a (presented at the December 1966 meetings of the Econometric Society, San Francisco).
Stiglitz, J., "The Effects of Income, Wealth and Capital Gains Taxation on Risk-Taking", *Quarterly Journal of Economics*, May 1969b.
Stiglitz, J., "The Theory of Screening, Education, and the Distribution of Income", *American Economic Review*, June 1975.
Stiglitz, J., "Notes on Estate Taxes, Redistribution and the Concept of Balanced Growth Path Incidence", *Journal of Political Economy* (1978).
Stiglitz, J., *Information and Economic Analysis*, (forthcoming).

11 DISCUSSION

PAPER BY JOSEPH E. STIGLITZ

Professor Taubman said he was always delighted to discuss a very good paper by an outstanding theorist which emphasised the need to do good empirical work. He also agreed with the need to consider both efficiency and equity effects within a general equilibrium framework when examining alternative tax policies.

The paper presents a series of growth models which enables some of these issues to be explored, and identifies several potential sources of economic inefficiency arising from capital taxes. However, he felt that the model did not do justice to the complexities of the issues involved. The treatment of market consumption and production was too simple, and the paper had a naive view of the way in which tax payers and tax lawyers react to tax laws. General conclusions for transferring funds are based solely on a per capita transfer system. Finally, it overlooks the fact that inheritance taxes may be used to limit the power and influence of those born to wealth, as well as to raise government revenue.

Much of the analysis is conducted within the framework of a neo-classical growth model in which labour supply is inelastic. Professor Taubman had used a similar approach about ten years ago in a paper investigating the impact of capital incentives on income and its distribution. But such a model is open to criticism concerning the distortionary effects of various taxes on which Professor Stiglitz had himself recently written. Whether a consumption or an income tax is the more distortionary cannot be determined. An income tax distorts both consumption–saving choices and labour–leisure choices, whilst the consumption tax distorts only labour–leisure choices. However, with positive savings and equal tax yields, the income tax *rate* is lower and therefore has a smaller distortionary effect on the labour–leisure decision. If replacing an income tax with a capital tax induces an increase in labour but leaves the labour growth rate unchanged, the paper's conclusions on the equilibrium growth path and capital/labour ratio stand. But if labour is higher at all points of time, per capita income can increase even when the capital/labour ratio declines. In addition, the utility of income plus leisure can be greater or smaller with the tax, even if income falls.

The argument that labour supply should be considered, as well as the capital/labour ratio, also applies to the discussion on the division of investments between human capital and physical capital. An increase in human capital will increase labour in efficiency units and income per capita, to partially compensate for the loss of capital.

He went on to mention another dimension in which the model was incomplete.

For assets whose profits decline with age, taxes and subsidies alter the point of economic obsolescence. Often a proportional tax on capital or profits will reduce the useful life of such assets and increase the depreciation rate, thus slowing the growth rate of the economy. The paper also tends to obscure the fact that, if growth is partly due to technical progress, future generations will be wealthier and a policy that redistributes income now may be optimal even if the income per capita of future generations is reduced.

One interesting suggestion is that wealthy parents, above average in ability, leave bequests to their children, since they are less able on average than their parents. Whilst this argument is plausible, it appears to conflict with what information is available. In particular, evidence from a sample of estates suggests that children tend to receive equal shares, even though most children in the sample were already grown up and the parents must have had substantial information on their relative abilities.

Lastly, he pointed out that the paper assumes that everyone is affected by an estate or inheritance tax, although nowadays less than 5% of estates are eligible for the US Federal Estate Tax. A tax on wealth which raises relatively little revenue may nevertheless prevent one group from acquiring sufficient wealth to purchase power. Alternatively, it may be regarded as an indirect tax on the security and status which wealth generates. He would like to see models examining the effect of inheritance taxes which included these considerations as well as the consumption potential of wealth hoardings.

Professor Somermeyer was not convinced that an increase in the inheritance tax would increase income inequality and felt that more attention should be paid to substitution rather than income effects. It is possible that an inheritance tax may reduce the savings rate but, as the paper points out, the income and substitution effects may work in opposite directions. Even if savings is reduced, the rate of interest may increase and with it the return on capital. He also pointed out that the government may use the increased revenue to boost investment, thus compensating for the reduction in private savings. Finally, he mentioned that very little was known about the determinants of terminal wealth and the responses by individuals to tax changes.

Professor Pen welcomed the exercise in secondary effects but felt it concentrated too much on savings rather than investment. Even staying within the proposed framework he felt that many important factors had been omitted. As examples he mentioned the rate of profit, professional post-tax incomes, the stock market, house prices and the level of pensions.

Professor Wiles agreed with these comments, saying that secondary effects rarely both exceed and offset primary effects. For example, taxing the rich will indeed lead them to choose increasingly risky investments and therefore increases inequality, but this could only affect, say, P_{100} as all lower quantiles would gain from and lose to each other, whereas such an increase in dispersion could only push outward the very top. He agreed that taxes on tangible capital may lead to an increase in investment in education but suggested that the opportunities for this were very limited since the children of the rich already have many years of education and increasing it further cuts into working life.

Whilst he agreed that estates tend to be divided fairly evenly he suggested that due consideration had not been given to assortative mating, which recombines them. Finally, he asked whether it was a consequence of the paper that, if we want more equality, we should all subscribe to a personal fund for Rockefeller.

Professor Chiswick wondered if the importance of the secondary effects might depend on whether there has been a history of such inheritance taxes. As an analogy she cited the fact that since certain epidemics had been eliminated, parents have become so careless about inoculating their children that the diseases are reappearing. Although initially inheritance taxes may have had their intended effects, after 2 or 3 generations the (possibly perverse) second-order effects appear to be important. She welcomed Professor Stiglitz's analysis and found it both useful and stimulating.

Mr. Layard accepted that a ban on inheritance might be disequalising, but suppose instead there was a tax of less than infinity. Then, if the income effect is strong, rich people cut back on their own consumption and the conclusion is not so apparent, particularly since the children will also have higher than average incomes and will cut back their consumption in response to the same tax.

Professor von Weizsäcker said that the steady state comparisons in the paper did not take account of the government's ability to save and maintain growth on the golden rule or another good path. When dynamics are included, any effect the tax may have on savings may be offset by government policy.

Some of the conclusions relied on a low elasticity of substitution between capital and labour and this raised the question whether a marginal productivity theory of wages and interest was tenable when the elasticities were small. In the extreme case when there is no substitution, the theory clearly falls down.

Returning to the points raised in his own paper, he asked whether real inequality increased if the imposition of an inheritance tax led to more risky investments. He also believed that the concept of lifetime income could be extended to encompass the income of family dynasties. In this case, if there is a strong positive correlation between the well-being of parents and children, the equalising effect of bequests vanishes.

Dr. Shorrocks approved of the fact that the models based on stochastic processes included many economic variables. This went some way to countering the criticism that stochastic models have little economic content. He pointed out that the continuous time formulation eliminated the possibility of having transfers both from parents to children and in the opposite direction. With regression towards the mean, parents on low incomes may expect their children to have higher relative incomes and rely on them for support in old age. If these are called positive and negative bequests, it is interesting to note that in the UK the tax treatment is quite symmetrical, with positive estate taxes levied on positive bequests and income tax refunds allowed against income transfers to parents. The proportional tax schedule assumed in the paper was clearly unrealistic, at least for the UK and the US, and other tax schedules could be considered.

He agreed with Professor Wiles that the composition of wealth holdings was important and wondered whether this type of analysis might be related to some of the other empirical evidence, for instance the use of educational expenditure to

Discussion

sustain inter-generational inequality. Assortative mating has indeed an important influence and the effects of various mating patterns has been considered by Atkinson and Harrison, amongst others, in their book on the UK wealth distribution.

Professor Stiglitz said that some of the discussants had complained about omissions from the paper. Many of these – induced changes in the savings rate, for example – could be incorporated relatively easily, but make the model even more complicated. The impact of a lump-sum redistribution of tax revenue had been investigated, and this leads to a reduction in savings, since it effectively converts wealth into income. However, he was not convinced that the savings effect was important for the reasons raised in the discussion – it could be offset by governmental action.

He agreed that in general equilibrium analysis, we are used to thinking that secondary effects may reduce primary effects but not completely offset them, so that the total impact is in the opposite direction. But when secondary effects are considered, they are usually aimed at the same variable as the primary effects. Here, we are dealing with margins, and examining the change in the distribution of returns. Had savings or bequests been the object of interest, it is unlikely that the secondary effects would have caused this reversal.

On the question of marriage patterns, Professor Stiglitz pointed out that the paper implicitly assumes perfectly assortative mating, and therefore tends to exaggerate the degree of inequality.

12 ENTROPY AND THE ANALYSIS OF INCOME DISTRIBUTION

BERTIL NASLUND

I. Introduction

In neo-Keynesian distribution theory, one is able to give an explicit form for the distribution of income between profit and labour, and under certain circumstances between workers and capitalists. Since randomness plays a very important role in the Keynesian analysis, we shall try to extend the neo-Keynesian distribution theory by introducing uncertainty.

In a market economy, opportunities, disasters, capabilities, and success are to a large degree random. This generates inequalities which have been used to derive the functional form of the distribution. Examples of these types of theories of the distribution of income are Champernowne (1953), Aitchison, and Brown (1957), and Rashevsky (1951).

In this type of analysis some authors have used the concept of entropy, e.g. Rashevsky (1951), Theil (1967), Murphy (1965), and generated exponential distributions of income. There are two main problems associated with these latter theories, namely
(a) The exponential distribution does not fit empirical data very well, since too little income is allocated to high income units.
(b) The theories use very few concepts from economic theory and therefore they are not always useful for further analysis of economic problems.

By introducing entropy into neo-Keynesian analysis we will try to overcome problems (a) and (b).

II. Neo-Keynesian distribution theory

Under the assumptions of full employment and autonomous investment, total income Y and investment I will be given. Kaldor (1956) divided the population into workers, with income W and a propensity to save s_w, and capitalists with income W and a propensity to save s_w, and capitalists with income from capital P and a propensity to save s_p. By using the following two equations, Kaldor was able to determine the functional distribution of income

$$W + P = Y, \tag{1}$$

$$s_w W + s_p P = I. \tag{2}$$

Eliminating W, we obtain the following expression for the share of capital

$$\frac{P}{Y} = \frac{1}{s_p - s_w} \frac{I}{Y} - \frac{s_w}{s_p - s_w}. \tag{3}$$

The result (3) is stable, if prices are more flexible than wages.

The fact that workers save implies that they become entitled to income from profits on these investments. This has the effect that the identity between the functional income categories (profits and wages) and social categories (workers and capitalists) no longer exists. This situation has been analysed by Pasinetti (1962) and others, as summarised by Harcourt (1972).

The analysis of Pasinetti (1962) required the introduction of financial markets in a simple form and extensions of his work by Kregel (1971, 1973) and others have pointed out the need to analyse the income distribution between many different social groups in society with different propensities to save. Kregel (1973) discusses the personal distribution of income and assumes that the propensity to save is an increasing function of income. Higher incomes will have a higher proportion of profits and claim a higher proportion of profit income than lower income groups. This is taken as a starting point for an analysis of the effects of a higher growth rate on various income groups, as well as the effects of monetary policy in general. This so called post-Keynesian theory still uses (1) and (2) but since there are now many income groups, e.g. different income classes, two equations are no longer sufficient for the derivation of a more precise form of the distribution of income.

To derive the personal distribution of income using (1) and (2), we shall introduce another major feature of the Keynesian theory, namely uncertainty. Uncertainty plays a critical role in, for instance, the Keynesian theory of money, investment and consumption. Money is said to be important because the future is uncertain and money provides the most certain link between the present and the future. This is because it is the most liquid of all assets used as a store of value over time. Investment decisions are assumed to be influenced more by uncertainty and expectations than by price movements, and can therefore be made an independent variable as in equation (2). In the theory of consumption, precautionary balances play an important role and may be built up at the expense of current consumption when uncertainty increases.

Due to the reasons above and others, uncertainty plays an absolutely central role in Keynes' critique of the neo-classical system. Given the important Keynesian assumption of autonomous investment (equation (2)), we shall here use the fact that uncertainty and randomness play a critical role in a market economy, and use uncertainty as an additional principle to derive an explicit form of the income distribution when society comprises many groups. We will introduce the effects of uncertainty by using entropy.

III. Entropy

Entropy has been used in many different situations for the analysis of distributions under uncertainty. Denote the probability of state i by $p_i (i = 1, 2, \ldots, k)$ and let

$p = (p_1, p_2, \ldots, p_k)$. If we have to estimate p given some known constraints C, application of the entropy concept implies that we determine the unknown distribution p by solving the problem

$$\max_{p \in C} H(p), \qquad (4)$$

where

$$H(p) = -\sum p_i \ln p_i \qquad (5)$$

is the entropy of p.

Two different ways have been used to justify this:

(A) When determining the distribution p, we seek an estimate which is in accordance with what is known about our system. This is the constraint set C or, in our economic problem, equations (1) and (2). The entropy measure $H(p)$ due to Shannon (1949) provides a unique criterion for the degree of uncertainty, which corresponds to the notion that a distribution which is broad indicates more uncertainty than one which is peaked. Shannon has proved that the entropy $H(p)$ increases with increasing uncertainty and is additive for independent sources of uncertainty. By maximising the entropy with respect to p under constraints (1) and (2), we can derive the distribution of income consistent with what is known about the economy, and do not allow anything else to influence it.

(B) Another justification for the entropy measure is as follows. We divide the economy into k income classes and assume that it consists of N income units. The probability that Np_i individuals are located in income class i can be written[1]

$$P(p, N) = \frac{N!}{\prod_i Np_i!} \prod_i \left(\frac{1}{k}\right)^{Np_i}. \qquad (6)$$

We then use Stirling's formula

$$r! = (2\Pi)^{1/2} r^{r+1/2} \exp\left[-r + o\left(\frac{1}{r}\right)\right]$$

and rewrite (6) by taking natural logarithms and dividing by N

$$\frac{1}{N} \ln P = \frac{1}{2N} \ln 2\Pi + \left(1 + \frac{1}{2N}\right) \ln N - 1 - \frac{k}{2N} \ln 2\Pi - \sum \left(p_i + \frac{1}{2N}\right) \ln N$$

$$- \sum \left(p_i + \frac{1}{2N}\right) \ln p_i + \sum p_i + \sum p_i \ln \frac{1}{k}$$

We then obtain the following approximation for large N

$$P(p, N) = \exp NH(p) + N \ln \frac{1}{k}. \qquad (7)$$

---

[1] We have assumed that the probability of any income unit being found in a particular income class is the same for all income classes ($1/k$). This assumption is further discussed in MacQueen and Marschak (1975) and in Näslund (1977).

Therefore, instead of maximising P we can maximise $H(p)$ subject to the constraints (1), (2) and $\sum p_i = 1$, to derive the most likely state of the system given the randomness and constraints.

A more detailed presentation of the micro-economic processes is given in the Appendix.

The entropy concept has been used in various ways in economics. See, for example, Finkelstein and Frieberg (1967), Theil (1967, 1969), Philippatos and Gressis (1975), Wilson (1970), Georgescu-Roegen (1972), Herniter (1973), Näslund (1970), Rashevsky (1951), Murphy (1965), Commoner (1976). The entropy concept of information theory is not often used in the original physical sense of a gradual decrease in the quality of energy and matter except in Georgescu-Roegen (1972) and Commoner (1976). Instead, the entropy concept is used as a measure of uncertainty, and economic problems are frequently formulated in ways that are analogous to the physical problems for which the concept was originally introduced – as is the case here – without references to any physical magnitudes. A critical examination of the application of entropy is given in MacQueen and Marschak (1975).

We shall now apply the methodology presented here to the problem stated in section II. Since we give a presentation of the microeconomics in the Appendix more in line with justification (B), we shall use (A) as an illustration in the next section.

IV. The personal distribution of income

Let us allocate the income units of a country into income classes and assume that equations (1) and (2) must always hold. Thus we have the following information about our economy
(a) The total number of income units N
(b) Full employment income Y
(c) Autonomous investment I

Let $f(x)$ be the distribution of income and $s(x)$ the savings function. We can then rewrite conditions (a)–(c) in the following way

$$\int_D f(x)\,dx = N, \tag{8}$$

$$\int_D xf(x)\,dx = Y, \tag{9}$$

$$\int_D s(x)f(x)\,dx = I, \tag{10}$$

where D is the domain of integration. If we divide $f(x)$ by N, we see from (8) that $f(x)/N$ can be interpreted as a probability density function. Therefore, (9) and (10), when divided by N, can be interpreted as expected values of x and $s(x)$ respectively.

We seek an estimate of $f(x)$ which avoids bias and which satisfies the rules governing the economy (equations (1) and (2)). We can write the entropy measure (5) in the following way.

$$-C \int_D \frac{f(x)}{N} \ln \frac{f(x)}{N} \, dx. \tag{11}$$

Maximising (11) with respect to $f(x)$ under the constraints (8)–(10), we derive the distribution of income that is consistent with what we know about the economy and do not allow anything else to influence it.

Using the calculus of variations and applying Euler's theorem, we obtain the following necessary conditions

$$f(x) = K e^{-\mu x - \lambda s(x)}, \tag{12}$$

where K, μ and λ are multipliers which can be determined by (8)–(10) as soon as the savings function $s(x)$ is known. One feature of (12) is that it connects two important areas of economics, namely the theory of income distribution and the theory of savings behaviour. Furthermore, the argument against the use of entropy for deriving income distributions, namely that it generates exponential distributions, is no longer valid, since the exact form of the distribution depends upon $s(x)$. For example, if the savings function is of the form

$$s(x) = -\frac{\mu}{\lambda} x + \frac{c}{\lambda} \log x,$$

then

$$f(x) = K x^{-c}, \tag{13}$$

which is the Pareto distribution.

The analysis of the effects of different growth policies have often been undertaken in terms of only two social classes, workers and capitalists. Using (12), we can now explicitly analyse such effects on the personal distribution of income as soon as the propensity to save is specified.

V. Conclusions

In recent years, there have been various attempts to extend the neo-Keynesian distribution theory to more than two groups in society. These attempts have not produced explicit forms of the distribution of income. By introducing the effects of uncertainty in a market economy, it is possible to use the main assumptions of neo-Keynesian distribution theory as relevant economic information and derive the distribution of income when social relations and savings behaviour are more complex.

Appendix: A formulation considering explicit market transactions

Consider an income unit of given size x_i at time t. This unit reacts directly or indirectly with another income unit, if part of its income is taken away or given to another income unit. These transfers take place at random due to variations in consumer preferences, technical developments etc.

The number of exchanges between a specific income unit of size x_i and any income units of size x_j is assumed to depend on the frequency of income units x_j and their size. Thus

$$g(x_i, x_j) f(x_j, t) \, dx_j, \tag{A1}$$

where f denotes the frequency of units of size x_j. We do not know the exact form of the function g. Since it seems reasonable that more of these types of interactions take place if their size is large,[2] we make the following specification for the function g

$$g(x_i, x_j) = g(x_i + x_j) \geqslant 0. \tag{A2}$$

We can now write (A1) as follows:

$$g(x_i + x_j) f(x_j, t) \, dx_j. \tag{A3}$$

The rate by which income units of size x_i move out of that size class is then obtained by integrating (A3) over all sizes x_j and multiplying by the frequency of income units of size x_j. Therefore we obtain the following expression for the rate A

$$A = f(x_i, t) \int g(x_i + x_j) f(x_j, t) \, dx_j. \tag{A4}$$

When two income units of size x_i and x_j interact this way, they change to new sizes x'_i and x'_j, respectively.

We can now study the interaction which is the reverse of the one shown above, namely

$$x'_i, x'_j \rightarrow x_i, x_j$$

and, in exactly the same way as above, we can determine the rate by which income units of size x_i are created. (This occurs when units smaller than x_i obtain income from other units and when units larger than x_i lose income to such an extent that the size becomes x_i.)

$$\bar{A} = f(x'_i, t) \int g(x'_i + x'_j) f(x'_j, t) \, dx'_j \tag{A5}$$

Due to the conservation of total income we must have

$$g(x_i + x_j) = g(x'_i + x'_j).$$

---

[2] This has to do with both the possibility of interactions taking place if people with high income are more exposed to random events, and the fact that more kinds of interactions are possible.
An income unit with high income can lose little *and* much, whereas an income unit with little income can only lose little.

We can now write $\partial f_i/\partial t = \bar{A} - A$ as follows:

$$\frac{\partial f}{\partial t} = \bar{A} - A = \int g(x_i + x_j)[f(x'_i, t)f(x'_j, t) - f(x_i, t)f(x_j, t)]\,dx_j. \tag{A6}$$

The equilibrium distribution is obtained when $\partial f/\partial t = 0$. This means that

$$0 = \int g(x_i + x_j)[f(x'_i)f(x'_j) - f(x_i)f(x_j)]\,dx_j, \tag{A7}$$

where x_i is a given income unit.

The sufficient condition for $f_0(x)$ to be a solution to (A7) is

$$f_0(x'_i)f_0(x'_j) - f_0(x_i)f_0(x_j) = 0. \tag{A8}$$

We will now show that this condition is also necessary. Define

$$H(t) = \int f(x, t) \log f(x, t)\,dx, \tag{A9}$$

where the distribution function $f(x, t)$ satisfies (A6).

Differentiating (A9) gives

$$\frac{dH}{dt} = \int \frac{\partial f(x, t)}{\partial t}[1 + \log f(x, t)] \tag{A10}$$

Thus we have that $\partial f/\partial t = 0$ implies $dH/dt = 0$ and we have shown that a necessary condition for $\partial f/\partial t = 0$ is $dH/dt = 0$.

Theorem[3]. *If f satisfies (A6) then $dH/dt \leq 0$.*

Proof. If we substitute (A6) into the integrand of (A10), we obtain

$$\frac{dH}{dt} = \iint g(x_i + x_j)(f'_i f'_j - f_i f_j)(1 + \log f_i)\,dx_i\,dx_j. \tag{A11}$$

Interchanging i and j does not alter (A11) and we get

$$\frac{dH}{dt} = \iint g(x_i + x_j)(f'_i f'_j - f_i f_j)(1 + \log f_j)\,dx_i\,dx_j. \tag{A12}$$

Adding (A11) and (A12) and taking one half of the sum, we obtain

$$\frac{dH}{dt} = \frac{1}{2}\iint g(x_i + x_j)(f'_i f'_j - f_i f_j)(2 + \log f_i f_j)\,dx_i\,dx_j. \tag{A13}$$

The integral (A13) does not change if we interchange (x_i, x_j) and (x'_i, x'_j) since $g(x_i + x_j) = g(x'_i + x'_j)$ due to the conservation of total income.

$$\frac{dH}{dt} = \frac{1}{2}\iint g(x_i + x_j)(f_i f_j - f'_i f'_j)(2 + \log f'_i f'_j)\,dx_i\,dx_j \tag{A14}$$

---

[3] This theorem is an economic application of a well known theorem in physics, see Huang (1963).

Adding (A13) and (A14) and taking one half of the sum we have

$$\frac{dH}{dt} = \frac{1}{4} \iint g(x_i + x_j)(f_i f_j - f_i' f_j')(\log f_i' f_j' - \log f_i f_j)\, dx_i\, dx_j \qquad (A15)$$

The integrand of (A15) is never positive and therefore $dH/dt \leq 0$. We also see that $dH/dt = 0$ if and only if the integrand of (A15) vanishes.

Thus regardless of the initial conditions

$$f(x, t) \to f_0(x),$$
$$t \to \infty.$$

We have found that the equilibrium distribution is determined by (A8). In order to find the form of the solution we take the logarithm of both sides of (A8)

$$\log f_0(x_i') + \log f_0(x_j') = \log f_0(x_i) + \log f_0(x_j). \qquad (A16)$$

Since (x_i', x_j') and (x_i, x_j) are chosen arbitrarily, (A16) has the form of a conservation law. Thus if $h(x)$ is any quantity associated with the size of income such that $h(x_i) + h(x_j)$ is constant, then a solution of (A16) is

$$\log f_0(x) - h(x) \qquad (A17)$$

If there are several quantities $h_1(x), h_2(x) \ldots h_n(x)$ that are conserved, we have the solution of the form

$$\log f_0(x) = h_1(x) + h_2(x) + \ldots + h_n(x). \qquad (A18)$$

The general solution can be written

$$\log f_0(x) = -\sum_{i=1}^{n} A h_i(x) + \log c_1,$$

where A is a constant:

$$f_0(x) = c_1 \exp\left[-\sum_{i=1}^{n} A h_i(x)\right]. \qquad (A19)$$

If the conservation law is that the total number of individuals is constant, total income is constant, and that saving must equal investment, then f_0 takes the form

$$f_0(x) = e^{\lambda - \mu x - \gamma g(x)}, \qquad (A20)$$

where λ, μ, and γ are constants.

The analysis above assumes that movement towards equilibrium can take place without disturbance or conscious interference. If the total income W to be distributed is not constant (due to economic growth), if the population N varies, and if these variations are small, the analysis shown here can be used as a starting point for an analysis of situations of disequilibrium. The reader can find such an attempt in Näslund (1977).

References

Aitchison, J. and J.A.C. Brown, *The Lognormal Distribution*, Cambridge, 1957.
Champernowne, D.G., "A Model of Income Distribution", *Economic Journal*, 1953.
Commoner, B., *The Poverty of Power*, New York, 1976.
Finkelstein, M.O. and R.M. Frieberg, "The Application of an Entropy Theory of Concentration to the Clayton Act", *The Yale Law Journal*, 1967.
Georgescu–Roegen, N., *The Entropy Law and the Economic Process*, Harvard University Press, 1972.
Harcourt, G.C., *Some Cambridge Controversies in the Theory of Capital*, Cambridge, 1972.
Herniter, J.D., "An Entropy Model of Brand Purchase Behavior", *Journal of Marketing Research*, 1973.
Huang, K., *Statistical Mechanics*, London, 1963.
Kaldor, N., "Alternative Theories of Distribution", *Review of Economic Studies*, 1955–56.
Kregel, J.A., *Rate of Profit, Distribution and Growth: Two Views*, MacMillan, 1971.
Kregel, J.A., *The Reconstruction of Political Economy, An Introduction to Post–Keynesian Economics*, MacMillan, 1973.
MacQueen, J. and J. Marschak, "Partial Knowledge, Entropy and Estimation", Working Paper 228, Western Management Science Institute, UCLA, 1975.
Murphy, R.E., *Adaptive Processes in Economic Systems*, New York, 1965.
Näslund, B., "Size Distributions and the Optimal Size of Firms", *Zeitschrift für Nationalökonomie*, 1970.
Näslund, B., *An Analysis of Economic Size Distributions*, Heidelberg, 1977.
Pasinetti, L.L., " Rate of Profit and Income Distribution in Relation to the Rate of Economic Growth", *Review of Economic Studies*, 1962.
Philippatos, G.C. and N. Gressis, "Conditions of Equivalence among E–V, SSD and EH Portfolio Selection Criteria", *Management Science*, 1975.
Rashevsky, N., *Mathematical Biology of Social Behavior*, Chicago, 1951.
Shannon, C.E. and W. Weaver, *The Mathematical Theory of Communication*, University of Illinois Press, 1949.
Theil, H., *Economics and Information Theory*, Amsterdam, 1967.
Theil, H.," The Use of Information Theory Concepts in the Analysis of Financial Statements", *Management Science*, 1969.
Wilson, A.G., "The Use of the Concept of Entropy in Systems Modelling", *Operational Research Quarterly*, 1970.

12 DISCUSSION

PAPER BY BERTIL NASLUND

Professor von Weizsäcker was concerned about the treatment of uncertainty in the paper. Income classes have one important characteristic, namely that they have a natural ordering on the real line. The concept of entropy seems to have been devised for more general situations where no simple measure of distance between classes was present. He therefore asked whether the entropy concept was applicable in the present context, and whether it enabled uncertainty to be appropriately measured.

Dr. Mustert appreciated attempts to integrate different theories and was therefore sympathetic to the paper's synthesis of an economic theory of distribution and the random event approach to the personal income distribution. He was prepared to accept the choice of a neo-Keynesian distribution theory, but was puzzled by the fact that it is the Shannon definition of entropy that is maximised. The same procedure is used elsewhere by Theil to construct two measures of income inequality. The one preferred for empirical work is defined for relative income shares; the other uses relative income frequencies and takes into account the income classes chosen. He interpreted the paper as looking for the income distribution with the lowest income inequality given the restrictions imposed by the economy. This accords with the notion that a distribution which is relatively flat indicates more uncertainty than one with a sharp peak. However he did not understand which of the definitions of income inequality would be more appropriate for the procedure followed in the paper.

Finally he pointed out that equation (12) requires λ and μ to be positive. Given a positive value for c, it is impossible to choose a positive μ which keeps savings non-negative at very high income levels. This is not the intention of the author, and the question therefore remains whether this model generates a Pareto distribution or whether we still have an exponential distribution.

Dr. Kuipers thought the paper elegant but felt it had less to do with the Kaldorian theory of income distribution, which was concerned with factor shares, than with the approach taken by Pasinetti, which was directed at the income distribution over social groups. He was puzzled by the fact that a change in savings caused by a change in the parameter μ had no effect on the income distribution, whilst a savings shift induced by a change in the other parameter c does alter the distribution. He did not understand how this difference could arise and wished to know more about the mechanism underlying the theory of income distribution.

Dr. Wagner thought that the Kaldorian theory and the stochastic approach were fundamentally incompatible at the micro level and therefore believed they could not be integrated within a single model.

Professor van Praag could not understand why entropy should be maximised, but suggested that this procedure should be able to generate functions other than those considered in the paper, for example the normal and log-normal distributions.

Mr. Bartels said that work along the lines suggested by Professor van Praag had already been done by Mogridge in several papers. Mogridge even generates a gamma function and presents empirical tests for goodness-of-fit. It was strange that these references had been omitted, particularly since the approach adopted in the appendix corresponds closely to that followed by Mogridge.

A crucial assumption in the appendix supposes that interactions between individuals increases with their total income. Why this assumption is chosen is not clear. He would have preferred to assume that the interaction increases with the difference between the individual's rank order in the distribution. Finally, he pointed out that the paper uses the Shannon definition of entropy which is a special case of Renyi's α-order entropy. This wider class would give rise to other entropy definitions which might well be more attractive.

Professor Krelle wondered about the precise objective of the paper. If a description of the income distribution was intended, then tests for the empirical fit of the derived distribution should have been included. If the aim was to explain how the income distribution was generated, more attention should be paid to the determinants of personal incomes.

Professor Wiles said the popularity of entropy was another characteristic feature of the "Dutch School". He felt it fitted in with their ideological belief in a continual egalitarian trend. There was something inevitable about the word entropy: to "heat death" in thermodynamics there corresponds "inequality death" in economics. But of course this was the merest analogy, and it was ironical that the inventor of the analogy, also a Dutchman, had used it in order to disparage equality – and then emigrated.

Professor de Wolff also wondered about the meaning of the paper which he felt had little to do with economics. In physics, entropy plays a very important role as a measure of disorder. For the world as a whole, it can never go down. But what is the economic justification for the author's assumption that economic entropy tends to a maximum?

Mr. Buenrostro-Hernandez mentioned a paper by Klas entitled "The Power Element in the Control of an Economy" which he believed justified the use of the maximum entropy approach.

Professor Naslund was unable to attend the conference and the discussion therefore took place in his absence. He was invited by the editors to address himself briefly to the points raised during the discussion. His reply is as follows:

As Professor von Weizsäcker points out, it is correct to regard the entropy concept as quite general. A more extensive justification for using it in connection with income distribution is given, for example, in Theil's book *Economics and Information Theory*. Mr. Mustert refers to the measures of income inequality proposed in this book. Theil's measure for relative income shares is similar to the one used here.

The savings function which is used to derive the Pareto distribution is only suggested as an illustration. As Dr. Mustert points out, a more complete analysis would require a discussion of the signs of the parameters and the domain over which the savings function gives non-negative values.

Professor van Praag and Mr. Bartels raise issues dealt with in a paper by Mogridge. Unfortunately I am not familiar with this work.

Professor Krelle is concerned about the objective of the paper, which is to show how income distributions are generated by randomness under certain macro-economic constraints. Ultimately this theory must be tested against empirical data.

Professor de Wolff asks if entropy always goes up in economics. It seems that the entropy concept and information theory have been quite useful for the analysis of various economic problems, even if the economic system as a whole does not evolve towards a state of maximum disorder.

13 PRODUCTION AND THE APPROPRIATION OF PERSONAL INCOMES

LOUIS LEVY-GARBOUA

The organisation of production and the distribution of personal incomes are inter-related. The problem is to discover whether this relationship is one of causality or interdependence. Functional theories of distribution have resolved it in the simplest way, by making one aspect subordinate to the other. The marxist theory goes as follows: the distribution of wealth is given as datum, and this determines the organisation of production and the structure of property rights which perpetuates it from one period to another. Neo-classical theory suggests the opposite conception: technical conditions and the productivity of individuals are given, and the associated factor payments sum to the total value of output. Whether they emphasise the technical process of production or the social process of appropriation, these two theories equally presuppose that the process in question is outside the control of factor-owners on whom the productive effort depends. This minimises the role played by individual and collective *behaviour* in the determination of productive contributions and incomes. Now, theories of personal distribution have shown that modelling the behaviour of agents enables real phenomena to be understood, which economic analysis had previously treated unsatisfactorily. It is tempting to follow this approach in analysing the interdependence that exists between the organisation of production and personal income distribution. This line of research has so far been little explored, probably because statistics rarely investigate the process of production.

I. Demonstrations

Production needs the cooperation of several factors, or, to be more accurate, of all the *persons* (groups) who exert a direct control over these factors and whom I shall call *factor-controllers*. These include factor-owners, factor-users and (factor) employers. The central point of this article is that factor-controllers have considerable scope to vary, both now and in the future, the quantity and quality of the productive factors they control, thus influencing their own income. However, the actions through which this behaviour manifests itself belong to two distinct categories, which may be called *investments* and *demonstrations*.

Investments directly change the productive contribution of the factors in which they are embodied, reducing it initially, only to increase it later. Thanks to the theory of human capital,[1] we now agree that people may increase their incomes by rationally choosing their education, health, information, geographical and professional mobility, and so on. What we find behind the unified concept of human investment is a great variety of activities all aiming to increase earnings and the quality of labour in the future. As well as these activities, the purpose of which is to directly increase productivity, there are a number of others that aim at increasing the income of a person or group without interfering with the maximum productivity that factors could possibly attain. I wish to focus, in this article, on this second category of actions, called demonstrations, and to explain the mechanisms through which they influence production and factor payments.

Demonstrations may be at least as varied as investments. They include such things as mobility (quits and layoffs), shirking, bargaining, unionisation and striking, etc. There are also actions that take place over a longer term such as rationing the supply of substitute factors, or establishing various constraints on social mobility. The only connection between these demonstrations is the fact that they are designed to influence factor payments, and it is also this aspect that distinguishes them from consumption activities.

The kinds of demonstrations which could alter the distribution of output amongst factors, are effective only insofar as they give one of the factor-controllers cooperating in production (entrepreneurs, factor-owners, or factor-users) the power to control part of the productive effort. I shall examine below the actual circumstances in which agents succeed in acquiring incomes as a result of the demonstrations undertaken. To begin with, I shall briefly consider two conventional models of production and distribution in order to illustrate their features and limitations.

II. Two conventional models of production and income distribution

Let us assume that each person attempts to maximise the *net* income associated with his productive contribution. The gross income of factor-owners is proportional to the productive effort of the factors they control:

$$R_i = w_i x_i, \qquad i = 1, 2, \ldots, n, \tag{1}$$

where R_i denotes the gross income of the ith owner, x_i the total productive effort of the controlled factors and w_i the average return to such effort.

For their part, entrepreneurs keep any residual profit that may remain after all factors have been paid. Gross profit is expressed thus:

$$P = pf(x_1, \ldots, x_n) - (w_1 x_1 + \ldots + w_n x_n), \tag{2}$$

where the letters P and p represent gross profit and the price of goods produced by the firm, and f is the production function, with marginal products assumed to be diminishing. The price p is determined by competition.

The simplest model assumes that entrepreneurs have full control over all the

---

[1] See Becker (1975).

productive efforts of useful factors purchased in the external market at market prices. They stop hiring factors when they achieve the maximum gross profit. Human capital theory modifies this argument by incorporating the quality of the productive efforts of factors and by estimating it using the aggregate investment embodied in these same factors. The cost of investments by various agents is then deducted from their gross incomes. Expressions (1) and (2) become respectively:

$$R'_i = w_i x_i - \Gamma_i(h_i), \qquad i = 1, \ldots, n, \tag{3}$$

$$P' = pf(x_1, \ldots, x_n, H_1, \ldots, H_n) - (w_1 x_1 + \ldots + w_n x_n) - \mathscr{C}(h_1, \ldots, h_n), \tag{4}$$

where

$$h_i = \dot{H}_i = \frac{dH_i}{dt}, \qquad i = 1, \ldots, n, \tag{5}$$

and where Γ_i and $\mathscr{C}$ stand for the investment expenditure in the factors, paid by owners and entrepreneurs, which we may assume, for the sake of simplification, to have been completely incurred during the period in question. We may add that marginal returns are inversely related to the quantity and quality of productive efforts and that the marginal cost of investment is non-decreasing. In this new model, the external market determines as many factor prices as there are heterogeneous qualities, according to the expressions:

$$w_i = w(H_i) \qquad \text{with } w'_{H_i} \geq 0, \qquad i = 1, \ldots, n. \tag{6}$$

Now the entrepreneurs choose the quantity and quality of all useful factors to maximise their long-run profits:

$$\int_0^\infty P'(t) e^{-rt} dt,$$

where r stands for the discount rate. Euler's equations provide the following two conditions of dynamic equilibrium:

$$pf'_{x_i} = w_i, \qquad i = 1, \ldots, n, \tag{7}$$

$$pf'_{H_i} = x_i w'_{H_i} + r\mathscr{C}'_i, \qquad i = 1, \ldots, n. \tag{8}$$

The human capital model extends the simple model, by adding equation (8) to equation (7). Equality between the price and marginal productivity of a factor (depending both on its quality and quantity, which we have so far artificially separated) is no longer always respected when there are investment activities. And, in fact, changes in the factor's productivity stream cost the entrepreneur an amount which he recovers by capturing part of the productivity gains. Human capital theory thus contradicts the conventional theory, according to which the income distribution is totally determined by the technical process of production. However, in the simplified version presented, it is not yet a satisfactory theory of appropriation, because it lacks a relationship determining how the increase in the factor price depends on the additional costs imposed on the various factor-controllers.

It is only by expressing *costs and productive output* as a function of the demonstration efforts of persons that theories concerning the process of income appropriation can be formulated. It is not just a question of improving conventional models, but of defining theories that may be refuted and verified as the classical theory, despite its ambiguities, could be. Factor markets are, in fact, characterised by fundamental "micro-imperfections". By omitting them "for the sake of simplification" we alter the essential features of income distribution, since we are unable to make a positive judgement on phenomena as important and varied as occupational mobility, internal markets within each firm, trade union action, subsistence wages and social classes.

III. Adjustment costs and personal incomes

The models examined above assume that entrepreneurs have full control over the productive effort of useful factors purchased in the external market. They thus disregard alternative internal market opportunities which are available the moment the two factor groups (internal and external) become imperfect substitutes. The most valid point the theories of personal distribution have taught us recently is that, in production, persons are not identical. The vintage models come to essentially the same conclusion for machinery. Replacement of a factor (by a substitute) and, in general, every *adjustment* of productive effort entails an additional cost for all those cooperating in production.

A precise analysis of such costs is very complex, but it has to be centred on two concepts: the *specificity* of factors, reflecting their technical specialisation and the consequent segmentation of internal markets; and *illiquidity*, which is a characteristic of their external market. Within the first concept, we may include the costs of searching for and evaluating new factors, costs of transport and migration, costs of specific training, and the cost of reorganising the production line, part of which is the disutility associated with a break in routine. The second concerns the non-availability of replacement factors, whose supply is inelastic, or increases in their price. These two types of micro and macro-imperfections describe the fundamental heterogeneity and diversity of individuals and goods.

III.1. *External control and productive efforts*

The above models neglect replacement and adjustment costs, limiting their application to perfectly general and malleable factors, which have the same productivity wherever they are used, and which may always be replaced without cost. In these circumstances, none of the factor-controllers cooperating in production can affect the behaviour of others by imposing on them a demonstration, or simply by threatening one, since an immediate replacement can be made without cost. Factors are perfectly mobile and competition does what it can to dictate their rewards. The results of the simple model then apply to each homogeneous factor. Demonstrations of mobility allow factor-owners to capture all the productivity gains accruing to their factors. On the other hand, when the replacement of a factor (or the adjustment of productive efforts) entails additional costs for certain agents, it is no longer in their interest to turn to the external market, since they would suffer a loss in that market. What, then, is exactly happening?

Let us examine the case when there are two agents, first assuming that both bear the cost when one of them is mobile, then assuming only one bears the cost. Both possibilities lead to significantly different results. The first situation applies when replacement costs depend on factor specificity. As the entrepreneur and the owner lose something if the other replaces them, it is in their interest to contract together to restrict the mobility of the factor, by sharing costs and productivity gains, which depend on the specificity of the latter.[2] Alternatively, if the factor market is in disequilibrium, the replacement cost is borne exclusively by the agent on whose side the excess supply is to be found; and if only one of the two enjoys a monopoly position, the cost will entirely fall on whoever has the least monopoly power. However general the factor in question may be from the technical standpoint, it is illiquid, difficult to transfer.[3] The agent that bears the whole replacement cost must agree to a unilateral reduction in his income to encourage the other not to exercise the mobility from which he suffers.

The most favourable situation for an agent is one in which he can transfer the cost of illiquidity to others, i.e. make himself difficult to replace. The collusion of employers and the unionisation of owners of substitute factors are the conflicting means used by each agent to achieve that result. By reinforcing the solidarity of members of the association, and by extending it to the largest possible number of similar people, it becomes possible for the most united group to control the supply in the external and internal markets, making the replacement cost much higher for members of the opposing group.

III.2. *Internal control of productive efforts*

Let us suppose that the factors employed by a firm are specific, or that their owners (direct users) form a powerful union. When the cost of an external control of the productive efforts of his factors becomes very high, the entrepreneur naturally turns to internal control as a solution. Can he then obtain the desired efforts corresponding to maximum profit? Despite the power he has to buy his own machinery, to modify the timetables and work rate, to lay off employees, to develop training courses on the job etc., he is not *entirely* free to use labour and capital as he wishes. This would be true even in a slave economy. For the activities of slaves usually go partially unchecked, and supervision of their productive efforts is not continual. And if the masters use their labour too intensively, sooner or later they pay for it through physical exhaustion and premature death of the slaves, who thus deprive them of part of the expected returns. For even stronger reasons, it is

---

[2] Parsons (1972) analyses this division within the framework of a two-period model.
[3] In his analysis of specific training, Becker (1975, pp. 26–37) confuses this situation with specificity. As he does not explicity introduce the replacement cost of human capital by the employee and his employer, his argument neglects this distinction, despite its importance for the study of distribution.

impossible, in a free society, to prevent workers from shirking, going absent or striking, if they wish to do so. Physical capital itself is not a completely inert factor, insofar as its services may be hired; and even when it has been bought, it is used by free workers. Thus, the entrepreneurs cannot directly control all the demonstrations of owners (direct users) of internal factors. Since these cannot be replaced, the production possibilities depend on the effort constraint[4] associated with the group of individuals that cooperate. This may be expressed thus:

$$E_x + E_h + E_X \leq \bar{E}, \tag{9}$$

where $\bar{E}$ is the maximum (exogenous) effort made by the collaborating group and E_x, E_h, E_X those efforts allocated to production, investment and demonstration respectively. The concerted efforts of the members of this group are assumed to be proportional to the factors it controls, with the coefficient of proportionality indicating the average degree to which these factors are embodied in the owner (or the degree of control over the factors he uses). The productive effort of any human factor can in fact be measured accurately via the workers endowed with it, while the productive effort of land or machinery depends little on the capitalist who owns them. Thus, we may write

$$E_x = ex \quad (0 \leq e \leq 1); \qquad E_h = kh \quad (0 \leq k \leq 1), \tag{10}$$

where the degree of embodiment (or control), e and k, becomes closer to one as the factor in question is more extensively incorporated within (or better controlled by) persons. It should be emphasised that x and h express the productive and investment efforts of factors, while E_x and E_h are the efforts of their *owners* (direct users). One feature of demonstration efforts is that they always concern persons, rather than factors, so that:

$$E_X = X, \tag{11}$$

where X measures the demonstration effort of the owners (direct users) of the factors.

If we substitute (10) and (11) into (9) we obtain

$$ex + kh + X \leq \bar{E}. \tag{12}$$

Equation (12) shows that by varying individual demonstration efforts (X) or investment (kh), it is possible to modify the productive effort of controlled factors (x). This enables the factor-owners (direct users) to bring production and residual profit down to a level below the expected optimum, with the aim of persuading entrepreneurs to increase their remuneration rate.

III.3. *Adjustment costs, demonstrations and the distribution of output*

Let us incorporate these arguments in a model that takes into account replacement or adjustment costs and the relevant control variables.[5] To simplify the exposition

---

[4] The effort constraint will be equivalent to a pure time constraint when the efforts are uniformly distributed over the duration of the period. This has been noted by Becker (1965).

[5] If we include investment behaviour, we must add investment effort to the demonstration effort.

and analysis, let us consider only one homogeneous input. The net incomes of the group of factor-owners (direct users) and the entrepreneurs, satisfy the following expressions:

$$R'' = wx - \gamma(y), \tag{13}$$

$$P'' = pf(x) - wx - C(y). \tag{14}$$

γ and C are the factor replacement (or adjustment) costs for both agents in question. Marginal costs are assumed to be increasing. In addition, y indicates the productive effort of replacement factors. When the entrepreneur tries to compute his maximum (net) profit, he must take into account a market constraint. All increases in the productive effort ($\dot{x} = dx/dt$) throughout a particular period are determined by the balance between the extra effort from replacement factors (y) and the reduction due to the group of internal collaborators[6] (X). We therefore have:

$$\dot{x} = y - X \tag{15}$$

Equation (15) summarises the problem faced by the two groups which cooperate in production, while at the same time each try to make the highest net income. On the whole, the entrepreneur has better control over replacement efforts, while owners (direct users) have better control over demonstration activities. The first is therefore able to neutralise the action of the second and make it less effective, except when collective action manages to control replacement efforts. In such circumstances, the entrepreneur is no longer able to determine the productive effort, unless he persuades the opposing group to moderate its demonstrations in return for higher rewards. In the general case, where no factor has absolute control over productive effort, the existence of replacement costs encourages the two groups to reduce mobility and other demonstrations simultaneously. And in fact, if the firm relies less on replacement factors, the opposing group's risks will diminish. Consequently the group may in turn agree to moderate its demonstrations (including the voluntary withdrawal of the factors it controls), causing a drop in adjustment costs and productive inefficiency. If the group behaves properly the entrepreneur's risks will decrease and output rise as a result of this action. He may consequently agree to share the gains by granting the group a higher remuneration rate.

When the entrepreneur has poor control over productive efforts, he has to influence them indirectly through demonstration efforts – by affecting the factor price. This is indicated in equation (16):

$$X = X(w), \qquad X'_w = \frac{dX}{dw} < 0. \tag{16}$$

By expressing y as a function of $\dot{x}$ and X in equation (15), and then expressing X as a function of w using (16), equation (14) becomes:

$$P'' = pf(x) - wx - C[\dot{x} + X(w)]. \tag{17}$$

---

[6] A similar model is used by Pencavel (1972) to study the connection between occupational mobility and salary policy of enterprises, and the quantity of specific training.

This time, the entrepreneur controls the mix of productive effort and factor price in an attempt to maximise his long run net profit. Using Euler's equations, we obtain the following two conditions of dynamic equilibrium:

$$pf'_x = w + rC', \tag{18}$$

$$-C'X'_w = x. \tag{19}$$

(18) generalises equations (7) and (8) of the previous models. The right hand side represents the user cost of the factor, comprising the market price and adjustment cost.[7] But, above all, the new equation establishes a marginal relation between the sensitivity of demonstrations to the factor price ($-X'_w$) and the replacement cost (C'). Formula (19) shows that the firm chooses the optimal mix (x, w) in such a way that, if the factor price is increased by one monetary unit, the additional reward of productive effort compensates for the induced decline in the replacement (or adjustment) cost of the factor.

This general relationship may be used to illustrate two hypotheses that occupy a central place in economic theory: the Walrasian and Classical models. First of all, it is immediately obvious that, if the adjustment cost is zero, for (19) to hold it is necessary that the demand for demonstrations be perfectly elastic near the point of equilibrium, and therefore that the factor price be entirely fixed by the market, rather than by the firm. Thus we rediscover the simple model of our starting point. Another interesting special case arises when the supply of a factor is assumed to be inelastic. This is well suited to the case of exhaustible natural resources, such as labour or land. Because of the intrinsic scarcity of the factor, the owners are able to influence their income by rationing their supply. Let us suppose that rationing decreases uniformly when the price of the factor goes up, until it reaches a threshold at which it stops completely. As soon as rationing begins, the entrepreneurs are subjected to a replacement cost that is actually the reproduction cost of the labour force, or else the cost of developing new land. However, this cost disappears when supply is sufficient. In such conditions the application of (19) shows that, on the one hand, the equilibrium price is fixed at the threshold value that just avoids rationing, while, on the other, this value must be such that it enables the labour force to reproduce itself and the land-owners to cover the cost of clearing the least fertile land.[8] The classical theories of subsistence wages and land rent thus re-

---

[7] We would also need to add the investment cost if we wished to take investment behaviour into account.

[8] Our hypothesis should be formally expressed as follows:

$$\begin{aligned} x &= \bar{x}, \\ y &= X, \end{aligned} \quad \text{(inelastic factor supply)}$$

$$X = \text{factor rationing} = \begin{cases} \bar{x} - \dfrac{\bar{x}}{s}w, & \text{if } w < s, \\ 0, & \text{if } w \geq s, \end{cases}$$

$$C(X) = \begin{cases} 0, & \text{if } X = 0, \\ \dfrac{\bar{C}}{\bar{x}}X, & \text{if } X > 0. \end{cases}$$

appear, if we add that wage earners ration the future supply of labour by reducing their offspring, and that landowners increase the supply of land by clearing new terrain.

IV. Revealing productive contributions

The efficacy of a demonstration as a means of increasing a factor price depends on the manner in which the entrepreneur associates it with the quantity produced. As most known production processes are complex, it is not easy to isolate the effect that variations in certain factors have on the volume of output, i.e. to evaluate their productive contributions.

IV.1. *Estimating productivities*

In order to pose the problem, let us imagine that an observer tries to estimate the production function of a complex process involving n factors, and suppose that he knows how to measure the productive efforts of all factors with great accuracy. The first thing he will undoubtedly do, is place himself at the exit of the factory to count the number of units produced in a particular period. If we add the sign ^ above the estimated sizes, we can state, on the basis of the above hypotheses, that:

$$\hat{x}_1 = x_1, \ldots, \hat{x}_n = x_n, \tag{20}$$

$$\hat{f}(\hat{x}_1, \ldots, \hat{x}_n) \equiv f(x_1, \ldots, x_n). \tag{21}$$

Let us bring the value of $\hat{x}_1$ into identity (21) by using (20), then differentiate (21). This gives

$$\hat{f}'_{x_1} dx_1 + \ldots + \hat{f}'_{x_n} dx_n \equiv f'_{x_1} dx_1 + \ldots + f'_{x_n} dx_n,$$

or

$$(\hat{f}'_{x_1} - f'_{x_1}) dx_1 + \ldots + (\hat{f}'_{x_n} - f'_{x_n}) dx_n \equiv 0 \text{ for all feasible } dx_1, \ldots, dx_n. \tag{22}$$

If, for all factors, any variation in productive effort is allowed, we may deduce from (22) that:

$$\hat{f}'_{x_1} - f'_{x_1} \equiv \ldots \equiv \hat{f}'_{x_n} - f'_{x_n} \equiv 0 \tag{23}$$

The observer is therefore in a position to evaluate exactly the marginal productivities of all factors.

From this it follows that

$$-C'_x X'_w = -\frac{\bar{C}}{\bar{x}}\left(-\frac{\bar{x}}{s}\right) = \frac{\bar{C}}{s}.$$

Equation (19) embodies the classical expression: $\dfrac{\bar{C}}{\bar{x}} = s$. The average replacement cost of the factor is equal to the rationing threshold.

But let us imagine from now on that certain variations are technically impossible or, more generally, unobservable. For example, the first factor appears to be fixed, and the others variable. Therefore,

$$dx_1 \equiv 0, \quad \text{in all observations.} \tag{24}$$

The first term disappears in equation (22), so only $(n - 1)$ productivities may be estimated with great accuracy. *The one associated with the invariant factor remains unknown.*

Now, if we solve the entrepreneur's program (17), adding the constraint that the first factor is invariant, we come up again with expression (18) for all variable factors, and a modified equation for the fixed one:

$$w_1 = (pf'_{x_1} - \sigma) - rC'_1, \qquad \sigma > 0, \tag{25}$$

where σ is the dual value of the constraint: $x_1 = x_1^0$.

The price of the constant factor corresponds to that of a similar variable factor with a (perfectly estimated) lower marginal product:

$$p\hat{f}'_{x_1} = w_1 + rC'_1, \tag{26}$$

and comparing (25) and (26):

$$pf'_{x_1} - p\hat{f}'_{x_1} = \sigma. \tag{27}$$

In other words, the productivity of the constant factor is *underestimated* by an amount equal to the dual value of the constraint on its productive effort. In such cases, the appropriation of income depends only to a limited extent on the technical process.

This suggests that the role played by certain demonstrations is merely that of revealing a factor's productivity, by allowing it to change relative to the others. The actions that fulfil this function must convey as accurately as possible, to both owners and entrepreneurs, information on the true productivity of the factor. Consequently, the kinds of demonstrations chosen are those which may be perceived and interpreted quite clearly. If we analyse the human factor in greater detail, strikes and obvious temporary work-stoppages should be more appropriate than underhand shirking behaviour.

Productivity-revealing demonstrations therefore contrast with *covert demonstrations*, which Alchian and Demsetz (1972) have explained in a particularly interesting way.[9] *Concealed demonstrations* follow simply from the previous argument if we suppose that it is very expensive to separately estimate the productive efforts of workers belonging to the same team. In such circumstances, these employees cannot reveal their individual productivities. The apparent reward structure penalises some of them and encourages them to reduce their productive effort. The demonstrations chosen in such cases will be hidden and difficult to detect, because there is a lower risk of them resulting in a reduction (or a very slight increase) in salary. Not being able to be paid cash for the productivity they would

---

[9] The literature on the X-efficiency factor is equally interested in "concealed demonstrations". See, on this subject, Leibenstein (1976).

be prepared to offer, these employees pay themselves in kind by shirking, by abusing work facilities (e.g. taking goods and using the office telephone), by allowing themselves small privileges (e.g. the freedom to come and go as they please – like that enjoyed by civil servants). Certain visible demonstrations, such as absenteeism and irregular work attendance, should be included in this category insofar as the employee may contend that these are events beyond his control. This is what Arrow (1963) calls "moral hazard".

Productivity-revealing demonstrations are different from covert ones, not only because they are visible. This characteristic makes it clear that their effects may well be anticipated. Therefore, they do not always need to actually occur: the threat of action is sufficient, at the right moment, to cause the desired reaction. Conversely, a feature of covert demonstrations is that they actually occur, because employers cannot be directly influenced, either by demonstrations or anything else. Productivity-revealing demonstrations tend to be infrequent, concealed ones continual.

Let us return to productivity-revealing demonstrations. They are undertaken when the disclosed productivity gain is higher than the marginal cost of factor substitution. However, the owners (direct users) of a factor ignore the former as long as they cannot vary the productive effort of that factor. Therefore, they will probably initiate searching behaviour and estimate the size of the increase they may obtain through a series of experimental demonstrations.

IV.2. *Factor invariance and Social classes*

The process indicated by equation (15) may be used to keep the productive effort of a factor constant over time. Given that this causes the owners (direct users) to lose part of their full income, only the entrepreneurs could be interested in controlling this input. They in fact take whatever the opposing group leaves, as the following equation states:

$$P''(x_1^0, \sigma) = P''(x_1^0, 0) + \sigma x_1^0, \tag{28}$$

This, however, only ensures maximum profit if

$$P''(x_1^0, 0) + \sigma x_1^0 > P''(x_1^*, 0),$$

where x_1^* stands for the optimal productive effort of the fixed factor when it recovers the freedom to vary. The above equation may also be written:

$$P''(x_1^*, 0) - P''(x_1^0, 0) < \sigma x_1^0. \tag{29}$$

In other words, the entrepreneurs have an incentive to make a factor invariant when the income they extract from the opposing group is higher than the fall in profit caused by productive inefficiency.

Relation (29) can be interpreted with greater accuracy when $x_1^0 \approx x_1^*$. If we assume that the profit function is locally continuously differentiable around x_1^*, it becomes:

$$P''(x_1^*, 0) - P''(x_1^0, 0) = (x_1^* - x_1^0) \frac{\partial P''}{\partial x_1}(x_1^0 + \theta), \quad (x_1^0 + \theta) \in \,]x_1^0, x_1^*[. \tag{30}$$

By substituting (30) into (29), we obtain the following condition:

$$\left(\frac{x_1^*}{x_1^0} - 1\right)\frac{\partial P''}{\partial x_1}(x_1^0 + \theta) < \sigma, \tag{31}$$

which shows that complete control of the productive effort of a factor is, to the entrepreneurs, a means of increasing their profits, at least when the fixed quantity is close to the optimum quantity. If the employer is in a better position than the owners (direct users) of the factor to judge productivity, he has the opportunity to estimate the quantity he has to keep invariant, and to increase his profits substantially. He then realises abnormally high profits close to σx_1^0, by *exploiting* the fixed factor. We must however stress that the aggregate net income of all contributors falls.

Let us now restrict attention to two factors: labour and capital. We have just shown that the entrepreneurs can *increase* their profits at the expense of a group of earners, by making their productive efforts invariant. This also requires that the group of earners does not change over time: variations in the mobility of the fixed factor are zero (in a stationary economy).[10] The result is the same if earners constitute several heterogeneous groups. This can be interpreted as a *social class equilibrium*.

The entrepreneur class (and that of capital owners) has several means of attaining and preserving such a situation and a comprehensive review is beyond the scope of this article. However, it can be established by preventing the proletariat from achieving inter-generational accumulation of non-human capital, or, in other words, by paying him a subsistence wage (I include in this term the cost of training). In this way, additional earnings of skilled workers would be entirely absorbed by the extra costs of their children's education and would not be employed to acquire physical capital.[11,12] Those who belong to the proletariat could not transfer from it. In fact, the range of preferences and individual abilities reduces, perhaps considerably, the effectiveness of such a mechanism. The most able people, those who enjoy risk, have access to the capitalist class despite the handicap of their background.[13] In order to maintain their position as long as possible from one generation to another, members of the capitalist class collectively establish barriers aimed at excluding wage-earners from their club: imperfect credit and information markets, a variety of discriminating signals (especially cultural), etc.

If the employers' group (the capitalist class) succeeds in controlling the productive efforts of certain factors for a long time, a social class equilibrium develops. Thus,

---

[10] The result may be extended to balanced growth, for scale changes can no longer disclose the productive contribution of factors.

[11] These points are elaborated in Lévy–Garboua (1972, pp. 40–42, and 134–140).

[12] Because it is embodied in people, the marginal product of human capital declines much faster than that of physical capital. Provided that human capital is more profitable than non-human capital for the first units of investment, we must note that only those people with the greatest inherited abilities and/or wealth acquire the second source of income in the course of their lifetime. This point is made by Becker (1975, p. 132).

[13] Schumpeter (1951) has even based his social class system on differences between individual abilities.

since the fixed productive contributions of factors cannot be revealed, the income appropriation process may depend little on technical conditions.

Fixing the productive efforts of another group is a general means of capturing a larger share of total income. A priori, such behaviour does not only apply to the capitalist class. A powerful trade union may also be able to increase the wage rate of its members beyond the group's marginal productivity, by linking the productive efforts of an "inferior" group to those of its members and by making both invariant. The same conceptual tools are used in understanding exploitation of one class by another, and discrimination of one group of wage-earners by another, provided the assumption of variability of productive efforts is questioned.

References

Alchian, A.A. and H. Demsetz, "Production, Information Costs, and Economic Organization", *American Economic Review*, 1972.
Arrow, K.J., "Uncertainty and the Welfare Economics of Medical Care", *American Economic Review*, 1963.
Becker, G.S., "A Theory of the Allocation of Time", *The Economic Journal*, 1965.
Becker, G.S., "*Human Capital*", 2nd edition, New York, 1975.
Leibenstein, H., *Beyond Economic Man: A New Foundation for Microeconomics*, Harvard University Press, 1976.
Lévy–Garboua, L., *Une Analyse Economique de la Distribution des Revenus Individuels*, Thèse de Doctorat, Université de Paris I, 1972.
Parsons, D.O., "Specific Human Capital: An Application to Quit Rates and Layoff Rates", *Journal of Political Economy*, 1972.
Pencavel, J.H., "Wages, Specific Training, and Labor Turnover in U.S. Manufacturing Industries", *International Economic Review*, 1972.
Schumpeter, J., *Social Classes in an Ethnically Homogeneous Environment*, New York, 1951.

13 DISCUSSION

PAPER BY LOUIS LEVY-GARBOUA

Professor Krupp began by suggesting that the paper was directed at the functional income distribution rather than the personal income distribution. He felt it would be useful to consider the following framework. Denote the distribution of income over persons by a vector vy, whose elements indicate the share of income received by a single person or group of persons and consequently sum to one. Such distribution vectors may also be defined for the distribution of income over persons from a single factor (vf) and for the functional distribution of different factors incomes over factors (vY). If the factor distribution vectors vf_f are regarded as columns of a distribution matrix VYF we have the following identity

$$vy = VYF \times vY$$

The paper really assumes that vY can be used as a proxy for vy, which is not the case for most industrialised countries, since the off-diagonal elements of the matrix VYF are often non-zero.

When, as in the paper, a theory of subsistence is introduced, it is the distribution of household incomes which is relevant and this requires a further step. Some method must be found of aggregating personal incomes into household incomes, to obtain the household distribution vector hy. Further manipulation enables the distribution of per capitalised household income ky to be derived. Empirically the distributions vy, vY, hy and ky differ considerably and it is not clear with which of these the paper is concerned. However it appears that the main objective is the functional distribution vY, in which case personal incomes are not explained and the relevance to questions of subsistence is not established.

He thought this approach could be regarded as an appealing theory of revealed marginal productivity. A factor owner can reveal the value of the factor by demonstration. However he wondered how this works in practice, particularly when the demonstrations are hidden. In addition, a number of problems have to be solved to make the approach operational. It was not clear which variables should be measured, which data could be used and how problems of estimation, such as multi-collinearity, might be solved.

He went on to ask whether this approach had any advantages over traditional theories such as those of collective bargaining. Theories of collective bargaining also deal with open demonstrations and allow a wider variety of non-economic factors to be incorporated. The new feature in the paper seemed to be the notion of covert demonstrations, and he asked how these could be made operational.

Finally he felt that the approach could be applied to a number of different issues, but more details of the precise applications should be given before any attempt is made to test the model. The paper suggests that the classical subsistence theory of wages can be accounted for, but he did not believe it very useful for the explanation of modern income distribution. Another suggested application is the interpretation of social classes as an equilibrium of fixed factor endowments. He would like to know what level of disaggregation the author had in mind.

Dr. *Psacharopoulos* congratulated Professor Lévy–Garboua for attempting to marry neo-classical income distribution theory to the Marxian concepts of the organisation of production and the social class structure. This is a very difficult task, involving not only economics but the reconciliation of two conflicting political ideologies. He was not to be blamed for not having succeeded in the difficult task undertaken.

The paper itself was extremely complex but essentially it assumes that personal incomes are determined by (a) productivity increments due to past investment, such as human capital, and/or (b) some kind of "demonstrations", for example strikes or unions. He was not clear on the effect of a "demonstration" on personal income distribution. Suppose there exist four persons (or groups of persons) sharing total income in the way depicted in the following figure, namely that the two proletarians (p_1 and p_2) have much lower incomes than the two capitalists (k_1 and k_2). According to the paper p_1 has two options for improving his fate:

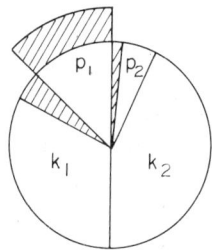

productive investment which increases both his income and the total pie (indicated by the shaded area outside the circle); or demonstration, which results in him taking part of the share of the first capitalist (indicated by the shaded area to the left of p_1). However, if the demonstration takes the form of unionisation, if p_2 is non-unionised and if the capitalists maintain their profits, the demonstration will result in p_1 taking his extra share from the other worker p_2 (shaded area to the right of p_1), making the income distribution more unequal.

Dr. Psacharopoulos continued by pointing out that the classification of demonstrations contained in the paper omitted what he believed to be the most important kind; power revealing demonstrations in situations where there is no need to persuade the employer that the union members have higher productivity. This point is further elaborated in Professor Pen's paper.

He doubted whether individuals would nowadays fall neatly into the social class categories defined in the paper. He suggested using an occupational classification instead, although even then there will be substantial earnings inequality within occupational groups, however these groups are defined. For this reason he tended to prefer an analysis based on individual earnings rather than those of groups. He was disturbed by the author's prediction of a "social class equilibrium", since this implies no mobility between social classes. Empirical evidence suggests that, whatever operational definition is given to social classes, the degree of mobility is substantial.

Finally he suggested that the relative importance of investments and "demonstrations" in determining personal, rather than group, incomes should be subjected to empirical tests. He believed that investments would turn out to be the more important factor, since there is already ample evidence that, say, human capital has a sizeable effect on earnings whilst unions have a much smaller effect.

Professor Michal hoped that the model might be subjected to statistical tests since it might help break the vicious cycle in neo-classical distribution theory – that the income distribution is explained by different marginal products and marginal products by relative incomes. On the point raised by Professor Krupp he felt that the dividing line between the personal income distribution and the factor distribution depended largely on the definition given to earners and factors.

Mr. Layard said that two questions were frequently posed in this type of analysis. The first was whether any particular group can raise its own wages, and the second whether it can raise wages above the marginal product. He suspected there would be general agreement that a group can raise its own wages, but doubted whether they could exceed the marginal product, since firms could always refuse to employ them. When regressions are run on individual characteristics he was always surprised at the relatively small residuals found for groups like the miners and power workers, who demonstrate their power quite forcibly. Miners, for example, earn something like 20 per cent more than individuals with similar personal characteristics. Given their obvious power he felt that they should be able to extract an even higher differential and the question therefore arises as to why they do not do so.

He went on to argue that the relative power of different occupational groups, if reflected in relative wages, should cause job rationing and therefore queueing in certain occupational categories. The extent to which this occurred could provide a test of theories such as that put forward by Professor Lévy–Garboua and he wondered whether any one had studied the degree of queueing. This related to the question whether workers can get more than their marginal product, since that is a question of whether they can influence the level of employment as well as the level of wages. Printing workers provide one example where this was certainly true, but this kind of power is not widespread.

He also felt that Professor Lévy-Garboua had failed to draw a crucial distinction between behaviour which could be undertaken by an isolated individual (e.g. quitting) and behaviour requiring cooperative action (e.g. a strike).

Professor Malinvaud said that for distribution theories it is important to specify the exact nature of competition between factor owners and employers. He emphasised the market imperfections arising from adjustment costs which cause indivisibilities or, in modern language, non-convexities. The paper, he felt, used the concept of non-cooperative equilibrium in game theory, or a Cournot equilibrium, to describe the imperfect competition in factor markets. He was a little surprised that a non-cooperative concept should be the most appropriate and wondered whether other speakers could provide alternatives.

He disagreed with Dr. Psacharopoulos' remark that social classes are difficult concepts and therefore cannot be used. Economists should recognise the fact that many people regard social classes as important concepts and take them into account. There had been progress towards describing socio-professional categories in which factors like occupation, educational requirements and the nature of income received, all contributed. Whilst the precise category definitions are still in dispute, the increasing use of these concepts is an indication of their relevance.

On the question raised by Mr Layard he suggested that evidence on the effect of minimum wage legislation on the demand for labour would give some indication of the extent of queueing that may result from wage increases obtained by labour unions.

Professor Taubman wondered whether the pay structure or organisation of a firm affects the ability of individuals to distinguish between productive effort and demonstration effort. For example, in a piece-work system individuals are only paid for their productive output. For hourly paid workers, on the other hand, firms have the additional problem of inducing their employees to work.

Dr. Kuipers recalled an article by Bruno in the *International Economic Review* (1968) which gave evidence that, in Israel in the post-war period, wages have exceeded marginal product. His own study of long-run production functions for the Netherlands found that the marginal product exceeded wages in the 1950s, but after about 1960 wages were progressively raised above the marginal product.

Professor Wiles thought there were two definitions of marginal productivity in the paper which should be more clearly distinguished. Most economic activity uses several inputs and they are almost always substitutable *at the margin*. With two inputs (A and B) it is desirable that

$$\frac{1}{w_a}\frac{\partial P}{\partial A} = \frac{1}{w_b}\frac{\partial P}{\partial B} = \frac{1}{p},$$

where w = input cost; P = output; p = output price. So, by Euler's theorem (and abstracting from such statistically minor considerations as the reward to enterprise).

$$Ap\frac{\partial P}{\partial A} + Bp\frac{\partial P}{\partial B} = w_a A + w_b B = pP.$$

But if an input owner withdraws all his services there will be, in the short run, a total shut down of output. This is because *strikes are not marginal:* each successive unit of A withdrawn has a higher marginal product than the one before. In fact

$$\frac{\partial P}{\partial A_1} + \frac{\partial P}{\partial A_2} + \ldots + \frac{\partial P}{\partial A_n} \approx P, \tag{1}$$

and similarly for B.

This shows, first, that the *go-slow* should not be classified as a "covert" demonstration of marginal productivity as is done implicitly in the paper. On the contrary, the go-slow reduces output by far more (per unit of input) than the marginal product; indeed, under "good" conditions it can reduce it almost to zero without abolishing a claim to wage payments. The reason is that *all "covert" demonstrations are collective* and organised.

Secondly he doubted whether the facts of power indicated by equation (1) were unknown to any trade union leader or employer. It is not equation (1) that is being demonstrated in a strike or go-slow, but the fact that the union has the will-power and funds to exploit it. Above all, it is not $\partial P/\partial A$ that is demonstrated, since that varies.

Professor Lévy-Garboua addressed himself first to Professor Krupp's suggestion that the paper was concerned more with the functional income distribution than the personal income distribution. He argued that the distinction between personal and functional theories of income distribution is not clear cut. Should human capital models, for example, be described as personal or functional theories? His model included important personal features and, in particular, distinguished between factors and factor-controllers.

On the points raised concerning the operational value of the model and the need for empirical testing, he said that the present paper was primarily theoretical and did not, therefore, discuss these issues. It suggested a simple framework in which assumptions about social classes, for instance, can be related to the contributions of factors in production. Moreover, it stressed the need to examine the operation of the production line in detail, instead of regarding the production process as a black box.

Several speakers had made useful remarks on the conditions required for the model to be valid; these were not completely explicit in the present formulation. In fact, this model can be applied when the production process is complex; when the number of individual factors and factor-controllers cooperating in production, is large; and when factors are partial substitutes. Under these conditions, demonstrations may have a marginal effect on production, and non-cooperative behaviour among factor-controllers is quite plausible.

On the question of the relative magnitudes of wage rates and marginal productivities of labour, raised by Mr. Layard, Dr. Kuipers and Professor Michal, Professor Lévy-Garboua said that his model demonstrates that the gap between wages and marginal products depends critically on the effect of demonstrations. This in turn depends on the technology being used, the means by which information is communicated, and the kind of behaviour taking place.

Finally, on the relevance of the demonstration concept, he made two remarks. Firstly, it should not be compared empirically with investment behaviour, as Dr. Psacharopoulos had suggested, because a demonstration is typically an activity aiming to appropriate income and, consequently, is always needed, even to capture the returns from investment. Secondly, there are many different types of demonstrations, probably too many to deal with them all in a single model. The paper had emphasised that the dividing line between various kinds of demonstrations (collective vs individual, revealing vs concealed) are associated with different kinds of market structure, information and technology. However, demonstrations are considered to be the unifying concept in the description of the process of appropriation.

14 THE ROLE OF POWER IN THE DISTRIBUTION OF PERSONAL INCOME: SOME ILLUSTRATIVE NUMBERS

JAN PEN

I. Power versus scarcity

Speaking of power and its impact on income distribution makes sense only if we try to separate this impact from the impact of other factors. At first sight there are at least three candidates for these "other factors": (a) scarcity, or the market, or, in a more specific way, marginal productivity; (b) personal characteristics or, more specifically, human capital;[1] (c) luck, which may lead us into stochastics or, as with Jencks (1972), into the blind alley of agnosticism. I would suggest that "power versus scarcity" is the best juxtaposition of explanatory variables, but I do not insist upon it. However, I do insist upon the following proposition: if someone rejects the first sentence of this paper, the power "theory" becomes a muddle. Those authors, mainly of marxist origin, who tell us that income distribution is nothing but the outcome of a power struggle, are bound to neglect the obvious influence of scarcity; or worse, they consider scarcity as a disguise of power, thereby stretching the latter concept into all-embracing meaninglessness. When the world is governed by power and by nothing else, traditional economics might as well be abolished. This is, of course, what the marxists have in mind.

On the other hand, some authors in the neo-classical tradition view power as a mere ripple on a lake; the ripple is of no consequence to the level of the water. These authors seem to be unaware of the facts of life. Trade unions do exert some influence on the wage structure and on the rate of increase of the money wage level (and, via wage inflation, on the profit squeeze). Some profits depend on monopoly power in product markets. At least some salaries are influenced by decision making within organisations. Governments do have some control over wages, in particular over real wages in times of inflation (for instance, compensation for price inflation to workers can be given in the form of lump sums – this technique has been applied several times in the Netherlands). These things should not be assumed away. It is difficult to understand how traditional supply and demand analysis could deal with them. The only escape route seems to lie with the hypothesis of perfect

---

[1] (a) and (b) are not mutually exclusive since ability and human capital command a price in the market.

shifting: the impact of power rolls forward and backward until the "natural" relationships between incomes are restored. Even if this were plausible in the long run – which it is not – we should be left with a considerable short-run problem, particularly when unions, governments, monopolists and administrative decision makers maintain their efforts continuously, by pulling and pushing at the income relationships.

Such extreme positions with regard to the significance of power bring the concept of power itself into disrepute. Words like "power structure" and "power struggle" become passwords revealing one's political stance. In some progressive circles the frequent use of these expressions is strictly *de rigueur*, and they are used to distinguish radical friend from conservative foe.[2] Among the practitioners of high theory the subject of power is considered to be the business of journalists or, worse, sociologists; I remember one mathematical economist who compared a treatise on power to "a sociologist's witty talk at a sherry party". And Bronfenbrenner (1971, page 439) says that the rivals of the Good Old Theory suffer from "highly specialised assumptions, tautological characteristics, confusions of cause and effect, shaky microfoundations, and/or general formlessness". Whilst I agree as far as kaldorist and marxist views are concerned. I do not agree with Bronfenbrenner's implicit argument that a theory of power is beyond the present capacity of the economist's mind.

Instead of all this metaphysical discussion we should try to disentangle quantitatively the role of power from the role of scarcity. I don't believe that we will succeed in this, given the present state of the art, but we should try. At least we should make the separation conceptually. Given this intention three things are imperative. First we should define power. My definition is that A is said to exercise power over B if A successfully threatens B into doing something contrary to B's preferences.[3] Second, we ought to distinguish between types of power. I suggest that three types are particularly relevant: political, economic and administrative power. Third, these categories should be defined by their sanctions, not by their outcomes. Economic power is power which rests on economic sanctions (the nature of these sanctions will be discussed below); it is not necessarily power over prices, wages, resource allocation etc. Political power is power exerted by political bodies with political sanctions; the result will certainly affect economic variables. Administrative power is based on the power wielder's position in an organisation. If we were to define the concept of economic power the other way round, with the impact on economic variables as a criterion, the distinction between scarcity and

---

[2] Fortunately, there are exceptions to the rule, which blur the demarcation lines. Tinbergen – most observers of the political scene would call him progressive – stresses the influence of scarcity up to the point where the long-term relevance of power is almost denied. He sometimes even regards power as a form of scarcity, which is the reverse of the marxist position (Tinbergen, 1975).

[3] B's frame of mind, including his system of preferences, is given, with one exception: his subjective evaluation of the probability that A will carry out his threat. If we do not allow for this exception, B cannot act contrary to his own preferences. If A succeeds in changing B's preferences, this is not power. The maximum probability which B will accept is called his propensity to fight. It can be analysed in terms of B's ophelimity functions, conflict ophelimity, etc. (This is done by Pen (1960)). The exercise is not particularly useful, apart from illuminating some basic concepts. The algebra is tautological, but it can be helpful in classifying the influential factors in a power struggle.

power would become fuzzy. Indeed, much confusion stems from the fact that people speak of economic power when they mean to refer to power over economic magnitudes.

II. Political power

Political power is easily defined in so far as it is exerted by governments. The sanctions of governments against trespassers are well known to all citizens, they are as visible as a policeman. But political power may also be exerted by pressure groups, political parties, voters etc., on governments, and so, via governments, on income distribution. The sanctions of pressure groups and political parties against governments are not always known, but in this paper we need not go into the workings of the political game; this can be left to our friends the political scientists. In discussing income distribution the acts of governments can be ascertained, and their impact on incomes should be estimated. That is the economist's problem. (Yet he should not be oblivious to the fact that behind governmental decisions there may lurk economic power!).

The impact of political power on income distribution is mainly twofold. The part which is probably less significant distorts the primary distribution of incomes by wage policy, price policy and monetary policy. (Indirectly government policy has many more effects. For instance, tariff policy in the sixties has favoured exporters and hurt domestic sellers in domestic markets. We shall come back to this). Little research effort of a quantitative nature has been put into estimation of the effects of these policies. A widely held view is that incidental measures – short-run wage restraints, price freezes etc. – have little lasting effects, whilst continual interference with wages, prices, rates of interest is supposed to be too uncommon to have any effect at all. Exceptions to this rule are perhaps minimum wage regulations. But repeated anti-inflationary intereference in wage determination may prove to be another exception; for instance, lump sum wage compensation for price increases, and the introduction of floors and ceilings in such wage adjustments, may lead to a reduction in wage differentials, provided that the operation is repeated every few years. The second impact of political power consists of redistribution by the budget and social security funds. This might be called budgetary power. The topic has, of course, been studied very extensively, and there has been a recent revival in research. We shall return to the differences between primary, secondary and tertiary income in the Netherlands. Recent estimates of these gaps exceed the figures for other countries. In the Netherlands political power seems to have been rather effective in reducing income inequality.[4]

---

[4] Political power has an important aspect which is not dealt with in this paper: the power of nations over other nations. This may, of course, influence income distribution within a country. The question is illustrated by the loss of colonial investments, which has been instrumental in lowering the share of capital in countries like the United Kingdom and the Netherlands. This problem is touched upon below in section X, but only in passing. It is remarkably absent from the traditional literature on income distribution. Here the radical criticism of mainstream economics certainly has a point.

III. Economic power

Even if we are thinking in terms of the sanctions, rather than the effects of power, the concept of economic power can be defined in various ways. I suggest that it consists of the power of withholding a marketable good or service, including labour, that the opponent wants. The sanction lies in the damage inflicted upon the weak party.[5] It is not necessary that the goods or services be actually withheld; the exertion of economic power uses the threat of retention. It is sufficient that the weak party *believes* that the threat can be made effective and that the strong party exploits this belief. The strike is the clearest example of a sanction which need not be applied to be successful. Usually the strong party is also hurt when the threat is applied; this makes the power relationships bilateral. The exercise of economic power is therefore usually a matter of bargaining, but the bargaining need not be overt; there are cases of unilateral price and wage setting based on economic power (and not on scarcity) with no preceding period of negotiation. Economic power presupposes the absence of perfect competition, because under conditions of perfect competition economic sanctions cannot be applied. Theoretically, all situations of imperfect competition imply economic power; but this element may be negligible, as in the case of product differentiation with many suppliers. The essential characteristic of the economic power relationship is that the weak party is more or less dependent upon one particular strong party. In a large labour market with sufficient mobility this condition is not fulfilled. If labour is abundant and capital and employment are scarce, the resulting low wages are a consequence, not of the power relationship (as the marxist view will have it), but of scarcity relationships. A concept like "power structure" is not helpful in understanding the situation.[6] But if a particular worker is dependent upon a particular employer, the latter can exercise economic power over the former; and vice versa, if the worker is difficult to replace. Power presupposes an element of play in the market; that is, it presupposes rents. Even if scarcity is contrived, I would not label the resulting high price a result of economic power.

The influence of economic power on income distribution has many aspects, but two of these seem to be quantitatively important. The first is power in the labour market, mainly exercised by unions. The matter is highly controversial – the partisans of the Barbara Wootton view (including, of course, most union leaders) opposing the pure economists. The latter have produced a flood of literature on the subject, partly concerned with the theoretical approach to bargaining (this is almost useless for our present purpose) and partly concerned with

---

[5] This damage depends, among other things, upon the scarcity of the good. Therefore economic power and scarcity cannot be completely separated from each other – not even conceptually, let alone quantitatively.

[6] This means that I reject the idea of defining the power structure by the elasticities of supply and demand, as has been suggested by Preiser (1952). Yet the elasticity of demand (for instance, the elasticity of demand for labour) may be relevant for the outcome of a power struggle. A strike will usually result in higher wages when the elasticity of demand is lower. In addition, elasticities of substitution between labour and capital, and between various types of labour, do matter. Generally speaking, the adherents of the power theory believe in low elasticities. Neo-Keynesian critics like Robinson and Kaldor are fond of complementarity.

marginal productivity in a strictly theoretical way. Some effort has been spent on the quantitative impact of unions on the wage structure. The latter type of research is within the down-to-earth tradition of labour economics, and will be referred to below.

The other field in which economic power is relevant for income distribution is that of profits. There can be no doubt that some part of total profits can be ascribed to the strong position of monopolistic sellers in product markets. But while the degree of monopoly explains part of profits, it is almost impossible to separate the fruits of power from the results of innovation, strong expansion, windfalls and the sluggishness of wage and interest adjustments in times of cyclical upswing (if such a sluggishness still exists, which is utterly doubtful). Profits remain a relatively unexplored area on the map of economic research, which has the unpleasant consequence that one of the most important facts of the mid-seventies – the profit squeeze – is still a riddle. We do not know whether it is mainly caused by power elements like the strong position of the unions (via wage inflation) and a decline in the degree of monopoly; or by non-power elements like saturation, an extended business cycle, changes in technology or shifts in the international division of labour.

IV. **Administrative power**

Apart from political and economic power we should distinguish administrative (or organisational) power. It is exercised within organisations, like government bureaucracies and firms. The sanctions are of the organisational type – one is outvoted, one is not promoted, one is called to order by the personnel department, in the last resort one is expelled from the organisation. Here again the procedure may consist in bargaining (within committees, or bilaterally between bureaucrats). This bargaining may certainly involve threats, but it differs from economic power: the goods or services which are threatened to be withheld are not marketable. Organisational rewards and punishments are a subject in themselves; our concern here is only with their effects on distribution.

Administrative power certainly helps to explain the wage and salary structure, particularly at higher income levels. Yet the abundant literature on organisational behaviour – abundant since Henry Simon – is not very helpful in separating the impact of this type of power from that of the market. The same is true for the Lydall–Beckmann approach, which explains the right-hand Pareto tail of an income distribution by pointing to the relationship between a person's salary and his or her place in the hierarchy. The theory may take the precise form of hypothesising a testable relationship between an executive's salary and the total amount of salaries paid out to the personnel one level below that executive. This is certainly a most interesting train of thought, but as Pareto-type tails are also found outside bureaucracies, the specific impact of organisational power remains an unsolved problem. For instance, Dutch figures show that the income differential between managers of corporations and the average income recipient has narrowed considerably in the post-war years: over the period 1952–1967 a reduction in the differential of about one third has been estimated (before tax). The question is whether this development has been caused by a shift in scarcity relationships, an increase in the supply of business economists, engineers, law school graduates, etc., a shift in the distribution of administrative power within the firms, or by a reduction in the total amount of salaries paid to the echelon just below the top managers. Some members of the administrative power school would probably deny that supply and demand relationships are applicable to the remuneration of top managers. Others would take a more moderate stand on the issue and accept that there is a combination of causal factors at work, including market forces. This view raises the question of the mix of these causal factors. The Lydall–Beckmann approach does not give much help in answering this type of question.

V. Social power

Political, economic and administrative power are not the only categories of power. Social power rests upon a subtle system of signals ranging from a slight frown to abuse and fisticuffs, and from a hardly perceptible affirmative nod to a decoration. This kind of power may have some relevance to income distribution. The great debate over justice may eventually lead to changes in social norms, and one might argue that it is the system of norms that basically determines income distribution. It is norms, among other things, that make a person decide as he does, and his exercise of power can be regarded as a manifestation of his value system. The trouble with social power is that, precisely because of its connection with norms, it is very hard to distinguish it from things which do not involve power. The concept of social power implies that a person is forced to do something against his own preferences. But social signals may change one's preferences; for instance, decision-makers within the firm may accept a moderate form of egalitarian ideology, and make decisions accordingly. Moreover, these signals and their effects on the human mind are all-pervading; they cannot be separated from other motives that influence people's actions and they cannot be separated from administrative and economic power. That is why I propose to leave social power aside.

VI. Complications

The three types of power and the influence of scarcity relationships are, of course, not mutually exclusive. One reason is that administrative power may result in contrived scarcity. Examples lie close at hand. Decisions taken over decades within Dutch universities have resulted in a permanent bottleneck in the training of dentists. The resulting scarcity is painfully clear to many patients, who find it difficult in some cities to get any treatment at all. The market has produced comfortable incomes for this particular profession. Given the contrived scarcity of dentists (plus the diffusion of costs by social insurance) we can understand these incomes without reference to any concept of power. But if we want to understand why this scarcity has been so persistent, we have to look into the power relationships behind the market. There is nothing in this situation that is mysterious, but the economist who refuses to consider the dealings of medical departments because he believes that this is outside his field, cannot fully understand income distribution.

In a more general sense scarcity depends on political decisions. If Tinbergen (1975) is right, and wage and salary differentials depend on the race between technology and education, government expenditure on schooling plays a crucial role. The educational system is, of course, the outcome of a long series of political decisions.

Another reason why the various categories intertwine is that economic power is sometimes used for political ends. Strikes against government measures are one example; another is threats to move an industry from a country or a city. It is my impression that, in the Netherlands, this indirect use of economic sanctions is almost negligible in its effect on income distribution. But I am aware of the fact that many people have different impressions.[7]

The relationships between types of power are complex in many other ways. Power may provoke countervailing power; but to what extent? Some believe in a rather prompt and ubiquitous reaction of this kind (Galbraith), but some do not (C. Wright Mills). In some cases (the Netherlands in the fifties) the economic power of the unions is counteracted by the political power of the government – a centralised wage policy. An evaluation of the ultimate role of power in society requires estimates of the promptness and intensity of these counter-reactions. Until now, we have had to rely on hunches, "views" and "beliefs"; preconceptions instead of scientific knowledge.

VII. Statics: The unattainable ideal

It is not difficult to identify specific and conspicuous events (a successful strike, an administrative decision to reduce a number of top salaries, a lump-sum wage increase) and see these as indications of power. This may be one reason why the power approach is popular with journalists and so-called realists. But what economics ought to do is something different; given the parameters of a certain income distribution, we should analyse what proportion of the Theil coefficient in a given year (or the Pareto coefficient, or some decile ratio) can be imputed to scarcity, what proportion to political power, to economic power, to administrative power. This is a heroic job which has, as far as I know, never been tackled. Therefore strategic questions remain unanswered. Is power relatively important? Would the income distribution in 1977 in the Netherlands, say, have been more or less equal if economic, political and administrative power had been absent?

It seems legitimate to doubt whether this type of static analysis is possible at all. A complete theory requires a comparison of a given world with a non-existent

---

[7] I have no quarrel with the popular idea that economic relations dominate politics. But this is not necessarily a matter of power. If politicians have economic goals in mind – employment, income distribution – there need not be any question of somebody doing something under duress. Even bribery does not necessarily imply the exercice of economic power in the sense of this paper – there may be agreement between the parties involved.

world – a world without unions, oligopolies, bureaucracies or governments. It requires a diagnosis of the degree to which power has led to countervailing power, and it requires a comprehensive analysis of the whole network of shifting. The impact of power on wages, interest and profits is partly shifted through the system, and added to the impact of taxation, government expenditure and social security. Economics has made little progress in estimating the quantitative aspect of shifting. Even the incidence of something as relatively simple as the corporation tax remains a moot point, and we are far from a comprehensive estimate of the more scattered forms of power on static equilibrium. Perhaps we should settle for less.

One way to do this is to look at the figures that are available, without bothering too much about their limitations and complications. A good example is the gap between various distribution criteria (Theil, Pareto, etc.) as shown by primary, secondary pre-tax, secondary after-tax and tertiary income. These gaps were estimated for the Netherlands.[8] The share of the top decile of income recipients in primary income in 1962 was 33%; in secondary pre-tax income 32%; in secondary post-tax income 27%. If we impute government services to income groups, the share is lowered to 26%. The total impact of budgetary power on the share of the top decile is the gap between 33 and 26, which amounts to about 20%. If we look at the share of the lowest decile – an even more precarious operation – we see that the percentage is raised from 0.9% to 2%, an increase of more than 100%.

If we take the income ratio between the top and bottom decile, budgetary power results in a reduction of inequality by two thirds. If we look not at the position of the extreme deciles but at the Theil coefficient, we find a lowering of the coefficient from 0.316 to 0.186: the reduction of inequality is 40% (in 1962). These figures show that income distribution is a different thing to different observers – inequality, and changes in inequality, differ according to the criterion by which they are measured. Perhaps the Theil coefficient deserves some recommendation (though it has no intuitive significance – it is relevant only if used in comparisons) and in that case a 40% gap might be a first approximation to the impact of budgetary power on distribution in 1962. It is a surprisingly high figure. Moreover, since 1962 subsidies to low income groups have increased; old age pensions are now relativity higher; compensation for the disabled has become more generous; and housing subsidies have been individualised. The gap will be probably higher for 1976.

One particularly vunerable aspect of this procedure is the imputation of benefits to income groups. If we leave these benefits and social security payments aside, the net effect of taxation remains. Here figures are available which show a remarkable similarity. For 1962, the pre-tax and post-tax Theil coefficients are 0.316 and 0.220, a gap of 33%. For 1964 the Pareto exponent α stood at 2.20 pre-tax and 2.79 post-tax, a gap of 25%. For 1972, the share of the top 1.25% stood at 10.1% pre-tax and 6.9% post-tax, a gap of 33%. For the same year the income ratio between the top decile and the lowest 60% of income recipients was 5.6 pre-tax and 4.2 post-tax, a gap of 25%. For 1975 the extreme decile ratio for employees of

---

[8] Sources: *Nota over de inkomensverdeling* (official government paper) (1969); Massizzo (1975).

the *Staatsmijnen* was pre-tax 3.5 and post-tax 2.5, a difference of about 33%. If we neglect shifting, the equalising power of the Dutch tax system lies somewhere between 25 and 33%.[9] This figure is quite consistent with a total impact of budgetary power of the order of 40%.

Crude and shaky as these estimates may be, they compare very favourably with our knowledge of political power over primary distribution. The government's wage, rent and interest policies have probably changed the Theil coefficient and the decile ratios, but nobody knows what these values would have been in equilibrium without government intervention. The impact has probably been in an equalising direction – mainly because of statutory increases in minimum wages and lump-sum compensation for price increases – but we don't know by how much. Moreover, we cannot separate this static influence from that of the unions, and from the impact of administrative decisions.

The research efforts in this field are, as far as I know them, of a more dynamic nature. They deal with such problems as: how much of the wage increase over a number of years can be attributed to union power? This line of approach does seem more promising than the static one. It can be seen as a second-best solution. The trouble with historic explanations of this type is that we have so much latitude in the number of years that we choose for our comparisons. Short periods may give different results from long periods; that is, the power element in the situation pertaining in the end years remains an unknown and disturbing factor. Moreover, history does not necessarily repeat itself.

VIII. Dynamics: Budgetary power and social security

Inequality changes over time and some of the changes are well-documented. For the Netherlands it was found that most indicators (coefficients of Pareto, Theil, decile ratios, the share of the top 1.25% of income recipients) show a reduction of inequality in post-tax income of at least 50% over the period since 1938 (Pen and Tinbergen (1976)). The question is the extent to which this dramatic change can be imputed to shifts in scarcity and to shifts in power, respectively.

A first step is to estimate the effect of increased taxation. We saw that the present (or, more correctly, 1964) equalising power of the tax system can be put between 25% and 33%. For 1938 the various parameters show a difference in their before and after tax values of about 7%. Excluding the effects of shifting, the equalising power of taxation over the forty year period lies between 18% and 26%, say 20%. This figure is based on the assumptions that the increase in the corporation tax is fully paid by consumers and that the Value Added Tax is regressive. The figure must be reduced if the recipients of high incomes were able to shift more of their increased tax burden than lower income recipients. There is no clear indication that the more affluent have been in such a favourable position. We all

---

[9] The pre-tax coefficient applies to taxable income, which is not identical to gross income. The difference is due to deductions which include some social insurance premiums, interest, medical expenses, and certain payments to relatives. The effect of these deductions is of course anti-egalitarian. Some authors argue that these anti-egalitarian effects are undesirable.

know examples of professional people who implicitly add their income tax to their outgoing bills, but wealthy shareholders and bond-holders can find no one to pay their increased taxes. The profit squeeze put many businessmen in the same boat as the passive investor: they had to carry their tax burden themselves. The same is true for most farmers. On the other hand, in the sixties and the seventies, wage negotiations aimed at increases in disposable income. In the average and minimum wage range, shifting has been a continuous game. If we lower the effect of taxation on inequality from 20% to 15% we stay on the safe side. The figure of 15% is the lowest that seems reasonable to me.

The second step is estimating the impact of the rise in social security and welfare payments. Their share in national income went up from a few percent in 1938 to 20% now. Part of the benefits go to the higher income brackets, but the net effect is egalitarian. According to Massizzo (1975), the Theil coefficient for the year 1962 is reduced by these payments from 0.220 to 0.192, a reduction of 13%. If we put the unknown prewar figure for the gap at 3% (which is a high guess, particularly if we exclude payments to the unemployed), the contribution of social security and welfare to the reduction in inequality was 10% in 1962. Since then it has probably increased somewhat.[10]

If we accept these guesses, taxation and transfer income – that is, budgetary power – has reduced inequality by 25% since 1938, about half of the post-tax income levelling that has taken place. The other half of the egalitarian trend reflects a change in the primary distribution.

IX. From capitalism to labourism

The third step is to explain the great eye-catcher: the fall in the share of capital. (The fourth step is to estimate the influence of this decreasing share on personal distribution. This white spot on the map of our knowledge is dealt with in section X).

Neo-classical theory has a particular claim to the explanation of changing shares. It looks at their development over time in the light of Hicks' Law: an increase in capital intensity K/L, combined with an elasticity of substitution between labour and capital σ less than unity, results in a smaller capital share. When dealing with this approach we have to make the following choice: shall we make a two-way division into labour income and capital income, or allow for more income categories? In the former case, profits are seen as capital income and Hicks' Law is supposed to be applicable to this type of income – which is a doubtful proposition. If we follow this procedure, the share of capital in the Netherlands fell by one third between 1938 and 1970, from 30% to 20%. Allowing for more categories, we may interpret capital income as the sum of dividends, interest, and rents – "passive" capital income – and the share then fell from 22.5% of national income to 5%,

---

[10] Within specific age groups the impact is much higher. Over the period 1950–1967 the Theil coefficient for people over 65 declined by 40%. Mustert (1973) explains almost this entire reduction by the introduction of the general old age pension scheme.

which is a 75% decline. In this latter case we have much more to explain than in the former: after applying Hicks' Law the residual will be greater.

Quantification goes as follows. The increase in K/L between 1938 and 1968 is at least 50%. (Source: unpublished study by Pen and Tinbergen). The elasticity ε of the share of capital κ with respect to the capital intensity K/L is given by $\varepsilon = (1 - \kappa)(1 - (1/\sigma))$. The value of σ is a moot point among econometricians. The belief in a Cobb–Douglas value of $\sigma = 1$ has been replaced by values between 0.4 (Tinbergen, in an unpublished study on translog production functions) and 1.2 (Berndt, 1973) – but the latter estimate applies to the industrial sector only. If $\sigma = 2/3$, a not uncommon estimate (Den Hartog, Tjan and Van den Klundert (1975)), and if we interpret κ in its broad sense (including profits), for the Netherlands we find $\varepsilon = 1/3$. If we follow Tinbergen and fix σ at 0.4, we find $\varepsilon = 1$. If we assume a compromise value $\varepsilon = 0.5$ and that K/L increased by 50% between 1938 and 1968, it follows that the share of capital will fall by 25%. The actual fall was 33.3%. Here neo-classical theory performs fairly well. It explains 75% of the distributional shift from capital to labour. The residual is the result of other causes, among which is a possible shift in power.

But this result hinges, among other things, on the fact that we interpreted κ in its broad sense. As I see it, profits should not be treated as part of the price of scarce capital, in the neo-classical sense. The profit squeeze cannot be explained by Hicks' Law. In other words, we should distinguish between the cost of capital, to which neo-classical theory applies, and pure profits. If we exclude profits from capital income, and look only at investment income, the picture changes drastically. Instead of $\varepsilon = 0.5$ we find $\varepsilon = 1$. A 50% increase in K/L causes κ to fall by 33%. The actual fall in the share of investment income was 75%. Less than half the shift from capital to labour is explained by a shift in scarcity relationships; more than half the shift is due to other causes.

These exercises are meant as illustrations of the explanatory power of neo-classical theory. It is clear that the numbers are the result of a good deal of rather arbitrary guess-work. The capital stock (and therefore K/L) and particularly σ are subject to wide margins of disagreement. Moreover, technical change is supposed to be neutral – not an insignificant restriction! These uncertainties are reflected in the residual and therefore in the role which we ascribe to other variables, including power.

The residual is not the result of power alone. Land rents declined from 3% of national income in 1938 to 0.5% in the sixties. This is partly due to the decline in agriculture, which cannot be classified as a power factor. But the falling share of rents is also due to ceilings on agricultural rents and this is a political factor. A similar cause has played a role in the movement of house rents. A more important change that should be quantified is the loss of Dutch investments in the former colonies – this explains part of the fall in dividends between 1938–1952. This aspect deserves more attention from income distribution specialists than it has had so far. In an interesting article Baudet and Wyers (1976) estimate that dividends from the colonies' interests, pensions, returns from shipping and exports to the East Indies accounted for 7% of national income in 1938. Part of this 7% is labour and profit income, included in the revenues from trade and shipping; perhaps 4%

falls under the heading of investment income. In that case, one quarter of the fall in the investors' share is explained by this political factor alone. The limited contribution of neo-classical theory becomes less disturbing.

We now broaden our view and look at the overall balance between labour and capital; and we include profits in property income. It is quite obvious that a general shift in economic power between labour and capital has taken place. It is clear that the unions are in a stronger bargaining position than in the thirties, which results in a substantial rate of nominal wage increases. This rate has been 13% per annum since 1963, whilst it was negative in the thirties. But unfortunately, it is debatable whether this stronger position is purely due to economic power (the threat of strikes). Adherents to the Phillips curve, even the more cautious among them, would prefer to explain wage inflation by market forces. Their theoretical position has been weakened by the course of events in the seventies: growing unemployment accompanied by continuous wage claims.[11] Here we meet another case where power and scarcity are intimately connected – even up to the point where sceptics would deny that they can be disentangled. (But these sceptics perhaps ignore Groenveld's 1976 approach, see below).

So much is sure, however: in the course of the sixties the nominal wage push became more and more difficult to shift to consumers. The story is well known. In the Netherlands the fifties were a period of high profits and strong expansion. Wage policy was centralised under strong government supervision. Power served to keep the spiral within bounds. The distributional result was a share of wages of about 60%, which was even lower than before the war. After 1963, when wage policy was left to employers and unions, wage inflation reached the two-digit stage. The money wage level rose by 13% per year in the period 1963–1973. This affected the real rate of interest, which gave business firms a little breathing space; in some years the rate became temporarily zero. The neo-classical effect of capital saturation on the share of capital was reinforced by the inflationary spiral, that is, by the bargaining power of the unions.

Eventually profits were also affected. The share of capital (including profits) fell to 20% at the beginning of the seventies. The real rate of return on total business capital, before tax, was 6% in 1960; it fell to 4% in 1972. This steady decline was the result of a rapid deterioration in profit margins which were, at first, compensated by a strong expansion in output. The margin fell over the period 1960–1972 by 3.8% per year (Source: *Jaarverslag van De Nederlandsche Bank* 1975 (1976)). Part of this decline can be interpreted as a shift in the balance of union power and the reduced power of semi-monopolistic firms in product markets.

This is one way of interpreting the process. It does not yet explain why business firms met with increasing resistance when they tried to roll the wage push forward. Several explanations are possible: (1) A decrease in the degree of monopoly in

---

[11] The outcome of the Dutch february strikes (1977) is significant. Although unemployment stood at 5% and profits were low, employers gave in after three days of well planned, scattered strike action. The unions obtained what the employers had said they would firmly resist: the continuation of automatic "price compensation" (a better term would be "wage compensation for price increases") plus two percent. These events seem to confirm the opinion of those who believe that the money wage level is determined unilaterally by the unions.

domestic markets, caused by lower tariffs within the Common Market. This is a political factor (although it leads to a change in scarcity relationships!) At the same time exporters benefited from these tariff reductions, so the overall effect on profits is uncertain. (2) Increased competition from overseas. (3) A counteracting force: increased mergers, which can be understood partly as reactions to increased competition. Here economic power is at work. (4) Saturation of some markets for durable consumer goods, including housing. This is an obvious scarcity element in the decline of profits. (5) A reallocation in favour of the service sector, where the increase in labour productivity is lower; an economic factor which cannot be labelled as power. Considering these five elements, we must conclude that the profit squeeze is partly due to shifts in scarcity and partly due to shifts in power. An exact quantitative separation of the causes appears almost impossible.

What is possible, however, is to give a quantitative impression of the gap between neo-classical theory and the complicated facts of life. The gap was estimated in a pioneering, but very tentative, paper by Groenveld (1976). He compared the elasticity of output with respect to labour and the share of labour in the private sector. The findings are remarkable. In the fifties, the share of labour was probably lower than the elasticity, but the gap was closing. The time series for the elasticity and the share of labour cross in 1965. Afterwards, the share of labour was higher than the elasticity and the difference was increasing. In the seventies the gap may have been quite substantial. The exact numbers are too uncertain to quote – they depend on the uncertain parameters of the production function – but the method itself seems to be promising.[12] And the analysis underlines the view that before 1965 the position of capitalists was strengthened by power, whilst after 1965 the opposite was true.

In the meantime the imputation of the fall in the share of capital to scarcity and power remains a matter of conjecture. Both elements have been at work. It is not unreasonable to suppose that a fifty-fifty division might be not far off the mark – but the guess is an invitation to further research and hardly the result of thorough quantitative studies.

X. The influence of changing shares on personal income distribution

We know that the share of capital in the broad sense (including profits) declined by one third. We may feel that about half of this fall was caused by a shift in scarcity and about half by a change in the balance of power. But we are still quite ignorant about the impact of changing shares on personal income distribution. So we have to take step four and ask which part of the 50% reduction of inequality is due to the share of capital falling from 30% to 20%. Here quantitative illustrations take the place of quantitative research. (Similar illustrations are found in Atkinson (1975)).

As the Theil coefficient for 1938 is unknown, we look at the share of the upper 1.25% of income recipients, before tax. The percentage was 15.4 in 1938 and 10 in

---

[12] A strange element in Groenveld's reasoning is that the elasticity of substitution between labour and capital is greater than one. In this case Hicks' Law works in the wrong (ie unrealistic) direction.

1972, a decline of one third. This corresponds neatly to the decline in the share of capital in the broad sense – also one third. The question is what proportion of Dutch wealth is owned by the top 1.25% of income recipients. This is unknown. The wealth tax applies to 10% of tax payers, but they are certainly not identical to the upper decile of income recipients. The reasons for this are that many wealth owners are retired people with modest or even low incomes; that the profit squeeze caused some small business-men and farmers to earn less than the average wage earner; and that the upper 1.25% contains many salaried people – from university professors upwards – and part of the professions. If we knew how much levelling had taken place within this upper bracket of the salary structure, we could isolate the role of the falling share of capital in the falling share of the top 1.25%, but we do not have this information. We have some indications, but they are contradictory. Managers of corporations suffered a 35% relative salary decline before tax during the years 1952–1967. But in the same period there were non-egalitarian trends favouring auditors, lawyers, architects, engineers, doctors and dentists; the figures are also of the order of 35%. It may look as if no clear income equalisation took place between the top labour incomes and the average Dutchman, but this view is inconsistent with the fall in the share of the top 1.25%. The latter cannot be explained by the fall in the share of capital income alone. The simplest explanation is that top salaries also suffered a relative decline of 35%, with salaries constituting half of the income of the top 1.25%. This is just another illustration of what might have been the case.

If we take these illustrative numbers for granted and assume, in accordance with the last section, that half the fall in the share of capital is due to political and economic power, it follows that one quarter of the equalisation of *primary* income since 1938, as measured by the share of the top 1.25%, is due to a shift in the balance of power. That is one eighth of *total* income equalisation. But this criterion – the share of the top 1.25% – exaggerates the trend; other criteria, like the Pareto α and perhaps the Theil coefficient, result in values which are lower by almost one third. If we go by these criteria, something like 10% of total equalisation since 1938 may have been due to the shift in the balance of power. Or, in terms of the initial 1938 values of our distributional criteria, income inequality diminished by 5% because unions became more powerful than business managers and by another 5% because capital became less scarce. (This is not a quantitative conclusion but an illustration.)

XI. Equalising labour income

This leaves us with 15% to be explained by what happened within the wage and salary structure.[13] Step five consists in disentangling power and scarcity in this

---

[13] This assumes that the only levelling factors at work are those enumerated in this paper. Actually, income differences between regions have diminished by a process of industrialisation, by a more even spread of government expenditures over municipalities, by the end of official regional salary differentials ("gemeenteclassificatie") and by the general decline in the vicious circle of local poverty. In this process again, political power and the market are subtly intertwined. But the contribution of the process to our 50% levelling is probably small.

type of levelling – a job that has often been tried with widely divergent results. One radical critic (Nell, 1972) calculated that marginal productivity applies to 3–4% of the labour force and the rest is a matter of struggle. At the other end of the spectrum, Tinbergen (1975) uses education (in the broad sense) as the main equalising force; he sees economic power as a retarding force which hampers long-run equilibrium. In between we find a number of empirical studies by labour economists. In particular Lewis (1963) has tried to separate market forces from union power (administrative power remains in the background). He divides the American economy into strongly organised and weakly organised sectors, writes wage differentials as exponential functions with union power (measured by the proportion of union members covered by wage agreements) as parameters, and estimates the functions $\log W = \log W_0 + \beta$, where W is the wage level in a sector and β the impact of union power. Lewis concludes that it is unlikely that unionisation has changed inter-industry inequality by as much as five per cent. This sort of conclusion is hardly applicable to the Netherlands, where union policy since the fifties has aimed at equal pay for equal work – we should see inter-industry differentials decline with union influence rather than increase, as in the American case. Moreover, Dutch unions supported the general equalitarian trend and our problem is to determine how far this trend can be ascribed to the various forms of power – including political power compressing vertical differentials by minimum wages and lump-sum wage increases.

The best approach is to start with supply and demand and see how far we can get.

Labour incomes have been subject to substantial equalisation. In 1938 a "referendaris" (principal in the Civil Service) earned four times the modal wage; now the ratio is two, before tax. (I concede that the status and rank of this person are not what they were in 1938). The ratio between the minimum wage and the modal wage increased by 50%. Over the period 1952–1964 the Theil coefficient for earnings fell by 12%. Over the same period the salary differential between managers of corporations and the average salaried person fell by 35%. On the other hand, the sixties witnessed an increase in a number of salary differentials, particularly in the Civil Service (so called "Toxopeus-rounds") and in education. In the sixties, professional people generally increased their pre-tax income as a reaction to higher taxation, higher insurance premiums etc. The net result for the period 1938–1976 is probably that pre-tax labour incomes were equalised less than primary incomes generally, i.e. less than 25%; the 15% residual in the first sentence of this section may be a more or less accurate guess of what actually happened.

At the same time the educational level of the Dutch population increased considerably. In Tinbergen's view, this is the great equaliser. In 1938 the proportion of graduates in the working population was well below 1%. (In 1947 the figure was 0.9%). In 1970 the proportion was twice as high. In Tinbergen's model (1975) this may have led to a decline in the relative position of graduates by about one third.

At the lower end we see a clear decline in the relative number of unskilled workers. It was 50% in 1960; 33% in 1970. In the sixties the tension in the labour market led to an influx of unskilled foreign labour; the share of foreign workers in the working population rose to 3.3% in 1973. This counteracted income equalisation, but at the same time the influx is a sure sign that the wage structure is not in equilibrium with domestic supply and demand relationships. Had wage differentials been more responsive to market forces, income levelling would have been greater. If this slow response is seen as a result of collective bargaining, we meet, for the first time, union power as a disequalising force.

In a more general sense, Kuipers (1973) concluded that over the period 1958–1966 there was a clear decline in the inequality of income earning skills. His estimate of the decline over this period is 30% (but the figure includes a somewhat peculiar element: the increase in productivity of unskilled workers resulting from more efficient capital goods).

These figures are quite consistent with the view that a good deal of the levelling of earnings can be explained by shifts in scarcity. This view was defended by Chiswick (1972) for the U.S. She explained the decrease in the salary ratio between white and blue collar workers over the period 1900–1963, from 2.5 to 1.6, by a change in scarcity relationships. The Dutch material might lead an advocate of the market theory to proclaim victory – the residual of income equalisation to be explained by power being probably very small.

But this belief is only warranted if power works in one direction. If the unions generally favour levelling, but at the same union power creates a less flexible wage structure, we only observe the net effect. Moreover, administrative power by decision makers within the firms may partly neutralise the equalising tendency of the unions wage policy. It could, therefore, be mere coincidence that the outcome of the total process of wage determination appears consistent with supply and demand.

There is an obvious need for more sophisticated methods. An example of a sophisticated exercise is the paper by Groenveld and Kuipers (1977). They estimate the influence of an increase in the supply of graduates on the wage ratio between graduates and other wage earners. Two crucial parameters turn up. One describes technical progress: will it be of the type that requires more and more graduates or will be opposite be true? (On this matter it seems, *a priori*, that the former possibility is more likely, although Kuipers and Groenveld find the opposite). The other crucial parameter is the elasticity of substitution between graduate and other labour. Here Tinbergen assumes that $\sigma = 1$, whilst Kuipers and Groenveld prefer higher values. But even with a rather high elasticity, the salary ratio declines rather rapidly over time. The model predicts a fall of at least 50% from 1930–1970 even if technical progress is of the "graduate labour using" type. In this sense, the paper supports the view that income levelling can be explained by the market and that power is a superfluous concept.

But the paper contains another element which points in the opposite direction. Kuipers and Groenveld find that the share of academic graduates in national income is lower than the elasticity of output with respect to this type of manpower, at least in the sixties. As I pointed out earlier in section IX, this discrepancy may reflect the exercise of power – in this case, the power of the unions to compress higher salaries by means of floors and ceilings in compensatory wage increases, "turning points" in salary scales, lump-sum wage rounds and other levelling techniques. But the gap between the share and the elasticity does not fit in with the Kuipers–Groenveld approach, which is essentially neo-classical; and they remove this anomaly by imposing restrictions on the parameters of their production function. The reader is left with a feeling of uncertainty, the more so because the exercise of union power over the wage and salary structure is difficult to understand when combined with elasticities of substitution between types of manpower which are relatively high. But the impression remains that a neo-classical model of the Kuipers–Groenveld type can explain a realistic amount of income levelling without having recourse to the power factor. As far as the econometrics of the Dutch case are concerned, power is not an important overall equaliser within the earnings category. We don't need the power hypothesis to understand the process we observe.

XII. The role of power in the Netherlands, 1938–1977

Putting together the various pieces of information in this paper, it seems to me that the following opinions and numbers are consistent with the observed facts. Our starting point is that income inequality in the Netherlands decreased by 50%, after tax, in the period since 1938.
(1) The political power of taxes and transfers accounts for half the decline in inequality, i.e. a reduction of 25% in the original inequality measure.
(2) Capital accumulation and economic factors behind the profit squeeze account for another 5%.
(3) A shift in economic and political power has accentuated the shift from capital to labour by something of the order of another 5%.
(4) The equalisation within the wage and salary structure – which reduces original inequality by 15% – can be explained by shifts in scarcity between types of labour.

All together, the explanatory power of power can be said to be 50% higher than the explanatory power of scarcity. This conclusion applies to the period and country under consideration. There is no reason to assume that this figure will apply in the future. On the contrary, I believe that in the coming decades the role of supply and demand will be more important than the role of power, but that is quite a different story. The share of capital has reached, or even exceeded, a critical limit and equalisation by taxation has almost reached such a limit. The future emphasis will be on levelling within the wage and salary bill, and market forces will, in accordance with Tinbergen's model, play a more important role than figures for the previous four decades suggest. Therefore the numbers presented in this paper, whatever their illustrative merits or demerits, do not pretend to be structural parameters. They refer to the recent past, not to the future.

References

Atkinson, A.B., *The Economics of Inequality*, Oxford, 1975.
Baudet, M.J. and G.J. Wyers, "De economische betekenis van Nederlands-Indië voor Nederland", *ESB*, 15-9-1976.

Berndt, E.R., "Reconciling Alternative Estimates of the Elasticity of Substitution", *Review of Econometrics*, 1973.
Bronfenbrenner, M., *Income Distribution Theory*, Chicago and New York, 1971.
Chiswick, C.U., "The Growth of Professional Occupations in the American Labor Force: 1900–1963", World Bank Paper, Washington D.C., 1972. A revised version is published in *Research in Human Capital and Development*, Vol I, 1977.
De Nederlandsche Bank N.V. *Jaarverslag 1975*, Amsterdam, 1976.
Den Hartog, H., H.S. Tjan en Th. v.d. Klundert, "De structurele ontwikkeling van de werkgelegenheid in macro-economisch perspectief", Pre-advies voor de Staatshuishoudkunde, Den Haag, 1975.
Groenveld, K., "Een toetsing en amendering van de neo-klassieke verdelingstheorie voor Nederland (1920–1975)", unpublished research paper, Groningen, 1976.
Groenveld, K. and S.K. Kuipers, "The Infleunce of Substitution and Technical Progress on Income Differences between Graduate and Other Labour" this volume, 1977.
Jencks, C., *Inequality*, New York, 1972.
Kuipers, S.K., "Personele verdeling en produktiestruktuur", Pre-advies voor de Vereniging voor de Staatshuishoudkunde, Den Haag, 1973.
Lewis, H.G., *Unionism and Relative Wages in the United States*, Chicago, 1963.
Massizzo, A.I.V., *De personele inkomensverdeling 1952–1967*, monografie no. 19 CPB, Den Haag, 1975.
Mustert G.R., "Enige statistische aspecten van de inkomensongelijkheid in Nederland in de jaren 1950–1967", Pre-advies voor de Vereniging voor de Staatshuishoudkunde, Den Haag, 1973.
Nell, E., "Two Review Articles on Two Books on the Theory of Income Distribution", *Journal of Economic Literature*, June, 1972.
Nota over de inkomensverdeling, Den Haag, 1969.
Pen, J., *The Wage Rate under Collective Bargaining*, Cambridge (Mass.), 1960.
Pen, J. and J. Tinbergen, "Hoeveel bedraagt de inkomensegalisatie sinds 1938?", *ESB* 15-9-1976.
Preiser, E., "Property, Power and The Distribution of Income" in *Power in Economics*, edited by K. Rothschild, Harmondsworth 1971.
Tinbergen, J., *Income Distribution*, Amsterdam, 1975.

14 DISCUSSION

PAPER BY JAN PEN

Professor Lecaillon agreed with the suggestion at the beginning of the paper that there are special problems involved in analysing the influence of power on the personal income distribution. In many cases it is difficult to distinguish what is due to scarcity from that which is due to power. In other cases various economic agents, in their conflicting efforts, neutralise each other's influence, so the ultimate result is of little, or no, consequence, even though the forces of power, conflicting interests and the resulting actions may have proved considerable. There are still other cases, where the same group of economic agents may have contradictory objectives. For example, unions may aim to reduce inter-industry wage differentials at the same time as maintaining vested interests. Similarly the state may reinforce tax progression in order to reduce inequality in disposable income, and simultaneously increase indirect taxation, which often proves regressive, to fulfil budget needs. The final results of these numerous pressures are so unpredictable and erratic that he doubted whether they were amenable to economic analysis.

The approach outlined in the paper is one possible way of examining the consequences of the balance of powers on the income distribution. Professor Lecaillon began with the functional income distribution, first considering the opposition between capital and labour and then the distributions within the capitalist and worker groups. The paper suggests that the reduction in the share of income attributable to capital can be interpreted as evidence of the strenthening of union power and a weakening of the employers' position. He believed two comments were in order. For the share of wage income to increase, real wages (i.e. the ratio of nominal wages to prices) must increase more rapidly than labour productivity. Unions, however, mainly exercise their power on nominal wages and, even if they succeed in raising wages above the competitive level, they cannot influence prices or productivity, which depends primarily on technology and investment. Secondly, the increase in the share of wage income observed in most countries of the world may arise from a higher proportion of wage earners in the labour force and a decline in those self-employed, particularly in agriculture. Everywhere there is a high correlation between these two variables and this might be one of the reasons why, in the Netherlands since 1965, the labour share has been higher than the elasticity of production with respect to labour. But in many other cases the whole labour share, including income from the self-employed, may prove to be relatively stable or even decreasing.

On the distribution of income within the capitalist group, he pointed out that inactive income (dividends, interest payments, rents) had experienced a fall caused by inflation. Thus, in so far as price rises are due to union pressure for rising wages and employers' actions to protect their margins, capitalists may be said to have been the indirect victims of the power of unions and employers. In addition, the development of self-financing has resulted in a smaller proportion of profits being distributed to stockholders and although undistributed profits are included in the functional distribution, they are omitted in the personal distribution of income. This may distort the differences between household incomes, probably in an equalising direction.

Regarding the distribution of wage income, wage differentials have tended to diminish in industrialised economies in recent years. But he questioned whether this was attributable to power. Union demands have often been successful only when market forces tended to operate in the same direction. In France, for instance, an increase in the minimum wage has meant a shift of the whole wage structure. When there has been a shortage of skilled labour, wage differentials were maintained and even widened. The reduction in differentials over the past ten years has coincided with an excess supply of graduates in the labour market. This suggests that the interplay of supply and demand has been the major factor, with the influence of different power elements having little effect.

The passage from functional to personal distribution is relatively easy when each social group has only one source of income. This is not the case in modern economies, when many households receive income from both capital and labour. As a result the influence of power may have different consequences depending on the structure of personal incomes. Suppose, for example, that unions succeed in reducing the share of capital in aggregate income. This leads to a greater equalisation of personal incomes, if capital is concentrated in the hands of the very rich, but has little effect, if any, in an economic system in which capital is more widely distributed. When income from capital accrues to rentiers or to older, lower income, members of the community, such union pressure may even lead to greater inequality, and the state may have to increase transfer payments, counteracting union pressure with political action.

Finally Professor Lecaillon considered the impact of fiscal policy and social security benefits, which have had a stronger egalitarian bias since the last war and which clearly contain an element of political power. He said that personal income redistribution through fiscal policy and social security programmes seems to be more efficient the less unequal is the initial distribution. From this he concluded that the influence of political power is not autonomous: it depends on the economic structure and social customs, which may be more or less favourable to distributional equality. He also pointed out that redistribution affects only the two highest deciles (unfavourably) and the two or three lowest deciles (favourably) but is apparently neutral for the main part of the distribution, which comprise the bulk of both total households and aggregate income.

He concluded by saying that the influence of power on the distribution depends on the economic structures and the general economic situation, so that the results obtained through political, economic or administrative pressures are far from being consistent with the conflicting efforts of different social groups. If the impact of power is to be measured, its influence must be separated from other factors.

Professor Chiswick wondered about the definition of power used in the paper. It seemed to imply that *A* does not exercise power over *B* unless it can be demonstrated that *B* is acting contrary to his preferences. This left open the question of whether power would be exercised if *A* and *B*, each acting to their own advantage, together reduced the opportunity set faced by *C*. It may not be possible to show that *C* is acting contrary to his preferences but nevertheless this is the type of real world situation to which the concept of power is often applied.

Dr. Thomas was interested in the impact of power on the international economy – the power of nations over nations. Here the separation of power from scarcity becomes a dubious exercise. A particularly forceful illustration is the abundance of labour in the Third World which, at the same time, is powerless. He asked whether this was not analogous to inter-industry or inter-enterprise differences in developed countries.

Professor Lévy-Garboua said that on reading section III he was struck by the similarity with his own paper. But it should be mentioned that scarcity can sometimes be artificially created.

Mr. Groenveld said the paper questioned his own estimate for the elasticity of substitution, which turned out to be greater than one. He could not see why this was regarded as strange. Of course Hicks' Law then works in the wrong direction, but this leaves more room for the power variable to explain income distribution. He was interested in Professor Pen's opinion on the relationship between the role of power and the value of the elasticity of substitution.

Professor Taubman wondered why the explanation of the 50% reduction in inequality since 1938 required the assumption that the increase in corporation tax was fully paid by consumers and that the Value Added Tax is regressive. Since the 50% reduction referred to post tax incomes, he saw no reason to be worried about shifting.

On the breakdown of the 50% reduction, the loss of dividends from previous colonies was said to be a major factor. He asked whether the corresponding loss of capital was taken into account when calculating the capital-labour ratio. If this was so, he felt the analysis was questionable since domestically used capital was more appropriate. Finally he asked whether the reduction in monopoly power in the Netherlands, due to its inclusion in the Common Market, had also had an impact on the total figure of 50% or its composition.

Professor Wiles found the paper fascinating but terribly neo-classical. He believed that the effects of pure chance or administrative power on groups of factor incomes played a large role. "Mandarin power" had been mentioned on page 7 in connection with administrative power and he felt something similar arose within business enterprises. Both in Yugoslavia and in capitalism there was an "Illyria of the élite", where the officials distribute the surplus amongst themselves.

He thought that tax loop-holes had not been given sufficient attention, nor administratively privileged access to markets not cleared by equilibrium prices. In the Soviet Union queues were the source of administrative privilege, and necessary to the prosperity of the élite; this was the basic relationship between power and economic prosperity.

Professor Morrisson said that he had studied the percentage of net profit in French industry during the period 1967–76 and found this followed the fluctuations in the proportion voting conservative in elections, as well as the influence of rightist elements within the conservative majority.

Professor Bentzel liked the paper but found the conclusions stimulating rather than reliable. The discussion of the profit squeeze overlooked the substantial drop in real capital costs. A zero real rate of interest has allowed wages to increase to such a level that the profitability on old capital has been almost eliminated. However, the high level of profitability on new investment enabled most unemployment to be avoided. In Sweden the combination of high wages and low capital costs had been made more pronounced by a decline in the labour force and by investment subsidies.

He felt that more interesting results would have been produced had the analysis been based on vintage models. A squeeze on profits is then associated with the scrapping of old capital. Moreover, since the labour share tends to be higher for new vintages, the aggregate labour share depends on the vintage structure and would therefore have been expected to increase in recent years.

Mr. Layard would have liked more information on the time path of the changes, in order that the changes could be better understood. Manufacturing industry in Great Britain had seen the share of profits fall permanently by one-third within a three year period beginning in 1968. It is difficult to imagine how this could be explained by production functions.

Professor Pen was in agreement with much of what Professor Lecaillon had said and, in particular, he shared the view that power depends on structure. But he did not accept the idea that the numerous pressures are too erratic to be analysed; economists should try to give a quantitative view of the shifts in the power relationships. Nor did he agree that the share of labour, if it includes the incomes of the self-employed, has proved to be stable; in most industrialised countries it shows an upward trend.

To Professor Chiswick he said it was important to know how the actions of A and B affect C, but he would not classify this as power. Similarly, many signals emanate from the market, but this could not be called power either. In his definition of power – economic, administrative or political – the essential element is that the weak party believes that he will be adversely affected by deliberate action on the part of the power-wielder. A typical characteristic of economic power is the possibility of retention of goods by the stronger party – marketable goods which have a price. Here indeed scarcity and power are intertwined.

To Mr. Groenveld he replied that the impact of power can be felt if elasticities are low; if the elasticities are high, the influence of threats is dissipated by the market process. This applies particularly to the elasticity of substitution between labour and capital.

Professor Taubman had asked about the incidence of corporation tax. In the paper increases in the corporation tax raise prices and this affects the degree of shifting under the various alternative assumptions. The increase in the tax burden is an element in the profit squeeze. The reduction in the degree of monopoly in the Netherlands is also partly due to the Common Market.

To Professor Wiles he replied that the impact of tax loop-holes and tax evasion is a highly controversial issue in the Netherlands. Some observers believe the impact to be disequalising (deduction of interest and medical expenses), others hold the opposite (moonlighting). Further research on this matter is in progress.

Finally, on the point raised by Mr. Layard, he said that the reduction in inequality had been almost continuous since 1938, except for part of the sixties, although the components parts are different for the different subperiods. The fall in the share of rentier incomes occurred particularly between 1938 and 1950; the impact of taxation was also strongest during this period. Social Security made its influence felt from 1955 onwards. Levelling within the wage structure began in 1950, initially at a slow pace and later accelerating. The profit squeeze has been operating since 1965. The trend towards equalisation is still continuing.

15 A GENERAL MARKET MODEL OF LABOUR INCOME DISTRIBUTION: AN OUTLINE

W.H. SOMERMEYER*

I. Purpose of the paper and framework of the theory

I.1. *Purpose and plan of the paper*

This paper[1] presents a theory of income distribution resulting from the demand and supply of labour of varying qualities. Although the number and types of the characteristics distinguished are not essential for the theory in question, intelligence, age and education are singled out as major representatives of income-determining factors.

The model presented below leans heavily on the theory of income distribution developed by Tinbergen (1956). In particular, the labour supply behaviour of (potential) workers in the model set out below is largely borrowed from him; in one of the simpler models presented below, however, it is somewhat condensed and simplified. On the other hand, the demand side of the labour market is dealt with in a slightly more elaborate manner: like (potential) suppliers of labour, firms, as (potential) employers, are assumed to maximise utility functions;[2] the latter may simply be viewed as long-term (if not short-term) profit functions, possibly modified by the incorporation of risk and uncertainty. For their own benefit, the firms may also take account of the optimisation performed by their (potential) employees.

The outcome of this double-optimisation process is a scale of prices (wage rates) corresponding to differences in the qualities of the services rendered and used.

The present paper outlines how variations in remuneration between economically active people, according to the quality of the labour they (might) offer, are affected by the labour market mechanism: sections II, III and IV, respectively deal with the demand side, the supply side, and both sides of the market related by the equilibrium conditions. Section V shows how changes in exogenous variables may

---

* The author is indebted to the discussants and to Dr. J. van Daal of the Econometric Institute for their stimulating and constructive criticisms.

[1] A prior (pilot) version of the present paper was attached to the author's Ph.D. thesis (Somermeyer (1965), Appendix XIII); an English version of this piece of research, originally published in Dutch, was presented in Somermeyer (1966). For the present paper, those earlier versions were overhauled and streamlined, i.e. condensed in some respects, and elaborated in others.

[2] Thus, the theory developed below may be considered as a generalisation of Tinbergen's pioneering study.

affect the (labour) income distribution. This may be of particular importance for those factors that might be used – by a Government or others – as instruments, with the express or subsidiary purpose of modifying that distribution; tax parameters are among that privileged set.

Finally, section VI outlines how the theory explained in the earlier sections might be extended, by relaxing the restrictions imposed on the model and the assumptions underlying it. An extension of this model incorporating an output market sub-model is presented in Somermeyer (1977).

I.2. *Framework of the theory*

The most important assumptions and other restrictions constituting the framework of the model are:
 (1) optimisation by the "actors" in the labour market;
 (2) limitation of the theory to labour income, i.e. to the exclusion of other kinds or sources of income;
 (3) freedom of choice on both sides of the labour market;
 (4) perfect competition on both sides of the labour market;
 (5) turnover of firms independent of wage rates;
 (6) disregard of possible relationships between wage rates, on the one hand, and productivity and costs, on the other;
 (7) absence of market imperfections due to lack of information or frictions;
 (8) absence of disequilibrium from the labour market;
 (9) static nature of the behavioural equations;
 (10) deterministic nature of the relationships;
 (11) individualistic nature of market behaviour;
 (12) partial and closed character of the labour market model.

The theory is presented in terms of discrete changes: those who prefer a treatment with continuous variations are referred to Somermeyer (1977).

I.3. *Notation*

Decision units (employees and employers or firms) have been identified as suppliers or demanders of inputs (*inter alia*, labour) and outputs by left-hand and right-hand subscripts, respectively. Other identification (of jobs, personal characteristics and possibly commodities) is made by means of (additional) right-hand subscripts. Point subscripts denote summation over the letter subscripts at the places otherwise assigned to the letter. For the sake of simplicity lower and upper limits of summation are omitted; it extends over the entire range of the subscript in question. For the same reason, time subscripts are suppressed; all variables are supposed to relate to a particular period of time. Functions "contracted" or "condensed", as the result of replacing all, or some, of the arguments because of their relationship with other variables, are denoted by $\tilde{\ }$.

II. Labour demand

The accounting equation for firm h may be written

$$\Pi_h = V_h - D_h, \tag{1}$$

where Π_h = profits; V_h = "value added"; and D_h = direct labour costs. Direct labour costs are defined

$$D_h = \sum_j \sum_k \sum_l \sum_m n_{hjklm} p_{jklm}, \tag{2}$$

where n_{hjklm} is the amount of labour with intelligence level $k(=1, \ldots, K)$, education level $l(=1, \ldots, L)$ and of age $m(=1, \ldots, M)$[3] required by firm $h(=1, \ldots, H)$ to perform job $j(=1, \ldots, J)$; and p_{jklm} is the rate of remuneration corresponding to n_{hjklm}, assumed to be the same for all firms h. "Value added" is defined

$$V_h = R_h - 0_h \tag{3}$$

with R_h = revenue and 0_h = other costs not directly connected with labour, but possibly indirectly related, e.g. for operations requiring space, tools and machines. Hence R_h and 0_h may depend on the size and composition of the labour force, as well as the jobs performed by employees according to the production functions:

$$V_h = V_h(n_{h1111}, \ldots, n_{hjklm}, \ldots, n_{hJKLM}), \tag{4}$$

which are assumed to satisfy

$$\frac{\partial V_h}{\partial n_{hjklm}} \geqslant 0, \tag{5}$$

$$\frac{\partial V_h}{\partial n_{hjk'l'm'}} \geqslant \frac{\partial V_h}{\partial n_{hjklm}} \quad \text{for all } h, j \text{ and } (k', l', m') \geqslant (k, l, m), \tag{6}$$

while the Hessian corresponding to (4),

$$\left[\frac{\partial^2 V_h}{\partial n_{hjklm} \partial n_{hj'k'l'm'}}\right], \tag{7}$$

is negative semi-definite.[4]

The first-order conditions for profit maximisation are

$$\frac{\partial \Pi_h}{\partial n_{hjklm}} = \frac{\partial V_h}{\partial n_{hjklm}} - p_{jklm} - \sum_{j'} \sum_{k'} \sum_{l'} \sum_{m'} \frac{\partial p_{j'k'l'm'}}{\partial n_{hjklm}} n_{hj'k'l'm'} = 0$$

$$\text{for all } h, j, k, l, m. \tag{8}$$

To ensure non-negativity of remunerations (i.e. $p_{jklm} \geqslant 0$), the inequalities

---

[3] Intelligence, education and age categories are ranked so that, for instance, intelligence level $k + 1$ is higher than intelligence level k.

[4] Properties (5), (6) and (7) are assumed to hold at least for the relevant (i.e. profit-maximising values) of the variables $n_{hjklm} \geq 0$.

$$\frac{\partial V_h}{\partial n_{hjklm}} \geq \sum_{j'}\sum_{k'}\sum_{l'}\sum_{m'} \frac{\partial p_{j'k'l'm'}}{\partial n_{hjklm}} n_{hj'k'l'm'} \geq 0 \qquad (9)$$

should hold good by virtue of (8) and (5). Provided that (5) is satisfied, the second inequality of (9) holds when labour supply is inflexible.[5]

In simple specifications of labour supply behaviour, no distinction is made with respect to jobs. In that case, the subscript j and summation over j may be dropped in equations (2) and (4)–(9). Alternatively, firms may require certain minimum levels $\underline{k}_j, \underline{l}_j, \underline{m}_j$ to be reached before assigning particular jobs j to potential employees; more rarely, maximum levels $\bar{k}_j, \bar{l}_j, \bar{m}_j$ may be imposed on one or more of these characteristics (precluding "over-qualification"); or some degree of mutual compensation, between a deficit on one characteristic and an excess of another, may be allowed for, e.g. by requiring $\rho_j(k, l, m) \geq \underline{\rho}_j$, where the ρ_j are monotonically increasing functions of k, l and m.[6]

From the first-order conditions (8), the number of workers with specific capabilities k, l, m for performing job j at firm h can be written in terms of $HJKLM$ demand equations:

$$n_{hjklm} = n_{hjklm}(p_{1111}, \ldots, p_{JKLM}). \qquad (10)$$

Generally we may expect

$$\frac{\partial n_{hjklm}}{\partial p_{j'k'l'm'}} < 0 \text{ when } (j', k', l', m') = (j, k, l, m), \qquad (11)$$

$$\geq 0 \text{ otherwise.}[7]$$

and total demand for labour is given by

$$n_{.jklm} = \sum_h n_{hjklm} = n_{.jklm}(p_{1111}, \ldots, p_{JKLM}). \qquad (12)$$

If the distinction according to job is dropped, and if employees are paid only according to their ability irrespective of the job they perform (or, equivalently, if jobs are adapted to their abilities), then $p_{jklm} = p_{klm}$ and (12) simplifies to

$$n_{.klm} = n_{.klm}(p_{111}, \ldots, p_{KLM}). \qquad (13)$$

On the other hand, if people are paid only according to the type of job performed, provided their capabilities satisfy the job requirements

$$p_{jklm} = p_j \text{ when, say, } (k, l, m) \geq (\underline{k}, \underline{l}, \underline{m}) \qquad (14)$$

---

[5] It is assumed that the second order conditions for a local maximum corresponding to (8) are satisfied. Inflexible labour supply together with (7) provide sufficient (but not necessary) conditions for such a local maximum.

[6] Possible variation in (minimum) requirements between firms could be incorporated by attaching the firm subscript h to the $\underline{k}_j, \underline{l}_j, \underline{m}_j$ to get $\underline{k}_{hj}$ etc.

[7] For a given output, the second order conditions for maximum profit require semi-definiteness of the matrix with (11) as its typical element. This implies that all elements on the main diagonal have to be negative, except at most one which can be zero, and a *tendency* of the off-diagonal elements to be positive, i.e. "on average".

The demand functions (10) are homogeneous of degree zero in the wage rates.

and the demand for workers to perform job j becomes

$$n_{.j} = \sum_{k \geqslant \underline{k}} \sum_{l \geqslant \underline{l}} \sum_{m \geqslant \underline{m}} \tilde{n}_{.jklm}(p_1, \ldots, p_J) = \tilde{n}_{.j}(p_1, \ldots, p_J), \tag{15}$$

with $\tilde{n}_{.j}$ the "condensed" function $n_{.jklm}$ arising when the $JKLM$ wage rates p_{jklm} are replaced by the J rates p_j.

Which of these alternative functional forms for the demand for labour is appropriate depends on the particular specification used for labour supply.

III. Labour supply

The utility function of the (potential) supplier of labour may be written

$$_i\omega = {_i\omega}(_iY^-; {_in_1}, \ldots, {_in_J}; {_ik}, {_il}, {_im}; \underline{k}_1, \underline{l}_1, \underline{m}_1, \ldots, \underline{k}_J, \underline{l}_J, \underline{m}_J), \quad \text{for } i=1,\ldots,I \tag{16}$$

where, for individual i, $_i\omega$ is the utility level attained; $_iY^-$ is net income received; $_in_j$ denotes the amount of labour supplied in job j; and $_ik$, $_il$, $_im$ are the levels of the individuals own characteristics.

For the time being, it is assumed that either the potential supplier of labour is indifferent to the surroundings (or firm) in which he works, or – more realistically – that he or she has already chosen the best available and suitable (firm); alternatively, additional subscripts h can be attached to the $_in_j$. The marginal utility of money may be assumed positive, and the marginal (dis)utility of labour negative:

$$\frac{\partial_i\omega}{\partial_iY^-} > 0, \quad \frac{\partial_i\omega}{\partial_in_j} < 0, \tag{17}$$

at least for the relevant (i.e. utility maximising) values of the variables $_in_j$.

The inclusion of individual ability levels $_ik$ etc. as well as (job-specific) minimum requirements $\underline{k}_j$ etc., may be regarded as an extension of Tinbergen's (1956) theory of income distribution: in his view, differences between available and required capabilities – irrespective of the sign of these discrepancies – reduce people's sense of well-being.

To prevent the utility function being swamped by an excessive number of arguments, other potentially relevant factors are provisionally omitted from (16); some of them may re-appear as instruments or parameters, as outlined in section V of this paper. Moreover, one of those factors – (income from) personal wealth – is already incorporated in the income variables $_iY^-$. Actually, this type of variable, as well as the $_in_j$ (but unlike the "data" $_ik$, $_il$, $_im$ and $\underline{k}_j, \underline{l}_j, \underline{m}_j$) is normally endogenous.

To begin with, net incomes are linked to gross incomes institutionally

$$_iY^- = {_iY} - {_i\tau}(_iY), \tag{18}$$

where, for the ith individual, $_iY$ is gross labour income received; $_iY^-$ is net labour income, i.e. gross income minus direct taxes plus transfers; and $_i\tau(_iY)$ is the net tax payable on $_iY$, which varies with the individual's characteristics (marital status, age, sex, etc.) and those of his or her taxable income (primarily size, and possibly also composition by source).

The gross income accounting equation for individual i can be written:

$$_iY = {_iB} + {_iA}, \tag{19}$$

with labour income $_iB$ given by

$$_iB = \sum_j {_in_j} {_ip_j}, \tag{20}$$

where $_ip_j$ is the payment for working at job j. The term $_iA$ represents the annuity[8] on current personal wealth less planned terminal wealth, $_iW_0 - {_iW_{iT}}$, which may be positive or negative. This annuity is defined implicitly by

$$_iW_0 - {_iW_{iT}} = \sum_{t=1}^{_iT} {_iA}(1+r)^{1-t} = {_iA}(1+r)^{1-{_iT}} \cdot \frac{(1+r)^{iT} - 1}{r}, \tag{21}$$

where r represents the rate of interest used to discount future values and $_iT$ is the individual's life expectancy, depending, *inter alia*, on i's age and sex. The personal wealth term is the main link between the distributions of labour income and wealth (or unearned income).

Maximisation of $_i\tilde{\omega}$ with respect to the $_in_j$ subject to (18), (19), (20) requires

$$\left. \frac{d_i\tilde{\omega}}{d_in_j} \right|_{_in_{j'} \text{ constant for all } j' \neq j} = \frac{\partial_i\tilde{\omega}}{\partial_in_j} + \frac{\partial_i\tilde{\omega}}{\partial_iY^-} \frac{\partial_iY^-}{\partial_iY} \frac{\partial_iY}{\partial_in_j}$$

$$= {_i\tilde{\omega}_{in_j}} + {_i\tilde{\omega}_{iY_-}}(1 - {_i\tau_Y}) {_ip_j} = 0, \tag{22}$$

where the two terms on the right-hand side of (22) indicate the direct and indirect effects of labour supply on utility; $_i\tilde{\omega}$ is the utility function after substituting (18), (19), (20); and the subscripts $_in_j$, $_iY$ denote the partial derivates with respect to these variables.

The corresponding second-order conditions can be derived and these, together with the first-order conditions (22), are invariant to an arbitrary (increasing) transformation of the ophelimity function $_i\omega$. However the non-negativity constraints

$$_in_j \geq 0, \quad \text{for all } j \tag{23}$$

restrict, and possibly invalidate, the application of calculus. It may therefore be necessary to resort to mathematical programming techniques.

Either way, the optimal solution $_in_j^*$ to the maximisation problem will depend, directly or indirectly, on the remuneration rates $_ip_j$ as well as the exogenous variables

$$_in_j^* = {_in_j^*}({_ip_1}, \ldots, {_ip_J}; {_iA}; {_ik}, {_il}, {_im}; \underline{k}_1, \underline{l}_1, \underline{m}_1, \ldots, \underline{k}_J, \underline{l}_J, \underline{m}_J; \mu_{ci}), \tag{24}$$

---

[8] This is done to avoid the restrictions imposed on the model by its static nature. In turn, current personal wealth depends upon past (net) income and expenditure; the latter depends also on the pattern of income in the past, as well as time preference with respect to consumption (see, for example, Sommermeyer and Bannink (1972)). To deal with these satisfactorily requires an appropriate dynamic model; however, within the present static model, personal wealth (and hence the annuity) is treated as data.

where μ_{c_i} represents the vector of the tax function parameters, which vary with the characteristic-mix c_i relevant to taxation (age, sex, marital status).

When the constraints (23) are binding, $_i n_j$ may be unresponsive to changes in the function arguments and, in particular, may remain zero. If this is not the case, the signs of the partial derivatives of $_i n_j$ with respect to the remuneration rates depend on the balance between (non-positive) income effects and (non-negative) substitution effects.

Anyhow, the second-order derivative of the supply of labour with respect to its remuneration rate is negative, or at most zero. This reflects the tendency of the income effect to approach, if not to overtake, the substitution effect as the wage rate increases and/or the number of hours worked per week nears the maximum physiological and psychological level. Thus, the sign of the effect of the wage rate on individual labour supply may change from positive to negative.

The model becomes much simpler if only the levels k, l, m of the individual's characteristics determine remuneration and if the individual's preferences depend only on the payment for these skills rather than the kind of work performed. Then the utility function (16) could be condensed to

$$_i\omega = {_i\omega}(_iY^-; {_in}), \tag{25}$$

where $_in = \sum_j {_in_j}$ (i's total labour supply), and the accounting equation (20) becomes

$$_iB = {_in} \, {_ip}. \tag{26}$$

Furthermore, the job-subscripts can be dropped in (22), (23), so that the individual's supply function (24) becomes

$$_in = {_in}(_ip; {_iA}; \mu_{c_i}). \tag{27}$$

Using (24), we may derive the aggregate supply functions for jobs j and capabilities k, l, m by appropriate summation. Starting with the joint distribution

$$\tilde{n}_{jklm} = \sum_{i \in I_{klm}} {_i\tilde{n}_j}(p_{1klm}, \ldots, p_{Jklm}; {_iA}; \underline{k}_1, \underline{l}_1, \underline{m}_1, \ldots, \underline{k}_J, \underline{l}_J, \underline{m}_J; \mu_{c_i})$$

$$= \tilde{n}_{jklm}(p_{1klm}, \ldots, p_{Jklm}; A_{klm}; \underline{k}_1, \underline{l}_1, \underline{m}_1, \ldots, \underline{k}_J, \underline{l}_J, \underline{m}_J; \mu_{klm}), \tag{28}$$

where I_{klm} denotes the subset of individuals with capabilities k, l, m; A_{klm} is an aggregate annuity value derived from the annuities $_iA$ of all individuals i in the subset I_{klm}; and μ_{klm} is a similar aggregate vector of tax parameters derived from the μ_{c_i}.[9] If (net) remuneration does not depend on the precise values of k, l, m, in other words that (13) applies provided the minimum requirements of the job are satisfied, then

$$n_j = \sum_{k > \underline{k}_j} \sum_{l > \underline{l}_j} \sum_{m > \underline{m}_j} \tilde{n}_{jklm}(p_{1klm}, \ldots, p_{Jklm}; A_{klm}; \underline{k}_1, \underline{l}_1, \underline{m}_1, \ldots, \underline{k}_J, \underline{l}_J, \underline{m}_J; \mu_{klm})$$

$$= \tilde{n}_j(p_1, \ldots, p_J; A; \underline{k}_1, \underline{l}_1, \underline{m}_1, \ldots, \underline{k}_J, \underline{l}_J, \underline{m}_J; \mu) \tag{29}$$

---

[9] This presupposes that the "contracted" functions $_i\tilde{n}_j$ are separable with respect to $_iA$, μ_{c_i} and the other arguments.

where A is an aggregate derived from all values of A_{klm} for which $(k, l, m) \geqslant (\underline{k}_j, \underline{l}_j, \underline{m}_j)$ and μ is a similar aggregate vector obtained from the μ_{klm}.[10]

Alternatively if no distinction is made according to job but only according to the capability-mix, the aggregate labour supply functions reduce to

$$n_{klm} = n_{klm}(p_{klm}; A_{klm}; \mu_{klm}). \tag{30}$$

The simplest case is naturally the one in which labour supply, distinguished according to quality, is considered to be exogenous – at least in aggregate, if not at the individual level:

$$n_{klm} \text{ given.} \tag{31}$$

IV. Labour market equilibrium and personal income distribution

IV.1. Labour market equilibrium

As outlined in section I, the labour market is assumed to be in equilibrium. Thus we have either

$$n_{.jklm} = n_{jklm}, \quad \text{for all } j, k, l, m, \tag{32}$$

which, equating (12) and (28), gives

$$p_{jklm} = p_{jklm}(A_{klm}; \underline{k}_1, \underline{l}_1, \underline{m}_1, \ldots, \underline{k}_J, \underline{l}_J, \underline{m}_J; \mu_{klm}), \tag{33}$$

or

$$n_{.j} = n_j, \quad \text{for all } j, \tag{34}$$

which, equating (15) and (29), gives

$$p_j = p_j(A; \underline{k}_1, \underline{l}_1, \underline{m}_1, \ldots, \underline{k}_J, \underline{l}_J, \underline{m}_J; \mu) \tag{35}$$

or

$$n_{.klm} = n_{klm}, \quad \text{for all } k, l, m, \tag{36}$$

which, using (13) and (30), results in

$$p_{klm} = p_{klm}(A_{klm}; \mu_{klm}). \tag{37}$$

If (30) is replaced by (31) we have instead

$$p_{klm} = p_{klm}(n_{111}, \ldots, n_{KLM}; A_{klm}; \mu_{klm}) \tag{38}$$

Clearly, equations (32) imply both (34) and (36), but the reverse is not true. Corresponding pairs of "quantity" and "price" relationships (such as (32), (33)), together represent the "reduced form" labour market equations, expressing the values of the endogenous variables in terms of the exogenous variables.

---

[10] Again this presupposes separability of the "contracted" functions $\cdot \tilde{n}_j$ with respect to the A_{klm}, μ_{klm} and the other arguments.

IV.2. Personal income distribution

Having established functions for the market wage rates, we now turn to the labour incomes $_iB$ of individuals.

First, we apply the general wage rate formulae (33), (35), (38) to individuals. If (32) is relevant

$$_ip = p_{jklm}, \quad \text{for all } i \in I_{klm}. \tag{39}$$

If (36) applies

$$_ip = p_{klm}, \quad \text{for all } i \in I_{klm}, \tag{40}$$

and for (34)

$$_ip = p_j, \quad \text{if } i \in I_{klm} \text{ and } (k, l, m) \geqslant (\underline{k}_j, \underline{l}_j, \underline{m}_j). \tag{41}$$

These wage rates are then inserted into the individual supply functions (24) or (27) to determine $_in_j$ or $_in$. This allows the values of $_iB$ to be derived from (20) or (26). A frequency function for the labour income distribution can then be constructed by choosing appropriate income ranges and computing the corresponding number of individuals with earnings $_iB$ in each interval. From the definition of $_iB$, this distribution clearly depends on the joint distribution of the amount of labour performed and the payment per unit of labour (in terms of time, quantity processed or produced, occasional premiums, etc.).

In view of such a complicated genesis of labour income distributions, the only general conclusion to be drawn so far is that it would be little short of miraculous if such distributions were to have a simple form. The fact that incomes appear to be distributed rather regularly may be an optical illusion, at least in part. The tendency to cumulate income distributions, as opposed to presenting the frequencies, may have contributed to that mistaken belief: in any case, cumulated distributions are monotonic (non-decreasing).

V. The effects of changes in exogenous variables on labour income distribution

Suppose that exogenous variables – parameters, or "instruments" – $\lambda_\theta (\theta = 1, \ldots, \Theta)$ affect, in principle, both demand equations (such as (10)) and supply equations (such as (30)). Then their effects on the demand and supply of labour may be expressed

$$\hat{N}_{.\lambda} = N_{.\lambda} + N_{.p} P_\lambda, \tag{42}$$

$$\hat{\dot{N}}_\lambda = \dot{N}_\lambda + \dot{n}_p P_\lambda, \tag{43}$$

where the terms on the right-hand side of (42) and (43) represent the direct and indirect effects (through price changes) of variations in λ. Total effects are given by the matrices

$$\hat{N}_{.\lambda} = \left[\frac{dn_{.klm}}{d\lambda_\theta} \right], \quad \hat{\dot{N}}_\lambda = \left[\frac{d.n_{klm}}{d\lambda_\theta} \right],$$

provided all other parameters are kept constant, and partial effects by

$$N_{.\lambda} = \left[\frac{\partial n_{.klm}}{\partial \lambda_\theta}\right], \quad .N_\lambda = \left[\frac{\partial .n_{klm}}{\partial \lambda_\theta}\right], \quad P_\lambda = \left[\frac{\partial p_{klm}}{\partial \lambda_\theta}\right].$$

These five matrices are of order $KLM \times \Theta$, while

$$N_{.p} = \left[\frac{\partial n_{.klm}}{\partial p_{k'l'm'}}\right], \quad .\dot{n}_p = \left[\frac{\partial .n_{klm}}{\partial p_{klm}}\right],$$

are square matrices (of order KLM), the last one being diagonal.

To maintain equilibrium, changes in λ affect demand and supply of labour equally, so

$$\hat{N}_{.\lambda} = .\hat{N}_\lambda. \tag{44}$$

Equations (42), (43), (44) together give

$$P_\lambda = [N_{.p} - .\dot{n}_p]^{-1}(.N_\lambda - N_{.\lambda}), \tag{45}$$

provided that $[N_{.p} - .\dot{n}_p]$ is non-singular.

The effects of changes in λ turn out to be more interesting for (individual) wages

$$_iB = {}_inp_{klm}, \quad i \in I_{klm}, \tag{46}$$

than for wage rates. Fortunately, we have the simple relationship

$$\begin{aligned}
.B_\lambda &= \dot{p}.\hat{N}_\lambda + \dot{n}P_\lambda \\
&= \dot{p}.N_\lambda + (\dot{p}.\dot{n}_p + \dot{n})P_\lambda \\
&= \dot{p}.N_\lambda + (\dot{p}.\dot{n}_p + \dot{n})[N_{.p} - .\dot{n}_p]^{-1}(.N_\lambda - N_{.\lambda}),
\end{aligned} \tag{47}$$

with $\dot{p}$ and $\dot{n}$ denoting diagonal matrices with the elements of the vectors p and n ($= .n = n.$) on the main diagonal.

For those variables that affect only one side of the labour market directly, expression (47) may be somewhat simplified, by dropping $N_{.\lambda}$ or $.N_\lambda$. Thus, since income tax rates only influence the supply side of the market, the effects of changes in the μ's on labour incomes can be written

$$.B_\mu = \{\dot{p} + (\dot{p}.\dot{n}_p + \dot{n})[N_{.p} - .\dot{n}_p]^{-1}\}.N_\mu. \tag{48}$$

Considering (11) and the second order conditions corresponding to (22), we might expect negative elements to dominate in $[N_{.p} - .\dot{n}_p]^{-1}$ and hence also in $(\dot{p}.\dot{n}_p + \dot{n})[N_{.p} - .\dot{n}_p]^{-1}$, at least on the main diagonals of these matrices. However, this partial effect is compensated to some extent, and may even be dominated, by the non-negative matrix $\dot{p}$. On balance, the majority of the elements of the matrix between curly brackets in (48) are likely to be positive or negative depending on whether demand for the various qualities of labour is more or less elastic with respect to price, disregarding possible effects through output adjustments. Since the former alternative seems to be more likely (i.e. labour of various "qualities" is highly substitutable for labour of other, not too dissimilar, qualities) the elements of $.B_\mu$ may tend to have the same sign as the corresponding elements of $.N_\mu$.

If, for instance, one of the μ's indicates the "steepness" of the tax system, one may expect that this parameter will tend to increase supply of labour that is poorly paid, as opposed to labour supply at a higher wage level; supply of the latter may even eventually decrease. This means that increasing the progressiveness of the tax system may reduce the dispersion of labour income. Actually, this "instrument" is sometimes adopted, or at least proposed, precisely for serving that particular purpose – even if not always stated explicitly.

The matrix expression between curly brackets in (48) is independent of possible changes in the parameters; hence, the effects of other potential factors, as far as they apply to only the *supply* side of the labour market, may be examined in a similar manner. Still, it will be difficult to trace the effects of exogenous changes, for example changes in educational opportunities, on jobs with significantly different levels of payment for scholastic qualifications. However, if such a change eventually reduced the differences in labour supply between lower paid jobs and those better rewarded, this again may reduce labour income dispersion.

The influence of factors directly affecting only the *demand* side of the labour market, can be expressed even more simply than those affecting the supply side. Denoting these sets of factors of parameters by vectors v, the "effect" formula (47) becomes

$$B_v = -(\dot{p}\,\dot{n}_p + \dot{n})[N_{.p} - \dot{n}_p]^{-1} N_{.v}. \tag{49}$$

Following the same reasoning as above, we may now conclude – with less doubt than before – that corresponding elements of B_v and N_v will in general have the same signs, since positive elements will prevail in $(\dot{p}\,\dot{n}_p + \dot{n})$ and negative elements will dominate in $[N_{.p} - \dot{n}_p]^{-1}$. For instance, technological progress will presumably require increasing amounts of highly developed intelligence and skill, while the automation of simple manual operations will reduce the need for unskilled labour. Hence, trained labour will be accorded a higher premium than before, compared with untrained labour. In itself, this tends to increase labour income dispersion.

VI. Possible extensions of the model

VI.1. *Distribution theory for non-labour income*

Some elements of the theory outlined above could also be used to develop a theory for the distribution of payments to factors of production other than labour. In particular, this applies to capital income arising from personal wealth. Here, too, there is a (capital) market – or rather, a number of interrelated markets – where the price of the (capital) services is determined by demand and supply. Here, too, the services rendered (as well as the payment offered) depend on the quality of the factor. However, the main difference between capital and labour services lies in the nature of the characteristics: the risks involved (capital gains or losses), as well as transfer costs, availability and terms of redemption,[11] rather than intelli-

---

[11] Terms of redemption (termination) might also be one of the secondary conditions underlying labour contracts.

gence, schooling and experience. Accordingly, borrowers as well as lenders of capital (private persons, firms and government) could include these characteristics in their utility functions. In the individual's utility function, this means that the "annuities" may no longer be considered "given". However, as mentioned earlier, this calls for a dynamic model as well as a stochastic one.[12]

In a sense, income from non-productive sources (transfer income), will be even more difficult to deal with, since it is often awarded in an arbitrary, although institutionally determined, manner. Treatment is complicated by its dependence on the amount of income from other sources. Moreover, transfer income (such as unemployment benefit) may affect labour supply, usually as a disincentive (cf., for instance, Siddré (1976)).

Considering income of all types together, rather than from several separate sources, is, of course, more interesting from both a theoretical and a practical point of view. Finally, relating direct taxation to total income, rather than to separate components of income, increases the importance of that factor. From an empirical point of view, it is fortunate that covariances between the size of income components tend to be small compared with their variances. At least, this appears to be the case in the Netherlands (Somermeyer (1965, ch. 3), (1967)).

VI.2. *Freedom of choice on both sides of the labour market*

When restrictions are imposed on the jobs performed[13] by people (with particular characteristics), i.e. on the $_i n_{jklm}$, perhaps even fixing them for some if not all people, the corresponding supply functions no longer apply. The freedom of firms may also be curbed, in the sense that upper and/or lower limits may be placed on the numbers n_{hjklm}, if not the actual individuals, to be employed.

VI.3. *Perfect competition on both sides of the labour market*

This assumption is less restrictive than it might appear at first sight; the reason is, of course, the distinction between different "qualities" of labour. This means that (potential) workers tend to behave like "monopolistic-competitors" when facing potential employers. For a *given* quality of labour and *specific* jobs, both firms and private individuals are assumed to consider themselves individually unable to significantly affect market prices.

At the other extreme, the labour market may be viewed as the battle-field on which the employers' association (as the single representative of all firms) and the trade union (as the single representative of all workers) fight each other for the best terms. In this context "best" means a level and scale of wages that maximises both the joint profits of employers and a utility function for trade unions, which has the real wage level, employment and the size of the strike fund as arguments.

---

[12] cf. sub-sections VI. 8, VI. 9.
[13] Including the location where they have to be performed.

Whether the "perfect" competition model (as set out in sections II to V) or the "bilateral monopoly" model is more realistic, depends, of course, on the degree of organisation of employers and employees.

Other violations of the "pureness" of competition in the labour market may be caused by restrictions imposed on particular groups of people (such as women, minors and foreigners) concerning entry into the (national) labour market, or on all people for particular kinds of jobs, requiring specific qualifications or trade union membership ("closed shop").

IV.4. *Independence of firms' turnover and wage rates*

This hypothesis is related to the assumption that entrepreneurs – and private individuals – are not sufficiently important to have an appreciable impact on the market. Similarly, firms generally employ such a small part of the labour force (in a certain area) that they could hardly sell more of their products by boosting the wages of their employees (Henry Ford's "gospel of high wages"). However, if this was the case, the model could be supplemented by a relationship between demand for the firm's products and their employees' wages (or wage levels).

VI.5. *Disregard of possible relationships between wage rates, on the one hand, and productivity and costs on the other*

In the model presented earlier, wage rates are considered as "independent", rather than "dependent", variables in the equations for both the demand and supply of labour. However, wages may be linked to the quality and/or quantity per unit of time produced, as well as depending on possible savings in costs due to employees' diligence. This may be achieved by an appropriate specification of the wage rate functions used by firms (see, for instance, Langhout and Somermeyer (1975)). Such functions could be incorporated in the model. The parameters of the wage rate functions, rather than the wage rates themselves, would then have to be considered in the optimisation procedure.

VI.6. *Absence of market imperfections*

Without sufficient *communication* or *information*, inter-firm as well as inter-personal differences may arise between people with the same relevant characteristics mixes, performing the same kinds of jobs. As far as such differences are due to accidental factors, they can be taken care of by introducing stochastics into the model, originally construed as deterministic (see sub-section VI.9). To the extent that such differences are systematic, however, the underlying factors (e.g. of a geographical nature) should be incorporated explicitly. Even if such factors prove or appear to rest on firms' prejudices (e.g. the alleged "inferiority" of women) rather than facts, the model should include them, since they affect the maximising behaviour of entrepreneurs.

Part of the lack of communication is due to lack of information. Consequently, the model should also allow for the cost of obtaining information. On the demand side, this may be done by including such costs (to the extent they are borne by firms) among the "other" (indirect labour) costs O_h; on the supply side, information costs may be deducted from income as one of the arguments of the utility function of workers.

Finally, *frictions* may create additional costs, e.g. for transferring employees, or for employees moving from one place to another. In as far as they are purely financial, they can be incorporated in a way similar to that proposed for information costs. To the extent thay they are non-pecuniary (say, parting from familiar surroundings or people), they may be included in the utility functions of workers.[14]

The possibility of moving people or (establishments of) firms between locations, with the associated costs, would further complicate the model: it would require distinguishing regions between which movements can take place. Thus, a national labour market model would be replaced by an inter-regional model.

Job search procedures indicate a lack of communication in the labour market; the relevant theories, with the duration of unemployment linked to the highest (expected) wage offers in the utility functions of the job searchers, introduce both stochastic and dynamic elements into the labour market model. For another, more macro-economic, approach to disequilibrium in the labour market, see Lenderink and Siebrand (1976).

VI.7. *Absence of disequilibrium in the labour market*

Disequilibrium in the labour market can be regarded as a shortage of labour – of particular qualities, for specific jobs – at one firm or place, and (more often) a surplus of labour – of (other) particular qualities, for (other) specific jobs – at other (or the same) firms or places. The possible failure of the price (wage rate) mechanism to establish equilibrium (i.e. equality between demand and supply of some *specific* labour) may be due to the fact that *some* types of labour may not be demanded at *any* (non-negative) price. Its marginal revenue might not cover the additional costs (included in O_h) that its employment would entail; this may be the fundamental problem of "unemployables", whose abilities do not enable them to cope with modern technology. In mathematical terms this means that the inequality $p_{jklm} \geq 0$ becomes binding.

Alternatively, it is conceivable that demand for a particular kind of labour cannot be satisfied, however high the price becomes. This might be due to the time required to train people to perform jobs (cf., for instance, Ritzen (1977)), and reflects on the static nature of the model, to be considered in the next sub-section. Moreover, establishing equilibrium in factor markets, such as those for labour and capital, may be aggravated by the tug of war between "substitution" and "income" effects; this may cause labour supply curves to be "backward bending".

---

[14] Since firms are generally impersonal, or cannot afford to be sentimental, there is no need to "burden" their labour demand functions in a similar manner.

Disequilibrium in the labour market may also be interpreted in terms of mathematical programming: when particular non-negativity constraints become binding, some labour capacities may not be fully utilised.

VI.8. *Static nature of the model*

This restriction could be relaxed, at least in principle, by
(a) making the objective functions of workers and firms dependent on variables referring to future periods of time as well as the present.
(b) taking account of possible time lags, such as those required to train people to perform particular operations.

In particular, proposal (a) would complicate the model considerably, because it would multiply the number of single-period variables and relationships by the number of (future and present) periods of time distinguished. Moreover, some of the characteristics may change over time. This applies (in a simple manner) to experience; other characteristics, like "schooling", may fade away unless employees are brought up to date with refresher courses. Consequently, the influence of experience and schooling on the "desirability" of employees (for employers), and the pattern of their remuneration over time, may counteract each other to a certain extent.

Introduction of time lags into the model creates mathematical problems of a somewhat different nature, viz. the solution of a complicated set of difference equations, to trace autonomous, as well as induced, variations in the (labour) income distribution over time.

VI.9. *Deterministic nature of the model*

Stochastic factors play an important role, particularly with respect to entrepreneurial income; compared to others, "independent" workers rely heavily on the whims of weather, customers and government officials. Taking account of stochastic factors makes more sense in a dynamic version of the model than in a static one. The main reason is the auto-regressive nature of disturbances, which plays havoc with people's incomes.

A stochastic formulation of the labour market process may have an even more radical impact on the optimisation procedures adopted by potential employers and employees. To begin with, the introduction of "uncertainty" – as represented by stochastic elements – into the model implies that only linear transformations of utility functions are admissable, thus restricting us to a cardinal rather than ordinal utility concept. Here "admissable" refers to invariance when the *expected* value of utility is maximised (subject to constraints). Moreover, uncertainty may induce people to adopt decision rules other than those based on the maximisation of mathematical expectations: instead, minimax (or maximax, etc.) decision procedures may be preferred by the parties concerned.

VI.10. *Individualistic nature of the model*

Limiting the concern of workers to labour supply may appear too restrictive: a person's decisions may also depend on wants, expectations, urges and actions emanating from people in his or her surroundings.

This applies first to members of the household of which the individual is a part, unless he or she lives alone. Thus, labour supply by the (male) head of the household may also depend on his wife's employment opportunities, inclination towards working and the corresponding payments, as well as the number and ages of any children. Conversely, the wife's labour-force participation may depend on the earning ability of the husband and other household characteristics (see, for instance, Bouma and Somermeyer (1977)). This suggests extending the utility function of the individual person to entire households. The latter utility functions should include, *inter alia*, the working conditions for all (potential) income recipients within the household, as well as other household characteristics (see, for instance, Gronau (1973) and Gramm–Lee (1975)).

A further possible (sociological) extension of the model would also incorporate the characteristics of people or circumstances *outside* the household in the utility function of the household or individual.

The most radical way of altering the individualistic nature of the model is to adopt the diametrically opposite assumption mentioned in sub-section VI.2: that the labour market is ruled by a bilateral monopoly of trade unions and employers' associations.

VI.11. *Partial and closed nature of the model*

The model presented in earlier sections is partial in the sense that *demand* for output has not been considered explicitly. This limitation may be removed by adding an output market model to the labour market model (see Somermeyer (1977)). It enables us to simultaneously evaluate changes in wage rate scales and output price vectors resulting from changes in exogenous variables, particularly those affecting demand for output; VAT may be a case in point. The total effect includes both direct and indirect effects, through reactions of outputs and labour inputs to changes in output prices and wage rates induced by the parameter changes.

Relaxing the closed nature of the model would require the introduction of relationships describing the movement of commodities and workers between the country under consideration and other nations. This is the international counterpart of the inter-regional aspects mentioned in section VI.6.

References

Bouma, P. and W.H. Somermeyer, *De Werkende gehuwde vrouw in Nederland*, Kluwer b.v., Deventer, 1977.
Duesenberry, J.S., *Income, Savings and the Theory of Consumer Behaviour*, Cambridge (Mass.) 1949[1], 1967[2].

Gramm-Lee, W.L., "Household Utility Maximisation and the Working Wife", *American Economic Review*, 65, 1975.

Gronau, R., "Information and Frictional Unemployment", *Quarterly Journal of Economics*, 60, 1971.

Gronau, R., "The Intra-Family Allocation of Time: the Value of the Housewife's Time", *American Economic Review*, 63, 1973.

Langhout, A. and W.H. Somermeyer, "Optimal Specification of Incentive Remuneration Systems", *Zeitschrift für Operations Research*, 18, 1975.

Lenderink, R.S.G. and J.C. Siebrand, *A Disequilibrium Analysis of the Labour Market*, Rotterdam University Press, Rotterdam, 1976.

Ritzen, J.M.M., *Education, Economic Growth and Income Distribution*, North-Holland Publishing Cy., Amsterdam, 1977.

Siddré, W., *De duur der werkloosheid*, inaugural address, Erasmus Universiteit Rotterdam, 1976.

Somermeyer, W.H., "Een econometrische analyse van interregionale inkomensverschillen in Nederland", *Statistische en Economische Onderzoekingen*, (1960) blz. 66–95.

Somermeyer, W.H., "Inkomens-ongelijkheid; een analyse van spreiding en scheefheid van inkomensverdelingen in Nederland", *Statistische en Economische Onderzoekingen*, no. 7, Centraal Bureau voor de Statistiek, Den Haag, 1965.

Somermeyer, W.H., "Outline of a General Market Theory for the Distribution of Labour Income", Report 6606 of the Econometric Institute of the Netherlands School of Economics, Rotterdam, 1966.

Somermeyer, W.H., "An analysis of income variance in the Netherlands", *Statistische Informationen*, Statistisches Amt der Europäischen Gemeinschaften, Bruxelles/Luxembourg, 1967.

Somermeyer, W.H. and R. Bannink, *A Consumption-Savings Model and its Applications*, North-Holland Publishing Cy., Amsterdam, 1972.

Somermeyer, W.H., "A General Market Model of Labour Income Distribution – An Outline", Report 7708/E of the Econometric Institute of the Erasmus University Rotterdam, Netherlands, 1977.

Tinbergen, J., "On the Theory of Income Distribution", *Weltwirtschaftliches Archiv*, 77, 1956.

15 DISCUSSION

PAPER BY W.H. SOMERMEYER

Dr. Kuipers said the paper, like his own, relied heavily on the work of Professor Tinbergen and gave credence to the idea that a Dutch school of income distribution existed. One common characteristic was the focus of attention on the distribution of labour incomes. This is by far the most important component of total income, contributing more than 90% of national income in the Netherlands. A second feature is the belief that scarcity is the main determinant of relative earnings. There is also a common assumption that personal characteristics such as the level of education, age and innate abilities, have to be distinguished. The theory erected on these foundations is quite conventional. In its static form it falls somewhere between partial and general equilibrium analysis. For each type of labour relative wages adjust to equalise demand and supply.

The main part of Professor Somermeyer's paper specifies the choice-theoretic structure from which the demand and and supply equations can be derived. This enables both the strengths and weaknesses of this approach to be revealed. The paper discusses these weaknesses in some detail and suggests possible modifications. These may not be easy to carry out in practice. Attempts have been made, not always successfully, to amend the neo-classical model of the labour market to incorporate market imperfections, uncertainty and market disequilibrium. A good example is the work of Phelps and others (1970) on job search and the cost of gathering information. Another example is the research on disequilibrium analysis inspired by Clower (1962). Including these different aspects in the model developed in the paper, supposing that this is possible, would only result in a huge model in which all insights into its working are lost.

His main criticism of the model presented in the paper concerned the definition of the labour categories. These were selected with reference to both personal characteristics and the types of jobs demanded and offered. This implicitly assumes that jobs can be defined independently of the labour characteristics required and he could not imagine how this could be done.

The strange implications of Professor Somermeyer's approach can be seen from equation (13) which is concerned simultaneously with the demand for all jobs and the demand for a certain quality of labour. In his opinion this was logically impossible. Another strange result is equation (27) where the supply of labour for all jobs depends only on one factor price.

Dr. Kuipers preferred to define jobs according to the labour characteristics required. To derive labour supply equations in terms of factor prices, he recommended either abandoning the assumption that the level of education is determined exogenously or introducing "tension variables", to allow people with a certain combination of characteristics to do work which requires some different combination.

Finally, he pointed out that the demand and supply equations given in the paper are characterised by money illusion, contradicting neo-classical theory. On the demand side this is due to the fact that real rather than nominal output appears in the appropriate equations. On the supply side it results from defining utility functions in terms of money income instead of real income. A convenient way to solve this problem is to assume that a single output is produced and to use its price to deflate the factor prices.

Professor Chiswick, in the Chair, said the characteristics of the Dutch school of income distribution seemed to bear a close resemblance to the Chicago school of income distribution.

Professor Lévy-Garboua said that if a Dutch school existed, it seemed to be mainly empirically oriented. Whilst the Chicago school attempted to unify problems, this was not the case with the Dutch school. He felt that the kind of analysis present in the paper must have applications and wondered what specific empirical results had been obtained.

Professor Pen said the paper is presented as a generalisation of Tinbergen (1956). One of the important results, however, has been lost: that people with different capabilities can earn the same wage in a market economy. People are born with different abilities, schooling only makes them more unequal, and yet the free market can result in them having the same income.

Professor Taubman said he was sympathetic to the idea that many skills are rewarded in the market place but, contrary to the comments made by Professor Pen, this had no implications for the effect of education on earnings.

Professor Bentzel asked if the model could be made more realistic so that, for example, the existence of trade unions is recognised.

Mr. Bartels pointed out that the analysis covered only firms and wondered whether it might be extended to include the service and government sectors. Also, it may be more appropriate to use a disequilibrium approach, rather than the equilibrium framework adopted in the paper.

Mr. Hartog felt the system may be too general. It did not have enough restrictions to make empirical testing possible. This is illustrated clearly at the end of section IV, where it is said that it would be remarkable if the income distribution had any regular shape. However it does have a regular shape, and he argued that this should be taken as a starting point for any theory.

He had recently been applying a similar model to data from the United States. Three types of capabilities appeared to be most relevant in the determination of income differentials: a general intellectual ability, a social ability and a manual ability, with the associated relative prices in that order. The empirical evidence also suggested that the relative price of the manual capability rose significantly during the period 1950–1960. These results demonstrated that this kind of model could be subjected to empirical tests when further restrictions are imposed.

Professor Somermeyer, in his reply, said that none of the features of Tinbergen's model had been lost. The notion of "tensions" is reflected in the utility function (16), which includes both the characteristics of the individual and those imposed by employers. Firms have minimum requirements for any particular job and these give rise to the restriction mentioned on page 5. He did not believe that these requirements are as inflexible as others have suggested; frequently job characteristics are adjusted to accommodate those individuals who are available for employment.

The assumption that education is exogenously given had also been used by Professor Kuipers himself. In a dynamic version of the model he felt certain that education should be made endogenous. The reason for dealing with nominal rather than real wages was that the model had originally been developed to explain *single-period* income distributions only; an intertemporal analysis of income distributions would certainly need to take account of changes in price levels. This could be done by supplementing the labour market model with an output market, i.e. relating demand for the output of firms to incomes as well as output prices. Then demand for labour of various "qualities" depends on all wage rates and all output prices. (Some suggestions as to what might be done have been included in the additional section VI.11).

He agreed with Professor Lévy-Garboua that the Dutch School was empirically oriented; otherwise, he did not wish to be "pigeon-holed" in his theoretical approach. He also agreed with Mr. Bartels that the government sector, an (increasingly) important employer, had been inadvertently omitted. However, it could be introduced fairly easily by specifying a government utility function

$$u_G = u_G(V_{G1}, \ldots, V_{Gs}, \ldots, V_{GS}),$$

where the values added by the government departments are given by

$$V_G = V_G(n_{G1111}, \ldots, n_{GJKLM})$$

The optimisation by the government can then be dealt with in a manner similar to that adopted for firms. Replying to Professor Bentzel, he pointed out that some remarks on the potential effects of trade unions (as well as employers' associations) are included in section VI.3; a "mixed" model is possibly in order, depending, inter alia, on the relative strengths of those organisations compared with individual employees and employers, respectively.

Finally in answer to Mr. Hartog he suggested that the observed regularities in income distribution are spurious, resulting mainly from cumulating the function. The density function itself may be rather irregular. Professor Somermeyer's own study of wage differentials among construction workers in 1947 corroborates Mr. Hartog's results, in the sense that professional skill appeared to be the single most important wage determining factor.

PART V

THE DISTRIBUTION OF EARNINGS

16 THE RELATIVE INFLUENCE OF INHERITABLE AND ENVIRONMENTAL FACTORS AND THE IMPORTANCE OF INTELLIGENCE IN EARNINGS FUNCTIONS

*PAUL TAUBMAN**

In the human capital model in a competitive equilibrium and with no investment in on the job training, a person's real wage rate equals his marginal product.[1] The major questions posed in the human capital model are what determines a person's marginal product and what is the relationship between annual and lifetime earnings?[2]

In the human capital model, differences in the quantity, quality and composition of ability give rise to individual variation in marginal productivity. Each ability in turn is produced by combining initial or genetic endowments with schooling, on-the-job training and other elements of environment.[3] In some version of these models, individuals invest optimally, i.e. to the point at which the expected present discounted value of future benefits equals the cost of any investment.[4]

Mincer (1974) and others have estimated the returns to schooling and other investments and have calculated the proportion of the variance in earnings attributable to investment in human capital. However, both of these types of calculations are based on coefficient estimates which may be biased because of omitted variables such as genetic endowments and parts of family environment. In previous studies some colleagues and I have developed methodologies with which we can control for and estimate the contribution of *all* unmeasured dimensions of genetic endowments and common environment in a sample of twins.[5] We often substitute family for common environment though we recognize that "family" is only appropriate in a reduced form sense, since twins share some common environment outside of

---

* I would like to thank the Medical Follow-Up Agency of the National Academy of Sciences for making the data available and for collecting and editing the General Classification Test material. I am grateful for helpful comments on earlier drafts of this paper by Professors Behrman, Chamberlain, Goldberger, Hause and Scarr, and Dr. Hrubec. B. Atrostic and F. Slade supplied able research assistance. The research in this paper was supported by NSF Grants SOC 73–05543 and SOC 76–17673 and by the Hoover Institute.

[1] Sometimes there is an adjustment for non-pecuniary returns. See Thaler and Rosen (1976), and Taubman (1975).
[2] See Becker (1974), Mincer (1974) and, for a perceptive survey, Rosen (1976).
[3] See Meade (1973), Becker (1974) or Mincer (1974).
[4] See Becker (1967) and, for an important critique, Rosen (1976).
[5] See Taubman (1976a, b), Behrman, Taubman and Wales (BTW) (1977) and Behrman, Taubman, Wales and Hrubec (BTWH) (1977).

the home. However, neighborhood and size of city in which reared are attributable to parental decisions.

Our earlier results are based on several statistical methodologies which neither require nor allow us to identify the type of ability that affects earnings or is correlated with schooling. Recently we have obtained scores on the General Classification Test for those men in our sample who entered the Navy as enlisted men. With this data, we can redo our analysis in a form more comparable to other studies in economics and sociology and determine the extent to which cognitive skills affect earnings and bias the coefficient on schooling.[6] These results also help us understand how and why genetic and family environment affect earnings.

I. Genetic endowments and twins

We will assume that genetic endowments differ between individuals.[7] In humans a gene is found at a particular location on one of (normally) 23 chromosomes. Each gene has two members or parts one of which is contributed by each parent from her or his two members at the same location. Each egg and each sperm contains a randomly selected one of the two members of every gene of the mother and father. Thus in general, offspring of the same mother and father do not have all genes the same though their genetic endowments are correlated.

Fraternal twins, often called dizygotic or DZ, result when two spearate eggs are released in the same ovulation period and are fertilized by two separate sperm. From a genetic viewpoint they are siblings born at the same time. DZ twins share some pre- and postnatal environment.

Identical twins, often called monozygotic or MZ, occur when a single egg already fertilized by a single sperm splits. Unless there is a mutuation, the two pieces of the already fertilized egg contain all and only the information of the original fertilized egg.[8] MZ twins have the same genetic endowments and share pre and post natal environment. MZ twins are more alike than DZ twins because of the MZ's greater genetic similarity and perhaps because of the MZ's greater environmental similarity – an issue on which there is intense debate and little evidence.[9]

II. Some uses of twin samples

In this section we discuss briefly how data on twins can be used to control for and measure the effects of unmeasured genetic endowments and family environ-

---

[6] For a recent survey that covers both disciplines and a number of topics see Leibowitz, (1977).

[7] Many genes such as those that control blood type are known to come in several types in the population. Of course blood type need not influence earnings.

[8] For a fuller discussion, see Cavalli–Sforza and Bodmer (1971, ch. 9) or BTWH (1977, ch. 3).

[9] For a discussion of and opposing viewpoints on this topic, see BTW (1977) and references therein. For some more recent evidence that is in accord with the idea of no greater environmental similarity for MZ then DZ pairs, see Scarr (1977).

ment. More formal statements will be found in BTWH, chapter 4 or Taubman (1976a,b).

We begin with a semi-log equation for earnings in which we denote the ln of earnings by Y. The independent variable in this equation is ability (A) which is not observed. We assume that ability is produced by combining the observed innate ability with a variety of environments of which, for ease of presentation, only years of schooling is observed. Substituting the production function for ability, our basic equation for an individual is:[10]

$$Y = bS + cG + dN^C + eN^T + v, \qquad (1)$$

where:

S is years of schooling,
G is an unobserved index of genetic endowments,
N^C is an unobserved index of common environment,
N^T is an unobserved index of noncommon environment
v is a random error term, assumed uncorrelated with the other right-hand side variables.

Arrange the brothers within a pair randomly and denote the within pair difference as ΔY. Then we can write

$$\Delta Y = b\Delta S + c\Delta G + d\Delta N^C + e\Delta N^T + \Delta v. \qquad (1a)$$

Now let us consider the OLS estimate for b. For MZ pairs, neither ΔG nor ΔN^C can cause a bias since both will be zero for all observations. Hence if $\sigma^2_{\Delta S} \neq 0$ the estimate of b from within MZ pairs regressions will be unbiased if e is zero or ΔN^T and ΔS are uncorrelated. Within DZ pairs, there is an additional potential source of bias for the estimate of b since ΔG is not zero for all observations. In both (1) and (1a) measurement error in S can lead to a biased estimate for b, but the noise to signal ratio is likely to be larger and cause a bigger bias in the estimates for (1a).[11]

The classic analysis of variance models used in twin data is presented with some modifications in Taubman (1976a). This model expresses S in terms of (perhaps different) indices of genetics and environment and partitions the variance of a reduced form for Y. The model builds upon the fact that any difference in, say, earnings within a MZ pair can be attributed to differences in noncommon environment (ΔN^T) since ΔG and ΔN^C are zero. (The method assumes that there is no interaction between N^T and G, which assumption according to footnote 10 is not inappropriate for ln Y.) The variance in ΔY for MZ twins provides an estimate of the contribution of non-family environment to the variance in Y. To partition the remainder into genetic, family environment and covariance terms, we use information on the DZ twins and some identifying assumptions. Still the model used in Taubman (1976a) is underidentified even if some strong assumptions are made.

---

[10] This equation is specified so that there are no interaction terms between G and N^T This is a crucial assumption. A test described in Taubman (1976a) indicates that it is not an inappropriate assumption in our sample for the semi-log earnings equation.

[11] See Taubman (1976b).

BTW (1977), combine the Classical twin model with latent variable analysis to reduce the under-identification in the Classical twin model and to test the proposition that not controlling for non-common environment (N^T) does not bias the coefficient on education in (1a). In our work, however, there remains one crucial untested assumption which is that the cross twin covariance in environment is the same for MZs and DZs. Put another way we assume σ^2_{NC}/σ^2_N where $N = N^C + N^T + v$ is the same for both twin types.[12] However, with this assumption we can estimate the contribution of G (and N^C) to the variance in Y.

Of what use is the estimate of σ^2_G/σ^2_Y? Suppose genes come in only observable forms A and B. Suppose we separate people by gene type and plot the value of an ability or income as the environment varies. This plot is called the "reaction function", examples of which for A and B are given in figure 16.1. The simplest case occurs when the reaction functions are everywhere parallel.

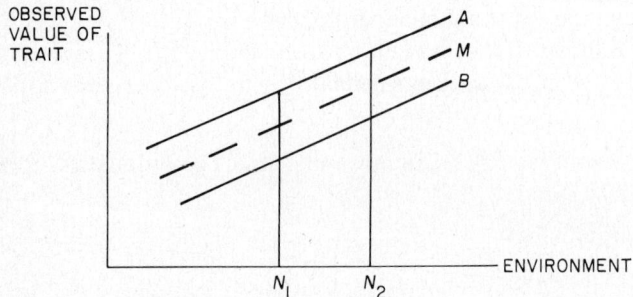

Figure 16.1. Hypothetical reaction functions.

In figure 16.1 the average value of ability in the population at each value of environment is obtained by averaging the reaction functions. Denote this by the line M. Suppose in a sample, the actual environments are restricted to N_1–N_2. The variance of the ability can be divided into the variance along M (from N_1 to N_2) and the variance around M (from A to M and M to B). Within the N_1–N_2 interval the proportion of the variance due to genetics will be greater the further apart are A and B. However, changing the bounds of the range of environment alters the proportion of the variance attributable to genetics. Thus if people in our sample are located on the N_1–N_2 interval, a large value for σ^2_G/σ^2_Y merely tells us that in the sample the variation in environment was small relative to the variation in genetics.

Knowledge of the relative size of σ^2_G does not convey any information about either the average level of G or the change in ability as N varies. For example, suppose everyone had the environment of N_1 in figure 16.1. Then all the variation in the trait would be due to variation in genotype. If everyone suddenly shifted the environment to N_2, the level of ability would change though the variation would still be solely genetic in origin. Moreover, the change in ability caused by a change in environment is given by the slope of M in figure 16.1. We can rotate

---

[12] See Goldberger (1977) or BTW (1977) for discussion of the evidence and implications of this assumption.

A, B and M without affecting the variance contributions, but the steeper is M the bigger is the effect of an environmental change on the mean level of ability.

Thus, our results on the contributions of the unmeasured variables of genetics, family and non-family environment to variance in earnings cannot indicate that changes in environment will be ineffective in altering the average level of earnings. Our results, however, do indicate something about the historical source of inequality as measured by variance. Moreover, all discussion of equality of opportunity, except those on racial and sexual discrimination, focus on differences associated with family environment. Our results on family environment, allow us to examine what would happen to inequality for white males if all differences in equality of opportunity between families were eliminated.

III. The NAS–NRC twin sample

The NAS–NRC Twin Sample has been described in detail in BTWH (1977) and Taubman (1976a,b). Briefly, the sample is drawn from a *panel* which consists of nearly all the white male twins – both veterans – born in the Continental U.S. between 1917 and 1927. In 1974 questionaires were sent to those members of the panel where both sibs were alive and had been cooperative in other recent inquiries. The responders to the survey are more educated and have greater earnings than the U.S. white population of the same age. However, if the U.S. data are weighted so as to correspond to our sample distribution by education class, the sample excess in average earnings is less than 10%. The two twin types have similar distributions on earnings, schooling and a variety of aspects of family background, except that DZs have a larger mean and variance for the number of sibs.

Shortly before and during World War II, the Navy gave the so-called General Qualifications Test (GCT) which is a verbal ability test and will correlate well with the standard so-called IQ tests given to those who entered as enlisted men.[13] The IQ data have been edited and adjusted. Details are available on request.

For about 1250 pairs in the *panel* for whom we can establish zygosity, both twins served in the Navy. IQ data were available for about 68.7% of these people while both members have scores in 55.2% of the pairs. If the probability of one sib having a score was independent of his sib's status, we would expect to find only 47.4% of the pairs with both having scores.

The mean and variance for the GCT in our subsample are 50.1 and 105.3 compared to the Navy population values of 50 and 100, respectively. These differences are not statistically significant nor are they large. While this is an encouraging finding, it is also somewhat surprising, at least for the mean, since the previously published results for twins indicate that twins average 5 points less on IQ tests and that the discrepancy is centered in the verbal or vocabulary test section.[14]

---

[13] The Army gave similar tests but about 80% of the Army's original personnel records were destroyed in a fire in 1972. Marines are not included because they use a different set of personnel records.

[14] See Mittler (1971) and Vandenberg (1968). Most of the previous studies are based on twins 11 years old or younger. Jencks and Brown (1977) report that in the Project Talent sample, IQ is the same for twins and their classmates in the 11th grade.

Possible reasons for this result are discussed in BTWH, chapter 5. Comparing the Navy and the remaining or "non-Navy" responders in the sample, BTWH find no noticeable differences in means and variances in schooling, earnings, and a host of background variables.

IV. Summary of previous results

The major findings in Taubman (1976a,b), BTW (1977) and BTWH (1977) include the following for the ln of earnings in 1973 when the twins were about 50 years old. First, when we estimate equation (1) in which we treat the twins as unrelated individuals and in which we omit any measures of G, N^C and N^T, the coefficient on years of schooling is 0.08.[15] (This coefficient is the same if age is included in the equation.) Using a set of controls even more extensive than that available in the U.S. Census, the coefficient on years of schooling only drops 12% to 0.07.[16]

Second, when we estimate equation (1a) within DZ pairs and control for common environment, the coefficient on schooling is statistically significant at about 0.06 which is 1/4 less than that obtained in equation (1).

Third, when we estimate equation (1a) within MZ pairs and control for genetic endowments and common environments, the coefficient on years of schooling is statistically significant, but less than 0.03 or 2/3 less than that obtained in equation (1). Because of measurement error, the bias of 2/3 is an upper bound, and a more realistic estimate of the bias may be 1/2. Thus, the set of family background measures we used is far from perfect as a control for genetic endowments and family environment in an earnings equation.

Fourth, we do not reject the hypothesis that specific environment (N^T) is not a latent variable. In other words, there is no bias from not controlling N^T in the within MZ equations.

Fifth, the sum of genetic endowments plus common (family) environment accounts for 57% and 75% of the variance in the ln of 1973 earnings and in years of schooling respectively.

Sixth, using the restrictions that σ^2_{NC}/σ^2_N is the same for MZ and DZ pairs and that $\sigma_{GN} = 0$, we estimate that genetic endowments account for about 45% and 56%, and family environment 12% and 41%, of the variance in the ln of 1973 earnings, and in years of schooling respectively.[17] (If σ^2_{NC} is greater for MZs, the estimate of genetic effects would decrease.) Thus, about half of the inequality in earnings at age 50 is attributable to genetics and not to investment in human capital. Of the remainder, some is not due to investment decisions.

Seventh, the genetic index that accounts for 36% of the variance in schooling

---

[15] This coefficient is similar to, though slightly lower than, those Mincer (1974) obtained in the 1960 Census and nearly identical to that Lillard and Willis (1976) obtained in the Michigan Income Dynamics Sample of the late 1960s and early 1970s.

[16] We include a number of sibs alive in 1940, father's and mother's years of schooling, father's occupational status and dummy variables for being Catholic, being Jewish, raised in a rural environment, and born in the South.

[17] If the restriction that $\sigma_{GN} = 0$ is dropped, the contribution of the additive effect of G is unchanged while the contributions of the additive effect of N is lowered.

Inheritable and environmental factors 387

only accounts for 9% of the variance in earnings, while the total genetic impact on earnings is 45%. In other words, some genetically based skills have differential importance for schooling and earnings.

V. The contributions of IQ

Because there is no guarantee that those in the Navy are a random drawing from the whole sample, in BTWH (1977) we estimated equations for those pairs both in the Navy and for the remainder of the sample. The estimates for the two groups are similar.

Table 16.1 contains results for those with both IQ and earnings data, a group who entered the Navy as enlisted men. In this table, the first line contains the coefficients of the independent variables and the second the "t" statistic. Equation (1) is the semi-log earnings equation similar to that advocated by Mincer and others, except that we have included age instead of Years of Work Experience. If the latter is defined as (Age – Years of Schooling Completed – 6), and if experience only enters linearly, which may be plausible for people around age 50, there is an exact linear transform between the two versions.

In this equation, the coefficient on years of schooling is a significant 0.055 when age is held constant and 0.032 if years of work experience is used. Both of these numbers are substantially less than those obtained when we use all those in our sample or all individuals in the Navy subsample. (See Table 16.2). Since the GCT data are only available for those who entered the Navy as enlisted men, it seems likely that those with high education who entered as enlisted men had less motivation or drive.[18] Thus, the availability of GCT data censors the sample and biases downward the education coefficient. (Compare equation (1) in table 16.2.)

While the estimate of the level of the schooling coefficient in the subsample with GCT data is not to be trusted, it is possible that the estimate of the *bias* from omitting IQ is appropriate. The necessary conditions are that the effect of cognitive skills on earnings, which is the slope coefficient on S in an IQ equation, be the same in the subsample and in the population.[19]

When in equation (2) we include our list of background variables, the coefficient on years of schooling declines by 0.010. In equation (3) we introduce the IQ or GCT variable, which has a highly significant coefficient. Each 10 points or 1 standard deviation increase in GCT is estimated to lead to a 13% increase in earnings. In comparison with equation (1), the coefficient on years of schooling in equation (3) declines by 0.023 points to 0.0317. When both IQ and family background measures are included as in equation (4), the coefficient on years of schooling is 0.0271 which is 0.028 less than in equation (1).

---

[18] There may also be some effects arising from truncation since those with very low cognitive ability and/or severe handicaps were not accepted into the military. Truncation at the upper end does not seem likely since some enlisted men subsequently became Ph. D's, LLB's, etc.

[19] When we include an officer dummy variable in equations for the full navy sample, the coefficient on education drops to about the same level as in table 16.1. Including this dummy in the equations (2) does not affect the change in the education coefficients when GCT is added. See Behrman, Taubman, Wales and Hrubec (1977), chapter (6).

Table 16.1. Equations for ln Y_{73}. Individuals with data on Y_{73} and GCT (609 persons).

Eq. number	ED	AGE	IQIND	EDNAVY	CATH	JEW	RURAL	SOUTH	SIBS	EDM	EDF	OCCF	Constant	R^2
(1)	0.055 (8.4)	−0.023 (2.8)											10.0 (23.9)	0.13
(2)	0.045 (6.7)	−0.016 (2.0)			0.026 (0.6)	0.58 (5.2)	0.032 (0.8)	0.068 (1.4)	−0.019 (2.3)	0.0090 (1.0)	−0.0094 (0.1)	0.00089 (1.0)	9.8 (22.6)	0.19
(3)	0.032 (4.2)	−0.024 (3.1)	0.013 (5.7)										9.7 (23.5)	0.17
(4)	0.027 (3.5)	−0.020 (2.5)	0.011 (4.8)		0.019 (0.4)	0.52 (4.8)	−0.013 (0.3)	0.096 (1.9)	−0.017 (2.0)	0.0040 (0.5)	0.00022 (0.03)	0.00075 (0.8)	9.6 (22.6)	0.22
(5)	0.033 (3.7)	−0.023 (2.9)	0.013 (5.5)	−0.0051 (0.3)									9.7 (23.5)	0.17
(6)	0.031 (3.5)	−0.018 (2.1)	0.011 (4.8)	−0.014 (0.9)	0.018 (0.4)	0.53 (4.8)	−0.013 (0.3)	0.093 (1.9)	−0.018 (2.1)	0.0044 (0.5)	0.00023 (0.03)	0.00075 (0.9)	9.6 (22.6)	0.21

[1] First row in each equation is coefficient.
[2] Second row in each equation is the value of the t statistic.
[3] R^2 is adjusted for degrees of freedom.
[4] See text for derivation of IQTWN.
[5] Definition of variables in tables:

CATH is a dummy variable = 1 if brought up Catholic.
JEW is a dummy variable = 1 if brought up Jewish.
RURAL is a dummy variable = 1 if raised in a rural area.
SOUTH is a dummy variable = 1 if born in Census definition of South.
ED is years of schooling as of 1974.
AGE is 1974 − year of birth.
SIBS is number of siblings alive in 1940.
EDM is mother's year's of schooling.
EDF is father's year's of schooling.
OCCF is Duncan Score for father's occupation, scaled 0 to 100.
EDNAVY is years of schooling at time of entry into Navy.
IQIND is GCT score for individual.
IQTWN is average GCT score for pair, some numbers are interpolated. See text for details.

Table 16.2. Equations for ln Y_{73} pair averages, both in Navy with Y_{73} for both sibs (404 pairs).

Eq. number	ED	AGE	IQTWN	EDNAVY	CATH	JEW	RURAL	SOUTH	SIBS	EDM	EDF	OCCF	Constant	R^2
(1)	0.076 (10.8)	−0.0063 (0.8)											9.0 (22.9)	0.23
(2)	0.059 (7.8)	−0.00034 (0.05)			0.057 (1.3)	0.55 (4.6)	−0.032 (0.7)	0.012 (0.2)	−0.025 (2.8)	0.0059 (0.7)	0.0067 (0.09)	0.0020 (1.9)	8.8 (22.4)	0.31
(3)	0.062 (7.5)	−0.0059 (0.8)	0.0087 (3.2)										8.7 (21.8)	0.25
(4)	0.051 (6.0)	−0.00056 (0.08)	0.0059 (2.2)		0.055 (1.2)	0.516 (4.3)	−0.029 (0.6)	0.024 (0.5)	−0.024 (2.7)	0.0048 (0.6)	0.0010 (0.1)	0.0019 (1.9)	8.6 (21.6)	0.31
(5)	0.051 (5.7)	−0.010 (1.4)	0.0085 (3.2)	0.023 (2.9)									8.8 (22.2)	0.26
(6)	0.046 (5.0)	−0.0033 (0.4)	0.0060 (2.3)	0.012 (1.4)	0.054 (1.2)	0.47 (3.7)	−0.028 (0.6)	0.028 (0.6)	−0.024 (2.7)	−0.0036 (0.4)	0.00013 (0.002)	0.0019 (1.9)	8.7 (21.6)	0.32

[1] Here each variable is the average for twin pair.
[2] For additional notes and definitions, see table 16.1.

If this 0.028 is an appropriate estimate of the bias from omitting IQ and measured aspects of family background, and if the 0.076 in table 16.2 is the correct estimate of the effect of schooling for those in the Navy or in the whole sample, when IQ and background are not controlled the percentage bias would be about 40%. The 0.028 or the 40% figures, however, may overstate the bias because the individuals had different amounts of schooling when the Navy administered the GCT tests. If prior schooling affected the test score results, then part of the total effect of schooling would be included in the effect of IQ.[20]

Griliches and Mason (1972) solved the same problem by noting that post test schooling cannot influence the previous GCT scores. Let the B and A subscripts indicate before and after the test date. Thus in an equation such as

$$Y = b(S_A - S_B) + cS_B + dIQ + u = b(S_A) + (c - b)S_B + dIQ + u \qquad (2)$$

The coefficient on $(S_A - S_B)$ would be an estimate of the total effect of schooling given previously attained levels of cognitive skills. In our data set, education at time of entry into the Navy and education as of 1974 correspond to B and A.

In equation (5), $(c - b)$ is -0.0051 with a "t" statistic of 0.3. Our estimate of b is now 0.033 which is only trivially different from the 0.031 in equation (4).[21] After adding in the background variables, the bias based on equation (6) would be estimated as about 30% of 0.076.

In table 16.2 we present regressions for all Navy pairs where both sibs have positive earnings in 1973. The observations used are the pair's average on each variable. The average IQ data were derived as follows. In the 224 pairs where each sib had a GCT score, we averaged them. In the 161 pairs where only one brother had a score, it was used as the pair average. In the 16 pairs where neither brother had a GCT score, both were assigned 52.5 which is the average for all Navy responders with GCT data.[22]

In the first equation the coefficient on schooling is 0.076 which is very similar to that obtained in the whole sample. The coefficient is reduced to 0.059 when the background variables are added in equation (2). In equation (3), when we add the GCT measure to equation (1), the GCT variable has a highly significant coefficient of 0.009 and the coefficient on schooling drops to 0.061. When the background variables are added in equation (4), the education coefficient falls to 0.0509 which is a decrease of 33% from equation (1). When in equation (5) we add premilitary education, the coefficient on education as of 1974 is unchanged.

Suppose that actual GCT scores are measured without error. Denote the cross twin correlation on GCT for those pairs where both have GCT data as r. Suppose

---

[20] Premilitary schooling and the GCT scores have a simple correlation of 0.55.

[21] Taubman and Wales (1974) also concluded that in the NBER–TH sample, pre-test differences in schooling had little effect on the variety of tests given to men in the Air Force in 1943. Griliches and Mason (1972) reached a similar conclusion.

[22] This methodology is subject to at least two criticisms. First it must cause random measurement error since the cross sib correlations for GCT for responders are only 0.76 and 0.46 for MZ's and DZ's respectively. Second, there may be a systematic measurement error since those who entered as officers were supposed to be above average in IQ. However, since only about 1/2 the men with no GCT scores left the service as officers and since the average GCT of the 161 sibs whose brother did not have a GCT score was about 54, some of the systematic error is eliminated.

this same r applies to the pairs where only one twin has an IQ measure. Denote the GCT score of the two twins by Q_1 and Q_2. The expected value of the variance of $\frac{1}{2}(Q_1 + Q_2)$ is $\frac{1}{2}$ var $Q(1 + r)$. When for some observations we substitute, say, Q_1 for Q_2, we overstate the above variance since for these substitute observations r is 1. The measurement error as a percentage of the variance in the true variable is about 0.16.[23] Assuming the measurement error is independent of earnings and schooling, in equation (3) the coefficient on years of schooling would fall by a trivial 0.004 while that on GCT would increase by 28%, which is very close to the corresponding coefficient in table 16.1.

The results in tables 16.1 and 16.2 suggest that the GCT test and certain aspects of family background are important determinants of earnings around age 50 and that omitting these variables induces a bias in the education variables of around 30% to 35%. Since GCT scores and the background measures are correlated, it is not possible to say precisely how much of the bias is attributable to background and how much to IQ. But the maximum contribution of the GCT scores is given by a comparison of equation (3) or (5) in tables 16.1 and 16.2 with equation (1) in table 16.2, which indicates a bias arising from not controlling GCT of about 30%. While this is a large bias, it still is small as compared to the 2/3 obtained in the within MZ equations.

The simple correlation between IQ and ln Y_{73} is about 0.36. Thus the maximum contribution of IQ to the variance of ln Y_{73} is 0.13. Some differences in IQ must arise from sources outside of the family, especially since the MZ cross sib covariance for IQ is only 0.76. Yet our estimate of the effect of genetics plus family environment on the variance of earnings is 0.57. Thus there must be some important skills which are not captured by the GCT test and which are derived from one's parents.

The equations in tables 16.1 and 16.2 use measured variables to control for genetic endowments and family environment. An alternative technique is to use within pair equations. Since the sample is small, we have included both MZ and DZ pairs though in some equations we allow for differences in coefficients by including a DZ = 1 dummy variable that interacts with the other variables. In these calculations the assignment of missing IQ scores does not affect the estimate of the IQ coefficient since in calculating both the covariance of IQ with education and the variance of IQ, an equal number of zeros are added to the sum of squares. In other words we estimate the IQ coefficient only on the basis of the pairs both of whom have IQ data. The education coefficient, however, is biased downward because the correlation of education and IQ will be understated since the sum of squares of education does not have the zeros. The effect however is trivial since the simple correlation of ΔED and ΔIQ is 0.367 in the sample with 404 pairs with the interpolated ΔIQ numbers, and 0.0467 in the sample with 224 pairs with no interpolated numbers.

The coefficient for ΔED is 0.031 when both twin types are included and nothing else is held constant. The introduction of ΔIQ leaves ΔED unchanged. ΔIQ has a

---

[23] For 80 MZ and 81 DZ pairs only one sib has such measurement error.

coefficient of 0.006 and a "t" value of 1.2, which of course is not significant at the 5% level though some 40% of the ΔIQ observations have been set at zero

When we introduce $\Delta EDNAVY$, the education and IQ coefficients are unchanged. When we introduce a dummy variable for DZ pairs which interacts with all the independent variables, the coefficient on ΔED declines while that on ΔIQ increases, but nothing is statistically significant.

As we noted earlier the coefficients in within pair equations are more affected by measurement error than equations for individuals. Still if one uses the estimated within MZ pairs equation of 0.023 ΔED + 0.001 ΔIQ and allows for independent measurement error of 10% in each, both coefficients would be increased by no more than 50%. If these tentative calculations are correct, controlling for family environment and genetics is more important in measuring the effect of education than controlling for within pair differences in IQ.

VI. Conclusions and implications

First, a measure of cognitive ability has a large, positive and significant coefficient in an earnings equation for white men about age 50 when the equation also holds constant education and a variety of measures of family background. A one standard deviation increase in the GCT leads to about a 10% increase in earnings.

Second, not controlling for the GCT in the earnings equation leads to about a 30% bias in the schooling coefficient. The size of this bias is in conformity with other studies, such as Fagerlind (1975), Olneck (1977) or Taubman and Wales (1974), in which the men in the sample have 10 or more years of work experience. It is not in conformity with the multitude of studies in which the men have 7 or less years of work experience. While none of the studies that have examined the importance of IQ and earnings are random samples of the population, and while a multitude of different IQ tests have been used, our new findings support the idea that the coefficient on IQ in an earnings equation is near zero only when people have few years of work experience. Thus conclusions on the importance of controlling IQ from samples of young men are inappropriate for later life cycle stages.

Third, the 30% bias on education from not holding IQ constant or perhaps 35% for not controlling for both IQ and our measured aspects of family background are roughly 1/2 the bias (of two/thirds) obtained from MZ within pair equations. However, as explained in Taubman (1976b) this 2/3 bias would be an upper bound if schooling is subject to measurement error. If the measurement error were 10% of the variance in the true differences in schooling, the coefficient on schooling would be 0.048, which is quite close to the estimates of about 0.052 in table 16.2. While the latter would also be biased downward by measurement error, it would appear that OLS estimates which control for IQ and the measured aspects of family background yield good estimates of the true effect on earnings. The 10% measurement error seems consistent with the results in Bielby, Hauser and Featherman (1976), if one assumes the larger error in the CPS occurs because only in that survey could spouses answer for the intended respondent. In other words, the measurement error in schooling causes a bias that approximately offsets the bias from the remaining omitted variables in tables 16.1 and 16.2.

Fourth, the total effect of the sum of genetic endowments and common environment is about 57% for earnings and 75% for both education and the GCT. The maximum contribution of GCT to the variance in the first two variables is 13% and 32% respectively. The IQ variable in conjunction with schooling and the measured background variables have at best an R^2 in the earnings equation equal to 0.32, which is 50% of that which can be attributable to genetics and common environment. Thus there remain unmeasured important aspects of ability and/or financing capability which, help explain the variance in earnings, and which are related to the family.

These conclusions are based on one sample of white males aged 50 who are not representative of the whole U.S. population. It is quite possible that different results would be obtained from more representative samples, from younger men, or from more recent cohorts. Still if our results are anywhere near being correct, our findings would have the following implications.

First, variations in schooling have much smaller effects on earnings than people have supposed once ability is controlled. In our sample, if we calculate the variance in individual's earnings explained by schooling using the coefficient estimate of 0.03, the R^2 would be less than 3%. Thus equalization of years of schooling would have little effect on the variance in earnings. Huge compensatory programs would be required to equalize the distribution.

Second, nearly 60% of the inequality in earnings is attributable to parental effects. Purely on grounds of equity, I find this a distressing situation. How parents create the inequality is far from clear. The IQ and schooling variables themselves explain less than 25% of the variance in earnings, and about 1/4 the variance in each of these variables is not due to the family.

Third, much of the parental effect on earnings appears to be genetic in origin. Policies of equality of opportunity that eliminate capital market imperfections and all other differences in family environment will reduce inequality by 12%. Those who are disturbed by the size of the remaining inequality will have to opt for unspecified compensatory training programs or income maintenance programs.

References

Becker, G., "Human Capital and the Personal Distribution of Income", *W.S. Woytinsky Lecture No. 1*, Ann Arbor: University of Michigan, 1967.
Becker, G., *Human Capital*, Columbia University Press, Second Edition, 1974.
Bielby, W., R. Hauser and D. Featherman, "Response Errors of Nonblack Males in Models of the Stratification Process", University of Wisconsin, mimeo, 1976.
Behrman, J., P. Taubman and T. Wales, "Controlling for and Measuring the Effects of Genetics and Family Environment in Equations for Schooling and Labor Market Success", in *Kinometrics: Determinants of Socioeconomic Success within and between Families*, P. Taubman, ed., North Holland, 1977.
Behrman, J., P. Taubman, T. Wales and Z. Hrubec, *Inter and Intragenerational Determinants of Socioeconomic Success: Genetic Endowments, Family and other Environments*, mimeo, 1977.
Cavalli-Sforza, L. and W. Bodmer, *The Genetics of Human Populations*, W.H. Freeman and Co., 1971.
Fagerlind, I., *Formal Education and Adult Earnings*, Stockholm: Almqvist and Wiksell, 1975.
Goldberger, A., "Structural Equation Models: An Overview", in *Structural Equation Models in the Social Sciences*, A. Goldberger and O. Duncan, ed., Seminar Press, 1973.

Goldberger, A., "Twin Methods; A Skeptical View", in *Kinometrics: Determinants of Socioeconomic Success within and between Families*, P. Taubman, ed., North Holland, 1977.

Griliches, Z. and W. Mason, "Education, Income and Ability", *Journal of Political Economy*, May/June 1972, part II.

Jencks, C. and M. Brown, "Genes and Social Stratification: A Methodological Exploration with Illustrative Data", in *Kinometrics: Determinants of Socioeconomic Success within and between Families*, P. Taubman, ed., North Holland, 1977.

Leibowitz, A., "Family Background and Socioeconomic Success: A Review of the Evidence", in *Kinometrics: Determinants of Socioeconomic Success within and between Families*, P. Taubman, ed., North Holland, 1977.

Lillard, L. and R. Willis, "Dynamic Aspects of Earnings Mobility", NBER Working Paper No. 150, 1976, mimeo.

Meade, J., "The Inheritance of Inequality: Some Biological, Demographic, Social and Economic Factors", *Proceedings of the British Academy*, 1973.

Mincer, J., *Schooling, Experience and Earnings*, Columbia University Press, 1974.

Mittler, P., *The Study of Twins*, Penguin, 1971.

Olneck, M., "On the Use of Sibling Data to Estimate the Effects of Family Background, Cognitive Skills and Schooling: Results from the Kalamazoo Brothers Study", in *Kinometrics: The Determinants of Socioeconomic Success within and between Families*, P. Taubman, ed., North Holland, 1977.

Rosen, S., "Human Capital: A Survey of Empirical Research", in *Research in Labor Economics*, R. Ehrenberg, ed., JAI Press, 1976.

Scarr, S., "Twin Method: Defence of a Critical Assumption", University of Minnesota, Psychology Department, 1977, mimeo.

Taubman, P., *Sources of Inequality of Earnings*, North Holland, 1975.

Taubman, P., "The Determinants of Earnings: Genetics, Family and Other Environments, A Study of White Male Twins", *American Economic Review*, December 1976a.

Taubman, P., "Earnings, Education, Genetics and Environment", *Journal of Human Resources*, Fall, 1976b.

Taubman, P. and T. Wales, *Higher Education as an Investment and as a Screening Device*, New York, McGraw Hill, 1974.

Thaler, R. and S. Rosen, "The Value of a Human Life", in *Household Production and Consumption*, N. Terleckjy, ed., Columbia University Press, 1976.

Vandenberg, S., "The Nature and Nurture of Intelligence", *Genetics*, D. Glass, ed., New York, 1968.

16 DISCUSSION

PAPER BY PAUL TAUBMAN

Professor de Wolff expressed admiration for Professor Taubman's many contributions in recent years and in particular for the present one, with which he was in general agreement. Mincer and other students of the human capital approach often measure the returns to investment in education by the gross regression coefficient of log earnings on schooling (in years), which is approximately equal to 0.08, and find that this coefficient shows little variation as other background factors are introduced. Taubman correctly points out that this coefficient may be overestimated due to latent factors. When a measure of intelligence is included, the coefficient shows a substantial fall. Taubman checked this result by comparing differences in earnings between fraternal twins, leading to a value of the coefficient of approximately 0.06, which is reduced still further when only identical twins are considered. The final value of around 0.05 is similar to the coefficient obtained for schooling when earnings are regressed against schooling, IQ and other variables. This he found a very interesting result.

The paper had also emphasised, correctly, that data based on only a few years of working experience lead to unreliable results. Swedish studies by Fägerlind and others using a longitudinal data sample covering almost 40 years had some relevance to this point. IQ, schooling and social background explained only 7 per cent of the variation in earnings at age 25. By age 35 this had risen to 36 per cent, and in the latest study, published only recently, the figure had risen to almost 50 percent. This supports very strongly the conclusion that the explanatory power of the variables depends on the period of working life.

He was particularly interested in comparing the figures given in table 16.1 with his own results for Sweden. Instead of measuring schooling by the number of years, he had grouped the schooling period into a small number of classes and used dummies for these variables. Such a procedure indicated a strong curvilinear relationship between schooling and earnings, with longer periods of schooling becoming progressively more important. This seemed to be consistent with the results in table 16.1, since the coefficient for the level of education prior to entering the navy was negative, whilst the overall coefficient was positive, therefore implying a higher contribution for education received after leaving the navy. Therefore he asked Professor Taubman if it would not have been better to use dummies in his investigation.

Another interesting point is that the Swedish data had IQ measurements at age 10 and also on entry to military service. The IQ at the older age was found to have a higher explanatory power, presumably because by then it was heavily influenced by schooling.

Professor de Wolff also referred to page 390, where it is stated that incomes below zero have been left out. He wondered if it would not have been better to exclude all excessive incomes. For the Swedish material this led to a considerable improvement and it might also be important for the US data since, after all, the correlation coefficient is rather low ($\simeq 0.20$).

He was puzzled by the 60 per cent of the total variation in earnings attributable to family background, which was substantially above comparable estimates in Sweden. Finally, he wondered about the highly significant coefficient attached to the Jewish variable, which indicated a 65 per cent income differential accounted for solely by this variable. This was equivalent to about 50 years of education and led him to ask if there was any possibility of an error.

Dr. Psacharopoulos was surprised by the results on page 390 which show that one half of the variance in earnings at age 50 is attributable to genetics. Intuitively he felt this was very high, considering the variety of influences which would have affected earnings by this age. He also wondered why, on page 390, a comparison is made between equations (1) and (4) of table 16.2 rather than (2) and (4), which he thought would be more relevant. Making this latter comparison he estimated the effect of IQ as reducing the coefficient on schooling by approximately 13 per cent.

Mr. Layard wished to pursue this point about the role of genetics. It is an interesting question since policies directed at income distribution can affect family environmental decisions but not the genetic component. But returns to genetic factors can be treated as rents. If, after allowing for all environmental influences, genetic factors made a substantial contribution to inequality, the conclusion he would draw is that a high degree of redistribution could be attained with little efficiency loss. However, he found the 50 per cent figure hard to accept. One point which he felt might be relevant was the assumption that identical and non-identical twins are subject to the same differences in environmental experience. This assumption might be questionable since identical twins do seem to be treated more identically.

Professor van Praag was concerned with the coefficient relating to the Jewish family background. With only 400 observations, a small sample of perhaps 8 or 10 Jewish twins might be expected. He thought the explanation of the high coefficient attached to this variable may lie in the fact that at that time it was very difficult for Jewish men to enter the navy.

His work with Tinbergen, estimating earnings functions, suggested that general and specialist schooling had different coefficients and should be distinguished. They had also used a variable to describe "leadership" and this made a substantial contribution to explaining variations in the logarithm of income. Using a sample of about 2000, the explanatory power of the functions and the significance of the coefficients were generally better than the results presented in the paper. He recommended the construction of intervening variables, notably leadership, which was itself determined partly by genetics. These intervening variables could then be used at a second stage to estimate the earnings process.

Professor Somermeyer was fairly happy with the results found in the paper, since they confirmed his own beliefs and were broadly consistent with his own results. He had found a coefficient for ability of roughly the same order of magnitude, but a smaller schooling effect. While Professor Taubman had suggested that the effects of ability and schooling were of the same order of magnitude, this might be due – at least partly – to a theoretically expected, and empirically supported, positive dependence of the ability coefficient on schooling or (equivalently) to a positive dependence of the schooling coefficient on ability. The coefficients for Jews and Catholics may be influenced by the fact that they are concentrated in the big cities. This is not captured in the rural–urban distinction as the *size* of the urban area is not taken into account.

Professor Lévy-Garboua felt there may be a strong positive correlation between education and some ability factors, particularly since IQ is measured after the completion of most schooling. He would have preferred a recursive model, as others had suggested, in which IQ and N_T are explained by education and other variables before the log earnings regression is performed.

Dr. Wagner liked the paper for reasons other than those already mentioned. He liked the policy conclusions, namely that income inequality cannot be achieved by changing factors on the supply side of the labour market. He took this to imply that policies directed at income redistribution should concentrate on the demand side of the labour market. Furthermore, he doubted whether intelligence was a scarce resource in our society. This would imply that the coefficient for the intelligence variable in the earnings function should be insignificant if the US labour market was working efficiently on a competitive basis.

Professor Pen commented on the small contribution attributable to education. He felt the system of equations being estimated did not take into account the fact that education changes the price structure, in particular relative wages, so the impact of education is still present.

Professor Stiglitz asked how sensitive the results were to the linear specification and to the strong separability assumptions assumed for the genetic and environmental influences. A second point concerned the impact of the supply of education on factor prices. There was no problem if education leads to higher productivity in the same jobs, but it may change the relative prices of skilled and unskilled labour.

Professor von Weizsacker understood that the paper suggests a strong genetic influence but a relatively unimportant family background effect. This raises an interesting question. If the same were true in the parental generation, the results lead us to expect a small correlation between the genetic endowments of parents and children. The family background should pick up the influence of the genetic endowment of parents on children. He also asked what hypotheses had been proposed concerning the impact of IQ and genetic endowments in general.

Professor Taubman replied first to the questions raised about the Jewish coefficient. Part of the explanation may be due to the small sample of those from a Jewish background. There may also have been more stringent selection into the Navy (although the proportion is similar to that in the military overall). Several other studies including the entire NAS–NRC sample give a 30–35% differential to those from Jewish homes, which he felt to be more reasonable than the 50% recorded here.

The reason why the effects of the other background variables (including IQ) were relatively small compared with the unmeasured factors was that the variables frequently used as proxies for family background were poor indicators. Thus, it seems there are a number of personal characteristics, not easily identified, which are related to family background.

Another general issue concerned the functional form. There was some evidence for non-linearity in the schooling effect, but this applied only to those with nineteen or more years of schooling, mainly doctors and lawyers. Another test indicates that it is not necessary to include an interaction between genetics and environment when the dependent variable is the log of earnings. While the analysis had used age rather than experience, other samples indicate that the experience effect is linear for men about age 50. When the experience effect is linear, age equals experience plus years of schooling (which is already held constant) plus a constant. He had not yet examined any possible interaction between schooling and ability, other than that implied by the semilog specification.

One crucial assumption is that σ_{NN^*} is the same for identical and fraternal twins. It appears there is greater similarity between identical twins in the way they dress, how much schooling they have and so on. These extra similarities are incorporated in the genetic effect, which is perfectly correct as long as these are mainly responses to genetic differences and are expected to continue in the future. He had experimented with different values of σ_{NN^*} for identical and fraternal twins. It turned out that the value of G fell, but the total family effect remained the same. Moreover, a recent study by Loehlin and Nichols showed that greater similarity in measured environment for identical twins was not related to difference in IQ for high school students.

Finally, in terms of the size of the genetic and family effects, it is worth noting that in a human capital model in which individuals choose the optimum amount of investments, variation in the present discounted value of lifetime earnings occurs because of variation in genetic endowments, in prices and in random events. For earnings about age 50, Professor Taubman attributes about 40% of the variation to random events and 45% to genetic endowments. If people want much more to be random, he asked why we should bother to have a theory.

17 THE INFLUENCE OF SUBSTITUTION AND TECHNICAL PROGRESS ON INCOME DIFFERENCES BETWEEN GRADUATE AND OTHER LABOUR

K. GROENVELD and S.K. KUIPERS*

I. Introduction

In his inspiring book *Income Distribution*, Tinbergen was the first to explicitly conceive income distribution as the result of both factor substitution and technical progress. It is not surprising that technical progress had hardly been recognised as a determinant of income distribution in earlier studies. Most of them are cross-section studies in which differences in technology are not taken into consideration, as a rule.[1] But in time series studies also, technical progress is not always introduced as one of the causal factors.[2]

Although Tinbergen's analysis of *The race between technological development and education* is a considerable step forward in our understanding of changes in income distribution, his analysis may still be considered rather restrictive, as it is based on the assumption that the elasticity of substitution between different categories of labour equals unity. As in most investigations a much higher substitution elasticity has been found,[3] there is reason to doubt Tinbergen's conclusion that technical progress is the only cause, on the demand side, of a rise in the income share of academically trained labour. If, for instance, such a rise is also due to an elasticity of substitution exceeding unity, the significance of technical progress for income inequality will be much less and it may even reduce, rather than augment, inequality. It is therefore important to understand the consequences of technical progress for the distribution of income, especially if governments try to influence its rate and direction in order to equalise incomes.

---

* The authors are indebted to Mr. M. Botman, graduate-assistant at Groningen, for computational assistance and to their colleagues at the Department of Economics for stimulating comments on an earlier draft of this paper.
 [1] See, for instance, Bowles (1969, 1970), Dougherty (1972a, 1972b), Fallon and Layard (1974), Kuipers (1976) and Psacharopoulos (1973). Exceptions are Groenveld and Kuipers (1976) and Tinbergen (1974, 1975d).
 [2] See, for instance, Berndt and Christensen (1974). In this respect a striking exception is Dresch (1975).
 [3] See Berndt and Christensen (1974), Bowles (1969, 1970), Dougherty (1972a, 1972b), Dresch (1975), Groenveld and Kuipers (1976), Kuipers (1976) and Psacharopoulos (1973). For some counter-evidence see Tinbergen (1974, 1975b, 1975d). However, see also Groenveld and Kuipers (1976) and the preliminary conclusion in Tinbergen (1975e). Support for Tinbergen's view can be found in Fallon and Layard (1974).

The aim of this paper is to present further evidence on how factor substitution and technical progress influence income distribution. The elasticity of substitution is assumed to be constant, but not necessarily equal to unity. Following in the footsteps of Tinbergen, labour will be broken down into only two categories: university-trained labour and other labour.

The paper is organised as follows. In section II estimated factor price equations will be presented, based on U.S. time series. In contrast with the United States, there are no time series available for wages of academically trained manpower in the Netherlands. This makes direct estimation of production functions inevitable. As is well-known, direct estimation of production functions may be quite troublesome, especially if more than two factor inputs are distinguished. Due to statistical difficulties, particularly multicollinearity, the estimation results may turn out to be unreliable. This is one of the main reasons why most authors confine themselves to estimating factor price equations, thus relying on the neo-classical postulate of equality between factor prices and marginal productivities. Section III reports on an attempt to estimate an aggregate production function for the Dutch economy. It turns out that this is impossible without the neo-classical postulate of equality between factor prices and marginal productivities. Finally, in section IV, some conclusions are drawn.

II. Estimates of factor price equations using U.S. time series

II.1. *The Tinbergen–Chiswick material*

In *Income Distribution* Tinbergen presents estimates of the shares of capital, university-trained and other labour in U.S. national product.[4] These estimates are based on material from Chiswick's (1972) study on "The Growth of Professional Occupations in the American Labour Force: 1900–1963." He also gives a time series for graduate labour as a percentage of the total labour force.[5] From these time series w_1/w_2 and N_1/N_2 can be calculated, where w_2, w_1 are yearly earnings of graduate and other labour and N_2, N_1 are academically trained and non-academically trained labour.[6] As has been mentioned in the preceding section, Tinbergen assumes the elasticity of substitution to be equal to unity on *a priori* grounds. Under such circumstances a rise in z_2, the share of graduate labour in national income, can only be due to technical progress. To test whether this is justified, the following equations have been estimated:[7]

---

[4] Tinbergen (1975a).
[5] See Tinbergen (1975a).
[6] The percentage of the labour force with university education in the years 1948, 1955, 1958 and 1963 have been obtained by linear interpolation between 1940–1950, 1950–1960 and 1960–1970 respectively.
[7] The terms in parentheses are t-values; R is the coefficient of correlation; DW is the Durbin–Watson statistic.

$$\log\frac{w_1}{w_2} = 0.9679 + 0.0006t + 0.4793 \log\frac{N_2}{N_1} \quad (1)$$
$$\phantom{\log\frac{w_1}{w_2} =\ } (0.5386)\ \ (0.0578)\ \ \ \ (1.0350) \quad\quad R = 0.9327$$
$$\phantom{\log\frac{w_1}{w_2} =\ (0.5386)\ \ (0.0578)\ \ \ \ (1.0350)\quad\quad } DW = 2.33$$

$$\Delta\log\frac{w_1}{w_2} = -0.0108 + 0.7276\,\Delta\log\frac{N_2}{N_1} \quad (2)$$
$$\phantom{\Delta\log\frac{w_1}{w_2} =\ } (-0.4369)\ \ (0.8816) \quad\quad R = 0.3386$$
$$\phantom{\Delta\log\frac{w_1}{w_2} =\ (-0.4369)\ \ (0.8816)\quad\quad } DW = 2.14$$

$$\log\frac{w_1}{w_2} = 1.0719 + 0.5057 \log\frac{N_2}{N_1} \quad (3)$$
$$\phantom{\log\frac{w_1}{w_2} =\ } (4.6741)\ \ (6.8404) \quad\quad R = 0.9327$$
$$\phantom{\log\frac{w_1}{w_2} =\ (4.6741)\ \ (6.8404)\quad\quad } DW = 2.31$$

$$\log\frac{w_1}{w_2} = 0.0065t + 0.2333 \log\frac{N_2}{N_1} \quad (4)$$
$$\phantom{\log\frac{w_1}{w_2} =\ } (4.2965)\ \ (9.5510) \quad\quad R = 0.8515$$
$$\phantom{\log\frac{w_1}{w_2} =\ (4.2965)\ \ (9.5510)\quad\quad } DW = 2.33$$

From these equations the following conclusions can be drawn. Due to a high degree of multicollinearity and a small number (9) of observations, the multiple regression of t and $\log N_2/N_1$ on $\log w_1/w_2$ is not very successful. None of the coefficients in equation (1) differs significantly from zero. The hypothesis of autocorrelation is, however, rejected at the 5% significance level. This also applies to the other specifications. Nor are the results satisfactory for a regression with first differences. From a statistical point of view the estimation results are acceptable only in the case when one of the coefficients in equation (1) is set equal to zero.[8] Consequently, no strong conclusions can be drawn. However, there is some evidence that the elasticity of substitution is not equal to unity. It varies from about 2 in equations (1) and (3) to roughly 4 in equation (4). Moreover, there is reason to expect that technical progress is graduate-labour saving in the sense of Hicks. In these circumstances the rise in the share of graduate labour in national income must be attributed to a high degree of substitutability. Instead of causing this income share to increase, technical progress has depressed it. So, contrary to Tinbergen's conclusion, income inequality is not a result of the race between technology and education. Instead technical progress affects income inequality in the same way as education.

To establish the consequences for the trend in income inequality, extrapolations have been made using equation (4). These calculations are made for the university-trained manpower predictions mentioned by Tinbergen.[9] The extrapolated values of w_2/w_1 and z_2, are presented in table 17.1.[10]

---

[8] Equation (4) is estimated as: $\dfrac{\log(w_1/w_2)}{\log(N_2/N_1)} = 0.2333 + 0.0065 \dfrac{t}{\log(N_2/N_1)}$.

[9] Tinbergen (1975a, table 6. VI).

[10] It has been assumed that the share of capital in national income has remained constant at 0.20 since 1963.

Table 17.1. Income inequality and income shares in the U.S.A. 1970, 1980 and 1990.

Year	Low proportion of university-trained labour		High proportion of university-trained labour	
	z_2	W_2/W_1	z_2	w_2/w_1
1970	0.095	1.03	0.095	1.03
1980	0.11	0.90	0.11	0.89
1990	0.12	0.79	0.13	0.76

Table 17.1 shows a much slower rise in graduate labour earnings, compared with those of other labour, than has been predicted by Tinbergen. The present estimates also lead to the conclusion that the share of graduate labour in national income is rising, but this rise is evidently smaller than that expected by Tinbergen. For 1990, for instance, Tinbergen predicts a graduate labour share in national income of about 0.17. The main cause of the more moderate rise in z_2 is the fact that technical progress, in contrast to Tinbergen's assumption, turns out to be graduate-labour saving. Although this bias in technical progress is accompanied by an elasticity of substitution exceeding unity, the ultimate consequence is a relatively small rise in z_2.

Under these conditions, it is not surprising that the income inequality existing in the sixties disappears very quickly. Later, in the seventies, a new kind of inequality arises when the income of graduate labour falls below that of other labour. In 1990, for instance, the average university-trained income recipient will be earning only 75%–80% of the average income of those not academically-trained. Although Tinbergen's analysis leads qualitatively to the same conclusion, his quantitative prediction of w_2/w_1 is somewhat higher. The difference has to be attributed mainly to his different assumption about the bias in technical progress.

It is not at all certain that the income of university-trained labour will indeed become so much lower than the income of other labour. It depends largely on the assumption that technical progress continues to be graduate-labour saving. If the bias in technical progress is at least partly endogenous in nature, it can be argued that the fall in w_2/w_1 will induce a transition of technical progress from graduate-labour saving to graduate-labour using. In turn, this may reverse the trend in w_2/w_1.

II.2. *The Griliches material*

Griliches (1970) offers a second source for American time series on wages and the number of workers with different levels of education. In this section university-trained manpower has to be defined as labour with more than one year of college education, since Griliches provides data on five and more years of college education only for a small number of years. The other category consists of labour with elementary and high school education. The time series of w_1, w_2, N_1 and N_2 (w_2 and N_2 refer to college trained and w_1 and N_1 to other labour) are presented in appendix 1.

The estimated equations are as follows:[11]

$$\log \frac{w_1}{w_2} = 0.3347 - 0.0142t + 0.4428 \log \frac{N_2}{N_1} \qquad (5)$$

$$(0.7020) \quad (1.6864) \quad (1.9844) \qquad R = 0.7449$$
$$DW = 2.01$$

$$\Delta \log \frac{w_1}{w_2} = -0.0344 + 0.9084 \, \Delta \log \frac{N_2}{N_1} \qquad (6)$$

$$(-2.2087) \quad (2.7181) \qquad R = 0.6339$$
$$DW = 2.58$$

$$\log \frac{w_1}{w_2} = -0.0084t + 0.2851 \log \frac{N_2}{N_1} \qquad (7)$$

$$(-15.2053) \quad (33.9058) \qquad R = 0.9750$$
$$DW = 1.85$$

In most of the equations (5)–(7) the coefficients differ significantly from zero at the 5% level. Only the constant term and the coefficient of t in equation (5) do not. The hypothesis of autocorrelation is again rejected. As in the preceding section, the elasticity of substitution is above unity. It varies between 1.1 in equation (6) and 3.4 in equation (7). In contrast with the preceding section, however, technical progress is college-trained labour using, in the sense of Hicks. This implies that college-trained manpower with less than five years of schooling is responsible for the college-trained using bias in technical progress. Tinbergen's conjecture concerning the bias in technical progress has, therefore, to be applied essentially to this category of labour.

The results show that both substitution and technical progress have a positive influence on college-trained labour's share in national income and hence lead to greater income inequality (a rise in w_2/w_1). Only a rising proportion of college-trained manpower can offset this tendency. As can be seen in table 17.2, the final result of these opposing forces is a slight reduction in the ratio of earnings for college-trained and other labour. In the 1960's however, this ratio shows a tendency to rise rather than fall. This contrasts clearly with the preceding section in which the ratio of graduate earnings to that of other labour showed a continual reduction. So, it is essentially the graduate-labour group whose income position has been weakened. The position of college-trained manpower is much stronger. Finally, table 17.2 shows that the fall in the ratio of factor prices is much less pronounced than the rise in the ratio of college-trained to other labour.

III. A time series analysis of income distribution in the Netherlands

In contrast to the United States, a time series for the earnings ratio between graduate and other labour is not available for the Netherlands. Tinbergen (1975a, 1975c) constructs such a series using an estimated time series equation for the

---

[11] Equation (7) has been estimated as: $\dfrac{\log(w_1/w_2)}{\log(N_2/N_1)} = 0.2851 - 0.0084 \dfrac{t}{\log(N_2/N_1)}$.

Table 17.2. Time series for the ratios of prices and quantities of college-trained to other labour in the U.S.A.

Year	w_2/w_1	N_1/N_2
1939	1.862	8.297
1940	1.849	9.018
1948	1.760	6.246
1949	1.760	5.896
1952	1.776	5.018
1956	1.770	4.612
1957	1.827	4.519
1958	1.878	4.288
1959	1.690	3.907
1962	1.699	3.367
1963	1.690	3.329
1965	1.728	3.255
1966	1.737	3.090
1967	1.744	2.937

U.S.A. and an estimated cross-section equation for some industrialised countries, relating the share of graduate labour in national income to per capita income. This is, however, a very rough approximation. There is, therefore, good reason to approach the distribution of income in another way, by directly estimating an aggregate production function for the Netherlands. As a time series of university-trained labour can be calculated[12] and time series of gross national product, other labour and the stock of capital are available, this approach is possible.[13]

The starting point of the analysis was a C.E.S.-production function,

$$X_t = \{a_{1,t}N_{1,t}^{-\rho} + a_{2,t}N_{2,t}^{-\rho} + a_{3,t}K_t^{-\rho}\}^{-1/\rho}, \qquad a_{1,t}, a_{2,t}, a_{3,t} > 0, \tag{8}$$

in which:

X_t : gross national product in millions of 1963 guilders;
K_t : the stock of capital in millions of 1963 guilders;
$N_{2,t}$: graduate labour in thousands of man-years;
$N_{1,t}$: other labour in thousands of man-years.

Different specifications of technical progress were estimated. Successive least squares estimations were performed for different values of $\sigma = 1/(1 + \rho)$ in the range $0.1 < \sigma < 10.0$, with steps of 0.2. However, the results were rather disappointing. Only those specifications in which a single parameter was variable through time were acceptable from a statistical point of view and satisfied the non-negativity restrictions on $a_{1,t}$, $a_{2,t}$ and $a_{3,t}$. But these specifications did not yield factor elasticities of production which corresponded with the factor shares. In particular the graduate labour elasticity turned out to be far too high (about

---

[12] For a description of the way in which this series is calculated, see appendix 2. In this appendix the other time series, as well as their sources, are presented.

[13] Instead of estimating a production equation for the whole economy, estimates for the private sector alone are preferable. However, as it is not known what proportion of graduate labour is employed in the private sector, this was not possible.

0.30) compared with Tinbergen's (1975a) estimated share of graduate labour income of 0.064 for 1962.

Direct least squares estimates of the Cobb-Douglas production function,

$$X_t = A_0 e^{\alpha t} N_{1,t}^{a_{1,t}} N_{2,t}^{a_{2,t}} K_t^{1-a_{1,t}-a_{2,t}}, \qquad (9)$$
$$0 < a_{1,t}, a_{2,t} < 1, \qquad a_{1,t} + a_{2,t} < 1,$$

produced the same results. Either the estimates failed to satisfy the parameter restrictions or the estimated factor elasticities differed substantially from the corresponding factor shares.[14]

For this reason restrictions were imposed on the parameters. As a starting point, it was assumed that the share of graduate labour in national income was equal to 0.064 (Tinbergen's figure) in 1962. Under this restriction the C.E.S. production function was re-estimated in the way described above. Only two specifications turned out to be statistically acceptable and fulfilled the non-negativity restrictions: one in which technical progress is solely capital augmenting and the other in which it is solely other-labour augmenting. In tables 17.3 and 17.4, estimates are given for the values of ρ when the non-negativity restrictions are satisfied.

Table 17.3. Estimates for $X_t = \{a_1 N_{1,t}^{-\rho} + \hat{a}_2 N_{2,t}^{-\rho} + (a_{31} + a_{32}t)K_t^{-\rho}\}^{-1/\rho}$.[15]

σ	ρ	a_1	a_{31}	a_{32}	R
0.300	2.333	0.001 (3.143)	21.209 (28.496)	−0.72059 (−4.853)	0.981
0.500	1.000	0.036 (4.165)	2.756 (13.083)	−0.062 (−5.121)	0.989
0.700	0.429	0.177 (4.764)	0.959 (6.463)	−0.015 (−5.409)	0.992
0.900	0.111	0.458 (5.129)	0.429 (3.348)	−0.003 (−5.609)	0.993

At first sight no discrimination between the different estimates seems to be possible. All correlation coefficients are high, and all estimates of the coefficients differ significantly from zero at the 1% level. So another criterion for discrimination is necessary. This is found in the degree to which distributive shares can be explained. From tables 17.3 and 17.4, it can be easily verified that, when elasticities of substitution are very low or very high, the capital elasticity of production significantly exceeds the capital share in national income as presented in appendix 2; whereas, if the elasticity of substitution approaches unity, either from above or below, the capital elasticity tends to the average value of the share of capital in national income (0.30). Thus there is evidence that the elasticity of substitution does not differ significantly from unity.

To investigate the sensitivity of this result to the value chosen for graduate labour's share in national income (z_2), the estimation was repeated for different

---

[14] The estimated graduate labour elasticity of production was again in the neighbourhood of 0.30.
[15] $\hat{a}_2 = 0.064/793^\rho$.

Table 17.4. Estimates for $X_t = \{(a_{11} + a_{12}t)N_{1,t}^{-\rho} + \hat{a}_2 N_{2,t}^{-\rho} + a_3 K_t^{-\rho}\}^{-1/\rho}$.[16]

σ	ρ	a_{11}	a_{21}	a_3	R
1.1	−0.091	0.694 (5.104)	0.003 (5.567)	0.312 (3.085)	0.994
1.3	−0.231	0.776 (4.897)	0.008 (5.426)	0.319 (4.246)	0.994
1.5	−0.333	0.844 (4.753)	0.014 (5.335)	0.311 (5.114)	0.994
1.7	−0.412	0.901 (4.645)	0.019 (5.272)	0.299 (5.787)	0.994
1.9	−0.474	0.949 (4.561)	0.024 (5.226)	0.288 (6.324)	0.994
2.1	−0.524	0.989 (4.492)	0.029 (5.190)	0.279 (6.761)	0.994
3.1	−0.677	1.222 (4.272)	0.049 (5.085)	0.247 (8.114)	0.994
4.1	−0.756	1.195 (4.152)	0.063 (5.035)	0.230 (8.812)	0.995
5.1	−0.804	1.240 (4.075)	0.072 (5.004)	0.220 (9.236)	0.995

values of z_2 in 1962 in the range $0.035 \leq z_2 \leq 0.095$, with steps of 0.005. Estimates of both equations turned out to be very insensitive to z_2. In addition, the property that the capital elasticity approaches the capital share when the elasticity of substitution approaches unity remains intact. One may conclude that this property does not depend on the value of z_2 chosen.

Two conclusions can now be drawn. First, there is evidence that the elasticity of substitution does not differ significantly from unity. Secondly, there is no reason to suppose that technical progress is either graduate-labour using or saving. Both conclusions together imply a constant share of graduate labour in national income.

The first conclusion suggests using a Cobb–Douglas production function. Different restricted least squares estimates of this function have been performed. Different specifications of the way in which technical progress enters into the equation have been tested under the restriction that $a_{2,t}$ is equal to 0.064 in 1962. Only the following specification satisfies the inequality restrictions and the statistical qualifications:

$$\log \frac{X_t}{N_{1,t}} = 1.27951 + 0.02521t + 0.064 \log \frac{N_{2,t}}{N_{1,t}} \quad (10)$$
$$\phantom{\log \frac{X_t}{N_{1,t}} = 1.27951} (3.19172) \ (5.67397)$$

$$+ 0.28906 \log \frac{K_t}{N_{1,t}}, \quad R = 0.99365,$$
$$ (2.34527) \phantom{\log \frac{K_t}{N_{1,t}},} \ DW = 1.22.$$

---

[16] $\hat{a}_2 = 0.064/793^\rho$.

Hence, technical progress is neutral and the capital elasticity of production is approximately 0.30. In order to test once again the neutrality of technical progress with respect to graduate labour, a Cobb–Douglas function has been estimated, in which the capital elasticity of production has been set equal to the capital share in national product (0.30). The result was:

$$\log\frac{X_t}{N_{1,t}} = \underset{(8.53945)}{1.23104} + \underset{(2.39538)}{0.02578t} + (0.064 + \underset{(0.08959)}{0.00023}(t-13))\log\frac{N_{2,t}}{N_{1,t}}$$

$$+ 0.30\log\frac{K_t}{N_{1,t}}, \quad R = 0.98705, \quad DW = 1.22. \tag{11}$$

Equation (11) shows that the hypothesis of neutral technical progress with respect to graduate labour cannot be rejected.[17]

If specification (10) is accepted as a description of the Dutch production structure, it can be used to establish the share of graduate labour in national income. That value will be chosen which equates the estimated value of the capital elasticity with the average value of the capital share in national product. To calculate this value, successive estimates have been performed for values of $a_2 = z_2$ in the range $0.035 \leq a_2 \leq 0.100$.[18] The results are shown in table 17.5.

Table 17.5 shows that the capital elasticity of production equals the capital share when $a_2 = 0.050$. Thus, university-trained labour has received 5% of gross national product in the postwar period. As this figure corresponds to about 5.5% of net national product, this estimate is somewhat lower than Tinbergen's 1962 estimate (6.4%).

The estimate corresponding to specification (11) is[19]

$$\log\frac{X_t}{N_{1,t}} = \underset{(7.9191)}{1.1529} + \underset{(2.5000)}{0.0272t} + (0.050 + \underset{(0.1757)}{0.0005}(t-13))\log\frac{N_{2,t}}{N_{1,t}}$$

$$+ 0.3000\log\frac{K_t}{N_{1,t}}, \quad R = 0.9873, \quad DW = 1.20, \tag{12}$$

so there is still no reason to reject the hypothesis of neutral technical progress.

The following conclusions can now be drawn. There is no reason to suppose that technical progress has been non-neutral with respect to graduate labour in the postwar period in the Netherlands. Neither is there evidence to suggest that the elasticity of substitution differed significantly from unity during this period.

---

[17] In equations (10) and (11) the Durbin–Watson test on autocorrelation is inconclusive at a 5% level of significance.

[18] Due to a high degree of multicollinearity a direct-estimate of

$$\log X_t = \log A_0 + \alpha t + (1 - a_2 - 0.30)\log N_{1,t} + a_2 \log N_{2,t} + 0.30 \log K_t$$

did not give acceptable results. Once again estimate of a_2 was too high.

[19] From equation (12) it follows that the hypothesis of autocorrelation cannot be rejected at a 5% level of significance; at a 1% level the test is, however, inconclusive. The same applies to the results in table 17.5 when $a_2 = 0.050$ ($DW = 1.19$).

Table 17.5. Successive estimates of Cobb–Douglas production functions for values of a_2 in the range $0.035 \leq a_2 \leq 0.10$.

a_2	$\log A_0$	α	$1 - a_1 - a_2$	R
0.035	1.065 (2.598)	0.0253 (5.5620)	0.3130 (2.4862)	0.9937
0.040	1.1019 (2.6988)	0.0253 (5.5818)	0.3091 (2.4627)	0.9937
0.045	1.1389 (2.8004)	0.0252 (5.6015)	0.3050 (2.4389)	0.9937
0.050	1.1759 (2.9026)	0.0252 (5.6209)	0.3008 (2.4148)	0.9937
0.055	1.2129 (3.0053)	0.0252 (5.6401)	0.2966 (2.3903)	0.9937
0.060	1.2499 (3.1087)	0.0252 (5.6590)	0.2924 (2.3654)	0.9937
0.065	1.2869 (3.2125)	0.0252 (5.6777)	0.2882 (2.3402)	0.9937
0.070	1.3239 (3.3170)	0.0252 (5.6961)	0.2840 (2.3146)	0.9936
0.075	1.3609 (3.4219)	0.0252 (5.7142)	0.2799 (2.2887)	0.9936
0.080	1.3979 (3.5273)	0.0252 (5.7320)	0.2757 (2.2624)	0.9936
0.085	1.4349 (3.6332)	0.0252 (5.7495)	0.2715 (2.2358)	0.9936
0.090	1.4719 (3.7396)	0.0252 (5.7667)	0.2673 (2.2088)	0.9936
0.095	1.5090 (3.8463)	0.0251 (5.7836)	0.2631 (2.1815)	0.9936
0.100	1.5460 (3.9535)	0.0251 (5.8001)	0.2589 (2.1538)	0.9936

Consequently the distribution of labour income between graduate and other labour must be considered remarkably stable.

The second conclusion clearly contradicts most factor-price studies, which almost always give elasticity of substitution estimates that exceed unity.[20] It also conflicts with the conclusions in section II of this paper. It supports, however, Tinbergen's conjecture concerning the value of the elasticity of substitution. On the other hand, the first conclusion conflicts with his assumption of graduate-labour using technical progress.[21]

The consequences for the trend in income inequality can be read from table 17.6. To determine the implications of the fact that technical progress is no longer neutral, w_2/w_1 and z_2 are presented both under the assumption that z_2 is constant and that $z_2 = 0.050 + 0.0005 \, (t - 13)$. Calculations for the years outside the

---

[20] See, for instance, Berndt and Christensen (1974), Bowles (1969, 1970), Dougherty (1972a, 1972b), Dresch (1975), Groenveld and Kuipers (1976), Kuipers (1976) and Psacharopoulos (1973).

[21] Tinbergen (1975a, ch. 6).

period 1950–1974 are based on Passenier's (1972) estimates for the number of graduate workers. As the production model has been estimated for the period 1950–1974, the values of w_2/w_1 and z_2 in 1900 and 1930 should also be considered as predictions.

Table 17.6. Trends in income inequality and the share of graduate labour in national income.

Year	$z_2 = 0.050$		$z_2 = 0.050 + 0.0005(t - 13)$	
	z_2	w_2/w_1	z_2	w_2/w_1
1900	0.050	14.0	0.019	5.1
1930	0.050	12.6	0.034	8.3
1950	0.050	8.0	0.044	7.0
1960	0.050	5.7	0.049	5.6
1970	0.050	4.2	0.054	4.6
1980	0.050	2.2	0.059	2.7
1990	0.050	1.5	0.064	1.9

Table 17.6 shows a steady reduction in income inequality. As expected, the fall in inequality is much more pronounced when technical progress is neutral than when it is graduate labour using. Furthermore, in the latter case, the race between technology and education has been won by education, to use Tinbergen's terminology. The only exception is the period 1900–1930 in which, due to a very small rise in university-trained manpower, technical progress dominates education and results in an increase in income inequality.

The figures for 1970 and 1980 correspond rather well to actual observations of gross wages for university-trained and other labour in the early Seventies. For the Netherlands the earnings ratio of university-trained labour to total labour employed in industry and services is about 2.[22] This group of university-trained labour excludes the free professions. Bearing in mind that these professions are at the top of the earnings distribution for graduate labour, the estimate of $w_2/w_1 \simeq 3$ seems perfectly reasonable.

To compare the above measure of income inequality (w_2/w_1) with that used by Tinbergen $(w_2/(X/N))$, the values of w_2/w_1 have to be multiplied by roughly 0.7. It then appears that there are only slight deviations from his estimates.[23] With regard to the differences, particular attention may be paid to the somewhat smaller income inequality predicted in this study for 1980 and 1990. These do not, however, affect Tinbergen's main conclusion, that a huge rise in university-trained labour had led to a substantial fall in income inequality between graduate and other labour. On the contrary, according to the results obtained in this study, income inequality will fall even faster than his predictions suggest.

[22] Central Bureau of Statistics of the Netherlands, *Statistisch zakboek* (Statistical Pocketbook), 1976.
[23] See Tinbergen (1975a, table 6. VII).

IV. Concluding remarks

If a successful study is defined as one which leads to an unambiguous answer to the question posed, this study does not fulfill that requirement. The evidence presented in the preceding sections is much too diverse for that. All previous studies give a different answer to questions concerning the influence of substitution and technical progress on income distribution. In particular, essential differences are found between estimates derived from factor price equations and those derived directly from production functions. In the former the elasticity of substitution turns out to be significantly different from one; whereas in the latter this does not appear to be the case. Moreover, the two factor-price estimations lead to two different conclusions regarding the bias in technical progress. According to one study there is evidence that technical progress is graduate labour-saving; according to the other it is probably college-trained labour using. Finally, neutrality of technical progress cannot be rejected on the basis of the direct production function estimates.

As has already been mentioned in sub-section II.2., the conflicting results on the bias in technical progress emerging from factor price equations may indicate a fundamental difference between college-trained and graduate labour, in the sense that it is mainly demand for the former category which has been induced by changes in technology in recent decades. Casual observation of the fast rate of growth of demand for computer operators and programmers, for example, does not contradict this conjecture. Differences in the results of factor-price and direct production function estimates are, however, more difficult to explain. There are various possibilities. First, due to problems such as multicollinearity, the direct estimates are unreliable. Secondly, there are too many measurement errors in the data used to estimate the factor price equations. Thirdly, the neo-classical assumption of equality between factor prices and marginal productivities is too strong. If, for instance, the rigidity in the wage structure does not correspond to the rigidity in the marginal rates of substitution, factor price estimates clearly exaggerate the elasticity of substitution. If this is indeed the case, marginal productivity theory alone can no longer explain income distribution. Other explanatory variables, such as the power structure and the degree of monopoly come into play. However, whether this is the case cannot be judged at this moment. Finally, the structure of the American and Dutch economies differ. There is evidence that the degree of substitutability in different countries is not the same.[24] In particular, substitutability in less-developed countries seems to be much lower than in advanced countries. Thus, differences in substitutability may also reflect differences in the stage of development of the two countries.

Diverse answers are not only characteristics of the present study. This diversity also characterises the main literature on this topic.[25] This inability to give definite answers is mainly attributable to the lack of reliable data. Because of this, too many assumptions have to be made which cannot themselves be tested. This gives

---

[24] See Groenveld and Kuipers (1976).
[25] See, for instance, Tinbergen (1975a) and Tinbergen (1975e).

ample opportunity for rival hypotheses to coexist. For a better insight into the determinants of income distribution, data on earnings and the numbers of people with different characteristics, for example with regard to schooling and occupation, must be considered indispensable.

Appendix 1

Table A.1. Time series of earnings and the proportion of college-trained and other labour in the American civilian work force.

Year	N_1	N_2	w_1	w_2
1939	89.4	10.7	1214	2260
1940	89.0	11.1	1385	2561
1948	86.2	13.8	2826	4974
1949	85.5	14.5	3001	5283
1952	83.3	16.6	3497	6212
1956	82.1	17.8	1226	7479
1957	81.8	18.1	4281	7823
1958	81.8	18.9	4344	8157
1959	79.7	20.4	5151	8706
1962	77.1	22.9	5218	8867
1963	76.9	23.1	5264	8897
1965	76.5	23.5	5899	10191
1966	75.6	24.5	6212	10792
1967	74.6	25.4	6531	11389

Sources: N_1 and N_2 are the proportions of elementary and high school labour, and college-trained manpower, in the total American civilian male work force aged between 18 and 64. From 1959 the figures refer to those employed. These time series are derived from Griliches (1970, table 1), by adding the proportions of those with various completed years in elementary and high school, on the one hand, and in college, on the other. The figures for 1939, 1949, 1956, 1958, 1963 and 1966 are derived by extra- or interpolation of the original series. For 1952 and 1956 the classification 5–7 and 8 years of schooling is chosen, whereas the 1949 figures are based on the classification, 5–6 and 7–8 years of schooling.

w_1 and w_2 are the annual mean earnings in dollars (total income in 1949, 1958, 1963 and 1966) of American males, aged twenty-five or over. These series are derived from Griliches (1970, table 2) by taking weighted averages of earnings corresponding to the different years of education, using the proportions in table 1 as weights. The figures for 1940, 1948, 1952, 1957, 1962, 1965 and 1967 are obtained by inter- or extrapolation of the original series.

Appendix 2

Table A.2. Time series of gross national product, capital stock, university-trained and non-university-trained labour and the share of capital in national income.

Year	X_t	K_t	$N_{2,t}$	$N_{1,t}$	q_t
1950	27279	106408	36	3737	0.329
1951	27020	109644	38	3750	0.338
1952	28067	112491	40	3732	0.348
1953	30393	115769	42	3798	0.357
1954	32152	119934	44	3900	0.354
1955	34996	124783	46	3970	0.366
1956	37309	130483	49	4030	0.351
1957	38080	136768	51	4050	0.341
1958	38026	142503	52	4010	0.332
1959	39945	147938	54	4050	0.349
1960	42951	154383	56	4126	0.349
1961	44356	161223	57	4187	0.333
1962	45975	168543	58	4270	0.320
1963	47484	175893	60	4328	0.299
1964	51265	184247	61	4403	0.295
1965	54076	193896	63	4438	0.286
1966	55579	204235	66	4470	0.261
1967	58617	215502	70	4452	0.268
1968	62844	227976	74	4490	0.269
1969	66200	240802	79	4562	0.265
1970	70361	254033	84	4612	0.248
1971	72538	268181	88	4640	0.235
1972	75988	281910	93	4597	0.243
1973	80952	295461	99	4571	0.247
1974	80967	308735	106	4627	0.223

Sources: X_t is gross national product at factor cost in millions of 1963 guilders. The nominal figures and the deflator are taken from *Statistical Yearbook of the Netherlands* and *National Accounts of the Netherlands* (various years).

K_t is the capital stock in millions of 1963 guilders. It is calculated by means of the formula

$$K_t = K_{t-1} + I_t,$$

where I_t is net investment in millions of 1963 guilders. Net investment figures at 1963 prices are taken from *Statistical Yearbook of the Netherlands* and *National Accounts of the Netherlands* (various years). The starting point is the capital stock in 1952 (in 1952 guilders) as given in Korn and Van der Weide (1960). Using a time series of investment good prices from *Statistical Yearbook of the Netherlands* and *National Accounts of the Netherlands* (various years), the capital stock has been adjusted to 1963 guilders. As the capital stock figures thus calculated are end of year figures, two year averages have been computed to get figures for the middle of the year. $N_{2,t}$ is the number of university graduates employed, in thousands. For 1947, 1960 and 1965 these figures are taken from the *Memorandum of the Commission for Statistical Research* of the Academic Council of the Netherlands (1968), whereas the figure for 1970 is taken from Passenier (1972). The number of graduates has been calculated in the following way. The number of university graduates in year t is equal to the number in year $t-1$ *plus* the number of students who finished their studies and found a job *minus* the number of university graduates that died or retired with a pension. The starting points are the numbers of university graduates in 1947, 1960, 1965 and 1970. The number of graduate students that finished their studies in a certain year can be derived from *Seventy Years of Statistics in Time Series* (1970), and from *Statistical Pocketbook* (various years). According to the 13*th Census of* 31*st May* 1960, 90 per cent of students who finished their studies obtained a job. To calculate the number of university graduates that leave the labour force, one has to know first the number of people that retire. Here it has been assumed that all university graduates retire at the age of 65. The number of people that retire can be calculated if the total number and age structure in a certain year are known. The age structure of employed university graduates can be derived from the 13*th Census of* 31*st May* 1960 (1966). This can then be used to calculate the number of university graduates that die in a certain year. In addition one needs death rates for the different age groups. These are given in *Seventy Years of Statistics in Time Series* (1970). Deviations between the predicted numbers of university graduates in 1960, 1965 and 1970 and the published numbers in these years have been redistributed proportionally over the previous years.

$N_{1,t}$ is the number of non university-trained labour in thousands. It is calculated as total employment *minus* employed university graduates. Total employment is given in *Working Population and Registered Unemployment*, 1950–1966 (1967) and *Central Economic Plan* (1975).

q_t is the share of capital in gross national product at factor cost. It has been calculated according to the formula

$$1 - \frac{\text{income of wage earners} + \text{wage income of self-employed}}{\text{gross national product at factor cost}}$$

Time series for the number of wage earners and self-employed are obtained from *Statistical Yearbook of the Netherlands* (various years), *Working Population and Registered Unemployment*, 1950–1966 (1966), and *Central Economic Plan* (1975).

Wage income of the self-employed has been calculated under the assumption that the wage rate of the self-employed equals that of wage earners. Total wage income of wage earners is given in *Statistical Yearbook of the Netherlands* (various years) and *Central Economic Plan* (1975).

References

Berndt, E.R. and L.R. Christensen, "Testing for the Existence of a Consistent Aggregate Index of Labor Inputs", *American Economic Review*, LXIV (1974).
Bowles, S., *Planning Educational Systems for Economic Growth*, Cambridge, Mass., 1969.
Bowles, S., "Aggregation of Labor Inputs in the Economics of Growth and Planning", *Journal of Political Economy*, LIIVIII (1970).
Central Bureau of Statistics of the Netherlands, *Jaarcijfers voor Nederland* (Statistical Yearbook of the Netherlands), 1959/1960, 1961/1962, 1965/1966, 1967/1968, The Hague, 1962, 1964, 1968, 1970.
Central Bureau of Statistics of the Netherlands, *Nationale rekeningen* (National Accounts), The Hague, 1975.

Central Bureau of Statistics of the Netherlands, *Statistisch zakboek* (Statistical Pocketbook), various years, The Hague.

Central Bureau of Statistics of the Netherlands, *12e Algemene Volkstelling – 31 mei 1947*, (12th Census of 31st May 1947), The Hague, 1949–1954.

Central Bureau of Statistics of the Netherlands, *13e Algemene Volkstelling – 31 mei 1960* (13th Census of 31st May 1960), The Hague, 1966.

Central Bureau of Statistics of the Netherlands, *Arbeidsvolume en geregistreerde arbeidsreserve, 1950–1966* (Working Population and Registered Unemployment 1950–1966), The Hague, 1967.

Central Bureau of Statistics of the Netherlands, *Zeventig Jaren statistiek in tijdreeksen* (Seventy Years of Statistics in Time Series), The Hague, 1970.

Central Planning Bureau of the Netherlands, *Centraal Economisch Plan 1975* (Central Economic Plan 1975), The Hague, 1975.

Chiswick, C.U., "The Growth of Professional Occupations in the American Labour Force: 1900–1963", World Bank paper based on Columbia University dissertation, Washington D.C. 1972. A revised version is published in *Research in Human Capital and Development*, Volume I, 1977.

Commissie voor Statistisch Onderzoek van de Academische Raad (Commission for Statistical Research of the Academic Council of the Netherlands), *Aantallen Academici to 1980, aanbod en behoefte*, (The Number of University Graduates in 1980, Supply and Demand), publication no. 10, The Hague, 1968.

Dougherty, C.S.R., "Estimates of Labor Aggregation Functions", *Journal of Political Economy*, LXXX (1972a).

Dougherty, C.R.S., "Substitution and the Structure of the Labour Force", *Economic Journal*, LXXXII (1972b).

Dresch, S.P., "Demography, Technology and Higher Education: Towards a Formal Model of Educational Adaptation", *Journal of Political Economy*, LXXXIII (1975).

Fallon, P.R. and P.R.G. Layard, "Capital-Skill Complementarity, Income Distribution and Output Accounting", Mimeographed Paper, Higher Education Research Unit, London School of Economics and Political Science, London, 1974.

Griliches, Z., "Notes on the Role of Education in Production Functions and Growth Accounting", in *Education, Income and Human Capital*, W.L. Hansen (ed.), New York and London, 1970.

Groenveld, K. and S.K. Kuipers, "Some Further Evidence on the Substitution Possibilities between Graduate and Other Labour", *Kyklos*, XXIX (1976).

Korn, B. and Th. D. van der Weide, "Het nationale vermogen van Nederland, 1948–1958", *Statistische en economische onderzoekingen*, Central Bureau of Statistics of the Netherlands, Zeist, 1960.

Kuipers, S.K., "Personal Income Distribution and Production Structure", *Economie Appliquée*, XXIX (1976).

Passenier, J., "Een arbeidsmarkt vol academici", *Intermediair*, VIII (27th October 1972).

Psacharopoulos, G., "Substitution Assumptions versus Empirical Evidence in Manpower Planning", *The Economist*, CXXI (1973).

Tinbergen, J., "Substitution of Graduate by Other Labour", *Kyklos*, XXVII (1974).

Tinbergen, J., *Income Distribution, Analysis and Policies*, Amsterdam, 1975a.

Tinbergen, J., "Substitution of Academically Trained by Other Manpower", *Weltwirtschaftliches Archiv*, CXI (1975b).

Tinbergen, J., "Een raming van de Nederlandse inkomensverdeling omstreeks 1990", *Liber Amicorum Prof. Dr. Gaston Eyskens*, Leuven, 1975c.

Tinbergen, J., "A Demand-Supply Theory of Incomes Tested by 1970 Census Figures", *Review of Income and Wealth*, XXI (1975d).

Tinbergen, J., *Income Differences: Recent Research*, Amsterdam, 1975e.

17 DISCUSSION

PAPER BY K. GROENVELD AND S.K. KUIPERS

Professor Chiswick first commented on the estimation of the elasticity of substitution σ using a CES production function. Taking equation (8) as the point of departure, the relative wage equation is

$$\frac{w_{2t}}{w_{1t}} = \frac{a_{2t}}{a_{1t}}\left[\frac{N_{2t}}{N_{1t}}\right]^{-(1+\rho)}, \quad \text{with } \sigma = \frac{1}{\rho+1}. \tag{1}$$

The paper assumes that technological development influences the efficiency of labour. If factors of production are measured in efficiency units and factor prices determined accordingly, then it can be shown that

$$\frac{a_{2t}}{a_{1t}} = \alpha\left[\frac{h_{2t}}{h_{1t}}\right]^{-\rho}, \tag{2}$$

where h_{1t}, h_{2t} denote the average efficiency levels (units per worker) of the two groups and α is a technical constant. Technological change affects the value of h_{2t}/h_{1t} and education raises the ratio N_{2t}/N_{1t}. The net effect of these two changes on relative earnings may be obtained by substituting (2) into (1):

$$\ln\left[\frac{w_{1t}}{w_{2t}}\right] = -\ln\alpha + \frac{1-\sigma}{\sigma}\ln\left[\frac{h_{2t}}{h_{1t}}\right] + \frac{1}{\sigma}\ln\left[\frac{N_{2t}}{N_{1t}}\right]. \tag{3}$$

When the elasticity of substitution σ exceeds unity, the last two terms in this equation have opposite signs; their net effect on relative earnings is the outcome of a "race" between technology and education. If the elasticity of substitution equals 1, the labour quality term vanishes and "technology" cannot affect wages; $\sigma = 1$ is thus incompatible with shifts in the composition of demand for labour generated by labour-embodied technical change. The case when $\sigma < 1$ is counter-intuitive since the coefficient of the quality variable would then be positive and improvements in the quality of high-level labour, *ceteris paribus*, would lead to a decline in their relative earnings.

She therefore raised the possibility that the time-series evidence reveals not a unit-elasticity relative demand curve shifting upwards over time, as suggested in the first part of the paper, but rather a high-elasticity curve which is, if anything, shifting downward over time. For the data examined in section III, she suggested that the lack of success in the empirical estimation may be due to the fact that the relative skills of the two groups of workers have not been specified explicitly.

Technological change affecting h_{2t}/h_{1t} may not be captured by the time-trend variable used in the estimates. (For the United States it is unlikely that technological change worked in this way.) If a better proxy were used for relative quality, a higher estimate of σ might perhaps have been found, with a corresponding improvement in the results.

Several problems arise from the use of the Griliches data which covers only a short time period. Since these data contain only six independent observations, there may be insufficient degrees of freedom for reliable significance tests. It is also possible that short-run fluctuations away from the long-run demand during this period may have led to the low estimates for the elasticity of substitution. She appreciated the desire to use time-series evidence when good cross-section data were not available, but suggested that techniques other than regression analysis may be more appropriate for such cases.

Finally, she was interested in the notion that different results applied to university graduates with degrees and those that had merely some college training. She was not, however convinced that this followed from the analysis, and suggested that further evidence would be needed to support this conclusion.

Mr. Bartels pointed out that the authors use equation (4) to conclude that technical progress is labour saving but equation (3) provides a better fit and does not support the same conclusion. Referring to the experiments with different Cobb–Douglas and CES functions, he suggested that the selection process might be easier if Box–Cox transformations were applied to all variables in the regression. This is the approach followed by Zarembka and allows explicit statistical tests both on the value of the substitution elasticity and the functional form of the production function.

Dr. Thomas said that no attention had been paid to the influence of the power structure on the value of σ. His own study of Yugoslavian data suggested that this caused the value of σ to be rather high. He had also found that time-series estimates of the elasticity of substitution tended to be substantially lower than those derived from cross-section data. The problem of identification had not been raised in the paper but this may cause difficulties since the determinants on the supply side had been completely excluded. Finally he questioned the interpretation given to the high elasticity of substitution and suggested that the issue of queueing had to be taken into account, particularly when there was high unemployment among highly skilled people.

Mr. Layard said that many people had found highly skilled labour and capital to be complementary. His own work, using a nested CES function and cross-section data, confirmed this complementarity. He had also found an elasticity of substitution between low and high skilled labour less than one. This was consistent with his own feeling that at least part of the fall in the relative wages of graduates was attributable to a decline in the growth of investment.

Professor Somermeyer thought that several problems needed solving before reliable estimates of the elasticity of substitution were possible. The analysis assumes N_1 and N_2 to be completely predetermined and did not therefore deal satisfactorily with the supply side. Secondly, the choice of just two labour categories implies too high a level of aggregation. With further disaggregation, higher elasticities of substitution are expected *a priori* since some of the categories are then more alike than in the present case.

Professor Stiglitz suggested that the estimates for the elasticity of substitution may be too low rather than too high. This followed from the assumption that the ratio of the qualities of labour in the two categories had been taken to be independent of the relative frequencies in the two groups. As the proportion in the more highly trained group increases, we would expect the average quality of this group to fall. Now suppose there is an infinite elasticity of substitution between the two groups, so relative wages remain constant. If the distribution of abilities is uniform, the regression proposed in the paper would give an estimate of the elasticity of substitution of unity, even though the true value is infinite. This he believed to be a general phenomenon, so the elasticity of substitution is always likely to be underestimated.

On the question of identification, he doubted whether the separate influences of factor-augmenting technical progress and the elasticity of substitution on the income distribution could be distinguished at all with the present data. At the very least, any attempt required strong additional assumptions.

Professor Bentzel could think of no reason why technological change would follow a systematic trend as represented by the time dummy. Analysis of time series data also required special attention to be paid to cyclical and trend influences, which were absent in the paper.

Professor Lévy-Garboua was concerned with the high level of aggregation, which meant the categories of labour were very heterogeneous. Furthermore, minimum wage legislation would tend to increase wages in the unskilled group relative to skilled workers. If there is regulation of minimum wages, he recommended considering only those above the minimum wage level when determining relative earnings, in order that this institutional factor is eliminated.

Professor Krelle said that the equations estimated in the first part of the paper take the supply of labour as given and assume that wage rates make the appropriate adjustments to equalise supply and demand. He suspected that in European countries the process operates quite differently. Wage rates are set somewhat independently of supply and demand, and are then given to employers who subsequently choose employment levels on the basis of the wages set. The valid regression procedure is therefore to express employment as a function of wage rates.

Professor Taubman commented on a point made by Professor Stiglitz. He had once studied the relative IQs of those entering college in the United States and of those who did not go to college. Contrary to expectations, the average IQ of those entering college had increased continually over the period 1920 to 1960, with the IQ of those not going to college showing a corresponding decline. The explanation of this phenomenon was that in the 1930s, for instance, very few people with high IQs managed to go to college. He also believed that the identification problem raised by Professor Stiglitz could be overcome if technical change occurs smoothly.

Dr. Kuipers said the problem raised by Professor Chiswick regarding a value of σ less than or equal to one, only arises if technical progress enters the production function solely via changes in the quality indices of the different categories of labour and, in addition, the levels of schooling influence output in the same way as factor inputs in natural units. The latter does not occur if the relation between a_{2t}/a_{1t} and h_{2t}/h_{1t} is assumed to be

$$\frac{a_{2t}}{a_{1t}} = \alpha \left[\frac{h_{2t}}{h_{1t}}\right]^{\beta},$$

where the parameter β is independent of σ. With regard to the other necessary condition, he thought it likely that at least part of technical change is not brought about by changes in h_1 and h_2, but by changes in α. For this reason, and also because reliable time series of efficiency levels are hard to construct, it is assumed that technical change can be represented by a simple trend in a_1 and a_2.

He questioned whether it was inconceivable that a change in h_{2t}/h_{1t} leads to an opposite change in w_{2t}/w_{1t}. The influence of h_{2t}/h_{1t} on w_{2t}/w_{1t} consists of two parts: a negative substitution effect and a positive "productivity" effect. With low substitutability, the overall effect may be negative, so the results of the time series analysis, with low elasticities of substitution, are quite reasonable. Although the data available were far from ideal, he felt that time series enabled the results to be more easily interpreted than was the case with cross-section data. On the other hand, he agreed with Dr. Thomas that a cross-section analysis may lead to better *long run* estimates than using time series, since short run fluctuations also influence the time series results, and the elasticity of substitution may therefore be underestimated.

Replying to Mr. Bartels, he said that the preference for relationship (4) over (3) was based on an *a priori* expectation that technical progress would be non-neutral. As the estimated equations are specified differently, the R^2 and t-values are not comparable.

With regard to the comment that no attention had been paid to the influence of the power structure, Dr. Kuipers said that σ is a technological variable which is not directly related to the power structure or other institutional factors. However, the *estimation* of σ relies on the assumption that marginal productivities equal the respective wage rates. This need not be true, and may cause the elasticity of substitution to be overestimated. However, it is very difficult to give due consideration to the role of the power structure, given the problem of separating it from scarcity elements. On a related point raised by Professor Wiles, Dr. Kuipers said that the Netherlands had a wage policy in the 1950s which continued to some extent into the present decade. But, he argued that these institutional factors have hardly altered relative wages; instead, they have caused a shift in the whole wage structure. The same applies, at least until 1973, to the measures designed to raise minimum wages. He agreed that labour markets are frequently in disequilibrium – otherwise the present high level of structural unemployment would be inexplicable. In the long run, however, these disequilibria tend to disappear. For this reason he did not think it necessary to omit minimum wage workers from consideration in a long run analysis, as Professor Lévy-Garboua had suggested. It is also the reason why he was not attracted by the suggestion that N_2/N_1 should be taken as the dependent variable.

The paper did assume labour supply to be fully predetermined. He agreed with Dr. Thomas and Professor Somermeyer that there are no *a priori* grounds for doing this. However, in another of their studies, they had found little evidence to indicate that labour supply is influenced by the real wage rate. Most of their supply function estimates gave very bad results. In particular, the supply elasticity always turned out to be negative. So factors other than wage rates may determine labour supply. He agreed that more disaggregated data would have been preferable, but these are not available for the Netherlands.

Finally, Dr. Kuipers said that Mr. Layard's suggestion, concerning the influence of investment growth on wage rates, did not apply to the Netherlands in the period under examination. The Netherlands experienced a very rapid rise in investment during the 1950s and 1960s.

18 LABOUR MARKET DUALITY AND INCOME DISTRIBUTION: THE CASE OF THE UK

*GEORGE PSACHAROPOULOS**

I. Introduction

Neoclassical economic theory has recently been confronted with an alternative explanation of the way in which labour markets operate. The new theory comes under the name of labour market duality or segmentation. It briefly means two things. First, the labour market is much less uniform than thus far envisaged; actually it is broken into two or more distinct segments, the upper segment exhibiting superior work conditions and pay relative to the lower segment. Second, education is a doubtful instrument for improving income distribution; instead, the policy emphasis should be shifted from the supply side to the demand side of the labour market, for example by reducing institutional mobility barriers.

The purpose of this paper is to empirically investigate several issues raised by the concept of labour market duality using data from the UK. For example, can one in the first place empirically identify the existence of a segmented labour market? Are there, perhaps, any other factors (such as age or health) that may account for the observed phenomenon that is labelled "duality"? And what is the role of a policy variable like schooling on income distribution?

In the section below I try to define the exact concept of a dual labour market and differentiate it from existing theories. In section III, I look at UK data in an effort to document the existence of labour market segmentation. The three tests I perform refer to the biomodality of the distribution of jobs and income, truncated earnings functions and socioeconomic mobility. In section IV I go a little beyond the concept of labour market duality and ask a more concrete question, namely what factors account for the observed income distribution and in particular what is the role of schooling in changing the observed distribution? In the last section I try to draw some conclusions on the analytical usefulness of the concept of labour market duality.

II. Defining a dual labour market

It might be useful at the outset to put the concept of the dual labour market in its proper perspective by providing a brief taxonomy of existing labour market

---

* I would like to thank Orley Ashenfelter, Richard Layard, David Metcalf and Mark Stewart for helpful discussions while writing this paper. I am also indebted to Tony Cornford for efficient research assistance.

theories (see Cain (1976)). These could be classified into four groups: classical, neo-classical, segmented (dual) and radical (Marxist). The first two are also known as "orthodox" and the other two as "alternative" (see table 18.1).

Table 18.1. A taxonomy of labour market theories.

Theory		Key element	Policy prescriptions	Principal exponent
Orthodox	Classical	Population dynamics, subsistence wage	Population control	Smith, Malthus, Mill, Marx
	Neoclassical	Supply and demand, marginal productivity, human capital	Productivity boosters, provision of education + training	Marshall, Schultz, Becker
Alternative	Segmented (Dual)	Demand side, institutional structure, mobility barriers	Reduction of barriers, institutional change	Bluestone, Doeringer, Piore, Harrison
	Radical (Marxist)	Social class conflict	Development of social class consciousness	Bowles, Gintis, Reich, Gordon, Edwards

(1) *Classical* economists adopted an aggregate view of labour as a factor of production and therefore were mainly concerned with the long-term share of wages in national income rather than personal income distribution. A typical example of their thinking is Malthus' dynamic model of food and population interaction leading to a subsistence wage. Improvement of labour conditions seemed beyond the control of the individual and, translated into modern terms, population control would be one of their policy prescriptions.

Of particular importance for this discussion is the classical concept of *non-competing groups*. This concept was developed by Cairnes (1874) and Mill (1900) in recognition of the fact that there exist distinct markets for different kinds of labour. Smith's proposition that wages vary inversely with the agreeableness of the job was thus modified (as early as 1850) to take into account the lack of mobility or opportunity: workers in dirty jobs were paid less than workers in more pleasant jobs because the latter were mainly recruited from their own ranks.

(2) *Neoclassical* labour theories are based on the bread and butter of modern economics, that is, supply and demand. Marginal productivity theory underlies the demand side, the state of technology being the main exogenous parameter. On the supply side, the human capital model is dominant, given consumer-worker tastes regarding leisure or time devoted to non-market activities. In contrast to the classical theories, neo-classical economists are optimistic regarding the capacity of the individual to improve his fate. The neoclassical solution is the provision of marketable skills via education and training.

As the classical economists introduced the concept of non-competing groups to deal with exceptions to Smith's basic theory, so neoclassical economists have introduced models of discrimination and screening to deal with market imperfections, thus trying to preserve their theoretical core.

(3) *Segmented* labour market theorists (or dualists) argue that although the neoclassical prescription may cure the patient in some cases, in other cases it might not. The reason is that institutional barriers prohibit all parts of the population from benefiting equally from education and training.

They view the labour market as being segmented into two pieces: the primary sector where employment conditions are good (e.g. high pay and pleasant jobs) and the secondary sector where employment conditions are bad. As the main reason for the existence of segmentation is lack of mobility, the policy prescription of dualists is the removal of institutional barriers.

Evidently, this theory echoes the classical concept of non-competing groups. Moreover, it is concerned with topics that have extensively been dealt with in the neoclassical literature as market imperfections (like discrimination). Therefore one has to look for the theoretical nuances that would make segmentation a distinct core theory in labour economics.

(4) *Radical* economists of the 1970s have much in common with dualists. For example, they share the view that labour markets are segmented. Where the two theories differ, however, is in the causes of segmentation and proposed remedies for the improvement of income distribution.

The radicals claim that the main cause of segmentation is monopoly capitalism: "employers actively and consciously foster segmentation in order to 'divide and conquer' the labour force" (Reich, Gordon and Edwards (1973)). In fact, it is the creation of human capital that further segments the labour force (Bowles and Gintis (1975)). Therefore, the radical policy prescription is for workers to become class conscious and fight to increase their class power and share in production.

Today, the main debate is between neoclassical theory and segmented labour markets. The reason is that, on the one hand, the profession has made some progress over classical economics. On the other hand, most of the radical prescriptions are not easily implementable, at least if one accepts the political regime as given.

The brief review above has shown that the theoretical seed of labour market segmentation is not new. The non-homogeneous character of labour as a factor of production, and thus labour markets as a whole, was mentioned by the classical economists and repeated by several contemporaries, like Dunlop (1957) and Kerr (1954). What is new, however, is the *emphasis* put on the non-homogeneous markets by writers in the late sixties. Therefore, let us have a closer look at what segmentation really means and in what respects it differs from existing theories.

Although there exist almost as many versions of segmentation as authors in this field (each giving special emphasis to a particular topic), the basic idea runs as follows:

(a) There exist two *distinct* labour markets, called primary and secondary.[1]

---

[1] See Gordon (1972). More than two markets have been distinguished as in Kerr's (1954) original classification of "open", "guild" and "manorial" markets, later elaborated by Alexander (1974); and Bluestone's (1970) "tripartite economy" consisting of the "core", the "periphery" and the "irregular" economy, further elaborated by Harrison (1972). Although there certainly exists a continuum between the "privileged" and "disadvantaged" sectors of the market, I have followed the common practice of identifying labour market segmentation with dualism.

(b) Workers compete *within* each market for jobs, wages and employment conditions in general.
(c) Workers in the secondary labour market are *treated in a much inferior way* relative to workers in the primary market.
(d) *Mobility barriers* prohibit the movement of workers from the secondary market to the primary market.

The employment conditions and worker characteristics in the two markets are described as follows. The primary market is characterised by high basic wages, high fringe benefits, high skills, possibility of acquisition of skills on the job, hierarchy and promotion, stable work habits and a high concentration of white, men and adult workers. On the contrary, the secondary market is characterised by low basic wages, lack of fringe benefits, low (easily obtainable) general skills, no promotion ladders, unstable work habits and a high concentration of coloured persons, women and youths.

Given these theoretical remarks, let us now look at some data and ask the question:

III. Is there really a dual labour market in the UK?

According to a recently published article in the *Economic Journal* (Bosanquet and Doeringer, 1973) the answer to this question is affirmative. However the evidence on which this conclusion is based is highly impressionistic. For example, they present as evidence for segmentation the fact that the age-earnings profiles of whites or men lie above those for blacks or women, respectively. This evidence is simply *descriptive* of income distribution conditions in the economy by sex or colour, and makes no mention of the many *causes* that may be responsible for the observed phenomenon. It also fails to standardise for many other worker characteristics that affect productivity, such as labour force participation, weeks worked during the year, experience with the firm, type of economic sector and state of health. Standardisation for these variables would greatly reduce the apparent differential attributed to discrimination or segmentation, and this is the procedure I shall follow in this paper.

The data on which my analysis is based come from the 1972 General Household Survey. I have concentrated on the earnings of male employees only, as differences in employment conditions between the two sexes might be due to a host of factors other than labour market segmentation. The resulting sample size was 6,873 males who were employees in their main occupation. A number of variables were constructed for each person referring to his particular personal characteristics and employment conditions. These variables are presented in the Appendix along with the means, standard deviations and zero-order correlation matrix.

The definition of the variables is straightforward. Perhaps the only variable that needs discussion is the one referring to the individual's occupation. This has been based on the Goldthorpe and Hope (1974) desirability scale for different occupations as established by a popular ranking assessment. Thus, it can be said that the occupation variable measures the "goodness" of the job held by the individual. Such a variable is crucial in studying the question of labour market duality as one does not have to rely on income which is only part of the total advantages associated with a given job. Note that this variable is superior to the Duncan scale used in US work as it is not constructed by direct reference to the mean income of a given job. The mean income of an occupation is only indirectly reflected in the Goldthorpe and Hope scale as the respondents must have taken this into account in ranking different jobs according to their desirability. Perhaps the major shortcoming of the occupation variable for the analysis undertaken here is its ordinal character.

Given this set of data and variables, let us now go through a series of tests attempting to discover the existence of labour market segmentation. Looking at the segmentation literature, these tests could be classified into the following groups:[2]

(a) The possible existence of bi- or multi-modality in the distribution of the goodness of jobs among individuals (modality test);
(b) The fact that schooling might be a more profitable investment for those who belong to the primary segment relative to those who belong to the lower segment (truncated earnings functions test); and
(c) The fact that those who belong to the lower segment of the labour market might not be able to move to the upper segment (socio-economic mobility test).

III.1. *The distribution of jobs and the distribution of earnings*

The range of the occupational variable in the sample is 18.36 to 79.53. In order to present the data in a digestable form, I constructed occupational classes by 5 point steps on the scale, as in table 18.2. Figure 18.1 shows a multimodal pattern in the distribution of jobs which, *prima vista* seems to be consistent with the theory of labour market segmentation.

However, a more careful look at this distribution reveals the following: in the first place, the second and third modes (points B and C in figure 18.1) correspond to less than one-half and one-third of the height of the dominant mode (point A). Therefore, the distribution could be interpreted as having a single mode. After all, it must be remembered that the occupational scale is an ordinal measure constructed by a popular ranking of different occupations. A different (arbitrary) scaling of this ranking could have produced either completely different "segments" from those shown in figure 18.1 or a continuous distribution with a single mode.

Even if one accepts point D as the frontier between two distinct segments of the labour market, then a look at who belongs to what segment makes the notion of dualism absurd. Table 18.3 presents the mean desirability rating of the jobs held by some specific socio-economic groups (the dotted line separating the two alleged segments according to figure 18.1). Yet we see that the upper segment includes

---

[2] One could also include a fourth category, namely the relative strength of supply versus demand factors in the determination of earnings (*à la* Wachtel and Betsey (1972)). However, I soon abandoned this alley due to my inability to classify variables into tight supply and demand compartments, as most observed variables are the result of both supply and demand forces.

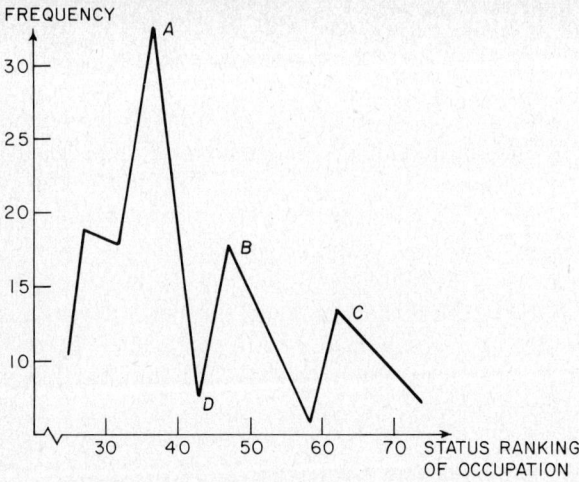

Figure 18.1 The distribution of jobs.

Table 18.2. The distribution of jobs according to their desirability, U.K. males, 1972.

Job desirability rating	Number of persons	Percentage
Up to 25	383	5.6
26–30	967	14.1
31–35	856	12.5
36–40	1,905	27.6
41–45	181	2.6
46–50	864	12.6
51–55	540	7.9
56–60	94	1.4
61–65	572	8.3
66–70	371	5.4
more than 71	140	2.0
Total	6,873	100.0

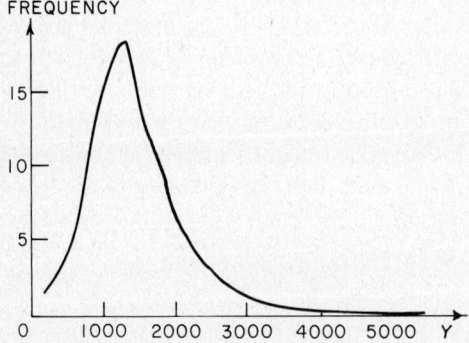

Figure 18.2. The distribution of earnings.

Table 18.3. Mean desirability rating and mean earnings of the jobs held by selected socioeconomic groups.

Segment[a] (1)	Socioeconomic group (2)	Mean job rating (3)	Mean annual earnings in £ (4)	Number of persons in the sample (5)
Upper	Managers in Government and large establishments	67.0	2,778	412
	Intermediate ancillary, non-manual workers	61.3	1,773	407
	Foremen, non-manual	55.5	1,886	73
	Managers in industry and small establishments	55.0	2,033	278
	Professional workers	48.8	2,517	315
	Members of the Armed Forces	48.5	2,100	75
	Foremen, manual	45.7	1,662	374
Lower	Junior workers, non-manual	40.8	1,339	877
	Skilled manual workers	38.8	1,317	2,475
	Semi-skilled manual workers	32.1	1,202	1,014
	Personal service workers	31.8	887	43
	Agricultural workers	31.6	892	91
	Unskilled manual workers	18.9	1,010	383

[a] The dividing line between the two segments corresponds to point D in Figure 18.1.

manual foremen (OCC = 45.7) who are mainly recruited from the ranks of skilled manual workers (OCC = 38.8) and who belong to the lower segment. But if such mobility exists between the two segments, the notion of segmentation or dualism is analytically useless.

What, I think, is a better way of tackling the problem is to start from the above *description*, i.e. the fact that there exist good jobs and bad jobs, and ask the question: who gets the good job, either initially or later in life? If, for example, age is a factor that causes someone to be initially in the secondary sector but later we observe him moving to the primary sector, then we are beginning to understand the causes of the observed phenomenon.

But before we turn to this procedure, let us compare the distribution of goodness of jobs to the distribution of earnings in the sample. After all, column 4 of table 18.3 suggests that the two segments could have been defined by looking at the mean earnings instead of the desirability of different jobs. A look at the earnings distribution (table 18.4 and figure 18.2) does not reveal any bimodality simply because earnings is a continuous cardinal variable, whereas the occupational scale was not. Since the two distributions roughly overlap, the non existence of gaps in the income distribution (here and elsewhere) could be interpreted as lack of duality.

Nevertheless, the descriptive statistics given above document the fact that there exist many people at the lower end of either distribution i.e. who are poor and/or have bad jobs. Therefore one should move beyond description and try to account for the causes of the observed phenomenon.

Table 18.4. The distribution of earnings, U.K. males, 1972.

Annual earnings	Number of persons	Percentage
Up to £250	188	2.7
251– 500	239	3.5
501– 750	347	5.0
751–1,000	837	12.2
1,001–1,250	1,133	16.5
1,251–1,500	1,275	18.6
1,501–1,750	913	13.3
1,751–2,000	717	10.4
2,001–2,250	380	5.5
2,251–2,500	278	4.0
2,501–2,750	175	2.5
2,751–3,000	116	1.7
3,001–3,250	63	0.9
3,251–3,500	47	0.7
3,501–3,750	35	0.5
3,751–4,000	23	0.3
4,001–5,000	58	0.8
5,001–6,000	17	0.2
6,001–7,000	10	0.1
More than 7,000	22	0.3
Total	6,873	100.0

III.2. *Differential earnings determination in the two sectors?*

Let us now move to another popular "test" for the existence of labour market duality, namely the possible discovery of a differential way in which earnings are determined in the two sectors.[3] These tests focus in particular on the effect of schooling on earnings in the two segments. For if schooling has a lower effect on the earnings of workers in the lower segment (relative to the upper segment), this is interpreted as either segmentation or inadequacy of a major supply-side variable to improve income distribution.

In the absence of a better measurable criterion of who belongs to what sector, the usual truncation criterion is earnings. But as pointed out by Cain (1976) it is not very surprising that the effect of schooling on earnings is lower in the lower segment since the high values of the dependent variable are cut off (see figure 18.3).

This approach can also be criticised on conceptual grounds. Splitting the sample into two segments amounts to standardising for occupation, as whatever split criterion one adopts (males versus females, whites versus blacks, etc.) the upper segment is bound to contain the highly paid occupations and the lower segment the low pay occupations. As earnings and the type of segment to which an individual belongs are highly correlated, it is very likely that the regression slope will be higher in the primary segment. Standardising for occupation in an earnings function underestimates the return to schooling as it denies the effect of schooling on

---

[3] For examples of truncated earnings functions referring to economic minority groups (blacks and women), see Weiss (1970), Harrison (1972) and Malkiel and Malkiel (1973).

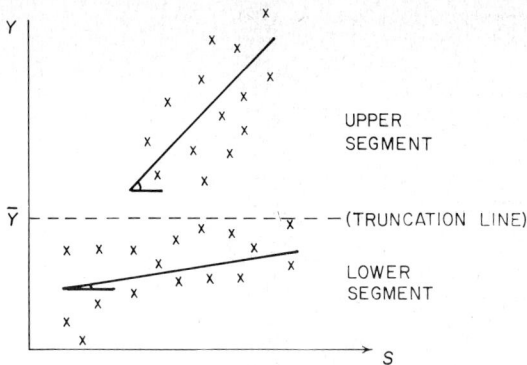

Figure 18.3. The effect of schooling on earnings in a truncated model.

earnings *via* changes in occupation (see Becker (1975)). To put it differently, the cards are already stacked before the exercise begins to show that segmentation exists, simply because it is supposed *a priori* to exist (for example, see Osterman (1975)).

In fact, this is exactly the case in our sample. The upper panel of table 18.5 shows that when mean earnings is used as the cut-off point in a model of the kind $\ln Y = a + bS$, schooling has a negative effect on the earnings of those who belong to the lower segment! Even so, when experience and its square enter as additional variables in a model of the kind $\ln Y = a + bS + cEX + dEX^2$, (lower panel of table 18.5), the effect of schooling on earnings is essentially identical in the two sectors. This "Mincerian correction" essentially amounts to bringing in age as an adjusting variable to correct the downward bias on the coefficient of schooling in the previous model, because those with high S have necessarily low EX.

In table 18.6 I have used an alternative truncation criterion, namely the median of the occupational scale.[4] Dualists would agree that this is a more appropriate truncation criterion than earnings, as the occupational scale reflects the whole

Table 18.5. Earnings functions results truncated according to mean earnings[a].

Variable	Lower segment	Upper segment	Whole sample
Constant term	7.217	7.223	6.603
S	−0.039	0.038	0.053
R^2	0.01	0.13	0.03
Constant term	5.619	6.752	5.200
S	0.050	0.051	0.097
EX	0.072	0.025	0.091
EX^2	−0.0012	−0.0004	−0.0015
R^2	0.22	0.21	0.32
N	4,059	2,814	6,873

[a] All coefficients are highly significant.

[4] The median has been used instead of the mean because of the ordinal character of the occupational scale.

Table 18.6. Earnings functions results truncated according to the median of the occupational scale[a].

Variable	Lower segment	Upper segment
Constant terms	6.573	6.944
S	0.043	0.035
R^2	0.01	0.02
Constant term	5.085	5.520
S	0.104	0.075
EX	0.085	0.092
EX^2	-0.0015	-0.0016
R^2	0.27	0.35

[a] All coefficients are highly significant.

wage package, i.e. it includes the non-pecuniary job conditions. Yet the results show that schooling is now a relatively more profitable investment in the lower segment. If the coefficients on the years of schooling variable are interpreted as private rates of return to schooling, then in the full model (which includes experience) schooling is a more profitable investment for those in the lower segment by about three percentage points. (Lower panel of table 18.6.) Therefore we conclude this section by having failed to document the existence of segmentation by the test of truncated earnings functions.

III.3. *Mobility*

So let us turn to a third test in an attempt to discover some kind of labour market duality in the UK, namely the extent of socio-economic mobility. There are two ways one can study mobility in a cross-sectional sample of this kind; first, by constructing age-occupational scale profiles; and second, by observing the amount and direction of mobility as measured by comparing the desirability rating of father's and son's occupation. These two ways of studying the problem roughly correspond to looking for evidence on intra- and inter-generational mobility.

III.3.1. *Intra-generational socio-economic mobility*

In figure 18.4 I have plotted the mean value of the occupational scale of the jobs held by people within single age groups in the sample. For comparison purposes I have also plotted the mean earnings within single age groups. Although the occupation profile exhibits a sawtooth pattern, its general shape closely follows that of the earnings profile. The most important aspect of the occupation profile is that it rises steeply until about the age of 27.[5]

What this means is that individuals advance in terms of the goodness of the job they hold as they grow older.

---

[5] So does the experience – OCC profile, not shown here.

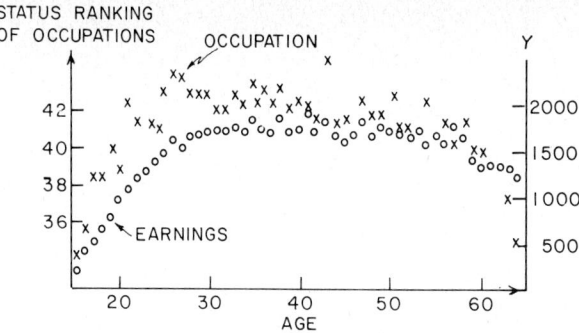

Figure 18.4. Age-earnings and age-occupational scale profiles.

To the extent that this cross-sectional profile is an approximation to the one that would have been obtained from true longitudinal data, I interpret this evidence as detrimental to the labour market segmentation hypothesis.[6] If a single exogenous demographic factor like age gives us a clue as to who gets initially a bad job, then where is the alleged segmentation?

To put it another way, the evidence shows the existence of a normal career pattern where young people enter *initially* less desirable jobs and later advance into better jobs. Also, the fact that the occupation profile closely follows that of earnings is evidence that in constructing a desirability scale one cannot avoid the implicit notion of income associated with a given job. The other side of the coin is that one may concentrate on a poverty, income distribution problem, rather than cast it in terms of dualism.

III.3.2. *Intergenerational occupational mobility*

What about intergenerational mobility? Of course its existence would be a much weaker test on the issue of dualism relative to the one presented in the previous section. Nevertheless, evidence of a considerable occupational transmission from generation to generation would favour recent radical theories on the role of schooling in our society. For example, it has been argued that schooling is used by the upper classes as a vehicle for the transmission of power and maintenance of the status quo (see Bowles (1972)). By the same token, evidence of low upward social mobility would strengthen the position of alternative labour market theories, including that of segmentation.

Because the measurement of father's occupation in this sample has been based on the collapsed version of the Goldthorpe and Hope scale (see Appendix), and because the resulting distribution of OCCF has a single mode containing 3,054 observations, the criterion I used for defining the upper and lower segments in the two generations is that the person had an OCC (or OCCF in the case of the father)

---

[6] Unfortunately, the literature on similar mobility studies is not very rich, the main reason being the scarcity of longitudinal data on the job histories of large samples of individuals, but see McCall (1973).

above or below any measure of central tendency in the two distributions.[7] The resulting number of observations was 2,441 persons who had the following characteristic in common: either themselves or their father had a job with a desirability rating above or below the median, mean or mode of the respective distribution. This procedure has eliminated the middle part of both distributions so that we may concentrate on the upper and lower tails. Figure 18.5 shows the resulting mobility matrix, the N on each arrow representing the number of people "moving" in different directions. I have also recorded the mean years of schooling of those who move (and the standard deviation of the mean years of schooling in parenthesis).

The study of this mobility table reveals the following facts: although there exists a fair amount of occupational transmission from one generation to the next ($N_{11} = 1,049$, $N_{22} = 503$), nearly as many people move upwards as those remaining in the lower segment ($N_{21} = 494$ versus $N_{22} = 503$). Once more, I consider this evidence as operating against the labour market segmentation hypothesis. For, as a weaker test, even if a person is, say, trapped by mobility barriers in the lower segment, then his son has a 50 per cent chance of escaping to the upper segment.

But what I consider to be a more important question in this respect, is: who will move to the upper segment and who will remain behind? The mean levels of schooling in figure 18.5 give the clue that it will be the one with more schooling who will move upwards, and, symmetrically, the one with less schooling who will move down. In fact, the difference between the mean levels of schooling (ΔS) of the two groups with the same starting point and who move in different directions are highly significant. (The t-ratios of the test of the difference between two means are of the order of 10.)

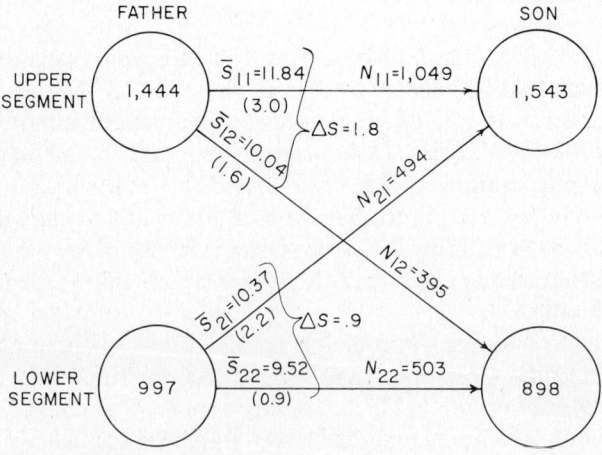

Figure 18.5. Intergenerational social mobility.

[7] I have also experimented with alternative truncation criteria using the whole sample such as the median and the mean and obtained the same general conclusions as those presented below.

Therefore, we conclude this section by having been unable to document the existence of labour market segmentation in the UK. We also have a clue that schooling has something to do with upward social mobility.

IV. Accounting for the sources of income inequality

Although the tests presented above have failed to support the existence of labour market segmentation in the UK, descriptive evidence has been given that some people have much lower earnings than others. To carry the argument a little further, let us now ask the question: who are those with low earnings? Is it those who allegedly belong to the secondary labour market or those who have some other characteristic in common that depresses their earnings? Figure 18.2 gave us the clue that age is an important factor associated with pay. What if someone were physically or mentally handicapped? Could one still claim that his low earnings or bad job were due to labour market duality?

Clearly, what one should do is first adjust the observed distribution of earnings for some *bona fide* factors that most people would agree do not relate to the structure of the labour market, and then interpret the residual income inequality as possibly due to dualism. Of course, the last estimate must be an extreme upper bound on the effect of labour market segmentation on income distribution due to the high residual variance of earnings in all known samples. But if the agreed exogenous standardising factors account for a large part of the observed earnings inequality, then the case for labour market segmentation (even if this thing exists) strongly diminishes.

This is exactly the procedure I follow in this section. First, I bring into the analysis additional personal characteristics and fit a general, *ad hoc* earnings function. Then I use this function to simulate the degree of earnings dispersion under certain conditions. This function is "*ad hoc*" in the sense that it is not based on any high-powered biological, sociological, human capital, R^2-maximisation or other theory. It is simply descriptive of the way personal characteristics relate to pay.

Table 18.7 presents the results of this function. Most coefficients have the sign one would expect, thus I limit my comments to a few variables that either need interpretation or apparently have the "wrong sign". The fact that one is married has one of the strongest effects on earnings. This is often used as an argument against neoclassical theory in the sense that wages are determined according to someone's social needs rather than his marginal productivity. Yet one could argue equally well that marriage acts as either a motive for higher earnings or that it is the better quality people who eventually get married in the process of mate selection. Married men might also be less prone to quit or they may work longer hours.

The negative coefficient on the British-born dummy comes as a surprise that could perhaps be rationalised by the possibility that recent immigrants work longer hours, a variable that is missing in this sample. Also, differences in annual hours worked might have biased the coefficients of Mining and Construction among the economic sector dummies.

Table 18.7. The descriptive earnings function[a].

Variable	Absolute earnings		Log earnings
	Coefficient	(Standard error)	Coefficient
Years of schooling	84.91	(4.70)	0.055
Age	85.55	(4.41)	0.050
Age squared	− 0.947	(0.053)	− 0.0009
Weeks worked	21.28	(1.03)	1.038
Apprentice	− 243.61	(74.51)	− 0.305
Disease	− 170.37	(28.26)	− 0.092
Married	217.75	(22.43)	0.195
Coloured	− 396.21	(62.56)	− 0.165
British	− 105.85	(41.46)	− 0.019
Urban resident	31.18	(19.62)	0.045
Seniority	123.86	(21.46)	0.090
Number of "O level" passes	37.59	(4.61)	0.020
Union	2.08	(0.93)	0.003
Occupational scale	15.30	(0.64)	0.007
Mining	− 1.97	(68.29)	0.122
Manufacturing	101.65	(59.11)	0.106
Gas, electricity	220.78	(71.02)	0.211
Administration	92.36	(59.03)	0.149
Construction	132.08	(57.02)	0.184
Services	94.17	(53.31)	0.107
Constant term	− 3,127.38	(118.28)	1.344
R^2	0.431		0.716
Number of observations	6,873		6,873

[a] Dependent variable is absolute annual earnings. Agriculture is the omitted economic sector dummy. See appendix for the exact definition of variables. All coefficients are highly significant in the log formulation.

Another coefficient with an apparent wrong sign (in this as in many other studies) is the one on the occupational scale. If Adam Smith's theory of equal advantage were correct, then earnings should vary inversely with the agreeableness of the job and thus obtain a negative coefficient on the occupation variable. It must be remembered, however, that the occupational scale indirectly reflects to a great extent the income associated with a given occupation. Therefore, the resulting positive coefficient is not very surprising.

Given this descriptive function, let us now account for the observed income distribution and see the impact of alternative policies to improve it. For this purpose the following procedure was followed: given the estimated coefficients of the earnings function in table 18.7 (first column), an arbitrary value was given to each independent variable, individual earnings were predicted according to the function, logged and (after repeating for each person in the sample) the variance of the log of earnings was recorded as a measure of earnings dispersion. The predicted Var ln $\hat{Y}$ of individual earnings in this fashion by the function (before adjustment) is equal to 0.374 and this will be the landmark to compare alternative distributions according to different assumptions.[8]

---

[8] For a similar procedure used in a different context, see Metcalf (1973).

Table 18.8. Earnings dispersion after adjustment for selected factors.

Adjusting factor	Adjustment meaning	Earnings dispersion (Var in $\hat{Y}$)	Reduction in earnings inequality (percentage)
None	–	0.374	–
Age	All mean age	0.140	62
	None less than 25	0.256	32
Disease	None with longstanding disease	0.360	4
Colour	None coloured	0.366	2
Apprenticeship	None apprenticed	0.365	2
Married	All married	0.289	23
Urban	All urban residents	0.359	4
O-level	All mean number of O-levels	0.336	10
Union	All mean percentage unionised	0.354	5
	None less than 50% unionised	0.346	7
Weeks	All worked mean weeks	0.144	61
Schooling[a]	All mean years of schooling ($\bar{S}$ = 10.49)	0.328	12
	None less than 9 years of schooling ($\bar{S}$ = 10.52)	0.368	2
	None less than 10 years of schooling ($\bar{S}$ = 10.88)	0.360	4
	None less than 11 years of schooling ($\bar{S}$ = 11.57)	0.316	16
	None less than 12 years of schooling ($\bar{S}$ = 12.41)	0.301	20

[a] $\bar{S}$ is the new mean years of schooling in the sample.

Table 18.8 shows that the biggest effect on income distribution comes from either an age or weeks adjustment. Adjustment for unionisation has a rather low effect on earnings dispersion.[9] Now, a single combination of adjustments for the two most exogenous factors I can pick, namely if none in the sample were sick and none less than 25 years old, earnings dispersion would be equal to 0.244.[10] If in addition none worked less than 48 weeks, earnings inequality would be equal to 0.078. Of course weeks worked is not an exogenous variable like age, but I have included it in the list of adjustments for the reader to make his own judgement on what he considers to be an "agreed" degree of correction of the crude earnings dispersion.

Schooling is different from age in the sense that it can be manipulated by policy. The last rows of table 18.8 show the effect of different hypothetical educational policies on earnings distribution,[11] and in figure 18.6 the relationship between mean years of schooling and earnings dispersion is plotted.[12] The conclusion we get from this simulation experiment is that, although small, the effect of increasing the mean level of years of schooling improves income distribution. This finding is consistent with that obtained using an alternative technique on US data (see Marin and Psacharopoulos, 1976).

---

[9] For the interpretation of the union variable in this analysis, see Metcalf (1977).

[10] The age adjustment here essentially corresponds to a lifetime income concept. For an alternative way of adjusting for age, using the same data, see Psacharopoulos (1977).

[11] For a more detailed simulation of the effect of alternative educational policies on lifetime income distribution using data from the 1971 General Household Survey, see Layard (1976).

[12] Clearly, the simulated distributions rest on the assumption that wages by level of schooling will remain the same after more people of a lower educational attainment obtain an extra year of schooling.

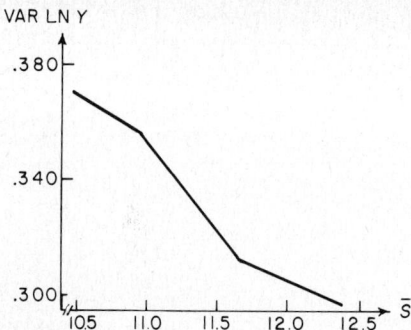

Figure 18.6. The relationship between mean years of schooling and earnings dispersion.

V. Concluding comments

In this paper we went through a melange of tests related to the concept of labour market segmentation. Let us now pull the threads together and see where we stand. Basically, we have been faced with two issues: one was the existence of labour market duality and the other was the relative strength of alternative policy instruments.

In discussing the first issue we have drawn a sharp distinction between a theory and a description of facts. It is an undisputed fact that there exist good jobs and bad jobs. Forgetting about semantics for a moment, any snapshot of the labour market at any given point in time would reveal that most of the characteristics advocated by the dualists do, in fact, exist. Where we need a theory, however, is in order to answer questions like: Why are some people in good jobs and other people in bad jobs? What causal factors allocate people into the different "segments" of the labour market? What are the reasons for immobility once a particular person has been in the secondary labour market?

In my opinion, the usefulness of models of duality (whether they refer to the labour market in advanced countries or to the traditional versus modern sector in LDCs) is limited, because they are mainly descriptive in character rather than analytical on the causes of the observed phenomenon. A more fruitful approach is to ask why dualism exists, instead of "explaining" poverty by the existence of dualism.

Now, the existing literature contains a variety of hypotheses purporting to explain the observed phenomenon. Economists, for example, would argue that people in primary jobs enjoy higher pay because, for a variety of reasons, they are more productive than people in secondary jobs. People in the two kinds of jobs are *dissimilar* in terms of their educational level, training, stability and tastes regarding leisure, motivation for work and willingness to accept responsibility. Persistent differences in pay or lack of mobility (that is, after correction for the above factors) are interpreted as *market imperfections* and treated by a series of sub-theories peripheral to the neoclassical core, such as that of discrimination (see Becker (1971)). Perhaps the only novel item in the segmentation literature is that stress has been put on the institutional factors impeding mobility, especially those coming under the heading of internal labour markets (a concept originally proposed by Kerr (1954)). Or, to cast it in terms of the theory of non-competing groups, the dualists have raised the question of how these groups are generated and what are the common characteristics of people who belong to them.

On the policy issue, neoclassical theory puts emphasis on the supply side of the labour market, namely on the provision of education and training, along with the improvement of information channels and the reduction of discrimination. By contrast, dualists seem to reject the role of education as a policy instrument because it does not work in the lower segment. Thus they shift their policy emphasis on measures that affect the demand side of the labour market, such as traditional Keynesian government expenditure (orientated towadrs the secondary sector) and novel ones like the direct transfer of workers from the secondary to the primary sector and the introduction of job ladders in secondary jobs. But one can always question the feasibility and practical aspect of these novel measures. To what extent can secondary workers be assigned to the primary sector without displacing the ones who are already there? To what extent can one introduce and enforce hierarchy and promotion sequences in secondary jobs?

There also exists the following contradiction in the segmentation literature: whereas the main worry of dualists is immobility (which is a long-term structural problem to eliminate), most of their policy measures are short-term in character. Human capital based policies (which are long-term in character) might better promote mobility than some of the policy measures of the dualists.

By way of summary, in this paper I have argued that, on the theoretical side labour market segmentation *analyses* are mainly descriptive in character and therefore do not qualify as alternative labour market *theories*. On the empirical side, I have found segmentation analyses deficient, in the sense of not having gone beyond neoclassical explanations of the observed differential treatment of workers and mobility barriers. However, their positive contribution lies in the emotional reporting of poverty conditions among minority groups so that *all* analysts (i.e. regardless of religious or political affiliation to a particular labour market theory) search harder to identify additional *causes* of the observed phenomenon.

On the policy front, one could perhaps compare the prescription of dualists with aspirin and that of the orthodox school with antibiotics. But then it should be remembered that poverty, which is the ultimate concern of all theories, is a complex long-term structural problem, and that policy prescriptions to deal with it should include sufficient doses of all kinds of known drugs. It is in this sense that the apparent alternative theories discussed in this paper might be complementary rather than competitive.

Appendix: Definition of selected variables

Annual earnings (Y): Earnings in the year preceding the interview divided by the monthly index of earnings in the month of interview to eliminate the effect of inflation (Central Statistical Office (1973, table 16)).

Years of schooling (S): Computed as terminal education age minus 5. But in cases where the terminal education age was inconsistent with the individual's qualifications, the terminal education age was adjusted downwards to an age consistent with the individual's qualifications. This apparent gap in full-time education applied to less than 4 per cent of the cases.

Experience (EX) = Age − S − 5.

Occupation (OCC): Measured on the Goldthorpe and Hope (1974, table 6.1) detailed occupational scale according to the individual's occupation unit group and employment status.

Father's occupation (OCCF): Measured on the collapsed version of the Goldthorpe and Hope (1974, table 6.6) as the unit group of father's occupation is not available in this sample.

Disease: A dummy having a value equal to 1 if the person suffers from a long standing disease which limits activity.

Urban: A dummy having a value equal to 1 if the person lives in a conurbation or other urban area.

British: A dummy having a value equal to 1 if the person was born in the British Isles.

Apprentice: A dummy having a value equal to 1 if the person is a trade apprentice.

Union: A continuous variable measuring the percentage union coverage (national plus local agreement) of the individual's industry.

Seniority: A dummy variable having a value of 1 if the individual has been two or more years with the present employer.

Table A.1. Sample variables: Overall means and standard deviations.

Variable	Mean or proportion	Standard deviation
Annual earnings (Y)	£1,513	866
Natural logarithm of earnings (ln Y)	7.159	0.660
Age	38.6	13.7
Experience in the labour force (EX)	23.1	14.4
Seniority with current employer	0.74	0.44
Years of schooling (S)	10.49	2.19
Occupation (OCC)	41.54	13.90
Father's occupation ($OCCF$)	41.20	10.85
Weeks worked	48.99	8.70
British born	0.94	0.24
Married	0.76	0.42
Coloured	0.03	0.16
Disease	0.09	0.29
Urban resident	0.79	0.41
Apprentice	0.01	0.11
Number of "O level" passes	0.87	2.13
Union	34.97	18.63
Economic sector dummies:		
Mining and quarrying	0.04	0.19
Manufacturing (S.I.C. 3 to 16)	0.41	0.49
Gas, electricity and water	0.03	0.16
Public administration	0.08	0.27
Construction	0.10	0.30
Services (S.I.C. 19 to 23)	0.32	0.47

Table A.2. Zero-order correlation matrix between selected variables.

	Y	ln Y	Age	EX	Sen.	S	OCC	OCCF	Weeks	Brit.	Marr.	Col.	Disease	Union	Mfg.
ln Y	0.799														
Age	0.189	0.256													
Experience	0.133	0.216	0.989												
Seniority	0.284	0.398	0.348	0.341											
Schooling	0.303	0.176	−0.265	−0.404	−0.072										
Occupation	0.416	0.326	−0.016	−0.067	0.133	0.337									
Fath. occ.	0.186	0.091	−0.028	−0.070	−0.001	0.287	0.215								
Weeks	0.371	0.686	0.151	0.142	0.421	0.010	0.149	0.005							
British	−0.006	0.002	0.007	0.021	0.045	−0.094	0.034	−0.097	0.013						
Married	0.305	0.397	0.389	0.378	0.221	−0.059	0.081	0.004	0.174	−0.032					
Coloured	−0.040	−0.040	−0.053	−0.068	−0.034	0.119	−0.024	0.086	−0.022	−0.581	−0.003				
Disease	−0.095	−0.098	0.173	0.178	0.008	−0.092	−0.052	−0.016	−0.128	0.011	0.025	−0.025			
Union	0.006	0.050	−0.005	0.016	0.044	−0.138	−0.081	−0.065	0.023	−0.010	0.020	0.034	−0.030		
Manufacturing	0.016	0.055	0.000	0.016	0.067	−0.103	−0.048	−0.054	0.031	0.001	0.023	0.022	−0.001	0.866	
Apprentice	−0.118	−0.164	−0.166	−0.159	−0.084	0.008	0.017	0.008	−0.038	0.005	−0.178	−0.001	−0.026	0.009	0.004

References

Alexander, A.J., "Income, Experience and the Structure of Internal Labour Markets", *Quarterly Journal of Economics* (February 1974).
Becker, G.S., *The Economics of Discrimination*, University of Chicago Press, second edition, 1971.
Becker, G.S., *Human Capital*, NBER, second edition, 1975.
Bluestone, B., "The Tripartite Economy: Labour Markets and the Working Poor", *Poverty and Human Resources* (July/August 1970).
Bosanquet, N. and B.P. Doeringer, "Is There a Dual Labour Market in Great Britain?", *Economic Journal* (June 1973).
Bowles, S., "Schooling and Inequality from Generation to Generation", *Journal of Political Economy* (May/June 1972 supplement).
Bowles, S. and H. Gintis, "The Problems with Human Capital Theory – A Marxian Critique", *American Economic Review* (May 1975).
Cain, G.G., "The Challenge of Segmented Labour Market Theories to Orthodox Theory: A Survey", *Journal of Economic Literature* (December 1976).
Cairnes, J.E., *Some Leading Principles of Political Economy Newly Expounded*, McMillan, 1974.
Dunlop, J.T., "The Task of Contemporary Wage Theory", in George W. Taylor and Frank C. Pierson, eds., *New Concepts in Wage Determination*, McGraw–Hill, 1957.
Goldthorpe, J.H. and K. Hope, *The Social Grading of Occupations*, Clarendon Press, 1974.
Gordon, D.M., *Theories of Poverty and Unemployment*, Heath Lexington, 1972.
Harrison, B., *Education, Training and the Urban Ghetto*, Johns Hopkins, 1972.
Kerr, C., "The Balkanisation of Labour Markets", in E. Wight Bakke et al., eds., *Labour Mobility and Economic Opportunity*, MIT Press, 1954.
Layard, R., "On Measuring the Redistribution of Lifetime Income", in M.S. Feldstein and R.P. Inman eds., *The Economics of Public Services. Proceedings of a Conference held by the International Economic Association at Turin, Italy*. MacMillan, 1976.
McCall, J.J. *Income Mobility, Racial Discrimination and Economic Growth*, Heath Lexington, 1973.
Malkiel, G.B. and J.A. Malkiel, "Male-Female Pay Differentials in Professional Employment", *American Economic Review* (September 1973).
Marin, A. and G. Psacharopoulos, "Schooling and Income Distribution", *Review of Economics and Statistics* (August 1976).
Metcalf, D., "Pay Dispersion, Information and Returns to Search in a Professional Labour Market", *Review of Economic Studies* (October 1973).
Metcalf, D., "Unions, Incomes Policy and Relative Wages in Britain", *British Journal of Industrial Relations* (July 1977).
Mill, J.S., *Principles of Political Economy*. Colonial Press, 1900.
Osterman, P., "An Empirical Study of Labour Market Segmentation", *Industrial and Labour Relations Review* (July 1975).
Psacharopoulos, G., "Family Background, Education and Achievement", *British Journal of Sociology* (September 1977).
Reich, M., D.M. Gordon and R.C. Edwards, "A Theory of Labour Market Segmentation", *American Economic Review* (May 1973).
Wachtel, H.M. and C. Betsey, "Employment at Low Wages", *Review of Economics and Statistics* (May 1972).
Weiss, R.D., "The Effect of Education on the Earnings of Blacks and Whites", *Review of Economics and Statistics* (May 1970).

18 DISCUSSION

PAPER BY GEORGE PSACHAROPOULOS

Dr. Thomas said that the paper was of particular interest to the conference since it dealt with one of the factors generating income inequalities. He intended to deal with two of the three main topics – theories of dual labour markets and empirical tests applied to such theories – leaving the exploration of factors that may influence existing income inequalities to the general discussion.

The paper contrasts those who adhere to a neo-classical labour market theory with others who concentrate on the segmentation of labour markets, and examines the relevance of the latter for the UK. The phenomenon of segmentation is reduced to a distinction between just two segments of the labour market – labour market duality – and the behaviour of people within each of these markets is considered. In his opinion such a description does not provide a theory of "dual labour markets". He would have preferred an analysis based, for instance, on the "screening hypothesis" or a theory of "job competition". Thurow's theory, as presented in his book *Generating Inequality*, could have been used as a framework for the multiple segmentation of labour markets. This offers a logically consistent theory in which changes in hiring characteristics rather than wage fluctuations, clear labour markets.

To a large extent wages are determined by rigid structures which generate a small number of very good jobs, a larger number of average quality jobs, very many bad jobs and, depending on the state of the business cycle, a number of unemployed. The key issue is the recognition that access to certain types of jobs is systematically denied to people with specific characteristics. Individuals then compete for a limited number of trainable opportunities, attempting to overcome their particular disadvantages. Longitudinal studies can be used to test hypotheses following from such a theory: whether mobility is indeed restricted to certain categories of people, and if so what are their characteristics; and whether hiring characteristics fluctuate rather than wage structures.

To investigate the validity of labour market duality for the UK, Dr. Psacharopoulos had concentrated on three different cross-sectional tests. The bi-modality test, reflecting the existence of "good" and "bad" jobs, cannot disprove the notion of labour market segmentation. The fact that some manual workers move from bad to good jobs, as indicated in Table 3, is used as an argument against market duality. But some workers in better jobs are always recruited from other segments of the labour market. The appropriate question is which groups get promoted and what are the characteristics of those left behind.

On the second test – truncating the sample to show that education has a different impact on the two segments of the labour market – he pointed out that truncation may cause a very serious bias in the estimates. In addition, the reported correlation coefficients were so low that he felt it unwise to draw conclusions concerning mobility patterns. Finally, the zero-order correlation of 0.189 between "age" and "earnings" given in the Appendix table A.2 is so low that it cannot be used as evidence that one variable has a dominant influence on the earnings structure, thereby invalidating the notion of labour market duality. In his opinion, therefore, none of the tests mentioned is sufficient to reject hypotheses connected with a theory of labour market duality.

He went on to suggest that a more successful approach would concentrate on the factors causing segmentation of labour markets and asked whether a logical framework existed under which segmentation would be consistent with profit maximisation. If indeed the organisation of production leads to segmentation of labour markets, one consequence would be that certain categories of people would have access to the best jobs, whilst other groups would be given no work at all. Recent research in the Netherlands by Bovenkerke supports such a hypothesis. The fact that in the Netherlands 50,000 people have been unemployed for more than a year and are given only a 7% probability of ever being employed again, indicates the seriousness of the problem. Segmentation of labour markets suggests that the present system of organising production at a national level seriously impedes any attempt to simultaneously achieve the objectives of equality, responsibility and freedom.

Professor Chiswick questioned whether bi-modality would be any reflection of dualism.

Professor Pen liked the paper, particularly since it attempts to refute a theory. In the Netherlands, he said, tri-modality had been discovered, but he did not feel this provided support for the dual labour market hypothesis, since it was due in part to differences in the number of hours worked. He agreed with the remark that the neo-classical and segmentation theories may become complementary rather than competitive. This is illustrated by the work of Professor Tinbergen, which combines neo-classical production functions with a total of nine market segments.

Mr. Groenveld wondered about the coefficients given in tables 5 and 6, which are said to be highly significant despite the fact that the correlation coefficients are extremely low.

Professor Lecaillon said it was easy enough to explain wage differentials by education, training and so on. However, when most people in a particular group stay in bad jobs, the risk of discrimination becomes very important and employers are no longer prepared to offer good jobs to those in the group with the required qualifications. He therefore felt that the problem needed to be tackled from the demand side of the market.

Professor Krelle said the status ranking of occupations seemed different to that in Germany which had seen significant changes over a short period of time. Such changes might alter the picture quite substantially. He also felt that the duality considered in the paper was only a special case of labour market segmentation and there may be several different types. It may be possible to use cluster analysis to see whether the same type of people get the same kind of jobs. This would provide information on, say, the difficulty of changing from one occupation to another.

In section IV of the paper it was suggested that unpleasant jobs do not get more pay. He felt that this would not be true in Germany at a more disaggregated level. For workers doing similar kinds of jobs, premiums are paid for the more unpleasant ones, although it is possible that this is not apparent when all occupations are aggregated.

Professor Wiles agreed that it was perfectly arbitrary to speak of *duality*. He felt the appeal of duality was Marxist in spirit though hardly in origin. A division between the "Lumpen-proletariat" and the "labour aristocracy" had been invested with all the emotion Marx had originally poured into his own dualism: that between proletariat and bourgeoisie. But although Marx had himself spoken of the labour aristocracy and the Lumpen-proletariat he had recognised them as parts of a continuum.

Even if consideration is restricted to dualism, Professor Wiles pointed out that references to the dual economy in development theory had an entirely different meaning. He was unimpressed by any of these sharp divisions when the situation was essentially one of imperfect competition, with a large number of distinct groups. Discontinuity however is still possible: the groups may overlap in a statistical sense and present the appearance of a continuum, while being very distinct social formations on the ground.

Professor Robinson raised the question of defining job desirability. Two entirely different approaches may be taken. People may be asked whether they would have preferred to be born with the qualifications to be the Queen or the Prime Minister; or they may be asked what job they would prefer given their own personal attributes. These could give rise to quite different rankings. He was sceptical as to the value of judgements made by individuals about jobs of which they had very little knowledge.

Professor de Wolff referred to the figure 18.3. If the relationship between earnings and schooling is linear, then truncation does not change the slope. However, if the true relationship is non-linear, with a higher contribution arising from later years of schooling, truncation means that a higher slope is obtained for the higher income groups.

Professor Morrisson referred to the significant coefficient of the number of weeks worked. He suggested that the number of weeks worked may divide workers between large corportions, where the risk of being fired is small, and medium and small firms, where the risk is greater.

Dr. Wagner, in line with the comments of some of the other discussants, felt that Dr. Psacharopoulos had put his dual labour market hypothesis to misleading tests using inadequate data.

Professor Lévy-Garboua liked the positive approach to duality. He believed it was right to explain duality theory mainly in terms of mobility barriers. This could be elaborated further, to examine why such barriers exist and what the consequences were for, say, wage determination.

He tended to agree with those who had emphasised the empirical difficulties involved with the type of data used. In particular the occupational ranking is not independent of earnings and for this reason the occupational classification used is open to question.

Professor Krupp was impressed with the tests and disagreed with those who had argued that the data were inadequate. The paper had exploited data from a variety of sources which contained a great deal of useful information. If this were not sufficient to do the required tests, he doubted whether they could ever be done. He suggested that factor analysis or analysis of variance may serve to separate the different groups. If the theories do not specify the dividing line between the separate groups, he felt it was quite valid to use statistical techniques to indicate the appropriate division, even though this was always open to the objection that this division was not the one intended by the theory.

Dr. Kuipers asked what conclusion should be drawn from table 7 where a strong correlation is found between colour and earnings. He felt this was evidence of discrimination in the labour market. This introduced an ethical aspect into the discussion as to which income differences are acceptable and which should be rejected.

Professor Taubman, in the chair, said it was correct to suggest that people who support the notion of dual labour markets think they have a separate theory, but Sherwin Rosen, in reviewing a book by Gordon, had come to the conclusion that it contained nothing which was inconsistent with neo-classical theory. It merely elaborated one particular aspect, sometimes overlooked by people in this field.

Dr. Psacharopoulos disagreed with Dr. Thomas that the existence of a dual labour market could be equated with a small number of good jobs. In any country in the world there were only a small number of good jobs, so this definition is not useful. In developed countries it is immigrants who tend to do the worst jobs and then gradually move up the occupational hierarchy. However he did agree that longitudinal data would have been preferred for testing purposes, had it been available.

To Mr. Groenveld he replied that a low R^2 was quite satisfactory in cross section studies. Moreover it is not only the statistical significance of the coefficients which are important but also their size relative to costs.

On the question of the stability of the occupational structure raised by Professor Krelle, he replied that the status scores may change but not their ranking. He agreed that there was no particular reason to consider duality rather than some more general market segmentation, but warned against having too many groups. As the number of groups increases the closer we get to a continuum, and the essence of segmentation theories is lost.

19 THE EFFECT OF COLLECTIVE BARGAINING ON WAGES

R. LAYARD, D. METCALF AND S. NICKELL*

I. Introduction and summary

Britain is famous for its unions, but little is known about their effects. In this paper we ask:
(1) How do unions affect relative wages?
(2) How has this effect varied over time, and what, if anything, does this tell us about the role of unions in wage inflation?
(3) How do unions affect relative real incomes, allowing for the non-pecuniary rewards of work?

To answer these questions we use recently-collected information on the fraction of workers in each occupation and industry who are covered by collective agreements.[1] For manual workers, this 'coverage' is positively correlated with the wage level, both across occupations and industries. However, this correlation may of course be due to the correlation of both wages and coverage with the quality of the workers involved. Elsewhere, attempts have been made to control for some dimensions of quality,[2] but these studies have not been able to control for many of the relevant variables. In the present paper we are able, using individual data, to control for many more quality variables, and still find evidence that for manual workers of a given quality the wage is affected by coverage. Holding quality constant, the wage in a wholly covered manual occupation is some 25 per cent higher than in one that is not covered.[3] In other words the wage of a worker of given quality is some 25 per cent higher if he is paid the covered wage than if he is not. Among non-manual workers we find no reliable evidence of an effect of collective bargaining on relative wages.

So how has collective bargaining affected inequality? Among manual workers

---

* We are extremely grateful to Roger Cooley, Tony Cornford and Kathy Pick for first-rate computing and research assistance. We have had very helpful discussions of the paper with Orley Ashenfelter, Jim Heckman and Marcus Miller. We are also grateful to the Esmee Fairbairn Charitable Trust, the department of employment and the Nuffield Foundation for financing the different parts of the study.

[1] Overall 75 percent of men are "covered", compared with 57 percent belonging to a union (1973 data).

[2] See Mulvey (1976), Mulvey and Foster (1976), Nickell (1977) and Metcalf (1977). Also, on the effects of union membership, Pencavel (1974). All these analyses rely on group data.

[3] This estimate is based on regressions excluding agriculture and mining where non-pecuniary factors play a special role. For U.S. estimates, see e.g. Ashenfelter (1976).

it has increased it. For coverage is, roughly speaking, independent of the other causes of wage variation. So it merely introduces a further source of variation. If 83% of male manual workers are covered and earn 25% more than other similar workers, it follows that the variance of log hourly earnings is thereby increased by approximately 0.01 (or by 6 per cent of the variance not arising from that cause).[4] Of course it does not follow that further extensions of coverage would further increase inequality among manual workers. This would depend on whether such extensions were concentrated on the higher or lower paid workers. So much for effects on inequality among manual workers. Unfortunately we cannot say anything about the effects of collective bargaining on overall inequality among all workers. To do so we should need to know how collective bargaining has altered the mean manual wage relative to the mean non-manual wage, and, for reasons explained later, we have no reliable evidence on this.

The preceding remarks relate to 1973. But how long has this state of affairs existed? According to the evidence of section III, for manual workers in manufacturing the effect of coverage rose sharply by about a half of itself between 1968 and 1972. This change was accompanied by a rise in the share of wages in manufacturing, a fall in relative employment in covered industries and a rise in unemployment. All of this is consistent with a model of cost-push inflation put forward in section III.

But surely unions affect more than the wages of their members? What about non-pecuniary returns? In section IV we develop a very preliminary and experimental approach to the measurement of real income. This uses the Goldthorpe-Hope scale of the desirability of occupations, normalised to be a standard normal variable. Regressions explaining this variable suggest once again that unions have no effect on the relative real income of white collar workers. But for manual workers they suggest that the effect of unions on relative real incomes may be greater than on relative money incomes. The whole analysis in the paper is confined to male employees.

II. The effects of unions on relative wages in 1973

II.1. *Theory*

We first want to know how collective bargaining has changed the inequality of hourly wages from what it would otherwise have been. This does not require any information about how collective bargaining has altered the mean level of real wages, which clearly cannot be discovered from any cross-sectional study of individuals. It does require us to know how collective bargaining has altered the level of each individual's wage relative to the mean.

The simplest model is one in which, after collective bargaining is introduced,

---

[4] $0.83 (0.25 - 0.21)^2 + 0.17 (-0.21)^2 \simeq 0.01$. The overall variance of male manual log hourly earnings is 0.15.

all individuals with given characteristics are paid the same except for those who are covered by a collective agreement. The latter receive We^m, where W is the uncovered wage and m is the proportional mark-up (for small m). Hence, for the ith individual,

$$\ln W_i = a + bX_i + mT_i, \qquad (1)$$

where W is hourly wages, X is a vector of personal characteristics and T is a dummy variable indicating whether the individual receives the union wage. Two possible complications suggest themselves. First, the wage of the uncovered workers in a sector of the economy might be affected by the strength of collective bargaining (as measured by coverage), due to the threat effect. However, this does not seem likely. For any effect of unionisation on the wages of non-union workers are already reflected in the fact that many non-union workers are paid the covered (union) wage – while 57% of men are union members, 75% are covered by collective agreements. Second, the mark-up may well vary across sectors and in particular might be affected by the coverage in the sector. So

$$m = m' + cU_j,$$

where U_j refers to coverage in the jth bargaining group.
Thus

$$\ln W_{ij} = a + bX_{ij} + m'T_{ij} + cU_jT_{ij}. \qquad (2)$$

These effects comprise about as much of the effects of collective bargaining as one could possibly hope to identify. As Lewis (1963) has pointed out, there may well be others. In particular, forcible changes in unionised wages will affect the labour supply available to the uncovered sector, and this may alter the pattern of relative values which are placed on the different personal characteristics in the uncovered sector. For example, if uneducated workers become particularly heavily unionised, this could depress the relative wages of uneducated workers in the uncovered sector.[5] But there is little hope of measuring these effects.

II.2. Estimation

For Britain there is a further limitation. We have no comprehensive survey data that show whether an individual belongs to a union, nor whether he receives the union wage. But data are available which show the proportions of workers covered by the union wage in different groups (U_j). So two alternatives are open: (i) one can run inter-group regressions using group means of all variables; (ii) one can run regressions for individuals, using individual data for all variables, except for coverage where the group mean would be used. Method (i) leads to unbiased estimates. But due to the small number of observations much information is wasted. Method (ii) is in that sense more efficient, but leads to biased estimates.

---

[5] This effect could be reversed if they mainly became unionised in sectors not intensive in their services.

Thus, suppose we accept model (1). If we use group data to run

$$\ln W_j = a_0 + a_1 X_j + a_2 U_j,$$

a_2 gives us an unbiassed estimate of m. But if we use individual data to run

$$\ln W_{ij} = a_0 + a_1 X_{ij} + a_2 U_j,$$

the estimated value a_2 is

$$a_2 = b_{TU/X} \cdot m,$$

where $b_{TU/X}$ is the regression coefficient of T on U holding X constant. However, there is good reason to think that $b_{TU/X}$ is not substantially different from unity.[6] So we believe that, if model (1) is correct, our individual regressions ought to provide a reasonable estimate of m. If model (2) is correct, this could be estimated from group data by

$$\ln W_j = b_0 + b_1 X_j + b_2 U_j + b_3 U_j^2.$$

However at no stage in our work was the squared term ever significant, so the question of bias on the corresponding individual regressions is of little interest.

There are other notorious estimation problems in this area. Suppose high wages encourage low turnover and thus provide an incentive to unionisation. Then an OLS regression of wages on unionisation cannot identify the causal effect of unions on wages, even if the wage-determining equation is properly specified (Johnson (1975)). This problem is less serious when we are measuring the effect of coverage rather than unionisation. And in any case previous work suffers at least as seriously from inadequate specification of the wage equation to allow for quality differences between workers and for non-pecuniary differences between jobs. These are the problems on which we focus.

---

[6] If X is a single variable

$$b_{TU/X} = \frac{\sigma_T}{\sigma_U} \left[\frac{r_{TU} - r_{TX} r_{UX}}{1 - r_{UX}^2} \right]$$

If we assume $r_{TX} = r_{UX}$, we can estimate the degree of bias. The bias must on that assumption be downward since

$$\frac{\sigma_T}{\sigma_U} \cdot r_{TU} = 1$$

and $\sigma_T > \sigma_U$. To get a feel for orders of magnitude, a typical correlation between U and an important variable like years of schooling is 0.1. Let us assume the correlation between U and the relevant product bX would also be 0.1. For manual workers σ_U is just under 0.1 and $\sigma_T = \sqrt{(p(1-p))} \simeq \sqrt{(0.8)(0.2)} = 0.4$. So

$$b_{TU/X} = \frac{0.4}{0.1} \left[\frac{0.25 - 0.1^2}{1 - 0.1^2} \right] = 1.$$

II.3. Individual regressions

We shall begin with the individual regressions (see table 19.1). These are based on the General Household Survey (1973), and are incidentally the first male hourly wage equations run for Britain. The variables for which we control are described in full in Appendix 1. They include, first, various educational variables – qualification, length of full-time schooling, type of school, apprenticeship completed and current educational activity. Next comes work experience. All these variables normally take the expected signs. So does father's occupation. Interestingly, of our two variables for colour (West Indian and 'other') the West Indian dummy has a coefficient of around minus 10 per cent, but with a standard error making it hardly significantly different from zero. 'Other' (mainly Asian) is insignificantly different from zero, as is the variable for Irish-born (Ireland). As expected, long-standing illness reduces wages. Marital status is included mainly as a quality variable, and appears to perform as such.

The next set of variables are somewhat inadequate for their purpose. They are two variables intended to pick up the fact that wages are higher for people working in large city centres, and consequently faced with higher rents for any given travel costs – or with higher travel costs for given rents. Unfortunately, we have no information on where people work. We only know the region where they live. When we included the full set of regional dummies, we found that all regions had very similar coefficients except for the South-East. So the only dummy we include is for the South-East. However, following the previous line of argument we have also included as a continuous variable the percentage of the population in the region who live in urban areas. This proved to have a positive effect for white-collar workers, but (surprisingly) a negative effect for manual workers.

Finally, we come to variables connected with the 2-digit industry in which the person works. In the light of recent debate in Britain, it is interesting to find that whether the industry is predominantly public seems to make little difference to wages ('on average'). For manufacturing industries we also examine the effect of plant size and concentration ratio but neither have any significant impact.

We have deliberately commented on the effects of other variables so that we can henceforth concentrate on the effect of coverage. The available data on coverage come in two forms.[8] One statistic shows the percentage of workers in each

---

[7] See office of population censuses and surveys (OPCAS) (1973). The GHS is an annual survey of some 10,000 households throughout Britain. We are extremely grateful to the OPCAS for making the tapes available to us. Other related papers that have used these data are Layard (1976), Psacharopoulos and Layard (forthcoming), Psacharopoulos (forthcoming), Stewart (1977) and Greenhalgh (1977).

[8] The data are from the *New Earnings Survey 1975*, which is a roughly 1 percent sample of all employees.

The survey asks the employer in respect of each member of the sample: "Please indicate the type of negotiated collective agreement, if any, which affects the pay and conditions of employment of this employee, either directly or indirectly: (1) National agreement and supplementary company/district/local agreement; (2) National agreement only; (3) Company/district/local agreement only; (4) No collective agreement." The survey report comments, "Even though an employee may have more favourable terms and conditions from those in an agreement, or may be employed by an employer who is not

Table 19.1. Regression equations explaining individual log hourly earnings (1973, males)[a].

Type of occ: → Sector: →	All All	Manual All	Manual All excl. primary	Manual Manufacturing	Non-manual All
Variables					
Coverage	−0.25 (8.3)	0.56 (10.9)	−0.33 (5.3)	0.27 (2.7)	−0.32 (6.4)
Schooling yrs.	0.05 (10.6)	0.04 (4.7)	0.04 (4.6)	0.04 (1.1)	0.05 (7.8)
Degree	0.41 (9.1)	0.05 (0.2)	0.04 (0.5)	0.04 (0.1)	0.38 (6.6)
Advanced	0.40 (16.6)	0.30 (5.4)	0.32 (5.6)	0.31 (3.8)	0.35 (10.6)
A level	0.21 (9.2)	0.13 (4.7)	0.14 (4.7)	0.06 (1.6)	0.22 (6.0)
O level	0.16 (8.5)	0.10 (4.7)	0.11 (4.6)	0.09 (2.8)	0.14 (4.3)
Other qual.	0.08 (3.2)	0.03 (0.9)	0.04 (1.1)	0.03 (0.6)	0.10 (2.6)
No. quals.	−	−	−	−	−
Sel. school	0.13 (8.9)	0.07 (3.4)	0.07 (3.4)	0.10 (3.5)	0.12 (5.2)
Ex-apprent.	0.03 (2.1)	0.05 (3.5)	0.06 (3.9)	0.06 (2.7)	0.01 (0.4)
Aim qual.	−0.08 (3.4)	−0.06 (2.2)	−0.05 (1.9)	−0.10 (2.4)	−0.08 (2.1)
Exp. 0–5	0.14 (16.6)	0.15 (16.2)	0.16 (16.1)	0.15 (11.1)	0.11 (7.4)
6–10	0.04 (7.2)	0.03 (5.1)	0.03 (4.9)	0.04 (4.0)	0.06 (5.4)
11–20	0.01 (4.4)	0.01 (2.8)	0.01 (2.9)	0.01 (1.3)	0.01 (2.4)
21–30	0.00 (0.9)	0.00 (1.7)	0.00 (1.7)	0.00 (0)	0.00 (0.5)
31–40	0.00 (0.1)	0.00 (0.5)	0.00 (0.9)	0.00 (0.4)	0.00 (0.2)
41+	−0.01 (4.1)	−0.01 (3.0)	−0.01 (3.0)	−0.01 (2.3)	−0.01 (2.1)
Father 1	0.10 (5.0)	0.04 (1.6)	0.03 (1.0)	0.09 (2.9)	0.14 (2.8)
Father 2	0.07 (3.6)	0.02 (0.7)	0.01 (0.6)	0.06 (1.9)	0.12 (2.5)
Father 3	0.09 (5.3)	0.05 (3.0)	0.03 (1.8)	0.05 (1.8)	0.11 (2.5)
Father 4	−	−	−	−	−
W. Indies	−0.11 (2.4)	−0.07 (1.5)	−0.07 (1.5)	−0.13 (2.1)	−0.14 (1.2)
Other coloured	−0.05 (1.8)	0.00 (0.2)	−0.01 (0.7)	−0.05 (1.4)	−0.06 (1.3)
Ireland	0.07 (1.3)	0.09 (1.6)	0.08 (1.3)	0.05 (0.5)	0.18 (1.1)
Other white	−	−	−	−	−
Sick	−0.09 (5.8)	−0.08 (4.8)	−0.09 (5.0)	−0.04 (1.6)	−0.10 (3.2)
Married	0.09 (6.3)	0.07 (4.4)	0.07 (4.4)	0.07 (3.2)	0.14 (4.6)
S. East	0.13 (9.4)	0.08 (5.6)	0.09 (6.0)	0.08 (3.4)	0.15 (5.9)
Urban	0.00 (0)	−0.13 (2.5)	−0.15 (3.0)	−0.30 (4.3)	0.25 (2.6)
Public	0.06 (4.4)	0.04 (0.7)	0.01 (0.7)	NA	0.03 (1.1)
Non-manuf.	−0.01 (0.5)	−0.02 (0.6)	−0.01 (0.2)	NA	−0.11 (1.5)
Plant size	0.00 (0.3)	0.00 (0.1)	0.00 (0.1)	0.00 (0.1)	0.00 (0.6)
Conc. ratio	0.14 (1.2)	−0.19 (1.7)	0.18 (1.5)	0.19 (1.6)	−0.18 (0.6)
Constant	−1.87 (22.8)	−2.29 (19.5)	−2.11 (16.7)	−1.97 (11.6)	−1.86 (12.6)
R^2	0.510	0.429	0.426	0.410	0.512
S.E.	0.32	0.29	0.27	0.27	0.36
N	4,306	2,829	2,598	1,385	1,476

[a] Source: General Household Survey tapes.
  t-statistic in brackets.
  The population covered included male employees normally working 30 hours a week or more, in non-seasonal and non-military employment, aged under 65.
  For definition of variables see Appendix 1.

a member of an association which is a party to the agreement, the employee's pay and/or conditions of employment may nevertheless be affected by an agreement." We interpret this to mean that any employer, whether a party to an agreement or not (by membership of an employer's federation), is covered if he is basing his pay on the agreement. We are grateful to Dave Winchester for advice on this and other points.

'occupation' (3-digit level) who are covered. The other shows the percentage of workers in each 'industry' (3-digit level) who are covered (separately for manual and non-manual workers). But unfortunately our individual data only identify the person's 2-digit industry. So in the individual regressions there is no problem of choice: we measure coverage by its level in the person's 3-digit occupation. The overall proportion of male workers covered are shown in table 19.2.

Table 19.2. Proportion of workers covered by collective agreements (1973, males)[a].

	Manufacturing	Non-manufacturing	All sectors	(All sectors, proportion unionised)
White-collar	0.46	0.67	0.60	(0.45)
Manual	0.84	0.83	0.83	(0.65)
All occupations	0.74	0.76	0.75	(0.57)

[a] Source: Coverage: D.E. *New Earnings Survey 1973*, tables 110 and 112.
Unionisation: Price and Bain (1976).

Before looking at the multiple regressions it is a good idea to look at the simple regression of log hourly wages on coverage for different groups of the population (see table 19.3). As this shows, if all workers, manual and non-manual together, are considered, there is a negative correlation of coverage and wages. However this chiefly reflects the fact that manual workers are more highly covered and get

Table 19.3. Simple regressions of log hourly wages on "coverage" (male employees, 1973)[a].

Occupation: → Sector: →	All All	Manual All	Manual All excl. primary	Manual Manufacturing	Non-manual All
Individual data					
Coefficient (*t*)	−0.56 (16)	0.67 (11)	0.40 (5)	0.34 (3.1)	−0.34 (5.7)
R^2	0.046	0.038	0.009	0.005	0.020
N	4,307	2,830	2,593	1,386	1,477
Group data (occupations)					
Coefficient (*t*)	0.22 (1.4)	0.64 (4.4)	0.26 (1.5)		
R^2	0.030	0.240	0.040		
N	79	65	61		
Group data (industries)					
Coefficient (*t*)				0.19 (2.9)	
R^2				0.013	
N				121	
(Standard deviation of "coverage")	0.176	0.107	0.088	0.075	0.212

[a] Sources: Coverage: D.E. *New Earnings Survey* 1973, tables 110 and 112.
Wages: Individual data: General Household Survey.
Group data on occupations: *New Earnings Survey* 1973, table 80.
Group data on industries: see table 19.9.
t-statistic in brackets.

lower wages. Within the working class, coverage and wages are positively correlated, particularly when the highly-paid and highly-unionised miners are included as well as the low-paid and little-unionised agricultural workers. Among non-manual workers there is once again a negative correlation between coverage and wages.

Turning to the multiple regressions in table 19.1, among manual workers coverage works wonders if all sectors are included. However if coverage is excluded and residuals are grouped by occupation, much the largest deviations are among miners (positive) and agricultural workers (negative). Non-pecuniary factors must also be important in both these cases, and neither of these groups form part of the ordinary urban labour market, for which alone it is probably feasible to assess union wage effects. So we shall henceforth concentrate on estimates excluding agriculture and mining. Coverage now seems to raise wages by some 33 per cent for manual workers.[9] We looked for various interactive effects, but without success. One cannot of course be certain that the measured effect does not in fact reflect, in part anyway, the effect of unmeasured quality differences – which must in fact account for the spurious negative effect of coverage among non-manual workers. We are, however, inclined to take a 25–30 per cent estimate as reasonable.

In table 19.4 it is confirmed by regressions run on occupational group data, which, for manual workers yields very similar estimates to the individual regressions. Many of the individual quality variables do not in this case acquire significant coefficients, presumably due to multicollinearity and lack of degrees of freedom.

In table 19.5 we present another similar analysis, this time using group data on 3-digit manufacturing industries. The coverage effect is somewhat less.

An obvious issue is: If data are to be grouped, which grouping is preferable: occupation or industry? If we believe model (1), it ought to be possible to partition the population into groups in any way one likes and obtain unbiased estimates of m. However, if model (2) were true, the sample ought to be partitioned into groups such that the U_j measured the relevant influences on the union mark-up. This points to the use of data on occupations, for the following reason. The normal bargain relates to an occupation within an industry. This is so, even though it may be contained within an industry settlement (e.g. the engineering industry manual workers' settlement). And the influence which affects the union mark-up is the level of coverage (or unionisation) in the occupation within the industry. But unfortunately we have no data on coverage within the occupation within the industry. So which variable will be a better proxy for this – unionisation within the occupation or unionisation within the industry? Fairly clearly the latter, since the variation of coverage across industries within occupations is likely to be less than the variation of coverage across occupations within industries. As regards the individual regressions, similar arguments apply. For this reason we are somewhat more inclined to accept the results of regressions where coverage is measured at the level of the occupation.

---

[9] The standard deviation of coverage in this group is 0.088.

Table 19.4. Regression equations explaining occupational group log hourly earnings (1973, male employees)[a].

Type of occ: → Sector: →	All All	Manual All	Manual All excl. primary
Variables			
Coverage	0.16 (1.2)	0.49 (2.6)	0.28 (1.4)
Schooling yrs.	0.10 (0.7)	−0.00 (0.0)	−0.29 (1.2)
Degree	0.00 (2.6)	−0.43 (0.1)	1.06 (0.2)
Advanced	−0.08 (0.1)	0.66 (0.6)	2.15 (1.8)
A level	0.12 (0.2)	−0.24 (0.2)	−0.14 (0.2)
O level	0.07 (0.3)	0.17 (0.4)	0.37 (0.8)
Other qual.	−0.33 (0.8)	−0.25 (0.4)	1.09 (1.5)
No. quals.	—	—	—
Sel. school	0.26 (0.7)	0.16 (0.3)	0.43 (0.9)
Ex-apprent.	0.28 (1.8)	0.20 (1.1)	0.17 (1.0)
Exp. 0–5	0.01 (0.0)	−0.11 (0.3)	−0.20 (0.5)
6–10	0.11 (0.4)	0.05 (0.2)	0.22 (0.7)
11–20	0.00 (0.0)	0.03 (0.2)	0.06 (0.3)
21–30	−0.16 (0.8)	−0.24 (1.0)	−0.44 (1.6)
31–40	−0.23 (1.5)	−0.23 (1.2)	−0.30 (1.5)
41+	—	—	—
Father 1	0.08 (0.3)	−0.00 (0.0)	−0.52 (1.6)
Father 2	0.12 (0.3)	−0.41 (1.0)	1.13 (2.4)
Father 3	0.55 (3.5)	0.30 (1.6)	−0.31 (1.2)
Father 4	—	—	—
Sick	−0.47 (1.5)	−0.39 (1.2)	−0.20 (0.6)
Married	0.11 (0.6)	0.17 (0.9)	0.02 (0.1)
Urban	−0.01 (0.9)	−0.00 (0.0)	−0.01 (1.2)
Constant	3.06 (2.2)	3.66 (1.6)	8.10 (3.2)
R^2	0.77	0.73	0.69
S.E.	0.11	0.10	0.09
N	79	65	61

[a] Sources: Wages: *New Earnings Survey, 1973*, table 80.
Coverage: *New Earnings Survey, 1973*, table 112.
Other variables: General Household Survey, 1973.

t-statistic in parentheses.
The experience variables measure the proportions in each experience category.

III. Changes in union effects over time

We now ask: Have unions always had these effects or is this something new? Phelps-Brown (1975) and others have suggested that the events of Paris 1968 heralded a new era of union militancy. They argue in support of this that the share of wages has risen in a number of countries. But there is of course no reason why the mechanism of recent inflation need be the same in all countries and we shall confine our remarks to Britain.

The only units of observation for which one can estimate a long time-series of coverage effects are 3-digit manufacturing industries (manual workers). In table 19.6 we present two such time-series. Both use coverage data for 1973. The first series

Table 19.5. Regression equation explaining industrial group log hourly earnings (3–digit manufacturing industries, male, manual employees, 1973)[a].

Coverage	0.19 (3.0)
Proportion skilled	0.15 (2.2)
Proportion unskilled	−0.08 (0.5)
Proportion 20–24	−0.93 (2.4)
Proportion 25–54	1.20 (6.4)
Proportion in S.E. and Midlands	0.02 (0.4)
Proportion in Conurbations	0.04 (0.7)
Constant	3.50 (22.9)
R^2	0.39
S.E.	0.089
N	121

[a] t statistics in parentheses.

Definition of variables

Skilled: proportion of male manual workers in S.E.G. 8 and 9 (foremen and skilled) – Census 1971. (S.E.G. = Socio-Economic Group).

Unskilled: proportion of male manual workers in S.E.G. 11 (unskilled) – Census 1971.

Age 20–24: proportion of male manual workers aged 20–24 – Census 1971.

Age 25–54: proportion of male manual workers aged 25–54 – Census 1971.

S.E. and Midlands: proportion of male workers in the industry working in the South-East and Midlands – Census 1971.

Conurbation: proportion of male workers in the industry working in a conurbation (Census definition) – Census 1971.

Hourly earnings: see table 19.6.

is comparable with the data presented in table 19.5. It is based on the 1968 Standard Industrial Classification and uses independent variables relating to the 1970s, the same values of the variables being used in all years. The second series is based on the 1958 Standard Industrial Classification and uses independent variables relating to the mid-60s, the same values of the variables being used in all years. For each series we show the partial regression coefficient of log average hourly earnings on coverage, holding constant the variables listed in table 19.5.[10]

As the table shows, the effect of coverage grew sharply between 1968 and 1972.[11] In column (2) the difference in effects from 1968 to 1972 is significant.[12] Lest this

---

[10] Simple regression coefficients are shown in the Appendix table, columns (1) and (2). In this case the changes in column (1) are rather more striking.

[11] In the Appendix table, columns (3) and (4) we also present the long time series using coverage data adjusted for changes in unionisation over time. The 1968–72 increase in the effect of coverage is much more dramatic, but it may be an artifact of the method of adjustment used.

[12] We have

$$\ln W_{72} = a_0 + a_1 X + a_2 U,$$
$$\ln W_{68} = b_0 + b_1 X + b_2 U,$$
$$\text{So } \Delta \ln W = (a_0 - b_0) + (a_1 - b_1)X + (a_2 - b_2)U,$$

where X is the other independent variables. In this regression the coefficient on U turns out to be significant.

might be due to increasing measurement error in the coverage series as we go back from 1973, we repeated the analysis using as independent variable the level of unionisation in 1966. A similar pattern of effects was found.

This only tells us that the effect of unions on relative wages has changed. Does it tell us anything about the effect on absolute wages? Taken on its own this evidence does not. However, we begin to have a set of data that is highly consistent with the notion of cost-push inflation, at any rate in the period 1968–72, when we combine this evidence with evidence on the time path of unemployment, of the employment pattern and of the share of wages.

Let us take the *unemployment* series first. At the same time that the union mark-up increased, unemployment also increased (see table 19.6). This is what any normal model of cost-push inflation would predict. For example, consider the following simple model. The only input is one type of labour, which can be employed in a unionised industry (U workers) or in a non-unionised industry (N workers). In each industry one worker produces one unit of output. The economy is closed, and the ouput mix is determined according to a social utility function $u(U, N)$ such that the relative marginal utility of the two outputs equals their relative prices, which equals the relative wages in the two sectors,

$$\frac{u_U(U, N)}{u_N(U, N)} = \frac{W_U}{W_N}. \tag{1}$$

The system is completed by an equation which equates monetary demand (Y) to the wage bill

$$Y = W_U U + W_N N. \tag{2}$$

Suppose we begin with $W_U = W_N$ and $Y = Y^0$ such that there is full employment:[13]

$$U + N = \bar{L}$$

This is illustrated at point P in figure 19.1.

Now the unions push up their wages by a factor λ to W_U'. Monetary demand remains unchanged. So consumption moves to say P'. Unemployment emerges. To relieve this the government starts to 'validate' the wage increase by expanding monetary demand. How far monetary demand has to be expanded depends on the behaviour of unionised workers. If unionised workers who lose their jobs are willing to take non-unionised jobs at less than the union rate, the government will only have to expand monetary demand by somewhat less than λ times the original share of unionised workers. In this case the mark-up is maintained (as in table 19.6), and employment in high-coverage industries falls permanently relative to employment in low-coverage industries (as also happens in table 19.6).[14] The alternative is that previously covered workers refuse to move into the uncovered sector and remain unemployed. To restore full employment the government must

---

[13] As will appear later, we could have full-employment with $W_U \neq W_N$. But this initial assumption simplifies the exposition without altering the structure of the argument.

[14] In column (4) the coverage level in each industry has been assumed constant at its 1973 level throughout. This is deliberately done so that the employment measure in column (4) is not confounded with one that is affected by union recruitment.

Table 19.6. Time series: 1961–1975[a].

	Partial regression coefficient of ln W on U		Unemployment (%)	Covered employment ÷ uncovered employment	Share of wages (%)	% change in hourly earnings (annual rate)
	1968 SIC industries	1958 SIC industries				
	(1)	(2)	(3)	(4)	(5)	(6)
1961 April		0.17 (2.5)	1.5		75.0	7.3
October		0.17 (2.5)	1.6			7.0
1962 April		0.15 (2.2)	1.9		75.4	5.1
October		0.19 (2.8)	2.2			4.1
1963 April		0.19 (2.7)	2.6		74.7	3.6
October		0.15 (2.2)	2.1			4.1
1964 April		0.17 (2.5)	1.8		73.4	7.4
October		0.16 (2.3)	1.5			8.2
1965 April		0.20 (3.0)	1.5		74.9	8.4
October		0.19 (2.6)	1.4			10.1
1966 April		0.21 (3.1)	1.2		76.7	9.8
October		0.17 (2.4)	1.7			6.2
1967 April		0.17 (2.4)	2.2		76.4	2.8
October		0.17 (2.5)	2.3			5.3
1968 April		0.18 (2.5)	2.4		77.0	8.1
October		0.20 (2.8)	2.3			7.2
1969 April		0.21 (2.8)	2.3		80.2	7.1
October	0.14 (2.3)	0.21 (2.9)	2.4			8.0
1970 October	0.16 (2.5)	0.26 (3.4)	2.5	2.30	84.2	15.3
1971 October	0.17 (2.5)	0.26 (3.1)	3.7	2.31	83.4	12.9
1972 October	0.19 (2.9)	0.31 (3.8)	3.4	2.25	82.9	15.0
1973 October	0.19 (2.9)	0.31 (3.7)	2.2	2.27	83.1	14.1
1974 October	0.19 (3.3)	0.25 (3.2)	2.8	2.26		21.4
1975 October	0.26 (4.0)	0.31 (3.3)	4.7	2.26		26.9
Sample size (N)	121	96				

[a] Sources: Cols. (1) and (2). See text. Based on group data on 3–digit manufacturing industries, male manual employees. Hourly earnings data from Department of Employment (*DE*) *Gazette*, articles on "Earnings and Hours of Manual Workers in April or October" (only October after 1969). April data are usually published in the following August; October data are usually published in the following February. Coverage data from DE, *New Earnings Survey 1973*, table 110. For column (2) the independent variables are the same as in table 19.5 except that the 1966 Census is used.

Col. (3). *DE Gazette* and DE, *British Labour Statistics: Historical Abstract 1886–1968*. When possible, school-leavers and adult students are excluded.

Col. (4). *DE Gazette*. June Census of Employment.

Col. (5). King (1975), table II. The data relate to the calendar year. They show labour costs as a percentage of labour costs plus pre-tax profit less capital consumption and stock appreciation, in manufacturing.

Col. (6). *DE Gazette*. Data relate to percentage changes since previous period (annual rate).

t-statistics in parentheses.

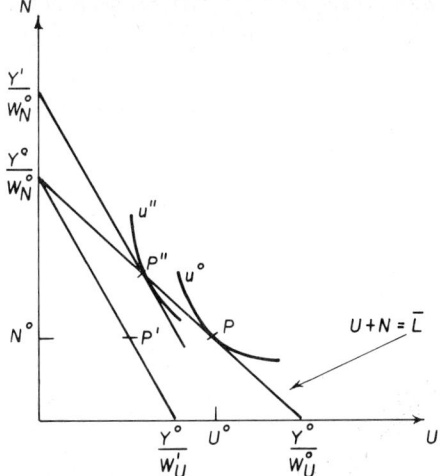

Figure 19.1. Cost-push inflation.

then raise Y by the full multiple λ. In this case the mark-up gets eliminated. We see no evidence of that in our time series.

We have just given a cost-push interpretation of the positive relationship between the mark-up and the level of unemployment.[15] However such a relationship is found since the First World War in the U.S. (Lewis (1963); Wachter (1974)). Lewis offers a different explanation. He says that union wages are sticky, so they rise less fast in the boom and fall less fast in the slump. This may do for periods when there was not sustained inflation. But in Britain over the last ten years inflation has been sustained. It is not clear how stickiness of union wages can lead to higher union wage increases in a slump (rather than smaller union wage decreases).

In our preceding account there was only one push (e.g. in 1968–72). However the model is also consistent with further pushes, offset by a simultaneous bidding-up of the uncovered wage. According to our evidence this may or may not have been happening since 1972.[16] However the picture since 1972 is exceptionally difficult to interpret, since, apart from 1974/5, there has been a continuous sequence of incomes policies. By contrast there were none between 1969 and 1972.

The final piece of evidence in table 19.6 concerns the time path of the share of wages, again in manufacturing. This rose sharply between 1968 and 1970 and remained at the new high level till the end of our series. Without developing a model, it seems intuitively reasonable that the share of wages should go up in a period of cost-push, and unreasonable that it should go up in a period of demand-pull.

The picture of a continuing mark-up from 1973 to 1975 is confirmed by group regressions on 3-digit occupations for manual males (excluding agriculture and

[15] By a cost-push process of wage setting, we mean one where the wage is set above the market-clearing level.
[16] At a later stage we intend to test a more formal time-series model of cost-push inflation, in which nominal demand will be explicitly included, as well as unemployment analysed by industry.

mining). These yield the following simple regression coefficients and partial regression coefficients (using the same independent variables as table 19.4) with t-statistics in parentheses.

		Simple regression coefficient	Partial regression coefficient
1973	April	0.26 (1.4)	0.28 (1.5)
1974	April	0.24 (1.4)	0.32 (1.8)
1975	April	0.32 (2.1)	0.47 (2.9)

These provide some support for the view that the 1975 increase in unemployment may have been connected with a further round of cost-push (see also table 19.6).

IV. Effects of unions on real income

We now attempt to see whether unions influence not only relative wages but also other sources of real income (e.g. conditions of work). What follows reports our first experimental steps in this slippery field. In their study of the *Social Grading of Occupations* Goldthorpe and Hope (1974) claim that when individuals are asked to rank occupations by 'social standing', they in fact rank them by 'general desirability'.[17] This provides an ordinal ranking of occupations. Presumably a person's characteristics determine what position in the scale of desirability (D) he can command – and for a given person whether he is covered by collective bargaining may also affect this.

In order to investigate this we need to adopt some cardinalisation of D, and in fact we make its log a standard normal variable. The rationale for this is as follows. For simplicity, let us assume that all men have the same tastes, so that we can talk about '*the*' non-pecuniary attractions of different jobs. We shall also assume that utility is of the form

$$u = f(W_i^\gamma \Phi_i^\delta), \quad \gamma + \delta = 1, \quad f' > 0,$$

where Φ_i represents the pleasantness of the occupation (apart from its monetary returns). This makes the amount of income a man is prepared to sacrifice for better conditions proportional to his wage. It also makes the income elasticity of demand for pleasantness unity.

Building on this, the first step is to look at occupations all paid the same particular level of wages (W). These jobs are ranked according to Φ_i, or, more conveniently, according to

$$W^\gamma \left(\frac{\Phi_i}{\overline{\Phi|W}} \right)^\delta = W^\gamma V_i^\delta \quad \text{(as a definition of } V\text{).}$$

---

[17] Their study is based on interviews of a national sample of 620 men and women aged 20–64 in England and Wales in 1972.

By construction V has a mean of unity. A natural scale for measuring the desirability of occupations paid W might be D, where

$$D_i = W^\gamma V_i^\delta.$$

So far the procedure is unobjectionable. We have simply chosen a cardinalisation of the ranking of occupations which is bound to preserve the correct ordering. The problem comes when we want to compare the desirability of occupations at different wage levels. If j refers to the wage and ij to the occupation i at wage j, occupations are ranked by

$$W_j^\gamma \Phi_{ij}^\delta \quad \text{or by} \quad W_j^\gamma (\bar{\Phi}|W_j)^\delta \left(\frac{\Phi_{ij}}{\bar{\Phi}|W_j}\right)^\delta = W_j^\gamma (\bar{\Phi}|W_j)^\delta V^\delta,$$

where V is independent of W. If $(\bar{\Phi}|W_j) = \alpha W_j^\beta$, the index of desirability (D) is now defined by

$$D = \alpha^\delta W_j^{\beta\delta + \gamma} V^\delta,$$

or

$$\ln D = \delta \ln \alpha + (\beta\delta + \gamma) \ln W_j + \delta \ln V.$$

We know that $\ln W$ is normal; and, if $\ln V$ is also normal, then so is $\ln D$. This provides some crude justification for taking the Goldthorpe–Hope ordinal scale of occupations and making it into a normal variable.

Apart from the arbitrariness of the three assumptions made, a remaining practical problem is what standard deviation to assume for the variable $\ln D$. If one knew the value of $(\beta\delta + \gamma) = (1 - \gamma)\beta + \gamma$, one could choose that standard deviation of $\ln D$ which gave the right regression coefficient when $\ln D$ is regressed on $\ln W$. If $\beta = 1$, the correct coefficient is of course unity, but we do not know the value of β. So, for the present purposes, we have normalised $\ln D$ to have a standard deviation of approximately unity (compared with 0.43 for $\ln W$). The regression coefficient implied is in fact 1.18. This we find when we take men aged 30–55 (to deal with problems of prospects affecting occupational desirability), and regress $\ln D$ on $\ln W$:

$$\ln D = 0.33 + 1.18 \ln W, \quad R^2 = 0.37,$$
$$\text{Standard error of estimate} = 0.72,$$
$$(SE = 0.04)$$

This seems to make reasonable sense, allowing for the fact that the error term includes not only errors due to V but to other sources.

We now run ordinary multiple regressions of $\ln D$ on coverage and our other variables (see table 19.7). (The simple regressions are in table 19.8.) As before, there is no significant effect for non-manual workers. For manual workers once again coverage appears to have a very striking effect. As expected, the effect (on desirability) is now *larger* when mining and agriculture are omitted. If one interprets D as a measure of adjusted money income, then (excluding mining and agriculture) coverage seems to have more than ten times as large an effect on this as on money wages. This counsels caution in the interpretation. An alternative approach is to

Table 19.7. Regression equations explaining the desirability of the individual's occupation (1973, males).[a]

Type of occ: → Sector: →	All All	Manual All	Manual All excl. primary	Manual Manufacturing	Non-manual All
Variables					
Coverage	−0.62 (9.4)	1.14 (10.5)	2.32 (17.1)	3.18 (18.0)	−0.14 (1.5)
Schooling yrs.	0.08 (7.9)	−0.01 (0.6)	−0.00 (0.2)	0.02 (1.3)	0.06 (4.5)
Degree	0.82 (7.9)	−0.27 (0.6)	−0.20 (0.4)	−0.14 (0.3)	0.70 (5.8)
Advanced	1.01 (18.5)	0.40 (3.3)	0.41 (3.3)	0.32 (2.3)	0.78 (11.5)
A level	0.56 (10.7)	0.34 (5.4)	0.32 (5.0)	0.26 (3.9)	0.53 (6.9)
O level	0.42 (9.9)	0.26 (5.3)	0.23 (4.7)	0.17 (3.2)	0.37 (5.5)
Other qual.	0.31 (5.6)	0.02 (0.4)	0.02 (0.4)	−0.00 (0.0)	0.34 (4.1)
No quals.	−	−	−	−	−
Sel. school	0.19 (5.8)	0.06 (1.4)	0.06 (1.3)	0.11 (2.1)	0.03 (0.6)
Aim qual.	0.32 (6.2)	0.38 (6.2)	0.36 (5.9)	0.33 (4.4)	0.22 (2.8)
Exp. 0–5	0.02 (0.9)	0.01 (0.5)	0.01 (0.4)	0.02 (0.7)	0.02 (0.5)
6–10	0.01 (0.1)	0.00 (0.1)	0.00 (0.1)	0.02 (1.1)	0.01 (0.6)
11–20	0.01 (1.8)	0.00 (0.1)	0.00 (0.7)	0.01 (0.9)	0.01 (1.4)
21–30	−0.00 (0.0)	−0.00 (0.6)	−0.00 (0.5)	0.00 (0.5)	−0.01 (0.8)
31–40	0.01 (1.5)	−0.00 (0.2)	−0.00 (0.7)	−0.02 (2.9)	0.01 (1.5)
41+	−0.02 (2.8)	−0.00 (0.0)	−0.00 (0.2)	0.02 (2.1)	−0.05 (3.7)
Father 1	0.14 (3.1)	0.01 (0.2)	0.08 (1.6)	0.08 (1.5)	0.09 (0.9)
Father 2	0.06 (1.3)	−0.05 (1.1)	−0.01 (0.3)	−0.04 (0.7)	0.02 (0.2)
Father 3	0.08 (2.0)	−0.04 (1.2)	0.03 (0.9)	0.01 (0.2)	0.06 (0.6)
Father 4	−	−	−	−	−
W. Indies	−0.21 (2.0)	−0.10 (1.0)	−0.10 (1.0)	−0.15 (1.3)	−0.12 (0.4)
Other coloured	−0.27 (4.6)	−0.19 (3.2)	−0.16 (2.7)	−0.13 (1.8)	−0.09 (0.9)
Ireland	−0.14 (1.1)	−0.24 (1.9)	−0.22 (1.7)	−0.07 (0.5)	0.32 (1.3)
Other white	−	−	−	−	−
Sick	−0.10 (2.7)	−0.02 (0.6)	−0.01 (0.3)	−0.06 (1.4)	−0.26 (3.8)
Married	0.15 (4.4)	0.08 (2.3)	0.08 (2.4)	0.06 (1.6)	0.26 (4.1)
S. East	0.14 (4.4)	0.04 (1.3)	0.03 (0.9)	0.08 (2.2)	0.11 (2.0)
Urban	0.04 (0.4)	−0.06 (0.6)	0.02 (0.2)	0.06 (0.5)	0.14 (0.7)
Non-manuf.	−0.04 (1.8)	−0.14 (6.3)	−0.18 (7.3)	−	−0.08 (1.7)
Constant	−0.98 (5.8)	−1.17 (4.7)	−2.36 (8.9)	−3.53 (12.1)	−0.72 (2.7)
R^2	0.34	0.11	0.17	0.26	0.28
S.E.	0.73	0.61			0.75
N	4,307	2,830	2,599	1,386	1,477

[a] Source: General Household Survey, see Appendix 1.
t-statistic in parentheses.

show some scepticism about the units of measurement. We can then ask: how do the effects of coverage on desirability and on wages differ when we measure the effect in units of the standard deviations of each dependent variable. The comparison is best made using the group data in table 19.3 and the quasi-group data in table 19.8. The answer (for manual workers outside mining and agriculture) is that increasing coverage by one standard deviation of itself raises ln W by 0.20 standard deviations and ln D by 0.32 standard deviations. This provides some preliminary but highly tentative support for the view that unions raise the relative non-

Effect of collective bargaining

Table 19.8. Simple regressions of log "desirability" on "coverage" (individual data, male employees, 1973).[a]

Occupation: → Sector: →	All All	Manual All	Manual All excl. primary	Manual Manufacturing	Non-manual All
Coefficient (t)	−1.23 (16	1.20 (11)	2.41 (17)	3.29 (18)	−0.07 (0.6)
R^2	0.059	0.040	0.102	0.195	0.000
N	4307	2830	2599	1386	1477

[a] Source: GHS tapes. For the desirability variable see text.

Both the desirability variable and the coverage variable relate to the 3-digit occupation group. So these regressions are the same as weighted regressions on group data.

pecuniary rewards of their workers as well as or more than their pecuniary rewards.[18]

Appendix 1: List of variables used in regressions using individual data

Coverage	Proportion of workers in the 3-digit occupation covered by any collective agreement.
Schooling years	Years of full-time education (measured by age on completing full-time education minus 5).[19]
Degree	First or higher degree (dummy).
Advanced	Non-graduate qualification above the standard of GCE Advanced Level (dummy).
A level	1 or more passes at GCE Advanced Level[20] (typically taken at age 18) or equivalent technical qualification (dummy).
O level	1 or more passes at GCE Ordinary Level (typically taken at age 16) or City and Guilds craft/ordinary technical qualification (dummy).
Other qual.	Some other qualification (dummy).
No quals.	No qualifications (excluded category).
Sel. school	Selective school (grammar or fee-paying) (dummy).
Ex-apprent.	Successfully completed apprenticeship (dummy).
Aim qual.	Currently apprenticed or studying for a qualification (dummy).
Exp. 0–5 6–10 11–20 21–30 31–40 41+	Age minus years of schooling minus 5. (The coefficients indicate the effect of *one* additional year within each experience category.)

[18] For confirmation of this with respect to provisions for sickness and old age, see Nickell (1977).
[19] In about 3 percent of cases the reported value of this figure was so large relative to the person's qualifications that the person had clearly re-entered education and a number was assigned based on the individual's qualifications.
[20] GCE = General Certificate of Education.

Father 1	Father professional or managerial (dummy).
Father 2	Father other white-collar (dummy).
Father 3	Father skilled or semi-skilled manual (dummy).
Father 4	Father unskilled (excluded category).
W. Indies	Coloured and born in British West Indies (dummy).
Other coloured	Other couloured (interviewer's classification) (dummy).
Ireland	Born in Ireland (Eire) (dummy).
Other white	Other white (excluded category).
Married	Married (dummy).
Sick	Suffers from a long-standing illness, disability or infirmity which limits activities compared with most people of the same age (dummy).
S. East	Living in South-East region (dummy).
Urban	Proportion of residents in the region living in conurbations or urban areas (as defined in GHS).
Public	Working in a 2-digit industry in which majority of employment is public sector, including nationalised industries.
Non-manuf.	Working outside manufacturing (dummy).
Plant size	Average number of employees in each plant in the individual's 2-digit industry (manufacturing only) (zero in non-manuf.).
Conc. ratio	Proportion of employment in 2-digit industry accounted for by largest five firms (manufacturing only) (zero in non-manuf.).

Sources: All variables except the four defined immediately below are from Office of Population Censuses and Surveys (OPCAS) *General Household Survey*, 1973 (data tapes). Urban variable is from GHS, 1972. Plant size and concentration ratio from Department of Trade and Industry, *Census of Production*, 1968, summary table 158. Coverage data from the *New Earnings Survey*, 1973, table 112.

Appendix 2: Derivation of time series on coverage

In the Appendix table, columns (3) and (4), the coverage variable for years other than 1973 is computed as follows. Price and Bain (1976) report that male unionisation rose not at all between 1948 and 1964, by 0.92 per cent per annum between 1964 and 1970 and by 0.58 per cent per annum between 1970 and 1974 – and by 8.67 per cent overall. They also report the change in unionisation in each industry between 1948 and 1974. We assume

(i) that the fraction of the 48–74 change in unionisation in each industry that occurred in 1964–70 and 1970–74 was the same as for overall unionisation.
(ii) that within each of these periods the change was linear, and
(iii) that the proportional changes in coverage were the same as the proportional changes in unionisation.

If these adjustments are made, the time series effects comparable to those shown in table 19.6, column (2), are as shown in Appendix table column (4). The table also shows the simple regression coefficients with the adjusted data in column (3). Columns (1) and (2) of the table show simple regression coefficients using the same data as are used for the partial regression coefficients of table 19.6. We are extremely grateful to Munia Awan and Stephen King for extracting all the time series data.

Appendix table. Effects of coverage on group log hourly earnings (3-digit manufacturing industries, male manual employees).[a]

		Simple regression coefficients		1958 SIC industries (adjusted coverage data)	
		1968 SIC industries	1958 SIC industries (unadjusted)	Simple coefficients coefficients	Partial regression coefficients
		(1)	(2)	(3)	(4)
1961	April		0.33 (3.9)	−0.07 (1.5)	−0.02 (0.6)
	October		0.31 (3.7)	−0.06 (1.2)	−0.01 (0.2)
1962	April		0.28 (3.3)	−0.06 (1.3)	−0.01 (0.2)
	October		0.32 (3.8)	−0.05 (1.0)	−0.01 (0.2)
1963	April		0.30 (3.4)	−0.05 (1.0)	−0.01 (0.3)
	October		0.29 (3.3)	−0.05 (1.1)	0.00
1964	April		0.32 (3.2)	−0.05 (1.1)	0.00
	October		0.31 (3.6)	−0.05 (1.0)	0.00
1965	April		0.36 (4.1)	−0.04 (0.7)	0.00
	October		0.33 (3.9)	−0.04 (0.3)	0.00
1966	April		0.36 (4.2)	−0.02 (0.3)	0.02 (0.5)
	October		0.31 (3.7)	−0.03 (0.6)	0.00
1967	April		0.30 (3.7)	0.00 (0.0)	0.02 (0.5)
	October		0.32 (3.9)	0.01 (0.2)	0.02 (0.5)
1968	April		0.32 (3.8)	0.06 (0.8)	0.06 (1.1)
	October		0.33 (4.1)	0.09 (1.2)	0.08 (1.5)
1969	April		0.33 (4.0)	0.14 (1.8)	0.12 (2.0)
	October	0.16 (2.3)	0.33 (3.9)	0.15 (1.8)	0.13 (2.1)
1970	October	0.21 (2.9)	0.37 (4.1)	0.24 (2.7)	0.19 (2.6)
1971	October	0.24 (3.1)	0.36 (3.8)	0.28 (2.9)	0.22 (2.8)
1972	October	0.28 (3.8)	0.43 (4.6)	0.39 (4.1)	0.29 (3.6)
1973	October	0.26 (3.9)	0.42 (4.7)	0.42 (4.7)	0.31 (3.7)
1974	October	0.27 (4.1)	0.35 (4.1)	0.36 (4.1)	0.26 (3.4)
1975	October	0.36 (5.0)	0.44 (4.4)	0.45 (4.9)	0.31 (3.5)

[a] Source: see text.

References

Ashenfelter, O., "Union Relative Wage Effects: New Evidence and a Survey of Their Implications for Wage Inflation", Industrial relations section, Princeton University, working paper 89, 1976.
Goldthorpe, J.H. and K. Hope, *The Social Grading of Occupations*, Oxford, 1974.
Greenhalgh, C., "Is Marriage an Equal Opportunity", LSE mimeo, 1977.
Johnson, G.E., "Economic Analysis of Trade Unionism", *American Economic Review*, May 1975.
King, M., "The U.K. Profits Crisis: Myth or Reality", *Economic Journal*, March 1975.

Layard, R., "On Measuring the Redistribution of Lifetime Income", in M.S. Feldstein and R.P. Inman, (eds.) *The Economics of Public Services*, Macmillan, 1976.

Lewis, H.G., *Unionism and Relative Wages in the United States*, Chicago, Chicago U.P., 1963.

Metcalf, D., "Unions, Incomes Policy and Relative Wages in Britain", *British Journal of Industrial Relations*, July 1977.

Mulvey, C. and J. Foster, "Occupational Earnings in the U.K. and the Effects of Collective Agreements", *Manchester School*, September 1976.

Mulvey, C., "Collective Agreements and Relative Earnings in U.K. Manufacturing in 1973", *Economica*, November 1976.

Nickell, S., "Trade Unions and the Position of Women in the Industrial Wage Structure", *British Journal of Industrial Relations*, July 1977.

Office of Population Censuses and Surveys (OPCAS), *General Household Survey, 1973*, London, HMSO, 1976.

Pencavel, J., "Relative Wages and Trade Unions in the U.K.", *Economica*, May 1974.

Phelps-Brown, E.H., "An Non-Monetarist View of the Pay Explosion", *The Three Banks Review*, March 1975.

Price, R. and G.S. Bain, "Union Growth Revisited: 1948–1974 in Perspective", *British Journal of Industrial Relations*, XIV, 3, 1976.

Psacharopoulos, G., "Family Background, Education and Achievement: A Path Model of Earnings Determinants in the U.K. and Some Alternatives", *British Journal of Sociology*, December 1977.

Psacharopoulos, G. and R. Layard, "Human Capital and Earnings: British Evidence and a Critique", *Review of Economic Studies*, forthcoming.

Stewart, M., "The Determinants of Earnings in Britain: An Occupation-Specific Approach", LSE mimeo, 1977.

Wachter, M.L., "Phase II, Cost-Push Inflation, and Relative Wages", *American Economic Review*, June 1974.

19 DISCUSSION

PAPER BY R. LAYARD, D. METCALF AND S. NICKELL

Professor de Wolff found the paper of great interest, although he was not sure whether the results for the UK could be extended to other countries, since comparisons between countries on these issues tend to be rather difficult. He was pleased to see that the material available for the UK contained observations on a variety of factors, such as education, experience and family background, for a large group of individuals. These variables were used as controls for the factor in which the paper was primarily interested, union coverage. Whilst the data did not give details of individual union membership, and coverage within broader groups had to be used instead, the results on unionisation were nevertheless very interesting; in particular, the fact that the difference between full and no coverage seems to lead to a difference of some 35% in wages.

One point which puzzled him in table 19.1 was the negative coefficient for coverage in the non-manual group. This was surprising, particularly since the coefficients for the control variables conformed to expectations. He agreed with the suggestion that it may be necessary to distinguish between groups in the non-manual category, but wondered why no attempt had been made to rerun the regressions without, say, the top 10% of individuals in the earnings distribution. He felt the coefficient on coverage might be zero, but did not see how it could be negative. He also asked how the negative coefficient in table 19.1 could become positive in table 19.4, when the only change had been to replace individual variables with group variables.

In the second part of the paper, changes in the logarithm of the wage level over time are related to coverage and the coefficient is found to increase strongly after the years 1969/70. However, the data on coverage only apply to one year and this may lead to serious biases. He pointed out that quite different results are given in the annex table, where an attempt is made to correct for the coverage data of earlier years.

He was not convinced that the comparison with unemployment was acceptable, since the theory of wages and cost-push inflation was far too simple. An increase in wages is not necessarily inflationary if productivity is also rising, and there are other factors to be taken into account, such as whether a sheltered or an unsheltered industry is considered. He had made a scatter of the level of unemployment against the regression coefficient of log w on the degree of unionisation. As the value of the regression coefficient increases, the average level of unemployment is roughly constant, but the variance of the unemployment level increases quite substantially.

On another diagram he had plotted the wage rate against the regression coefficient and found the points to fall into two distinct groups, corresponding to the years before and after 1970. This led him to believe there may be something in the suggestion, attributed to Professor Phelps Brown, that the result is due to a general development which started with the French experience in 1968.

Finally he made some remarks on the part dealing with occupational desirability. It is a very interesting attempt to measure the importance attached by trade unions to the non-pecuniary labour conditions. Whilst unions attempt to affect wages, they do not in general try to move people from less desirable jobs to more desirable ones. However, the results are not very convincing. The arguments used to derive the coefficient of desirability are rather weak and the contrast between tables 19.1 and 19.7, which are based on the same individual data, is striking. In table 19.1 most of the coefficients of the additional variables are very plausible; in table 19.7 they are practically all insignificant. This led him to recommend caution in interpreting the results.

Dr. Kuipers said the paper took account of many personal characteristics and the results therefore seem strong, but he was not convinced that unionisation caused higher wages. There may be some spurious correlation, resulting perhaps from the tendency of those with a higher productivity to be unionised.

On the cost-push element of inflation, the conclusion that coverage has an impact on the total level of wages was based on the simultaneous rise in unemployment and fall in coverage during the 1970s. He pointed out, however, that since 1972 an incomes policy had been in existence in the UK. During periods of incomes policy in the Netherlands, unionisation has fallen as the role of the unions in wage negotiations diminished. Table 19.6 seemed to be consistent with this experience, indicating a decline in coverage after 1972 which might be attributable to the incomes policy.

Professor Pen asked what the T.U.C. was doing. As he understood the paper, trade unions were increasing inequality amongst workers horizontally. This creates conflict within the working class, undermining the class struggle. In the Netherlands the trade union movement co-ordinates wages to avoid this kind of conflict.

Professor Wiles suggested a possible explanation for the negative coefficient on coverage for non-manual occupations in table 19.1. People may join a union when their real incomes fall or suffer a relative decline, so the upper non-manual groups are being caught at a moment when they are falling behind but nevertheless becoming more unionised.

Professor Krelle suggested that coverage was perhaps related to the industrial structure. The textile industry in Germany, for example, contained a high proportion of women and had consequently both low unionisation and low pay. Thus, in this example, coverage measures the proportion of women. On the point raised by Professor Pen, he said that in Germany the unions always attempt to establish parity for similar kinds of work, in contrast to the employers who try to maintain differences. In Germany it is also true that once the contract is signed all workers are paid that amount regardless of whether they belong to the union.

Professor Lecaillon was surprised that coverage could raise wages by 25%. He asked whether there was not some demonstration effect progressively extending advantages obtained in one sector to the whole labour force. In France this solidarity is an important inflationary factor, with the initial disequalising effect of collective bargaining followed by a secondary equalising tendency.

He also suggested there was a systematic relationship between high productivity, high profitability, strong unions and high wages. If this were the case, he asked what the relative contributions of productivity and collective bargaining were on wage differentials.

Professor Robinson wondered whether he was right in believing that the paper was only concerned with males. In some industries there is a clear division between those jobs done by males and those by females, but in other industries the dividing line is not so clearly established. An increase in the wages of males in the latter case may tend to substitute women for men in the workforce. The important criterion in such cases is not whether males are organised, but the extent to which the whole workforce is unionised. He asked whether the analysis was being extended to women. If so, he suggested it would be useful to find the combined effects.

Professor Krupp said that, in this type of study, a range of results is normally obtained depending on which variables are included and excluded. He asked about the sensitivity of the coefficients to these kinds of modifications. Secondly, he emphasised the difficulties involved in using cross-section evidence to support a causal relationship. As had been indicated in the discussion, other interpretations were possible.

Mr. Bartels agreed with Professor Krupp's reservations concerning the use of cross-section studies as evidence for causal relationships. He also warned that the results might change if certain omitted variables were correlated with those included.

He had difficulties similar to those of Professor de Wolff in comparing the results for individuals in table 19.1 with those for groups in table 19.4. He understood the link to be a simple linear aggregation, in which case the estimation technique on the grouped data will not be efficient unless generalised least squares is used.

Professor Chiswick was intrigued by the attempt to capture the dimension of job desirability. However, there are two possible ways in which job desirability could vary with income. Unions may seek to improve working conditions once wages have risen to a certain level, suggesting a positive relationship. On the other hand, there is the notion that unions try to extract compensatory wage differentials for unpleasant work, suggesting a negative relationship. In the first case, high coverage would be expected to be associated with pleasant occupations, whilst the second possibility suggests that attempts to unionise would be strongest where working conditions are worst.

Professor Taubman, in the chair, said that the paper concentrated on wages. It is possible that the effects are different for wages and annual incomes and this may have to be taken into account. He also pointed out that some US studies had examined changes in the coefficient of variation by occupation and industry over the business cycle. When the labour market is tight there tends to be a smaller coefficient of variation and this may affect comparisons over time. Finally, he wondered whether table 19.7 merely indicated which jobs were unionised. It is possible that the figures only reflect the fact that higher craft jobs are more unionised than lower craft jobs.

In reply *Mr. Layard* said that the most difficult issue raised was that of causality: were they saying something over and above the simple fact that highly paid occupations are more likely to be covered by union agreements? He believed they were, although, as always, there are the problems of omitted variables and simultaneous equation bias discussed in section II of the paper. The fact that individual data were used makes these problems less serious than if group data had been used.

Turning to the detailed comments, he intended to take up Professor Robinson's suggestion and attempt to examine the effects of coverage of *all* workers (both male and female). He also thought it would be interesting to try omitting those with high predicted incomes in order to see whether white collar unionism has an effect. But it seemed to him unlikely that the white collar groups who are unionised are those whose wages are transitorily low, as Professor Wiles had suggested.

In the time series work it was unfortunate that they did not have a different measure of coverage for each year, but it was striking that they obtained similar results over time using data on unionisation in 1966. The attempt (in the Annex) to derive an index of coverage that varied from year to year clearly introduced more error than it removed. Professor Kuipers' interpretation of table 19.6 was not correct. Column (4) does not reflect changing levels of unionisation within industries, but simply changes in the mix of employment between industries (see footnote in text).

As regards Professor Pen and the T.U.C., Mr. Layard said that their model implies that once 50 per cent of the labour force is covered, further extensions of coverage will be equalising. This follows since, ignoring other sources of inequality,

$$\ln W = a + mT$$

and

$$\text{Var}(\ln W) = m^2 \bar{U}(1 - \bar{U})$$

where $\bar{U}$ is the fraction of the workforce covered. Thus inequality is at its minimum when all workers or none are covered.

Finally, on the question of the desirability of jobs, unions clearly do not try to shift workers from one job to another, but they do try to influence working conditions as well as wages. However, he was not sure whether Professor Chiswick's remarks recognised that the index of general desirability used in the analysis took account of both working conditions *and* wages. One would of course expect that, holding general desirability constant, wages would vary inversely with working conditions. But there is no prior expectation about the simple relation between wages and desirability.

PART VI

ECONOMIC POLICY AND INCOME DISTRIBUTION

20 GROWTH POLICY AND THE DISTRIBUTION OF INCOME

*CARMEL ULLMAN CHISWICK**

I. Introduction

The size distribution of income within nations has received a great deal of attention in the economic literature in recent years. The unprecedented availability of household survey and census data for many LDCs has greatly stimulated this literature, increasing not only our ability to measure the distribution of income but also – and consequently – increasing the sophistication with which we define our interest in this subject.[1] Alternative hypotheses about poverty and wealth are often capable of being tested with such data, and the subjects most relevant for policy analysis can be selected for more intensive study.[2] At some point, however, it is seemly that we back off from these studies and return to the broader questions with which we started. It is in this spirit that this paper discusses the implications of growth policy for the distribution of income.

Our interest in income distribution derives from our concern with equity. A sampling of five-year development plans from a wide variety of LDCs suggest that this is indeed the underlying concern, and that equity may be characterized by three propositions: (1) equal pay for equal work (2) "fair" skill differentials, and (3) the absence of a situation in which extreme poverty for some is accompanied by extreme wealth for others.[3] The formal exercise which this paper undertakes

---

* Participation in this conference was made possible by an NSF Travel Support Grant SOC 77–06829.

[1] The empirical studies of income distribution in particular countries are by now too numerous to list. As a start, however, the interested reader can refer to the studies collected in *Income Distribution, Employment and Economic Development in Southeast and East Asia* (Papers and Proceedings of the JERC–CAMS Seminar held in December 1974), Japan Economic Research Center, (Tokyo, 1975), and to P. Musgrove, *Income and Spending of Urban Families in Latin America*, Brookings, 1977 (ECIEL). Note also the many studies sponsored by the Income Distribution and Employment Programme, as part of the ILO's World Employment Programme Research.

[2] The recent spate of analyses of human resources in general and labor supply effects in particular would appear to belong in this category. Fairly detailed technical analyses of the relationships between earnings and wage rates on the one hand and education, fertility and migration on the other have become quite common in the literature on LDCs. Although these works are of uneven quality and focus on a variety of different problems, in general they tend to support the notion that labor supply is price-responsive in a wide range of economic circumstances. For a summary of the effects of earnings incentives on migration, for example, see L. Yap, "Internal migration in less developed countries: a survey of the literature", (World Bank Staff Working Paper No. 215, September 1975).

[3] United Nations economic and social council, *Social objectives and related policies and programmes in national plans of selected developing countries for the Second United Nations Development Decade, Report of the Secretary-General* (Document No. E/CN. 5/476, 27 October 1972), par. 56–60.

begins with a neoclassical free-market equilibrium in which only the last of these conditions is not satisfied. Three socio-economic groups are specified, corresponding to unskilled labor, skilled labor and high-level manpower, and the earnings of unskilled labor are presumed to be "too" low relative to the earnings of high-level manpower.

In order to improve the distribution of income, a "minimum wage" is targeted which is higher than the equilibrium wage for unskilled workers yet lower than the wage for skilled workers. It is assumed that such a target cannot be imposed by fiat but must reflect a genuine improvement in the productivity of unskilled labor. Thus the question is: what combination of investment incentives will raise the competitive earnings of unskilled labor to the target level with the least sacrifice in aggregate income, and how will factor prices in this case compare to the free-market equilibrium prices?

Since experience with modern technologies suggests that they are not well suited for employing truly unskilled labor, the analysis must take place in the context of a dual economy. The modern and the traditional sectors are characterized by two different technologies and each firm is assumed to belong to one sector or the other. Acquisition of middle-level skills is a prerequisite – but not a guarantee – for employment in the modern sector. The unskilled must work with non-modern, "traditional" technologies which are generally incompatible with the use of high-level manpower. Firms in both sectors compete in the factor markets for middle-level manpower as well as for non-human resources. Factor-market dualism may be defined as a market situation in which the factor can command a different price depending on the sector in which it is employed. For this to occur, it is not sufficient that the demand for factors be different in the two sectors; there must also be some mechanism on the supply side to check the private incentive to "migrate" from one sector to the other. Clearly such a dualism is impossible for both unskilled and high-level manpower since each of these is employed in only one sector. Dualism in the middle-level labor market or in the market for non-human resources is possible but may be difficult to sustain in a competitive free-market economy.[4] One important implication of this paper, however, is that some government intervention in the factor markets in order to sustain such a dualism is part of the optimal policy package for meeting the "minimum wage" target.

The policy framework for the more formal analysis to follow is outlined in section II and a simplified model is presented in section III. Section IV develops the full model from which the policy conclusions are derived. Section V concludes with a summary of policy implications and a short discussion of some dynamic aspects of this analysis. The optimal solution of the model is defined as that which meets all three equity criteria with the least sacrifice in income. This solution is

---

[4] There is a fairly large literature in dualism reconciling between sector price differentials with the existence of competitive markets. Without going into this matter in detail, it may be noted that nearly all such explanations imply that the differential is "compensating" for something – risk, uncertainty, cost of living differences, on-the-job formation of general skills, cost of search, etc. The assumption made in this paper is that all such supply-price differentials are already embodied in the competitive free-market equilibrium, and "dualism" is *additional* to this.

shown to be unique for an important class of production functions, so that the trade-off between the minimum-wage target and foregone income may be clearly defined. Assuming that production functions for both sectors are characterized by constant returns to scale, diminishing marginal products and the usual convexity conditions, and assuming that in the absence of specific interventions the factor markets would be competitive, firms pay factors according to their (marginal) productivity, earnings differentials just equal the differential values of prior investment in skill-formation, and the marginal product of unskilled labor is just equal to the minimum-wage target. A set of policies for achieving the optimal solution might include non-intervention in the modern-sector factor markets, subsidies for any type of education that effectively converts unskilled labor into middle-level manpower and hence reduces the need for the traditional sector, and subsidies to all factors other than unskilled labor actually employed in the traditional sector. These factors should be subsidized up to the point where the total value of the subsidy just equals the cost of converting all remaining unskilled workers into middle-level manpower, and the subsidies should be such that relative factor prices (marginal products) are the same in both sectors.

II. Development strategies and income distribution

Consider a country with a two-technology economy and a labor force composed primarily of people without modern skills. Most of these people work in comparatively small enterprises with varying degrees of "informality" in their business arrangements; we may suppose that they are for the most part remote from the centers of government, socially as well as perhaps geographically. In contrast, the comparatively small proportion of the labor force which works in modern-technology firms is typically quite close to the political center of the country. Thus one of the political facts which will affect the choice of government policies for both income distribution and growth is the comparative remoteness from direct contract between the government and the large body of people depending on the traditional sector for their incomes.

Consider also in this country that unskilled, traditional-sector workers are very poor and that the government wishes to devise some policy for raising their incomes. Direct redistribution schemes are not practical; administration costs may be very high for programs involving direct contact with poor people, while the better-off among the poor, or even the non-poor, are most likely to be first in line to receive the benefits of such a program. Moreover for philosophical, ideological or aesthetic reasons it is deemed that self-help programs are more appropriate than direct redistribution schemes, and the government therefore decides that it must devise some way to improve the earnings of the poor.

There are several development strategies which must be considered, all aimed at improving the earnings of people in the traditional sector. One of the most influential focuses on the modern-sector growth rate (of aggregate income) in the expectation that the modern sector will either absorb the traditional sector eventually or that there will be a "trickle-down" effect triggered by a high income elasticity for traditional-sector output. Another important strategy is to concentrate on modern-sector capital accumulation (which may or may not be growth-maximizing) as the solution to the poverty problem; by building more modern-technology factories to employ people who would otherwise be poor, modern-sector employment will be expanded and hence traditional-sector employment will be reduced. Adherents of yet another strategy insist that education is the best hope for the poor, pointing out (correctly) that hardly anyone with a high school education is poor, regardless of family background. The education faction notes that children from families with modern-sector employment (and incomes) are much more likely to be sent to school by their families than children from traditional backgrounds; although it may approve of the objective of universal literacy, its main concern is that poor children have the opportunity to compete for higher education on the basis of ability rather than family income. Finally, a fourth viewpoint is that while each of the above proposals has merit, the magnitude of the problem is such that even if the government does everything possible, there will still be a large number of people relying on traditional-sector technology for their income and this income will still be too low. Proponents of this point of view see direct technical assistance as the only hope for these people, assistance that enables them to take advantage of new knowledge (and to some extent new skills) with marginal modifications in traditional production techniques.

Certainly from a practical point of view the government must acknowledge that it will be impossible to eliminate the poverty problem during the relevant planning period insofar as this problem is associated with the existence of unskilled traditional-sector labor. The larger the proportion of the population in this category the longer the time period that would be needed before any scheme for absorbing these people into the modern sector would have an appreciable impact. In the short run, some sort of assistance appears to be essential for raising the incomes of the poor through self-help. This assistance may be aimed at improving the knowledge and/or skills of the individual, at providing the individual with a package of complementary resources (together with knowledge about its use), or by employing a technical advisor who effectively acts as a productive input complementary to those already in use. It is also possible to provide assistance in the form of subsidized loans to traditional-sector enterprises without specifying the manner in which these loans are to be used. These policies all have the effect of reducing the cost of resources complementary to unskilled labor in the traditional sector and hence provide an incentive to expand their use. Following such policies will not only result in higher incomes for the poor but also in an expansion of the traditional sector at the expense of the modern sector, since these complementary resources would otherwise be employed in modern-sector activities.

Although a traditional-sector household may improve its income situation noticeably with the help of a good assistance program, an individual member of a poor household can dramatically change his or her earnings prospects through education. Government policy towards education is thus an important aspect of its income distribution policy and it must take into account the variety of mechanisms through which education can affect incomes. To the extent that education is associated with the formation of productive skills it constitutes a special type of capital formation and from this point of view the incentives to invest in education are similar to the incentives to invest in non-human capital. It may be presumed that if there is a competitive market for financing all types of investment, the distribution of education would be such that the present value of expected income (net of investment costs) is maximized for each household and aggregate income is maximized for the economy as a whole.

Apart from its effect on human capital formation, education is the prerequisite for employment in modern-sector firms. An individual employed in the modern sector is no longer part of the poverty problem, and if family ties are sufficiently strong it is possible that within-family transfers can actually raise the entire household out of poverty. To the extent that income is positively associated with education within the modern sector, the higher the education level the farther out of poverty the family can get. Thus education is clearly an investment considered from the point of view of the individual and the household, whether or not it is associated with the formation of human capital in the sense of productivity-increasing skills.[5] To the extent that education reduces the number of people in poverty, it is also appropriately considered as an investment on the part of a government concerned with reducing poverty. As such, it competes with other types of investment for financing both in the private capital markets and in the government's budget.

Because of this double function, the private incentives to invest in education may be "too low" in a free-market economy. It may be socially productive to decrease the number of people in poverty even after investments in education are no longer competitive with investments of other types. Note, however, that such a possibility arises only for those types of education which actually convert traditional-sector labor into either modern-sector labor or into a more skilled (and hence better paid) traditional-sector resource; if education serves only to change the skill level of a person who would otherwise not be in poverty anyway, it does not contribute directly to the objective of reducing poverty and there is no need to argue that the private incentive to invest is "too low."

"Over-investing" in the type of basic education required for access to modern-sector jobs raises the earnings of the poor in two distinct ways: reducing their numbers, *ceteris paribus*, would relieve crowding and thus raise marginal productivity; and increasing the number of skilled workers in the traditional sector, *ceteris paribus*, raises the marginal productivity of unskilled workers (like any other increase in capital). In contrast, a policy of "over-investing" in capital-formation for the modern sector would reduce the complementary resources available to unskilled labor by drawing away both investment and skilled labor from the tradi-

---

[5] The "screening hypothesis", which has received much attention in the recent literature, argues that there is *no* human capital formation associated with schooling even though for various reasons earnings are positively associated with educational attainment. In such a case investment in education may be subdivided into two distinct components: resources devoted to skill-formation and resources devoted to other means of increasing incomes. Without denying the possible importance of the latter for a specific country and time period, this paper deals only with the distribution of earnings of productive factors and the analysis is thus limited to the former.

tional sector. Moreover this impoverishment of the traditional sector need not be accompanied by any improvement of earnings *within* the modern sector, and there is the possibility that the income distribution effects may even be perverse if the policy encourages the expansion of capital-intensive technologies instead of expanding modern-sector employment.

Indeed, it is distinctly possible that strategies focusing on growth rates in the modern sector are missing the main development objective. No matter how wealthy the modern sector may be, a country will still have development problems as long as a large proportion of its labor force is effectively excluded from that sector. It would seem more reasonable to maximize the growth rate of total income, regardless of the sector in which it is generated, and to let the optimal allocation of income, investment and employment between sectors be derived from this objective. If lack of skills constitutes a barrier to employment in the modern sector, skill-formation is the only way to expand employment in that sector; and if "over-investment" in education is not sufficient to eliminate poverty, technical assistance type programs will be necessary as well.

III. The simplified model

The simplest case with which to illustrate the relationship between income distribution and growth policy is that of a three-factor, two-sector economy. The traditional sector employs physical capital and unskilled labor, and the modern sector employs physical capital and skilled labor. Each sector is characterized by constant returns to scale and diminishing marginal productivity of each factor. These relationships may be summarized by the following equations:

$$Y_T = L_T f(K_T/L_T), \qquad f' > 0, \quad f'' < 0, \tag{1}$$

$$Y_M = L_M g(K_M/L_M), \qquad g' > 0, \quad g'' < 0. \tag{2}$$

where:

Y_T, Y_M = value added in the traditional and modern sectors, respectively;
K_T, K_M = physical capital employed in the traditional and modern sectors, respectively;
L_T = unskilled labor; and
L_M = skilled labor.

Equilibrium of the firms in each sector requires that factors be paid their marginal products:

$$r_T c_T = MPK_T = f', \tag{3}$$

$$r_M c_M = MPK_M = g', \tag{4}$$

$$w_T = MPL_T = f - (K_T/L_T)f', \tag{5}$$

$$w_M = MPL_M = g - (K_M/L_M)g', \tag{6}$$

where:

r_T, r_M = rates of return on investments in K_T and K_M, respectively;
c_T, c_M = unit costs for investments in K_T and K_M, respectively; and
w_T, w_M = earnings of unskilled and skilled labor, respectively.

For the sake of simplicity, we can interpret the wage differential $(w_M - w_T)$ as the expected increment in earnings resulting from an investment of amount c_L in skill-formation, an increment which does not vary with the age of the worker and which extends into an infinite future. This permits the rate of return on an investment in human resources to be expressed as:

$$r_L = \frac{w_M - w_T}{c_L}. \tag{7}$$

Finally, there are two resource constraints since the total amount of labor (number of workers) and the total amount spent on capital formation are limited:

$$L = L_T + L_M, \tag{8}$$

$$K = c_T K_T + c_M K_M + c_L L_M. \tag{9}$$

If total income $(Y_T + Y_M)$ is maximized subject to the two resource constraints, we obtain as income-maximizing equilibrium conditions that the rates of return to all three types of investment be equalized. (i.e. $r_T = r_M = r_L$). But we are considering a situation where this solution of the model leaves the wages of unskilled labor at an unacceptably low level; we are looking for an investment policy which raises the productivity of unskilled labor to an acceptable level, $\bar{w}$, with the least sacrifice of total income.

This increase in the productivity of unskilled labor can be achieved in either or both of two ways: by increasing the amount of complementary resources (K_T) or by decreasing the actual amount of unskilled labor (L_T). The first can be achieved only at the expense of the modern sector because of the limit on total capital accumulation, whereas the second actually raises aggregate income in the modern sector by shifting resources to it. The optimal combination of policies obviously depends on the two production functions. Investing in the traditional sector is comparatively more attractive when the rate of diminishing marginal productivity of labor in the traditional sector is low, when the elasticity of substitution between capital and labor in the traditional sector is low, and when the elasticity of substitution between capital and labor in the modern sector is high. Investing in human resources, which has the effect of reducing the size of the traditional sector, is more attractive when the marginal productivity of unskilled labor is diminishing at a rapid rate, the elasticity of substitution between unskilled labor and capital is high, and when the elasticity of substitution between skilled labor and capital is low.

It may be helpful to consider a graphic illustration of this simplified model. Figure 20.1a shows the labor markets in both the modern (reading from left to right) and the traditional (reading from right to left) sectors; the horizontal axis represents the total labor force L and wages are graphed on the vertical axes. D_{LM}^0 and D_{LT}^0 are the traditional and modern sector demand schedules for labor, respectively, corresponding to the levels of physical capital K_M^0 and K_L^0 characterizing the growth-maximizing equilibrium. S_L^0 divides the labor force into L_M^0 and L_T^0, the growth-maximizing allocation of workers between sectors. The capital markets are graphed in figures 20.1b-1d. When all three rates of return are equal to the income-maximizing equilibrium rate of interest, r^0, the total capital constraint is just satisfied and the wage differential between the two sectors is just sufficient to cover the value of investment in human capital.

Still referring to figure 20.1, suppose that a minimum wage constraint $\bar{w}$ is imposed, this poverty line being higher than w_T^0 but lower than w_M^0. A full-employment solution in which the traditional-sector wage w_T^* meets this constraint can be obtained by increasing the capital-labor ratio in the traditional sector, either by investing more than K_T^0 in physical capital or by reducing the number of workers below L_T^0 (i.e. investing more in human capital). Figure 20.1a illustrates the case where the optimal solution is a combination of both of these: the additional investment in K_T raises the traditional-sector labor demand schedule from D_{LT}^0 to D_{LT}^* while the additional investment in human capital shifts supply from S_L^0 to S_L^*. Because of the total capital constraint, these shifts cannot be accomplished without a reduction in investment in modern-sector physical capital below its growth-maximizing level, so that the demand schedule for modern-sector labor shifts downward from D_{LM}^0 to D_{LM}^*. The magnitude of these shifts in demand curves for any given reallocation of investment clearly depends on the elasticities of substitution between capital and labor in the appropriate sector.

For any given division of labor between the two sectors, the demand schedules D_{LM}^* and D_{LT}^* imply a smaller wage differential than do the demand schedules D_{LM}^0 and D_{LT}^0 and hence a lower return to investment in human capital; it follows

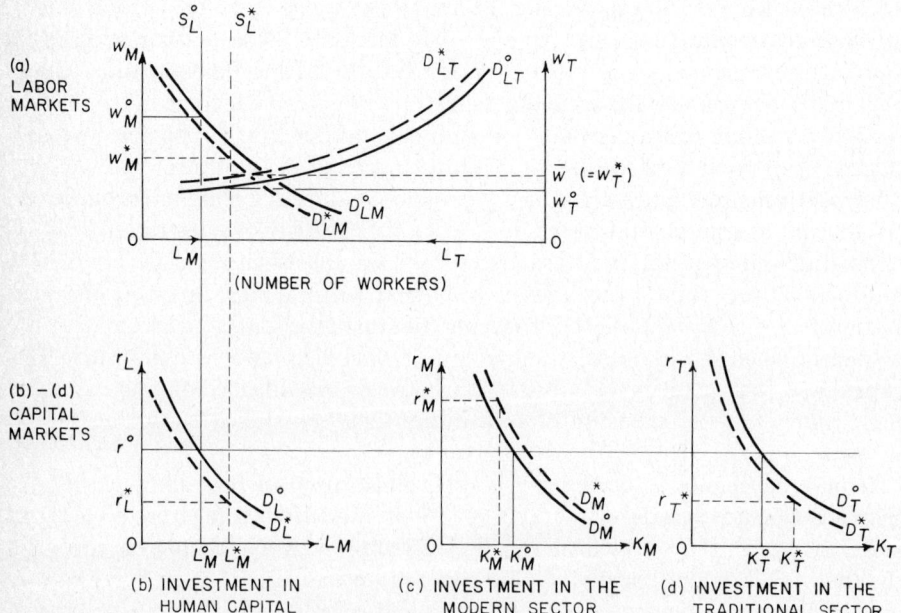

Figure 20.1. Factor markets: The simplified model.

that the rate of return schedule for human capital, D_L^*, must be lower than D_L^0 in figure 20.1b. At the same time, the rightward shift of the labor supply curve S_L implies that D_M^* is higher than D_M^0 in figure 20.1c (since there is more modern-sector labor) and that D_T^* is lower than D_T^0 in figure 20.1d (since there is less traditional-sector labor). This combination of shifts in supply and demand is incompatible with equalization of rates of return in the capital market; it is clear from figures 20.1b and 20.1c, for example, that increasing L_M and decreasing K_M with respect to their growth-maximizing levels requires that r_M^* be higher than r^0 while r_L^* must be lower than r^0. Similarly, figure 20.1d shows that increasing K_T and decreasing L_T with respect to their growth-maximising levels implies that r_T^* must also be lower than r^0. If the investment market is competitive, some policy intervention that effectively taxes K_M and subsidizes both K_T and L_M is necessary in order to attain the appropriate resource allocation.

To derive the optimal combination of policies, the problem may be formulated as a constrained income maximization: what is the highest possible income $(Y_T + Y_M)$ consistent with the total labor and investment constraints, which permits the earnings of unskilled labor to reach the target wage level? We set up the Lagrangian function:

$$\mathcal{L} = Y_T + Y_M - \lambda_1(L_T + L_M - L) - \\ - \lambda_2(c_T K_T + c_M K_M + c_L L_M - K) - \lambda_3(MPL_T - \bar{w})$$

and set its first partial derivatives equal to zero:

(i) $MPK_T = \lambda_2 c_T + \left[\dfrac{\partial^2 Y_T}{\partial K_T \partial L_T}\right]\lambda_3$

(ii) $MPK_M = \lambda_2 c_M$

(iii) $MPL_T = \lambda_1 + \lambda_3 \left[\dfrac{\partial^2 Y_T}{\partial L_T^2}\right]$

(iv) $MPL_M = \lambda_1 + \lambda_2 c_L$

The Lagrangian multipliers λ_1 and λ_2 represent shadow prices for labor and capital, respectively; to see this, multiply each factor by its marginal product and sum across factors. Since constant returns to scale implies that this sum will just equal total income and also that

$$0 = K_T\left\{\dfrac{\partial^2 Y_T}{\partial K_T \partial L_T}\right\} + L_T\left\{\dfrac{\partial^2 Y_T}{\partial L_T^2}\right\},$$

this procedure yields:

$$\begin{cases} Y_T = \lambda_1 L_T + \lambda_2 c_T K_T \\ Y_M = \lambda_1 L_M + \lambda_2(c_M K_M + c_L L_M) \\ Y_T + Y_M = \lambda_1 L + \lambda_2 K \end{cases}$$

The Lagrangian multiplier λ_3 may be thought of as the "price" of a unit increase in the minimum wage evaluated as the sacrifice in income necessary to obtain such an increase. The equilibrium conditions (i) – (iv) thus yield a solution for which the shadow price of capital is the modern-sector interest rate r_M^*. The shadow price of labor is that portion of the wage of skilled labor not attributable to investment in human capital, where that investment is valued at its shadow price. We also obtain the equilibrium condition:

$$\frac{(r_M - r_L)c_L}{(r_M - r_T)c_T} = \frac{-\partial^2 Y_T/\partial L_T^2}{\partial^2 Y_T/\partial K_T \partial L_T} \tag{10}$$

which established the optimal combination of subsidies for r_L and r_T. This is the combination for which the cost of an additional unit of K_T-formation relative to an additional unit reduction in L_T is just equal to the relative value of these two investments in raising the marginal productivity of unskilled labor. In the case of constant returns to scale, this relative value is simply the capital–labor ratio in the traditional sector and equation (10) can be rewritten:

$$(r_M - r_L)c_L L_T = (r_M - r_T)c_T K_T \tag{10a}$$

The opportunity cost of employing in the traditional sector a factor (K_T) which could earn more in the modern sector must be equal to the total cost of converting all unskilled labor (L_T) into modern sector labor.

In summary, then, a policy of subsidizing both investments in traditional-sector physical capital and investments in human capital will permit the two-sector economy to meet its income-distribution objectives with the least sacrifice in income. The tax on the remaining type of investment, even if it is only implicit, will raise the unit price of modern-sector capital. The degree of dualism in the economy may be measured by the difference in the rates of return on physical capital in the two sectors, $r_M - r_T$, which is non-zero in this solution. The difference in the earnings of workers in the two sectors is not attributable to this dualism but rather to skill differences, and this skill differential in earnings is lower than it would be in the free-market solution.

Perhaps the most noteworthy implication of this analysis is that the optimal policy involves a "tax" on the price of modern-sector physical capital rather than a subsidy. In part this is the result of our income distribution policy, but it is also in part the result of our formulation of growth policy with respect to total income rather than just modern-sector income. Although the equilibrium conditions imply a policy of modern-sector expansion at the expense of the traditional sector, this expansion is defined in terms of employment rather than income. A set of graphs similar to those in figure 20.1 may be used to analyze the implication of a policy which subsidizes the price of K_M: S_L and the demand functions for investment in K_T and K_M would shift in the same direction as in the equilibrium solution discussed above, the demand schedules for L_T and L_M, and hence demand for investment in human capital, would shift in the opposite direction. If the elasticities of substitution were low enough and the elasticities of supply and demand for labor were high enough, it might still be possible to raise the wage of unskilled labor to w and at the same time to reduce the earnings differential in comparison with the free-market solution. This cannot, however, be the least-cost solution since we have seen that income maximization requires that r_M be higher than its free-market level.

IV. The development model

The full version of the model has three types of labor instead of two and both production functions have three factors. Unskilled labor, L_0, is used only in the traditional sector, while high-level manpower, L_2, is used only in the modern sector. Middle-level manpower, L_1, may be used in either sector; like physical capital, the subscripts "T" and "M" will be used to denote that portion of L_1 employed in the traditional sector (L_{1T}) and modern sectors (L_{1M}), respectively. Each sector is characterized by constant returns to scale, diminishing marginal productivity for each factor, and mutual complementarity of all factors. Thus we have the production functions:

$$Y_T = F(L_0, L_{1T}, K_T), \qquad F_1, F_2, F_3 > 0; \quad F_{11} < 0; \quad F_{12}, F_{13} > 0 \tag{11}$$

$$Y_M = G(L_{1M}, L_2, K_M), \qquad G_1, G_2, G_3 > 0 \tag{12}$$

with factor prices equal to marginal products:

$$r_T c_T = F_3 \tag{13}$$

$$r_M c_M = G_3 \tag{14}$$

$$w_0 = F_1 \tag{15}$$

$$w_{1T} = F_2 \tag{16}$$

$$w_{1M} = G_1 \tag{17}$$

$$w_2 = G_2 \tag{18}$$

and the two resource constraints:

$$L = L_0 + L_{1T} + L_{1M} + L_2 \tag{19}$$

$$K = c_T K_T + c_M K_M + c_1 (L_{1M} + L_{1T}) + c_2 L_2 \tag{20}$$

where c_1 is the cost of converting a worker from unskilled into middle-level manpower and c_2 is the total investment embodied in a unit of high-level manpower.

The appropriate rates of return for various investments in human capital in this model depend on our assumptions about the investment process itself. For example, the sector in which a middle-level worker is employed affects the rate of return realized on an investment in skill-formation. If this sector is known at the time the investment decision is being made, the creation of L_{1T} and L_{1M} should be thought of as two separate investments with two separate rates of return, r_{1T} and r_{1M}, respectively. Following the procedure of section III, we shall assume that wage differentials between two types of workers represent the expected increment in earnings resulting from an investment in human capital and that this increment extends into an infinite future without varying over time. This permits the rates of return on investments in middle-level manpower to be expressed as:

$$r_{1T} = \frac{w_{1T} - w_0}{c_1} \tag{21}$$

$$r_{1M} = \frac{w_{1M} - w_0}{c_1} \tag{22}$$

In the typical case where the future sector of employment is not known at the time of the investment, the appropriate rate of return (if investors are risk-neutral) is the expected value

$$r_1 = s_T r_{1T} + s_M r_{1M} \tag{23}$$

where

$$\left. \begin{array}{l} s_T = L_{1T}/L_1 \\ s_M = L_{1M}/L_1 \end{array} \right\}, \quad s_T + s_M = 1.$$

The rates of return for investments in higher education may also be specified under various assumptions. Since the relevant characteristic of this type of manpower is that it can be employed only in the modern sector, it is not necessary to assume that it represents "more" human capital than does middle-level manpower. If the creation of L_2 were appropriately viewed in this manner, the rate of return on an investment of this type would be:

$$\hat{r}_2 = \frac{w_2 - w_0}{c_2}. \tag{24}$$

Since the educational process is sequential, however, middle-level manpower may be thought of as an intermediate product in the creation of high-level manpower. At some stage in the educational process (after an expenditure of c_1) a decision is made as to whether or not to continue the investment; if not, the worker finds employment as middle-level manpower. If this decision is made with knowledge about the sector in which the worker would be employed if his or her education is not continued, the rate of return to higher education would vary by sector:

$$r_{2T} = \frac{w_2 - w_{1T}}{c_2 - c_1} \tag{25}$$

$$r_{2M} = \frac{w_2 - w_{1M}}{c_2 - c_1}. \tag{26}$$

If the decision to continue were made without knowledge of the sector of employment, the expected rate of return would be

$$r_2 = s_T r_{2T} + s_M r_{2M}. \tag{27}$$

The assumptions which will be used for the remainder of this paper will be that education is sequential, that at the time of the initial decision to invest in human capital the future sector of employment is not known, but by the time the decision is made whether or not to continue education to the higher level the sector of employment as middle-level manpower is known. Thus when we are concerned with the incentives for investment, workers in L_0 face a rate of return r_1 to convert themselves into middle-level manpower and workers in L_{1T} or L_{1M} face a rate of return of r_{2T} or r_{2M}, respectively, to convert themselves into high-level manpower.

The rates of return r_{1T}, r_{1M} and $\hat{r}_2$ are the "realized" rates for workers in L_{1T}, L_{1M} and L_2, respectively; although they may not be directly relevant for investment decisions, they may be useful when we are evaluating the efficiency of resource allocation.

Table 20.1. Summary of variables.

Factor of production	Factor price per unit	Investment in factor — Cost of investment per unit	Rate of return
I. *Physical capital*			
a) Modern sector (K_M)	$r_M c_M$	c_M	r_M
b) Traditional sector (K_T)	$r_T c_T$	c_T	r_T
II. *Human capital*			
a) Unskilled labor (L_0)	w_0	None	None
b) Middle-level manpower			
1) Modern sector (L_{1M})	w_{1M}	c_1	$r_1 = \dfrac{(s_T w_{1T} + s_M w_{1M}) w_0}{c_1}$
2) Traditional sector (L_{1T})	w_{1T}		
c) High-level manpower (L_2)	w_2	c_2	
1) Investment in modern-sector worker			$r_{2M} = \dfrac{w_2 - w_{1M}}{c_2 - c_1}$
2) Investment in traditional-sector worker			$r_{2T} = \dfrac{w_2 - w_{1T}}{c_2 - c_1}$

Equations (11)–(20), (23), (25) and (26) constitute a thirteen-equation system in seventeen variables: six factors of production, six factor prices, three rates of return on investment in human capital, and two levels of output, Y_T and Y_M. These are summarized in table 20.1, along with the cost of production for each factor and the rate of return on an investment in that factor. If the market for middle-level manpower is competitive, earnings for that factor should be equalized between the two sectors ($w_{1T} = w_{1M}$) from which it follows by definition that $r_{2T} = r_{2M} = r_2$. Competition in the investment market would result in the equilization of all rates of return, so that $r_T = r_M = r_1 = r_2$. Competition in the factor markets thus yields four additional equations and closes the system. A similar result is obtained if income ($Y_T + Y_M$) is maximized subject to the resource constraints in equations (19) and (20). (In contrast to an income-maximizing problem where labor is not subject to investment, the solution of this system is unique; the one degree of freedom to which we are accustomed is lost when the relative wage is related to the equilibrium rate of interest by the possibility of investing in human capital.)

Now consider the case where a minimum wage target is specified. Let this wage be denoted $\bar{w}$, and assume that $\bar{w}$ is higher than the competitive equilibrium wage for low-level manpower (w_0^0) but lower than the competitive wage for middle-level labor (w_1^0). The income-maximizing allocation of resources may be obtained by setting up the Lagrangian:

$$\mathcal{L} = Y_T + Y_M - \lambda_1(L_0 + L_1 + L_2 - L)$$
$$- \lambda_2(c_M K_M + c_T K_T + c_1 L_1 + c_2 L_2 - K)$$
$$- \lambda_3(F_1 - \bar{w})$$

and taking its partial derivatives with respect to each of the six factors of production. Setting these partial derivatives equal to zero yields the following relationships:

$$F_1 = \lambda_1 + \lambda_3 F_{11} \tag{28}$$

$$F_2 = \lambda_1 + \lambda_2 c_1 + \lambda_3 F_{12} \tag{29}$$

$$F_3 = \lambda_2 c_T + \lambda_3 F_{13} \tag{30}$$

$$G_1 = \lambda_1 + \lambda_2 c_1 \tag{31}$$

$$G_2 = \lambda_1 + \lambda_2 c_2 \tag{32}$$

$$G_3 = \lambda_2 c_M \tag{33}$$

As was the case with the simple model in Section II, the Lagrangian multipliers λ_1 and λ_2 represent shadow prices for labor and capital, respectively. To see this, multiply each factor of production by its marginal product and sum across factors. Since constant returns to scale in each sector means that this sum will just equal total income and also that $0 = F_{11}L_0 + F_{12}L_{1T} + F_{13}K_T$, this procedure yields the results:

$$\begin{cases} Y_T = \lambda_1(L_0 + L_{1T}) + \lambda_2(c_1 L_{1T} + c_T K_T) \\ Y_M = \lambda_1(L_{1M} + L_2) + \lambda_2(c_1 L_{1M} + c_2 L_2 + c_M K_M) \\ Y_T + Y_M = \lambda_1 L + \lambda_2 K \end{cases}$$

Equation (33) implies that in equilibrium the rate of return on an investment in modern-sector capital, r_M^*, is the shadow price of capital. Equations (31) and (32) imply that in equilibrium the wage of either type of modern-sector labor is equal to the shadow price of labor plus the value of human capital, this value being determined by the size of the investment and the shadow rate of return on that investment.

The Lagrangian multiplier λ_3 is the price of a unit increase in the minimum wage. To see this, solve equations (28)–(33) to obtain:

$$-\lambda_3 = \frac{\bar{w} - \lambda_1}{-F_{11}} = \frac{w_{1M} - w_{1T}}{F_{12}} = \frac{(r_M - r_T)c_T}{F_{13}}.$$

In equilibrium, the marginal rates of substitution for each factor between the minimum-wage objective and the maximum-growth objective are equalized. These two conditions may also be expressed as:

$$\frac{w_{1M} - w_{1T}}{(r_M - r_T)c_T} = \frac{F_{12}}{F_{13}} \tag{34}$$

$$\frac{(r_M - r_{1M})c_1}{(r_M - r_T)c_T} = \frac{-F_{11}}{F_{13}} = \left(\frac{F_{12}}{F_{13}}\right)\left(\frac{L_{1T}}{L_0}\right) + \left(\frac{K_T}{L_0}\right) \tag{35}$$

In the case of a separable production function F (where the marginal rate of substitution between any two factors is independent of the amount of the third factor) we have the especially simple result that $F_{12}/F_{13} = F_2/F_3$ and hence:

$$\frac{w_{1T}}{r_T} = \frac{w_{1M}}{r_M} \tag{34a}$$

$$(r_M - r_{1M})c_1 L_0 = (w_{1M} - w_{1T})L_{1T} + (r_M - r_T)c_T K_T. \tag{35a}$$

The first equilibrium condition is that factors employed in both sectors must have the same relative prices in each sector. The second condition says that the opportunity cost of factors employed in the traditional instead of the modern sector, evaluated as the difference in factor prices between sectors times the amount of each factor, must just equal the cost of eliminating the traditional sector entirely, by converting all unskilled labor into middle-level manpower. The third equilibrium condition may be obtained directly from equations (31)–(33):

$$r_{2M} = r_M; \tag{36}$$

the rate of return on an investment which converts one type of modern-sector worker into another must be equal to the rate of return on investments in non-human capital in the modern sector.

The total employment and investment constraints in equations (19) and (20) may be solved for L_{1M} and L_{1T} as a function of the factor proportions within each of the two sectors: L_{1T}/L_0, K_T/L_{1T}, L_2/L_{1M}, and K_M/L_{1M}. Thus once factor proportions are known, the equilibrium amount of middle-level manpower and its allocation between the two sectors are determined; from this may be derived the absolute values of all factors and hence of all factor prices (marginal products) as well as income in each sector. But factor proportions depend on relative factor prices, and for an important class of traditional-sector production functions (including the CES and the generalized Cobb–Douglas) the unskilled-labor wage-rental ratio is sufficient to determine uniquely relative factor prices in both sectors.[6] Thus there is a one-to-one relationship between the ratio w_0/r_T and the value of w_0, and in general we may expect only one value of this ratio to be consistent with $w_0 = \bar{w}$. The equilibrium allocation of resources between sectors and between factors of production and the degree of dualism characterizing the income-maximizing solution are effectively determined by the choice of a minimum-income target. Thus it is possible within this framework to determine trade-offs between the minimum income target and each of the variables in this system, including of course aggregate income.

The similarities between this equilibrium solution and that of the simplified model presented in Section III are evident. Income maximization constrained by a minimum-wage target requires more investment in traditional-sector factors and in skill-formation aimed at low-level manpower than does income-maximiza-

---

[6] To see this, observe that specifying $w_0 = \bar{w}$ determines uniquely the share of unskilled labor in traditional-sector income and thus permits the wage-rental ratio for skilled labor, w_{1T}/r_T, to be solved as a function of $\bar{w}/r_T$. Equations (34a) and (36) then yield $w_{1M}/r_M = w_{1T}/r_T$ and $w_2/r_M = w_{1M}/r_M + (c_2 - c_1)$, respectively.

tion without that constraint. The Lagrangian multipliers have the same interpretations in both models: λ_1 and λ_2 are shadow prices for labor and capital, respectively, and λ_3 is the price of imposing the minimum-wage target. In equilibrium, the shadow price of capital is the rate of interest in the modern sector and the shadow price of labor is the modern-sector wage net of the value of investments in human capital. In equilibrium, the cost of an investment converting all remaining unskilled labor into middle-level manpower, thereby eliminating the traditional sector entirely, must just equal the opportunity cost of complementary resources employed in the traditional rather than the modern sector.

Some additional implications for growth policy arise here, however, that were not evident in the simplified model. In equilibrium, relative factor prices in each sector must be the same for factors which are actually used in both sectors. This means that in order to attain the maximum income if the rate of return on physical capital is lower in the traditional sector than in the modern sector, the wage of middle-level manpower must also be lower in the traditional than in the modern sector by the same proportion. This in turn implies that the rate of return on an investment in higher education will be lower for people who would otherwise be employed in the modern sector than for people who would have worked as middle-level manpower in the traditional sector. Subsidizing the traditional-sector interest rate thus introduces two stresses into the middle-level labor market: it increases the incentive for migration of skilled labor from the traditional to the modern sector and it raises the rate of return to an investment in higher education. Both of these stresses are relieved if the wage of middle-level workers actually employed in the traditional sector is subsidized to the point where the between-sector earnings differential is small despite the lower marginal product in the traditional sector. Income is maximized if this subsidy is proportionately the same as that on the interest rate.

V. Policy implications

The model developed in this paper provides a framework within which to analyze the relative merits of some important development strategies. The combined objectives of high growth rates and equity in the distribution of income has been formulated as attaining a minimum-productivity target for individual workers with the least sacrifice in aggregate income. It has been shown that a combination of assistance and education programs aimed specifically at improving the earnings prospects of the poor involves the least sacrifice in aggregate income. Three alternative strategies for reducing poverty have been considered explicitly and shown to be inferior: subsidizing capital formation in the modern sector; concentrating exclusively on growth rates in the modern sector; and laissez-faire non-intervention in both sectors. The conclusion that these are inferior is quite general, although the actual differences in aggregate income depend on the parameters of the factor demand and supply functions.

The optimal development strategy requires more investment in the traditional sector, and hence less in the modern, in comparison with the competitive free-market equilibrium and, *a fortiori*, with the other development strategies considered. At the same time, however, it calls for some expansion of modern-sector employment since reducing the number of unskilled workers implies increasing the supply of middle-level labor available to the modern sector. This is in effect the *only* subsidy appropriate for the modern sector. Since increased supplies of middle-level labor can be expected to result in a lower wage rate and hence an increased rate of return to investments in higher education, the supply of high-level manpower will probably also rise although no additional subsidy is called for. The combined effect of this increase in supply of high level manpower and the decrease in the number of unskilled workers is to reduce the relative income difference between these two groups at the same time that the absolute wage level for unskilled workers is rising.

Although the model has been developed within a static framework, the policy recommendation clearly has some dynamic implications. The long-run minimum wage target need not be achieved in a single planning period but may instead be specified as a rising sequence of targets for a succession of planning periods. A strategy of this sort is clearly indicated if factor proportions at the beginning of the period differ greatly from those indicated by the optimal solution of the model. If the educational process is irreversible, so that once a person has been converted from one type of labor to another he does not revert to his former state, "over-investment" for one planning period in the type of education that removes people from poverty will result in fewer people remaining in poverty for subsequent periods. Moreover, the degree of dualism which characterizes the optimal policy solution is smaller the smaller the proportion of the labor force in the poverty group. This suggests that a dynamic analysis would provide for a reduction and eventual phasing out of subsidies as the optimal distribution of the labor force is approached.

References

Japan Economic Research Center, *Income Distribution, Employment and Economic Development in Southeast and East Asia*, (Papers and Proceedings of the JERC–CAMS Seminar held in December 1974), Tokyo, 1975.

Musgrove, P., *Income and Spending of Urban Families in Latin America*, Brookings, 1977 (ECIEL).

United Nations Economic and Social Council, *Social Objectives and related policies and programmes in national plans of selected developing countries for the Second United Nations Development Decade, Report of the Secretary General* (Document No. E/CN. 5/476, 27 October 1972), par 56–60.

Yap, L., International Migration in Less Developed Countries: A Survey of the Literature, World Bank Staff Working Paper No. 215, September 1975.

20 DISCUSSION

PAPER BY CARMEL V. CHISWICK

Professor Stiglitz found the paper very interesting but had some reservations about applying the model to developing countries. These reservations mainly concerned the description of the labour market and the market for education.

He felt the neglect of unemployment in the model was a serious omission. Migration from rural to urban areas depended not only on wage differentials but also on employment opportunities. Recent models had drawn attention to the fact that workers who move from rural areas usually join the ranks of the urban unemployed. Searching for jobs required capital to survive, and it may be this, rather than wage differentials, which is the main factor determining migration. Rural development may lead to more capital, enable more people to search for jobs in towns, and result in *higher* unemployment among the poorest groups.

The role of education depends critically on whether it is provided by the government or purchased by the individuals themselves. In the latter case, there is no lifetime income inequality amongst homogeneous groups of workers. Higher incomes reflect a greater expenditure on earlier education, so any observed inequality is spurious, representing income foregone. However, education always involves some gift element to those being taught, and this should be modelled.

Apart from increasing skills, education also has a credentials function and a screening function. The credentials aspect may currently be very important in developing countries. For instance a degree may guarantee a variety of jobs and give a higher probability of getting a job. These features are taken into account in "bumping" models, where the private and social benefits of education can be vastly different. The private return is normally very high, but the social return can even be negative, since someone else is eliminated from the queue.

On the policy side, it is argued that direct transfers are too costly due to the large number of people involved. This suggests using inefficient transfer mechanisms which are more selective and consequently less expensive. However, this argument does not always follow – it depends critically on the elasticity of substitution.

Professor Stiglitz went on to point out that the traditional discussion of the effects of inflation and differential savings propensities on growth is absent from the paper. He said that, when migration is included, attention should be directed towards distortions in the labour market rather than the savings problem, since changes in the level of urban employment have no effect on the savings rate.

Some issues were raised concerning the focus on distributional objectives. There is considerable evidence of a large volume of private transfers from the urban to the rural sector. To the extent that private redistribution is taking place, inequality may not be as important as it appears. Secondly, if people have a choice between remaining in the rural sector or going to the urban sector and facing a probability of unemployment, movement from the rural areas is a risky investment with the same ex ante expected utility. The distributional objective should take account of this fact.

Finally, he welcomed the conclusion that wage differentials between different sectors of the economy were desirable, but added that other reasons related to the efficiency-wage hypothesis, quality differences, informational problems and labour turnover considerations, also gave support to the notion of optimal wage differentials.

Professor Bentzel, in the chair, suggested it might be valuable to have some discussion of the "screening hypothesis" and related issues.

Dr. Psacharopoulos said there was no hard evidence to support the screening or credentials hypotheses and defended the paper for not taking them into account. He admitted that people may initially be paid more for having a degree, but could not see why earnings later in life would depend on anything except productivity in that particular job.

Professor Taubman disagreed with Dr. Psacharopoulos. The screening hypothesis, he said, is as capable of explaining all the features of earnings functions as human capital models. In particular, it is consistent with the more able receiving a greater premium over the less able as the years of work experience increase. Since the screening hypothesis is appealing and not contradicted by empirical evidence, he supported the suggestion that this should be incorporated.

Professor Pen believed the credentials hypothesis to be an anti-education ideology, invented to show that education is a complete waste of time.

Professor van Meerhaeghe thought that too much emphasis had been placed on education. Since many school and university leavers in less developed countries are now unemployed, many believe that there is over-investment in education. He also suggested that insufficient weight had been given to the problems of population growth.

Mr. Layard said it was important to distinguish different types of education. In developing countries, individuals who undertake education to alter their job prospects frequently end up in the public sector. The impact on the income distribution then depends heavily on the wage policy followed in that sector. The fact that job rationing is important in countries such as India suggests that inequality could be reduced by lowering public sector wages in addition to changing education policy. However, another function of education is to improve basic skills in the rural sector and here education policy could have a significant impact on inequality.

Professor Krelle thought that the demand side should be given more attention and that technical progress should be introduced explicitly as a function of education, which in turn depends on the expenditure on education. The levels of employment of the two kinds of labour will depend on the elasticity of substitution.

Professor Chiswick believed there were countries for which the credentials hypothesis applied, but this should not be confused with education. She had avoided identifying education with the school system of a particular country. Instead it was defined as investment in human capital – the formation of productive skills – and this left open the question of how efficient the educational structure is as an instrument for skill formation.

Dr. Thomas said that the whole concept of a dual economy needs more investigation. For example, the assumptions of the dual economy are incompatible with much of the recent literature on development.

Dr. Kuipers believed that many of the policy conclusions depended heavily on the model specified. In particular, he referred to the implicit assumption that the two sectors are producing an identical product. In section III, the wage rates in the modern and traditional sectors are expressed in terms of the sector outputs, and later on these wage rates are added and subtracted. This led him to conclude that it is really a one sector model, in which case there is no problem of changes in the terms of trade.

Professor Taubman said that the paper was essentially a comparative static analysis. It may be of some importance for policy decisions to know the time needed to get from one equilibrium to another and how this varies with different policies.

Professor Hogan supported those who had argued that the structure of the labour market and migration were critical for the policy implications. He drew attention to the role of extended families in providing accommodation and other assistance to relatives seeking work in the urban areas.

Even if a distinction can be made between pure subsistence farming and modern farming, this is not an adequate description of the rural situation. The subsistence group may have access to cash income through contract outworking and may therefore be linked to the modern sector. The cash income may be used for education or equipment. The work provides some training and perhaps a basis for later migration to full-time industrial employment.

Professor Chiswick was surprised by the comments that her paper overemphasises education, or even that it encourages more education. The topics dealt with are much broader than mere skill "improvement". If technological "progress" can be described as an expansion of modern-technology employment at the expense of the traditional sector, and if the choice of technology by modern-sector firms is affected by factor prices in that sector, then it follows that the optimal educational policy and the optimal rate of technological change or "progress" are not only mutually dependent, but are also endogenous to a system in which government objectives are specified in terms of growth maximisation subject to a distribution constraint. Education is not an object of policy *per se*, but rather a type of capital formation for which government policy typically plays an important role and for which the distributional implications are clearly important. Moreover the conclusions of the analysis do not necessarily support "more" investment in education; it is clear that public subsidy of higher education is a poor use of resources, and it is also clear that public resources devoted to primary schooling (of a level that is not sufficient to give workers at least the option of competing for modern-sector jobs) may have little or no impact on either growth or income distribution.

In her definition of a two-sector economy as one in which there are two alternative technologies for producing the same output, Professor Chiswick was following the approach recommended by T.W. Schultz for understanding agricultural development. The development problem is one of "transforming" farmers (or other producers) currently using traditional techniques into farmers using modern techniques. As long as the products of the two sectors are close substitutes in consumption, there is no loss of generality in measuring the output of both sectors in value-added units. This approach has the additional advantage that it clearly distinguishes between the "transformation" process and geographical migration. Although Professor Chiswick agreed that a realistic extension of the model could impose a non-zero cost of transfer from the traditional to the modern sector, the conclusions of the analysis would not be altered. Such a cost would have to be balanced in the free-market equilibrium solution by a compensating wage differential; but this differential would also have to be included in the optimal solution of the model, in addition to the "dualism" which the latter requires. Similarly, a between-sector wage differential compensating for the various factors mentioned by Professor Stiglitz, would characterise both the optimal and free-market solutions, but the policy conclusions are based on the fact that the former solution requires a larger wage differential than the latter.

Professor Chiswick welcomed Professor Taubman's suggestion that it could be useful to introduce a time dimension into the analysis, and consider explicitly the growth path implied by different distribution policies. This would highlight the sensitivity of the policy conclusions to the elasticity of substitution. If the elasticity of substitution in the traditional sector is low, reducing the number of people in that sector would be an efficient way not only of raising current earnings in that sector, but also of reducing the total time needed to modernise the economy. If this elasticity is high, so that large transfers of investment to the traditional sector would have little effect on relative wages, a factor price subsidy would be an efficient means of inducing large transfers of private investment. She also suggested that, with a time dimension, modern-sector unemployment could be brought into the model as part of the equilibriating process, without changing the full-employment assumption.

21 TRANSFER POLICY AND CHANGES IN INCOME DISTRIBUTION

HANS-JUERGEN KRUPP[1]

I. Competing goals of income policy

The increasing amount of data available in the field of income distribution, as well as the discussion of different policy objectives raised by the Social Indicator Movement, have contributed to the recognition that incomes policy may have a number of different goals which may not be compatible. Changes in the income distribution may reflect quite different considerations.[2] These changes can only be discussed by introducing these different goal dimensions.

This paper will restrict attention to three of the relevant considerations:
(a) The adequacy of a person's income with respect to the contributions he makes in the production process (for brevity called *Adequacy*).
(b) The degree of equality of consumption possibilities (for brevity referred to as *the Degree of Equality*).
(c) *The Level of Poverty*.

The adequacy of income relative to contributions in the production process can only be judged by the individuals themselves. It has an objective and a subjective component. Subjectively, one asks whether the individual considers his income to be just, given the work he performs; objectively, one compares the incomes of different people with the work they perform. There exist no scientifically based, objective criteria to judge the adequacy of an individual's income.

A different question is raised if one is interested in the degree of equality of consumption possibilities. This question can only be answered on the basis of "families", "households" or "spending units". The size of these units, as well as the number of earners within them, determine both the needs and income of each unit.

A third dimension is the level of poverty. The aim of eliminating poverty is widely accepted. The unit of analysis is again families, households or spending units. A unit is considered to be poor if it is incapable of covering its basic needs, as defined by social convention.

---

[1] The author is a member of the Sozialpolitische Forschergruppe Frankfurt/Mannheim which develops a socio-political decision and indicator system for the Federal Republic Germany (SPES-Project). He wishes to thank his colleagues in this research group for many discussions and ideas. He is especially grateful to Dr Frank Klanberg for many helpful comments and to Klaus Kortmann and Gunther Schmaus for the empirical results that they contributed to this paper.

[2] See Glatzer and Krupp (1975) and Krupp (1975), especially chapter 2.

There exist various indicators which reflect these different goal dimensions, but these will not be systematically developed in this paper.

Usually, transfer policy concerns the second and third of the above considerations. Eliminating poverty and equalising consumption possibilities are the basic objectives of transfer policy. It is frequently held that this may endanger the first goal mentioned – the adequacy of income relative to contributions to production. Transfer policy is therefore usually regarded as a policy which may succeed with respect to two goals, but which may adversely affect another goal of income distribution.

II. **The influence of transfer policy on the distribution of income**

Before discussing the possibilities of influencing the distribution of income by transfer policy, it may be useful to ask the extent to which transfer policy affects the income distribution. This will be examined with a few examples. However, this is only possible if one discusses the different concepts used for income and transfers.

II.1. *Different Concepts of Income and Transfers*

A relatively simple concept is provided by the monetary variables defined in national accounts. It is relatively easy to statistically implement a concept of this kind. There may, however, be objections to it, since only a fraction of the transfer process is taken into account. Moreover, the part included is defined very arbitrarily. A social security system which prefers to make transfers in kind, is not comparable to a system which prefers monetary transfers. So it is usually argued that transfers in kind should also be included. This problem can be solved (at least logically) for those transfers that can be allocated to a person or a unit. The concept runs into logical difficulties, however, in the case of public goods whose benefits cannot be attributed to specific persons or units without arbitrary assumptions. These measurement difficulties will not be discussed here. But it should be mentioned that there still exist major problems which have not yet been solved.[3] Besides, this discussion is primarily theoretical. Data difficulties even arise with very modest concepts of transfers. In the following we will confine ourselves, in most cases, to the monetary concept as defined by the national accounts.

II.2. *Indicators of the Distribution of Factor and Disposable Income*

The first question posed is how the distribution of factor incomes received by individuals is changed by transfer incomes. The analysis will be restricted to direct effects. Feedbacks to the production system caused by transfer payments will be neglected. The answer depends on the groups which are considered. One reason-

---

[3] For an overview, see Lampman (1975).

able approach is to restrict attention to income earners whose main income arises from employment. Since some transfer and property incomes cannot be related to individuals, but only to a family or household unit, it is necessary to make the assumption that these incomes can be allocated to the head of the household. A second approach is to consider all individuals who receive any kind of factor income as their main income. The resulting group is not very homogeneous, but changes in the inequality that results from the production process due to transfer policy, can be determined.

A third approach would include persons whose main income is transfer income. However, this does not make sense, since there are people who are not connected with the production process. Their income cannot be related to factors which they contribute to production. The best examples are young students and those in retirement.

The indicators used are very simple ones: the multiple of mean income; the concentration ratio or Gini Index; the shares of the top 5 and the lowest 20 per cent. One disadvantage of these indicators is that their welfare implications are not explicit. Atkinson (1970)[4] has shown that there exist different degrees of inequality aversion which lead to different measures of inequality. Even if these measures are theoretically more easily interpreted, it is very difficult to give comprehensive information in this form.

Table 21.1 shows these indicators for the distribution of factor incomes (i.e. incomes before taxes and transfers) and disposable incomes (i.e. incomes after taxes and transfers). The values are calculated from a merge file for the Federal Republic of Germany, called IMDAF 1969.[5] It is based on a large income and expenditure survey (EVS), the micro-census and information from tax data.

Whereas the indicators of table 21.1 may reflect the aspect of income adequacy, it may be more useful to judge the effects of transfer policy by looking at indicators related to "equality". The basic unit used in the following analysis is the household. The simplest approach is to compare indicators for the distributions of factor and disposable income of households.

It may be even more useful to compare the distributions of factor and disposable household income per household member.

A further possibility is to define the basic needs of households depending on their size. Then the income may be related to the amount required for basic needs. Factor and disposable income may be compared for households on the basis of the so-called "income welfare ratios". This has the advantage that the size of the household is taken into account in a more appropriate way than in the two previous approaches. For basic needs, a medium standard was chosen, since a very low poverty standard could underestimate the needs of large families, especially with regard to housing. The main differences between this and the poverty standard used later is that housing needs are taken at an average level rather than at a poverty level. Table 2 shows indicators for these three types of comparisons.

Regarding the poverty aspect, one has to compare the share when only factor

---

[4] For an application see Watts and Peck (1975).
[5] See Kortmann, Krupp and Schmaus (1975) and Kortman and Schmaus (1975).

Table 21.1. Indicators for the distribution of factor income and total disposable income for employed and self-employed persons whose main income is factor income, Federal Republic Germany 1969.

	Multiple of mean income		Concentration ratio (Gini index)		Share of the top 5% (in %)		Share of the lowest 20% (in %)	
	Factor income	Disposable income	Factor income	Disposable income	Factor income	Disposable income	Factor income	Disposable income
All recipients whose main income is factor income	1.000	1.000	0.410	0.400	23.7	21.7	4.8	5.1
Main income from employment	0.817	0.817	0.318	0.321	13.9	14.1	5.7	5.9
Wage earners	0.712	0.715	0.263	0.260	9.8	10.1	6.2	6.6
Salaried employees	0.867	0.851	0.362	0.370	15.7	16.0	5.0	5.2
Civil servants	1.166	1.225	0.249	0.242	11.2	10.9	9.3	9.5
Main income from self-employment	2.199	2.200	0.545	0.462	34.6	28.0	3.1	4.4
Self employed	3.048	2.830	0.546	0.468	36.3	27.8	3.7	4.8
Farmers	1.229	1.464	0.347	0.326	13.7	12.6	4.8	5.3
Others	0.855	1.249	0.514	0.465	31.4	27.6	4.3	4.8

Source: Calculations by G. Schmaus of the SPES–Project Frankfurt/Mannheim based on the Integrated Microdata-File (IMDAF) 1969. Population base: German nationals in private households

Table 21.2. Indicators for the distribution of factor income and disposable income for households, Federal Republic Germany 1969.

		Concentration ratio (Gini index)		Share of the top 5% (in %)		Share of the lowest 20% (in %)	
		Factor income	Disposable income	Factor income	Disposable income	Factor income	Disposable income
Household income[1]	1962	0.497	0.360	24.9	18.8	0.4	6.1
	1969	0.500	0.352	23.3	17.9	0.4	6.5
Household income per head[1]	1962	0.455	0.320	24.3	18.1	2.8	8.5
	1969	0.452	0.324	23.0	17.5	2.9	8.5
Welfare ratio[2]	1969	0.415	0.229	15.9	12.3	1.2	10.8
Household income Head of household:[1]							
Wage earner	1962	0.220	0.202	10.4	10.0	10.2	11.1
	1969	0.214	0.206	9.9	9.9	10.1	10.7
Salaried employee	1962	0.291	0.284	15.7	14.7	8.7	8.7
	1969	0.277	0.271	13.4	13.1	8.4	8.7
Civil servant	1962	0.212	0.202	10.6	10.2	11.2	11.5
	1969	0.219	0.211	10.9	10.6	10.9	11.2
Self employed	1962	0.542	0.459	36.9	27.9	4.1	5.3
	1969	0.510	0.418	34.2	24.4	4.6	6.2
Farmer	1962	0.286	0.261	14.0	13.3	8.4	9.7
	1969	0.262	0.235	12.0	10.7	8.1	9.3
Retired person	1962	0.746	0.408	39.9	17.4	0.0	4.6
	1969	0.728	0.364	38.0	15.8	0.0	6.2

Sources: Calculations by F. Klanberg and G. Schmaus of the SPES-Project Frankfurt/Mannheim based on the Integrated Microdata-File (IMDAF) 1962 and 1969.
[1] Population in German and foreign households and population in institutions.
[2] German nationals in private households only.

incomes exist with that occuring when a transfer policy is in operation. First we will indicate the share of those in poverty in the working population; secondly the share of those in the whole population, including those who are not integrated into the production process. For this purpose a very low poverty standard[6] is used. Table 21.3 gives the results.

Table 21.3. The share of poor households in the population, Federal Republic of Germany 1969 (low poverty standard: Public Assistance (BSG) and effective rent).

	All	Poor	% Poor
Households, working head			
factor income only	14,805,969	163,068	1.10
disposable income	14,805,969	24,646	0.16
All Households			
factor income only	21,517,976	5,244,294	24.37
disposable income	21,517,976	179,898	0.84

Source: Calculations by K. Kortmann of the SPES-Project Frankfurt/Mannheim. Database: IMDAF 1969. Population base: German and foreign nationals in private households.

The indicators presented in the preceding tables show very clearly that the transfer policy in the Federal Republic of Germany changes the distribution of income to a considerable extent. A comparison between table 21.1 and table 21.2 shows that the effect of transfer policy is relatively small when only those in the production process (i.e. people whose main income is factor income) are considered. The concentration ratio in this case does not decrease significantly – in some cases it even increases slightly. In addition, the impact of transfers, expressed as a proportion of income, varies between different social groups.

The whole impact of transfer policy is seen if one also includes that part of the population which is not integrated into the production process, and uses the household as the basic unit. Table 21.1 shows that, for all indicators, considerable changes are caused by transfer policy. This is particularly true if one considers the indicators based on the welfare ratio.

The reduction of poverty due to transfer policy is also remarkable. Again it can be shown that the effect is relatively small if one includes only the population integrated into the production process. Without transfers one would have a poor population comprising some 25 per cent, even using a very low poverty standard.

Similar results can be seen by glancing at the data of comparable countries. For the United States a reduction is reported in the concentration ratio from 0.4595 to 0.3998 for the year 1966[7] and, using a different source, from 0.417 to 0.361 for the year 1969.[8] A similar result is available for the United Kingdom where the reduction is from 0.403 to 0.326 in the period 1961 to 1963, and from 0.423 to 0.326 in the period 1971 to 1973.[9] The question whether a transfer policy can be

---

[6] For the definition of the poverty standard see Kortman (1976).
[7] Okner (1975, p. 65).
[8] Taussig (1973, p. 17).
[9] Royal Commission on the Distribution of Income and Wealth (1975, p. 62).

Transfer policy

successful at all is therefore easily answered. It is more important to ask whether a transfer policy is an efficient means of changing the income distribution in its different dimensions.

II.3. *The Efficiency Transfer Policy*

Theoretically the efficiency of transfer policy could be judged by comparing the volume of transfers and the changes in the income distribution induced by these transfers.[10]

Since the volume of transfers has dimensions other than the different goal dimensions of income distribution, there exists no maximum value for efficiency. One can only rely on intertemporal or interregional comparisons. Both of these are difficult to make, however. Institutional differences between countries make comparisons difficult and there exist no time-series on the different aspects of income distribution.

Even if it is impossible to use a single measure of efficiency, some methods of judging efficiency can be developed. These are derived from:
(a) The relationship between the impact of transfer policy on the income distribution and the aggregate volume of transfers.
(b) An analysis of the transfers within social groups or households.
(c) The relationship between the distributions of disposable income and factor income.

Table 21.4 shows some aggregate measures of transfer efficiency. Movements in the distribution of factor income towards the distribution of disposable income, as measured in table 21.2, are related to the share of positive transfers to households in the net national product. With regard to the concentration ratio, the transfer efficiency shows no change. Nearly the same is true for the impact on the share of the lowest 20 per cent. Only for the share of the top 5 per cent can a decrease in the aggregate efficiency value be observed.

The result presented here is not very meaningful, since only two years are compared and these are very close. More interesting results could be derived from a longer time-series, but this is not available if one requires some comparability over time.

On a more disaggregated level it may be useful to measure efficiency by asking the extent to which transfers are paid and received by the same social group. Usually, transfer policy is regarded as a policy of transfers between different persons, or at least between people belonging to different social groups. If a transfer policy finally produces a situation where the same person pays and receives transfers, it is questionable whether this is consistent with the original goal of transfer policy. It is often believed that transfer policy in modern societies is inefficient, since a considerable proportion of income transfers are transfers within the same social group, rather than between different groups. However, the

---

[10] Questions regarding the measurement of efficiency are considered in Lindbeck (1975), especially pp. 356–361.

Table 21.4. Transfer volume and the impact of transfer policy in million DM/percent.

	1962	1969
1. Net national product (market prices)	327430	541250
2. Indirect taxes less subsidies	49170	80600
3. Net National Product (factor prices)	277450	460650
4. Direct taxes	37830	50090
5. Social Security contributions	37700	69780
6. Sum of negative transfers (2 + 4 + 5)	124700	200470
7. Positive transfers to households	45050	80380
8. Net revenue (6–7)	79650	120090
9. Positive transfers as a % of Net National Product (factor prices) (7/3)	16.2	17.45
10. Impact of transfer policy on the concentration ratio of household income (rate of change as a % of the concentration ratio of factor income)	27.6	29.6
11. Aggregate transfer efficiency with respect to the concentration ratio of household income (10/9)	170	170
12. Impact of transfer policy on the share of the top 5 percent (rate of change as a percentage of the share of the top 5 percent in factor income)	24.5	23.2
13. Aggregate transfer efficiency with respect to the share of the top 5 percent (12/9)	151	133
14. Impact of transfer policy on the share of the lowest 20 percent (rate of change as a percentage of the share of the lowest 20 percent in factor income)	−1425	−1525
15. Aggregate transfer efficiency with respect to the share of the lowest 20 percent (14/9)	−8800	−8740

Source: Table 21.2. and National Accounts.

data base for judging this issue is very weak. The change in the overall distribution of income, mentioned in the last section, indicates that there are at least some transfers between social groups. The government of the Federal Republic of Germany has decided to found a special commission, the "Transfer-Enquête-Kommission", which will enquire into problems related to this question.

The traditional way of measuring this type of efficiency is to define groups which are regarded as homogeneous, so that transfers within these groups can be called inefficient and transfers between the groups can be called efficient. Then it is possible to calculate the transfers within each group. The value of this indicator, however, will depend largely on the classification chosen. A correlation is expected between the number of groups and the corresponding efficiency. When the number of groups increases the share of the within-group transfers will decrease.

The development of micro-analytical methods allows this type of efficiency to be measured, even at the individual level. By using a Microfile, it is possible to calculate the transfers paid and received by each individual, and to determine the amount of transfers regarded as inefficient (i.e. transfer payments, when taxes and contributions are higher than transfer payments; and the sum of taxes and contributions, when transfer payments are higher than taxes and contributions).

Table 21.5 gives the "inefficient" transfers as a percentage of the "efficient" transfers for six social groups and eleven factor income classes. The columns A show that the classification chosen for groups does not clearly separate households with net positive transfers from those with net negative transfers. Even in the highest income class, 0.7% receive higher transfer payments than they pay in direct taxes and social security contributions. Columns A show the percentage of such households with higher positive transfers than negative transfers, i.e. households which receive a net transfer.

For these households, column B indicates the proportion of "inefficient" transfers (the percentage of direct taxes and contributions paid, compared to the transfers received). This percentage increases with factor income, since the negative transfers are positively correlated with factor income. 44% of the households receive higher transfers than they contribute. Nevertheless, they finance 12.4% of the transfers received by themselves. In the higher income brackets, particularly, a considerable proportion (40-60%) is financed by the same households.

Columns C indicate the situation of households which pay more direct taxes and contributions than they receive as positive transfers. Again, "inefficient" transfers are given as a percentage of "efficient" transfers (i.e. positive transfers as a percentage of negative transfers). 15.1% of direct taxes and contributions are returned to the same households. There is a negative correlation with the amount of factor income for the same reasons as before – the increase in taxes and contributions with income. This effect, however, is distorted for those social groups which pay little or no social security contributions. This applies to civil servants, the self-employed and farmers. For households headed by a retired person, column C should be interpreted cautiously, since negative transfers exceed positive transfers for only a fraction of these households (2.1%).

In general, positive and negative transfers are received and paid to a considerable extent by the same households. This is particularly true in the middle income intervals.

The results presented in table 21.5 are not compatible with the hypothesis that the German transfer system essentially follows a negative income tax schedule. Even in low income classes there are still payments of taxes and social security contributions, and considerable transfers payments are made to high income recipients.

The amount of within-household transfers is particularly remarkable, since the analysis is done at the level of an individual household during one time period. Intertemporal transfers by the same person are not included here. Social security contributions which are later repaid as social security benefits, are regarded as efficient in this type of analysis. This is consistent with the basic rationale of social security systems, which is to make a person pay and receive transfers at different points of time. One is tempted to broaden the analysis to include this type of intertemporal transfer. However, it is almost impossible to incorporate this aspect. Only data sets which give the social and income histories of individuals over their life, can provide reliable information on this problem. Studies have shown that

Table 21.5. Within-household transfers for households defined by factor income ranges and the status of the head of the household, Federal Republic of Germany 1969.
A: Households with positive transfers larger than negative transfers as a % of all households.
B: Negative transfers as a % of positive transfers, if positive transfers are larger than negative transfers.
C: Positive transfers as a % of negative transfers, if negative transfers are larger than positive transfers.

Status of head of household	Wage-earner			Salaried employee			Civil servant			Self employed			Farmer			Retired			All		
Factor income	A	B	C	A	B	C	A	B	C	A	B	C	A	B	C	A	B	C	A	B	C
below 300	100.0	3.2	0.0	100.0	2.7	0.0	100.0	5.1	0.0	71.7	4.3	0.0	89.6	1.8	0.0	99.9	2.4	33.0	99.8	2.4	31.3
300– 600	76.1	16.6	34.5	87.7	14.1	35.4	100.0	11.2	0.0	86.3	3.2	25.0	78.6	2.5	0.0	99.1	6.0	26.9	93.8	6.9	33.2
600– 800	43.0	33.4	28.8	50.9	26.0	21.9	46.4	14.8	16.3	73.9	8.7	4.0	86.2	1.8	0.0	95.4	10.8	70.9	65.6	15.1	28.9
800–1000	29.6	42.4	22.7	22.7	34.8	13.5	42.3	42.2	18.8	58.8	9.1	12.3	79.9	6.5	41.8	96.1	18.8	39.4	42.3	25.9	20.1
1000–1200	19.1	47.1	25.3	17.7	42.8	18.0	33.3	34.1	23.1	47.5	14.5	27.7	77.4	9.6	3.2	92.9	23.2	50.1	28.4	32.0	23.4
1200–1500	15.2	51.3	23.7	15.6	47.8	21.8	29.6	41.3	22.3	46.2	22.3	16.7	61.1	13.5	25.8	88.7	26.4	43.5	23.9	36.6	23.3
1500–1800	10.6	57.3	22.2	10.3	46.2	20.6	23.4	43.2	24.8	32.1	29.9	13.1	64.7	12.1	28.2	86.6	31.6	51.3	17.9	39.8	21.9
1800–2500	8.3	58.6	18.3	8.5	50.7	18.2	20.2	48.0	24.2	23.8	34.0	14.7	61.6	15.5	29.6	77.9	33.9	57.7	17.1	40.9	19.1
2500–5000	6.4	63.7	15.6	6.8	56.0	15.7	14.1	55.2	22.7	12.0	47.7	12.2	56.4	19.7	29.2	63.8	39.2	50.3	15.6	44.6	16.6
5000–10000	0.0	0.0	12.0	2.1	67.6	11.7	4.3	90.0	14.4	4.6	48.8	7.1	21.8	16.5	4.9	38.0	68.2	29.6	5.5	54.3	8.6
more than 10000	–	–	–	0.0	0.0	8.6	–	–	–	0.8	61.6	1.2	0.0	0.0	0.0	0.0	0.0	22.2	0.7	61.6	1.9
All income ranges	18.0	43.2	21.3	13.6	42.2	17.6	23.3	45.1	23.2	21.4	31.4	3.8	62.6	13.5	21.0	97.9	6.6	38.3	44.8	12.4	15.1

Source: Calculations by K. Kortmann of the SPES-Project Frankfurt/Mannheim.
Database: IMDAF 1969. Population base: German nationals in private households, institutions excluded.

there is considerable social mobility in modern societies. It is not, therefore possible to use cross section information alone.

On the other hand, the volume of within-household transfers can be partly explained by the aggregation of different types of transfer payments within a single household. An analysis based on single people would lead to lower values. It is, however, appropriate to centre attention on the household, since this is the basic unit of economic activity.

The next point to be considered is the relationship between factor and disposable income. Figure 21.1 shows factor income and disposable income for all households and some groups of households. The curve for all households is misleading. It shows a decline in disposable income with increasing factor income. This decline, however, is caused by aggregation. For all social groups, it can be shown that marginal disposable income increases with factor income. This diagram is, in fact, a good example of how crudely aggregated data can be misleading. In this context it should be remembered that even the curves for the individual sub groups presented in figure 21.1 may include a bias due to aggregation.

On the other hand, it is impossible to analyse this relationship for single households, since only one observation is available for each household. An alternative approach would be to use official schedules to construct this relationship for hypothetical households. Figures 21.2 and 21.3 are examples of this approach, not directly comparable to figure 21.1 since they are based on the year 1975.[11] The

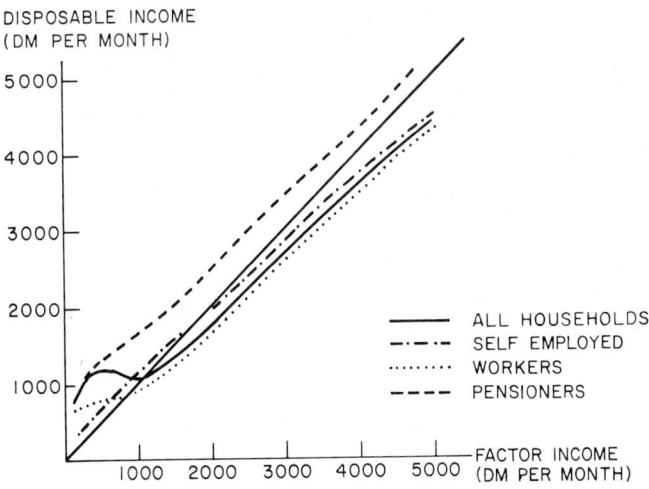

Figure 21.1. Disposable and factor income of households, Federal Republic of Germany 1969.

---

[11] For an exact description of the assumptions made and further examples see Sarrazin (1976).

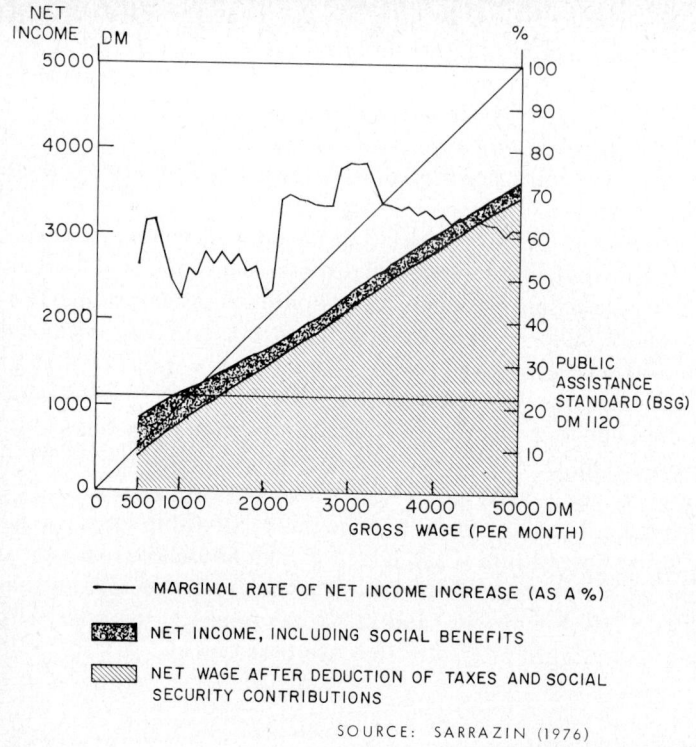

Figure 21.2. Impact of official provisions regarding taxes, social security contributions and social benefits without educational allowances (BAFOG) on the income of a married employee with two children whose wife is not working, Federal Republic of Germany 1975.

example chosen takes a married couple with two children, where the wife is not working. However, the outcome is similar to that observed for workers and the self-employed in figure 21.1.

The comparison between figures 21.2 and 21.3 clearly demonstrates that particular types of transfers may change the picture considerably. Figure 21.2 excludes the educational assistance given by the State to low income households (BAFOG). Figure 21.3 includes these payments. The marginal increase in disposable income depends very strongly on this factor. The decision to make transfers directed at a single social goal is therefore very likely to distort the general rules being followed in a simple negative income tax schedule.

The results presented so far apply to the German transfer system, where a considerable portion of the transfer volume contains some within-household transfers. Nevertheless disposable income still increases with factor income. Figure 21.4 shows that other systems are also possible. An illustration for Denmark, again calculated for a hypothetical household, indicates that disposable income actually decreases with factor income.

These results show that it is not possible to judge a transfer system solely by its ability to change net income values. There are many social goals which the

Transfer policy

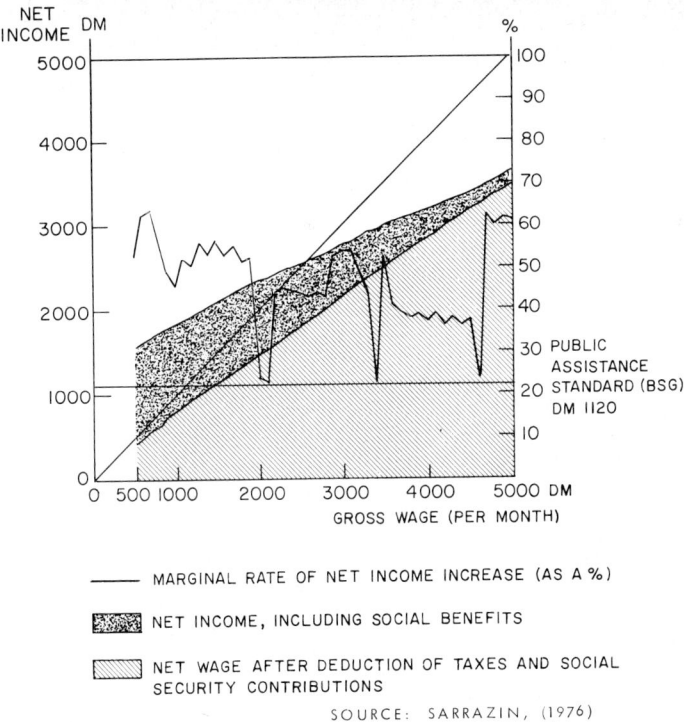

Figure 21.3. Impact of official provisions regarding taxes, social security contributions and social benefits including educational allowances (BAFOG) on the income of a married employee with two children whose wife is not working, Federal Republic of Germany 1975.

transfer system also has to fulfil and these may generate within-household transfers that are efficient as far as these other goals are concerned.[12]

Finally, some of the within-household transfers can be justified by the need to legislate a system of transfers. In order to be just, it is necessary to treat comparable situations in a similar way, even if this results in within-household transfers.

Even if we restrict our concept of efficiency to the goal of net income transfers, the judgement of the degree of efficiency is a matter of opinion. In particular, within-household efficiency depends on institutional factors which may result in the same pattern of disposable income, but which may differ in the volume of transfers. One example is the change in the treatment of child allowances in the German transfer system. Before 1975 there were tax exemptions for children which could be deducted from taxable income. This resulted in higher tax savings for higher income classes. Criticism of the additional benefit to higher income classes led to a change in the system. One possibility would have been to substitute deductions from taxes paid instead of deductions from the bax base. In this way the extra advantage for higher income classes could be avoided. It was decided,

---

[12] For an example of the practical problems related to a policy of this kind see the different contributions in Lurie (1975).

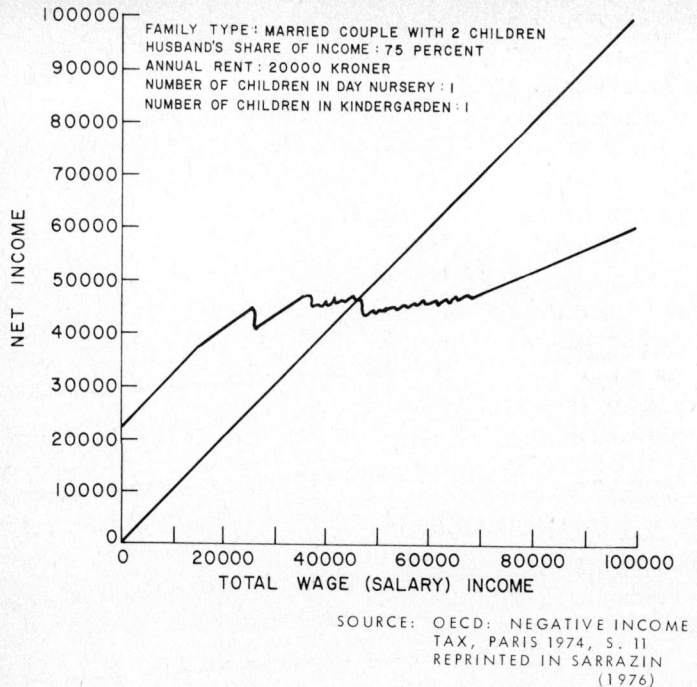

Figure 21.4. The combined effect of the tax burden and the loss of selected social benefits for a Danish household of 4 persons.

however, to replace the system by general transfer payments for children. All tax exemptions for children were eliminated, and allowances were paid for each child.

This change in the tax system had a considerable impact on the efficiency of the transfer system as defined above. There was some improvement in the income distribution, since the advantage to higher income classes was reduced. On the other hand, most of the transfer payments for children were within-household transfers. Most people pay at least as much tax as they receive in child allowances. If the social security system is taken into account, the situation is even worse. One could argue that the net effect of a system where tax exemptions are deducted from tax liability, and of a system where special transfers are paid, is very similar. However, the proportion of within-household transfers increases substantially.

But even if the effects are very similar, it is debatable which system should be preferred. At least from the viewpoint of administrative costs it can be questioned whether the special transfer system is really advantageous. Besides, one may ask what effects this type of system has on the relationship between the Individual and the State. A more thorough investigation could therefore suggest that, even in simple cases, the concept of within-household efficiency is useful in judging a transfer system.

Measures of efficiency based on the net effect of positive and negative transfers between individuals (or households or groups) neglect the fact that the transfer system consists of different components. When issues like those mentioned above are discussed, the picture may change for each of the sub-groups. The basic question of an integrated social and economic policy has to be raised again.

However, this question means that we can not restrict considerations of efficiency to single goals. A combination of goals, which includes the different dimensions of social welfare, has to be developed. The empirical results presented here show that it is also necessary to define the goal dimensions at a more disaggregated level. One example may help to clarify this. Whereas the impact of transfer policy on the overall income distribution is relatively large, the indicators that reflect the situation of the working population show that the effect of transfer policy on this group is relatively small. A similar result holds for the transfer system of the United States.[13] It is the combination of desired goals which determines whether this type of transfer policy is regarded as useful. However, this question cannot be answered without an analysis of transfer incomes. It is related to the question of work incentives and, consequently, to traditional economic goals. These also have to be included in the analysis.

The empirical results presented were not aimed at a socio-economic framework of this kind. This does not yet exist. It is therefore not possible to present a general theory of transfer policy which allows the development of a goal orientated, rational transfer policy.

III. A framework for the development of transfer policy

In the previous section it was shown that the impact of transfer policy on income distribution is considerable even if the efficiency, as indicated by different concepts, is perhaps sub-optimal. If we turn to the normative question as to how transfer policy should be further developed, no clear answer is possible. Following the general theory of economic policy, one has to define the goals, the instruments and the data which determine a rational transfer policy. Large simulation systems based on micro-files allow actual observations and assumed instruments to be used to calculate values for the different goal dimensions. Attempts have been made to develop this type of system. Some parts of a general system of this kind are available and in use. Systems of this type do not allow, however, general conclusions. It is not, therefore, possible to develop an overall strategy for transfer policy. It is only possible to indicate a few of the significant opinions as to the appropriate goals, data and instruments. They have to be followed if one develops a simulation or decision system on which to base a rational transfer policy. They are also useful if one wishes to discuss the development of a transfer system, even if such a system is not yet available.

III.1. *Goal Dimensions*

The elimination of poverty belongs to those goals which have widespread support within society. This goal can be restricted to the population that is not integrated

---

[13] See Watts and Peck (1975), especially p. 113.

into the working process. It can also be defined in such a way that it includes low income earners.

A second main goal is the degree of equality in consumption opportunities. In transfer policy, the low income aspect is of particular importance. So the concentration ratio and the share of the lowest 20% are useful measures. Family composition may be taken into account using welfare ratios. Again, the situation of the working and non-working population can be examined separately.

Fluctuations in the income flow also have to be taken into account. It is very difficult to develop operational measures, since time-series of micro-files are needed to observe the variability of income. Except for a few examples, from which no general conclusions can be drawn, this type of data is not available.[14]

One crucial goal dimension is related to the question whether the goal of transfer policy should be restricted to the objective of income maintenance, or whether attempts should also be made to integrate or reintegrate people who receive transfer payments into the production process.

The inclusion of this goal raises the question of work incentives affected by the transfer system. Our empirical knowledge of this problem is relatively weak. However, experiments carried out in the United States show that transfer policy may have some impact on the degree of participation in the labour market.[15] The empirical results can not be generalised in a simple way. One example shows that transfer payments – following a negative income tax pattern – produce a slight disincentive to work, which is, however, partly due to the fact that earnings per hour are significantly higher for the group that receives transfer payments than for the control group without transfers. In contrast to what is widely believed, the disincentive effects are greater for families at the lowest level of transfers. There are some reasons to support the hypothesis that work incentives may be reduced if very low income levels could be avoided. It might be useful to construct a transfer system in such a way that the decision to join the labour force is made in circumstances where the individual may hope to reach the middle income classes.

This might be encouraged by schemes which include transfer payments that are independent of incomes earned in the production process. An example would be the child allowances reported above, which are independent of other income receipts. On the other hand, the sum of child and educational allowances could prove to be a substantial fraction of household income.

Traditional economic goals also have to be taken into account. The inclusion of economic growth raises the question of work incentives at higher income levels. The overall burden of taxes and social security contributions, as well as marginal tax rates, may increase the disincentives for higher income groups. But there is little empirical evidence available. By introducing the dimension of the adequacy of incomes, the role of very high incomes in a society could be discussed.

There is one piece of empirical evidence, however, which should be reported. The history of public finance shows very convincingly that the tax burden, which has risen constantly during the period for which obtained statistical observations

---

[14] For an interesting example see Cohen et al. (1975).
[15] See Shore and Scott (1973).

are available, has always been regarded as the maximum burden that could be imposed.

The objectives of economic stabilisation also have to be taken into account. The unemployment rate affects employment prospects in the labour market. Price increases may have a negative impact on the poor or low income population. The effects of inflation on the poor, however, are still unknown. This goal dimension is influenced by the balance of transfer flows.

III.2. *Data: Parameters that are not determined by Transfer Policy*

An assessment of transfer policy also requires an analysis of factors that are not easily influenced by government policies. One example of the utmost importance is the population structure. Intergenerational transfers depend particularly on the composition of the population. Transfers to the young and old must be financed by the active population. These transfers necessarily depend on the number of young people eligible for education and the size of the old age population. Within each period, there is a balance between these groups, which can not be lightly ignored without running the risk of adversely affecting other economic goals.

The fact that the population structure has a considerable impact on transfer policy has to be taken into account when a system of transfers is designed. Demographic processes have to be included in this type of system. Thus a high degree of disaggregation is not only indispensable for distinguishing the different goals; it is needed to incorporate different demographic processes. Simulation models used to assess transfer policy are therefore large-scale socio-economic systems which apply the micro-analytical simulation approach.

Whether the primary income distribution should be considered to be given as data is an issue discussed in other papers in this volume. If it can be changed by integrated social policy, it should not be regarded as data. For many purposes, however, it may be useful to take it to be data, even if some influence of transfer policy on the primary income distribution is known to exist. But in many cases it will be reasonable to neglect this type of feed-back.

III.3. *Instruments: Parameters that can be used for Transfer Policy*

A rational transfer policy has many instruments at its disposal. They can be combined in very different ways. The number of degrees of freedom is therefore very large. This is true even if one considers the goal system as a whole.

One of the central parameters to be chosen is the overall transfer volume. This has to be related to the net revenue regarded as necessary. It might be argued that both values are not exactly parameters. This is correct. On the other hand, these variables are crucial to the political discussion of transfer systems. The political acceptability of a transfer system depends to a great extent on the transfer volume which it generates.

Considerations regarding the net revenue of the system have to be included, partly because the system requires financing and partly because the supply of public goods has a bearing on the transfer system. In this context, the degree to which transfers in kind should be used in the system has to be decided.

An important group of policy parameters can be related to the degree to which the transfer system is directed towadrs different social sub-goals. A more diversified transfer system enables individual goals to be reached with more precision. One must decide whether transfer sub-systems should exist for child allowances, educational allowances, health care, old age pensions, employment security and similar objectives. It was noted earlier that this decision may greatly influence the relationship between disposable and factor income and, therefore, the consumption opportunities as well as work incentives.

The problem of diversification of the system is linked to the question of using negative income tax schedules. On the one hand, one can imagine a system where all the objectives of transfer policy are achieved with a single negative income tax formula. On the other hand, transfer payments may vary with individual circumstances and depend on laws directed at specific situations. Diversified systems may be of this latter type.

A broad group of parameters are those of the tax and transfer schedules. The degree of proportionality, progressiveness or regressiveness has to be worked out. The basis for tax and transfer payments has to be fixed. Exemptions and allowances have to be defined. Special provisions for particular groups have to be considered.

These are only some of the parameters that can be used when designing a transfer system. However, it is not very useful to discuss these or other parameters at this general level. The empirical section of this paper has shown that transfer policy may change the income distribution considerably (though there can be differences in efficiency). This section has suggested a framework which might serve as a basis for the construction of a transfer system. If this is to be done rationally, it will be necessary to develop a decision system which is suitable for this purpose. Since there are so many goal dimensions and parameters, there is no point in speculating on the development of transfer systems in a more general way. The work to be done within the next years is the development of systems that are directed towards this objective.

Efforts are being made in a number of places throughout the world, although various problems still await solution. In Germany a research group at the Universities of Frankfurt/Main and Mannheim is in the process of developing a decision and indicator system of this type, called the SPES-Project. The system has been described elsewhere.[16] The flow chart given in figure 21.5, may convey a rough impression of the system. At the moment, the system only allows a partial analysis of single questions. At a later stage it will be possible to also tackle problems arising from an integrated social policy.

---

[16] For a short description of the system see Brennecke and Krupp (1976) and Krupp (1976).

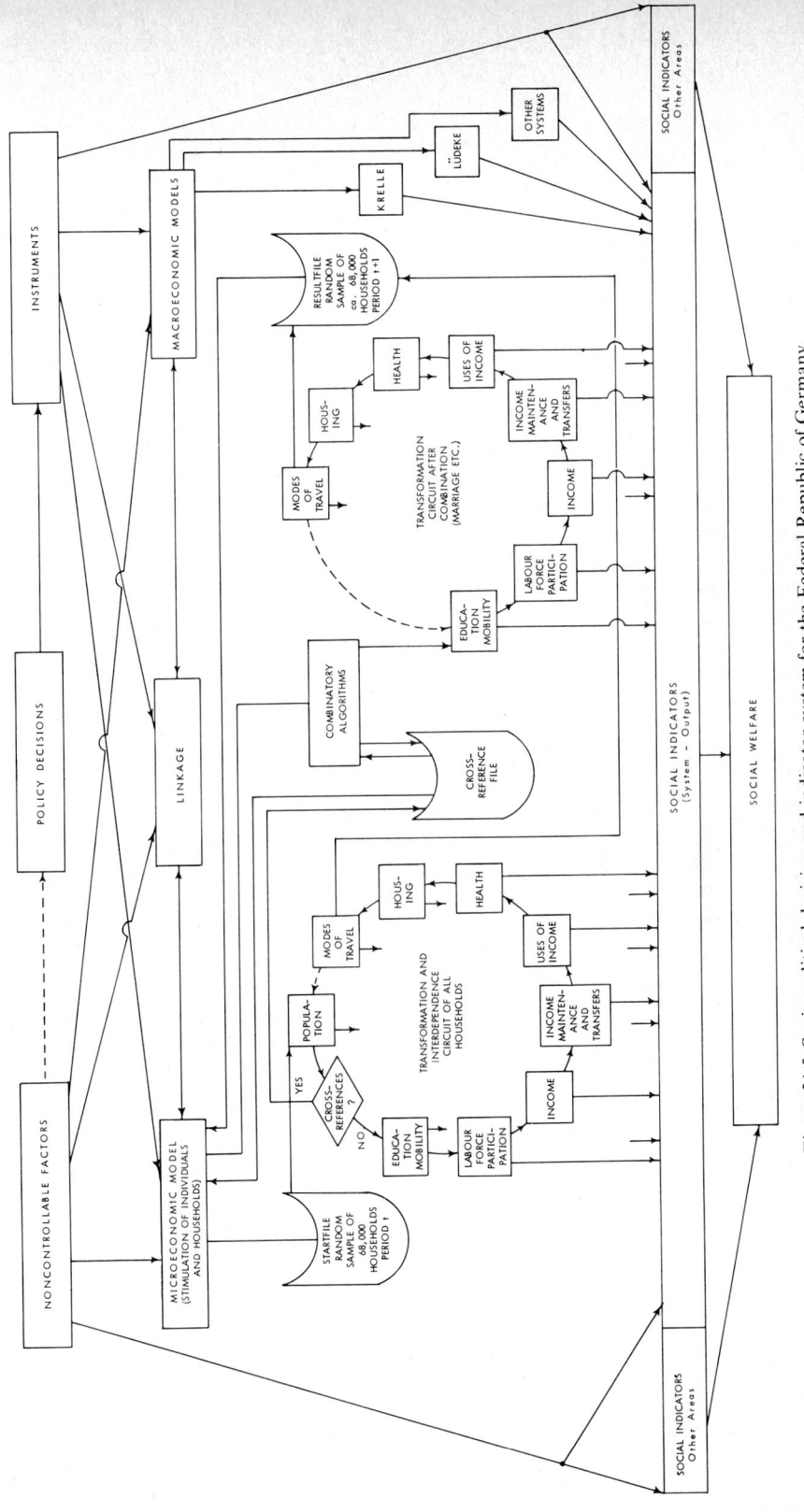

Figure 21.5. Socio-political decision and indicator system for the Federal Republic of Germany.

References

Atkinson, A.B., "On the Measurement of Inequality", *Journal of Economic Theory*, 1970.
Brennecke, R. and H.-J. Krupp, "Das Sozialpolitische Entscheidungs- und Indikatorensystem für die Bundesrepublik Deutschland – Genesis, Ziele, Struktur und Stand des Forschungsprojektes", in H.J. Hoffman – Nowotny (ed.), *Soziale Indikatoren – Internationale Beiträge zu einer neuen praxisorientierten Forschungsrichtung*. Frauenfeld and Stuttgart, 1976.
Cohen, A.I., H.S. Parnes and J.R. Shea, "Income Instability among Young and Middle-aged Men" in Smith (1975).
Glatzer, W. and H.-J. Krupp, 'Soziale Indikatoren des Einkommens und seine Verteilung für die Bundesrepublik Deutschland", in Zapf (ed.), *Soziale Indikatoren. Konzepte und Forschungsansätze III*, Frankfurt/Main 1975.
Kortmann, K., "Zur Armutsdiskussion in der Bundesrepublik Deutschland – Kritischer Vergleich vorgelegter Studien auf der Grundlage des Bundessozialhilfegesetzes", in *Deutscher Verein für öffentliche und private Fürsorge*, Nachrichtendienst. Heft 5/1976.
Kortmann, K., H.-J. Krupp and G. Schmaus, "Strukturen der Einkommensverteilung 1969", in *WSI Mitteilungen*, no. 10, Köln 1975.
Kortmann, K. and G. Schmaus, "Generierung des Mikrodatenfiles 1969 für die Bundesrepublik Deutschland (IMDAF 69)", SPES Working Paper, No. 39, Frankfurt/Main, November 1975.
Krupp, H.-J., *Möglichkeiten der Verbesserung der Einkommens – und Vermögensstatistik*. Kommission für wirtschaftlichen und sozialen Wandel, Vol. 50, Göttingen 1975.
Krupp, H.-J., "The Use of Microanalytic Simulation Methods in the Theory of Income Distribution", a paper delivered to an International Symposium on "Income Distribution and Economic Inequality", Bad Homberg, 1976.
Lampman, R.J., "Social Accounting for Transfers", in Smith (1975).
Lindbeck, A., "Inequality and Redistribution Policy Issues – Principles and Swedish Experience", in *Education, Inequality and Life Chances*, Volume 2, OECD, Paris 1975.
Lurie, I., (ed.), *Integrating Income Maintenance Programs*, New York, San Francisco, London 1975.
Okner, B.A., "Individual Taxes and the Distribution of Income", in Smith (1975).
Royal Commission on the Distribution of Income and Wealth, *Report No. 1, Initial Report on the Standing Reference*, London 1975.
Sarrazin, T., "Kumulative Effekte der Finanz und Sozialpolitik auf die Einkommensverteilung", in *Finanzarchiv*, N.F., Volume 34, 1976.
Shore, A.R. and R.A. Scott, "Work Response and Family Composition Changes in a Negative Income Tax Experiment: Preliminary mid-experiment results", in E.B. Sheldon (ed.), *Family Economic Behaviour, Problems and Prospects*, Philadelphia, Toronto, 1973.
Smith, J.D. (ed.), *The Personal Distribution of Income and Wealth. Studies in Income and Wealth*, Vol. 39, New York, 1975.
Taussig, M.K., *Alternative Measures of the Distribution of Economic Welfare*. Princeton, 1973.
Watts, H.W. and J.K. Peck, "On the Comparison of Income Redistribution Plans", in Smith (1975).

21 DISCUSSION

PAPER BY HANS-JUERGEN KRUPP

Mr. Groenveld felt the paper provided interesting and reliable information on the efficacy of a transfer system as an instrument for personal income redistribution. He thought that the calculations for West Germany allowed general conclusions to be drawn for other Western European countries.

Essentially the paper compares income inequality before and after taxes and transfers are made, and relates changes in the measures of income inequality to the volume of transfers. This is an obvious approach to take, but a number of difficulties arise. There are problems involved in the selection of inequality measures, the concepts chosen for income and transfers, and the level of aggregation used, although none of these are critical. A more serious problem occurs if the distribution of factor incomes is itself influenced by transfers. The existence of a transfer system with egalitarian motives will probably increase inequality in factor incomes, since the transfers are taken into account in the bargaining process determining gross incomes. He suggested that this type of feedback may partially explain the increase in the pre-transfer concentration ratios for Great Britain given on page 498 of the paper. The ratio was 0.403 for the period 1961–1963 and increased to 0.423 for the years 1971–1973. If no allowance were made for such feedbacks, the effectiveness of a transfer system will be overestimated. The precise degree of over-estimation could only be guessed at, but he would not accept that it was negligible. When this feedback is taken into account it may perhaps turn out to be impossible to devise a transfer system which is effective as a levelling instrument. For this reason he preferred in the long run to rely on policies affecting supply and demand in the factor markets to decrease income inequality.

He went on to comment on specific points raised in the paper. Professor Krupp had stated that there exist no completely objective criteria for judging the adequacy of a person's income in relation to the contribution made in production. Mr. Groenveld felt that the marginal productivity of different kinds of labour could be calculated from estimated production functions, although this was a difficult task. The paper also stated that the poor are to be regarded as those unable to cover basic needs as defined by social convention. Since figures for the proportion of poor households in the population are given in table 21.3, the appropriate social convention had clearly been chosen and he wondered exactly which definition had been used.

A third point concerned figure 21.1, which indicates a decline in disposable income when factor income increases. Since disposable income increases with factor income for each of the social groups, the decline found for all households combined was explained as an aggregation bias. Another interpretation is possible: that income earners transfer from one social group to another. He therefore felt it would be unwise to rely on the hypothetical relations underlying figures 21.2 and 21.3 when judging a transfer system.

Finally he questioned the desirability of replacing the transfer system with a negative income tax. This may improve administrative efficiency and the incentive to work for the lower paid, but research in the US has been unable to determine unambiguously the effects of a negative income tax on labour supply. Another disadvantage is the impersonal character of such a system. Attempting to overcome this impersonality would make it very close to the traditional transfer system.

Professor Hogan said that Australia had not experienced the noticeable reduction in inequality through the tax structure reported for the Federal Republic. The available evidence suggests that this may be due to the fact that the thrust of tax policies in Australia has been less directed towards equalisation than in the Federal Republic. Since it is generally supposed that Australia has the more equitable distribution of income, it might be argued that there would be less concern with distributional issues. He felt that this view should be treated with caution, owing to the probable over-statement of German inequality in the comparative studies provided by the OECD, and the fact that the OECD study relies on relatively old Australian data for 1966/67, since when issues bearing upon income distribution and poverty have come into prominence.

The paper links transfer policies mainly with goals associated with the degree of equality in consumption opportunities and the level of poverty, although the adequacy of income from the production process is also considered. It appears that the impact has been substantial for the overall income distribution, but not for the working population (or more correctly, the working population of German nationals). Thus the main beneficiaries have been those outside the workforce, primarily those in retirement. On the assessment of the efficiency of transfer policies, the paper suggests that transfers within relatively homogeneous groups are inefficient compared with transfers across groups. The final section deals with the development of a transfers policy, with attention focused on the issues to be explored. Professor Hogan emphasised the need to remember that, in advanced industrial societies, low income recipients rarely remain in this category for long. If the basis for these transitions changes, detailed administrative procedures for attacking problems of poverty may suddenly become inappropriate.

He went on to query a number of specific points. Whilst the general impact of the transfer policies considered in the paper may tend to shift the distribution in favour of those outside the workforce, it appears that some working groups are better rewarded than others. Table 21.1 provides estimates for the net gains from the transfer arrangements, and these figures indicate that civil servants fare better than wage and salary earners. Moreover, table 21.5 shows that those who make a net gain extend well up the salary scale. He asked whether Professor Krupp could explain these anomalies. He also argued that a social welfare spending programme cannot be considered independently of the political process in which it takes place. Transfer systems cannot be divorced from the broad goals of the community for which they are designed, some of which may not necessarily be concerned with social welfare objectives as seen in terms of social or economic justice.

Finally he expressed concern about the position of the migrant workforce in the Federal Republic. The analysis was directed towards German nationals and their households, and it therefore appeared that migrant workers had been excluded from the calculations. This led him to ask whether the net transfer pattern examined in the paper had not been extracted from the factor incomes of these "guest workers". This question is by-passed since the analysis is based on the relationship between factor rewards as a datum and the net impact of the transfer system.

On his interpretation of the evidence, the migrant worker group does not necessarily share in the transfer payments. This illustrates the difficulties involved in concepts of social and economic justice advanced in support of social welfare programmes. Much depends upon the strength of those initiating programmes and their command of the policy instruments for the execution of policies. Those not participating in the formulation of policies may draw few rewards and there may be discrimination against migrants, particularly when there are cultural and educational gaps between the national workforce and the foreign entrant. The Australian experience points to such discrimination and he suggested that the problems may be more severe when the immigrant workforce have only short term contracts.

Professor Wiles said that Mr. Groenveld had spotted an interesting point on page 10, that pre-tax income in the UK had become more unequal. Sweden had also experienced something similar. However the period 1962–72 is recognised as being an exceptional period for the UK, during which no shift in inequality occurred. In the years before and after this period, taxes and expenditure on social services did have an effect; and from 1972 onwards, as in the Netherlands recently, increases in taxes and expenditure on social services seem to have accompanied equalisation of incomes.

Professor Michal liked to see a paper which combined empirical observations with policy questions but felt that the paper underestimated the effect of transfer policy on the equalisation of consumption opportunities and the alleviation of poverty. This was due to two reasons: the choice of the Gini coefficient to measure inequality, which is not as sensitive to the bottom of the distribution as other measures which might have been selected; and the choice of household income as the measurement unit, rather than household income per capita.

Professor van Praag said it would be useful to have a similar analysis conducted for the Netherlands. He pointed out that the apparent effectiveness of transfers policy might well be sensitive to the implicit family equivalence scales used in the construction of the welfare ratio and the poverty line. He also believed that estimates of administrative costs need to be taken into account in the discussion of efficiency.

Professor Somermeyer was interested in the scope and coverage of the tables. He assumed that transfers referred to cash payments only and wondered whether the Federal Republic had other kinds of transfers like, for example, the food stamp programme in the United States. The analysis might be extended to include *all* forms of government activity, as had been done for the Netherlands. With reference to the conclusion that between-group transfers were efficient but within-group transfers were inefficient, he pointed out that the criterion of efficiency depends on the policy objective. Finally, he believed that the influence of transfer policy had been over-estimated, since only the direct effects had been included, and the indirect effects of transfers will generally have a negative effect.

Professor Taubman said it was very difficult to decide the appropriate definition for transfers, but some work in the US had extended the scope to include tax allowances against tax-deductable expenses. It was his impression that the total value of these tax allowances exceeded the value of all other forms of transfers. He understood that there were similar tax allowances in Germany and asked about their total value and distribution. Secondly, the fact that individuals respond to taxes and transfers raises two issues: the extent of the resulting loss in average income (or welfare); and what assumptions should be made about these individual responses in order that the approach can be integrated into the macro framework described at the end of the paper.

Professor Bentzel found the figures presented in the paper both interesting and illuminating, but wondered whether the most important and interesting figures had not been omitted. For instance the disaggregated figures on which table 21.5 is based would be very useful. This would enable the marginal effects of different types of transfers to be investigated and consequently the distributive efficiency of different kinds of transfers. This is more interesting than the question of what happens when all transfers are removed, which is the only question which can be answered with the figures reported.

Dr. Wagner was very much in sympathy with the approach adopted in the paper but thought there was a basic conceptual problem in deciding what the world would look like in the absence of a transfer system. The figures provided only show the situation before and after transfers, and no attempt is made to predict the distribution which would arise if all transfers were abolished. Nevertheless, it is useful to examine the effects of particular transfers which seem to have little feedback on the primary distribution of income. This type of analysis is carried out in an interesting way in figures 21.2 and 21.3 in the paper. He also supported Professor Hogan in stressing that economic justice may stop well short of national or community boundaries.

Professor Krupp, in his reply, agreed that the feedback of the transfer system on factor incomes should be taken into consideration. This point had been mentioned briefly in the paper. However, almost nothing is known about this feedback and it is very difficult to determine what the income distribution would look like if no transfers existed. But, even accepting this argument, transfers have no significant levelling effect for the working population; it is the non-working population who are primarily affected, especially the older age groups.

He admired Mr. Groenveld's belief that marginal productivity provides an objective criterion to judge the adequacy of a person's income. However, there is no scientific justification for this belief, nor is there universal agreement. Poverty lines are established by convention – they are not derived scientifically. Consequently, estimates of those in poverty in Germany range from 1 per cent of the population up to 10 per cent. In the paper two different standards are used. For the poverty calculations a very low standard had been chosen, which suggests about 1 per cent of the population are poor. For the welfare ratio, which allows family size to be taken into account, a higher poverty standard is used.

Professor Krupp was generally in agreement with Professor Hogan. For statistical reasons his results did not cover the guest-workers. Including them would have introduced a major source of errors. However, their omission can also be justified on logical grounds. Their current transfer position does not reflect the true situation since it neglects the pension liability of the government, which is not yet due for payment.

He shared Professor Michal's preference for household income per capita, but pointed out that using welfare ratios in the calculation of concentration measures is an even more powerful way of including the influence of family size. He was also sympathetic to the very broad programme suggested by Professor Somermeyer. However, the difference between analyses at the macro- and micro-levels has to be observed. It will take a long time before this type of analysis is feasible at the micro-level. The questions raised by Professor Taubman were very interesting, but further research would be necessary before an answer could be given.

Finally, he stressed the restricted objective of the paper. If an analysis at the micro-level is to be useful for answering distributional questions, the numerous difficulties found at this level have to be taken into account.

INDEX

Entries in the index in bold type under the names of participants in the Conference indicate their papers or discussions of their papers. Entries in italic type indicate contributions by participants to the discussions.

Abbing, P.J.R., 1, 2, 3, 6, 7, **59–77, 78–80**
Abele, H., *138*, 141n.
Adelman, I., *139, 160, 195, 239, 260–1, 266*
Aitchison, J., and Brown, J.A.C., 115n., 136n., 305, 313n.
Alchian, A.A., and Demsetz, H., 326, 329n.
Alexander, A.J., 423n., 440n.
Anand, S., 243n., 245n., 259n.
Arrow, K.J., 8n., 31n., 81n., 87, 90n., 92n., 125, 133, 136n., 327, 329n.
Ashenfelter, O., 421n., 445n., 463n
d'Aspremont, G. and Gevers, L., 87, 92n.
Atkinson, A.B., 18, 31n., 81, 82, 83, 84, 87, 89n., 92n., 101, 102, 104, 105, 130, 132, 133, 134, 135, 136n., 141n., 143n., 146n., 158n., 200, 201, 202, 224n., 271n., 299n., 347, 351n., 512n.

Bain, G.S. and Price, R., 462, 464n.
Bannink, R. and Somermeyer, W.H., 364n., 375n.
Bartels, C.P.A., *97, 159–60, 226–7, 315, 377, 416, 467*
Barth, K., 6, 7, 31n.
Bartholomew, D.J., 156n., 158n.
Baudet, M.J. and Wyers, G.J., 345, 351n.
Becker, G.S., 29, 31n., 318n., 321n., 322n., 328n., 329n., 381n., 393n., 429, 436, 440n.
Behrman, J., Taubman, P., Wales, T. and Hrubec, Z., 381n., 383, 384, 385, 386, 387, 393n.
Bentham, J., 8, 31n.
Bentzel, R., 78–9, 81n., 92n., *96, 109, 195, 227, 267, 356, 377, 417, 489, 516*
Bergson–Samuelson, social welfare function, 81, 91
Berkouwer, J., 46, 49n.
Berndt, E.R., 352n.; and Christensen, L.R., 399n., 408n., 413n.
Betsey, C. and Wachtel, H.M., 425n., 440n.
Bevan, D., 271n.
Bielby, W., Hauser, R. and Featherman, D., 392, 393n.
Blaug, M., 259n.
Bluestone, B., 423n., 440n.

Bockle, F. (ed.), 5, 31n.
Bodmer, W. and Cavelli–Sforza, L., 382n., 393n.
Boersma, W., **xiii-xix**
Bosanquet, N. and Doeringer, P., 424, 440n.
Boulding, K., 30
Bouma, N., 46n.; Van Praag, B.M.S. and Tinbergen, J., 45, 49n.
Bouma, P. and Somermeyer, W.H., 374
Bourguignon, F., 255n., 259n.
Bowles, S., 399n., 408n., 413n., 431, 440n.; and Gintes, H., 423, 440n.
Brandt, R.B., 11, 12, 31n., 76n.
Brennecke, R., and Krupp, H.-J., 510n., 512n.
Britto, R., 199n.
Bronfenbrenner, M., 336, 352n.
Brown, J.A.C., and Aitchison, J., 115n., 136n., 305, 313n.
Brown, M. and Jencks, C., 385n., 394n.
Brumberg, F. and Modigliani, F., 105n.
Brunner, E., 6, 7, 16, 31n., 76n.
Buchanan, J.M. and Bush, W.C., 154n., 158n.
Buenrostro–Hernandez, J., *315*
Burck, C.G., 49n.
Burk, R., and Gehrig, W., 92n.
Bush, W.C. and Buchanan, J.M., 154n., 158n.
Butts, R. and Hintikka, J. (eds.), 93n.

Cain, G.G., 422, 428, 440n.
Cairncross, A. and Puri, M. (eds.), 50n.
Cairnes, J.E., 422, 440n.
Cartter, A.M., 176n., 182, 183, 184, 190n.
Carnoy, M., 259n.; and Thias, H., 259n.
Cavelli–Sforza, L. and Bodmer, W., 382n., 393n.
Chakravarty, S., 83n., 92n.
Champernowne, D.G., 149n., 158n., 200n., 225n., 274, 299n., 305, 313n.
Chau, L., and Hsia, R., 242n., 259n.
Chiplin, B. and Sloane, P.J., 142n., 158n.
Chiswick, B.R., 49n.
Chiswick, C.U., 29, 30, 47, 49n., *160–1, 261–2, 266, 302,* 350, 352n., *355, 377,* 400, 414n., *415–6, 442, 467,* **471–87, 488–91**

Christensen, L.R. and Berndt, E.R., 399n., 408n., 413n.
Cohen, A.I., Parnes, H.S. and Shea, J.R., 508n., 512n.
Commoner, B., 308, 313n.
Conrad, A.H., 176n., 190n.
Consumption expenditures, inequality of, 187–9

Daal, J. van, 359n.
Dalton, H., 18, 31n., 81, 82, 83, 84, 92n., 130, 133, 134, 135, 136n.; and Atkinson, A.B., 114
Dasgupta, P., 146n.; Sen, A.K. and Starrett, D., 82n., 87, 92n., 158n.
David, M., and Morgan, J., 259n.
David, P.A. and Reder, M.W. (eds.), 136n.
Demonstrations, revealing productive contributions by, 317–29
Demsetz, H. and Alchian, A.A., 326, 329n.
Den Hartog, H., Tjan, H.S. and Van den Klundert, T., 345, 352n.
Deschamps, R. and Gevers, L., 87, 88n., 92n.
Development strategies, implications for income inequality, 486–7
Distribution of earnings, a general theoretical framework, 24–9, 359–74
Doeringer, B.P. and Bosanquet, N., 424, 440n.
Domar, E. and Musgrave, R., 296, 299n.
Dougherty, C.R.S., 399n., 408n., 414n.
Dresch, S.P., 399n., 408n., 414n.
Dual labour market, 421–30; in a developing economy, 471–86
Duesenberry, J.S., 121, 136n., 374n.
Duncan, B., Duncan, O.D. and Featherman, D.L. 46, 49n.
Duncan, O.D., Featherman, D.L. and Duncan, B., 46, 49n.; and Golberger, A. (eds.), 393n.
Dunlop, J.T., 423, 440n.
Dworking, R., 91, 92n.
Dynamic equity, definition of, 146

Earnings functions, 433–6, 449–53, 459–61
Easterlin, R.A., 121, 136n.
Education, estimated rates of return to, 328–87; and technological development, 47–9; in a developing economy, 471–86
Edwards, R.C., Reich, M. and Gordon, D.M., 432, 440n.
Elasticity of substitution between graduate and other labour, estimates of, 400–8
Eltető, O. and Láng, G., 212n., 225n.
Encarnacion, J., 245n., 259n.
Engels, F. and Marx, K., 93n.
Entropy, 306–9
Equitable distribution, definition of, 36–8, 60–7, 82–92; and theological ethics, 7; and Utilitarianism, 7–15; and optimal distribution, 37–8; feasibility of, 47–9
Esteban, J.M., 87n., 92n.

Fagerlind, I., 393n.
Fallenbuchl, Z. (ed.), 225n.

Fallon, P.R. and Layard, P.R.G., 399n., 414n.
Featherman, D., Bielby, W. and Hauser, R., 392, 393n.; Duncan, B. and Duncan, O.D., 46, 49n.
Feldstein, M.S. and Inman, R.P. (eds.), 440n., 464n.
Feller, W., 143n., 147n., 158n.
Fellner, W., 222, 225n.
Ferge, Z., 212, 225n.
Finkelstein, R.M. and Fieberg, M.O., 308, 313n.
Flemming, J., 271n.
Foster, J. and Mulvey, C., 445n., 464n.
Frankema, W.K., 76n.
Frieberg, R.M. and Finkelstein, M.O., 308, 313n.
Friedman, M., 101, 105n.; and Savage, L.J., 136n.
Frisch, R., 18, 31n., 133, 136n.
Furubotn, E.G. and Pejovich, S., 154n., 158n.

Galan, C. de, Tinbergen, J. and Van den Doel, J., 50n.
Galbraith, J.K., 69, 341
Gehrig, W. and Burk, R., 92n.
Georgescu-Roegen, N., 308, 313n.
Gerloch, V., 225n.
Gevers, L. and d'Aspremont, G., 87, 92n.; and Deschamps, R., 87, 88n., 92n.
Gibrat, R., 23, 31n.
Ginneken, W. van, 244n., 245n., 259n.
Gintes, H., and Bowles, S., 423, 440n.
Glatzer, W. and Krupp, H.J., 493n., 512n.
Goldberger, A., 384n., 393n.; and Duncan, O. (eds.), 393n.
Goldthorpe, J.H. and Hope, K., 424, 425, 431, 440n., 446, 458, 459, 463n.
Gollas, M., *261*
Gordon, D.H. 423n., 440n.; Edwards, R.C. and Reich, M., 423, 440n.
Graaff, J. de V., 81, 92n.
Gramm-Lee, W.L., 374, 375n.
Greenhalgh, C., 449n., 463n.
Gressis, N. and Philippatos, G.C., 308, 313n.
Griliches, Z., 402, 411, 414n.; and Mason, W., 390, 394n.
Groenveld, K., 346, 347, 352n., *355, 442, 513–4*; and Kuipers, S.K., 350, 351, 352n., **399–414, 415–9**
Gronau, R., 374, 375n.
Groves, T. and Ledyard, J., 8n., 31n.

Halberstadt, V., 46; and de Kam, C.A., 49n.
Hammond, P.J., 81, 87, 92n.
Hanoch, G., 259n.
Hansson, B., 81n., 83, 84, 93n.
Harcourt, G.C., 306, 313n.
Hardy, G., Littlewood, J. and Polya, G., 88n., 93n.
Hare, R.M., 93n.
Harrison, J., 423n., 428n.
Harsanyi, J.C., 9, 11, 12, 31n., 32n., 85n., 86, 93n., 123
Hart, H.L.A., 91, 93n.

Index

Hauser, R., Featherman, D. and Bielby, W., 392, 393n.
Haveman, R.H., 46, 49n.
Henry, R., 242n., 259n.
Herniter, J.D., 308, 313n.
Hicks, J., 344, 347n., 348, 401, 403; and Weber, W. (eds.), 32n.
Hinrichs, J. and Radner, W., 176
Hintikka, J. and Butts, R. (eds.), 93n.
Hogan, W.P., *265, 490, 514–5*
Hope, K., and Goldthorpe, J.H., 424, 425, 431, 440n., 446, 458, 459, 463n.
Hrubec, Z., Behrman, J., Taubman, P. and Wales, T., 381n., 383, 385, 386, 387, 393n.
Hsia, R. and Chau, L., 242n., 259n.
Huang, K., 311n., 313n.
Human capital, investment in, 319–20; impact of taxation on, 291–5

Imputation mechanism, importance of, 141–2; a model of, 143–50, 153–6; short- and long-run aspects of, 150–3
Income distribution, organising data on, 17–23; and the level of development, 185–6; impact of age on, 244–9; by socioeconomic group, 255–8; impact of length of life on, 264–8; neo-Keynesian theory of, 305–9; impact of transfers on, 493–9
Incomes policy, **xiii–xix**
Inman, R.P. and Feldstein, M.S. (eds.), 440n., 464n.
International comparison of income inequality, 190–1
IQ, contribution to income inequality, 387–93

Jencks, C., 158n., 352n.; and Brown, M., 385n., 394n.
Johnson, G.E., 463n.

Kaldor, N., 23, 305, 313n., 338n.
Kam, C.A. de, 46; and Halberstadt, V., 49n.
Kanger, S., 91, 93n.; and Kanger, H., 93n.
Kapteyn, A., 117n.; and Van Praag, B.M.S., 50n., 85, 94n., 116n., 119, 120, 136n.; Van Praag, B.M.S. and Van Herwaarden, F., 119, 121, 136n.
Kerr, C., 423, 437, 440n.
Keynes, J.M., 306
King, M., 463n.
Klanberg, F., 493n., 497n.
Knight, J., 255n., 259n.
Kolm, S.-C., 18, 82n., 86, 87, 93n., 113, 114, 128, 136n., 147n., 158n.
Kordas, J. and Stroinska, Z., 188n., 190n.
Korn, B. and Weide, T.O. van der, 414n.
Kortmann, K., 498n., 512n.; Krupp, H.J. and Schmaus, G., 495n., 512n.
Kramer, R., 6, 32n.
Krelle, W., **1–32**, *51–2, 96, 138, 162, 227, 262, 267, 315, 417, 442–3, 466, 489*
Kruijtbosch, E.D.J., **xix–xx**

Krupp, H.-J., 30, *109, 139–40, 195, 330–1, 444, 467*, **493–512, 513–7**; and Brennecke, R., 510n., 512n.; and Glatzer, W., 493n., 512n.; Schmaus, G., and Kortman, H., 495n., 512n.
Kuipers, S.K., 29, *97, 162, 239, 314, 333,* 350, 352n., *376–7, 444, 466, 490*; and Groenveld, K., 350, 351, 352n., **399–414, 415–9**
Kurihara, K. (ed.), 105n.
Kuznets, S., 172, 175, 176n., 177, 181, 182, 184, 185, 192n., 242, 243, 246, 256, 259n.

Lampman, R.J., 494n., 512n.
Láng, G., and Eltétö, O., 212n., 225n.
Langhout, A. and Somermeyer, W.H., 371, 375n.
Langoni, C., 245n., 259n.
Layard, R., 28, *55, 97, 106–7, 138–9, 196, 266–7, 302, 332, 356, 396, 416,* 421, 440n., 464n., *489*; and Fallon, P.R., 399n., 414n.; Metcalf, D. and Nickell, S., **445–64, 465–8**; and Psacharopoulos, G., 449n.
Lean, L., 246, 259n.
Lecaillon, J., *194, 353–5, 442, 466–7*
Ledyard, J. and Groves, T., 8n., 31n.
Leibenstein, H., 122, 136n., 326n., 329n.
Leibowitz, A., 382n., 394n.
Lenderink, R.S.G. and Siebrand, J.C., 372, 375n.
Lerner, A.P., 76n.
Levy-Garboua, L., 28, 29, **317–29, 330–4**, *355, 377, 397, 417, 443–4*
Levcik, F., 188n.
Lewis, H.G., 349, 352n., 447, 457, 464n.
Lifetime consumption, impact of taxation on, 283–4
Lifetime income inequality, 101–3, 249–54; impact of taxation on, 275–83
Lillard, L. and Willis, R., 386n., 394n.
Lindahl, L., 93n.
Lindbeck, A., 499n., 512n.
Little, I.M.D., 86, 93n.
Littlewood, J., Polya, G. and Hardy, G., 88n., 93n.
Love, R. and Wolfson, M.C., 188n., 192n.
Lurie, I. (ed.), 505n., 512n.
Lydall, W., 143n., 158n., 177n., 182, 185, 192n., 220, 225n., 255n., 259n., 339, 340

Macauley, A., 191n., 192n.
Mach, J., 210n.
MacQueen, J. and Marschak, J., 307n., 308, 313n.
Maikiel, G.B. and Maikiel, J.A., 428n., 440n.
Malinvaud, E., *332–3*
Malthus, T., 422
Mandelbrot, B., 274, 299n.
Marin, A. and Psacharopoulos, G., 435, 440n.
Markowski, S. and Wiles, P.J.D., 188n., 189n., 191n., 192n.
Marschak, J. and MacQueen, J., 307n., 308, 313n.
Marx, K., 90n., 193n.; and Engels, F., 93n.
Maskin, E., 87, 93n.
Mason, W. and Griliches, Z., 390, 394n.
Massizzo, A.I.V., 344, 352n.

Maton, J., Paukert, F., and Skolka, J., 256n., 259n.
McCall, J.J., 156n., 158n., 431n., 440n.
McCloskey, H.J., 76
Measures of income inequality, 18, 200–3, 221–3; based on social welfare functions, 81–6, 101–3, 122–35; descriptive and prescriptive aspects of, 87–9
Meerhaeghe, M.A.C. van, *95–6, 160, 227–8, 489*
Mehran, F., 89n., 93n.
Mera, K., 225n.
Metcalf, D., 421n., 344n., 435n., 440n.; Nickell, S. and Layard, R., **445–64, 465–8**
Michal, J.M., 18, 23, *110*, 186n., 190, *193–4*, **199–225, 226–8**, *239, 332, 515*
Mill, J.S., 8, 32n., 422, 440n.
Mincer, J., 156n., 158n., 381, 386n., 387., 394n.
Mirrlees, J., 271n.
Mitter, P., 141n.; and Wagner, M., 153n., 158n.
Mittler, P., 385n., 394n.
Mobility, socio-economic, 430–3
Morrisson, C., 22, *228*, **241–59, 260–3**, *356, 443*
Modigliani, F., 101; and Brumberg, F., 105n.
Morgenstern, O. and Neumann, J., 141n., 158n.
Mossin, J., 296, 299n.
Muellbauer, J., 89n., 93n.
Mueller, E. and Sarma, I.R.K., 186n., 192n.
Muller, H., 41, 49n.
Mulvey, C., 445n., 464n.; and Foster, J., 445n., 464n.
Murphey, R.E., 305, 308, 313n.
Musgrave, R. and Domar, E., 296, 299n.
Musgrove, P., 471n., 487n.
Mustert, G.R., 47, 49n., *162, 314*, 344n., 352n.

Naslund, B., 23, **305–13, 314–6**
Neumann, J., and Morgenstern, O., 10n., 104, 141n., 158n.
Nickell, S., Layard, R., and Metcalf, D., **445–64, 465–8**
Niebuhr, R., 69
Nozick, R., 91n., 93n.

Observed income distributions, for North America, 168–81; the U.K., 182–5; Socialist countries, 203–21, 229–38; less developed countries, 241–58
O'Higgins, M., 167n.
Okner, B.A., 498n., 512n.; and Pechman, J.A., 191n., 192n., 254n., 259n.
Okun, A.M., 30, 32n.
Olneck, M., 394n.
Osterman, P., 429, 440n.

Paglin, M., 244, 245n., 259n.
Pareto, V., 18, 49n., 51, 342
Parnes, H.S., Shea, J.R. and Cohen, A.I., 508n., 512n.
Parsons, D.O., 321n., 329n.
Pasinetti, L.L., 306, 313n.

Passenier, J., 409, 412, 414n.
Paukert, F., Skolka, J. and Maton, J., 256n., 259n.
Peacock, A.T. (ed.), 190n.
Pechman, J.A. and Okner, B.A., 191n., 192n., 254n., 259n.
Peck, J.K., and Watts, H.W., 495n., 507n., 512n.
Pejovich, S. and Furubotn, E.G., 154n., 158n.
Pen, J., 28, 30, 46, 76n., *161, 194, 227, 239, 301,* **335–52, 353–57**, *377, 397, 442, 466, 489*; and Tinbergen, J., **xiv**, 46, 48, 49n., 136n., 173, 343, 345, 352n.
Pencavel, J.H., 323n., 329n., 464n.
Percapitalised income distributions, 168–85, 210–3
Personal welfare, measurement of, using survey data, 42–3, 114–22; based on individual behaviour, 43–6
Pfaff, M. (ed.), 30, 32
Phelps-Brown, E.H., 453, 464n.
Philippatos, G.C. and Gressis, N., 308, 313n.
Pierson, F.C. and Taylor. G.W. (eds.), 440n.
Pigou, A., 84
Polya, G., Hardy, G., and Littlewood, J., 88n., 93n.
Powell, A.A. and Van Hoa, T., 225n.
Power, political, 337; economic, 338–9; administrative, 339–40; estimate of impact on income inequality, 342–51
Pracy, R.S., 188n.
Pratt, J.W., 125, 136n.
Preiser, E., 338n., 352n.
Price, R. and Bain, G.S., 462, 464n.
Projections for future income inequality, 48–9, 408–9
Psacharopoulos, G., 29, *107, 331–2, 396,* 399n., 408n., 414n., **421–40, 441–4**, 449n., *489*; and Layard, R., 449n.; and Marin, A., 435, 440n.
Puri, M. and Cairncross, A. (eds.), 50n.
Pyatt, G., 259n.

Rabkina, N. and Rimashevskaya, N.M., 187, 188n., 192n.
Radner, W. and Hinrichs, J., 176
Rashevsky, N., 305, 308, 313n.
Rawls, J., 9, 32n., 75, 76, 78, 80, 86, 91n., 93n.
Reder, M.W. and David, P.A. (eds.), 136n.
Reich, M., Gordon, D.H. and Edwards, R.C., 423, 440n.
Reiner, H., 77n.
Rimasheveskaya, N.M. and Rabkina, N., 187, 188n., 192n.
Risk-taking, as a source of spurious inequality, 104–5; impact of inheritance and capital taxation on, 296–8
Ritzen, J.M.M., 372, 375n.
Robbins, L., 86, 93n.
Roberts, K.W.S., 87, 93n.
Robinson, E.A.G., *110, 262, 266, 443, 467*
Robinson, J.V., 338n.
Rosen, S., 381n., 394n.; and Thaler, R., 381n., 394n.

Rothschild, M. and Stiglitz, J.E., 87, 93n., 153, 158n., 271n., 272n., 299n.

Samuelson, P.A., 59, 77n., 81, 83n.; Samuelson–Bergson, social welfare function 81, 91; and Swamy, S., 18, 32n.
Sarma, I.R.K. and Mueller, E., 186n., 192n.
Sarrazin, T., 503n., 512n.
Savage, L.J. and Friedman, M., 136n.
Sawyer, M., 192n.
Scarr, S., 382n., 394n.
Schmaus, G., 497n.; and Kortman, K., 495n., 512n.; Kortman, K., and Krupp, H.-J., 495n., 512n.
Schumpeter, J., 71, 328n., 329n.
Scott, R.A. and Shore, A.R., 508n., 512n.
Segmented labour markets, 320–9
Selfishness and altruism, 67–70
Selten, R., 9, 32n.
Sen, A.K., 2, 3, 16, 18, *53–4, 79–80,* **81–94, 95–8,** *108,* 123, 136n., *140,* 147n., 155, 158n., *160,* 168, *227, 265–6;* Starrett, D. and Dasgupta, P., 82n., 87, 92n., 158n.
Shannon, C.E. and Weaver, W., 307, 313n.
Shea, J.R., Cohen, A.I. and Parnes, H.S., 508n., 512n.
Sheshinski, E., 87, 93n.
Shore, A.R. and Scott, R.A., 508n., 512n.
Shorrocks, A.F., *110,* 143n., 153, 154, 158n., *161, 267–8, 302–3*
Siddré, W., 370, 375n.
Siebrand, J.C. and Lenderink, R.S.G., 372, 375n.
Simon, H., 339
Skolka, J., Maton, J. and Paukert, F., 256n., 259n.
Sloane, P.J. and Chiplin, B., 142n., 158n.
Smith, A., 422, 434
Smith, J.D. (ed.), 512n.
Söderstrom, L., 191n., 192n.
Somermeyer, W.H., 24, 28, *53, 108, 161, 195–6, 301,* **359–75, 376–8,** *396–7, 416–7, 515–6;* and Bannink, R., 364n., 375n.; and Bouma, P., 374; and Langhout, A., 371, 375n.
Spånt, R., 191n.
Starrett, D., Dasgupta, P. and Sen, A.K., 82, 87, 92n., 158n.
Steindle, J., 149n., 158n.
Stewart, M., 421n., 449n., 464n.
Stiglitz, J.E., 29, 30, 32n., 54, *108–9, 139, 162,* **271–99, 300–3,** *397, 417, 488–9;* and Rothschild, M., 87, 93n., 153n., 158n., 271n., 272n., 299n.
Stoft, S., 89n., 94n.
Stoikov, V., 244, 259n.
Stroinska, Z. and Kordas, J., 188n., 190n.
Suppes, P., 86, 94n.
Swamy, S., and Samuelson, P.A., 18, 32n.

Taubman, P., 28, 46, 47, *109, 139, 194–5, 227, 267, 300–1, 333, 355,* **381–94, 395–8,** *417, 444, 467–8, 489–90, 516;* and Wales, T., 49n., 390n., 393n.; Wales, T. and Behrman, J., 381n., 384, 386, 393n.; Wales, T., Hrubec, Z. and Behrman, J., 381n., 383, 385, 386, 387, 393n.
Taussig, M.K., 498n., 512n.
Tautscher, A., 5, 32n.
Taylor, G.W., and Pierson, F.C. (eds.), 440n.
Technological development and education, 47–9
Terleckjy, N. (ed.), 394n.
Thaler, R. and Rosen, S., 381n., 394n.
Theil, H., 18, 244, 246, 256, 305, 308, 313n., 342, 344, 347, 349
Thias, H. and Carnoy, M., 259n.
Thielicke, H., 6, 7, 32n.
Tjan, H.S., Van den Klundert, T. and Den Hartog, H., 345, 352n.
Thomas, H., *227, 355, 416, 441–2, 490*
Tinbergen, J., **xix**, 1, 2, 3, 9, 32n., **35–50, 51–7,** 73, 77n., 82, 94n., *95, 98, 194, 227,* 336n., 349, 350, 352n., 359, 363, 375n., *399–413* pass.; and Pen, J., **xiv**, 46, 48, 49n., 113, 136n., 343, 345, 352n.; Bouma, N. and Van Praag, B.M.S., 45, 49n.; Van den Doel, J. and de Galan, C., 50n.
Transfer policy, objectives of, 493–4, 507–11; efficiency of, 499–507
Twin samples, use of, 382–93

Unionisation, impact on relative wages, 445–58; impact on real incomes, 458–61

Vandenberg, S., 385n., 394n.
Van den Doel, J., de Galan, C. and Tinbergen, J., 50n.
Van den Klundert, T., Den Hartog, H. and Tjan, H.S., 345, 352n.
Van der Weide, T.D. and Korn, B., 414n.
Van Herwaarden, F., Kapteyn, A. and Van Praag, B.M.S., 119, 121, 136n.
Van Hoa, T. and Powell, A.A., 225n.
Van Praag, B.M.S., 16, 18, 40, 42, 43, 45, 47, 50n., 85, 89, 90, 94n., *108,* **113–36, 137–40,** 133, 136n., *161–2,* 224, *227, 315, 396, 515;* and Kapteyn, A., 50n., 85, 94n., 116n., 119, 120, 136n.; Tinbergen, J. and Bouma, N., 45, 49n.; Van Herwaarden, F. and Kapteyn, A., 119, 121, 136n.
Veldhuis, R., 77n.
Velluso, J., 259n.
Vickrey, W., 86, 94n.
Vielrose, E., *109,* 23, 190, *226,* **229–38, 239–40**

Wachtel, H.M. and Betsey, C., 440n.
Wachter, M.L., 457, 464n.
Wagner, M., 23, *55–6, 96, 137, 138,* **141–58, 159–63,** *195, 228, 267, 314–5, 397, 443, 516;* and Mitter, P., 153n., 158n.
Wales, T. and Taubman, P., 49n., 390n., 394n.; Behrman, J. and Taubman, P., 381n., 384, 386, 393n.; Hrubec, Z., Behrman, J. and Taubman, P., 381n., 383, 385, 386, 387, 393n.
Watts, H.W. and Peck, J.K., 495n., 507n., 512n.
Weaver, W. and Shannon, C.E., 307, 313n.
Weber, H., 32n.
Weber, W., 6n., 124; and Hicks, J., (eds.), 32n.

Weddigen, W., 77n.
Weizsäcker, C.C. von, 3, 16, 18, *55, 96*, **101–5**, **106–11**, *266, 302, 314, 397*
Weiss, R.D., 428n., 440n.
Welfarism, 89–91
Wiedemann, P., 188n.
Wighte Bakke E. et al. (eds.), 440n.
Wiles, P., 17, 22, 54–5, 81n., 94n., *96, 109–10, 137*, **167–92**, **193–7**, *239, 264–5, 266, 301–2, 315, 333–4, 355, 443, 466, 515*; and Markowski, S., 188n., 189n., 191n., 192n.

Willis, R. and Lillard, L., 386n., 394n.
Wilson, A.G., 308, 313n.
Winchester, D., 450n.
Wolff, P. de, *315, 395–6, 443, 465–6*
Wolfson, M.C. and Love, R., 188n., 192n.
Wright Mills, C., 341
Wünsch, G., 6, 7, 16, 32n.
Wyers, G.J. and Baudet, M.J., 345, 351n.

Yap, L., 471n., 487n.
Yu, F., 199n.